THE

Parade
Cookbook

by the Editors of Parade Magazine

SIMON AND SCHUSTER · NEW YORK

Copyright © 1978 by Parade Publications, Inc.
All rights reserved
including the right of reproduction
in whole or in part in any form
Published by Simon and Schuster
A Division of Gulf & Western Corporation
Simon & Schuster Building
Rockefeller Center
1230 Avenue of the Americas
New York, New York 10020

Designed by Irving Perkins
Manufactured in the United States of America
1   2   3   4   5   6   7   8   9   10

Library of Congress Cataloging in Publication Data

Main entry under title:
The Parade cookbook.

   Includes index.
   1. Cookery.   I. Parade.
TX715.P1968   641.5   78-18300

ISBN 0-671-22579-0

A NOTE TO THE READER

All temperatures given are Fahrenheit.

Contents

Foreword

HERE, IN a single volume, are all the recipes *Parade* has published for the past thirty years, edited to bring them up to date as to terminology and modern methods of recipe writing.

We feel sure that you will be happy to have these recipes all in one book. So many of you have written asking us to replace a favorite recipe that was lost, mislaid, or unintentionally thrown away. In many cases, an unbelievable number of years had passed since the recipe was published! Naturally, it made us happy to know that one of our recipes had been cherished so long, and we were more than willing to search until we found it!

This is truly a family cookbook, with recipes for everyday use, for company meals, and for special occasions. As we all know too well, food prices, though constantly fluctuating, are high. However, there are very few extravagant recipes in this book, but once in a while it is good for the soul to prepare a dish that is truly special, even though it means cutting down for the rest of the week!

We are confident that this book will help you to take advantage of "specials," to use seasonal foods, and to plan meals within your budget. Use the Contents and the Index to give you ideas. Do a little comparison shopping, watch for advertised bargains, and, if you have a freezer, cook ahead and store some of the dishes whose main ingredients you have bought on sale (see Shopping Hints, page 13).

With this book go our best wishes and the hope that you will find cooking a pleasure rather than a routine ordeal. Add a little love along with the other ingredients. It makes all the difference!

Yours sincerely,
Editors of Parade Magazine

Shopping Hints

1. Don't shop when you're hungry; you will almost surely buy more food items than you really need.

2. If possible, plan your menus for the entire week before you go to the supermarket.

3. Make a shopping list and follow it closely.

4. Buy foods that are in season.

5. Compare the labels on the products to be sure you are getting the most nutritional value.

6. Use unit pricing so that you know exactly how much you pay for an item.

7. Use open dating to be sure you're getting the freshest product. If, in spite of your efforts, you get something unusable, take it back to the store for a refund or credit.

8. Set a specific budget for food items and stay within that budget.

9. Use "consumer power" in the marketplace, resisting overpriced foods.

10. When you're buying meat, take into account the amount of fat, gristle, or bone which can't be eaten and which creates a false impression of the real price per pound you are paying.

11. Use your home freezer to help you take advantage of specials on bread, meats, and other perishable items.

12. Practice comparison shopping—check the ads and get the bargains.

13. Get the best protein buy for your dollar. Good sources of protein are meat, poultry, fish, milk, cheese, eggs, and soybeans.

14. If you're not satisfied that your retailer is giving you all the assistance you need, demand better assistance.

15. Join an organized consumer group that focuses attention on getting answers to your questions and action on the problems you face in the marketplace.

CHAPTER 1

Appetizers

WHETHER OR not an appetizer is served depends on the occasion and on the meal that follows. For example, if a salad or a sandwich is to be the main course, a hearty soup makes an excellent first course. For a company dinner, appetizers served in the living room while the hostess adds the finishing touches to the meal relieve her of hurry and stress. You will find recipes to meet every need in the pages that follow.

HAM-AND-LIVER PÂTÉ

1 large can (4½ ounces) deviled ham
1 cup chopped ripe olives, divided
1 can (4½ ounces) liver spread
1 tablespoon lemon juice

Combine deviled ham with ½ cup chopped ripe olives; pack in oiled 1½-cup mold. Combine liver spread with lemon juice and remaining ½ cup chopped ripe olives; pack on top of ham layer in mold. Chill several hours. Unmold by dipping in warm water. If there is no time for chilling, the ham and liver mixtures may be served separately in small bowls. Serve with crackers. Makes approximately 1½ cups.

PARTY PÂTÉ

2 cups finely chopped onions
1 cup butter or margarine
2 pounds chicken livers
1 cup chicken broth
2 teaspoons salt
¼ teaspoon freshly ground black pepper
½ cup dry sherry
2 envelopes unflavored gelatin
½ cup cold water

Cook onions in butter over low heat until soft but not brown. Add chicken livers, broth, salt, and pepper; cover and cook over low heat 30 minutes. Cool. Stir in sherry. Blend about ¼ at a time in electric blender until smooth, or put through food mill or sieve. Soften gelatin in cold water; dissolve over hot water; add to pâté mixture; mix well. Pack in oiled 4-cup mold; chill thoroughly. Unmold; serve with crackers.

SHRIMP DIP

¾ cup catchup
⅓ cup lemon juice
1½ tablespoons grated onion
2 tablespoons minced celery

3 tablespoons drained prepared horseradish
⅓ cup mayonnaise
1½ teaspoons Worcestershire sauce
Few drops hot-pepper sauce
Salt to taste

Combine all ingredients; chill thoroughly. Makes about 1¾ cups.
ACCOMPANIMENT: Chilled cooked shrimp.

AVOCADO DIP FOR SHRIMP

2 ripe avocados
1 cup dairy sour cream
½ teaspoon salt
2 tablespoons drained prepared horseradish
1 small onion, grated

Wash and peel avocados; cut each lengthwise and remove the seed. Mash avocados to smooth pulp with wooden spoon or in electric blender. Whip in remaining ingredients. Makes about 2 cups.
ACCOMPANIMENT: Chilled cooked shrimp.

DIP FOR VEGETABLES

4 packages (3 ounces each) chive cream cheese
2 teaspoons Dijon mustard
1 tablespoon prepared horseradish
1 teaspoon Worcestershire sauce
Few drops hot-pepper sauce
½ cup mayonnaise

Blend chive cream cheese with remaining ingredients. Makes about 2 cups.
ACCOMPANIMENTS: Celery curls, carrot sticks, cherry tomatoes, or your favorite party vegetables.

PIQUANT CHEESE SPREAD OR DIP

1 jar (5 ounces) pineapple–cream cheese spread
1 jar (5 ounces) pimiento–cream cheese spread
1 jar (5 ounces) relish–cream cheese spread
⅓ cup finely chopped pecans
Whipping cream

Combine cheese spreads; beat until fluffy. Stir in pecans. Add enough cream for spreading or dipping consistency, as preferred. Makes about 2 cups.

BLUE CHEESE SPREAD

2 packages (3 ounces each) cream cheese
¼ cup crumbled blue cheese
¼ teaspoon Worcestershire sauce
2 teaspoons grated onion
Whipping cream

Combine cream cheese, blue cheese, Worcestershire sauce, and onion. Mix thoroughly; beat until fluffy, adding enough cream to make easy spreading consistency. Makes about 1 cup.

GARNISHES

Carrot Curls: Cut thin lengthwise strips from carrots with vegetable peeler. Roll up tightly; secure with wooden picks. Drop into ice water with ice cubes. Chill several hours. To serve, remove picks.

Celery Curls: Cut celery stalks into 3-inch lengths. Fringe ends with sharp knife. Drop into ice water with ice cubes. Chill several hours.

Stuffed Celery: Use the little heart stalks, leaves and all. Fill with any of the many cheese spreads that are available.

Radish Roses:
1. Cut a thin slice from each side of each radish; cut thin slices, not quite through to stem, behind each white spot. Drop into ice water with ice cubes. Chill several hours.
2. With sharp paring knife cut 4 thin red petals not quite through to stem. Then cut a white petal behind each red one. Chill as for 1.

Radish Fans: Cut each radish crosswise into thin slices, not quite through to stem. Chill as for 1, above.

SAVORY CHEESE SPREAD

1 carton (8 ounces) creamed cottage cheese
2 packages (3 ounces each) chive cream cheese
1 tablespoon prepared mustard
½ teaspoon Worcestershire sauce
Dash hot-pepper sauce
½ teaspoon curry powder
1 teaspoon prepared horseradish
¼ cup chopped stuffed olives

Blend cottage cheese and cream cheese. Add remaining ingredients; blend well. Makes about 1½ cups.

COTTAGE-CHEDDAR MOLD

2 envelopes unflavored gelatin
½ cup cold water
2 teaspoons instant minced onion
2 cups milk
2 cups creamed cottage cheese
2 cups grated sharp Cheddar cheese
¼ teaspoon hot-pepper sauce
1 teaspoon Worcestershire sauce
1 tablespoon prepared horseradish
¼ teaspoon coarsely ground black pepper
1 teaspoon celery salt

Soften gelatin in cold water. Add minced onion to milk; heat to scalding; add to gelatin; stir until gelatin dissolves. Chill until slightly thickened. Put cottage cheese through fine sieve; combine with remaining ingredients; fold into thickened gelatin mixture. Spoon into 5-cup mold. Chill until firm. Unmold. Serve as a spread for crackers.

CANAPÉS

1. Spread Melba toast rounds with liver pâté. Sprinkle crumbled crisp bacon around edge of each.
2. Spread Melba toast strips with cream cheese. Top each with a small strip of smoked salmon and gherkin slices.
3. Spread Melba toast strips lightly with prepared mustard. Top each with thin strips of ham and halved pineapple tidbits.
4. Spread Melba toast rounds lightly with mayonnaise. Top each with a cucumber slice, 2 tiny deveined shrimp, and 2 slices stuffed olive.
5. Spread Melba toast rounds lightly with thick sour cream. Top each with a thin slice of cucumber, a smoked oyster, and a slice of pitted black olive.
6. Spread Melba toast strips with anchovy paste. Top each with a mixture of chopped hard-cooked egg and mayonnaise, then 2 lengthwise slices of gherkin.
7. Mash ¼ pound blue cheese; add 1 package (3 ounces) cream cheese and 2 tablespoons French dressing; whip until smooth and creamy; blend in 1 tablespoon finely cut chives. Spread on fingers of pumpernickel bread; garnish with sliced sweet gherkins.
8. Mash ½ pound liverwurst; add ¼ cup dairy sour cream, 1 tablespoon mayonnaise, ½ teaspoon Worcestershire sauce, dash hot-pepper sauce; whip until smooth and creamy. Spread on square salted crackers; garnish with sliced stuffed olives.
9. Spread Melba toast rounds with mayonnaise. Top each with thinly sliced smoked salmon; garnish with crumbled crisp bacon.
10. Spread round crackers with cream cheese. Place rolled anchovy fillet in center of each; surround with strips of pimiento.

NOTE: Pumpernickel, whole wheat, rye, or enriched white bread may be cut in rounds or strips and used instead of Melba toast.

CRISP BREADSTICKS

Trim crust from bread slices. Cut each slice in narrow strips. Brush strips with melted butter or margarine. Roll some of the strips in grated Parmesan cheese, others in celery seed. Toast at 350° for 15 minutes.

TOASTED ANCHOVY ROLLS

Combine equal amounts anchovy paste and softened butter or margarine; cream thoroughly. Spread trimmed bread slices with anchovy mixture. Roll up each slice; fasten with 3 wood picks. Cut each roll in thirds. Brush with melted butter or margarine. Toast under preheated broiler just before serving. Garnish with slices of stuffed olives.

CHEDDAR PENNIES

¼ pound (1 stick) butter or margarine
1 jar (5 ounces) sharp Cheddar cheese spread
¾ cup flour

Blend butter and cheese spread; add flour. Chill. Shape into balls about 1 inch in diameter. Freeze. Remove from freezer to baking sheets, spacing 2 inches apart. Bake at 425° for 8 to 10 minutes. Makes about 40.

CUCUMBER RINGS

2 cucumbers, 6 to 7 inches long
1 can (4½ ounces) chicken spread
1 hard-cooked egg, chopped
3 tablespoons minced pimiento
½ teaspoon seasoned salt
24 bread rounds (approximately)
Mayonnaise

Cut cucumbers in half crosswise. Remove strips of peel for striped effect. Hollow centers with apple corer. Combine next 4 ingredients; fill cucumbers; wrap and chill for 2 to 3 hours. Cut bread with round cookie cutter the same diameter as cucumbers. Spread rounds lightly with mayonnaise. Slice cucumbers crosswise in slices about ½ inch thick. Place slice on each bread round. Makes approximately 24.

SHRIMP ASPIC CANAPÉS

1 envelope unflavored gelatin
1½ cups chicken broth, divided
1 cup Rhine wine
Dash hot-pepper sauce
¼ teaspoon Worcestershire sauce
½ teaspoon salt
30 small deveined shrimp, cooked or canned
30 Melba toast rounds
Mayonnaise

Soften gelatin in ¼ cup cold chicken broth. Heat remaining broth; add to gelatin; stir until dissolved. Cool. Add wine, hot-pepper sauce, Worcestershire sauce, and salt. Oil 30 tiny muffin cups (1¼-inch bottom diameter). Place 1 shrimp in each. Add just enough gelatin mixture to barely cover shrimp. Chill until firm. Unmold. Spread toast rounds with mayonnaise; top with shrimp in aspic. Makes 30 canapés.

SAVORY NIBBLES

½ pound butter or margarine
2 garlic cloves
2 tablespoons Worcestershire sauce
6 cups bite-size shredded rice biscuits
4 cups spoon-size shredded wheat biscuits
4 cups O-shaped puffed oat cereal
1 small box (8 ounces) thin pretzel sticks
1 can (6½ ounces) salted peanuts
1 teaspoon celery salt
1 teaspoon onion salt
2 teaspoons seasoned salt

Melt butter; add garlic; cook over low heat 10 minutes (do not let butter brown). Remove garlic; add Worcestershire sauce. Combine cereals, pretzel sticks, and peanuts in large shallow baking pan; mix well. Pour butter evenly over this mixture. Toast at 250° for 30 minutes, stirring often. Remove from oven. Combine salts; sprinkle over mixture in pan, blending well. Cool.

Store in tightly covered containers. Makes about 4½ quarts.

ASPARAGUS ROLL-UPS

Trim thin slices of white bread. Roll as thin as possible with rolling pin. Spread with mayonnaise. Roll each slice around a cooked asparagus spear; cut to fit. Wrap and chill until ready to serve.

BEEFED-UP SNACKS

1 package (3 ounces) cream cheese
1 can (12 ounces) or leftover roast beef with gravy
1 egg, slightly beaten
1 can (4 ounces) mushroom stems and pieces, drained
2 tablespoons cracker crumbs
1 teaspoon Worcestershire sauce
1 package refrigerated crescent rolls
Garnish: stuffed olives, sliced

Soften cream cheese at room temperature. Flake chunks of roast beef; combine with gravy, softened cream cheese, egg, mushrooms, cracker crumbs, and Worcestershire sauce; mix well. Separate crescent roll dough into 2 segments; do not separate individual rolls in each segment. Roll out each segment to make a rectangle 5 x 13 inches; place on lightly greased baking sheet. Spread each rectangle with half the beef mixture, spreading almost but not quite to edges. Bake at 375° for 20 minutes or until edges of dough are browned and beef mixture is bubbling. Remove from oven; cool slightly. Cut each rectangle in half lengthwise, then cut each half into 6 pieces. Garnish with slices of stuffed olives. Serve hot. Makes 24.

BEEF BALLS

½ pound round steak, ground
1 egg
2 tablespoons flour
2 teaspoons finely chopped onion
¼ teaspoon Worcestershire sauce
Few drops hot-pepper sauce
Salt and pepper to taste
Packaged cracker crumbs
Fat for frying

Combine first 7 ingredients; mix well; form into small balls. Roll balls in cracker crumbs. Fry until brown in deep fat heated to 375°. Drain on absorbent paper. Serve hot on picks. Makes 20 to 24 depending on size of balls.

HAM BALLS

1 pound cooked ham, ground
¼ cup prepared mustard
Few drops hot-pepper sauce
1 teaspoon Worcestershire sauce
1 egg
½ cup fine dry packaged bread crumbs
½ teaspoon onion powder
Vegetable oil for frying

Combine first 7 ingredients; mix thoroughly. Shape into balls about ¾ inch in diameter. Heat vegetable oil, 2 inches deep, to 375°; fry balls until golden brown. Drain on absorbent paper. Serve with cocktail picks. Makes about 4 dozen.

LITTLE SMOKED BOWKNOTS

Roll pie pastry ⅛ inch thick; cut in strips 6 inches long and ½ inch wide. Tie each strip around a smoked cocktail sausage. Bake at 425° for 18 to 20 minutes or until pastry is golden brown.

MARINATED SHRIMP

1½ pounds shrimp
¾ cup vegetable oil
¼ cup wine vinegar
¼ teaspoon salt
½ teaspoon sugar
Few drops hot-pepper sauce
½ teaspoon Worcestershire sauce
1 small onion, grated

Cook shrimp; peel; devein; chill. Combine remaining ingredients; beat with rotary egg beater until well blended; pour over shrimp; chill several hours; drain shrimp before serving.

DEVILED EGGS

6 hard-cooked eggs
¼ teaspoon salt
Few grains pepper
2 tablespoons sour cream
1 tablespoon mayonnaise
1 teaspoon prepared mustard

Cut eggs in half lengthwise; remove yolks. Mash yolks; add remaining ingredients; whip until fluffy; refill whites with mixture. Makes 12 halves.

MINI QUICHES

Cream Cheese Pastry*
1 can (2¼ ounces) liverwurst spread
1 can (2¼ ounces) deviled ham
1 small onion, minced
1 teaspoon butter or margarine
¼ cup grated American or Swiss cheese, divided
1 egg, slightly beaten
¼ cup milk
Dash nutmeg
Few grains pepper

Line 24 small muffin cups (2-inch top diameter) with Cream Cheese Pastry. Put equal amount liverwurst spread in each of 12 pastry-lined cups. Put deviled ham in remaining 12 cups. Cook onion in butter until soft but not brown. Remove onion; combine with 2 tablespoons grated cheese; scatter over liverwurst and deviled ham spreads. Combine remaining cheese, egg, milk, nutmeg, and pepper; mix well. Spoon into cups. Bake at 450° for 10 minutes. Lower heat to 350°; bake 10 minutes longer or until custard is set. Makes 24.

*CREAM CHEESE PASTRY

1 cup butter or margarine
2 packages (3 ounces each) cream cheese
2 cups sifted all-purpose flour

Soften butter at room temperature. Add cream cheese; beat until smooth and creamy. Add flour, ½ cup at a time, blending well after each addition. Work with fingers to smooth dough. Wrap; chill thoroughly.

PICKLED MUSHROOMS

2 cans (6 ounces each) broiled mushroom crowns
½ cup tarragon vinegar
½ cup dark brown sugar
¼ teaspoon salt
½ teaspoon peppercorns
1 bay leaf
1 garlic clove, slivered

Drain mushrooms, saving broth. Combine ½ cup broth with remaining ingredients in small saucepan. Bring to boil, stirring until sugar dissolves. Pour over mushrooms. Cover tightly; chill for at least 24 hours. Drain. Serve with cocktail picks.

QUICHE LORRAINE

1 teaspoon butter
3 slices Canadian bacon, ¼ inch thick, diced
1 medium onion, finely chopped
9-inch unbaked pie shell
½ cup grated Swiss cheese, divided
4 eggs, slightly beaten
1 cup milk
1 cup whipping cream
Pinch nutmeg
½ teaspoon salt
¼ teaspoon pepper

In a small, heavy saucepan, heat butter. Add bacon; cook 5 minutes or until bacon is golden brown. Remove bacon; set aside. Add onion to pan; cook 5 minutes. Remove onion; set aside. Cover bottom of pie shell with bacon, onion, and ¼ cup grated cheese. Combine remaining cheese, eggs, milk, cream, nutmeg, salt, and pepper. Mix well. Pour over bacon mixture. Bake at 450° for 15 minutes. Reduce heat to 350°; continue baking 15 minutes longer or until custard is well set. Serve warm, cut in 1-inch wedges.

SALMON LOG

1 can (1 pound) salmon
1 large package (8 ounces) cream cheese, softened
1 tablespoon lemon juice
2 tablespoons grated onion
1 teaspoon prepared horseradish
¼ teaspoon salt
1 teaspoon liquid smoke seasoning
½ cup chopped walnuts
3 tablespoons snipped parsley

Drain and flake salmon, removing skin and bones. Combine salmon with next 6 ingredients; mix well. Chill several hours. Combine walnuts and parsley. Shape salmon mixture in an 8 x 2-inch log; roll log in nut mixture. Chill well. Serve with crisp crackers.

SEA SCALLOP SOUFFLÉ SNACKS

1 pound sea scallops (about 12)
¼ cup mayonnaise

2 tablespoons drained pickle relish
1 tablespoon minced parsley
1½ teaspoons lemon juice
⅛ teaspoon salt
¼ teaspoon Worcestershire sauce
Few grains pepper
1 egg white

Cook sea scallops in about 1 cup water in covered saucepan, keeping water below boiling point, until just tender (about 10 minutes). Drain; cool; cut in halves crosswise. Combine mayonnaise and remaining ingredients except egg white; mix well. Beat egg white stiff; fold into mayonnaise mixture. Place scallop halves on baking sheet or in shallow pan; top each with mayonnaise mixture. When ready to serve, run under broiler, with surface of food 3 inches below broiler heat. Broil about 3 minutes or until golden brown. Serve at once. Makes about 24.

SHRIMP BALLS

2 cans (about 5 ounces each) peeled, deveined shrimp, rinsed and drained
½ teaspoon onion powder
½ cup mayonnaise
¼ cup chopped stuffed olives
2 teaspoons prepared horseradish
Fine dry packaged bread crumbs
Fat for frying

Combine first 5 ingredients and ½ cup bread crumbs; mix well. Shape into balls about ¾ inch in diameter. Roll in additional bread crumbs. Heat fat, about 2 inches deep, to 375°; fry balls until golden brown. Drain on absorbent paper. Serve with cocktail picks. Makes about 4½ dozen.

STUFFED BACON ROLLS

Save some bread stuffing used for stuffing poultry. Roll up 1 tablespoon stuffing in a bacon strip. Continue until all stuffing is used. Secure with wooden picks. Broil until bacon is crisp, turning once.

SHRIMP TOAST

1 can (5 ounces) water chestnuts
1 cup (packed) minced raw shrimp
1 teaspoon powdered ginger
1 egg, slightly beaten
1 tablespoon cornstarch

1 tablespoon dry sherry
1 teaspoon salt
Few grains pepper
10 slices white bread
Vegetable oil for frying

Drain water chestnuts; mince; combine with shrimp and ginger. Stir in egg, cornstarch, sherry, salt, and pepper; mix well. Trim crust from bread slices. Spread shrimp mixture evenly on slices; cut each slice into 4 squares or 4 triangles. Heat vegetable oil, 2 inches deep, to 375°. Place bread squares or triangles on slotted spoon, shrimp side down; lower into oil. Fry a few pieces at a time until bread is golden (about 1½ minutes); turn and fry a few seconds longer. Drain on paper towels. Serve hot. Makes 40 pieces of shrimp toast.

APPLE SALAD APPETIZER

2 red apples
2 small yellow onions
1 cup diced celery
½ cup mayonnaise
¼ cup chili sauce

Quarter and core apples (do not pare); slice thin; cut each slice in half. Slice onions; separate into rings. Combine apples, onion rings, and celery. Combine mayonnaise and chili sauce; add to apple mixture; mix well. Makes 12 small servings.

GRAPEFRUIT SPECIAL

3 grapefruit
6 teaspoons sherry
6 teaspoons sugar
6 teaspoons butter or margarine

Cut grapefruit in halves, crosswise. Sprinkle each half with 1 teaspoon sherry and 1 teaspoon sugar. Dot each with 1 teaspoon butter. Place grapefruit on broiler rack; broil 15 to 20 minutes or until fruit browns delicately and is heated through. Or, if preferred, heat grapefruit in a moderately hot oven the same length of time. Serve hot as a first course. Makes 6 servings.

CHAMPAGNE FRUIT CUP

1 can or jar (11 ounces) mandarin orange
   sections, chilled
1 can (1 pound) Queen Anne cherries, pitted
   and chilled
1 cup diced unpeeled red apple
1 cup halved, seeded Tokay grapes
1 bottle pink champagne, chilled

Drain mandarin orange sections and cherries; combine with diced apple and grapes. Spoon into saucer champagne glasses. Just before serving, fill glasses with champagne. Makes 8 to 10 servings.

PROSCIUTTO-APPLE APPETIZER

Roll up tissue-thin slices of Italian prosciutto ham and serve with apple slices and white grapes for a different and delicious first course.

FRUIT GINGER SPARKLE

3 eating apples
6 tangerines
6 maraschino cherries
Chilled ginger ale

Core and dice apples. Combine with tangerine sections in sherbet glasses. Top with maraschino cherries. Fill glasses with ice-cold ginger ale. Serve as a first course. Makes 6 servings.

CHAPTER 2

Beverages

THE AIR is hot and still and humid. Suddenly there is the tinkling sound of ice in tall glasses filled to the brim with a refreshing cold drink. An oasis appears in a desert land—whether it be porch, patio, or shady lawn—once a tray is set down and eager hands reach for frosty glasses!

Or, on a cold winter evening, when the chill penetrates the warmest clothing, contentment and comfort come into the room with a tray of some favorite hot beverage.

It once was quite a chore to make good cocoa or hot chocolate. Now with instant products, already containing milk and sugar, and a kettle of boiling water, mugs of delicious frothy hot chocolate can be made in a matter of seconds. A treat no one can refuse!

Two beverages, served either hot or cold, are favorites, even necessities, in every household—coffee and tea. All too often they are not all that they could be if they were properly prepared. The rules are simple, and if they are followed, perfect tea or coffee, hot or iced, can be the joy of your home.

POINTERS FOR PERFECT COFFEE

Pick the grind that is right for your type of coffee maker. For a percolator, use regular grind; for a drip pot, drip grind; for a vacuum-style coffee maker, drip or fine grind. The grind is important because coffee must be fine enough for the water to circulate freely to extract the coffee's flavor. If coffee is too coarse, it permits water to pass through too quickly, resulting in underextraction. Good coffee is a clear, rich brown.

Whether you like a rich or a mild blend of coffee, it must be made full strength. Coffee cannot be "stretched." For each serving of coffee, you need 1 approved coffee measure (or 2 level measuring tablespoons of coffee) and ¾ of a measuring cup (6 fluid ounces) of water. Amounts of ground coffee and water needed to make a given number of servings of coffee are shown in the table below. Proportions apply to all brewing methods, all coffee makers, automatic or not.

Use fresh coffee. It will keep fresh for about a week when container is kept tightly closed in a cool, dry place—such as the refrigerator. Try to purchase coffee in amounts that can be used within a week after opening. Water, too, should be fresh. Freshly drawn cold water is preferred for making coffee because hot-water pipes have mineral deposits that affect coffee's flavor.

When You Brew Coffee: Start with a clean coffee maker and never brew less than three-fourths of the coffee maker's capacity. For lesser quantities, use a smaller coffeepot. If your coffee maker isn't automatic, timing is important. When using a percolator on the range, usual gentle perking time for best results is from 6 to 8 minutes.

When You Serve Coffee: Try to serve it freshly brewed and piping hot. If coffee must stand before serving, hold it at serving temperature by placing the pot (nonautomatic) in a pan of hot water or over very low heat. Here's an important point: Never boil coffee after it has brewed. Boiling ruins coffee's flavor.

When You Clean Your Coffee Maker: A clean coffee maker is essential to good coffee. After each use, wash all parts in hot water using a light-duty detergent. Rinse thoroughly with clear water. Before using the pot again, scald with boiling water. From time to time, disassemble all parts and scrub each thoroughly, using a thin brush to clean hard-to-reach places. Occasionally, you may want to use one of the coffee-maker cleansers.

BASIC COFFEE-TO-WATER MEASURE

Number of 5½-Ounce Servings	Approved Coffee Measures*	Tablespoon Measure (Level)	Measuring Cups of Water+	Fluid Ounces of Water
2	2	4	1½	12
4	4	8	3	24
6	6	12	4½	36
8	8	16	6	48

FOR LARGE QUANTITIES OF COFFEE

20	½ pound coffee	1 gallon water
40	1 pound coffee	2 gallons water

For Demitasse Service: Brew coffee by any of the three basic methods, but make it half again as strong as regular coffee. For three 4-ounce servings, you would use 3 approved coffee measures of coffee to 1½ measuring cups of water.

Percolator Method: Measure fresh cold water into percolator. Place on heat until water boils. Remove from heat. Measure regular-grind coffee into basket. Insert basket into percolator, cover, return to gentle heat, percolate slowly 6 to 8 minutes. (Note: Water level should always be below the bottom of coffee basket.) Remove coffee basket before serving.

*Equal 2 level measuring tablespoons of coffee.
+Three-fourths of a measuring cup (6 fluid ounces) of water yields about 5½ ounces of coffee, an average serving.

Drip Method: Preheat pot by rinsing with very hot water. Measure drip-grind coffee into filter section. Place upper container over filter section. Measure fresh boiling water into upper container. Cover. When dripping is completed, remove upper section. Stir brew vigorously before pouring or brew will be uneven in strength.

Vacuum Method: Measure fresh cold water into lower bowl. Place on heat. Place filter in upper bowl. Add drip or fine grind coffee. When water boils, reduce heat or turn off electricity. Insert upper bowl with slight twist. Let most of water rise into upper bowl. Stir water and coffee thoroughly. In 1 to 3 minutes, remove from heat. When brew returns to lower bowl, remove upper bowl and serve.

HOW TO MAKE PERFECT ICED COFFEE

One of the most attractive and timesaving methods of making iced coffee calls for coffee ice cubes. At breakfast, brew a few extra cups of coffee and freeze them into coffee ice cubes in the refrigerator tray. Then it is a simple matter to pour regular-strength hot coffee over the cubes at any time. For each serving of regular-strength coffee, you will need ¾ measuring cup of water and 1 standard measure (or 2 level measuring tablespoons) of coffee.

When you are in a hurry, excellent iced coffee can be made by using extra-strength coffee and regular ice cubes. Make coffee extra strength by using ½ measuring cup of water to each standard measure of coffee. Pour the hot coffee over lots of ice cubes in tall glasses. The extra-strong coffee allows for the dilution caused by the melting ice.

Instant coffee also may be used to make delicious iced coffee. Simply mix twice the usual amount of instant coffee with a little water (hot or cold, according to brand) in each glass. Add ice cubes and more water. Stir thoroughly.

RULES FOR MAKING PERFECT TEA

Follow these simple rules for perfect results:
1. Preheat teapot by rinsing it out with hot water.
2. Use 1 tea bag or teaspoon of tea for each cup.
3. Bring freshly drawn cold water to a full rolling boil and pour over the tea.
4. Brew by the clock—3 to 5 minutes.

To Serve a Large Crowd: Make a hot tea concentrate. Bring 1½ quarts of cold fresh water to a full rolling boil. Remove from heat and immediately add ¼ pound loose tea. Stir to immerse leaves. Cover. Let stand 5 minutes. Strain into teapot until ready to use. (This makes enough concentrate for 40 to 45 cups; double recipe for 85 to 90 cups of tea.) When ready to serve, bring out a potful of piping-hot water. Pour about 2 tablespoons of concentrate into a cup and fill cup with water.

HOW TO MAKE PERFECT ICED TEA

Follow the rules for hot tea but use half again as much tea to allow for melting ice, i.e., use 6 tea bags for 4 glasses of iced tea.

To Make Iced Tea by the Pitcherful: Use this easy open saucepan method. Bring 1 quart of freshly drawn cold water to a full rolling boil in a saucepan. Remove from the heat and immediately add ⅓ cup loose tea or 15 tea bags. Brew 5 minutes, uncovered. Stir and strain into a pitcher holding another quart of freshly drawn water. Do not refrigerate. Pour over ice cubes when ready to serve. Makes 2 quarts of tea.

Never refrigerate iced tea; it may become cloudy. If this happens, a dash of boiling water will restore clarity.

PARADE SKI-BALL

4 level tablespoons black tea
1 level tablespoon whole cloves
1 level tablespoon allspice berries
8 cups briskly boiling water
8 cinnamon sticks
Sugar
8 lemon slices

Measure tea into teapot; add cloves and allspice berries. Pour in boiling water. Steep 5 minutes. Strain into mugs holding cinnamon-stick "muddlers." Use sugar and lemon to taste. Makes 8 generous servings.

LAMB'S WOOL

In certain localities in England a hot drink called lamb's wool is always served on Twelfth Night. The English use ale with apples in this beverage, but cider is an excellent alternative. Presumably the name derives from the rather thick, fluffy consistency of the beverage.

8 large baking apples
2 quarts apple cider
1 cup firmly packed brown sugar

½ teaspoon nutmeg
1 teaspoon powdered ginger
2 tablespoons mixed pickling spices
Garnish: 1 red apple; whole cloves

Wrap each apple securely in a double thickness of heavy-duty aluminum foil (do not pare or core). Place in baking pan. Roast at 450° until very soft, about 1½ hours. Put through food mill or sieve (there should be 5 to 6 cups of pulp). Meanwhile, combine cider, brown sugar, and spices in kettle. Stir over low heat until sugar dissolves; bring to boil. Lower heat; simmer for 30 minutes; strain; add to apple pulp; mix well. Garnish with a red apple studded with whole cloves. Serve hot, in sturdy mugs. Makes about 3½ quarts.

HOT SPICED CITRUS PUNCH

1 cup sugar
2 cups water
1 teaspoon whole cloves
1 3-inch piece stick cinnamon
4 cups strong tea
2 cans (6 ounces each) frozen orange juice concentrate, reconstituted
1 can (6 ounces) frozen grapefruit juice concentrate, reconstituted
Garnish: orange slices; whole cloves

Combine sugar, water, cloves, and cinnamon in saucepan; simmer 10 minutes; strain. Add to combined tea and fruit juices. Reheat; serve hot. Stud orange slices with additional cloves; float on top of punch. Makes 15 cups.

FRISKY SOURS

1 can (10½ ounces) condensed beef broth
¼ soup can water
4 ice cubes
2 to 3 tablespoons lemon juice

Put all ingredients into a shaker or a jar with tight-fitting cover. Cover and shake well. Serve in chilled glasses. Makes 3 to 4 servings.

CONCORD APPLEADE

1 quart apple juice or cider
2 cups grape juice
¼ cup lime juice

Combine all ingredients. Pour over ice in 6 tall glasses.

APPLE SPARKLE

For each serving, squeeze juice from ½ lime over ice in tall glass. Fill glass with equal amounts apple juice and club soda. Stir gently to mix.

LIME-GINGER COOLER

1 can (6 ounces) frozen limeade concentrate
2 bottles (7 ounces each) ginger ale, chilled
1 cup ice-cold water
Green food coloring (optional)
Crushed ice
Garnish: sprigs of mint

Reconstitute limeade with ginger ale and water. If desired, tint pale green with few drops green food coloring. Half fill 6 tall glasses with crushed ice; pour in limeade mixture. Garnish with mint sprigs. Makes 6 servings.

FRUIT SPARKLE

Lemonade ice cubes
1 cup mint jelly
2 cups water, divided
3 cups unsweetened pineapple juice
½ cup lemon juice
1 bottle (28 ounces) dry ginger ale, chilled
Garnish: lemon slices; sprigs of mint

To make lemonade ice cubes, dilute frozen lemonade concentrate as directed on cans; pour into ice cube trays; freeze firm. Combine mint jelly and 1 cup water in saucepan. Stir over low heat until jelly is melted. Cool. Add pineapple juice, remaining 1 cup water, and lemon juice. Chill thoroughly. Place lemonade ice cubes in tall glasses; fill half full with fruit mixture. Fill to top with ginger ale. Garnish with lemon slices and sprigs of fresh mint. Makes about 10 servings.

1-2-3 FRUITADE

1 can (46 ounces) red fruit punch, chilled
3 cups cold tea*
1 can (6 ounces) frozen lemonade concentrate
Garnish: lemon slices

In a large pitcher or small punch bowl combine all ingredients; stir. Pour into 9 to 10 ice-filled glasses. Garnish with lemon slices.

*Pour 3 cups boiling water over 4 tea bags; steep about 5 minutes. Remove bags; cover tea; cool.

DIETER'S SPECIAL

1 cup strong coffee
Sugar substitute of choice
1 teaspoon vanilla
Club soda

Sweeten coffee to taste with preferred sugar substitute. Stir in vanilla. Divide equally among 4 tall glasses. Add ice cubes. Fill glasses with club soda. Stir gently to mix. Makes 4 servings.

WHITE WINE COOLER

2 limes, grated peel and juice
½ cup sugar
1 cup sliced strawberries
White wine, chilled

Combine grated peel and juice of 2 limes. Add sugar and strawberries. Set over low heat, stirring until sugar is dissolved. Purée in electric blender. Fill 6 medium-sized glasses with ice cubes. Pour equal amount hot berry mixture into each glass. Fill glasses with chilled wine. Stir gently to mix. Makes 6 servings.

GINGER TEA PUNCH

4 cups strong hot tea
1 cup light corn syrup
3 cups orange juice
¾ cup lime juice
Red food coloring
2 quart-size bottles ginger ale

Combine hot tea and corn syrup. Stir until syrup dissolves. Chill. Add juices; mix well. Add a few drops red food coloring and mix thoroughly. Pour over ice in punch bowl; just before serving add ginger ale. Makes 25 punch cup servings.

SUMMER SUNSET SODA

2 cups red raspberries
Sugar or sugar substitute
½ cup heavy cream
4 large scoops orange sherbet
Club soda

Put raspberries through sieve to remove seeds. Sweeten pulp to taste with sugar or sugar substitute; place equal amount of sweetened pulp in each of 4 tall glasses. Add 2 tablespoons heavy cream and 1 generous scoop orange sherbet to each glass. Fill glasses with club soda; stir gently to mix. Makes 4 servings.

CHERRY COOL

1 package cherry sugar-sweetened soft drink
  mix
1 teaspoon almond extract
½ pint (1 cup) cherry ice cream

Prepare drink mix as directed on envelope. Stir in almond extract. Pour 2 cups into blender; add ice cream. Blend until thick and foamy. Makes 2 to 3 servings depending on size of glass. Repeat to make desired number of servings.

PITCHER COOLER

1 pint strong cold tea
¼ cup lemon juice
½ cup orange juice
¼ cup sugar
1 pint cranberry juice cocktail
2 cups water
Chilled ginger ale

Combine all ingredients except ginger ale in a large pitcher. Chill. Pour over ice in tall glasses, filling ⅔ full. Fill glasses to top with ginger ale. Stir gently to mix. Makes 10 servings.

STRAWBERRY SHAKE

1 can (6 ounces) frozen orange juice
  concentrate
1 cup chilled evaporated milk
2 ripe bananas, cut up
½ cup crushed fresh strawberries
Garnish: 6 whole strawberries

Reconstitute orange juice according to label directions. Put juice in electric blender or small bowl of electric mixer with remaining ingredients except whole strawberries. Blend or beat until light and frothy. Pour into 6 tall glasses. Garnish each with whole strawberry. Makes 6 servings.

TROPICAL EGGNOG

2 eggs, separated
2 tablespoons molasses
2 cups milk
Garnish: nutmeg

Beat together egg yolks and molasses; gradually stir in milk. Beat egg whites until stiff but not dry; fold half the beaten egg whites into molasses mixture. Pour into two 10-ounce glasses. Top each serving with remaining egg white. Sprinkle with nutmeg. Makes 2 servings.

HAWAIIAN TWIST

Ice cubes containing lemon, lime, and orange
  peel twists
1 can (46 ounces) red fruit punch, chilled
1 can (6 ounces) frozen lemonade concentrate
1 quart club soda, chilled

Freeze ice cubes containing lemon, lime, and orange peel twists. Pour fruit punch into a bowl. Add lemonade concentrate; mix well. Just before serving, add club soda. Pour punch over the citrus cubes in tall glasses. Makes about twelve 8-ounce servings.

STRAWBERRY FLIP

¼ cup quick strawberry-flavor beverage mix
1 tablespoon lemon juice
⅓ cup cold water
2 scoops lemon sherbet
Club soda

Combine in a 16-ounce glass the strawberry-flavor beverage mix, lemon juice, and cold water. Stir briskly until blended. Add lemon sherbet; fill slowly with chilled club soda. Makes 1 serving.

FROSTY PINK FIZZ

For each serving, place 1 scoop of lemon sherbet and 1 scoop of raspberry sherbet in each tall glass. Fill glass with carbonated lemon-lime beverage.

DELUXE STRAWBERRY SODA

⅓ cup quick strawberry-flavor beverage mix
½ cup milk
2 scoops vanilla ice cream
Club soda
Garnish: whipped cream; 1 whole strawberry

Combine in a 20-ounce glass the strawberry-flavor beverage mix and milk. Stir briskly until blended. Add vanilla ice cream; fill slowly with chilled club soda. Garnish with whipped cream and a strawberry. Makes 1 serving.

CHOCOLATE-ORANGE SODA

For each serving, fill each glass about half full of chocolate milk. Add a scoop of orange sherbet. Fill glass with chilled club soda. Stir gently to mix.

SPICY CHOCOLATE FLOAT

¼ cup quick chocolate-flavor beverage mix
1 cup milk
¼ teaspoon cinnamon
1 large scoop vanilla ice cream

Combine in a 12-ounce glass the chocolate-flavor beverage mix, milk, and cinnamon. Stir briskly until thoroughly blended. Top with a generous scoop of vanilla ice cream. Makes 1 serving.

QUICK SODAS

1 tablespoon instant cocoa
1 tablespoon milk
1 scoop (¼ pint) vanilla or chocolate ice cream
Ginger ale *or* cola

Combine cocoa and milk in a tall glass. Add ice cream. Fill to top with ginger ale or cola. Makes 1 serving.

COLA FROSTED

1 tablespoon instant cocoa
1 tablespoon instant coffee
1 pint partially melted vanilla or chocolate ice cream
2 bottles (12 ounces each) chilled cola beverage
Garnish: instant coffee

Mix together cocoa and 1 tablespoon instant coffee in electric blender or small bowl of electric mixer. Add ice cream and cola beverage. Blend or beat until thick and frothy. Pour into 6 tall glasses. Sprinkle each with additional instant coffee. Makes 6 servings.

BLACK-AND-ORANGE SODAS

1 can (6 ounces) frozen orange juice concentrate, thawed
1½ cups quick chocolate-flavor beverage mix
1 quart ice cream (vanilla, chocolate, or orange ice)
1 quart chilled club soda

Combine orange juice concentrate and quick chocolate-flavor beverage mix; stir until smooth. Divide among 8 soda glasses. Add a scoop of ice cream to each glass. Add club soda slowly. Makes 8 servings.

BROADWAY SODA

8 tablespoons chocolate syrup
Cream
Coffee ice cream
Club soda

Put 2 tablespoons chocolate syrup in each of 4 tall glasses. Add approximately the same amount of cream, according to taste, and a generous scoop of ice cream. Fill glasses with ice-cold club soda. Stir gently to mix. Makes 4 servings.

ORANGE CRUSH

1 can (6 ounces) frozen orange juice concentrate
½ pint orange sherbet
1 bottle (7 ounces) ginger ale, chilled
1 cup shaved ice
Garnish: sprigs of mint

Reconstitute orange juice according to label directions. Put juice in electric blender or shaker. Add sherbet, ginger ale, and shaved ice. Blend or shake until thick and frothy. Pour into 6 tall glasses. Garnish with mint. Makes 6 servings.

VIENNESE VELVET

1 quart vanilla ice cream
6 cups hot double-strength coffee

Place 1 large scoop vanilla ice cream in each of 6 tall glasses. Pour coffee carefully over ice cream until glass is about ⅔ full. Add a second scoop of ice cream and fill glass with coffee. Makes 6 servings.

STRAWBERRY SMASH

⅓ cup quick strawberry-flavor beverage mix
¼ cup applesauce
Vanilla ice cream
Club soda

Blend strawberry-flavor beverage mix and applesauce. Alternate layers of vanilla ice cream and strawberry mixture in a 20-ounce glass until ¾ full. Fill with chilled club soda; stir gently. Serve with a spoon. Makes 1 serving.

SYLLABUB

Syllabub came to us from England, the recipe imported by early colonists who settled in the South. The name came from Sillery, in the wine region of France, added to "bub," Elizabethan slang for a bubbly drink.

Peel of 2 lemons
1 cup sweet white wine
1 cup Madeira wine
1 quart whipping cream
⅓ cup lemon juice
Sugar to taste
Nutmeg

Soak lemon peel in the combined wines for several hours. Discard peel. Whip cream until it barely holds its shape. Gradually whisk in the wines, lemon juice, sugar, and a dash of nutmeg until frothy. Spoon into small glasses and serve with spoons. Whisk occasionally to keep frothy. Makes 12 servings.

HALLOWEEN PUNCH

Orange and black are the colors associated with Halloween. So with this orange-colored punch serve packaged or homemade dark chocolate cookies and have some ready for the trick or treaters who ring your doorbell.

1 quart cold tea
1 quart orange juice
1 can (46 ounces) red fruit punch
Garnish: lemon slices

Combine first 3 ingredients. Pour over ice in punch bowl. Garnish with lemon slices. Makes 36 punch cup servings.

OPEN-HOUSE PUNCH

6 pieces loaf sugar
Aromatic bitters
1 bottle Burgundy
2 cups canned cranberry juice cocktail
1 cup pineapple juice
½ cup orange juice
Juice of 3 limes
2 quarts club soda
Garnish: orange slices; maraschino cherries

Dip sugar in bitters; place in large bowl; add next 5 ingredients in order given. Chill thoroughly. Pour over ice in punch bowl; add club soda. Garnish with orange slices and maraschino cherries. Makes 35 to 40 punch cup servings.

HALLOWEEN CHOCOLATE PUNCH

2½ quarts milk
2 cups quick chocolate-flavor beverage mix
1½ teaspoons cinnamon
12 marshmallow "ghosties"*

Heat milk in 4-quart saucepan. Add quick chocolate-flavor beverage mix and cinnamon. Stir briskly or beat with rotary beater until blended. Float marshmallow "ghosties" in hot punch. Serve in mugs. Makes 12 servings.

HOLIDAY PUNCH I

1 quart Cranberry Sherbet*
1 bottle sauterne

Combine ingredients in small punch bowl; stir until sherbet is melted. Serve at once. Makes 18 punch cup servings.

*CRANBERRY SHERBET

2 cups sugar
2 cups water
4 cups fresh cranberries
Juice and grated peel of 1 orange
Juice and grated peel of 1 lemon

Combine sugar, water, and cranberries in saucepan; cook until cranberries are soft and mushy (about 15 minutes). Cool. Put through sieve or food mill. Add fruit juices and grated peels. Pour into freezing trays. Freeze firm. Makes 1 quart.

HOLIDAY PUNCH II

2 cans (1 pound each) jellied cranberry sauce
1 cup lemon juice
1 tablespoon almond extract
1 bottle white wine
1 quart dry ginger ale

Blend cranberry sauce, lemon juice, and almond extract with electric blender or rotary egg beater. Add wine. Pour over ice in punch bowl. Just be-

*For marshmallow "ghosties," use whole cloves to make faces on marshmallows.

fore serving add ginger ale. Makes about 30 punch cup servings.

HOLIDAY PUNCH III

1 bottle Concord grape wine
3 cups chilled canned pineapple juice
2 cups orange juice
½ cup lemon juice
1 quart-size bottle pale dry ginger ale

Combine wine and fruit juices. Pour over ice in punch bowl. Just before serving add ginger ale. Makes about 35 punch cup servings.

EGGNOG SAUTERNE

1 bottle sauterne, chilled
1 can (6 ounces) frozen concentrated apple-flavor red fruit punch, thawed
4 eggs, well beaten
2 cups (1 pint) whipping cream, chilled
1 teaspoon ground nutmeg

Combine sauterne and fruit punch concentrate. Beat eggs with cream and nutmeg; stir into wine mixture. Chill until ready to serve. Serve in small punch cups. Makes about 16 half-cup servings.

CREAM SHERRY EGGNOG

4 eggs, separated
1 cup sugar, divided
2 quarts milk
1 bottle cream sherry (oloroso type)
Garnish: nutmeg

Beat egg yolks until thick and lemon-colored. Beat in ¾ cup sugar slowly. Continue beating until sugar is dissolved. Add milk and sherry; chill. Beat egg whites until stiff; beat in remaining sugar. Spoon into punch bowl. Pour sherry mixture into punch bowl; sprinkle with nutmeg. Makes about 24 punch cup servings.

GOLDEN EGGNOG

8 eggs, separated
⅔ cup sugar
4 cups chilled apricot nectar
3 cups chilled muscatel
1 pint soft ice cream
Garnish: nutmeg

Beat egg whites until stiff. Gradually beat in sugar. Beat yolks well; fold into egg white mix-

ture. Stir in apricot nectar, muscatel, and ice cream; pour into chilled bowl. Sprinkle with nutmeg. Makes about 4 quarts.

WATCH NIGHT PUNCH

On Watch Night (New Year's Eve), open house is a pleasant custom. Friends drop in on their way to parties or dances, others drop in and stay! A big punch bowl filled with colorful, refreshing punch and thin slices of fruitcake are good refreshment companions, and you may wish to add bowls of salted nuts and mints.

1 jar (10 ounces) preserved kumquats
1 cup sugar
⅛ teaspoon powdered ginger
1 cup boiling water
Juice of 6 lemons, strained
2 cups cranberry juice cocktail, chilled
1 quart apple cider, chilled
1 bottle rosé wine, chilled
Kumquat Ice Cubes*
1 quart-size bottle club soda, chilled

Drain kumquats; save syrup. Combine sugar and ginger; add boiling water; bring to boil; stir until sugar dissolves. Cool. Add strained lemon juice and kumquat syrup. In punch bowl combine sugar-lemon mixture, cranberry juice, cider, and wine. Just before serving add Kumquat Ice Cubes and club soda. Makes 35 to 40 punch cup servings.

*KUMQUAT ICE CUBES

Cut kumquats in halves. Fill ice cube tray sections half full with water; freeze. Place ½ kumquat in each section; fill to top with ice water; freeze.

MULLED HOLIDAY PUNCH

6 cans (12 ounces each) apricot nectar
⅔ cup sugar
2 teaspoons whole cloves
2 teaspoons whole allspice
2 3-inch sticks cinnamon
Coarsely grated peel of 1 lemon
1 large bottle (⅘ quart) Chablis or sauterne
1 cup muscatel

Combine nectar, sugar, spices, and lemon peel; simmer 15 minutes. Strain. Add wines; heat thoroughly but do not boil. Serve hot. Makes about 3½ quarts.

PARTY PUNCH

2 cups orange juice
½ cup lemon juice
2 pints cranberry juice cocktail
2 cups pineapple juice
4 large bottles sparkling lemon-lime beverage

Combine first 4 ingredients; mix well. Pour over ice in large bowl. Fill bowl with lemon-lime beverage. Makes about 50 punch cup servings.

TWELFTH NIGHT PUNCH

3 cups strong tea
2 cups apple cider
2 cups grapefruit juice
1 cup lime juice
1 cup orange juice
1 cup pineapple juice
3 cups Sugar Syrup*
2 quarts dry ginger ale
Fruited Ice Ring† (optional)

Combine tea, cider, fruit juices, and Sugar Syrup; chill. Pour into large punch bowl. Add ginger ale. Add Fruited Ice Ring, if desired. Makes about 50 punch cup servings.

*SUGAR SYRUP

Combine 2 cups each sugar and water; stir over low heat until sugar dissolves; bring to boil; boil 5 minutes. Cool.

†FRUITED ICE RING

Arrange red and green maraschino cherries in bottom of 8-inch ring mold. Add just enough water to cover bottom of mold; freeze firm. Fill mold with crushed ice, then gently pour in cold water until it reaches the top. Freeze firm. To remove wreath let stand at room temperature a few minutes, or run lukewarm water over bottom of mold.

WASSAIL BOWL

In Herefordshire, Devonshire, and Cornwall the old custom of "wassailing" the apple orchards on Christmas Eve still persists. Farmers walk in procession to a chosen tree in each orchard, an incantation is spoken, and a bowl of cider is dashed against the trunk of the tree. Supposedly this insures a fruitful harvest.

It is also customary in many places in England to serve a wassail bowl on Twelfth Night.

1 can (16 ounces) pineapple juice
4 cups cranberry juice cocktail
4 cups sweet cider
2 cups strong tea
1 quart ginger ale

Combine pineapple juice, cranberry juice, cider, and tea. Just before serving pour mixture over ice in punch bowl and add ginger ale. Makes 35 punch cup servings.

FESTIVAL FRUIT PUNCH

¼ cup sugar
1 cup water
2 pints fresh strawberries, halved
2 tablespoons whole allspice in cheesecloth bag
1 can (6 ounces) frozen lemonade concentrate, thawed
1 can (6 ounces) frozen limeade concentrate, thawed
1 can (6 ounces) frozen orange juice concentrate, thawed
¼ cup lemon juice
3 cups cold water
1 quart ginger ale, chilled
Strawberry Wreath Ice Ring* (optional)

Pour sugar and 1 cup water over strawberries in a bowl. Add allspice tied in cheesecloth bag. Let stand in refrigerator overnight. Just before serving remove allspice and put strawberries with liquid through fine sieve, food mill, or electric blender. Mix in punch bowl with lemonade, limeade, and orange juice concentrates, lemon juice, 3 cups water, and ginger ale. Add Strawberry Wreath Ice Ring, if desired. Makes 24 punch cup (4 ounce) servings.

*STRAWBERRY WREATH ICE RING

Wash enough strawberries (do not hull) to make a wreath in bottom of 8-inch ring mold. Pour in just enough water to anchor berries; freeze firm. Carefully fill mold with ice water. (This can be done in installments, if preferred, freezing firm after each addition. In this way the wreath is less likely to be disturbed.) Freeze firm. To unmold, dip in warm water.

WITCH'S BREW (HALLOWEEN)

1 cup sugar
1 teaspoon cinnamon
1 teaspoon allspice
1 teaspoon nutmeg
2 quarts cider, divided
2 cans (6 ounces each) frozen orange juice concentrate
1 quart ginger ale, chilled
Garnish: orange slices; whole cloves

Mix sugar, cinnamon, allspice, and nutmeg in saucepan; add 1 cup cider and heat until sugar dissolves. Add remaining cider and orange juice concentrate; chill. Just before serving stir in ginger ale. Garnish with orange slices decorated with whole cloves to make pumpkin faces. Makes about 14 cups (20 to 24 punch cup servings).

HOLLY PUNCH BOWL

4 cups cranberry juice cocktail
½ cup firmly packed brown sugar
4 cups grapefruit juice
2 large bottles carbonated lemon-lime beverage
Garnish: sprigs of holly (optional)

Heat cranberry juice. Dissolve brown sugar in hot juice; add grapefruit juice; mix well; chill. Pour over ice in punch bowl. Add ice-cold lemon-lime beverage. Stir gently to mix. Surround punch bowl with sprigs of holly, if desired, for a festive touch. Makes about 30 punch cup servings.

FLAVOR FILLIPS

- Try lime instead of lemon with iced tea.
- Add a handful of fresh mint sprigs to the tea in the teapot. Add boiling water and brew 3 to 5 minutes.
- Try a few drops of brandy flavoring in a tall glass of iced coffee—or add aromatic bitters to taste.

ICED TEA GARNISHES

Orange Aids: Cut wedge from unpeeled orange. With cocktail pick, pin watercress sprig and kumquat to peel. Slit peel from point to pick and slip over rim of glass, peel side out.

High Moon: Cut small wedge from unpeeled cantaloupe. Fasten watermelon ball to inside of wedge with cocktail pick. Slit cantaloupe from point to pick. Slip over rim of glass, peel side in. Add mint sprig.

Berry Sentry: Press large strawberry, point down, over rim of glass; tuck mint sprig into glass.

Lemon-Tea Cubes: Thaw 2 cans (6 ounces each) lemonade concentrate; pour into mixing bowl. Bring 1½ quarts water to a full rolling boil. Remove from heat; immediately add ⅓ cup loose tea or 15 tea bags. Brew for about 4 minutes. Stir; strain into lemonade concentrate. Pour into ice cube trays; freeze.

CHAPTER 3

Soups

"SOME LIKE it hot, some like it cold"—but soups can be delicious either way.

No need to tell you that the shelves of your supermarket offer an infinite variety of soups— condensed, ready-to-serve, frozen, dehydrated. There is never any reason to skip the soup with the excuse that you can't think of what to serve. A walk through the soup section will give you a dozen ideas in as many seconds.

Prepared soups can cut down on time and effort and add a blend of delightful flavors when you make a kettle of "homemade" soup. Many of the following recipes use prepared soups in this way. And there are some recipes that start from scratch and end up as a kind of soup not yet available at the supermarket.

So begin with any recipe that appeals to you, and go on from there until you've tried them all!

A QUARTET OF COLD SOUPS FOR SUMMER

Chilled Tomato Soup: Top with whipped cream enlivened with a dash of chili powder; or thin, scored slices of unpared cucumber; or a blend of dairy sour cream, grated horseradish, and chopped parsley.

Chilled Green Pea Soup: Top with thin slices of cooked frankfurter; or a generous sprinkling of crumbled crisp bacon; or dairy sour cream blended with minced pickled beets.

Chilled Asparagus Soup: Top with cheese croutons (bread cubes sprinkled with grated cheese and toasted); or dainty square cheese crackers; or chopped egg and diced pimiento.

Cream of Spinach Soup: Top with a blend of whipped cream and curry powder; or slivers of canned spiced ham or bologna; or thin wedges of unpared red apple.

AVOCADO SOUP

2 cans (11½ ounces each) condensed green pea soup, chilled
2 tablespoons dry sherry
1 large avocado, peeled, stoned, and diced
2 tablespoons lemon juice
2 soup cans milk
Garnish: avocado slices; lemon slices

Combine first 5 ingredients in blender. Blend about 2 minutes. Serve cold, garnished with slices of avocado and lemon. Makes 8 to 10 servings.

CHILLED CUCUMBER SOUP

1 medium cucumber, peeled
1¼ cups water
1 can (10¾ ounces) condensed cream of
    chicken soup
Garnish: cut chives, fresh or freeze-dried

Dice cucumber; cook in water until tender (about 10 minutes). Do not drain. Blend in soup. Chill. Garnish with cut chives. Makes 3 to 4 servings.

CHILLED GARDEN SOUP

1 medium potato
1 medium onion
1 cucumber
1 large stalk celery with leaves
1 tart apple
1 teaspoon salt
1 pint chicken broth or bouillon
1 cup light cream
1 tablespoon butter or margarine, melted
1 teaspoon curry powder
Few grains pepper
Garnish: cut chives, fresh or freeze-dried

Peel and chop potato, onion, cucumber, celery, and apple. Add salt to chicken broth or bouillon; add the chopped vegetables and apple. Simmer until vegetables are tender. Put through food mill or fine sieve, or blend in electric blender, until smooth. Stir in cream, butter, curry powder, and pepper. Chill thoroughly. Sprinkle with chives. Makes 6 servings.

CHICKEN-BROCCOLI SOUP

1 package (10 ounces) frozen chopped
    broccoli
Vegetable water and milk to make 1 cup
½ teaspoon salt
⅛ teaspoon pepper
¼ teaspoon dry mustard
1 can (10¾ ounces) condensed cream of
    chicken soup
1 cup whipping cream, chilled

Cook broccoli according to package directions until tender-crisp. Drain vegetable water into 1-cup measure; add milk to make 1 cup. Place broccoli, milk mixture, salt, pepper, and dry

mustard in electric blender. Cover; blend about 30 seconds. Add chicken soup; chill thoroughly. When ready to serve add chilled cream; mix well. Makes 4 servings.

CHILLED RIPE OLIVE SOUP

¼ cup butter or margarine
¼ cup flour
1 envelope chicken broth mix
1 teaspoon celery salt
⅛ teaspoon white pepper
2 cups instant nonfat dry milk
5 cups water
½ cup pitted ripe olives, finely chopped
3 tablespoons chopped parsley
Garnish: paprika, parsley sprigs

Melt butter in saucepan over medium heat. Blend in flour, chicken broth mix, celery salt, and pepper. Stir instant milk into water; add gradually to mixture in saucepan. Cook and stir until mixture thickens and boils 1 minute. Stir in olives and chopped parsley; cover; chill. Sprinkle each serving with paprika; garnish with parsley sprigs. Serves 8.

COLD BORSCHT

1 can (1 pound) shoestring or julienne beets
2 tablespoons minced onion
1 cup finely shredded cabbage
Water
1 teaspoon salt
1 teaspoon sugar
1 tablespoon vinegar
Dairy sour cream

Drain beets; save liquid. Combine beets, onion, and cabbage. Measure beet liquid; add enough water to make 4 cups; add to beet mixture with salt, sugar, and vinegar. Simmer, covered, 15 to 20 minutes. Chill thoroughly. Top each serving with a generous amount of sour cream. Makes 6 servings.

CREAM OF AVOCADO SOUP

1 ripe avocado
1½ cups chicken broth
2 tablespoons lemon juice
1 cup light cream
Salt and pepper to taste
Dash cayenne pepper
Garnish: 4 thin slices lemon

Peel avocado; remove stone; cut pulp into fairly small pieces; place in blender. Add chicken broth and lemon juice; blend until puréed. Add cream, salt, pepper, and cayenne pepper. Stir well. Chill several hours. Garnish each serving with a lemon slice. Makes 4 servings.

CHILLED LOBSTER SOUP

3 cups water
½ teaspoon Worcestershire sauce
½ cup nonfat dry milk
3 tablespoons flour
1 teaspoon salt
⅛ teaspoon pepper
1 tablespoon grated onion
1 can (7 ounces) lobster meat, diced
2 tablespoons lemon juice
Garnish: cut chives, fresh or freeze-dried

Pour water and Worcestershire sauce into top of double boiler. Sprinkle nonfat dry milk, flour, salt, and pepper over surface of water. Beat with rotary beater only until blended. Cook over boiling water, stirring constantly, until slightly thickened. Stir in onion and lobster meat. Remove from heat. Chill thoroughly. Stir in lemon juice just before serving. Garnish each serving with finely cut chives. Makes 4 servings.

FROSTY SOUP FLOAT

1 can (11½ ounces) condensed green pea soup
1 soup can milk
Dash of aromatic bitters
3 tablespoons dairy sour cream
Salt
1 grated lemon peel
Paprika

Combine chilled condensed soup, milk, and bitters; whip to a froth. Top each serving with a spoonful of sour cream seasoned to taste with salt, grated lemon peel, and paprika. Makes 3 generous servings.

CHILLED PEANUT BUTTER SOUP

½ cup finely chopped scallions
2 chicken bouillon cubes
2 tablespoons butter, melted
¼ cup flour
¾ cup creamy peanut butter
1 cup nonfat dry milk
1 quart water
Garnish: chopped peanuts or parsley

Add scallions and bouillon cubes to melted butter in saucepan. Cook slowly until bouillon cubes dissolve and scallions are tender; blend in flour and peanut butter, stirring constantly to avoid scorching. Stir dry milk into water; add to mixture in saucepan. Cook and stir over medium heat until soup thickens and boils. Cover; chill. Sprinkle with peanuts or parsley. Makes 8 servings.

ACCOMPANIMENT: Lemon wedges.

GREEN-AND-WHITE SOUP

1 cup chicken broth
1 can (10¾ ounces) condensed cream of
    potato soup
½ cup dairy sour cream
½ cup diced cucumber
Garnish: 1 tablespoon snipped parsley; 4
    large stuffed olives, sliced

Heat chicken broth and cream of potato soup over low heat, stirring to blend. Cool. Beat until smooth with electric blender or rotary beater. Blend in sour cream and cucumber. Chill for at least 4 hours. Garnish with parsley and sliced stuffed olives. Makes 4 servings.

ICED GARDEN BROTH

2 cans (10½ ounces each) condensed beef
    broth
2 cups tomato juice
1 can (1 pound) shoestring beets, undrained
½ cup dry red wine
Dash garlic powder
¼ teaspoon onion salt
1 teaspoon sugar
Salt and black pepper to taste

Combine all ingredients; simmer 5 minutes; cover; chill. Serve over ice. Makes 6 to 8 servings.

ACCOMPANIMENTS: Surround soup tureen or bowl with several small bowls holding diced unpeeled cucumber, chopped sweet red onion, packaged croutons, slivered toasted almonds, and chopped black olives. Let each person add a spoonful of these accompaniments to his serving of soup.

CRÈME VICHYSSOISE

4 leek bulbs, thinly sliced
¼ cup finely chopped onion

3 tablespoons butter or margarine
5 medium potatoes, peeled and thinly sliced
4 cups chicken bouillon or stock
2 cups milk
1 cup light cream
Salt and white pepper
Garnish: cut chives, fresh or freeze-dried

Cook leeks and onion in butter until lightly browned. Add potatoes and chicken bouillon. Bring to boil; lower heat; simmer about 30 minutes or until potatoes are very soft. Put mixture through food mill or sieve or purée in an electric blender. Add milk; heat. Add cream. Season to taste with salt and pepper. Chill thoroughly. Garnish each serving with cut chives. Makes 6 to 8 servings.

ICED SOUP PUNCH

1 large can (1⅔ cups) evaporated milk
1 can (10¾ ounces) condensed cream of mushroom soup
1 can (11½ ounces) condensed green pea soup
2 cans (10½ ounces each) condensed bouillon or consommé
1 cup ice cubes
Garnish: chopped chives

Add evaporated milk to combined cream of mushroom soup and pea soup; mix well. Stir in bouillon or consommé. Beat with rotary or electric beater until blended and frothy. Turn mixture into punch bowl; add ice cubes; stir until melted. Sprinkle with chopped chives. Makes 10 to 12 punch cup servings.

SUGGESTION: Set punch bowl in crushed ice; border with carrot curls, celery curls, radish roses, ripe and stuffed olives, etc.

ICED TOMATO GUMBO

1 can (10½ ounces) condensed chicken gumbo soup
1 can (10¾ ounces) condensed tomato soup
1 soup can water
1 cup thinly sliced cucumber
1 garlic clove, minced
3 tablespoons wine vinegar
1 tablespoon olive oil
Garnish: watercress

Combine all ingredients except watercress. Chill thoroughly. Garnish with sprigs of watercress. Makes 6 servings.

ICED WATERCRESS SOUP

1 bunch watercress, saving sprigs for garnish
2 cans (10¾ ounces each) condensed cream of celery soup
2 soup cans milk
1 slice onion
6 sprigs parsley
Salt and pepper
Dash of ground cloves
Garnish: lemon twists

Wash and drain watercress. Combine all ingredients except lemon twists in electric blender. Blend 1 minute or until watercress disappears into smooth greenness. Chill. Garnish with sprigs of watercress and twists of lemon peel. Makes 6 servings.

JELLIED CHICKEN BOUILLON

1 envelope unflavored gelatin
¼ cup cold water
4 cups chicken broth
1 teaspoon celery salt
½ teaspoon salt
Few grains pepper
Garnish: lemon slices; minced parsley

Sprinkle gelatin on water. Add hot chicken broth; stir until gelatin dissolves. Add seasonings; chill until set. Beat slightly with a fork; serve in bouillon cups; garnish with lemon slices dipped in minced parsley. Makes 4 to 6 servings.

MADRILENE AUX FINES HERBES

1 can or jar consommé madrilene
1 tablespoon each chopped parsley and cut chives
Garnish: cucumber slices, peeled and scored

Open can or jar of consommé madrilene. Chill in refrigerator until syrupy. Empty into bowl. Fold in parsley and chives. Return to can or jar and chill until set. Break up with fork to serve. Garnish with scored cucumber slices. Makes 3 to 4 servings.

SAVORY JELLIED SOUP

5 instant chicken bouillon cubes
2½ cups hot water
2 packages (3 ounces each) lemon-flavor gelatin

2 cans (8 ounces each) tomato sauce
3 tablespoons vinegar
1 teaspoon salt
Few grains pepper
Dairy sour cream
Chopped chives or parsley

Dissolve chicken bouillon cubes in hot water; add gelatin; stir until dissolved. Add tomato sauce, vinegar, salt, and pepper. Chill until firm. Break up with fork. Serve topped with sour cream and chives or parsley. Makes 8 servings.

SHERRIED CONSOMMÉ MADRILENE

½ cup dry sherry
¼ cup lemon juice
1 teaspoon Worcestershire sauce
¼ cup cold water
1 tablespoon unflavored gelatin
2 cans (12½ ounces each) consommé
    madrilene
Garnish: dairy sour cream; freeze-dried cut
    chives

Combine sherry, lemon juice, Worcestershire sauce, and cold water. Pour over gelatin; let stand 5 minutes. Heat consommé; add to gelatin mixture; stir until gelatin dissolves. Chill several hours or overnight. Break up with a fork. Serve in soup cups; garnish with sour cream and chives. Makes 8 servings.

SOUP SWIRL

1 can (10¾ ounces) condensed tomato soup,
    chilled
2 soup cans ice-cold milk, divided
1 can (10¾ ounces) condensed cream of
    asparagus soup, chilled
Garnish: sprigs of mint

Combine chilled tomato soup with 1 soup can of ice-cold milk. Whip to a froth. Combine chilled cream of asparagus soup with remaining soup can of ice-cold milk. Whip as above. Fill 4 large parfait glasses by pouring whipped soups, alternately in small amounts, into glasses. Garnish with sprigs of fresh mint. Serves 4.

SPICY SOUP

1 garlic clove, peeled
1 can (16 ounces) tomato juice
½ cup diced cucumber

½ cup diced celery
2 tablespoons chopped parsley
1 tablespoon chopped scallions
1 tablespoon lemon juice
½ teaspoon salt
Few drops hot-pepper sauce
Dash black pepper
Garnish: dairy sour cream; cut chives

Rub large bowl with garlic; discard garlic. Combine tomato juice with next 8 ingredients in a bowl. Cover; chill at least 3 hours. Garnish with dairy sour cream and cut chives. Makes 4 servings.

QUICK VICHYSSOISE

3 tablespoons minced dried onion
1 cup light cream
2 cups milk
½ teaspoon salt
Few grains pepper
¼ cup instant mashed potato (dry)
1 can (10¾ ounces) condensed cream of
    chicken soup
Garnish: 2 tablespoons cut chives, fresh or
    freeze-dried

Add onion to light cream; let stand 10 minutes. Meanwhile, combine milk, salt, and pepper. Bring to scalding point; stir in mashed potato; cook over low heat, stirring until smooth and slightly thickened. Combine with cream mixture and soup. Cool. Pour into electric blender or bowl of electric mixer. Blend or beat until smooth and creamy. Chill thoroughly. Serve garnished with cut chives. Makes 6 servings.

SPANISH GAZPACHO

1 large sweet onion, chopped
2 medium cucumbers, peeled and chopped
4 large or 6 medium-sized tomatoes, peeled
    and chopped
1 garlic clove
1 can (4 ounces) pimientos, drained
3 cups chicken broth or bouillon
2 tablespoons olive oil (optional)
¼ cup red-wine vinegar
1 teaspoon sugar
2 teaspoons salt (or to taste)
Ice cubes

Blend onion, cucumbers, tomatoes, garlic, and pimientos in electric blender until fairly smooth, or put through food chopper, using fine blade. Add chicken broth, oil, vinegar, sugar, and salt. Mix well; chill thoroughly. When ready to serve place an ice cube in each soup bowl. Ladle in the soup. Serve with any or all of the accompaniments below. Makes 6 generous servings.

ACCOMPANIMENTS: Garlic croutons (packaged or homemade), diced unpeeled cucumber, chopped parsley, sliced scallions, diced green pepper, chopped sweet onion, peeled and chopped tomatoes.

SUMMER BORSCHT

1 can (1 pound) julienne or shoestring beets
1 can (10½ ounces) condensed beef broth
1 tablespoon grated orange peel
½ cup orange juice
Garnish (optional): dairy sour cream; orange
    slices, quartered

Combine beets with their juice, broth, orange peel, and orange juice. Chill at least 4 hours. Serve in chilled bowls, garnished, if desired, with a spoonful of sour cream and quartered orange slice. Makes about 3½ cups.

WINE SOUP ON THE ROCKS

1 can (10½ ounces) condensed beef broth
2 to 4 tablespoons dry sherry or vermouth
Garnish: lemon peel

Combine soup and wine; pour into glasses over ice. Garnish with a twist of lemon peel. Makes 4 servings.

BEEF-TOMATO SOUP

1 can (10¾ ounces) condensed tomato soup
1½ cups water
½ pound lean beef, ground
½ cup soft bread crumbs
¼ cup milk
½ teaspoon salt
1 teaspoon grated onion
⅛ teaspoon hot-pepper sauce

Combine tomato soup and water in saucepan; bring to boiling point. Mix together remaining ingredients; shape into small balls about ¾ inch in diameter. Add to hot soup; simmer for approximately 10 minutes. Makes 4 servings.

COPAIN BLACK BEAN SOUP

2 cups black beans
3 quarts water
1 bay leaf
1 ham bone
1 grapefruit
1 beef bouillon cube
1 small green pepper, minced
1 garlic clove, crushed
2 ounces (¼ cup) dry sherry
1 cup fluffy buttered rice
½ cup finely chopped onion

Wash beans; cover with cold water; soak overnight; drain. Add 3 quarts water, bay leaf, and ham bone. Boil gently until the beans are completely soft and the liquid fairly thick, adding more water from time to time if necessary. Do not purée or sieve. Add the pulp from the grapefruit, the bouillon cube, green pepper, garlic, and sherry. Simmer ½ hour longer. Remove bay leaf and ham bone. Let each dinner guest garnish his soup with rice and chopped onion. Makes 8 servings.

EASY BLACK BEAN SOUP

2 tablespoons butter or margarine
¼ cup minced onion
1 can (11 ounces) condensed black bean soup
1½ cups water
1 tablespoon lime juice
3 frankfurters

Melt butter in saucepan; add onion; cook until tender but not brown. Add soup and water; bring to boiling point. Add lime juice. Slice frankfurters into ¼-inch rounds; add to soup; heat thoroughly. Makes 4 generous servings.

ORANGE-PUMPKIN SOUP

1 tablespoon butter or margarine
2 tablespoons minced onion
2 cups canned pumpkin
2½ cups orange juice
¼ teaspoon salt
½ teaspoon powdered ginger
1 teaspoon grated orange peel
¼ teaspoon pumpkin pie spice
1 cup light cream

Melt butter in saucepan. Add onion; cook until tender. Add remaining ingredients except cream; mix well. Simmer 10 minutes. Cool slightly. Stir in cream slowly; heat but do not boil. Makes 6 to 8 servings.

CREAM OF PUMPKIN SOUP

2 tablespoons grated onion
2 tablespoons butter or margarine
2 cups chicken broth
¼ cup instant mashed potato (dry)
1 teaspoon salt
¼ teaspoon pepper
¼ teaspoon nutmeg
1 cup milk
1 cup light cream
1 cup canned pumpkin
Garnish: ½ cup dairy sour cream

Sauté onion lightly in butter or margarine in large saucepan. Add broth; heat to boiling; remove from heat. Beat in instant mashed potato, salt, pepper, and nutmeg until creamy. Combine milk and cream; stir in. Beat in pumpkin. Simmer, stirring often, 15 minutes. Garnish with dairy sour cream. Soup may be served hot or chilled. Makes 6 servings.

CURRIED MUSHROOM SOUP

1 teaspoon curry powder
1 large can (1⅔ cups) evaporated milk
1 can (10¾ ounces) condensed cream of
    mushroom soup
1 teaspoon minced dried onion
Garnish (optional): paprika; pitted ripe olives,
    chopped

Blend curry powder to a smooth paste with a little of the evaporated milk. Add remaining milk slowly; combine with soup and onion in saucepan. Heat to serving temperature (be careful not to boil). Garnish with a dash of paprika and a few chopped ripe olives, if desired. Makes 3 to 4 servings.

GREEN PEA AND BACON SOUP

1 can (11½ ounces) condensed green pea soup
1 cup milk
½ cup whipping cream
⅓ cup white wine
1 instant chicken bouillon cube
1 tablespoon grated onion
Garnish: crumbled crisp bacon

Combine soup, milk, cream, and wine in a saucepan, stirring until perfectly smooth. Add bouillon cube and onion. Heat to simmering, stirring until bouillon cube dissolves. Top each serving with crumbled crisp bacon. Makes 3 or 4 servings.

MONTEREY JACK CHEESE SOUP

½ cup finely chopped onion
1 large ripe tomato, peeled and diced
2 large canned or fresh green chilies, veins
    and seeds removed, chopped
½ garlic clove, minced
1 cup chicken stock
1½ cups medium white sauce (p. 220)
1½ cups milk
¼ teaspoon salt
Dash freshly ground black pepper
1½ cups grated Monterey Jack cheese (or any
    semisoft mild Cheddar)

Put the chopped onion, diced tomato, chopped chilies, and minced garlic in a saucepan with chicken stock and simmer until the vegetables are tender; remove from heat. Slowly stir in white sauce, stirring constantly. Add the milk slowly. Add salt, pepper, and cheese. Simmer over low heat, stirring, until cheese melts. Serve immediately. Makes 6 servings.

CRAB MEAT SOUP

1 can (11½ ounces) condensed green pea soup
1 soup can rich milk or light cream
2 cans (10¾ ounces each) condensed tomato
    soup
1 can (6½ ounces) crab meat, flaked
3 tablespoons dry sherry

Combine pea soup, milk, and tomato soup in saucepan; blend thoroughly. Add flaked crab meat and sherry. Cook over low heat, stirring, until hot. Makes 4 servings.

SHRIMP BISQUE

1 tablespoon minced onion
2 tablespoons finely chopped green pepper
3 tablespoons butter or margarine
1 tablespoon flour
½ teaspoon salt
1 cup grated American Cheddar cheese
4 cups milk
1 can (about 5 ounces) shrimp
¼ teaspoon aromatic bitters

Simmer onion and green pepper in butter for 5 minutes; do not brown. Blend in flour and salt. Add cheese, milk, shrimp, and liquid from shrimp. Heat until cheese is melted and soup is hot. Add bitters and serve at once. Makes 6 servings.

SOUP NOG

5 cans (10¾ ounces each) condensed tomato soup
5 soup cans milk
5 eggs
Garnish: nutmeg *or* cinnamon

Combine soup and milk. Heat, stirring often. Meanwhile, beat eggs. Stir heated soup slowly into eggs. Serve from a tureen after sprinkling with nutmeg or cinnamon. Makes 3 quarts, or about 15 servings.

TOMATO CREAM SOUP

2 cans (10¾ ounces each) condensed tomato soup
1 can (10½ ounces) condensed consommé
1 cup dairy sour cream
⅓ cup sherry
1 teaspoon grated onion
Few grains celery salt
2 tablespoons chopped parsley
Garnish: sour cream; paprika

Combine tomato soup, consommé, 1 cup sour cream, and sherry in saucepan, stirring until perfectly smooth. Add onion, celery salt, and parsley. Heat to simmering. Top each serving with spoonful of additional sour cream; sprinkle with paprika. Makes 4 or 5 servings.

TUNA MAXISTRONI

2 tablespoons vegetable oil
1 small onion, minced
1 celery stalk, minced
1 garlic clove, minced
1 can (10½ ounces) condensed chicken broth
1 soup can tomato juice
1 teaspoon dried leaf basil
¼ teaspoon powdered thyme
1 teaspoon salt
¼ teaspoon pepper
1 package (10 ounces) frozen mixed vegetables
2 cans (6½ or 7 ounces each) tuna, drained
Garnish (optional): grated Parmesan cheese

Heat oil in saucepan; add onion, celery, and garlic; cook until soft but not brown. Add undiluted chicken broth and remaining ingredients except cheese; bring to a boil. Reduce heat; simmer, covered, 10 minutes. Ladle into heated soup bowl; sprinkle with Parmesan cheese, if desired. Makes 6 servings.

VIRGINIA BISQUE

6 tablespoons creamy peanut butter
4 tablespoons flour
1 can (10¾ ounces) condensed tomato soup
1 quart (4 cups) milk
Garnish: dairy sour cream

Blend peanut butter and flour in top of double boiler. Stir in soup and milk; blend thoroughly. Cook over hot water, stirring constantly until smooth and thickened. Cover; cook 10 minutes longer. Garnish each serving with a spoonful of dairy sour cream. Makes 6 generous servings.

HEARTY WINTER SOUP

2 quarts water
1 medium onion, quartered
1 tablespoon salt
¼ teaspoon coarse black pepper
1½ pounds beef chuck
2 tablespoons vegetable oil
1 medium onion, sliced
1 garlic clove, minced
1 tablespoon chopped parsley
2 stalks celery, sliced
2 cups shredded cabbage
2 cups sliced carrots
1 can (1 pound) tomatoes
1 can (1 pound) kidney beans, undrained
¼ teaspoon oregano
½ cup pastina
¼ cup grated Parmesan cheese

Combine water, quartered onion, salt, pepper, and beef in deep kettle. Bring to boil; lower heat; simmer 2 hours. Remove beef; strain stock; measure; add water to make 2½ quarts. Dice beef. Heat oil in skillet; add sliced onion, garlic, parsley, and celery; cook 10 minutes over medium heat, stirring frequently. Return diced meat to stock; add contents of skillet, cabbage, carrots, and tomatoes. Cover; simmer 1¼ hours. Add kidney beans, oregano, and pastina. Cook 15 minutes longer or until pastina is tender. Stir in cheese; mix well. Serve at once. Makes 8 to 10 servings.

QUICK WINTER SOUP

2 cans (10½ ounces each) condensed beef
    bouillon
1½ cups water
2 tablespoons barley
1 cup each cubed carrots, parsnips, celery
    root, turnips, potatoes
1 teaspoon sugar
Salt and pepper to taste

Combine bouillon and water; bring to boil. Add barley; cook 20 minutes. Add vegetables, sugar, salt, and pepper. Simmer 35 minutes or until vegetables are tender. Makes 4 hearty servings.

PEANUT SOUP

1 medium onion, finely chopped
2 tablespoons vegetable oil
¾ cup creamy peanut butter .
3 cups chicken broth
Salt and pepper to taste
Garnish: freshly ground black pepper;
    croutons

Cook onion in oil until soft and golden brown. Lower heat; blend in peanut butter. Add chicken broth slowly, stirring constantly until mixture is smooth. Bring to boil; season to taste; lower heat; simmer 10 minutes. Garnish with freshly ground pepper or croutons. Makes 4 or 5 servings.

CAPTAIN'S CHOWDER

2 pounds haddock or cod (or any firm white
    fish), fresh or frozen
⅛ pound bacon, diced
1 large onion, finely cubed
5 medium potatoes, sliced thin
1 quart milk
1 cup light cream
⅓ cup Chablis
Salt and pepper to taste

Cover fish with salted water; simmer gently for about 10 minutes. Strain, saving stock for later use; debone and skin fish. Fry bacon in large kettle until crisp and lightly browned; remove to absorbent paper. Sauté onion in drippings until golden brown. Add potatoes, fish, and approximately 2 cups fish stock. Simmer, covered, 10

minutes. Add milk, cream, and wine; reheat without boiling. Season to taste; sprinkle bacon over soup. Makes 6 servings.

CHICKEN CHOWDER

1 large stewing chicken
4 medium-sized onions, quartered
¼ bay leaf
4 cups diced potatoes
1 package (10 ounces) frozen corn
1 tablespoon salt pork, diced
2 quarts milk
1 tablespoon salt
1 teaspoon freshly ground black pepper

Place whole chicken, which has been cleaned, into large kettle; add enough boiling water to barely cover. Add 1 of the onions and the bay leaf. Bring to boil; skim; reduce heat. Continue cooking slowly until chicken is tender and meat falls off the bones easily. Strain soup into large bowl. Let chicken cool enough to handle; remove skin and bones. Dice chicken; return to stock. Add remaining onions, potatoes, and corn. Cook until vegetables are tender. Fry pork until crisp; pour off fat; add pork and milk to chowder; add salt and pepper; heat through but do not boil. Makes 6 portions as a main course, 8 to 10 as a first course.

JUMBO GUMBO

To Prepare Chicken:

1 whole broiler-fryer chicken
4 cups water
1 medium onion, sliced
4 celery tops
1 teaspoon salt
¼ teaspoon pepper

Put chicken in kettle with 4 cups water; add remaining ingredients. Bring to a boil; cover tightly. Reduce heat; simmer 1 hour or until tender. Remove from heat; strain and save broth. Refrigerate chicken and broth at once. When chicken is cool, remove meat from bones; cut in large pieces. Skim fat from broth. Reserve chicken and broth.

To Prepare Gumbo:

3 tablespoons butter or margarine
1 medium onion, chopped
1 green pepper, chopped

1 cup sliced celery
2 tablespoons flour
Reserved stock (from above)
1 bay leaf
½ teaspoon dried leaf thyme
1 teaspoon salt
¼ teaspoon pepper
2 cans (1 pound each) tomatoes
1 teaspoon Worcestershire sauce
1 package (10 ounces) frozen okra, thawed
Reserved chicken (from above)

Heat butter in a deep kettle. Add onion, green pepper, and celery. Cook, stirring occasionally, about 5 minutes. Blend in flour. Gradually add reserved stock and cook, stirring occasionally, until mixture comes to a boil. Add remaining ingredients except okra and chicken. Bring to a boil; reduce heat and simmer 1 hour. Remove bay leaf. Add okra and reserved chicken pieces; simmer 15 minutes longer. Makes 6 servings.

SHRIMP CHOWDER

2 cans (10¾ ounces each) condensed cream of
    chicken soup
1 teaspoon curry powder
2 soup cans light cream
1 can (about 5 ounces) small shrimp, drained
Butter
Garnish: paprika; chopped parsley

Add a little of the soup to curry powder; blend; add remaining soup. Blend with cream. Heat gently; do not allow to boil. About 5 minutes before serving, add shrimp. Serve in bowls with a dot of butter. Sprinkle with paprika and chopped parsley. Makes 6 servings.

CORN CHOWDER

1 can (1 pound) cream-style corn
2 cups milk
1 can (10¾ ounces) condensed cream of
    mushroom soup
½ teaspoon salt
¼ teaspoon hot-pepper sauce
Garnish: paprika

Empty can of corn into saucepan; add milk. Add soup; blend thoroughly. Bring to boiling point over low heat, stirring frequently. Just before serving, stir in salt and hot-pepper sauce. Sprinkle each serving with paprika. Makes 6 servings.

CORN AND KIDNEY BEAN CHOWDER

2 large sweet onions, thinly sliced
2 tablespoons vegetable oil
2 cans (10¾ ounces each) condensed tomato
    soup
1½ cups water
1 large can (1⅔ cups) evaporated milk
2 cans (1 pound 4 ounces each) kidney beans
2 cans (12 ounces each) kernel corn
¼ teaspoon oregano
Salt and pepper to taste

Cook onions in oil until soft and light brown. Combine soup, water, and evaporated milk; add to onions. Add undrained kidney beans and corn; simmer 10 minutes; add oregano, salt, and pepper. Simmer 5 minutes longer. Makes 8 generous servings.

VEGETABLE CHOWDER

2 cans (10¾ ounces each) condensed
    mushroom soup
2½ cups milk
1 package (10 ounces) frozen mixed
    vegetables, cooked
Salt and pepper

Combine soup, milk, and vegetables; heat but do not boil. Season to taste with salt and pepper. Makes 4 main dish servings or 8 first course servings.

MANHATTAN SCALLOP CHOWDER

4 tablespoons butter or margarine*
1 teaspoon dried thyme
1 cup sliced onions
3 cups diced potatoes
1 cup sliced celery
8 cups hot water
2 teaspoons salt
⅛ teaspoon pepper
2 cans (1 pound each) tomatoes
1½ cups diced carrots
2 pounds sea scallops, fresh or frozen (thaw, if
    frozen)

Melt butter in deep kettle. Add thyme and onions; cook, stirring frequently, until onions are tender but not brown. Add potatoes, celery,

*Or dice ⅛ pound salt pork; fry until crisp; remove and save pork scraps for garnish; use drippings instead of butter.

water, salt, and pepper. Cover; simmer 5 minutes. Add tomatoes and carrots. Simmer, uncovered, 1 hour. Halve scallops crosswise; add. Simmer 5 to 10 minutes longer or until scallops are done. Add salt if necessary. Makes 8 servings.

TELEGRAPH HILL CHOWDER

1 can (11½ ounces) condensed green pea soup
¾ cup water
1 tablespoon minced dried onion
1 can (3 ounces) broiled mushroom crowns
3 tablespoons sherry
Salt
1 can (6½ ounces) crab meat, drained

Combine soup, water, and onion. Heat to boiling. Add mushrooms (including broth), wine, and salt to taste. Just before serving, add crab meat separated into chunks (reserve a few chunks for garnish, if desired). Heat thoroughly; serve at once. Garnish with reserved chunks of crab meat. Makes 3 to 4 servings.

CHAPTER 4
Meats

It USED to be that the price of meat varied with the seasons, but this is no longer true. Many factors influence meat costs and quality, among them the availability of grain, and the expense and time it takes to ready grain-fed animals for the market.

A special word about beef: Grass-fed beef describes meat from cattle that have been fed only on range or pasture or have received a *limited* amount of grain before being marketed. This type of beef is usually cheaper per pound than grain-fed beef, and has less fat covering and marbling. Therefore it may be slightly less flavorful and juicy. It has somewhat fewer calories, but lean for lean, the nutritive value is the same.

In cooking any type of meat, if you are doubtful of its tenderness, don't forget natural meat tenderizer. It is available seasoned or unseasoned, and when used according to package directions, results are excellent.

LONDON BROIL

1 flank steak, 2 to 2½ pounds
Unseasoned natural meat tenderizer
1 can (3 ounces) broiled sliced mushrooms
1 can (10½ ounces) beef gravy

Treat meat with tenderizer as directed on label. Place on broiler rack in preheated broiler oven with top surface of meat 3 inches below source of heat. Broil 4 minutes on each side. Slice diagonally in thin slices across the grain of meat. Add mushrooms with their broth to gravy; heat; pour some of the gravy over the beef slices; serve rest separately. Makes 6 servings.

MINUTE STEAKS, WESTERN STYLE

½ cup diced green pepper
½ cup chopped onion
1 pimiento, chopped
2 tablespoons vegetable oil
1 can (6 ounces) tomato paste
½ cup chopped black olives
¼ cup grated sharp Cheddar cheese
¼ cup fine dry bread crumbs
1½ teaspoons salt
2 teaspoons chili powder
¼ teaspoon pepper
6 individual minute steaks
¾ cup water

Cook green pepper, onion, and pimiento in oil until onion is tender but not brown. Add tomato paste, olives, cheese, bread crumbs, salt, chili powder, and pepper. Mix well. Spread steaks with half the tomato mixture; roll as for jelly roll. Fasten with wooden picks. Place, folded side down, in shallow, ungreased baking pan. Mix remaining sauce with ¾ cup water; pour over steaks. Bake at 375° for 45 minutes or until steaks are tender. Makes 6 servings.

STEAK COUNTRY STYLE

1 pound round steak
Unseasoned natural meat tenderizer
¾ cup fine dry bread crumbs
¼ teaspoon pepper, divided
½ cup evaporated milk
⅓ cup vegetable oil
1 can (1 pound) tomatoes
1 can (1 pound) whole kernel corn
1 medium onion, sliced
1 green pepper, cut in strips

Treat meat with tenderizer as directed on label; cut into ¼-inch strips. Combine bread crumbs and ⅛ teaspoon of the pepper. Dip meat strips in bread crumb mixture, then in evaporated milk and then in bread crumbs again. Brown meat, about ¼ at a time, in hot oil over medium heat. Return browned meat to skillet; cover tightly; cook over very low heat 8 minutes. Remove to warm platter; keep hot. Drain tomato and corn liquids into skillet; add onion and green pepper. Boil liquid rapidly until reduced to about ½ cup. Add tomatoes, corn, and remaining ⅛ teaspoon pepper; heat to serving temperature. Serve with steak. Makes 4 servings.

BEEF STROGANOFF

3 Bermuda onions
2 pounds top round steak
1 pound mushrooms
1 cup butter or margarine
1 can (10¾ ounces) condensed tomato soup
1 can (6 ounces) tomato paste
1 cup dairy sour cream
1 teaspoon salt
Few grains pepper
1 teaspoon Worcestershire sauce
Hot cooked rice

Put onions through food chopper, using coarse knife; then drain, saving juice. Cut meat in very thin slices; trim off excess fat. Slice mushrooms. Brown meat and mushrooms in butter or marga-

rine. Add onions; remove from heat. Combine soup, tomato paste, sour cream, seasonings, and onion juice; add to meat mixture. Cover; simmer 1 hour. Serve in ring of fluffy rice. Makes 6 servings.

OVEN-BROILED STUFFED STEAK

3-pound top round of beef, in 1 piece, 1½ inches thick
Unseasoned natural meat tenderizer
1 small garlic clove, minced
1 small onion, sliced thin
1 small green pepper, slivered
2 tablespoons butter or margarine
1 can (10¾ ounces) condensed cream of celery soup
1 can (3 ounces) sliced broiled mushrooms
2 tablespoons sliced stuffed olives
½ cup packaged bread stuffing
1 tablespoon minced pimiento
Few grains coarsely ground pepper

Cut beef in half, crosswise, to make 2 slices, each 1½ inches thick. Treat with meat tenderizer as directed on label. Cook garlic, onion, and green pepper in butter until soft but not brown. Blend in soup. Drain mushrooms; add to soup with olives, bread stuffing, pimiento, and pepper. Heat to boiling. Remove from heat; cool slightly. Spread mixture over one slice of beef; top with other slice of beef; fasten with skewers. Place on rack in shallow roasting pan. Roast at 450° for 15 minutes. Lower heat to 350°; roast 30 minutes longer (medium rare). Makes 6 to 8 servings.

STEAK LOUISIANA

1½-pound round steak, cut 1 inch thick
Seasoned flour
3 tablespoons vegetable oil
2 medium-sized onions, thinly sliced into rings
1 can (1 pound) tomatoes
1 cup tomato juice
1 tablespoon grated Parmesan cheese
1 green pepper, cut into rings
4 medium-sized yams, peeled and sliced ¾ inch thick
Salt and pepper to taste

Dredge meat in seasoned flour. Heat oil over low heat; add onion rings; cook until golden brown; remove. Brown meat well on both sides. Add tomatoes, tomato juice, cheese, and green pepper rings. Top with onion rings. Cover; cook over low heat until meat is tender (about 1 hour). Add yam slices. Cover; continue cooking until yams are tender (about 15 minutes). Season to taste with salt and pepper. Makes 4 to 6 servings.

OVEN-BARBECUED STEAK

2-pound round steak, in 1 piece, 1½ inches
    thick
Unseasoned natural meat tenderizer
2 tablespoons vegetable oil
½ cup catchup
2 tablespoons wine vinegar
1 cup water
1 teaspoon salt
½ teaspoon nutmeg
Few drops hot-pepper sauce
¼ teaspoon basil

Treat the round steak with meat tenderizer as directed on label. Brown meat on both sides in hot oil. Transfer to shallow roasting pan or baking dish. Combine remaining ingredients; pour over meat. Bake at 350° for 1½ hours, basting occasionally with sauce in pan. To serve, cut in thin slices on the diagonal. (Save sauce in pan for use in soups and stews.) Makes 6 to 8 servings.

GLAZED LONDON BROIL

1 flank steak, 2 to 2½ pounds
2 teaspoons unseasoned natural meat
    tenderizer
1 tablespoon sugar
2 tablespoons dry sherry
2 tablespoons soy sauce
1 tablespoon honey
1 teaspoon salt

Treat flank steak with tenderizer as directed on label. Combine remaining ingredients. Pour over steak. Let stand at room temperature 1 hour, turning occasionally. Broil with surface of meat about 3 inches below source of heat, allowing 3 minutes for each side. To serve, slice with sharp knife into thin slices, carving at an angle, against the grain. Makes 8 servings.

PEPPER STEAK

1½ pounds beef round, cut 2 inches thick
¾ teaspoon unseasoned natural meat
    tenderizer

3 tablespoons vegetable oil
2 large green peppers, cut in 1-inch squares
3 scallions (with tops), thinly sliced
1½ cups diagonally sliced celery
1½ cups water, consommé, or bouillon
1 tablespoon cornstarch
⅓ cup light molasses
3 tablespoons soy sauce
¾ teaspoon salt
1 teaspoon garlic powder
1½ teaspoons ginger
2 teaspoons lemon juice
4 cups hot cooked rice

Cut beef into paper-thin slices; treat slices with tenderizer according to package directions. Heat vegetable oil in large skillet over high heat; add beef slices; cook briefly just until red color disappears. Add peppers, scallions, and celery; cook 3 to 5 minutes, stirring frequently. Blend water with cornstarch; stir in remaining ingredients except rice. Stir quickly into beef mixture. Stir constantly until slightly thickened and boiling. Serve with rice. Makes 6 servings.

BRUNCH BEEFSTEAK PIE

3 pounds lean steak, round or chuck, about
    2½ inches thick
2 cups boiling water
½ teaspoon thyme
2 tablespoons finely chopped parsley
¼ teaspoon pepper
2 medium-sized onions, thinly sliced
4 mushrooms, sliced; *or* 6 hard-cooked eggs,
    sliced
2 tablespoons cornstarch
⅓ cup cold water
1 teaspoon salt
1 tablespoon Worcestershire sauce
Pastry for single piecrust

Cut steak into thick slices about 3 inches long; put in a large skillet; add boiling water. Cover; simmer 20 minutes; add thyme, parsley, pepper, and onions. Simmer until meat is tender (about 45 minutes). Add sliced mushrooms, if used, and cook for 5 minutes longer. Remove meat to ungreased casserole or deep pie pan, alternating layers of meat with egg slices, if used. Blend cornstarch with cold water, salt, and Worcestershire sauce; stir into skillet. Stir over medium heat until thickened. Pour gravy over meat and mushrooms or meat and eggs. Roll out pastry and place on top; cut slit in pastry. Bake pie at 425°

until crust is brown, 12 to 15 minutes. Makes 6 servings.*

STEAK TURNOVERS

Rich pastry dough
8 frozen steak patties
3 tablespoons butter or margarine, divided
1 teaspoon salt
Few grains pepper
Dash garlic salt
2 tablespoons flour
1 can (4 ounces) mushroom stems and pieces
Salt and pepper to taste

Roll out pastry dough ⅛ inch thick. Cut into eight 7-inch circles, one for each steak. Pan-broil steaks in 2 tablespoons butter or margarine, 1 minute each side. Season with salt, pepper, and garlic salt. Place on pastry rounds. To same skillet add remaining 1 tablespoon butter. Blend in flour. Drain mushrooms; measure liquid; add enough water to make 1 cup; add to skillet; cook over low heat, stirring, until smooth and thickened. Add mushrooms; season to taste with salt and pepper. Place spoonful of sauce on each steak. Fold pastry over steaks; crimp edges. Bake at 425° for 20 minutes or until brown. Heat remaining sauce; spoon over turnovers. Makes 8 servings.

AUSTRALIAN BEEFSTEAK-AND-KIDNEY PIE

1 pound beef, chuck or round
2 lamb kidneys
1 tablespoon flour
½ teaspoon salt
¼ teaspoon pepper
3 tablespoons vegetable oil
1 slice onion
2 cups cold water or stock (canned consommé
    or bouillon may be used)
Flaky pastry for pie topping
1 egg, beaten; *or* 1½ tablespoons milk

Cut beef in 1-inch cubes; slice kidneys. Dip meats into flour blended with salt and pepper. Sauté in hot oil until slightly brown. Add onion slice and water or stock. Simmer 30 to 45 minutes; thicken liquid if desired. Cool; pour into

*Pie can be prepared in advance and baked or reheated on the day of serving. Allow extra time in the oven if baked after being refrigerated.

1-quart casserole. The liquid should come nearly to top of casserole. Top with pastry; brush with egg or milk. Bake at 425° until golden brown (about 20 minutes). Reduce heat to 350°; bake 45 minutes longer. Makes 4 servings.

BURGUNDY BEEF

2 pounds beef round, cut 1 inch thick
1 garlic clove
3 medium onions, sliced thin
4 tablespoons butter or margarine
2 cans (10½ ounces each) beef gravy
Salt and pepper to taste
¼ teaspoon marjoram
¼ teaspoon oregano
½ cup Burgundy
½ pint dairy sour cream, divided
Hot cooked rice or noodles

Cut beef into 1-inch cubes. Sauté garlic and onions in butter slowly until onions are soft and lightly browned; discard garlic; remove onions from pan. Brown meat cubes slowly in drippings left in pan. Add beef gravy, salt, and pepper. Return onions to pan; simmer 1 hour or until beef is tender. Add herbs and wine; simmer 15 minutes longer. Stir in half the sour cream. Turn into serving dish; garnish with remaining sour cream. Serve with rice or noodles. Makes 6 servings.

STUFFED FLANK STEAK BURGUNDY

1 flank steak, 2 pounds
4 cups soft bread crumbs
½ cup melted bacon fat, divided
1 small onion, minced
1 teaspoon poultry seasoning
Salt and pepper to taste
¼ cup water
Seasoned flour
1 cup Burgundy
1 can (10¾ ounces) condensed cream of
    mushroom soup

Score flank steak in diagonal lines with a sharp knife. Mix bread crumbs, ⅓ cup melted bacon fat, onion, poultry seasoning, salt, pepper, and water; spread evenly over steak. Roll up steak with stuffing inside (from one wide edge to the other). Tuck ends in; fasten with wooden picks; tie with white string. Cut roll in 2 pieces; dust each with seasoned flour. Heat remaining bacon fat in large, heavy skillet; brown steak rolls. Add Burgundy; cover; simmer 1½ hours or until meat is tender, turning rolls occasionally. Remove wooden picks; slice steak rolls; place on hot platter. Add mushroom soup to drippings in pan; blend well; bring to a boil; serve with sliced steak rolls. Makes 6 servings.

RIBS OF BEEF AND INDIVIDUAL YORKSHIRE PUDDINGS

    1 3-rib roast of beef, 6 to 7 pounds
    1 cup sifted flour
    ½ teaspoon salt
    3 eggs
    1 cup milk

Place roast fat side up in shallow open pan. The rib bones serve as a rack to keep roast off bottom of pan. Insert meat thermometer into center of thickest part of roast, avoiding fat and bone. Do not season; do not add water; do not cover. Roast at 325° until thermometer registers the desired degree of doneness (140°, rare; 160°, medium; 170°, well done). Approximate cooking time for a 6-pound roast: 2¼ hours, rare; 2½ hours, medium; 3 hours 20 minutes, well done.

To Make Yorkshire Pudding Batter: Combine flour and salt. Beat eggs well; beat in milk. Pour egg mixture into flour; continue beating until the thin batter is smooth. About half an hour before roast is done, remove from oven. Raise oven temperature to 400°. Grease 6 large or 8 small popover cups or custard cups; fill each ⅓ full of Yorkshire pudding batter. Put cups into oven. Return roast to oven. In 30 minutes remove roast from oven to "set" before carving. Let puddings bake another 10 minutes or until puffed and dry. Remove from custard cups. Place on platter around roast to catch and absorb the meat juices from carving. Makes 6 to 8 servings.

POT ROAST MARINADA

    4-pound piece of beef, chuck or brisket, for
        pot roast
    1½ cups sliced onion
    1 cup diced celery
    1½ teaspoons salt
    ⅛ teaspoon pepper
    6 sprigs parsley
    1½ cups dry red wine
    ¼ teaspoon salt
    Dash pepper
    ¼ cup flour
    Butter or margarine

About 18 to 24 hours before cooking, marinate the beef in a mixture of the next 6 ingredients. Cover and place in refrigerator. Turn occasionally. Just before cooking, remove meat, reserving marinade, and rub the meat with a mixture of salt, pepper, and flour. Brown meat in large skillet on all sides in a small amount of butter or margarine. Add reserved marinade. Cover; simmer slowly until tender (about 3 hours), basting occasionally. Add a little water if needed. Makes 6 to 8 servings.

PHILADELPHIA POT ROAST

    1 blade pot roast, 3 to 5 pounds, 2 inches thick
    Salt, pepper, paprika, flour
    ½ pound bacon, diced
    ½ cup sliced sweet gherkins
    1 large onion, sliced
    1 can (8 ounces) tomato sauce
    1 cup water
    ½ cup dairy sour cream

Rub pot roast on both sides with salt, pepper, paprika, and flour. Fry diced bacon in large skillet until crisp and brown; drain on absorbent paper. Pour off all but about 2 tablespoons bacon fat. Brown pot roast in bacon fat left in skillet. Add gherkin and onion slices, tomato sauce, and water. Cover; simmer 2½ to 3 hours, adding more water as needed. When meat is tender remove to platter. Thicken gravy; add bacon bits and sour cream; blend well. Serve at once with the meat. Makes 6 to 8 servings.

POT ROAST INDIENNE

    4-pound piece of lean beef, chuck or round
    1 teaspoon salt
    2 tablespoons lemon juice
    3 slices bacon
    1 garlic clove, minced
    ⅔ cup chopped onion
    ¼ cup chopped parsley
    4 whole cloves
    ½ teaspoon cinnamon
    ½ bay leaf
    1 cup canned tomatoes
    1 teaspoon sugar
    1 cup orange juice

Season beef with salt and lemon juice. Cook bacon in large, heavy skillet until crisp; remove from skillet. Add beef to bacon drippings. Brown on all sides. Combine garlic, onion, parsley, cloves, cinnamon, bay leaf, tomatoes, and sugar. Add to beef. Crumble bacon over beef. Bring to boil; reduce heat and cover; simmer 10 minutes. Remove cloves and bay leaf. Add orange juice; simmer, covered, about 3 hours or until tender. If necessary, add water to keep moist. Makes 6 to 8 servings.

CAPE COD POT ROAST

2 tablespoons vegetable oil
4-to-5-pound beef chuck, boned and rolled
½ cup seasoned flour (salt and pepper added)
1 cup fresh cranberries
4 cups water
3 tablespoons brown sugar
¼ teaspoon nutmeg
Salt and pepper to taste

Heat oil in large kettle; dredge beef with seasoned flour; brown well on all sides. Add cranberries and water. Bring to a boil. Cover; simmer 3 hours or until beef is tender. Strain gravy; measure; thicken with flour mixed to a smooth paste with equal amount of cold water, using 1 tablespoon flour for each cup liquid. Add brown sugar and nutmeg; stir over low heat until sugar dissolves. Season to taste with salt and pepper. Serve gravy separately with meat. Makes 4 to 5 servings.

CALIFORNIA POT ROAST

1 boned and rolled beef chuck pot roast, 3 to 4 pounds
1 bottle Italian salad dressing
1 can (10½ ounces) condensed beef bouillon
1 cup hot water
4 to 6 carrots, cut in chunks
1 package (10 ounces) frozen green beans

Marinate pot roast in salad dressing 1 hour, turning every 15 minutes. Remove meat from marinade; reserve marinade. Brown meat in large skillet on all sides. Add beef bouillon and water; cover; simmer 2 hours, adding more water as needed. Add carrots; cook 5 minutes. Add green beans; cook 5 minutes. Add marinade. Cook, uncovered, until liquid cooks down and vegetables are tender. Arrange meat and vegetables on platter. Thicken gravy; serve separately. Makes 4 to 5 servings.

CALIFORNIA SAUERBRATEN

½ cup dry red wine
1½ cups wine vinegar
1 cup water
3 tablespoons light brown sugar
1 cup dried pitted prunes
8 small onions, halved
1 teaspoon whole black pepper
¼ teaspoon powdered bay leaves
8 whole allspice
2-inch stick cinnamon
8 whole cloves
2 teaspoons salt
4-pound boned and rolled beef chuck
3 tablespoons vegetable oil

Combine first 12 ingredients; pour over meat. Marinate in refrigerator 24 to 48 hours, turning several times. Remove meat; reserve marinade; pat meat dry. Remove prunes from marinade; set aside. In large, heavy skillet brown meat slowly on all sides in vegetable oil. Pour off any remaining oil. Add marinade. Cover; simmer 2½ to 3 hours or until meat is tender. Remove meat; keep warm. Strain meat stock; thicken with flour mixed smooth with an equal amount of cold water, using 1 or 2 tablespoons per cup of stock according to thickness desired. Garnish meat with prunes. Serve gravy separately. Makes 4 to 6 servings.

QUICK SAUERBRATEN

4-to-5-pound pot roast, chuck, round, or rump
¼ cup vegetable oil
½ cup chopped onion
2 teaspoons salt
2 tablespoons mixed pickling spices
1 cup red wine vinegar
3 cups water
½ cup firmly packed brown sugar
12 gingersnaps, crumbled

Brown pot roast slowly on all sides in oil in heavy kettle or Dutch oven. Pour off excess oil. Add next 6 ingredients. Simmer 3 to 4 hours or until tender. Remove meat; keep warm. Strain liquid left in kettle; measure 4 cups. Add gingersnaps. Cook and stir until smooth and slightly thickened. (If a thicker gravy is desired, stir in 3 tablespoons flour blended with ⅓ cup cold water.) Cook, stirring often, 5 minutes longer. Serve gravy separately with meat. Makes 5 to 6 servings.

BRAISED CHUCK WITH FRUIT

4-pound beef chuck
2 teaspoons salt
¼ teaspoon basil or marjoram
1 tablespoon vegetable oil
½ cup water
1 can (1 pound) grapefruit sections
2 tablespoons cornstarch
1 can (14 ounces) pineapple chunks
1 tablespoon lemon juice
Garnish: 6 maraschino cherries, drained

Sprinkle beef with salt and basil or marjoram. Heat oil in large, heavy skillet. Brown beef slowly and evenly on all sides (30 minutes). Add water; cover tightly. Simmer over low heat on top of range about 3 hours or until meat is tender. Remove meat to a hot platter. Drain ¼ cup syrup from grapefruit into small dish; stir in cornstarch until smooth. Drain remaining syrup from grapefruit and syrup from pineapple; add to liquid in skillet; heat. Gradually add cornstarch mixture, stirring constantly. Add grapefruit sections and pineapple chunks; cook until mixture is thickened and fruit is heated. Stir in lemon juice. Spoon fruit sauce over and around meat. Garnish with cherries. Makes 6 servings.

BOILED BEEF INTERNATIONAL

2 envelopes instant beef broth mix
3 cups boiling water
3 sprigs parsley
2 teaspoons celery flakes
Dash hot-pepper sauce
4 peppercorns
3 medium onions, halved
2 garlic cloves
1 bay leaf
1 teaspoon oregano
2 teaspoons salt
1 teaspoon sugar
1 can (12 ounces) beer
6-to-7-pound boned and rolled beef for
    boiling, chuck or round
Horseradish Gravy*

Dissolve beef broth mix in boiling water in a large, heavy skillet. Add all remaining ingredients but beef and gravy. Bring to boil. Add meat and lower heat; simmer about 3 hours or until meat is tender. Chill meat in broth overnight. Remove any fat that has risen to surface. Reheat.

Remove meat to platter and keep warm while making gravy. Makes 6 to 8 servings.

ACCOMPANIMENTS: Surround meat with mounds of well-seasoned cooked vegetables of your choice. Serve gravy separately.

*HORSERADISH GRAVY

3 cups broth in which meat was cooked
6 tablespoons butter or margarine
6 tablespoons flour
1 cup dairy sour cream
¼ cup prepared horseradish

Strain broth through wet cheesecloth or very fine sieve. Measure 3 cups (save any extra broth for cooking purposes; if broth is to be kept for more than a day or two, freeze). Melt butter; blend in flour. Add stock; stir over medium heat until smooth and thickened. Stir in sour cream slowly. Add horseradish. Makes 4 cups.

BEEF RAGOUT

6 slices bacon
2½ pounds lean boned chuck, cut in 1½-inch
    cubes
Salt and pepper
1 can (10½ ounces) condensed beef broth
1¼ cups water, divided
½ cup dry red wine
2 large garlic cloves, minced
1 large bay leaf
1 can (8 ounces) small white onions
1 can (about 1 pound) baby carrots
1 can (6 ounces) sliced broiled mushrooms
2 tablespoons flour

Fry bacon in a large skillet; drain and crumble, saving drippings. Brown beef on all sides in bacon drippings; pour off excess. Sprinkle beef with salt and pepper. Add broth, 1 cup water, wine, garlic, and bay leaf. Cover; simmer 1½ hours or until beef is tender. Remove bay leaf. Drain vegetables; add. Simmer ½ hour. Blend remaining ¼ cup water into flour. Push meat and vegetables to one side; stir flour mixture slowly into sauce. Cook and stir until thickened. Stir in crumbled bacon. Transfer to serving dish. Makes 4 to 5 servings.

QUICK STEW WITH OATMEAL DUMPLINGS

3 to 4 cups cooked cubed beef or lamb
2 tablespoons vegetable oil

1 can (1 pound) onions, drained
1 can (1 pound) white potatoes, drained and sliced
1 can (15 ounces) tomato-herb sauce
1½ cups water
2 cans (10½ ounces each) beef gravy
1 teaspoon salt
¼ teaspoon pepper
1 package (10 ounces) frozen peas
⅓ cup dry red wine
Oatmeal Dumplings*

Brown meat in oil in kettle. Add all but last 3 ingredients. Bring to boil; reduce heat; simmer, covered, 20 minutes. Add frozen peas and wine to stew; bring quickly to boil, breaking up peas with a fork. Spoon dumpling batter by tablespoons into boiling stew. Be sure batter rests on pieces of meat or vegetable. Reduce heat until stew is barely bubbling. Cook, uncovered, 10 minutes. Cover; cook about 10 minutes longer. Makes 6 to 8 servings.

*OATMEAL DUMPLINGS

1½ cups sifted all-purpose flour
1½ teaspoons baking powder
¾ teaspoon salt
½ cup quick or old-fashioned oats, uncooked
1 cup milk
1½ tablespoons vegetable oil

Mix and sift flour, baking powder, and salt. Stir in oats. Add milk and oil. Stir until all ingredients are thoroughly combined. Add to stew as directed above. Makes about 1 dozen.

IN-A-MINUTE STEW

1½ pounds ground beef
¾ cup quick or old-fashioned oats, uncooked
2 tablespoons parsley flakes
1 teaspoon salt
¼ teaspoon pepper
⅛ teaspoon garlic powder
¼ cup milk
1 egg
3 tablespoons vegetable oil
2 cans (10½ ounces each) condensed beef broth
1 can (8 ounces) tomato sauce
1 can (1 pound) small white potatoes, drained
1 can or jar (1 pound) small white onions, drained
1 can (1 pound) baby carrots, drained

1 package (10 ounces) frozen lima beans
¾ teaspoon marjoram
¼ teaspoon powdered thyme
½ teaspoon salt
3 cups water, divided
½ cup dry red wine
½ cup flour

Combine first 8 ingredients; shape into 24 small meatballs. Brown in hot vegetable oil. Pour meatballs and pan juices into large saucepan or Dutch oven. Add beef broth and tomato sauce. Add vegetables, herbs, salt, and 2 cups water. Bring to boil; lower heat; simmer 20 minutes. Remove meatballs and vegetables to heated deep serving dish. Combine remaining 1 cup water, wine, and flour; stir until smooth; pour into beef broth mixture. Bring to boil, stirring constantly. Cook and stir until thickened; pour over meatballs and vegetables. Makes 6 servings.

QUICK STEW

1 pound ground beef
1¼ teaspoons salt, divided
¼ teaspoon pepper
2 tablespoons vegetable oil
1 can (1 pound) red kidney beans
1 can (1 pound) tomatoes
1 medium onion, chopped
1 green pepper, diced
1 can (12 ounces) kernel corn, with juice
1 teaspoon chili powder

Sprinkle beef with ¾ teaspoon of the salt and ¼ teaspoon pepper. Toss gently with fork to distribute seasonings. Form into balls about 1½ inches in diameter. Brown in hot oil in skillet, turning to brown evenly. Remove from skillet. Drain liquid from beans and tomatoes into skillet. Add onion and green pepper; cook until liquid is reduced to about half. Add meatballs, drained vegetables, corn, chili powder, and remaining ½ teaspoon salt. Heat to serving temperature. Makes 4 servings.

HAMBURGER PINWHEEL STEW

3 cups cubed raw potatoes
2 cups sliced raw carrots
1 large onion, chopped
4 tablespoons vegetable oil, divided
1 can (1 pound) tomatoes, with juice
1 cup water
3 tablespoons flour

¼ cup water
1 pound ground beef
1 teaspoon salt
Few grains pepper
6 strips sliced process Swiss cheese

Cook potatoes and carrots until almost tender; drain. Brown onion lightly in 2 tablespoons oil; add tomatoes and 1 cup water. Blend flour and ¼ cup water until smooth; stir into tomato mixture; cook and stir until thickened. Add tomato mixture to potatoes and carrots. Combine beef, salt, and pepper. Form into small balls; brown in remaining 2 tablespoons oil. Layer vegetable mixture and meatballs in 2-quart ungreased casserole. Bake at 350° for 20 minutes. Arrange cheese strips pinwheel-fashion on top. Continue to bake until cheese begins to melt. Makes 4 to 6 servings.

BEAN-POT STEW

2 pounds stewing beef
¼ cup flour
2½ teaspoons salt
½ teaspoon pepper
3 tablespoons vegetable oil
1 garlic clove, minced
1 quart boiling water
6 medium carrots, halved
10 small onions
½ teaspoon paprika
5 stalks celery, cut in 2-inch pieces
1 tablespoon lemon juice
1 teaspoon Worcestershire sauce
1 teaspoon sugar
Dash ground cloves

Cut beef in 1-inch cubes. Combine flour, salt and pepper; roll meat in flour mixture to coat. Brown meat on all sides in hot oil. Put all remaining ingredients and beef into 2½-quart bean pot or casserole. Cover. Bake at 350° for 2½ to 3 hours. Makes 6 to 8 servings.

OVEN BEEF-VEGETABLE STEW

1½ pounds top round, cut into 1½-inch cubes
2 tablespoons seasoned flour
2 tablespoons vegetable oil
½ cup hot water
1 can (8 ounces) tomato sauce
2 tablespoons lemon juice
¼ cup sugar
2 whole cloves

½ pound small white onions, peeled
1 cup cut green beans
½ cup sliced carrots
½ cup sliced celery

Dredge meat in seasoned flour; brown on all sides in oil; place in ungreased casserole. Combine water, tomato sauce, lemon juice, sugar, and cloves; pour into casserole. Cover; bake at 300° for 1 hour. Add vegetables; continue baking until meat and vegetables are tender. Makes 4 servings.

SAVORY MEAT LOAF

2 pounds beef chuck, ground
2 cups soft bread crumbs
2 eggs
2 teaspoons salt
½ cup catchup
1 tablespoon prepared mustard
½ cup chopped suet
3 tablespoons prepared horseradish
1 large onion, minced

Combine all ingredients; mix well. Pack into greased loaf pan, 8 x 4 x 3 inches. Bake at 350° for 1 hour 15 minutes. Serve hot or cold, as desired. Makes 6 servings.

LAYERED MEAT LOAF

4 cups soft bread crumbs
1 small onion, grated
2 teaspoons poultry seasoning
½ teaspoon salt
Few grains pepper
½ cup melted butter or margarine
Hot water
2 pounds lean beef, ground
½ teaspoon salt
Few grains pepper
1 egg

Combine first 6 ingredients; mix well. Add enough hot water to hold ingredients together. Combine remaining ingredients; mix well. Pack half meat mixture in greased 9 x 5 x 3-inch loaf pan. Add bread crumb mixture. Top with remaining meat mixture. Bake at 375° for 1 hour. Makes 8 servings.

PINWHEEL MEAT LOAF

½ cup chopped onion
2 tablespoons vegetable oil

2 pounds lean beef, ground
1 teaspoon salt
1 cup soft bread crumbs
2 teaspoons Worcestershire sauce
¼ cup milk
Bread Stuffing*

Cook onion in oil until soft; combine with beef, salt, crumbs, Worcestershire sauce, and milk; mix well. Roll out between 2 sheets of waxed paper in an oblong about 10 x 14 inches. Remove top paper; spread surface with stuffing. Roll up firmly. Place on heatproof platter seam side down. Bake at 325° for 1 hour 15 minutes. Makes 6 servings.

*BREAD STUFFING

½ cup minced onion
¼ cup butter or margarine
4 cups soft bread crumbs
½ teaspoon salt
Few grains pepper
1 teaspoon poultry seasoning

Brown onion in butter or margarine; add remaining ingredients. Mix well.

FROSTED MEAT LOAF

2 pounds lean beef, ground
2 cups soft bread crumbs
2 eggs
1 teaspoon salt
1 tablespoon prepared mustard
¼ cup well-drained prepared horseradish
1 large onion, minced
1 teaspoon oregano
1 tablespoon Worcestershire sauce
2 tablespoons chili sauce
3 cups hot well-seasoned mashed potatoes

Combine all ingredients except potatoes. Mix thoroughly. Pack into greased 9-inch pie pan. Bake at 350° for 45 minutes. Just before serving top with hot mashed potatoes. Cut in wedges to serve. Makes 6 to 8 servings.

PEANUT MEAT LOAF

2 slices whole wheat bread, crumbled
1 package (2¾ ounces) mild-flavor meat
    extender
1 egg
1 cup milk
¼ cup finely chopped onion
1 tablespoon Worcestershire sauce
¼ cup crunchy peanut butter
1 pound ground beef
½ teaspoon salt
¼ teaspoon pepper

Combine bread and meat extender. Beat in, with a fork, the egg, milk, onion, and Worcestershire sauce. Combine peanut butter, ground beef, salt, and pepper; mix well with a fork; combine with first mixture. Spoon into well-greased small loaf pan, 8 x 4 x 3 inches. Bake at 350° for about 1 hour. Let cool in pan 5 to 10 minutes. Pour off any juices that may not have been absorbed. Remove loaf to serving platter. Garnish as desired. Makes 6 servings.

OATMEAL-RAISIN MEAT LOAF

1 pound lean beef, ground
1 cup rolled oats, quick or old-fashioned,
    uncooked
½ cup chopped onion
1½ teaspoons salt
⅛ teaspoon pepper
1 teaspoon prepared mustard
1 egg, beaten
1½ cups milk
1 cup seedless raisins

Measure all ingredients into mixing bowl; mix well. Pack firmly in small greased loaf pan, or shape into loaf and place in shallow greased baking pan. Bake at 375° for about 1 hour. Serve hot or cold. Makes 6 servings.

SUMMER MEAT LOAF

1 pound lean beef, ground
½ pound ground pork
½ pound ground veal
½ cup wheat germ
2 eggs
1 medium onion
1 garlic clove
1 teaspoon salt
⅛ teaspoon ground pepper
2 tablespoons catchup
1 teaspoon Worcestershire sauce
Dash hot-pepper sauce
1 bay leaf
¼ teaspoon thyme
6 strips bacon

Combine ground meats in large mixing bowl. Stir in wheat germ. Place all other ingredients, except bacon, in electric blender;* liquefy. Pour liquid over meat; knead with fingers until well blended. Place 3 strips bacon in bottom of lightly greased loaf pan, 9 x 5 x 3 inches. Put meat loaf mixture in pan, patting down. Place 3 strips of bacon lengthwise across top. Bake at 350° for 1½ to 1¾ hours or until meat is cooked through. Makes 6 to 8 servings.

SAVORY FREEZE-AHEAD MEAT LOAF

1 can (8 ounces) tomato sauce
1 cup water
3 tablespoons minced dried onion
3 tablespoons parsley flakes
1 teaspoon thyme
1 tablespoon salt
¼ teaspoon pepper
3 cups soft bread crumbs
3 eggs
6 pounds ground beef

Empty tomato sauce into large mixing bowl. Add next 7 ingredients. Mix thoroughly. Add eggs; blend well. Mix in ground beef. Turn into 3 ungreased loaf pans, 8 x 4 x 3 inches. Bake at 350° for 1 hour. *To serve hot*, pour juices from pan. Turn loaf out on baking sheet; place upside down on serving platter. Use juices to make gravy, if desired. *To serve cold*, remove from pan; cool; wrap in foil or plastic film; store in refrigerator. *To freeze*, remove from pan; cool to room temperature; package in freezer wrappings; store in freezer until ready to use. Each loaf makes 5 to 6 servings.

RICE MEAT LOAF

1 package (7 ounces) precooked rice
1 tablespoon minced dried onion
1 teaspoon curry powder
1 tablespoon melted butter or margarine
1 tablespoon chopped parsley
½ cup finely diced bread
½ cup evaporated milk
1 pound ground beef
1 egg, slightly beaten
1 teaspoon salt
Few grains pepper
1 teaspoon Worcestershire sauce

*If electric blender is not available, use a mortar and pestle after chopping onion and crushing garlic.

Prepare rice as directed on package, adding onion to water used in preparation. Blend curry powder, melted butter, and parsley; add to finished rice; mix well. Combine bread, evaporated milk, beef, egg, salt, pepper, and Worcestershire sauce; mix well. Spread ⅓ of meat mixture in bottom of ungreased loaf pan, 9 x 5 x 3 inches; top with ½ rice mixture. Repeat, ending with meat mixture. Bake at 350° for 45 minutes. Makes 6 servings.

INDIVIDUAL FROSTED MEAT LOAVES

3 tablespoons molasses
3 tablespoons prepared mustard
3 tablespoons vinegar
¼ cup catchup
1¼ cups milk
2 eggs, unbeaten
1 envelope onion soup mix
1 package bread stuffing mix
½ teaspoon hot-pepper sauce
½ teaspoon leaf oregano
3 pounds lean beef, ground
4 cups hot well-seasoned mashed potatoes
Melted butter or margarine

Blend molasses and mustard in a large bowl. Add next 6 ingredients; stir well to moisten and break up large pieces of stuffing mix. Add next 3 ingredients; mix thoroughly. Let stand 10 minutes, stirring occasionally. Pack into 9 or 10 large greased muffin cups (3-inch top diameter), rounding well above rim of cups. Bake at 350° for 50 to 60 minutes, depending on degree of doneness desired. Heap mashed potatoes on top; brush with melted butter or margarine. Broil or bake at 500° for a few minutes, until potatoes are tipped with brown. Makes 9 or 10 individual loaves.

THREE-RING DINNER

1½ pounds ground beef
1 cup evaporated milk
2 cups soft bread crumbs
6 tablespoons finely chopped onion, divided
2¼ teaspoons salt, divided
¼ teaspoon pepper, divided
1 can (1 pound) green beans
1 can (10¾ ounces) condensed tomato soup
2 teaspoons vinegar
3 cups hot mashed potatoes

Combine beef, evaporated milk, bread crumbs, ½ the onion, 2 teaspoons of the salt, and ½ the pepper. Pack into well-greased 5-cup ring mold. Bake at 375° for 45 minutes. During last 20 minutes' baking time, drain beans, reserving liquid. Add remaining onion to bean liquid; boil rapidly until liquid is reduced to ¼ cup. Add soup, vinegar, remaining salt and pepper; simmer 10 minutes. Add beans. Heat to serving temperature. To serve, unmold meat; turn bean mixture into center; surround with mashed potatoes. Makes 6 servings.

CHEESE-STUFFED MEAT LOAF

½ pound mozzarella cheese, not sliced
2 pounds lean beef, ground
2 eggs
½ cup packaged seasoned bread crumbs
1 cup tomato juice
½ teaspoon salt
1 teaspoon oregano
Few grains pepper
2 small onions, minced
Vegetable oil
8 paper-thin slices boiled ham

Grate cheese; set aside. Combine beef, eggs, bread crumbs, tomato juice, salt, oregano, and pepper. Sauté onions in a little vegetable oil until golden brown; add to meat mixture; mix well. Turn out on sheet of aluminum foil; flatten into oblong about 1 inch thick. Place ham slices on oblong, keeping them about 1 inch from edge. Sprinkle grated cheese on ham. Use the foil to fold meat mixture over ham and cheese, closing all openings. Turn loaf from foil into a greased loaf pan, 8 x 5 x 3 inches. Pat with fingers to fill corners of pan and shape loaf, which will completely fill pan and be rounded slightly on top. Bake at 325° for 60 to 75 minutes, depending on degree of doneness desired. Makes 6 servings.

FOUR-STAR CHEDDAR MEAT LOAF

3 pounds lean beef, ground
1½ cups rolled oats, quick or old-fashioned, uncooked
½ cup chopped onion
½ cup chopped green pepper
1 cup grated sharp Cheddar cheese
2 teaspoons salt
¼ teaspoon pepper
2 eggs
2 cans (8 ounces each) tomato sauce

Combine all ingredients; mix well. Pack into 9 x 5 x 3-inch loaf pan. Bake at 350° about 1½ hours. Let stand 5 minutes. Makes 8 to 12 servings.

MEAT LOAF BRAZIL

1 medium onion, minced
2 stalks celery, diced
2 tablespoons butter or margarine
2 pounds lean beef, ground
2 teaspoons salt
¼ teaspoon pepper
¼ pound liverwurst
1 tablespoon catchup
1 teaspoon prepared mustard
1 package piecrust mix

Cook onion and celery in butter or margarine until soft but not brown. Add to beef with salt and pepper. Shape in a roll about 10 inches long. Mash liverwurst; blend in catchup and mustard. Prepare piecrust mix as directed on package; roll out in rectangle about 10 x 12 inches. Spread center of rectangle with liverwurst mixture covering an area the size of meat roll; place meat roll on liverwurst mixture; bring pastry up over meat; seal, leaving ends open. Place roll seam side down on ungreased baking sheet. Cut gashes along top to indicate slices. Bake at 400° for 30 to 35 minutes or until pastry is lightly browned. Makes 8 to 10 servings.

SURPRISE MEAT LOAF

1 egg, slightly beaten
1 cup tomato juice
2 cups soft bread crumbs
1 medium onion, minced
1 teaspoon salt
Few grains pepper
1 teaspoon poultry seasoning
3 pounds ground beef
4 frankfurters

Combine all ingredients except beef and frankfurters; let stand 10 minutes. Add beef; mix well. Fill 11 x 4½ x 2½-inch pan half full of beef mixture. Place frankfurters on top lengthwise, in pairs. Add remaining beef mixture. Bake at 350° for 1½ hours. Makes 8 servings.

MACARONI MEAT LOAF

2 pounds lean beef, ground
2 cans (8 ounces each) tomato sauce

1½ cups soft bread crumbs
½ cup chopped onion
2 eggs
2½ teaspoons salt, divided
¼ teaspoon pepper
1 cup elbow macaroni, cooked and drained
1 cup shredded process American cheese
¼ cup sliced stuffed olives
Mushroom sauce (page 57; optional)

Combine beef, 1 can tomato sauce, bread crumbs, onion, 1 egg, 1½ teaspoons salt, and pepper. Beat remaining egg until frothy; blend in macaroni, cheese, olives, remaining can of tomato sauce, and remaining salt. Pack half the meat mixture firmly into ungreased 9 x 5 x 3 loaf pan; spread macaroni mixture on top. Cover with remaining meat mixture; pack down firmly. Bake at 350° for 45 minutes; pour off fat. Let stand 10 minutes; unmold carefully on hot serving platter. Serve with Mushroom Sauce, if desired. Makes 6 servings.

DELUXE MEAT LOAF

2 medium stalks celery, chopped
1 medium onion, minced
1 medium carrot, minced
2 strips bacon, finely diced
1 can (3 or 4 ounces) mushrooms, diced
1 medium green pepper, minced
½ teaspoon each celery flakes, dry mustard, sage, and salt
¼ teaspoon each garlic powder and pepper
1 tablespoon soy sauce
1 tablespoon Worcestershire sauce
1 cup milk
2 eggs
1 cup packaged fine dry bread crumbs
1 pound lean beef, ground
1 can (8 ounces) tomato sauce (optional)

Combine all ingredients except beef and tomato sauce; mix well; let stand 30 minutes to 1 hour. Add beef; mix thoroughly. Spoon into greased 8 x 4 x 3-inch loaf pan. Bake at 350° for 1 hour and 15 minutes. If desired, top with tomato sauce for last 15 minutes of baking time, or serve hot tomato sauce separately. Makes 5 to 6 servings.

GLORIFIED MEAT LOAF

2 pounds ground beef
¼ cup chopped onion
2 teaspoons salt

¼ teaspoon pepper
¼ teaspoon marjoram
2 eggs, beaten
1 can (8 ounces) tomato sauce
1 cup rolled oats, quick or old-fashioned, uncooked
Mushroom Rice (page 169)
Curry-Ginger Sauce*

Combine first 8 ingredients. Pack into 1½-quart ring mold. Bake at 350° about 45 minutes. Unmold; fill center with Mushroom Rice. Serve Curry-Ginger Sauce separately. Makes 6 to 8 servings.

*CURRY-GINGER SAUCE

3 tablespoons butter or margarine
3 tablespoons flour
1½ cups milk
⅛ teaspoon ginger
1½ teaspoons curry powder
¼ teaspoon salt
⅛ teaspoon pepper
2 tablespoons sliced stuffed olives

Melt butter in saucepan; add flour; stir until well blended. Add milk gradually, stirring constantly until thickened. Add remaining ingredients except olives; cook over low heat about 15 minutes. Stir frequently; add olives just before serving. Makes about 1½ cups.

SPICED-UP MEAT LOAF

2 pounds ground beef, round steak or chuck
1 cup ground suet
1 cup finely chopped onions
2 cups soft bread crumbs
2 teaspoons salt
2 tablespoons Worcestershire sauce
2 eggs
¼ cup drained prepared horseradish
1 teaspoon dry mustard
1 green pepper, finely chopped
¼ to ⅓ cup catchup

Combine all ingredients except catchup. Mix thoroughly. Spoon into greased loaf pan, 8 x 5 x 3 inches, mounding slightly in center. Spread catchup over top. Bake at 350° for 1 hour and 15 minutes. Can be served hot or cold. Makes 6 to 8 servings.

MEAT LOAF DELUXE

3 eggs
1 cup evaporated milk
2 cups soft bread crumbs
1½ teaspoons salt
¾ teaspoon dry thyme leaves
½ teaspoon hot-pepper sauce
½ cup finely chopped onion
3 pounds ground beef
1 package piecrust mix
Tomato-Mushroom Sauce* (optional)

Beat eggs and milk with rotary beater until blended. Remove 3 tablespoons of this mixture; reserve to use as a glaze. Add bread crumbs to remaining mixture; beat with rotary beater until blended. Add remaining ingredients except piecrust mix and sauce; stir with a fork until thoroughly blended. Pack into ungreased loaf pan, 9 x 5 x 3 inches. Bake at 375° for 1½ hours. While loaf is baking, make pastry according to package directions and roll into a rectangle slightly larger than 10 x 13 inches. Trim to make a rectangle exactly 10 x 13 inches. Roll out scraps; cut with leaf canapé cutter for garnish. Remove meat loaf from pan to foil-lined baking sheet, making rim 1 inch high with foil. Cover loaf with pastry rectangle; press bottom edges with fork; prick sides. Press leaf shapes around edge. Brush pastry with reserved egg-milk mixture. Bake at 400° for 20 to 25 minutes longer, brushing with glaze several times. Serve hot, with Tomato-Mushroom Sauce, if desired, or cold. Makes 8 to 12 servings.

*TOMATO-MUSHROOM SAUCE

Combine 2 cans (8 ounces each) tomato sauce and 1 can (3 ounces) sliced broiled mushrooms. Heat.

BARBECUED MEAT LOAF

¼ cup light molasses
¼ cup prepared mustard
¼ cup vinegar
½ cup tomato juice
2 eggs
2 cups soft bread crumbs
½ cup minced onion
2 teaspoons salt
¼ teaspoon thyme
2 pounds lean beef, ground
1 can (1 pound 14 ounces) peach halves, drained

Combine molasses and mustard; blend thoroughly. Add vinegar; mix well. Measure ⅓ cup of molasses mixture; combine with tomato juice, eggs, and bread crumbs in large mixing bowl; mix until blended. Mix in onion, salt, and thyme. Add ground beef; mix well. Form into loaf in shallow ungreased baking pan. Brush with part of remaining molasses mixture. Bake at 350° for 1 hour, brushing occasionally with molasses mixture. Add peach halves to pan; spoon molasses mixture into hollows; bake 15 minutes longer. Serve loaf with barbecued peaches. Makes 8 servings.

MEAT-AND-VEGETABLE LOAF

1 tablespoon minced dried onion
2 teaspoons Worcestershire sauce
1 can (10¾ ounces) condensed vegetable soup
1 egg, unbeaten
2 pounds ground beef chuck

Add onion and Worcestershire sauce to soup. Let stand about 10 minutes. Add egg and soup mixture to meat. Mix thoroughly. Bake in greased loaf pan, 8 x 5 x 3 inches, at 350° about 1 hour 15 minutes. Makes 6 servings.

MEAT LOAF ITALIAN STYLE

2 pounds lean beef, ground
¾ cup wheat germ
½ cup finely chopped onion
¼ cup catchup
2 eggs
1 tablespoon Worcestershire sauce
1½ teaspoons salt
1 teaspoon oregano
1 teaspoon basil
¼ teaspoon pepper
¼ pound mozzarella cheese, cut in ¼-inch cubes
3 square slices (3½ inches) mozzarella cheese, cut in half diagonally (optional)

Combine all ingredients except cheese; mix well. Add cubed cheese; mix well. Pack into greased loaf pan, 8 x 5 x 3 inches. Push all cheese cubes into loaf, smoothing off top of loaf. Bake at 350° for about 1 hour or until done. Remove from oven; overlap slices of cheese down center of loaf, if desired. Return loaf to oven for 1 or 2 minutes to soften cheese. Serve hot or cold. Makes 6 to 8 servings.

MEXICALI MEAT LOAF

1½ pounds ground beef
¾ cup quick or old-fashioned oats, uncooked
½ cup tomato juice
1 egg, beaten
1 teaspoon salt
¼ teaspoon pepper
1 teaspoon chili powder
2 teaspoons minced dried onion
3 tablespoons butter or margarine
3 tablespoons all-purpose flour
1 teaspoon salt
1½ cups milk
8 slices (½-pound package) process American cheese, cut in pieces
1 can (12 ounces) Mexican-style whole kernel corn, drained
2 small green peppers, cut into 8 rings

Combine first 8 ingredients thoroughly. Pack in bottom of ungreased 9-inch square baking pan or shallow, oblong 2-quart baking dish. Bake at 350° for 20 minutes. Drain off excess juices. Meanwhile, melt butter in saucepan. Blend in flour and salt until smooth. Add milk; bring to boil; cook 1 minute. Add cheese; stir until melted. Stir in corn. Pour over partially cooked meat loaf. Top with green pepper rings. Return meat loaf to oven. Bake an additional 20 minutes. Cool 10 minutes before cutting. Makes 8 servings.

BEEF ROLLS

2 tablespoons butter or margarine
2 medium onions, chopped fine
1 garlic clove, minced
3 pounds beef chuck, ground
3 eggs
1 tablespoon prepared mustard
1½ teaspoons salt
Few grains pepper
3 tablespoons vegetable oil
½ cup dry red wine
1 tablespoon tomato paste
1 teaspoon cornstarch (optional)
Garnish (optional): mushroom caps

Melt butter or margarine in frying pan; add onion and garlic. Cook over low heat 5 minutes. Combine beef and eggs; add mustard and onion mixture, salt and pepper. Divide mixture in half; shape into 2 rolls about 3 inches in diameter. Place in roasting pan with oil. Bake at 325° for 45 minutes to 1 hour. Remove rolls to hot platter;

keep warm. Add wine and tomato paste to drippings in roasting pan; stir smooth; thicken with 1 teaspoon cornstarch blended with 1 tablespoon cold water, if desired; pour over loaves. Garnish with mushroom caps, if desired. Makes 12 servings.

STUFFED MEAT ROLL WITH MUSHROOM SAUCE

4 tablespoons butter or margarine
2 tablespoons minced onion
4 cups soft bread crumbs
½ cup finely diced celery
2 tablespoons chopped parsley
1 teaspoon salt, divided
¼ teaspoon pepper, divided
1 pound ground beef
¼ cup milk
Mushroom Sauce*

Melt butter in saucepan; add onion; cook until tender but not brown. Add bread crumbs, celery, parsley, ½ teaspoon salt, and half the pepper. Mix lightly; reserve. Combine beef, milk, remaining salt and pepper; mix in 1 cup of the crumb mixture. Put waxed paper on breadboard; place meat on paper. Flour rolling pin; roll meat into rectangle 9 x 11 inches. Spread remaining crumb mixture on meat; roll as for jelly roll. Place in shallow ungreased baking pan; bake at 350° for 45 minutes. Remove meat roll to warm platter while making sauce. Serve sauce separately. Makes 4 to 6 servings.

*MUSHROOM SAUCE

1 can (4 ounces) button mushrooms
1 tablespoon flour
¼ teaspoon salt
Drippings (from Stuffed Meat Roll, above)

Drain mushrooms; add enough water to mushroom liquid to make 1 cup. Add flour and salt to drippings in baking pan; stir smooth. Add liquid; cook, stirring constantly, until mixture thickens and comes to a boil. Add mushrooms; heat to serving temperature.

PATIO SUPPER

2 tablespoons butter or margarine
1 large onion, chopped
2 pounds ground beef
2 cans (1 pound each) tomatoes

2 cans (10¾ ounces each) condensed tomato
    soup
1 teaspoon paprika
¼ teaspoon cayenne
1 bay leaf
2 tablespoons chili powder
1 garlic clove
1 teaspoon salt
2 cans (1 pound each) kidney beans
Corn Bread*

Melt butter over medium heat. Add onion and
meat; cook until brown, stirring often. Add tomatoes with juice, soup, paprika, cayenne, bay
leaf, and chili powder. Simmer 1 hour, adding
water if mixture gets too thick. Mash garlic and
salt together; stir into mixture. Stir in beans (do
not drain). Heat thoroughly. Serve on squares of
hot Corn Bread. Makes 12 servings.

*CORN BREAD

Prepare 2 packages corn muffin mix as directed
on package. Bake in well-greased oblong pan, 8
x 11 x 2 inches, at 350° for about 35 minutes or
until golden brown. Cut in squares and serve
piping-hot.

HAMBURGER TURNOVERS

Pastry for 2-crust pie
1½ pounds round steak, ground
2 cups finely diced cooked potatoes
1 large onion, finely chopped
⅓ cup chopped parsley
1½ teaspoons salt
⅛ teaspoon pepper
⅛ teaspoon rosemary
⅓ cup butter or margarine
⅓ cup lemon juice
1 teaspoon grated lemon peel
1 egg, beaten

For 12 turnovers, roll pastry ⅛ inch thick; cut
into twelve 6-inch circles. Mix ground steak, potatoes, onion, parsley, salt, pepper, and rosemary. Place a layer of meat mixture on each
round of pastry to within ½ inch of edge. Dot
with butter; sprinkle with lemon juice and grated
lemon peel. Dampen edges of pastry with water;
fold over; press edges together and flute. Brush
with beaten egg. Make 2 small slits in top of each
turnover. Bake at 400° for 1 hour.

ACCOMPANIMENT: Serve hot with a tomato
sauce or cold with relish.

MOCK STEAK

2 teaspoons Worcestershire sauce
1 teaspoon salt
Few grains pepper
½ cup catchup
2 pounds ground beef
1 cup bread crumbs
¼ cup chopped onion
3 cups mashed potatoes
1 can (4 ounces) button mushrooms
2 cups cooked and seasoned green peas

Combine Worcestershire sauce, salt, pepper, and
catchup; blend with meat, crumbs, and onion.
Heat plank (or use heatproof platter) at 350°;
grease well. Shape meat mixture on plank to resemble T-bone steak. Bake at 350° for 45 minutes. Spoon border of mashed potatoes around
meat; garnish with drained mushrooms. Raise
oven to 450°; return plank to oven to brown potatoes. Spoon hot peas between meat and potatoes. Makes 6 servings.

CHOPPED BEEF CURRY

1 tart apple, peeled, cored, and chopped
2 medium onions, finely chopped
1 garlic clove, minced
1 tablespoon vegetable oil
1 pound lean beef, ground
2 tablespoons curry powder (or to taste)
1 teaspoon salt
½ cup diced celery
⅓ cup raisins
¼ cup flaked coconut
1 can (10½ ounces) beef gravy
1 can (8 ounces) tomato sauce
Hot cooked rice

Sauté apple, onions, and garlic in oil for 5 minutes. Add beef; break up with fork; brown
slowly. Sprinkle with curry powder and salt. Add
remaining ingredients except rice; mix well.
Simmer, covered, about 1 hour. Serve on hot
fluffy rice. Makes 4 servings.

ACCOMPANIMENTS: Any desired curry accompaniments such as chutney, peanuts, flaked coconut, diced cucumber, additional raisins, etc.

CABBAGE ROLLS

1 head cabbage
1 pound round steak, ground
2 green peppers, chopped fine

2 medium onions, chopped fine
2 tablespoons vegetable oil
⅓ cup chili sauce
1 tablespoon soy sauce
1 teaspoon salt
⅛ teaspoon pepper
1 can (10½ ounces) beef gravy

Core cabbage; cook 7 minutes in boiling salted water to cover. Drain; cool; remove 12 large leaves.* Meanwhile, cook ground meat, green peppers, and onions in oil until meat is browned; add chili sauce, soy sauce, salt, and pepper; mix well. Place equal amount meat mixture on each cabbage leaf; roll up; secure with wooden picks; place in large saucepan; add 1 cup water; cover; simmer about 1 hour; drain. Heat gravy; pour over rolls. Makes 6 servings.

MOCK ENCHILADA

1 pound hamburger
2 tablespoons vegetable oil
⅓ cup chopped onion
1 teaspoon salt
¼ teaspoon pepper
1 can (15 ounces) chili con carne
1 package corn chips
½ pound American Cheddar cheese, diced

Stir hamburger in hot oil until browned. Add onion; cook until soft. Add salt, pepper, and chili con carne. Mix well. Place alternate layers of corn chips, chili mixture, and diced cheese in greased casserole, ending with corn chips. Bake at 350° for 15 minutes. Makes 6 servings.

CHILI POTPIE

1½ pounds lean beef, ground
1½ teaspoons salt
⅛ teaspoon pepper
1 teaspoon Worcestershire sauce
1 medium onion, chopped
1 green pepper, cut in strips
3 tablespoons vegetable oil
1 tablespoon chili powder (or to taste)
1 can (1 pound) whole kernel corn, drained
1 can (1 pound) kidney beans, drained
1 can (1 pound) tomatoes, undrained
¼ cup sliced pitted ripe olives
Corn Meal Biscuit Topping*

*Serve remaining cabbage at a later meal, chopped and creamed or served in a cheese sauce.

Combine beef, salt, pepper, and Worcestershire sauce; mix well. Shape into 12 balls. Cook onion and green pepper in oil until tender; remove from pan. Brown meatballs in oil remaining in pan; remove meatballs to 2-quart ungreased baking dish. Stir chili powder into meat drippings; add corn, kidney beans, tomatoes, and ripe olives; mix well. Simmer 5 to 10 minutes. Stir in onion and green pepper; pour over meatballs. Prepare Corn Meal Biscuit Topping; arrange on top of contents of baking dish. Bake at 425° for 20 to 25 minutes or until biscuits are done. Makes 6 servings.

*CORN MEAL BISCUIT TOPPING

1 cup sifted all-purpose flour
½ cup enriched corn meal
2 teaspoons baking powder
1 teaspoon salt
1 teaspoon paprika
3 tablespoons shortening
½ cup milk

Sift dry ingredients into bowl. Cut in shortening until mixture resembles coarse crumbs. Add milk; stir lightly until mixture is dampened. Turn out onto lightly floured board or canvas; knead gently a few seconds. Roll out to ½-inch thickness. Cut with 2-inch floured cutter. Makes 10 to 12 biscuits.

AMERICAN PIE

1 pound ground beef
1 teaspoon vegetable oil
¼ cup sliced celery
1 small zucchini, sliced
1 small onion, chopped
½ green pepper, sliced
½ pound whole peeled canned tomatoes
1 teaspoon chili powder
1½ teaspoons Worcestershire sauce
1 teaspoon salt
Dash pepper
½ can condensed tomato soup
Pastry for 1-crust pie
½ pound sliced American cheese

Brown the meat in the oil. Add vegetables, seasonings; stir. Add tomato soup. Simmer and stir until vegetables are tender (about 15 minutes). Line 6 x 9-inch pan with pastry. Fill the pan with the vegetable mixture. Bake at 350° for about 30 minutes. Place cheese slices on top. Put pie back in oven for a few minutes to melt cheese. Makes 4 servings.

TOMATO CHEESEBURGER PIE

1½ pounds lean chuck, ground
1 tablespoon minced onion
⅓ cup packaged dry bread crumbs
¼ teaspoon pepper
Dash hot-pepper sauce
¼ cup catchup
½ teaspoon garlic salt
1½ teaspoons seasoned salt
1 egg, beaten
9-inch unbaked pie shell
1 medium tomato
¼ cup grated Cheddar cheese

Combine meat, onion, bread crumbs, pepper, hot-pepper sauce, catchup, garlic salt, seasoned salt, and egg; mix until blended. Spread meat mixture over bottom of pie shell. Cut tomato in ½-inch slices; cut each slice in half crosswise; arrange around edge of pie. Bake at 425° for 25 minutes or until meat is done. Sprinkle tomatoes with grated cheese; return to oven until cheese melts. Cut in wedges to serve. Makes 6 servings.

SAVORY RICE PIE WITH HAMBURGER CRUST

1 pound very lean ground beef
½ cup soft bread crumbs
¼ cup chopped onion
¼ cup chopped green pepper
1½ teaspoons salt, divided
⅛ teaspoon oregano
⅛ teaspoon pepper
2 cans (8 ounces each) tomato sauce, divided
1⅓ cups packaged precooked rice
1 cup water
1 cup shredded sharp Cheddar cheese, divided

Combine ground beef, crumbs, onion, green pepper, 1 teaspoon salt, oregano, pepper, and ½ cup tomato sauce; mix well. Pat mixture firmly over bottom and sides of 9-inch pie plate. Pinch 1-inch flutings around edge; set aside. Combine rice, water, ¼ cup cheese, remaining tomato sauce, and ½ teaspoon salt. Spoon into meat shell. Cover with aluminum foil. Bake at 350° for 25 minutes. Remove foil cover; sprinkle remaining cheese over top; bake 10 to 15 minutes longer. Cut in wedges. Makes 6 servings.

HAMBURGER-VEGETABLE PIE

1 medium onion, minced
1 pound ground beef
2 tablespoons butter or margarine
1 cup thinly sliced cooked potatoes
1 package (10 ounces) frozen mixed vegetables, cooked
⅓ cup flour
1 can (10½ ounces) beef bouillon
Pastry for 2-crust pie

Cook onion and ground beef in butter until onion is soft and meat is browned. Add potatoes and vegetables; mix gently with fork. Blend flour with enough bouillon to make a smooth paste; add remaining bouillon; cook, stirring, until thickened; add to meat and vegetables. Line 9-inch pie pan with pastry; fill with meat-vegetable mixture. Top with pastry; flute edges; cut slits in top. Bake at 425° for 35 minutes. Makes 4 generous servings.

HAMBURGER PIE

1 pound lean beef, ground
1 teaspoon onion salt
Few grains pepper
2 teaspoons prepared mustard
2 teaspoons Worcestershire sauce
2 tablespoons vegetable oil
1 can (10½ ounces) beef gravy
1 can (8 ounces) tomato sauce
1 can (1 pound) green peas, drained*
1 can (1 pound) onions, drained*
1½ cups biscuit mix

Combine first 5 ingredients; mix well; form into 8 patties; brown in oil. Remove patties; add gravy and tomato sauce to pan; heat. Arrange patties, peas, and onions in ungreased casserole. Add gravy. Make biscuits, using 1½ cups biscuit mix, according to package directions; place on casserole. Bake at 450° for 20 minutes. Makes 4 generous servings.

BEEF ROULADES

Pancakes:

1 cup sifted all-purpose flour
1 tablespoon sugar
Few grains salt
3 eggs

*Or use 3 to 4 cups leftover vegetables.

1 cup milk
2 tablespoons melted butter
½ teaspoon butter

To make pancake batter, mix and sift flour, sugar, and salt. Beat eggs; add to dry ingredients. Add milk; stir until smooth. Add 2 tablespoons melted butter. Strain through a fine sieve. Chill 2 hours. Melt ½ teaspoon additional butter in 7-inch skillet. Pour in a thin layer of batter. When set and brown on underside, turn and brown on other side (about 1 minute each side). Repeat until batter is used, making 8 large, thin pancakes.

Filling:

¾ pound ground lean beef
1 medium onion, finely chopped
1 can (4 ounces) mushroom stems and pieces, drained, minced
2 tablespoons butter or margarine
½ teaspoon salt
Few grains pepper
1 teaspoon dry mustard
2 garlic cloves, minced
½ cup catchup
1 tablespoon bottled steak sauce
1 teaspoon each snipped parsley, oregano, and rosemary
1 bay leaf, crumbled
2 cups coarsely crumbled sharp Cheddar cheese
1 cup shredded Parmesan cheese, divided
½ cup dry sherry
16 thin slices mozzarella cheese
Paprika
Melted butter or margarine

Brown beef, onion, and mushrooms in butter or margarine. Add salt, pepper, mustard, and garlic. Simmer 5 minutes. Add catchup and steak sauce. Combine herbs, Cheddar cheese, and ½ cup Parmesan cheese; add to meat mixture; cover; simmer until cheese is half melted; remove from heat. Spread beef mixture on pancakes; roll up; place in greased baking dish. Sprinkle with dry sherry and ½ cup shredded Parmesan cheese. Place 2 thin slices mozzarella cheese on each roll. Sprinkle with paprika and drizzle with a little melted butter. Heat at 400° about 5 minutes or until mozzarella is melted. If desired, brown under broiler. Makes 8 roulades, or 4 servings.

ITALIAN BEEF BALLS

1 garlic clove
2 teaspoons salt
2 pounds lean beef, ground
2 eggs
¼ cup packaged fine dry bread crumbs
¼ teaspoon cayenne
1½ cups sliced onions (about 2 medium onions)
⅓ cup vegetable oil, divided
3 tablespoons flour
1 bouillon cube
1 cup boiling water
¼ cup wine vinegar
1 can (1 pound) tomatoes, undrained
½ teaspoon oregano
½ teaspoon salt
2 medium green peppers, cut in 1-inch squares
2 packages (about 8 ounces each) thin spaghetti, cooked
¼ cup minced parsley
½ cup shredded Parmesan cheese

Crush garlic in salt. Combine with beef, eggs, bread crumbs, and cayenne; mix well. Shape into 24 balls. Cook onions in ¼ cup oil until tender; remove from pan. Add meatballs; brown on all sides. Remove from pan. Stir flour into drippings in pan. Dissolve bouillon cube in water; add to pan. Return onions to pan with vinegar, undrained tomatoes, oregano, and salt; stir to mix well. Cook, uncovered, 15 minutes. Return meatballs to pan. Add green peppers; cook another 5 to 10 minutes. Drain spaghetti; add parsley; toss with remaining oil and Parmesan cheese. Serve spaghetti and meatballs separately. Makes 8 servings.

PLANKED GROUND BEEF

Vegetable oil
2 pounds ground beef
⅔ cup quick or old-fashioned oats, uncooked
1½ teaspoons salt
¼ teaspoon pepper
⅔ cup milk
1 teaspoon Worcestershire sauce
¾ cup grated sharp Cheddar cheese
1 can (3 ounces) sliced broiled mushrooms, well drained

To Prepare Plank:

Brush plank with vegetable oil and heat at 225° for at least 1 hour. For best flavor, use an oak plank. A cutting board that has not been painted or varnished may also be used.

To Prepare Beef Patties:

Combine ground beef with next 5 ingredients. Divide mixture into 4 equal parts. Shape each to form a patty ½ inch thick. Place cheese and mushrooms on 2 patties. Top with remaining 2 patties; seal edges. Shape to form 2 patties about 6 inches in diameter. Place patties in broiler 5 to 7 inches from source of heat. Broil about 10 minutes. Turn; broil about 5 minutes longer.

To Assemble:

Place patties on prepared plank (or a cookie sheet with a rim or a heatproof platter). Make a border of hot mashed potatoes on edge of plank. Brush potatoes with melted butter. Brush exposed part of plank with vegetable oil. Place plank in broiler 5 inches from source of heat. Broil until potato border is golden brown. Remove plank from oven. Place hot green beans and baby lima beans around patties. Cut each patty sandwich into 3 wedges; serve immediately. Makes 6 servings.

SNACK BURGERS

1½ pounds ground beef
1½ teaspoons salt
¼ teaspoon pepper
40 miniature rolls* (made from 1 package hot-roll mix)
10 slices packaged sliced American cheese

Break up meat with fork in mixing bowl. Sprinkle salt and pepper over entire surface of meat. Toss gently with fork to distribute seasoning. Shape into 40 tiny patties. Cook in preheated, ungreased skillet about 1 minute on each side. Cut rolls in half crosswise. Place a miniature burger on bottom half of each. Cut each cheese slice in fourths; place quarter slice on each burger; cover with top of roll. Refrigerate. Before serving, heat at 350° for 6 to 8 minutes or until cheese melts.

*To make dough for miniature rolls, follow package directions for hot rolls. Shape dough into 40 tiny balls, rolling between palms of hands. Place on greased baking sheets; brush with melted butter and let rise according to directions. Bake at 400° about 12 minutes; cool.

WINEBURGERS

1 medium onion, minced
1 tablespoon butter or margarine
1 pound ground beef
2 tablespoons flour
1 can (10¾ ounces) condensed tomato soup
⅓ cup Burgundy or claret
1 teaspoon chili powder (or more, if desired)
Salt and pepper to taste
6 hamburger buns
Melted butter or margarine

Cook onion in butter until soft but not brown. Add meat; cook, stirring with fork, until meat is no longer red. Sprinkle flour over meat; blend well. Add soup and wine; cook, stirring constantly, until mixture boils and thickens. Add seasonings. Simmer, uncovered, for about 10 minutes, stirring frequently. Cut thin slice from top of each hamburger bun; hollow out inside of buns;* brush inside with butter or margarine; toast under broiler to a golden brown, heating bun lids at the same time. Fill shells with hot meat mixture; put lids in place. Serve at once. Makes 6 servings.

WEST COAST BURGERS

1½ pounds lean beef, ground
1½ teaspoons salt
⅛ teaspoon pepper
¾ cup chopped walnuts
1½ tablespoons finely chopped onion
3 tablespoons vegetable oil
Burger Sauce*
Garnish: onion rings; lemon slices
Cheese Muffins†

Combine ground beef with next 4 ingredients; shape into 6 patties. Brown patties on both sides in oil in skillet. Remove from skillet. Make Burger Sauce in skillet; return patties. Cover; cook 30 minutes. Serve on large heated platter with mounds of fluffy rice. Garnish with onion rings and lemon slices. Serve with Cheese Muffins. Makes 6 servings.

*BURGER SAUCE

1 can (10½ ounces) condensed consommé
¼ cup cold water mixed with 2 tablespoons cornstarch

*Save crumbs for casserole toppings, etc.

⅓ cup lemon juice
¼ cup brown sugar
½ teaspoon salt
½ teaspoon black pepper
1 teaspoon dry mustard

Combine ingredients in a skillet. Stir over low heat until slightly thickened.

†CHEESE MUFFINS

Split 3 English muffins; spread with melted butter; sprinkle with grated Parmesan cheese; toast golden brown.

SIRLOIN STROGANOFF

1½ pounds sirloin tip, ground
¾ cup finely chopped onion
¾ cup cracker meal
⅛ teaspoon garlic powder
1¾ teaspoons salt, divided
¼ teaspoon pepper
1½ cups milk
3 tablespoons butter or margarine
¼ cup flour
1 cup dairy sour cream
1 can (10½ ounces) condensed consommé
3 tablespoons tomato paste
1 teaspoon Worcestershire sauce
⅓ cup dry sherry
1 cup pitted ripe olives, cut in wedges
Hot cooked rice or noodles

Combine beef, onion, cracker meal, garlic powder, 1½ teaspoons salt, pepper, and milk. Shape into 10 or 12 cakes. Brown slowly in butter or margarine. Combine flour and sour cream; add undiluted consommé, tomato paste, Worcestershire sauce, and remaining salt. Pour over meat cakes. Cover; cook slowly 10 minutes. Add sherry and ripe olives; mix gently; heat 1 minute longer. Serve with rice or noodles. Makes 5 or 6 servings.

DECK STEAK

1 pound ground beef
4 slices (1 ounce each) sharp Cheddar cheese
Garnish: sprigs of parsley

Season ground beef to taste; shape into 8 thin square patties; put pairs together with cheese between; grill to desired degree of doneness. Garnish with parsley. Makes 4 servings.

CRUSTY HAMBURGERS

1½ pounds hamburger
1 egg, well beaten
3 tablespoons flour
1 teaspoon salt
½ teaspoon pepper
½ cup fine soft bread crumbs
4 tablespoons bacon fat

Season hamburger to taste; shape into 4 to 6 cakes. Dip in egg; roll in flour seasoned with salt and pepper; dip in egg again; roll in bread crumbs. Fry in hot bacon fat until hamburgers are golden brown. Makes 4 to 6 servings.

CHILI BURGUNDIES

1½ pounds ground beef
3 tablespoons bacon drippings or vegetable oil
2 can (15 ounces each) chili con carne with beans
⅔ cup Burgundy

Season ground beef to taste; shape into 6 cakes; brown well in bacon drippings. While cakes are browning, heat chili con carne to boiling; stir in wine. Pour chili mixture over browned meat cakes; cover; simmer 5 minutes. Makes 6 servings.

HIGH-HAT HAMBURGERS

2 cups sifted all-purpose flour
2 teaspoons baking powder
2½ teaspoons salt, divided
½ cup shortening
1 cup milk, divided
Poppy seeds
1½ pounds ground beef
¾ cup rolled oats, quick or old-fashioned, uncooked
½ cup chopped onion
¼ teaspoon pepper
¼ teaspoon oregano
Flour
Vegetable oil
Cheese Sauce*

Sift together flour, baking powder, and ½ teaspoon salt. Cut in shortening until mixture resembles coarse crumbs. Add ½ cup (about) of the milk, stirring only until flour is moistened. Roll out dough to ¼-inch thickness; cut in six 5-inch circles. Brush lightly with more milk. Sprinkle with poppy seeds. Bake on ungreased cookie sheet at 425° for 10 to 12 minutes or until golden brown. Meanwhile, combine ground beef with next 4 ingredients and remaining salt and milk; shape into 12 balls; chill. When ready to cook, roll meatballs in flour; brown in hot vegetable oil over medium heat. When browned, simmer over low heat about 15 minutes. To serve, place meatballs on pastry; top with Cheese Sauce. Makes 6 servings.

*CHEESE SAUCE

1 large can (1⅔ cups) evaporated milk
½ pound sharp Cheddar cheese, cubed
¼ teaspoon prepared mustard

Scald evaporated milk; add Cheddar cheese and mustard to hot milk. Cook about 5 minutes longer, stirring to blend well.

LITTLE-LEAGUE HAMBURGERS

2 pounds ground beef
1⅓ cups rolled oats, quick or old-fashioned, uncooked
⅔ cup catchup
⅔ cup finely chopped onion
2 eggs, unbeaten
¼ cup milk
2 tablespoons Worcestershire sauce
1½ teaspoons salt
½ teaspoon white pepper
12 hamburger buns
6 square slices packaged Cheddar cheese

Combine all ingredients except the last two. Mix well. Split buns in half. Spread each half completely with about ¼ cup ground beef mixture. Place meat side up on cookie sheet or broiler pan. Broil 10 to 12 minutes or until edges of beef mixture are brown. Cut each slice of cheese in 4 strips, then crosswise to make 8 short strips. Arrange 4 strips on hamburger to form an open diamond in the center. Broil until cheese is melted (about 1 minute). Serve hot. Makes 12 servings— the team plus 3 subs!

ORIENTAL BURGERS

4 eggs, beaten
½ pound ground beef
¾ cup quick-cooking rolled oats, uncooked
½ cup chopped onions
¼ cup chopped green pepper

1 teaspoon salt
¼ teaspoon pepper
¼ cup milk
1 tablespoon soy sauce
Vegetable oil
Hot cooked rice

Combine first 9 ingredients; mix thoroughly. Form into 8 flat patties. Fry patties in a little hot vegetable oil over low heat until brown on both sides. Serve with rice. Makes 4 servings.

SWEDISH MEATBALLS IN CAPER SAUCE

1 pound lean beef, ground
¾ cup wheat germ flakes
¼ cup minced onion
1 egg
1½ teaspoons salt, divided
Dash pepper
1 tablespoon Worcestershire sauce
1¼ cups milk, divided
2 tablespoons vegetable oil
2 tablespoons flour
1 cup half-and-half
2 tablespoons drained capers

Combine beef, wheat germ, onion, egg, 1 teaspoon salt, pepper, Worcestershire sauce, and ¾ cup milk; mix well. Shape into 36 balls (1 rounded tablespoon for each ball). Brown meatballs in hot oil, turning to brown all sides; remove from pan. Stir flour into pan drippings. Add remaining milk and salt, half-and-half, and capers. Cook slowly, stirring constantly, until thickened. Return meatballs to sauce. Cover; simmer about 10 minutes. Makes 4 to 6 servings.

MONTEREY MIX-UP

8 slices bacon, diced
2 pounds lean beef, ground
Salt and pepper
2 medium onions, sliced
2 medium green peppers, diced
4 cans (20 ounces each) red kidney beans
2 cans (1 pound each) Italian bell tomatoes, drained
3 tablespoons chili powder (or to taste)
1 teaspoon salt
1 pound sharp Cheddar cheese, grated
12 English muffins

Fry bacon crisp; drain on absorbent paper; reserve drippings. Season beef with salt and pepper; shape into 36 small balls; fry in 3 tablespoons of the bacon drippings until well browned and cooked to desired degree of doneness. Remove from pan. Cook onions and green peppers in 3 more tablespoons bacon drippings until soft but not brown. Add undrained kidney beans, tomatoes, chili powder, salt, and cheese. Stir over low heat until cheese melts. Add meatballs. Serve on split, toasted English muffins. Garnish with bacon bits. Makes 12 generous servings.

MEXICAN MELODY SUPPER

1 pound ground beef
½ cup quick-cooking rolled oats, uncooked
⅔ cup milk
1½ teaspoons salt
⅛ teaspoon pepper
1 teaspoon Worcestershire sauce
3 tablespoons flour
1 teaspoon paprika
2 tablespoons vegetable oil
¼ cup chopped onion
¼ cup chopped green pepper
1 can (8 ounces) tomato sauce
1 can (1 pound) whole kernel corn, drained

Combine ground beef, rolled oats, milk, salt, pepper, and Worcestershire sauce; shape into 12 balls. Combine flour and paprika; roll meatballs in flour mixture; brown in hot oil. Add onion; cook until tender but not brown. Add green pepper and tomato sauce; cover; simmer 20 minutes. Add corn; cook about 5 minutes longer or until corn is heated through. Makes 6 servings.

MEATBALLS BAVARIAN

2 pounds ground lean beef
½ garlic clove, crushed
1 medium onion, minced
½ teaspoon savory
1 teaspoon salt
1 cup soft bread crumbs
1 tablespoon prepared mustard
Dash hot-pepper sauce
2 teaspoons Worcestershire sauce
Flour
4 strips bacon, diced
1 cup strong coffee
1 teaspoon sugar
½ teaspoon salt
½ cup chili sauce

1 cup water
4 tablespoons flour
1 cup dairy sour cream

Combine first 9 ingredients; mix well. Shape into approximately 2½ dozen balls; dust with flour. Cook bacon until crisp; remove from pan. Brown meatballs in bacon drippings; remove meatballs from pan. Add coffee, sugar, salt, chili sauce, and water to pan; blend well. Mix flour to a smooth paste with an additional ¼ cup water; stir into pan. Cook and stir over medium heat until sauce is smooth and thickened. Return bacon and meatballs to pan; simmer 5 minutes longer. Add sour cream, a little at a time, blending well after each addition. Heat gently to serving temperature. Makes 6 to 8 servings.

MEATBALLS ITALIAN STYLE

1½ pounds ground round
1½ cups fine day-old whole wheat bread crumbs, divided
¼ cup finely minced onion
1 egg
½ teaspoon salt
⅛ teaspoon pepper
2 cans (15 ounces each) tomato-herb sauce, divided
2 tablespoons grated Parmesan cheese
½ pound sweet Italian sausage
½ cup red wine
½ cup water
¼ teaspoon sugar
½ pound elbow macaroni, cooked
Garnish: ¼ cup minced parsley

Combine beef, ½ cup bread crumbs, onion, egg, salt, pepper, and ½ cup tomato-herb sauce; mix lightly but thoroughly. Form into 18 balls. Roll meatballs in remaining bread crumbs mixed with Parmesan cheese. Place on rack in shallow baking pan. Bake at 400° for 25 minutes. Meanwhile, slice sausage in 1-inch pieces; brown lightly in large skillet; drain fat. Add remaining tomato-herb sauce, wine, water, and sugar to skillet; simmer gently 15 to 20 minutes. To serve, arrange meatballs in sauce on deep serving platter; ring with hot macaroni. Sprinkle with parsley. Serve any remaining sauce separately. Makes 6 servings.

HAMBURGER NESTS

1½ pounds lean beef, ground
⅓ cup finely diced celery

⅓ cup finely diced green pepper
1½ teaspoons salt
Few grains pepper
Dash hot-pepper sauce
1 teaspoon Worcestershire sauce
1 tablespoon prepared mustard
1 cup soft bread crumbs
6 thin slices Bermuda or Spanish onion
6 poached eggs *or* 6 scrambled eggs

Combine all ingredients except onion and eggs. Shape into 6 deep nests. Arrange on onion slices in shallow baking pan. Bake at 350° for 30 minutes. Just before serving drop a poached egg in center of each nest. Or fill with hot scrambled eggs. Makes 6 servings.

FARMHOUSE HAMBURGERS

1 tablespoon minced dried onion
1 tablespoon water
2 pounds lean beef, ground
2 eggs
2 tablespoons drained prepared horseradish
1 teaspoon salt
Few grains pepper
¼ teaspoon sugar
1 tablespoon lemon juice
½ cup finely chopped pickled beets
½ cup light cream or evaporated milk
1½ cups whole wheat bread crumbs
¼ cup vegetable oil
¼ cup butter or margarine

Combine dried onion and water; let stand until onion is soft; add to beef with eggs, horseradish, seasonings, lemon juice, and beets. Combine cream and bread crumbs; let stand 5 minutes; add to meat mixture. Mix thoroughly. Shape into 12 large patties. Heat oil and butter in large skillet. Cook patties over moderate heat until well browned on both sides, turning once (5 to 6 minutes on each side for medium rare). Makes 12 servings.

DINNER IN A DISH

1½ pounds lean beef, ground
Vegetable oil
1 can (about 15 ounces) spaghetti sauce with mushrooms
1 can (about 15 ounces) marinara spaghetti sauce
1 can (1 pound) tomatoes, undrained

1½ cups water
1 package (10 ounces) frozen mixed vegetables, thawed
2 cups packaged precooked rice
1 can (3 ounces) broiled mushroom crowns

Season ground beef as desired; shape into 18 balls; brown on all sides in hot oil. In same pan combine spaghetti sauces, tomatoes, and water; simmer 10 minutes, stirring often. In a 2½-quart ungreased casserole arrange alternate layers of vegetables, rice (just as it comes from package), meatballs and sauce until all ingredients except mushrooms are used. Arrange mushrooms on top. Bake at 350° for 1 hour. Makes 6 generous servings.

VIENNESE HAMBURGER

2 pounds lean beef, ground
1 egg
¼ cup packaged fine dry bread crumbs
¼ cup milk
2 teaspoons salt
1½ cups sliced onions
½ cup butter or margarine, divided
3 tablespoons flour
2 beef bouillon cubes
2 cups boiling water
2 tablespoons tomato paste
1 cup dairy sour cream
8 ounces broad noodles, cooked
½ teaspoon poppy seeds

Combine beef, egg, bread crumbs, milk, and salt; mix well. Shape into 24 small patties. Cook onions in ¼ cup butter or margarine until light golden in color and tender; remove from pan. Add meatballs; brown on all sides; remove from pan. Stir flour into drippings in pan. Dissolve bouillon cubes in water; add to pan. Return onion to pan; add tomato paste; mix. Stir gently over low heat until thickened; return meatballs to pan; simmer gently 20 minutes. Just before serving, stir in sour cream; heat carefully. Rinse cooked noodles well with hot water, then toss with remaining butter or margarine and sprinkle with poppy seeds. Serve beef mixture on noodles. Makes 8 servings.

STUFFED MEATBALLS WITH SPAGHETTI

1 pound ground lean beef
1 teaspoon salt
½ teaspoon oregano

4 slices bacon
2 hard-cooked eggs, finely chopped
2 slices bread, finely diced
2 cans (10¼ ounces each) meatless spaghetti
    sauce
1 package (8 ounces) thin spaghetti
Shredded Parmesan cheese

Combine beef, salt, and oregano; mix well. Fry bacon crisp; drain; crumble; save drippings. Combine chopped eggs, bread, bacon, and 2 tablespoons bacon drippings. Form egg mixture into 16 small balls. about ¾ inch in diameter. Press meat mixture firmly around egg balls; brown well on all sides in remaining bacon drippings. Add browned meatballs to spaghetti sauce; simmer 10 minutes. Cook spaghetti in boiling salted water until just tender (about 7 minutes); drain; arrange on platter. Pour sauce and meatballs on top of spaghetti. Sprinkle with shredded Parmesan cheese. Makes 4 servings.

YORKSHIRE BURGERS

1½ pounds ground beef
1 package onion soup mix
2 tablespoons chopped parsley
¼ teaspoon pepper
¼ teaspoon poultry seasoning
¼ cup chili sauce
1 egg, slightly beaten
1 tablespoon water
1½ cups sifted all-purpose flour
1½ teaspoons baking powder
1 teaspoon salt
4 eggs
1½ cups milk
3 tablespoons melted butter or margarine

Combine ground beef, soup mix, parsley, pepper, poultry seasoning, and chili sauce. Blend egg with water; add to meat mixture. Mix thoroughly. Form into 24 balls. Place in well-greased shallow baking dish, 12 x 8 inches. Mix and sift flour, baking powder, and salt. Beat remaining eggs until foamy. Add milk and butter; mix well. Add dry ingredients all at once to egg mixture. Beat with rotary beater (or low speed on mixer) until smooth and well blended. Pour batter over meatballs. Bake at 350° for 50 to 60 minutes or until golden brown. Serve hot, with canned beef gravy, if desired. Makes 8 servings.

SAUSAGEBURGERS

3 medium onions, sliced thin
3 tablespoons vegetable oil
1 pound lean beef, ground
¼ pound pork sausage (bulk)
1 cup soft bread crumbs
1 egg
1 can (8 ounces) tomato sauce
1 cup dairy sour cream

Cook onions in oil until soft and golden brown; remove from pan. Combine ground beef, sausage, bread crumbs, and egg; mix well; shape into 8 patties. Brown on both sides in oil remaining in pan. Pour off any excess oil. Place onions on top of meat cakes; pour tomato sauce into pan; cover; simmer 40 minutes. Remove meat cakes and onions to serving dish; keep warm. Add tomato sauce slowly to sour cream, mixing well after each addition. Return to pan; heat to serving temperature. Serve with meat cakes. Makes 4 servings.

SPANISH CHEESEBURGERS

1½ cups soft bread crumbs
Stuffed olives
¾ teaspoon water
Few grains pepper
1¼ pounds ground beef
Prepared mustard
1 package (8 ounces) sliced American cheese

Combine bread crumbs, ¾ teaspoon brine from olives, water, and pepper. Mix well. Let stand 5 minutes; add to beef; mix well. Form into 8 flat patties. Broil on one side about 5 minutes; turn; spread with mustard; cover with sliced stuffed olives; top with cheese slices. Broil 5 minutes longer or until cheese melts. Makes 8 cheeseburgers.

PARMESAN MEATBALLS WITH MUSHROOM SAUCE

1 pound lean beef, ground
1 egg
¼ cup fine soft bread crumbs
2 tablespoons grated Parmesan cheese
1 teaspoon salt
2 tablespoons butter or margarine
1 can (10¾ ounces) condensed cream of
    mushroom soup
⅓ cup dry sherry

½ cup water
2 tablespoons minced parsley

Combine beef, egg, crumbs, cheese, and salt; mix well. Take up mixture by rounded teaspoons; shape into balls. Melt butter in large, heavy skillet; add meatballs; brown on all sides. Remove meatballs; pour off all but about 1 tablespoon drippings. Blend mushroom soup, sherry, water, and parsley. Add meatballs. Cover; simmer 20 minutes. Stir occasionally during cooking, adding a little more water if sauce is too thick. Serve with noodles. Makes 4 servings

STUFFED BURGERS WITH MUSTARD SAUCE

1½ pounds lean beef, ground
1¼ teaspoons salt, divided
2 tablespoons butter or margarine
½ cup finely diced celery
3 tablespoons chopped onion
1 cup soft bread cubes
⅓ cup wheat germ
1 tablespoon chopped parsley
¼ teaspoon dry mustard
1 tablespoon water
Mustard Sauce*

Combine beef and 1 teaspoon salt. Shape into 8 thin patties. Melt butter in skillet; add celery and onion; sauté until onion is soft. Add the next 5 ingredients and the remaining ¼ teaspoon salt, mixing well. Spread stuffing on 4 patties. Top with remaining patties. Broil 4 inches from heat for 10 to 12 minutes or until done as desired, turning once. Serve hot with Mustard Sauce. Makes 4 servings

*MUSTARD SAUCE

3 tablespoons butter or margarine
3 tablespoons flour
¾ teaspoon salt
¼ teaspoon sugar
¾ teaspoon dry mustard
½ teaspoon paprika
½ teaspoon prepared horseradish
1½ cups milk

Melt butter in saucepan. Blend in flour and seasonings. Add milk gradually, stirring over medium heat until thick and smooth. Makes 4 servings.

STEAK PATTIES U.S.A.

2 pounds lean beef, ground
2 teaspoons salt
½ teaspoon pepper
1 teaspoon Worcestershire sauce
1 tablespoon steak sauce
¼ teaspoon hot-pepper sauce
1¼ cups finely chopped onions
3 cups shredded sharp Cheddar cheese
    (¾ pound)
8 hamburger buns, toasted

Combine beef, salt, pepper, and sauces; mix well. Shape into 8 patties. Broil 3 inches from source of heat for 8 to 10 minutes, turning once to brown both sides. Top each patty with onions and cheese. Return to broiler long enough to soften cheese. Serve between toasted bun halves. Makes 8 servings.

SWEET-AND-PUNGENT MEATBALLS

3 large green peppers
1 pound ground beef, seasoned with salt and
    pepper to taste
1 egg, beaten
2 tablespoons flour
1½ teaspoons salt, divided
Few grains pepper
¼ cup vegetable oil
1 cup chicken bouillon, divided
4 slices canned pineapple, diced
12 maraschino cherries
3 tablespoons cornstarch
2 teaspoons soy sauce
½ cup vinegar
½ cup light corn syrup

Cut green peppers in sixths. Form seasoned beef into 16 small balls. Combine egg, flour, ½ teaspoon salt, and pepper; dip meatballs in this batter. Heat vegetable oil; add remaining salt. Fry meatballs in hot oil, turning to brown on all sides. Remove meatballs; drain off all but 1 tablespoon oil. Add ⅓ cup bouillon, diced pineapple, cherries, and green peppers; simmer 10 minutes. Blend cornstarch, soy sauce, vinegar, corn syrup, and remaining bouillon. Add to pineapple mixture; cook slowly, stirring, until thickened. Pour over meatballs. Makes 4 servings.

SAUCY MEATBALLS

Meatballs:

1½ pounds lean beef, ground
¾ cup rolled oats, quick or old-fashioned, uncooked
¼ cup chopped onion
1 teaspoon salt
¼ teaspoon oregano
¼ teaspoon pepper
1 egg
½ cup milk
Vegetable oil

Combine first 8 ingredients thoroughly. Shape to form 12 meatballs. Brown in just enough vegetable oil to cover bottom of large skillet. Remove meatballs.

Sauce:

½ cup chopped onion
⅓ cup chopped green pepper
1 can (1 pound) tomatoes
1 can (8 ounces) tomato sauce
½ teaspoon salt
¼ teaspoon garlic powder
Dash cayenne
¼ teaspoon oregano
1 bay leaf

In same skillet lightly brown onion and green pepper in drippings. Add remaining ingredients; simmer over low heat 15 minutes.

To Assemble:

Add meatballs to sauce; cover; simmer about 30 minutes. Remove bay leaf. Makes 6 servings.
    ACCOMPANIMENT: Hot buttered noodles.

VEAL STEAK SAUTERNE

¼ cup flour
1 tablespoon paprika
1 teaspoon salt
1 veal steak, 1½ to 2 pounds, cut 1½ inch thick
1 Bermuda onion
3 tablespoons vegetable oil
¾ cup water
¼ cup sauterne
¼ teaspoon oregano
1 cup dairy sour cream

Combine flour, paprika, and salt; dredge veal thoroughly with this mixture. Slice onion thin;

cook in vegetable oil until soft and golden brown; remove onion from pan. Brown veal steak slowly on both sides in oil remaining in pan. Place onion on veal. Add any remaining flour mixture to pan. Add water; cover; simmer until veal is tender (about 1 hour). Remove veal and onion to platter; keep warm. Add sauterne, oregano, and sour cream to pan; blend well; heat slowly. Pour over steak. Makes 6 servings.

BARBECUED VEAL

1 pound boneless veal
½ pound cooked ham
¼ pound bacon
2 tablespoons vegetable oil
1 cup large stuffed olives
1 medium-sized tomato, cut in wedges
1 cup cooked or canned small white onions
1 medium-sized green pepper, cubed
½ pound fresh mushrooms
¼ cup vegetable oil
½ teaspoon paprika
¼ teaspoon salt
⅛ teaspoon pepper

Cut veal, ham, and bacon into 1½ x ½-inch pieces. Heat 2 tablespoons oil; add veal; cook until lightly browned on all sides. Arrange meats, olives, tomato, onions, green pepper, and mushrooms on skewers in any desired combination. Combine remaining ingredients; blend. Arrange skewers on broiling rack. Brush with oil mixture. Broil 3 to 4 inches from source of heat 10 minutes or until lightly browned. Turn; brush with oil mixture several times during the remaining broiling period (about 10 minutes). Makes 4 to 6 servings.

PEACH-GLAZED MEAT LOAF

1½ pounds veal shoulder, ground
1 pound fully cooked ham, ground
2 eggs, well beaten
1 cup milk
½ teaspoon salt
⅛ teaspoon pepper
1 cup packaged fine dry bread crumbs
Whole cloves
1 can (1 pound 13 ounces) cling peach halves
½ cup brown sugar, firmly packed
2 tablespoons vinegar

Combine first 7 ingredients. Shape into loaf in shallow ungreased baking pan. Insert whole cloves in diagonal pattern on top of loaf. Bake at 350° for 1½ hours. Meanwhile, drain peaches; mix peach syrup, brown sugar, and vinegar in saucepan; simmer 5 minutes, stirring until sugar is dissolved. Baste loaf every 20 minutes, using approximately half the syrup. Stud peach halves with cloves; heat in remaining syrup. Use as garnish. Makes 8 servings.

VEAL GOULASH

1½ pounds boneless veal
¼ cup flour
1 teaspoon salt
Dash pepper
¼ cup chopped onion
1 teaspoon paprika
½ cup vegetable oil
2 medium tomatoes
½ cup hot water
½ cup dairy sour cream
Hot buttered noodles

Cut veal in 1-inch cubes. Dredge with flour mixed with salt and pepper. Cook onion, veal cubes, and paprika in oil until meat is well browned, stirring frequently. Cut tomatoes into small pieces; add hot water and rub through sieve. Add to meat; cover; simmer 1½ hours or until veal is tender. Add sour cream; simmer 15 minutes longer. More paprika may be added to taste. Serve with buttered noodles. Makes 4 servings.

SAVORY VEAL STEW

3 pounds veal brisket, cubed
¼ cup flour
3 tablespoons vegetable oil
3 medium onions, sliced
1 can (8 ounces) tomato sauce
1 tablespoon lemon juice
1 cup water
1 cup diced celery
4 carrots, sliced
½ green pepper, diced
1 cup boiling water
½ teaspoon marjoram
½ teaspoon rosemary
2 teaspoons salt
¼ teaspoon pepper

Dredge veal in flour. Brown meat in oil; add onions, tomato sauce, lemon juice, and 1 cup of water; simmer 1 hour. Add remaining vegetables and 1 cup boiling water; simmer about 1 hour longer. Add seasonings 15 minutes before the completion of cooking time. Makes 6 servings.

CASSEROLE OF VEAL AND MACARONI

1 package (8 ounces) elbow macaroni
½ pound fresh mushrooms, sliced
½ cup chopped onions
¼ cup butter or margarine, divided
1 can (6 ounces) tomato paste
2 teaspoons sugar
¾ cup water
Salt and pepper
1½ pounds veal, sliced thin
1 cup crushed cornflakes

Cook macaroni in boiling, salted water until tender; drain; rinse with hot water. Sauté mushrooms and onions in 2 tablespoons butter or margarine. Add tomato paste, sugar, and water. Season with salt and pepper. Cook 5 minutes. Cut veal in 2-inch pieces; sauté in remaining butter or margarine until tender. Arrange alternating layers of macaroni, veal, and tomato mixture in ungreased casserole. Top with crushed cornflakes. Bake at 375° for ½ hour. Makes 6 servings.

VEAL JULIENNE

1½ pounds veal steak, cut in julienne strips
4 tablespoons butter or margarine, divided
½ cup water
1 teaspoon basil
1 medium green pepper, diced
1 cup thinly sliced onions
1 can (6 ounces) broiled sliced mushrooms, drained
1 can (15 ounces) special tomato sauce
½ cup canned water chestnuts, halved or chopped
Few drops hot-pepper sauce
1 teaspoon Worcestershire sauce
Salt and pepper to taste
½ cup dry sherry
1 cup dairy sour cream

Brown veal strips slowly in 2 tablespoons butter, stirring often to prevent burning. Add water and basil; simmer 20 minutes. Meanwhile, cook green pepper and onions in remaining 2 tablespoons butter until soft but not brown; add to veal with mushrooms, tomato sauce, and water chestnuts. Mix well. Simmer 15 minutes longer. Stir in hot-pepper sauce, Worcestershire sauce, salt, pepper, and sherry. Simmer 5 minutes. Lower heat; stir in sour cream slowly. Makes 6 servings.

LAMB MECHADA

1 garlic clove
½ teaspoon marjoram
½ teaspoon salt
2 tablespoons lime juice
¼ teaspoon hot-pepper sauce
2 strips bacon
20 small stuffed olives
7-to-8 lb. leg of lamb

Mash and mix garlic, marjoram, and salt together, or chop garlic very fine, then mix with marjoram and salt. Add lime juice and hot-pepper sauce. Cut bacon into ½-inch pieces. Makes holes with handle of wooden spoon about 1½ inches deep in about 10 places in lamb. Push small stuffed olive in hole, then piece of bacon, ½ teaspoon of garlic mixture, then another stuffed olive. Place roast fat side up on rack in open roasting pan. Roast at 325°, allowing 30 minutes per pound for medium or 35 minutes per pound for well done. Makes 8 to 10 servings.

ROLLED STUFFED LEG OF LAMB

¼ cup butter or margarine
½ cup minced onion
2 carrots, pared and finely chopped
¼ cup minced green pepper
¼ cup snipped fresh parsley
1 garlic clove, minced
½ pound link sausage, sliced
2½ cups tiny cubes of fresh bread
1 teaspoon salt, divided
¼ teaspoon pepper, divided
½ teaspoon dried leaf thyme
1 boned 7-pound leg of lamb, butterfly style

Melt butter in large skillet. Add minced onion, carrots, green pepper, parsley, garlic, and sausage. Cook over medium heat until vegetables are tender (about 10 minutes). Add bread cubes, ¾ teaspoon salt, ⅛ teaspoon pepper, and ½ teaspoon thyme. Cook 10 minutes, stirring occasionally. Sprinkle lamb with remaining ¼ teaspoon salt and ⅛ teaspoon pepper. Spread stuffing mixture over lamb; roll up. Tie with string. Place in roasting pan fat side up. Bake at

325° for 2 hours or until meat thermometer inserted in center of meat reaches 145°. (Lamb will be pink, not well done.) Makes 8 servings.

LAMB CROWN

1 crown roast of lamb (16 chops)
1 garlic clove, crushed
½ teaspoon salt
½ teaspoon pepper
1 tablespoon vegetable oil
Hot mashed potatoes
Garnish: watercress

Rub lamb crown with garlic; sprinkle with salt and pepper; rub with oil. Roast at 425° for 30 to 40 minutes. Fill center with hot mashed potatoes. Garnish with watercress. Makes 8 servings.

ROAST LAMB SUPREME

1 leg of lamb
2 garlic cloves
1 cup Burgundy, divided
Garnish: Peach Chutney (page 300) and parsley

Cut slits ½ inch long and ¼ inch deep along length of the leg of lamb, spacing them about 1 inch apart. Peel garlic cloves; cut in fourths lengthwise. Insert garlic in slits. Place lamb on rack in open roaster. Insert meat thermometer in thickest part of lamb, being sure it does not touch the bone. Roast at 350° for 1 hour. Remove garlic. Baste with ¼ cup Burgundy. Return to oven; roast until done, calculating 30 minutes per pound or until meat thermometer registers 180°. Baste 3 times during remaining roasting period, using ¼ cup Burgundy each time. Remove to platter. Surround with Peach Chutney and parsley.

GLAZED LAMB STEAKS

1 leg of lamb, cut into steaks
¾ cup honey
1 tablespoon brown gravy seasoning sauce
¼ cup brown sugar
3 tablespoons lemon juice
1 teaspoon dry mustard
½ teaspoon curry powder
Few grains salt
¼ teaspoon mint extract

Tell your meat dealer how many lamb steaks you will need; he will select the leg of lamb accordingly. (Use the shank meat and bones as the basis for a rich soup or stew for another meal.) Blend honey and seasoning sauce. Add brown sugar, lemon juice, mustard, curry, and salt. Cook and stir over low heat until sugar dissolves and ingredients are well blended. Cool slightly; stir in mint extract. Arrange lamb steaks on rack in large open roasting pan; brush generously with glaze. Roast at 350° for 1 hour or to desired degree of doneness, basting several times with glaze.

GRAND SLAM LAMB SHANKS

6 large lamb shanks, about 1 pound each
½ cup soy sauce
¼ teaspoon salt
¼ teaspoon oregano
¼ teaspoon rosemary
1 tablespoon paprika
1 cup dry red wine
Few grains pepper
Cornstarch

Place lamb shanks in shallow roasting pan. Combine remaining ingredients except cornstarch; pour over lamb shanks; let stand 1 hour, turning often. Roast at 325° for 2 hours, basting occasionally with marinade in pan. If desired, thicken marinade in pan with a little cornstarch (about 2 teaspoons) and serve as a sauce. Makes 6 servings.

EAST INDIAN CURRY

3 pounds boned lamb shoulder
3 tablespoons vegetable oil
1 medium onion, chopped
4 garlic cloves, minced
4 teaspoons curry powder
½ teaspoon powdered coriander
1 teaspoon paprika
2 tablespoons tomato paste
2 tablespoons finely crushed blanched almonds
1 cup light cream
2 tablespoons flaked coconut
2 tablespoons minced dill pickle
2 tablespoons minced watermelon pickle
Dash cayenne
Salt
Hot cooked rice

Remove all excess skin and fat from lamb; cut in small, thin slices. Cover with boiling water; simmer 5 minutes. Set aside. Heat oil in large, heavy skillet; add onion and garlic; cook over low heat, stirring often, until onion is soft but not brown. Stir in curry powder, coriander, paprika, tomato paste, and almonds. Stir in 1 cup of water in which lamb was simmered and light cream. Bring to boil. Add the coconut, pickles, and cayenne; stir until well blended. Add drained lamb slices to skillet. Bring to boil; lower heat; cover; simmer 45 to 60 minutes or until lamb is well done. Salt to taste. Serve with rice. Makes 8 servings.

ACCOMPANIMENTS: Peanuts, raisins, and chutney.

SKEWERED LAMB AND BACON

1½ pounds boned lamb shoulder
1 garlic clove
½ cup vegetable oil
¼ cup vinegar
1 teaspoon dry mustard
1 teaspoon Worcestershire sauce
⅛ teaspoon hot-pepper sauce
4 strips bacon

Cut lamb into 1½-inch cubes. Rub bowl with slashed garlic clove. Leave garlic in bowl. Blend oil, vinegar, and seasonings in bowl with garlic. Add lamb cubes. Chill several hours or overnight. Drain. Cut bacon strips in fourths. Alternate lamb and bacon on 4 skewers. Broil with surface of meat about 3 inches below source of heat for about 20 minutes. Turn frequently for even browning. Makes 4 servings.

SPRING LAMB CASSEROLE

1 medium onion, finely chopped
1 medium green pepper, minced
1 garlic clove, crushed
Pinch of thyme
¼ teaspoon rosemary
½ teaspoon dillweed
3 tablespoons butter or margarine
4 shoulder lamb chops
1 teaspoon salt
1 package (5½ ounces) scalloped potato mix

Combine onion, green pepper, garlic, and herbs. Cook in butter or margarine until onion is soft but not brown. Remove onion mixture from pan.

Sprinkle chops with salt; brown slowly on both sides in drippings left in pan. Prepare scalloped potato mix as directed on package, using shallow 1½-quart baking dish. Arrange lamb chops on top. Divide onion mixture in 4 equal parts; mound on chops. Bake at 350° for 30 to 35 minutes or until potatoes are golden brown and tender. Makes 4 servings.

LAMB CHOPS WITH DILL SAUCE

4 to 6 shoulder lamb chops
1 tablespoon vegetable oil
1 can (14 ounces) chicken broth
1 tablespoon snipped fresh dill *or* 1 teaspoon dried dillweed
1 tablespoon minced dried onion
Few grains pepper
1 teaspoon sugar
1 tablespoon lemon juice
Dill Sauce*

Brown chops slowly in oil, turning to brown both sides. Combine chicken broth, dill, minced onion, pepper, and sugar; pour over chops. Simmer 30 minutes. Remove from heat. Remove chops; keep warm. Stir lemon juice into broth mixture; strain; use in making Dill Sauce. Makes 4 to 6 servings.

°DILL SAUCE

3 tablespoons butter or margarine
3 tablespoons flour
1½ cups broth used in cooking chops
½ cup light cream or half-and-half
2 tablespoons snipped dill *or* 2 teaspoons dried dillweed
1 tablespoon lemon juice
2 teaspoons sugar
Salt to taste
1 egg yolk, slightly beaten

Melt butter; blend in flour. Combine broth and cream; stir into butter slowly. Cook and stir over medium heat until smooth and thickened; simmer 10 minutes. Add dill, lemon juice, sugar, and salt; mix well. Pour a little of this hot mixture on egg yolk; return to remaining sauce; blend. Heat, stirring for 1 minute (do not boil). Makes about 2 cups sauce.

SAVORY SHOULDER LAMP CHOPS

4 large shoulder lamb chops
2 tablespoons vegetable oil

1 cup honey
1 cup dry white wine
2 tablespoons Worcestershire sauce
1 large garlic clove, crushed
½ teaspoon powdered ginger
Few drops hot-pepper sauce
Hot buttered noodles
Croutons
Poppy seeds

Brown chops slowly on both sides in oil. Combine next 6 ingredients; mix well; pour over chops. Simmer over very low heat about 45 minutes. Serve chops and sauce over hot buttered noodles to which croutons and poppy seeds have been added. Makes 4 servings.

FRUITED LAMB CHOPS

6 canned Bartlett pear halves
¼ cup syrup drained from pears
¼ cup orange marmalade
¼ teaspoon ground ginger
6 lamb chops
2 unpeeled oranges, cut in 6 thick slices
Garnish: parsley

Drain pears. Heat pear syrup, marmalade, and ginger until marmalade melts. Broil lamp chops, 4 inches below heat, for about 10 minutes. Arrange pear halves and orange slices on broiler pan. Turn lamb chops. Brush chops and fruits with hot sauce and broil until lamb chops are done, basting occasionally with sauce. Garnish with parsley. Makes 6 servings.

IRISH STEW

2 pounds boneless lamb, cut in chunks
2 tablespoons flour
2 teaspoons salt
¼ teaspoon pepper
2 tablespoons vegetable oil
1 garlic clove, minced
1 onion, minced
½ cup thinly sliced celery
2 cups water
1½ teaspoons sugar
6 carrots, cut in 1-inch chunks
8 small white onions, peeled
4 potatoes, pared and quartered
1 package (10 ounces) frozen lima beans
1 tablespoon snipped fresh dill *or* 1 teaspoon dried dillweed
¼ cup dry white wine

Roll lamb in mixture of flour, salt, and pepper; brown in hot oil. Add garlic, onion, and celery; brown slightly. Add water and sugar. Simmer, covered, 1 to 1½ hours or until lamb is tender. Add carrots, onions, and potatoes; simmer, covered, about 30 minutes, adding more water if necessary. Add lima beans and dill; cook 15 minutes longer or until all vegetables are tender. Stir in wine; thicken gravy, if desired; heat to serving temperature. Makes 4 servings.

SPRING LAMB STEW WITH CHIVE DUMPLINGS

2 pounds boned stewing lamb
Seasoned flour
3 tablespoons vegetable oil
1 cup tomato juice
3 cups water
8 white onions
8 carrots
1 teaspoon salt
Few grains pepper
1 pound fresh asparagus
1 teaspoon savory
2 cups biscuit mix
2 tablespoons cut chives, fresh or freeze-dried

Cut lamb in 2-inch pieces; dredge with seasoned flour (salt and pepper added). Brown on all sides in deep kettle or Dutch oven in vegetable oil. Add tomato juice and water; simmer 1 hour. Add onions; simmer ½ hour. Add carrots, salt, and pepper; simmer ½ hour. Cut asparagus in 1-inch pieces; add with savory; simmer 10 minutes. Make dumplings, using 2 cups biscuit mix, according to package directions; stir in chives. Drop into simmering stew, being sure each dumpling rests on a piece of meat or vegetable. Simmer, uncovered, 10 minutes. Cover tightly; cook 10 minutes longer. Add more salt and pepper if necessary. Makes 6 servings.

LAMB SKILLET STEW

2 pounds boned lamb shoulder
Seasoned natural meat tenderizer
2 tablespoons vegetable oil
1 large onion, thinly sliced
2 cups water
¼ teaspoon marjoram
½ teaspoon paprika
½ teaspoon garlic salt
1 package (1½ ounces) stroganoff sauce mix

1 cup dairy sour cream
2 cups cooked or canned peas

Trim all excess fat from lamb shoulder. Treat with seasoned meat tenderizer as directed on label. Cut meat into 1-inch cubes. Heat oil in large skillet; brown meat cubes and onion. Add water; bring to boil; reduce heat; simmer until lamb is done (about 45 minutes). Remove lamb. Measure liquid left in skillet; add water, if necessary, to make 2 cups. Return liquid to skillet; add marjoram, paprika, garlic salt, and stroganoff sauce mix; stir to blend. Return lamb to skillet. Simmer 15 minutes. Blend in sour cream and peas; heat to serving temperature. Makes 6 servings.

NEW ENGLAND LAMB STEW

2 pounds boneless lamb, cut in chunks
2 tablespoons flour
1½ teaspoons salt
¼ teaspoon pepper
2 tablespoons vegetable oil
1 garlic clove, minced
1 onion, minced
½ cup thinly sliced celery
1 teaspoon tarragon
1 pint cranberry juice cocktail
1½ teaspoons sugar
6 carrots, cut in 1-inch chunks
8 small onions, peeled
4 potatoes, pared and quartered
1 package (10 ounces) frozen green peas

Roll lamb chunks in mixture of flour, salt, and pepper; brown in hot oil. Add garlic, onion, and celery; brown slightly. Add tarragon, cranberry juice cocktail, and sugar. Simmer, covered, 1 to 1½ hours or until lamb is tender. Add carrots, onions, and potatoes; simmer, covered, about 30 minutes. Add peas, cook 15 minutes longer or until tender. Thicken gravy with additional flour, if desired. Makes 4 servings.

RAGOUT OF SPRING LAMB

3 tablespoons butter or margarine
2½ pounds boneless shoulder of lamb, cubed
½ teaspoon sugar
1½ tablespoons flour
3 cups lukewarm water
1½ cups consommé
1 large onion, studded with cloves
1 bay leaf

Pinch of thyme
¾ teaspoon salt
¼ teaspoon pepper
½ cup dry red wine
Herb Dumplings*
1 tablespoon cornstarch blended with 2
    tablespoons cold water (optional)

Melt butter in Dutch oven or large, heavy saucepan. Add lamb; brown on all sides. Add sugar; cook 3 minutes, stirring constantly. Pour off fat. Sprinkle meat with flour; cook until brown, stirring constantly. Stir in water and consommé. Add onion, bay leaf, thyme, salt, and pepper. Bring to boil. Cover; simmer 2 hours. Remove onion and bay leaf. Add wine; bring to boil. Drop dumpling dough from spoon on pieces of meat. Cook, uncovered, over low heat 10 minutes. Cover; cook 10 minutes longer (liquid should just bubble gently). If desired, remove dumplings; keep warm; thicken gravy with 1 tablespoon cornstarch blended with 2 tablespoons cold water. Makes 6 servings.

*HERB DUMPLINGS

1 teaspoon each poultry seasoning, minced
    dried onion, celery flakes, and parsley
    flakes
2 cups biscuit mix

Add seasonings to dry biscuit mix. Prepare biscuit mix according to directions for dumplings on package. Makes 12 dumplings.

SPRINGTIME STEW

2 pounds boneless lamb, cut in chunks
2 tablespoons flour
2 teaspoons salt
¼ teaspoon pepper
2 tablespoons vegetable oil
1 garlic clove, minced
1 onion, minced
½ cup thinly sliced celery
2 cups water
1½ teaspoons sugar
6 carrots, cut in 1-inch chunks
8 small white onions, peeled
4 potatoes, pared and quartered
1 package (10 ounces) frozen lima beans
1 tablespoon snipped fresh dill *or* 1 teaspoon
    dried dillweed
¼ cup dry white wine

Roll lamb in mixture of flour, salt, and pepper; brown in hot oil. Add garlic, onion, and celery; brown lightly. Add water and sugar. Simmer, covered, 1 to 1½ hours or until lamb is tender. Add carrots, onions, and potatoes; simmer, covered, about 30 minutes; add more water if necessary. Add lima beans and dill; cook 15 minutes longer or until all vegetables are tender. Stir in wine; thicken gravy, if desired; heat to serving temperature. Makes 4 servings.

LAMB STEW WITH GINGER

3 pounds lamb neck slices
Flour
2 medium onions, sliced
2 tablespoons butter or margarine
2 cups chicken broth
1 can (8 ounces) tomato sauce
1 bay leaf
1 teaspoon salt
¼ teaspoon pepper
¼ cup vinegar
⅓ cup gingersnap crumbs
¼ cup warm water
⅛ teaspoon ground ginger

Roll neck slices in flour until coated. Brown lamb and onions in butter in Dutch oven over medium heat. Add broth, tomato sauce, seasonings, and vinegar. Bring to boil; cover; simmer 1½ hours or until meat is tender. Add more water while simmering, if necessary. Remove bay leaf. Soften gingersnap crumbs in warm water; stir into gravy with ginger. Simmer until gravy is thickened. Makes 4 servings.

RING-O-GOLD LAMBURGERS

Sauce:

¼ cup brown sugar
½ teaspoon dry mustard
2 tablespoons vinegar
2 tablespoons pineapple juice

Combine all ingredients. Cook over low heat until sugar is dissolved. Use to glaze burgers. Makes about ¼ cup.

Burgers:

1 pound lean lamb, ground
½ cup rolled oats, quick or old-fashioned, un-
    cooked
1 tablespoon prepared mustard

1½ teaspoons Worcestershire sauce
⅛ teaspoon pepper
1 egg, beaten
6 pineapple slices

Mix together all ingredients except pineapple slices. Form mixture into 6 flat patties. Press a pineapple slice into each patty. Broil slowly until brown on both sides. Turn burgers pineapple side up in pan. Baste with sauce. Broil until glazed. Serve hot with additional sauce. Makes 6 lamburgers.

CREAMY-CAPPED LAMB PATTIES

1½ pounds ground lamb
2 eggs, beaten
¾ cup rolled oats, quick or old-fashioned,
    uncooked
2 teaspoons salt
¼ teaspoon pepper
⅔ cup milk
1 can (4 ounces) mushroom stems and pieces,
    drained
½ pint dairy sour cream
1 teaspoon crushed mint leaves
Garnish: pimiento

Combine lamb with next 6 ingredients. Shape into 8 patties. Chill. Broil 4 to 5 inches from source of heat 6 to 8 minutes on each side. For sauce, combine sour cream and crushed mint leaves. Garnish with pimiento. Makes 4 servings.

FIFTEEN-MINUTE BROILER DINNER

1½ pounds ground lamb
½ cup rolled oats, quick or old-fashioned,
    uncooked
¼ cup chopped onion
⅛ teaspoon ground marjoram
1 teaspoon salt
⅛ teaspoon pepper
½ cup milk
6 strips bacon
2 cans (1 pound each) small whole Irish
    potatoes, drained
Melted butter
6 bananas, peeled

Combine lamb, oats, onion, seasonings, and milk. Shape into 6 patties. Wrap 1 strip bacon around each patty; secure with wooden picks; place on rack. Place potatoes on rack; brush tops with melted butter. Broil 7 to 8 minutes 5 to 6

inches from source of heat. Turn patties and potatoes; add bananas to rack; brush potatoes and bananas with melted butter. Broil 7 to 8 minutes longer. Makes 6 servings.

BREADED LAMB CHUNKS

½ cup packaged fine dry bread crumbs
½ cup freshly grated Parmesan cheese
½ teaspoon dried parsley
¼ teaspoon oregano
¼ teaspoon dried rosemary
½ teaspoon salt
Freshly ground pepper to taste
1½ pounds lean lamb, cut in small chunks
1 egg, beaten
⅓ cup vegetable oil

Combine bread crumbs, cheese, herbs, and seasonings; mix well. Dip each piece of lamb in the beaten egg; roll in the cheese-crumb mixture until coated on all sides. Place lamb in oil in skillet over low heat. Lightly sauté over low to medium heat until lamb is golden brown on the outside, still pinkish inside (about 12 minutes). To test for doneness, cut a small slit in one chunk and observe color. Makes 4 servings.

STUFFED ROAST LOIN OF PORK

1 whole or half pork loin
Apple rings (see below)
1 package (17 ounces) corn bread top-of-stove
    stuffing mix
Honey
Lemon juice

Have meat dealer loosen backbone from ribs and cut loin into 6 to 8 chops, but not all the way through to the bone. Pare and core apples; slice crosswise into ½-inch-thick rings, one fewer than number of chops. Prepare stuffing mix according to directions for making a moist mixture. Place an apple ring and a spoonful of stuffing between chops, beginning and ending with a chop. Tie chops together with clean white string or hold firmly in place with long skewers. Place in roasting pan (no rack is required, as bone serves this purpose). Roast at 325° for about 2 hours or until meat thermometer inserted in chops reaches 170°, basting occasionally with honey mixed with a little lemon juice. Remove string or skewers and serve at once. Makes 6 to 8 servings.

LOIN OF PORK HAWAII

Pork loin, 8 to 10 chops
1 can (18 ounces) pineapple juice
Hot water
8 whole cloves
1 bay leaf
12 peppercorns
4 to 5 slices canned pineapple
½ cup brown sugar

Place pork loin in large kettle; add pineapple juice and enough hot water to cover. Add cloves, bay leaf, and peppercorns. Bring to boil; lower heat; simmer 2 hours. Let stand in broth until cool enough to handle. Place fat side up in shallow roasting pan. Cut deep slits between chops. Insert a half slice of pineapple in each slit, rounded side up. Sprinkle with brown sugar. Bake at 375° about 1 hour or until pork is browned and thoroughly done. Makes 8 to 10 servings.

PORK CROWN

6 to 8 pounds center cut loin of pork
¼ cup each minced celery and onion
3 cups soft bread crumbs
¼ cup melted butter or margarine
¾ teaspoon salt
⅛ teaspoon pepper
1 teaspoon rosemary
¼ cup milk
1 can (1 pound) tomatoes with juice
½ teaspoon salt
⅛ teaspoon pepper
1 tablespoon aromatic bitters
1 can (4 ounces) button mushrooms with juice
Brussels sprouts

Have pork cut in double chops with deep pockets. Combine next 7 ingredients; stuff pockets in chops with this mixture. Arrange chops in a circle; tie securely. Roast, uncovered, at 325° allowing 45 minutes per pound. Meanwhile, combine tomatoes with next 4 ingredients. Simmer until thick. When roast is done, pour fat from pan. Add tomato mixture to drippings in pan; stir over low heat until blended. Fill center of roast with hot seasoned Brussels sprouts. Serve gravy separately. Makes 8 servings.

SAVORY BAKED PORK CHOPS

6 pork chops, 1 inch thick
3 large baking apples
1 medium onion, finely chopped
3 cans (8 ounces each) spaghetti sauce with mushrooms

Brown chops on both sides in skillet. Peel apples; core and slice. Place browned chops in baking dish. Place apple slices and chopped onion over chops. Spoon spaghetti sauce over all. Cover tightly; bake at 350° for 45 minutes. Uncover; bake 15 minutes longer. Makes 6 servings.

SWEET-AND-PUNGENT PORK CHOPS

6 to 8 loin pork chops
1 can (13¼ ounces) pineapple chunks
1 can or jar (11 ounces) mandarin oranges
½ cup light molasses
½ cup vinegar
½ teaspoon salt
¼ teaspoon ginger
½ teaspoon soy sauce
2 teaspoons cornstarch
1 teaspoon cold water or pineapple syrup
½ green pepper, diced
6 maraschino cherries

Trim excess fat from chops; place on rack in baking pan. Bake at 325° about 1 hour or until thoroughly done. Drain pineapple chunks and oranges; reserve ½ cup of the pineapple syrup. (Reserve remaining fruit syrup for future use in fruit drinks, punches, etc.) Combine molasses, vinegar, and ½ cup reserved pineapple syrup in saucepan. Stir in salt, ginger, and soy sauce. Blend cornstarch and cold water until smooth; add to molasses mixture. Add green pepper. Place over medium heat. Bring to boil; stir and simmer 5 minutes. Add pineapple chunks, oranges, and maraschino cherries. Simmer 2 minutes longer. Serve over pork chops. Makes 6 to 8 servings.

PORK CHOP SKILLET DINNER

6 loin pork chops
4 cups pared, sliced potatoes
6 carrots, scraped and quartered lengthwise
1 cup sliced onions
⅔ cup coarsely diced green pepper
2 teaspoons salt
1 can (10¾ ounces) condensed tomato soup
½ cup water
¼ teaspoon hot-pepper sauce

Brown pork chops over high heat in skillet. Cover; cook over low heat 15 minutes. Remove chops; spoon out fat. Starting with potatoes, put vegetables in layers in skillet; sprinkle each layer with part of the salt. Place pork chops on top; sprinkle with remaining salt. Combine tomato soup, water, and hot-pepper sauce; pour over meat and vegetables. Cover; cook over medium heat 45 minutes or until tender. Makes 6 servings.

PORK CHOP DINNER

6 double-rib pork chops
1 can (1 pound) sauerkraut
1 tart apple, peeled and finely chopped
1 tablespoon brown sugar
1 tablespoon melted butter or margarine
Flour
Garnish: 6 fried apple rings

Have meat dealer make a pocket for dressing inside each chop, with opening between the 2 bones. Drain sauerkraut; reserve juice. Cut sauerkraut into short lengths with sharp knife or kitchen scissors. Combine sauerkraut, chopped apple, brown sugar, and melted butter; toss lightly but thoroughly. Stuff pork chops with sauerkraut mixture. Place chops in baking dish or skillet; sprinkle with flour. Pour in sauerkraut juice. Add water, if necessary, to reach a depth of about ½ inch. Cover; bake at 350° for about 2 hours or until chops are tender. Remove cover for the last ½ hour. Garnish with fried apple rings. Makes 6 servings.

PIQUANT PORK CHOPS

6 loin pork chops
3 tablespoons butter or margarine
½ cup minced onions
1 tablespoon flour
Few grains pepper
¾ cup chicken broth or bouillon
½ cup Rhine wine
2 teaspoons wine vinegar
¼ cup sliced sweet gherkins
1 tablespoon sherry

Brown chops slowly in butter or margarine over medium heat for about 30 minutes. Add onions; cook until golden brown. Remove chops. Sprinkle flour and pepper into skillet; stir until brown. Add broth gradually, stirring constantly. Add Rhine wine, vinegar, and gherkins; simmer 1 minute. Return chops to skillet; simmer 10 minutes longer. Stir in sherry. Makes 6 servings.

GLAZED PORK CHOPS

6 thick loin pork chops
½ teaspoon salt
½ cup water
½ cup syrup from canned pineapple slices
6 canned pineapple slices
6 canned cling peach halves
Chutney
Flaked coconut
Curry Sauce*

Sprinkle pork chops with salt. Stand chops on fat side in hot skillet until enough fat cooks out to brown chops. Brown chops on both sides. Pour off fat; reserve 4 tablespoons for Curry Sauce. Add water to skillet; cover and cook over low heat about 1 hour, until pork chops are tender and liquid has evaporated. Add syrup from pineapple slices to skillet. Glaze chops on both sides in hot syrup; remove. Glaze pineapple slices and peach halves. Arrange chops, topped with pineapple slices, on hot platter. Garnish with peach halves filled with chutney and sprinkled with coconut. Serve with Curry Sauce. Makes 6 servings.

*CURRY SAUCE

4 tablespoons reserved pork fat
1 medium apple, peeled, cored, and chopped
1 medium onion, chopped
1 tablespoon flour
1 teaspoon curry powder
½ teaspoon salt
1 cup milk

Heat fat. Add apple and onion; cook slowly until very tender but not brown. Blend in flour, curry powder, and salt. Stir in milk. Cook, stirring constantly, until thickened. Makes about 2 cups sauce.

FRUITED PORK CHOPS

6 pork chops, 1¼ inches thick
Salt and pepper
½ cup seedless raisins
½ cup minced celery
½ cup minced green pepper
2 tablespoons minced onion
1 cup chopped apple
Vegetable oil
1 cup apple cider
1 tablespoon cornstarch
2 tablespoons cold water

Slit chops from side to bone. Sprinkle with salt and pepper. Soak raisins in hot water; drain. Combine raisins, celery, green pepper, onion, and apple. Fill slits in chops generously with mixture. Fasten with wooden picks. Brown chops on both sides in a little oil. Place in open roasting pan. Sprinkle remaining stuffing around the chops. Pour cider over all. Bake at 350° for 1½ hours. Thicken gravy with cornstarch blended with cold water. Makes 6 servings.

BAKED SAVORY PORK CHOPS

    6 pork chops, cut 1 inch thick
    Seasoned flour
    1 large onion, very thinly sliced
    ⅛ teaspoon each thyme and rosemary
    ¾ cup dry white wine
    2¼ cups water, divided
    3 tablespoons flour

Dredge pork chops with flour seasoned with salt and pepper. Brown well on both sides in Dutch oven. Cover with onion slices; sprinkle with thyme and rosemary. Pour wine and ½ cup water over all. Cover; bake at 350° for 1½ hours, basting occasionally. Remove chops to heated platter. Mix flour and remaining water until smooth; add to juices in Dutch oven. Cook, stirring constantly, until mixture boils and thickens. Season gravy to taste with salt and pepper; serve with chops. Makes 6 servings.

SAVORY PORK CASSEROLE

    6 pork chops, cut ½ inch thick
    4 tablespoons vegetable oil, divided
    Salt and pepper
    1 package (6 ounces) yellow rice (saffron)
    ½ cup chopped onion
    ¼ cup chopped celery
    ¼ cup seedless raisins
    2½ cups boiling water
    6 apple rings
    Melted butter or margarine
    ¼ teaspoon nutmeg

Trim excess fat from chops. Brown chops slowly in 2 tablespoons oil; season with salt and pepper; set aside. Sauté yellow rice, onion, and celery for 5 minutes in remaining 2 tablespoons oil. Add raisins and stir to mix thoroughly. Add boiling water and stir. Turn into oblong casserole; top rice with chops; cover tightly. Bake at 350° for 40 to 45 minutes. Top pork chops with apple rings brushed with melted butter and sprinkled with nutmeg. Cover; bake 15 minutes longer. If desired, run under broiler to brown apple rings. Makes 6 servings.

PORK CHOPS ORIENTAL

    6 thick pork chops
    Salt and pepper
    1 can (10¾ ounces) condensed chicken broth
    1 soup can boiling water
    1 tablespoon dehydrated green pepper flakes
    ¼ cup cornstarch
    2 tablespoons soy sauce
    1 can (about 1 pound) pineapple chunks
    2 bananas, peeled, scored, and cut in chunks
    Hot cooked rice

Brown chops slowly in large skillet; sprinkle with salt and pepper. Combine broth and boiling water; add green pepper flakes; pour over chops. Cover; simmer for 25 to 30 minutes. Remove chops; keep warm. Blend cornstarch with soy sauce and syrup from pineapple. Add to skillet; stir until thickened. Stir in pineapple chunks and bananas; bring to boil. Serve over pork chops and hot cooked rice, with any additional sauce served separately. Makes 6 servings.

PAN-AMERICAN PORK CHOPS

    ½ teaspoon oregano
    1 tablespoon minced parsley
    1 garlic clove
    2 teaspoons salt, divided
    1 teaspoon lemon juice
    ¼ cup vegetable oil, divided
    4 center loin pork chops, 1 inch thick
    1 cup chopped onion
    1 pimiento, chopped
    2 tomatoes, diced
    1 cup regular raw rice
    2 cups tomato juice
    1 envelope instant vegetable broth mix

Crush oregano, parsley, garlic, and 1 teaspoon salt together until thoroughly blended. Add lemon juice and 1 tablespoon oil; mix well. Brush on both sides of chops; let stand at least 15 minutes. Heat remaining oil in skillet; brown chops slowly on both sides (about 15 minutes). Remove chops. Add onion, pimiento, and tomatoes to skillet; cook until onion is soft. Add rice;

stir until well coated with oil. Sprinkle with remaining salt. Combine tomato juice and broth mix; pour over all. Return chops to skillet. Cover; bring to boil; lower heat; simmer until all liquid is absorbed (20 to 25 minutes). Makes 4 servings.

CAJUN FRUITED PORK CHOPS AND YAMS

6 pork chops, about ¾ inch thick
4 medium yams
4 cooking apples
⅓ cup orange juice
⅓ cup lemon juice
½ teaspoon cinnamon
¼ teaspoon cloves
2 small bananas

Brown chops on both sides in their own fat. Peel yams; cut each into 3 lengthwise slices. Core apples; do not peel; cut into 12 rings. Arrange yams and apple rings in shallow roasting pan. Top with chops. Combine fruit juices and spices; pour over chops. Bake at 350° for 45 minutes. Cut bananas into thick slices; add. Bake 15 minutes longer. Makes 6 servings.

GLAZED SPARERIBS

4 pounds spareribs, cut in serving pieces
3 tablespoons red wine vinegar
⅔ cup dry sherry
⅔ cup brown sugar, firmly packed
¼ cup soy sauce

Arrange spareribs in single layer in large, shallow baking pan. Mix remaining ingredients; pour over ribs. Bake, uncovered, at 325° for 2¼ to 2½ hours, turning and basting ribs frequently. When the ribs are done, most of the fat will have cooked out of them. Makes 6 servings.

OVEN-BARBECUED SPARERIBS

3 pounds spareribs, cut in serving pieces
1 teaspoon salt, divided
2 tablespoons Worcestershire sauce
¾ cup Basic Barbecue Sauce*

Place spareribs in shallow baking pan. Sprinkle with ½ teaspoon salt. Add Worcestershire sauce to Basic Barbecue Sauce; brush ribs with part of this sauce. Bake at 350°, brushing frequently with sauce. At the end of 45 minutes turn ribs; sprinkle with remaining ½ teaspoon salt. Brush with remaining sauce. Bake 45 minutes longer. Makes 4 servings.

*BASIC BARBECUE SAUCE

1 cup light molasses
1 cup prepared yellow mustard
1 cup cider vinegar

Combine molasses and mustard; mix well. Stir in vinegar. Makes 3 cups. (May be stored in covered container in refrigerator.)

SAVORY SPARERIBS

3 pounds spareribs
4 tablespoons molasses
3 tablespoons vinegar or lemon juice
4 tablespoons prepared mustard
2 tablespoons steak sauce
2 teaspoons hot-pepper sauce
1 can or bottle (12 ounces) beer

Have spareribs cut in serving pieces. Place in shallow pan. Combine remaining ingredients. Pour over spareribs. Bake at 350° for 1½ hours, basting frequently. Makes 6 servings.

SPARERIBS WITH DUMPLINGS

1 rack spareribs, cut into 2-rib portions
2 teaspoons salt
⅛ teaspoon pepper
Cold water
Dumplings*
¾ cup flour
Few drops hot-pepper sauce
2 teaspoons Worcestershire sauce
Brown gravy seasoning sauce

Wash ribs thoroughly in cold water. Place in decorative Dutch oven or large kettle suitable for both cooking and serving. Sprinkle with salt and pepper. Add enough cold water to cover; bring to boil; cook gently until tender (about 45 minutes). Lower heat to simmer. Do not pour off any fat. Simmer 15 minutes. Drop dumplings on top of ribs. Return to boil; cook 10 minutes. Cover; cook 10 minutes longer. Remove dumplings and spareribs. Measure liquid; return 6 cups to kettle. Blend ¾ cup flour with equal amount of cold water to smooth, thin paste. Pour slowly into kettle, stirring constantly. Cook and stir until gravy is thickened and smooth. Add more salt if necessary. Add hot-pepper sauce, Worcestershire sauce, and enough seasoning sauce to give the gravy an attractive color. Return ribs and dumplings to kettle; heat to serving temperature. Makes 4 servings.

*DUMPLINGS

2 cups biscuit mix
½ cup cold water (approximately)

Combine biscuit mix with enough cold water to make a soft dough. Roll out ½ inch thick on lightly floured surface. Shape into square or oblong. Cut into 12 squares with floured sharp knife.

HONEY-GLAZED PORK BUTT

1 boneless smoked pork butt, about 2 pounds
1 tablespoon mixed pickling spices
3 tablespoons light brown sugar
¼ cup honey
⅛ teaspoon powdered cloves

Remove casing from pork butt; place in kettle or Dutch oven with pickling spices and brown sugar. Add enough hot water to cover meat. Bring to boil; lower heat; simmer 45 minutes. Drain meat; place on rack in open roasting pan. Combine honey and powdered cloves; brush generously over surface of meat. Bake at 350° for 1 hour, basting occasionally with liquid from pan. Remove meat from pan. Chill. Makes 6 to 8 servings.

GLAZED BONELESS SMOKED PORK BUTT

1 boneless smoked pork butt
Water
½ cup light brown sugar
¼ teaspoon cloves
Prepared mustard
½ cup water

Simmer pork butt in water to cover 45 minutes; drain. Combine brown sugar and cloves with enough mustard to make a smooth, thick paste; spread over surface of meat. Place meat on rack in roasting pan. Pour ½ cup water in pan. Bake at 375° for 40 minutes. Makes 6 to 8 servings.

SKEWERED PORK WITH FRUITS

Lean boneless or boned pork
Marinade*
Small white onions
Apple chunks
Canned pineapple chunks

Cut pork into 1-inch cubes. Cover with Marinade; chill several hours or overnight. Drain; saving Marinade. Peel onions; parboil 5 minutes. To make apple chunks, peel and core firm cooking apples; cut in eighths; cut each eighth in half. String pork cubes, onions, and fruits on long skewers. Brush with Marinade. Broil 4 inches below heat for 30 minutes, turning frequently and brushing with Marinade. To serve, slide food off skewers.

*MARINADE

2 cups canned pineapple juice
¼ cup vegetable oil
2 tablespoons soy sauce
1 teaspoon powdered ginger
¼ teaspoon powdered cloves
½ teaspoon powdered cinnamon
2 medium onions, sliced
1 tablespoon lime juice

Combine all ingredients; mix well.

PORK AND FRIED NOODLES ORIENTAL

1 package (8 ounces) medium egg noodles
6 tablespoons vegetable oil, divided
1 egg, slightly beaten
1 pound lean pork, cut in 2 x ½-inch strips
1 cup thinly sliced celery
1 cup chopped onion
1½ cups chicken broth
1 tablespoon cornstarch
¼ teaspoon salt
¼ teaspoon pepper
¼ teaspoon ginger
1 tablespoon soy sauce

Cook noodles according to package directions until tender. Drain in colander. Rinse in cold water; drain again. Heat 1 tablespoon of the oil in large skillet; tilt to coat evenly. Add egg and tilt again. When egg is set, remove; cut in strips. Set aside. In same skillet cook pork in 2 more tablespoons of the oil until browned, stirring often to brown on all sides. Add celery and onion; cook about 2 minutes. Add chicken broth. Combine cornstarch, salt, pepper, ginger, and soy sauce; stir into pork mixture. Cook and stir until mixture thickens and boils 1 minute. Remove from skillet. Heat remaining oil in skillet. Add cooked noodles; cook over medium heat, lifting with spatula occasionally until lightly browned. Turn noodles into serving dish; pour pork mixture over top. Garnish with egg strips. Makes 4 servings.

SPRINGTIME HAM

1 ready-to-eat half ham, 6 to 8 pounds
Whole cloves
¼ cup molasses
¼ cup prepared mustard
¼ cup orange marmalade
Thin carrot slices

Place ham, fat side up, in shallow baking pan. Bake at 325° for 14 minutes per pound or until meat thermometer registers 130°. Forty-five minutes before ham is done, take from oven and remove rind, if necessary. Score fat surface and stud with cloves. Combine molasses, prepared mustard, and marmalade; brush part of mixture over ham. Continue baking, brushing frequently with remaining mixture. Just before serving, surround some of the cloves with thin overlapping slices of carrot; heat from ham will make carrot slices curl slightly, to resemble flower petals. Makes 8 to 10 servings.

HAM BAKED IN GRAND MARNIER SAUCE

Grand Marnier Sauce*
½ fully cooked bone-in ham, shank or butt, about 6 pounds
Whole cloves
½ cup prepared yellow mustard
1 cup firmly packed dark brown sugar
1 cup cream sherry

Prepare sauce. When sauce is ready to use, score fat surface of ham; stud with whole cloves. Combine mustard and brown sugar; spread over ham. Place ham in baking pan; add sherry to pan. Bake at 325° for 1½ to 2 hours or until meat thermometer registers 130°. About half an hour before ham is heated through, pour sauce over ham and finish cooking, basting several times with sauce. To serve, slice ham and pour sauce over slices. Allow ⅓ to ½ pound of bone-in ham per person.

*GRAND MARNIER SAUCE

1 orange, unpeeled, diced
1 cup firmly packed dark brown sugar
2 cups raspberry preserves or jam
2 tablespoons prepared yellow mustard
1 tablespoon Worcestershire sauce
1 cup cream sherry
½ cup Grand Marnier liqueur

Combine all ingredients; purée in blender; chill. Pour sauce back into blender, blend again; pour over ham and finish cooking as directed in recipe above.

ORANGE-GLAZED HAM

1 whole ham, 10 to 12 pounds, fully cooked or cook-before-eating type; rind removed
Orange Glaze*

Place square of heavy-duty foil in shallow baking pan. Place ham in center of foil; insert meat thermometer through fat side into center of thickest part of ham (do not touch bone). Pull foil up around ham, but do not close tightly. Bake at 325° to 130° internal temperature (about 2 hours) for fully cooked ham and to 160° (about 4 hours) for cook-before-eating ham. Remove from oven about 30 minutes before ham is done; brush with Orange Glaze; return to oven. Brush with glaze again in 15 minutes. Remove from oven; let ham stand for 30 minutes before carving.

*ORANGE GLAZE

1 can (6 ounces) frozen orange juice concentrate, undiluted
2 tablespoons each dry mustard, prepared mustard, and molasses
1 tablespoon Worcestershire sauce

Blend ingredients in saucepan until smooth; bring to boil. Use to brush on ham. Serve remaining glaze with ham. Makes about 1 cup.

ROTISSERIE OVEN-GLAZED PICNIC HAM

1 fully cooked picnic ham, 4 to 6 pounds
¾ cup firmly packed brown sugar
1 tablespoon prepared mustard
2 tablespoons cider vinegar
¾ cup canned pineapple juice
¼ teaspoon ground cloves

Run spit rod through center of picnic ham; skewer securely. Start motor. Cook 1¼ to 2 hours, depending on weight of ham. Combine remaining ingredients; heat until sugar dissolves. Use to brush ham often during last hour of cooking.

HAM WITH FRUIT GLAZE

1 canned ham, 6 to 12 pounds
Whole cloves
1 can (1 pound) cling peach halves

1 can (1 pound) pear halves
1 can (1 pound) sliced pineapple
½ cup sugar
2 tablespoons vinegar
2 tablespoons prepared mustard
2 tablespoons light molasses

Cut ¼-inch slice from ham; stud top edges of slice with whole cloves. Cut second slice; leave this slice plain. Finish slicing ham, alternating plain and clove-studded slices. Tie sliced ham in original shape with string; place in shallow baking pan. Drain fruits, combining syrups from cans. Add sugar and vinegar to syrups; bring to boil, stirring until sugar dissolves. Boil rapidly until reduced to half. Use to baste ham 2 or 3 times during baking. Bake ham at 350° for 1 to 2 hours, depending on size. Combine mustard and molasses; spread over ham for last 15 minutes of baking. For serving, remove string; run long skewer through ham. Add fruit to remaining syrup; heat; serve with ham.

EASTER HAM

1 ready-to-eat ham, about 8 pounds
Whole cloves
1 cup firmly packed brown sugar
1 teaspoon dry mustard
¼ teaspoon powdered allspice
1½ cups pineapple juice
Garnish: hard-cooked eggs, dyed or
    decorated; sprigs of parsley

Place ham on rack in open roaster; bake at 350° for 1 hour. Cool slightly; remove rind. Instead of scoring fat in the usual diamonds, use an Easter bunny cookie cutter, pressing in deeply. Use whole cloves for eyes. Combine brown sugar, mustard, and allspice; sprinkle over ham; return to oven; bake 1 hour longer, basting at 15-minute intervals with pineapple juice. Garnish with dyed or decorated hard-cooked eggs and parsley.

BEER-GLAZED HAM

1 ready-to-eat half ham, 6 to 8 pounds
½ cup firmly packed brown sugar
2 tablespoons prepared mustard
¼ cup beer or ale
Garnish: radishes; pitted black olives; chives

Place ham fat side up in shallow baking pan. Bake at 325° for 14 minutes per pound or until meat thermometer registers 130°. Forty-five min-

utes before ham is done, take from oven and remove rind, if necessary. Combine brown sugar and mustard; stir to a paste. Gradually add beer, stirring until blended. Brush part of mixture over ham. Continue baking, brushing frequently with remaining mixture. Garnish top of ham with "flowers" made with sliced radishes for petals, pitted black olive circles for center, and stems made with chives.

HAM STEAK WITH ORANGE SAUCE

1 thick (1½ inch) center slice ready-to-eat ham
Orange Sauce*
Garnish: pitted ripe olive

Preheat broiler. Slash fat edges of ham to prevent curling. Place ham on broiler rack 2 to 3 inches from heat. Broil 8 minutes on each side. While ham is broiling, prepare Orange Sauce. Place ham on heated serving platter; spoon some of the sauce over ham. Make a "sunflower" with some orange sections (saved from Orange Sauce recipe) and half a pitted ripe olive to garnish top of ham. Serve with remaining sauce. Makes 6 servings.

*ORANGE SAUCE

1 tablespoon cornstarch
½ cup sugar
¼ teaspoon salt
1 cup orange juice
2 teaspoons grated orange peel
2 oranges, sectioned (reserve a few sections
    for ham garnish)

Mix cornstarch, sugar, and salt in saucepan. Stir in orange juice and orange peel. Bring to a boil, stirring constantly, until thickened and clear. Add orange sections; heat.

PLANKED HAM SLICE

1 center slice ready-to-eat ham, about 1½
    inches thick
Whole cloves
3 to 4 cups mashed potatoes
⅓ cup grated sharp Cheddar cheese
8 canned grapefruit sections
½ teaspoon cinnamon
¼ teaspoon nutmeg
¼ cup molasses
¼ cup grapefruit juice from can

Slash fat edge of ham to prevent curling; stud fat with whole cloves at ½-inch intervals. Place on plank or large heatproof platter; set on broiler rack with surface of ham 3 inches below source of heat; broil 5 to 7 minutes or until lightly browned. Remove from broiler; turn ham. Arrange mashed potatoes in mounds around ham (an ice cream scoop does this neatly). Top potatoes with grated cheese. Arrange grapefruit sections on top surface of ham. Combine spices; sprinkle on grapefruit sections. Combine molasses and grapefruit juice; pour half over grapefruit sections. Return plank to broiler; broil until ham is lightly browned and cheese is melted and browned (about 7 minutes), basting once or twice with remaining molasses mixture. Makes 6 to 8 servings.

GRILLED HAM SLICE

1 center slice ready-to-eat ham, cut 1½ to 2 inches thick
½ cup honey
1 teaspoon brown gravy seasoning sauce
¼ cup lemon juice
½ teaspoon ground cloves

Slash fat edge of ham at ½-inch intervals. Place on broiler pan. Combine honey, seasoning sauce, lemon juice, and cloves; mix well. Brush top of ham with some of honey mixture. Broil with surface of meat 5 or 6 inches from source of heat for 5 minutes. Turn; brush with honey mixture; broil 5 minutes longer. Repeat twice again. Makes 6 servings.

BAKED HAM SLICES

2 ham slices, cut 1½ inches thick
Whole cloves
3 tablespoons vegetable oil
2 onions, sliced
1 bay leaf
2 tablespoons brown sugar
2 cups sweet cider
½ cup light corn syrup
½ cup seedless raisins
¼ teaspoon cinnamon
⅛ teaspoon nutmeg
2 teaspoons cornstarch

Score ham fat; stud with whole cloves. Brown ham slices on both sides in hot oil. Place in baking pan; add onions, bay leaf, sugar, and cider.

Cover; bake at 350° for 2 hours, basting often with cider in pan. Drain liquid from pan; measure ½ cup; combine with corn syrup and raisins; bring to a boil. Combine cinnamon, nutmeg, and cornstarch; blend with a little of the hot sauce; add to sauce. Cook, stirring constantly, until slightly thickened. Serve with ham. Makes 8 servings.

CRANBERRY HAM

2 slices ham, about ¾ inch thick
Whole cloves
2 cups fresh cranberries
1 cup honey
3 tablespoons prepared horseradish
Juice of ½ lemon

Slash fat edges of ham slices at ½-inch intervals to prevent curling. Stud fat with whole cloves. Put cranberries through food chopper, using coarse knife. Combine honey, horseradish, and lemon juice. Place 1 slice ham in baking dish; cover with half the cranberries. Top with second ham slice and remaining cranberries. Pour honey mixture over all. Bake at 325° for 1½ hours, basting often with liquid in pan. Makes 8 servings.

STUFFED HAM ROLLS WITH APPLE GRAVY

8 shredded-wheat biscuits
Hot water
8 thin slices cooked ham
Prepared mustard
1 package (8 slices) process American cheese
1 tablespoon cornstarch
1 tablespoon sugar
½ teaspoon cinnamon
¼ teaspoon nutmeg
2 cups apple juice
2½ tablespoons butter or margarine
Garnish: olives; sweet gherkins

Dip shredded-wheat biscuits one at a time in hot water. Drain immediately. Spread each ham slice with prepared mustard. Set a shredded-wheat biscuit on each ham slice; place ½ slice of cheese on biscuit. Roll ham around biscuit; top with another half slice of cheese. Fasten with wooden picks. Place ham rolls in shallow baking dish. Bake at 400° for 20 minutes. Meanwhile, mix cornstarch, sugar, and spices. Stir in apple juice. Cook, stirring constantly, until mixture boils. Continue to cook, stirring constantly, until mixture is thickened and clear. Stir in butter or margarine. Garnish ham rolls with olives and sweet gherkins on wooden picks. Serve hot apple gravy with the ham rolls. Makes 8 ham rolls.

DIXIE SHORTCAKE

6 tablespoons butter or margarine
1 cup thin strips green pepper
1 can (6 ounces) sliced broiled mushrooms, drained
½ cup flour
1 teaspoon salt
4 cups milk
½ cup thin strips pimiento
4 cups diced cooked ham*
1 package (10 ounces) frozen cut green beans, cooked and drained
8 packaged corn muffins, heated

Melt butter or margarine in saucepan. Add green pepper and mushrooms; cook over low heat until pepper is tender. Add flour and salt; stir to smooth paste. Add milk; cook, stirring constantly, until mixture thickens and comes to a boil. Add pimiento, diced ham, and green beans to sauce. Heat 10 to 15 minutes over very low heat. Serve over split corn muffins. Makes 4 generous servings.

WESTERN SHORTCAKE

¼ cup chopped onion
¼ cup diced green pepper
2 tablespoons butter or margarine
2 cups diced cooked ham
1 package (12 ounces) corn muffin mix
Mustard Eggs*
Garnish: 2 hard-cooked eggs

Cook onion and green pepper in butter or margarine until soft but not brown. Add ham; cook until lightly browned. Prepare muffin mix as directed on package. Stir in ham mixture. Bake in 2 square 8-inch greased cake pans at 425° for 20 to 25 minutes. Place one layer on serving plate; add half the Mustard Eggs. Add second layer; top with remaining Mustard Eggs. Garnish with 2 hard-cooked eggs, quartered. Makes 6 servings.

*Or leftover poultry or other meat.

*MUSTARD EGGS

2 tablespoons prepared mustard
2 cups well-seasoned medium white sauce
4 hard-cooked eggs, quartered

Stir prepared mustard into white sauce; add quartered hard-cooked eggs. Heat well.

CREAMED HAM, PEAS, AND MUSHROOMS

1 can (1 pound) peas
2 cans (3 or 4 ounces each) sliced mushrooms
Milk
¼ teaspoon hot-pepper sauce
⅓ cup butter or margarine
6 tablespoons flour
½ teaspoon salt
½ teaspoon dry mustard
1 can (4 ounces) pimiento, diced
3 cups diced cooked ham
Hot cooked rice

Drain peas and mushrooms; combine liquids and boil rapidly until reduced to 1 cup. Add enough milk to make 3 cups. Stir in hot-pepper sauce; reserve. Melt butter; add flour, salt, and dry mustard; stir to a smooth paste. Add reserved liquid; cook, stirring constantly, until mixture thickens and comes to a boil. Add drained peas, mushrooms, pimiento, and ham. Heat to serving temperature. Serve in rice ring. Makes 12 servings.

HAM AND SWEET POTATO LOAF

Filling:

2 cups mashed sweet potatoes
2 tablespoons brown sugar
½ teaspoon salt

Combine all ingredients; mix thoroughly.

Meat Loaf:

1 pound smoked boneless shoulder butt (lean)
½ cup quick rolled oats, uncooked
1 egg, beaten
¼ cup milk
1 tablespoon prepared mustard
¼ teaspoon pepper

Grind shoulder butt using coarse blade of food chopper. Combine ground meat thoroughly with remaining ingredients. Using about ⅔ of the meat loaf mixture, pack layer on the bottom and sides of greased loaf pan. Fill center of loaf with sweet potato filling; cover with the remaining meat mixture. Bake at 325° for 1 hour. Let stand 10 minutes before removing from pan. Makes 6 servings.

HAM PATTIES HAWAIIAN

1 cup seedless raisins
3 cups ground cooked ham
2 cups soft bread crumbs
1 cup thick white sauce
Few grains pepper
1 egg, slightly beaten
1 tablespoon water
1 cup packaged fine dry bread crumbs
Fat for frying
12 pineapple slices
¾ cup grated Cheddar cheese

Combine first 5 ingredients. Form into 12 patties. Mix egg and water. Dip patties in egg, then in crumbs; fry in shallow fat heated to 390° for 2 minutes. Place on heatproof platter; top with pineapple and cheese. Broil until cheese melts. Makes 6 servings.

HAM-ASPARAGUS BUNDLES

2½ cups ground cooked ham
1 medium onion, finely chopped
⅛ teaspoon cloves
1 egg, beaten
½ cup packaged fine dry bread crumbs
2 tablespoons milk
24 stalks cooked green asparagus
2 tablespoons butter or margarine
2 tablespoons flour
1 cup milk
¼ teaspoon salt
1 tablespoon prepared mustard

Combine ham, onion, cloves, egg, crumbs, and milk; mix well. Divide into 4 portions; shape each portion around 6 stalks of asparagus. Wrap each bundle securely in aluminum foil; place on baking sheet. Bake at 350° for 45 minutes. Meanwhile, melt butter or margarine over low heat; add flour; blend. Add milk; cook until thickened, stirring constantly. Add salt and mustard; mix well. Serve mustard sauce over asparagus-ham rolls. Makes 4 servings.

HAMETTES

2 cups ground cooked ham*
1 egg

*Or sausage meat.

¼ cup drained sweet pickle relish
1 teaspoon prepared mustard
2 cups mashed yams
2 tablespoons grated orange peel
½ teaspoon salt
⅛ teaspoon pepper
8 strips bacon
16 slices pineapple

Combine ham, egg, pickle relish, and mustard. Shape into 8 patties the same size as pineapple slices. Combine mashed yams, orange peel, salt, and pepper. Form into 8 patties, same size. With scissors, cut bacon strips in half lengthwise. Place a ham patty on pineapple slice, then a yam patty and another pineapple slice. Cross bacon strips; place a Hamette in center of cross. Bring ends of bacon up and over top; fasten with wooden pick. Make 8 patties in the same manner. Place in baking pan, about 1 inch apart. Bake at 350° for 1 hour or until bacon is crisp. Makes 8 servings.

HAM BALLS À L'ORANGE

1 egg
¼ cup orange juice
1 cup fine soft bread crumbs
2 cups ground cooked ham
1 tablespoon minced onion
½ teaspoon grated orange peel
¼ teaspoon dry mustard
½ teaspoon dried leaf sage
2 tablespoons butter or margarine
Orange Sauce*
Hot buttered shell macaroni

Beat egg in medium bowl. Add orange juice and bread crumbs; stir to combine; let stand 5 minutes. Add ham, onion, orange peel, dry mustard, and sage; mix well. Shape into 16 balls about 1 inch in diameter. Heat butter in skillet; add balls and brown lightly on all sides. Serve with Orange Sauce and buttered shell macaroni. Makes 4 to 6 servings.

*ORANGE SAUCE

2 tablespoons cornstarch
1½ cups orange juice
½ cup red currant jelly
½ teaspoon minced onion
¾ teaspoon salt
½ teaspoon dry mustard
½ teaspoon dried leaf sage

¼ teaspoon ginger
1 teaspoon vinegar
¼ teaspoon hot-pepper sauce
2 oranges, sectioned

Blend cornstarch with a small amount of the orange juice in a saucepan. Add remaining orange juice, red currant jelly, onion, salt, dry mustard, sage, ginger, vinegar, and hot-pepper sauce. Mix well. Cook, stirring constantly, until mixture thickens and comes to a boil. Add orange sections.

GLAZED CANNED HAM

1 canned ham, 6 to 12 pounds
¼ cup light molasses
¼ cup prepared mustard
⅛ teaspoon ginger
2 teaspoons vinegar

Score fat surface of ham. Combine molasses, mustard, ginger, and vinegar; brush top and sides of ham. Bake at 325° 15 minutes per pound, brushing several times with remaining glaze. Makes 3 to 4 servings per pound.

KIDNEY SAUTÉ

8 lamb kidneys
Seasoned flour
Vegetable oil
2 large onions, chopped
4 slices lean bacon (or Canadian bacon), diced
8 medium-sized mushrooms
1 bay leaf
3 bouillon cubes
Salt
Pepper
¼ cup dry sherry (or to taste)

Dust kidneys thoroughly with seasoned flour. Brown lightly in oil; add onions. Cook slowly for 30 minutes. Cut kidneys in small pieces. Add just enough water to cover them. Add bacon, mushrooms, bay leaf, bouillon cubes, and salt and pepper to taste; simmer slowly for 30 minutes longer. Remove bay leaf. (If you prefer a thicker gravy, add a little more flour.) Add sherry; simmer 5 minutes longer. Makes 4 servings.

ACCOMPANIMENTS: Serve with scrambled eggs and hot French bread.

SPICED TONGUE WITH SPECIAL SAUCE

1 smoked beef tongue, about 4 pounds
2 tablespoons mixed pickling spices
1 tablespoon minced dried onion
1 tablespoon celery seed
1 tablespoon parsley flakes
Special Sauce*

Cover tongue with cold water. Add remaining ingredients except Special Sauce. Cover. Cook slowly until tongue is tender (about 2 hours). Cool in broth; save broth for Special Sauce recipe. Remove root section and skin from tongue. Slice and serve with Special Sauce. Makes 8 to 10 servings.

*SPECIAL SAUCE

½ cup firmly packed brown sugar
3 tablespoons flour
2 cups strained broth from tongue
⅓ cup lemon juice (or to taste)
½ cup raisins
½ teaspoon salt
3 tablespoons butter or margarine

Combine brown sugar and flour. Add broth; stir smooth. Add lemon juice, raisins, and salt. Boil 5 minutes, stirring constantly, until thickened; then stir occasionally. Add butter; stir until butter melts. Makes 8 to 10 servings.

SWEETBREADS PARISIENNE

4 pairs sweetbreads
Ice water
1 tablespoon vinegar
2 tablespoons butter or margarine
1 carrot, sliced
1 onion, sliced
½ teaspoon thyme
2 parsley sprigs
1 teaspoon salt
Few grains pepper
½ cup white wine
1 cup bouillon
2 egg yolks
Cooked asparagus tips
1 cup grated cheese
Garnish: canned broiled mushroom crowns

Cover sweetbreads with ice water until ready to cook. Drain. Cover with fresh water; add vinegar; bring to boiling point; cover; boil 3 minutes.

Drain; plunge into ice water. Remove membrane and connective tissue. Melt butter in skillet; add carrot, onion, thyme, and parsley. Place sweetbreads on vegetables; sprinkle with salt and pepper. Cover; simmer 10 minutes. Add wine and bouillon. Cover; simmer 45 minutes. Drain off stock; save. Place vegetables in 4 individual ramekins; top with sweetbreads. Beat egg yolks; add stock. Cook, stirring constantly, until thickened. Arrange cooked asparagus tips in ramekins; pour sauce over all. Top with grated cheese. Bake at 450° until cheese melts and browns. Garnish with canned broiled mushroom crowns. Makes 4 servings.

SPICED VEAL TONGUE WITH SPECIAL SAUCE

    2 fresh veal tongues, about 1½ pounds each
    1 tablespoon mixed pickling spices
    1 teaspoon cardamom seeds
    2-inch stick cinnamon
    2 teaspoons celery seeds
    2 teaspoons parsley flakes
    Special Sauce (page 87)

Cover tongues with cold water. Add remaining ingredients. Cover. Simmer until meat is tender (about 1½ hours). Cool in cooking water. Remove root section and skin from tongues. Slice on the diagonal. Heat to serving temperature in Special Sauce. Makes 4 servings.

ALL-AMERICAN CASSEROLE

    1 pound frankfurters, cut in 1-inch pieces
    2 cans (20 ounces each) brick-oven baked
        beans
    ½ cup finely chopped onions
    ½ cup finely diced green pepper
    ⅔ cup bottled barbecue sauce
    Baking powder biscuits (optional)

Combine frankfurters with next 4 ingredients in bean pot or casserole that holds at least 2½ quarts. Bake at 400° for 35 minutes or until bubbling hot. At serving time, ring top of casserole with hot baking powder biscuits, if desired. Makes 8 servings.

FRANKS AND FETTUCINE

    2 packages (8 ounces each) fettucine noodles
        or medium egg noodles
    16 frankfurters

    2 egg yolks
    3 cups milk
    1 cup whipping cream
    4 tablespoons butter or margarine
    4 tablespoons flour
    ½ teaspoon salt
    1 cup ricotta cheese*
    ½ cup grated Parmesan cheese
    ½ cup grated Romano cheese
    2 to 3 tablespoons chopped parsley

Cook noodles according to package directions; drain. Cut deep gashes about ½ inch apart along length of frankfurters; broil or fry until deeply browned. Meanwhile, prepare sauce: Beat egg yolks slightly; add milk and cream; mix well. Melt butter; blend in flour and salt. Add milk mixture; stir over low heat until smooth and thickened. Add cheeses; stir until melted; pour over hot noodles; toss to mix. Sprinkle with parsley. Arrange with frankfurters on top. Makes 8 servings.

KRAUTFURTER TWISTS

    1 package hot-roll mix
    ¾ cup hot tomato juice
    ¼ cup hot water
    ¼ teaspoon onion salt
    2 tablespoons melted butter or margarine
    ¼ cup grated Cheddar cheese
    16 frankfurters
    1 can (27 to 29 ounces) sauerkraut
    Poppy seeds or caraway seeds

Prepare hot-roll mix according to package directions, substituting combined tomato juice and water for liquid. Add onion salt. Let rise according to directions. Roll dough on lightly floured surface in circle ¼ inch thick. Brush with butter; sprinkle with cheese. Cut circle, pie-fashion, into 16 wedges. Roll each wedge around frankfurter, starting at wide end and including a spoonful of sauerkraut in each. Brush with additional melted butter; sprinkle with poppy or caraway seeds. Bake at 375° for 12 to 15 minutes. Serve immediately with remaining sauerkraut, heated. Makes 16 twists.

HAWAIIAN FRANKFURTERS

    1 large can (1⅔ cups) undiluted evaporated
        milk

*Or any dry, fine curd cottage cheese.

¼ teaspoon salt
2 cups grated American cheese
1 tablespoon steak sauce
1 teaspoon dry mustard
4 cups cooked noodles
¼ cup canned slivered blanched almonds
1 cup drained pineapple chunks
2 cups (about 6) sliced frankfurters
2 tablespoons grated onion

Heat evaporated milk and salt in saucepan over low heat to just below boiling point (2 minutes). Add cheese; stir until thickened and smooth (1 minute). Stir in steak sauce and mustard. Combine noodles, almonds, pineapple, frankfurters, and onion in greased shallow casserole. Pour cheese sauce over all. Bake at 350° for 25 to 30 minutes. Makes 6 servings.

HALLOWEEN HOT DOGS

16 frankfurters
4 slices packaged sliced American cheese, cut into 16 strips
Chili sauce
Pickle relish
⅔ cup shortening
4 cups pancake mix
1⅓ cups milk
Prepared mustard

Split frankfurters almost all the way through. Fill each with a cheese strip, then cover cheese with chili sauce and pickle relish. Cut shortening into pancake mix until mixture resembles coarse crumbs. Add milk, stirring lightly only until mixture is dampened. (Add more milk if necessary to make a soft dough.) Turn dough out on lightly floured board; knead gently a few seconds. Divide in half; roll each half out to form a rectangle 12 x 8 inches. Using a pastry wheel, cut into 3 x 4-inch pieces. Spread each square with mustard. Wrap dough around frankfurters, sealing edges together. Place sealed side down on lightly greased cookie sheets. Bake at 425° for 12 to 15 minutes. Makes 16.

BUFFET FRANKS AND BEANS

¼ cup molasses
¼ cup prepared mustard
¼ cup vinegar
½ teaspoon hot-pepper sauce
6 cans (1 pound each) baked beans in tomato sauce

1 can (20 ounces) pie-sliced apples
2 medium onions, sliced
24 frankfurters
½ pound packaged pre-sliced process American cheese
4 medium dill pickles
24 slices bacon

Combine molasses, mustard, vinegar, and hot-pepper sauce; mix well; combine with baked beans, apples, and onions; turn into 2 shallow pans. Split frankfurters lengthwise but do not cut all the way through. Cut 6 slices of cheese into 4 strips each. Place 1 strip cheese in each frankfurter. Cut each dill pickle lengthwise into 12 strips; place 2 strips on each frankfurter to cover cheese. Cook bacon slowly, turning occasionally, until about half done. Wrap 1 slice bacon around each frankfurter. Place on beans. Bake at 350° for 30 minutes. Makes 12 servings.

FRANKFURTER-MACARONI LOAF

1 package (8 ounces) elbow macaroni
6 frankfurters
1 cup soft bread crumbs
1 cup milk
¾ cup grated sharp Cheddar cheese
2 tablespoons drained pickle relish
2 eggs, slightly beaten
1 teaspoon salt
1 can (8 ounces) tomato sauce
⅓ cup sliced stuffed olives

Cook macaroni as directed on package; drain. Cover frankfurters with boiling water; cover; let stand 10 minutes; drain. Combine bread crumbs, milk, cheese, pickle relish, eggs, and salt; add macaroni; mix. Turn half of macaroni mixture into greased loaf pan. 9 x 5 x 3 inches. Place frankfurters on macaroni mixture; cover with remaining mixture. Bake at 350° for 45 minutes. Heat tomato sauce; add olives. Unmold loaf; slice; serve with tomato-olive sauce. Makes 8 servings.

FRANKFURTER SPECIAL

1 cup butter or margarine
1 cup all-purpose flour
2 teaspoons salt
⅛ teaspoon pepper
6 cups milk
2 cans (8 ounces each) tomato sauce
1 pound sharp Cheddar cheese, grated

1 teaspoon thyme
1 teaspoon basil
12 frankfurters, sliced
4 cups cooked or canned green peas
Hot cooked rice or noodles

Melt butter or margarine; blend in flour, salt, and pepper. Add milk; stir over low heat until smooth and thickened. Add tomato sauce and cheese; stir until cheese melts. Add herbs, frankfurters, and peas. Cook 5 minutes longer. Serve on rice or noodles. Makes 12 servings.

SCALLOPED POTATOES AND FRANKFURTERS

6 tablespoons nonfat dry milk
2 tablespoons flour
1 teaspoon salt
⅛ teaspoon pepper
1½ cups water
¼ pound sharp Cheddar cheese, finely grated, divided
2 tablespoons grated onion
4 cups thinly sliced cooked potatoes (about 6 medium)
6 frankfurters, cut in ¾-inch pieces

Combine nonfat dry milk, flour, salt, and pepper. Sprinkle over water in top of double boiler. Beat with rotary beater until just blended. Cook over boiling water, stirring constantly, until mixture thickens. Add ¾ of the cheese; continue cooking, stirring constantly, until cheese melts. Stir in onion. Arrange layer of potatoes, frankfurters, and sauce in shallow baking dish. Repeat. Sprinkle top with remaining cheese. Bake at 350° until lightly browned (15 to 20 minutes). Serve at once. Makes 6 servings.

BROILER DINNER I

1½ cups bread stuffing
8 frankfurters
8 strips bacon
2 large tomatoes
¼ cup mayonnaise
1 tablespoon cut chives, fresh or freeze-dried
2 packages (10 ounces each) frozen asparagus, thawed
2 tablespoons butter or margarine
Grated cheese

Prepare stuffing as directed on package of stuffing mix. Split frankfurters lengthwise with a sharp knife, being careful not to cut all the way through; fill with bread stuffing; wrap each in bacon strip; secure with wooden picks. Halve tomatoes; combine mayonnaise and chives; spread on tomatoes. Place defrosted asparagus on heatproof glass platter; dot with butter; sprinkle generously with grated cheese. Arrange frankfurters, tomatoes, and platter of asparagus on broiler rack. Broil with surface of food 3 inches below heat for about 8 minutes or until bacon is crisp. Serve at once. Makes 4 servings.

DOGS IN BLANKETS

2 cups sifted all-purpose flour
½ teaspoon salt
⅔ cup shortening
¼ cup catchup
3 tablespoons cold water
1 pound frankfurters
2 tablespoons prepared mustard
1 egg, slightly beaten

Mix and sift flour and salt; cut in shortening. Combine catchup and water; add to flour mixture; blend lightly with fork. Divide dough in half. Roll out each half on floured surface to a 12 x 9-inch rectangle. Cut each into four 6 x 4½-inch rectangles. Grind frankfurters; blend with mustard and egg. Divide meat mixture equally on pastry rectangles. Fold over pastry so that 4½-inch edges are together; seal edges well. Place on ungreased baking sheets. Bake at 425° for 15 to 20 minutes. Makes 8.

PARTY BAKED BEANS

1 jar (20 ounces) brick-oven baked beans
1 cup drained pineapple chunks
2 tablespoons molasses
2 teaspoons prepared mustard
¼ cup firmly packed brown sugar
⅛ teaspoon cinnamon
Dash cloves
8 frankfurters
Melted butter or margarine

Combine baked beans, pineapple, molasses, and mustard in 1½-quart casserole. Combine brown sugar, cinnamon, and cloves; sprinkle over beans. Top with 8 scored frankfurters brushed with melted butter. Bake at 350° for 30 minutes. Makes 4 servings.

APPLE SUPPER TREAT

6 large baking apples
1 can (18 ounces) brick-oven baked beans
⅛ teaspoon nutmeg
2 teaspoons prepared mustard
3 tablespoons molasses
6 frankfurters

Core apples, being careful not to cut all the way through. Scoop out pulp, leaving firm shells. Dice pulp fine; combine with baked beans, nutmeg, mustard, and molasses. Cut frankfurters in half lengthwise, then cut each in half again crosswise. Spread cut surfaces with additional prepared mustard. Place 4 frankfurter quarters in each apple shell. Fill with baked bean mixture. Place in shallow baking dish with any remaining baked bean mixture. Add enough boiling water to cover bottom of dish to ¼ inch. Bake at 400° about 30 minutes or until apple shells are tender. Makes 6 servings.

CURRIED FRANKS ON RICE

1 medium onion, finely chopped
1 garlic clove, minced
1 tart apple, peeled and chopped
3 tablespoons vegetable oil
2 teaspoons each curry powder, brown sugar,
        and Worcestershire sauce
1 teaspoon paprika
½ teaspoon powdered ginger
¼ teaspoon each sugar and chili powder
6 frankfurters
2 cans (8 ounces each) tomato sauce
3 cups hot fluffy rice

Cook onion, garlic, and apple in hot oil until lightly browned. Stir in next 7 ingredients. Cut frankfurters into fourths, on the diagonal; add to onion-apple mixture together with tomato sauce. Heat thoroughly. Serve on rice. Makes 4 to 6 servings.

SKILLET FRANKS AND BEANS

8 frankfurters
8 strips bacon
2 tablespoons each molasses, prepared
        mustard, and vinegar
2 cans (1 pound each) kidney beans

Wrap each frankfurter in a strip of bacon. Place in cold skillet. Turn heat high. Cook, turning carefully, until bacon is uniformly crisp. Remove frankfurters; drain drippings from skillet. Combine molasses, mustard, and vinegar; add to beans; mix well; pour into skillet. Cook over medium heat, stirring occasionally, until slightly thickened. Place frankfurters on top; heat to serving temperature. Makes 4 to 6 servings.

FRESH CORN CHOWDER WITH FRANKS

2 tablespoons butter or margarine
1 large onion, sliced thin
3 cups diced raw potatoes
2 cups boiling water
3 cups corn stripped from cobs
2 teaspoons salt
⅛ teaspoon pepper
1 quart milk
6 frankfurters

Melt butter in Dutch oven or kettle; add onion; cook over medium heat until onion is soft but not brown. Add potatoes and boiling water; cover; simmer 10 minutes or until potatoes are fork-tender. Add corn, salt, and pepper; cook 5 minutes. Add milk. Cut frankfurters in fourths; add. Heat to serving temperature but do not boil. Makes 4 to 6 servings.

FRANKS AND SPANISH RICE

8 frankfurters
¼ cup vegetable oil
½ green pepper, diced
1 medium onion, chopped
1 package (7 ounces) precooked rice
2 cups hot water
2 cans (8 ounces each) tomato sauce
1 teaspoon salt
Few grains pepper

Brown frankfurters in a skillet over medium heat; remove from skillet. Heat oil in skillet; add green pepper, onion, and rice. Cook and stir over high heat until lightly browned. Add hot water, tomato sauce, salt, and pepper; mix well. Bring to a boil; cover; lower heat; simmer 15 minutes. Replace frankfurters; simmer 5 minutes longer. Makes 4 servings.

BOSTON FRANKS

2 cans (1 pound each) Boston brown bread
Catchup
4 frankfurters

1 can (18 ounces) brick-oven baked beans
Garnish: onion rings
Sweet pickle relish

Remove both ends from cans of brown bread; loosen bread with spatula; slide out; cut each crosswise into 3 pieces. Scoop out centers (save for later use in bread pudding) leaving ½-inch shells. Brush inside of shells with catchup. Cut frankfurters crosswise into thin slices; combine with baked beans; fill shells heaping full. Bake at 400° for 15 minutes. Heat remaining bean mixture. Remove bean cups to serving dish; spoon heated bean mixture around them. Garnish with onion rings. Serve with catchup and pickle relish. Makes 6 servings.

SAVORY FRANKS AND NOODLES

8 frankfurters
¼ cup grated onion
2 tablespoons vegetable oil
1 tablespoon flour
¼ cup catchup
1 cup dairy sour cream
2 teaspoons sugar
¼ teaspoon salt
⅛ teaspoon hot-pepper sauce
¼ cup water
1 package (8 ounces) medium noodles, cooked
Poppy seeds

Score frankfurters at ½-inch intervals. Brown with onion in hot oil. Remove frankfurters. Stir in flour, catchup, sour cream, sugar, salt, hot-pepper sauce, and water. Cook and stir until thickened. Return frankfurters; heat to boiling point. Serve over hot buttered noodles sprinkled with poppy seeds. Makes 4 servings.

FRANKS AMSTERDAM

1 small cabbage, cored and shredded
6 tablespoons butter or margarine, divided
1½ cups water, divided
2 teaspoons salt, divided
8 frankfurters
2 tablespoons flour
4 teaspoons each dry mustard and sugar
½ cup vinegar
¼ cup mayonnaise
½ cup drained sweet pickle relish
4 radishes, slices

Cook cabbage with 2 tablespoons butter, ½ cup water, and 1 teaspoon salt in skillet over medium heat for 10 minutes. Split frankfurters lengthwise; place on cabbage; cover; cook 5 minutes. Meanwhile, melt remaining butter; blend in flour, mustard, sugar, and remaining salt. Stir in remaining water and vinegar. Cook and stir until thick. Stir in mayonnaise, pickle relish, and radishes. Fill frankfurters with this sauce; serve on cabbage. Makes 4 servings.

CARNIVAL FRANKS

2 cups drained canned sauerkraut
¼ cup minced onion
½ cup finely chopped green pepper
8 frankfurter rolls
8 frankfurters
Prepared mustard
Sweet pickle relish
Catchup

Combine first 3 ingredients. Unless frankfurter rolls are already partially split, split them almost through, lengthwise; half fill with kraut mixture. Split the franks lengthwise, almost through. Spread cut surfaces with mustard; fill with relish; top with catchup; place on kraut mixture in rolls. Bake at 425° about 10 minutes or until piping-hot. Serve at once. Makes 4 servings.

FRANKFURTER CROWN

16 frankfurters
Savory Potato Salad*

Thread frankfurters through center, using heavy white string and keeping them close together. Tie ends. Stand frankfurters on end to form crown. Place upright in shallow baking pan. Fill center with Savory Potato Salad. Bake at 375° for about 25 minutes. Lift carefully to serving plate, using wide spatulas underneath crown. Makes 8 servings.

°SAVORY POTATO SALAD

9 medium potatoes, cooked and sliced thin
1½ cups chopped celery
3 tablespoons minced parsley
6 strips crisp bacon, diced
2 tablespoons bacon drippings
3 tablespoons cider vinegar
3 tablespoons tarragon vinegar
Salt, pepper, and sugar to taste

Combine all ingredients. (If not to be used in Frankfurter Crown, let stand over low heat until warm.) Makes 8 servings.

YANKEE POLENTA

6 cups water, divided
1 teaspoon salt
2 cups yellow corn meal
½ pound pork sausage meat
1 cup chopped onion
2 cans (10¾ ounces each) condensed tomato bisque
2 teaspoons sugar
½ teaspoon salt
Few grains pepper
Grated Parmesan cheese

Bring 4 cups water to boiling point; add salt. Combine remaining 2 cups cold water and corn meal; add to boiling water. Cook, stirring constantly, until thick; cover and cook over hot water 20 minutes. Pour into greased loaf pan; chill. Cook sausage meat until slightly browned. Pour off and set aside all but about 3 tablespoons sausage fat. Add onion; cook until sausage meat and onion are brown. Add soup, sugar, salt, and pepper. Bring to boiling point; lower heat; cover; simmer ½ hour. Meanwhile, unmold corn meal; cut in 12 slices. Sauté slices in reserved sausage fat. Arrange slices on platter; cover with sauce. Serve with grated cheese. Makes 6 servings.

SAUERKRAUT-SAUSAGE SKILLET

1½ pounds bulk pork sausage
½ cup minced onions
1 can (27 to 29 ounces) sauerkraut
2 medium-sized apples, cored and cut into rings

Combine sausage and onions; mix well. Shape into 6 patties. In a skillet, cook patties until browned on all sides; remove. Pour off all but 4 tablespoons drippings. Place sauerkraut in skillet; top with sausage patties and apple rings. Cover; cook over medium heat 1 hour. Makes 6 servings.

STUFFED GREEN PEPPERS

6 medium green peppers
¾ pound pork sausage meat
¼ cup chopped onion

3 cups soft bread crumbs, divided
2 tablespoons catchup

Wash peppers; cut slice from stem end; remove cores and seeds. Cook in boiling salted water 3 to 5 minutes; drain. Fry sausage; drain off fat and save. Cook onion in 2 tablespoons sausage fat. Combine onion, sausage, 2½ cups crumbs, and catchup. Fill peppers with mixture. Top with remaining crumbs mixed with 2 tablespoons sausage fat. Place in baking dish; cover bottom of dish with water. Bake at 400° for 15 minutes. Makes 6 servings.

BROILER DINNER II

4 thick slices bologna
4 thick slices liverwurst
2 large firm tomatoes
4 all-yellow or slightly green-tipped bananas
Melted butter or margarine
Salt

Have bologna and liverwurst slices cut about ⅜ inch thick; remove outer casing. Cut a small slit in center of bologna slices to prevent curling. Halve tomatoes; peel bananas. Arrange on broiler rack. Brush all foods with melted butter or margarine. Sprinkle bananas and tomatoes with salt. Place in broiler with surface of food 3 inches below heat. Broil 10 minutes, turning meats once. Makes 4 servings.

SAUSAGES IN GARDEN RELISH SAUCE

1 medium onion, chopped
1 green pepper, chopped
⅓ cup drained sweet pickle relish
¼ cup vinegar
1 cup chili sauce
2 tablespoons brown sugar
2 teaspoons prepared mustard
¼ teaspoon hot-pepper sauce
2 cans (4 ounces each) Vienna sausages
Hot cooked rice

Combine all ingredients except sausages and rice in skillet or saucepan. Add sausages; simmer 15 minutes. Serve on hot fluffy rice. Makes 4 servings.

CHEVRON CASSEROLE

1 package (5½ ounces) scalloped potato mix
2 tablespoons butter or margarine

1 can (3 ounces) sliced broiled mushrooms
Boiling water
⅔ cup milk
2 cans (5 ounces each) Vienna sausages

Empty potato slices into 1½-quart casserole; sprinkle with seasoned sauce mix from packet. Dot with butter. Drain mushrooms; save broth. Scatter mushrooms over top of casserole. Add enough boiling water to mushroom broth to measure 2½ cups. Stir into casserole; add milk; mix well. Drain sausages. Arrange on top of casserole in a chevron pattern. Bake at 400° for 30 to 35 minutes. Makes 4 generous servings.

CORNED-BEEF HASHBURGER

1 can (1 pound) corned-beef hash
Prepared mustard
4 thin onion slices
4 tomato slices
Salt, pepper, sugar
Catchup or chili sauce

Chill corned beef in refrigerator. Remove both ends from can of corned-beef hash and push hash out. Cut in 8 slices. Place 4 slices in lightly greased shallow baking pan; spread with prepared mustard; cover with onion and tomato slices; season with salt, pepper, and dash of sugar. Top with remaining slices of hash. Bake at 400° for 30 minutes. Serve with catchup or chili sauce. Makes 4 servings.

TOMATO MOUNDS

4 large firm tomatoes
1 can (1 pound) corned-beef hash
½ teaspoon celery seed
½ cup diced process American cheese

Wash tomatoes; cut ¼-inch slice from stem end of each; scoop out pulp. (Pulp may be used for sauce, added to soup, or stewed.) Combine corned-beef hash and celery seed; stir in diced cheese. Stuff each tomato with about ½ cup of the corned-beef mixture. Bake at 375° for about 30 minutes. Makes 4 servings.

SAVORY ACORN SQUASH

2 medium acorn squash
1 can (1 pound) corned-beef hash
½ cup chili sauce
1 tablespoon minced onion

1 teaspoon dry mustard
2 tablespoons molasses

Wash squash. Halve lengthwise; remove seeds and stringy portions. Place cut side down in greased shallow baking pan. Bake at 375° for 30 minutes. Combine corned-beef hash, chili sauce, minced onion, and dry mustard. Turn squash cut side up; brush inside with molasses. Fill with hash mixture. Bake 30 minutes longer or until hash is lightly browned and squash is tender. Makes 4 servings.

STUFFED BAKED APPLES

8 large baking apples
1 can (1 pound) corned-beef hash
¼ cup cream
1 tablespoon minced dried onion
¼ cup catchup or chili sauce
Grated Parmesan or Romano cheese
8 bacon strips, fried crisp

Core apples; peel about ⅓ of the way from the stem to the blossom end. Carefully scoop out some of the pulp, leaving a shell about ½ inch thick. Chop pulp; combine with corned-beef hash. Combine cream, onion, and catchup; let stand 10 minutes; add to hash mixture; mix well. Fill apple shells with hash mixture. Sprinkle with cheese. Bake at 350° for 30 minutes or until apples are tender. Garnish with bacon strips. Makes 8 servings.

CORNED-BEEF PIE

8 strips bacon
½ cup minced green pepper
¼ cup minced onion
2 cans (15½ ounces each) corned-beef hash
1 cup grated sharp Cheddar cheese
9-inch baked pie shell
½ cup catchup

Cook bacon until limp and transparent; shape into curls; set aside. Pour off all but 3 tablespoons bacon fat. Cook green pepper and onion in remaining bacon fat until soft but not brown. Add corned-beef hash and cheese; mix well. Cook over medium heat until warmed through; spoon into pie shell. Spread catchup to within 2 inches of rim. Place bacon curls around edge. Bake at 350° until bacon is crisp and pie is sizzling hot. Makes 6 to 8 servings.

CORNED-BEEF HASH STUFFED PEPPERS

4 large or 6 small green peppers
1 can (1 pound) corned-beef hash
¼ cup chopped onion
2 tablespoons sweet pickle relish
2 tablespoons vinegar
½ cup chili sauce
1 tablespoon brown sugar
1 teaspoon prepared mustard
⅛ teaspoon hot-pepper sauce

Wash peppers; cut slice from stem end of each; remove seeds. Cover with boiling salted water; cook 5 minutes; drain. Fill peppers with corned-beef hash. Combine remaining ingredients; bring to a boil. Reduce heat; simmer 5 minutes. Place filled peppers in casserole; pour sauce over all. Cover; bake at 400° for 30 minutes. Makes 4 to 6 servings.

CHILI CORNED BEEF

8 slices bacon, diced
2 medium onions, sliced
2 green peppers, diced
4 cans (1 pound each) red kidney beans, drained
2 cans (8 ounces each) tomato sauce
¼ cup chili powder
1 teaspoon salt
⅛ teaspoon pepper
2 tablespoons light brown sugar
1 pound sharp Cheddar cheese, grated
2 cans (12 ounces each) corned beef, cubed
English muffins

Fry bacon until crisp; drain on absorbent paper; set aside. Cook onions and green peppers in 2 tablespoons bacon drippings until onions are soft but not brown. Add kidney beans, tomato sauce, chili powder, salt, pepper, and brown sugar; stir to mix well. Add cheese. Cook and stir over low heat until cheese melts. Add corned beef. Heat. Serve on toasted English muffins; top with bacon. Makes 12 servings.

CHILI WITH CORN-MEAL–CHEESE TOPPING

2 cans (1 pound each) chili con carne
½ cup sifted all-purpose flour
½ cup enriched yellow corn meal
¼ teaspoon salt
1½ teaspoons baking powder
¼ cup shortening
½ cup grated American cheese
3 tablespoons milk

Heat chili con carne to serving temperature. Meanwhile, mix and sift flour, corn meal, salt, and baking powder. Cut in shortening and cheese with 2 knives or pastry blender. Stir in milk. Roll on lightly floured surface into oblong 10 x 4 inches. Cut into four 10 x 1-inch strips; cut 2 of the strips in half; reserve. Turn chili into baking dish, 10 x 6 x 2 inches. Place 2 long strips lengthwise on casserole; cross with 4 remaining small strips. Bake at 425° for 15 minutes. Makes 6 servings.

QUICK CHILI WITH CORN CAKES

½ cup yellow corn meal
½ cup sifted all-purpose flour
2 teaspoons sugar
¼ teaspoon salt
2 teaspoons baking powder
1 small egg
½ cup milk
3 tablespoons soft shortening, divided
2 cans (1 pound each) chili con carne

Mix and sift dry ingredients. Add egg, milk, and 2 tablespoons shortening. Beat with rotary beater until blended. Melt remaining tablespoon shortening in skillet. Make corn cakes in skillet, using ¼ cup batter for each cake; 2 cakes may be cooked at the same time. When cakes are brown on one side, turn and cook until done. Use additional shortening when necessary. Remove cakes from skillet. Add chili con carne to skillet; heat to serving temperature, stirring occasionally. Just before serving place corncakes on top; cover; heat thoroughly. Serve chili over corn cakes. Makes 6 servings.

HAM 'N' CHEESE PUFF

8 ½-inch slices day-old bread
2 small cans (2¼ ounces each) deviled ham
2 cups (8 ounces) grated process sharp Cheddar cheese
¼ teaspoon salt
½ teaspoon dry mustard
¼ teaspoon hot-pepper sauce
3 eggs
1 cup evaporated milk
1 cup water

Remove crusts from bread; spread with deviled ham. Cut slices in half lengthwise. Arrange half the bread on bottom of greased 8-inch square baking dish. Sprinkle with half the cheese; cover with remaining bread and cheese. Add salt, mustard, and hot-pepper sauce to eggs and beat until blended. Stir in milk and water and pour over bread and cheese. Let stand 1 hour. Bake at 325° for 45 minutes, until browned and puffy. Serve immediately. Makes 6 servings.

DEVILED MACARONI

1 package (8 ounces) elbow macaroni
1 large can (4½ ounces) deviled ham
1 can (10¾ ounces) condensed tomato soup
1 cup grated Cheddar cheese

Cook macaroni in boiling salted water until tender; drain. Rinse with hot water. In a greased casserole arrange a layer of macaroni, then a very thin layer of deviled ham, then a layer of undiluted tomato soup, then a layer of grated cheese. Repeat until all ingredients are used, ending with grated cheese. Bake at 350° for 30 minutes. Makes 6 servings.

HAM TRIANGLES

1 large can (4½ ounces) deviled ham
2 tablespoons chili sauce
1 package refrigerated crescent dinner rolls
1 tablespoon butter or margarine, melted
2 tablespoons crumbled canned French fried onion rings
2 teaspoons sesame seed

Combine deviled ham and chili sauce. Unroll refrigerated dough in 1 piece; cut into 4 rectangles. Place 2 rectangles on ungreased cookie sheet; pat each into a 4 x 6½-inch rectangle. Spread with ham mixture not quite to edges; top with remaining rectangles, matching dough edges. Brush tops with butter or margarine. Sprinkle half of each with onion and half with sesame seeds, gently pressing topping into dough. Bake at 375° for 15 minutes, until golden brown. Cool on wire rack about 5 minutes. Cut each into 4 triangles. Serve warm. Makes 8 servings.

DEVILED HAM NAPOLEONS

2 cups sifted all-purpose flour
½ teaspoon salt
¾ cup shortening, divided
5 tablespoons water
2 large cans (4½ ounces each) deviled ham
2 tablespoons chili sauce
1 teaspoon prepared mustard
Mushroom Sauce*

Sift flour and salt together. Cut in half of the shortening until consistency of corn meal. Cut in remaining shortening until size of small peas. Gradually add water, mixing with a fork until all dry particles are moistened. Shape dough into 2 balls. Roll each on a lightly floured surface into a 12 x 8-inch rectangle about ⅛ inch thick. Cut in 24 strips, 4 x 2 inches. Place on baking sheet. Prick with fork. Bake at 425° for 8 to 10 minutes or until lightly browned. Remove from sheet. Cool. Combine deviled ham, chili sauce, and prepared mustard. Spread a generous tablespoon of deviled ham mixture on each of 18 strips. Stack 3 deviled-ham-spread strips with deviled ham side on top. Top with fourth pastry strip. Repeat until all strips are used. Place on baking sheet and bake at 425° about 10 minutes or until very hot. Serve with Mushroom Sauce. Makes 6 napoleons.

*MUSHROOM SAUCE

Blend 1 can (10¾ ounces) condensed mushroom soup with ⅓ cup milk or cream. Heat well.

MEAT SALAD TOMATO STACKS

4 tomatoes
1 can (4½ ounces) ham spread
2 tablespoons drained pickle relish
1 teaspoon prepared mustard
1 can (4¾ ounces) liverwurst spread
1 tablespoon finely chopped celery
1 teaspoon minced onion
Lettuce leaves for cups
Garnish: ripe olives

Wash tomatoes. Cut thin slice from stem end; cut tomatoes in half. Combine ham spread, pickle relish, prepared mustard; reserve. Combine liverwurst spread, celery, and onion; spread 2 tablespoons on bottom half of each tomato. Top with remaining tomato half; spoon reserved ham mixture over tops. Serve in lettuce cups. Garnish with slivers of ripe olives. Makes 4 servings.

APPLE-BEAN BAKE

2 cans (12 ounces each) luncheon meat
Whole cloves
¼ cup light molasses
3 tablespoons prepared mustard
2 tablespoons vinegar or lemon juice
2 teaspoons Worcestershire sauce
2 cans (1 pound 4 ounces each) brick-oven
    baked beans
1 can (20 ounces) pie-sliced apples with juice

Remove luncheon meat from each can in one whole piece. Score top of luncheon meat; stud with whole cloves. Place together to form double loaf in center of shallow baking dish. Combine molasses and mustard in mixing bowl; stir in vinegar and Worcestershire sauce. Add baked beans and apple slices; toss. Spoon around luncheon meat. Bake at 350° for 45 minutes. Makes 8 servings.

TOUCHDOWNERS

1 can (12 ounces) luncheon meat
1 cup (¼ pound) grated American cheese
¼ cup drained pickle relish
1 tablespoon prepared mustard
2 tablespoons mayonnaise
8 hamburger rolls

Chop luncheon meat. Combine with cheese and pickle relish; toss lightly. Mix together mustard and mayonnaise; stir into meat mixture. Spread about ¼ cup of the mixture in each bun. Wrap each individually in aluminum foil. Bake at 375° for 20 minutes. Makes 8 servings.

PANTRY-SHELF DINNER

1 can (12 ounces) luncheon meat, cubed
2 cans (1 pound each) peas
¼ teaspoon onion salt
½ teaspoon celery salt
⅛ teaspoon pepper
½ teaspoon paprika
1 can (10¾ ounces) condensed cream of
    mushroom soup
1 can (4 ounces) pimientos, drained and
    chopped
Hot cooked rice

Brown cubed meat in skillet; remove. Drain liquid from peas into skillet; add seasonings; cook until liquid is reduced to about half. Stir in mushroom soup. Add meat, peas, and pimientos; heat to serving temperature. Serve on rice. Makes 6 servings.

SPICY APPLE-GLAZED MEAT LOAF

2 cans (12 ounces each) luncheon meat
Whole cloves
½ cup firmly packed brown sugar
¼ teaspoon cinnamon
⅛ teaspoon nutmeg
2 tablespoons vinegar
1 can or jar (1 pound) applesauce

Place meat side by side to form loaf in shallow baking pan. Score with sharp knife, making diagonal lines ¾ inch apart. Place whole clove in center of each square. Combine brown sugar, cinnamon, and nutmeg in saucepan; blend with vinegar to smooth paste. Add applesauce; blend well. Pour ¾ cup applesauce mixture over scored meat loaf. Bake at 350° for 45 minutes. Heat remaining applesauce mixture; serve with meat loaf. Makes 8 servings.

MEAT 'N' NOODLE NEST

½ package (4 ounces) egg noodles
1 can (4 ounces) sliced mushrooms
1 can (10¾ ounces) condensed cream of
    chicken soup
1 can (12 ounces) luncheon meat, cut in thin
    strips

Cook noodles according to directions on package; drain; turn into 1½-quart casserole. Drain mushrooms; blend liquid with soup. Add to casserole with mushrooms and half the luncheon meat; toss lightly. Place remaining luncheon meat in border around casserole. Cover. Bake at 375° for 30 minutes. Remove cover for last 15 minutes of baking time. Makes 4 servings.

KABOBS WITH SPAGHETTI

1 can (12 ounces) luncheon meat
1 can (20 ounces) pineapple chunks
2 tablespoons butter or margarine
2 cans (15 ounces each) spaghetti in tomato
    sauce
¼ teaspoon hot-pepper sauce

Cut luncheon meat crosswise in 4 slices. Cut slices in half lengthwise, then crosswise in fourths to make 32 cubes. Arrange meat cubes and pineapple chunks alternately on six 8-inch skewers. Melt butter in skillet. Add kabobs; brown over medium heat, turning occasionally. Remove from skillet; keep warm. Add spaghetti; stir in hot-pepper sauce. Heat to serving temperature. Arrange kabobs over top. Makes 6 servings.

CHAPTER 5

Poultry

Is THERE a corner of this earth where poultry is not popular? We doubt it. Chicken, duck, turkey, game hens—all of them are flavorful, versatile, and usually less expensive than other high-quality protein foods. Peruse the following pages and see for yourself how recipes like these prevent monotony and bring pleasure to all who share them with you.

ROAST CHICKEN, GARDEN STYLE

1½ cups cubed raw potatoes
½ cup sliced raw carrots
1 cup cooked or canned peas
1 cup diced celery
Salt and pepper
3 tablespoons melted butter or margarine, divided
1 roasting chicken
1 teaspoon grated onion
3 strips green pepper
1 cup hot water

Parboil potatoes and carrots 15 minutes; combine with peas and celery; season; add 2 tablespoons melted butter. Stuff chicken with vegetable mixture. Rub outside with onion; place pepper strips on top. Roast, uncovered, at 450° for 15 minutes. Reduce heat to 350°. Combine remaining melted butter and hot water; pour over chicken. Cover; bake until tender (about 30 minutes per pound). Makes 6 to 8 servings.

THANKSGIVING CHICKEN

1 broiler-fryer chicken, about 3 pounds
Seasoned flour
Stuffing of choice
3 to 4 tablespoons vegetable oil
1 cup dry white wine
1 cup giblet broth (page 107)
1 tablespoon wine vinegar
1 garlic clove, crushed
1 teaspoon brown seasoning sauce
1 teaspoon cornstarch
Vegetables of choice (see below)
Glaze*

Rub chicken inside and out with salt and pepper mixed with a little flour. Stuff with any favorite stuffing. (If any stuffing is left over, wrap it in foil

*To make glaze: Combine 2 tablespoons honey, ¼ cup wine or cider, and ½ teaspoon brown seasoning sauce.

and put in the oven during the last half hour.) Truss chicken; brown on all sides in hot oil in skillet. Place in flameproof casserole or roasting pan according to size. Pour off most of the oil left in skillet. Add wine, broth (made from giblets), wine vinegar, garlic, and brown seasoning sauce to skillet. Bring to a boil; lower heat; simmer until mixture is slightly reduced. Blend cornstarch with a little cold water; stir in. Strain sauce over chicken. Cover; roast at 350° for 30 minutes. Add vegetables such as small whole canned potatoes, canned baby carrots, frozen green beans (thawed), and frozen green peas (thawed). Cover; return to oven for 15 minutes or until chicken is tender and frozen vegetables are cooked. Remove from oven; raise heat to 400°. Spoon glaze over chicken (and vegetables, too, if you wish). Return to oven, uncovered, and roast about 10 minutes longer, brushing with glaze as needed. A 3-pound broiler-fryer serves 2 to 4.

ROAST CHICKEN BOMBAY

1 broiler-fryer chicken, 3½ pounds
½ teaspoon salt
Curry Stuffing*
Vegetable oil or shortening
Chutney Gravy†

Sprinkle neck and cavity of chicken with salt. Stuff with Curry Stuffing. Hook wing tips onto back to hold neck skin. Tie legs together, then tie to tail. Place chicken in shallow foil-lined pan. (It is not necessary to use a rack.) Brush with vegetable oil or shortening. Roast at 375° for 1½ hours. Serve with Chutney Gravy. Makes 4 servings.

*CURRY STUFFING

¼ cup butter or margarine
¼ cup chopped onion
1 small apple, peeled and chopped
½ cup raisins
1 to 2 teaspoons curry powder
⅛ teaspoon ginger
⅓ cup slivered toasted almonds
¼ teaspoon salt
1½ cups cooked rice

Melt butter in saucepan. Add onion, apple, raisins, and curry powder. Cook, stirring occasionally, until onion and apple are tender. Remove from heat. Stir in ginger, almonds, salt, and rice.

Mix well. Makes approximately 3 cups stuffing. (If any stuffing is left after neck and body cavities are filled, wrap in foil and heat in oven with chicken during last half hour.)

†CHUTNEY GRAVY

1 can (10½ ounces) chicken gravy
1 teaspoon curry powder
¼ cup chopped chutney

Combine all ingredients in saucepan. Heat to serving temperature, stirring occasionally. Makes approximately 1½ cups.

THREE LITTLE CHICKENS

3 broiler-fryer chickens, 3 pounds each
1½ teaspoons salt, divided
Walnut Stuffing*
Cranberry-Orange Glaze†

Sprinkle neck and body cavities of each chicken with ½ teaspoon salt. Stuff with Walnut Stuffing. Hook wing tips onto back to hold neck skin; tie legs together and then to tail. Place chickens in shallow roasting pan (it is not necessary to use rack). Roast 1½ hours at 375°. Brush with Cranberry-Orange Glaze; roast 15 minutes longer. Serve remaining glaze as sauce for chickens. Makes 12 servings.

*WALNUT STUFFING

Butter
1 package (8 ounces) stuffing mix
½ cup chopped celery
¼ cup chopped onion
1 tablespoon parsley flakes
1 cup coarsely chopped walnuts

Melt butter called for in stuffing mix package directions. Add celery and onion to butter in pan; cook until tender but not brown. Add water called for in package directions; bring to boil and remove from heat. Stir in stuffing mix, parsley flakes, and walnuts. Makes 5½ cups stuffing.

†CRANBERRY-ORANGE GLAZE

1 cup orange juice
3 tablespoons cornstarch
2 cups cranberry juice cocktail
¼ teaspoon each cinnamon, ginger, dry mustard, and hot-pepper sauce

2 tablespoons sugar
2 tablespoons butter or margarine

Blend orange juice and cornstarch in saucepan. Add cranberry juice cocktail, spices, hot-pepper sauce, and sugar. Stir until blended. Cook over medium heat, stirring constantly, until mixture thickens and comes to a boil. Remove from heat. Stir in butter. Makes 3 cups.

FOIL-ROASTED CHICKEN WITH VEGETABLES

1 broiler-fryer chicken, 2½ to 3 pounds
Salt and pepper
Heavy-duty aluminum foil
Paprika
1 pound unpared zucchini, cut into ½-inch slices
4 carrots, cut in half lengthwise
2 potatoes, cut in half
Chopped parsley

Wash and dry chicken. Sprinkle cavity with salt and pepper. Hook wing tips onto back to hold neck skin; tie legs together. Place chicken across center of a 24-inch piece of foil. Sprinkle with paprika. Arrange vegetables around chicken. Sprinkle all with more salt and pepper. Bring ends of foil together over chicken; make double fold at each end. Place in shallow roasting pan. Bake at 450° for 1 hour. Open foil and fold back; roast 20 minutes longer. Sprinkle with chopped parsley. Makes 4 servings.

MUSTARD-BROILED CHICKEN

1 broiler-fryer chicken, quartered
1 teaspoon salt
¼ teaspoon pepper
⅓ cup prepared mustard
1½ tablespoons chopped scallions
½ teaspoon dried leaf tarragon
2 tablespoons lemon juice
¼ cup packaged fine dry bread crumbs

Sprinkle both sides of chicken with salt and pepper. Place skin side down on broiler rack set 6 inches from heat; broil until lightly browned (15 to 20 minutes). Turn; broil 10 to 15 minutes longer, until lightly browned. While chicken is broiling, combine mustard with remaining ingredients. Spread half the mustard mixture on bone side of chicken; broil 5 minutes. Turn; spread remaining mustard mixture over skin side; broil

5 minutes longer or until chicken is tender. Makes 4 servings.

TARRAGON CHICKEN

½ cup butter or margarine
2 broiler-fryers, cut in serving pieces
Salt, pepper, and paprika
2 teaspoons tarragon, divided

Melt butter in shallow baking pan. Place chicken skin side down in pan; sprinkle with salt, pepper, paprika, and 1 teaspoon tarragon. Place under broiler 4 to 5 inches from heat. At end of 15 minutes, turn chicken and sprinkle again with salt, pepper, paprika, and remaining 1 teaspoon tarragon. Broil 15 minutes longer. Remove from broiler. Spoon pan drippings over chicken. Cover pan tightly with foil; bake at 300° for 20 minutes. Makes 6 to 8 servings.

CHICKEN BREASTS BENEDICT

4 chicken breasts, cut in half and boned
Seasoned coating mix for chicken
4 English muffins, split and toasted
4 slices cooked ham, cut in half
Mock Hollandaise Sauce (page 222)

Rinse chicken breasts. Sprinkle enough coating mix evenly on wet chicken breasts to coat all surfaces generously. Place chicken breasts skin side down on broiler pan; broil 20 minutes 6 inches from heat; turn; broil 7 minutes longer. Arrange muffins with a slice of ham and half a chicken breast on each. Cover generously with Mock Hollandaise Sauce. Makes 4 servings.

BONELESS FRIED CHICKEN

2 frying chickens, disjointed
2 eggs
2 tablespoons water
1 cup packaged pancake mix
Vegetable oil

Trim meat from chicken with sharp-pointed knife, keeping pieces as large as possible (save bones and bony pieces for making soup.) Beat eggs slightly; add water; mix well. Dip chicken pieces first in egg mixture, then in pancake mix. Sauté slowly in large frying pan in small amount of vegetable oil, turning often, until golden brown and done. Drain on absorbent paper. Makes 6 to 8 servings.

BEST-EVER FRIED CHICKEN

1¼ cups flour
2 teaspoons salt
2 teaspoons paprika
1 teaspoon thyme or sage
⅛ teaspoon pepper
2 broiler-fryer chickens, cut in serving pieces
Vegetable oil

Combine flour and seasonings. Rinse chicken in cold running water, but do not dry; immediately roll pieces in seasoned flour. Heat vegetable oil, ½ inch deep in skillet, until drop of water added to oil sizzles. Place chicken skin side down in skillet. Put larger, meatier pieces in first. Cook, uncovered, 15 to 25 minutes on each side, turning only once. Drain well on absorbent paper. Makes 8 servings.

OVEN-FRIED CHICKEN

1½ cups packaged cornflake crumbs
2 teaspoons salt
1 tablespoon paprika
2 tablespoons prepared mustard
4 teaspoons vinegar
1 teaspoon hot-pepper sauce
1 teaspoon Worcestershire sauce
1 cup evaporated milk
2 broiler-fryer chickens, cut in servings pieces

Combine cornflake crumbs with salt and paprika in pie pan or shallow baking dish. Blend together mustard, vinegar, hot-pepper sauce, and Worcestershire sauce; stir in evaporated milk. Line shallow baking pan with aluminum foil. Dip chicken pieces in evaporated milk mixture; roll immediately in seasoned cornflake crumbs. Place chicken pieces skin side up in foil-lined pan; do not crowd. Bake at 350° about 1 hour or until tender. Do not cover or turn chicken while cooking. Makes 8 servings.

OVEN-FRIED PARMESAN CHICKEN

¾ cup butter or margarine, divided
3 broiler-fryer chickens, cut in serving pieces
3 teaspoons salt, divided
¼ teaspoon pepper, divided
1½ cups flour
½ cup grated Parmesan cheese
½ teaspoon paprika
1½ teaspoons oregano
1 cup buttermilk

Line two 15 x 10 x 1-inch baking pans with aluminum foil. Divide butter between pans; put in 425° oven for about 5 minutes or until butter is melted. Sprinkle chicken pieces with half the salt and pepper. Turn chicken; sprinkle with remaining salt and pepper. Combine flour, Parmesan cheese, paprika, and oregano; put in shallow pan or pie pan. Pour buttermilk in second shallow pan. Dip chicken pieces in buttermilk; roll in flour mixture; place skin side down in melted butter, placing half the chicken pieces in each of two pans. Bake at 425° for 30 minutes. Turn chicken; reverse pans on shelves; bake 20 minutes longer. Makes 12 servings.

FRIED CHICKEN WITH CREAM GRAVY

1 can (1⅔ cups) evaporated milk
⅔ cup flour, divided
2¼ teaspoons salt, divided
½ teaspoon poultry seasoning
⅛ teaspoon pepper
1 broiler-fryer chicken, about 3 pounds, cut in pieces
Vegetable oil
1 cup giblet broth (page 107)

Pour evaporated milk into a bowl. Combine ½ cup of the flour, 1½ teaspoons of the salt, poultry seasoning, and pepper. Dip chicken pieces in milk (save milk); roll in flour mixture. Cook chicken slowly in hot oil, ½ inch deep, about 30 minutes, turning to brown on all sides. Remove chicken; keep hot; pour off all but 2 tablespoons oil. Stir in remaining flour and salt. Add giblet broth and reserved milk; heat, stirring, until thickened. Serve with chicken. Makes 4 servings.

BAKED CHICKEN, FRENCH STYLE

1 broiler-fryer chicken, 3 pounds, whole
2 teaspoons salt, divided
½ teaspoon dried leaf thyme
4 parsley sprigs
2 celery tops with leaves
1 yellow onion, peeled
2 tablespoons butter or margarine
12 small white onions, peeled
12 small potatoes, pared
¼ cup dry sherry or giblet broth (page 107)
Chopped parsley

Sprinkle inside of chicken with 1 teaspoon salt and thyme. Place parsley, celery tops, and yellow onion in cavity of chicken. Tie legs together, then to tail. Place chicken in heavy casserole with tight-fitting lid. Dot with butter. Cover and bake at 375° for 30 minutes. Add white onions and potatoes; sprinkle with remaining 1 teaspoon salt. Add sherry. Cover; bake 30 minutes longer. Remove cover; bake until chicken and vegetables are browned and tender, basting frequently with juices in casserole. Serve sprinkled with chopped parsley. Makes 4 servings.

BAKED GLAZED CHICKEN

1 can (6 ounces) frozen orange juice
    concentrate, thawed, undiluted
1 can (8 ounces) tomato sauce
1 tablespoon soy sauce
½ teaspoon powdered ginger
1½ teaspoons salt, divided
2 whole broiler-fryer chickens, about 3
    pounds each

Combine orange juice concentrate, tomato sauce, soy sauce, ginger, and ½ teaspoon salt; mix well. Sprinkle cavity of each chicken with ½ teaspoon salt. Fasten neck skin to back with wing tips. Tie legs together, then tie to tail. Place in shallow roasting pan; brush with sauce. Bake, uncovered, at 375° for 1 hour; brush with sauce. Bake ½ hour longer, brushing frequently with sauce and pan drippings. Makes 8 servings.

SAVORY BAKED BROILERS

2 broiler-fryer chickens, 2 to 2½ pounds each,
    halved
Salt
½ teaspoon hot-pepper sauce
1 tablespoon prepared mustard
1 tablespoon Worcestershire sauce
1 tablespoon molasses
3 tablespoons lemon juice
3 tablespoons butter or margarine

Sprinkle chicken halves on both sides lightly with salt. Place chicken halves skin side down in shallow baking pan. (Do not overlap.) Combine hot-pepper sauce, mustard, and Worcestershire sauce; mix well in saucepan. Add remaining ingredients; heat until butter is melted. Brush mixture over cut side of chicken. Bake at 350° for 1½ hours. At end of first ½ hour, turn chicken over and brush again with sauce. Bake 30 minutes; brush again with sauce. Bake 30 minutes; brush with remaining sauce. Makes 4 servings.

SAVORY BAKED CHICKEN

2 broilers, halved
Seasoned flour
¼ cup vegetable oil
1 cup water
2 whole cloves
1 bay leaf
Pinch of thyme
Pinch of marjoram
Few grains mace
¾ cup orange juice
Garnish: orange slices

Shake chicken in paper bag containing flour seasoned with salt and pepper. Brown on both sides in hot oil in frying pan. Remove to large roasting pan. Pour water into frying pan in which chicken was browned; add cloves, herbs, and mace; simmer 10 minutes; strain over chicken in roaster. Cover; bake at 350° for 1 hour. Add orange juice; bake ½ hour longer or until chicken is tender. Thicken gravy if desired. Garnish with orange slices. Makes 4 servings.

BAKED CHICKEN HALVES WITH PRUNE STUFFING

Salt and pepper
1 roasting chicken, about 3½ pounds, split in
    half lengthwise
Softened butter
1 teaspoon lemon juice
Prune Stuffing*
Melted butter

Rub salt and pepper into bony side of chicken halves; brush skin with softened butter and lemon juice. Place halves skin side up on double fold of greased foil in shallow roasting pan. Bake at 350°, uncovered, for 40 minutes. Remove from oven; quickly turn chicken on foil, hollow side up; fill hollows with Prune Stuffing. Brush with melted butter; bake 45 minutes longer. Baste occasionally with juices in pan. Makes 4 servings.

*PRUNE STUFFING

1 package (3 cups) bread stuffing mix
1 cup plumped* pitted prunes, quartered
1 egg, well beaten
3 tablespoons melted butter or margarine

*How to plump prunes: To 1 cup pitted prunes, add 1 cup cold water. Cover; simmer gently 20 minutes.

2 teaspoons each freeze-dried chives and
    shallots
2 tablespoons minced celery and few tiny
    leaves
¼ teaspoon each salt, thyme, and marjoram
¾ cup giblet broth (approximately) (page 107)

Combine all ingredients, adding enough giblet
broth to make stuffing moist but crumbly.

NEW FLAVORS FOR BAKED CHICKEN

2 broiler-fryer chickens, quartered
1½ teaspoons salt
Variation I, II, or III (see below)

Sprinkle chicken with salt. Combine ingredients
for dipping liquid in pie pan. Combine ingredients for crumb mixture in another pie pan. Dip
chicken quarters in dipping liquid; then roll in
crumb mixture to coat thoroughly. Place skin
side up on foil-lined baking sheets. Bake at 350°
for 40 minutes; reverse pans in oven; bake another 40 minutes. Do not turn chicken over.
Makes 8 servings.

VARIATION I

Dipping Liquid:

1 egg, beaten
1 can (6 ounces) frozen orange juice concen-
    trate, thawed
½ teaspoon ginger

Crumb Mixture:

1⅓ cups cornflake crumbs
1⅓ cups flaked coconut

VARIATION II

Dipping Liquid:

1 can (10¾ ounces) condensed cream of mush-
    room soup
⅓ cup water

Crumb Mixture:

1½ cups packaged fine dry bread crumbs
2 teaspoons dried thyme
2 teaspoons paprika

VARIATION III

Dipping Liquid:

1 can (10¾ ounces) condensed tomato soup
⅓ cup water

Crumb Mixture:

1½ cups cornflake crumbs
½ cup grated Parmesan cheese
2 teaspoons oregano

CHICKEN MARENGO

½ cup flour
¼ teaspoon thyme
½ teaspoon salt
1 frying chicken, 3 to 3½ pounds, quartered
¼ cup butter or margarine
8 small onions, parboiled
¼ pound mushrooms, sliced
1 small garlic clove, minced
1 cup chicken broth or bouillon
1½ tablespoons flour
2 tomatoes, sliced
1 tablespoon chopped parsley
Salt and pepper to taste
1 package (8 ounces) medium egg noodles,
    cooked

Combine first 3 ingredients; coat chicken with
this mixture. Brown chicken slowly on all sides
in butter or margarine; set aside. Add onions,
mushrooms, and garlic to drippings; sauté 5 minutes. Blend chicken broth into 1½ tablespoons
flour; add to skillet with tomatoes, parsley, salt,
and pepper; boil 1 minute, stirring constantly.
Arrange chicken, vegetables, and sauce in covered roasting pan; bake at 375° for 30 minutes.
Meanwhile, prepare noodles as directed on
package; drain. Arrange chicken, vegetables, and
sauce on noodles. Makes 4 servings.

VINEYARD CHICKEN

1 frying chicken, about 3 pounds, quartered
1 cup dry white wine
1 tablespoon lemon juice
3 teaspoons salt
¼ teaspoon ground pepper
½ teaspoon paprika
¼ cup butter or margarine, melted
¼ cup chopped scallions with tops
¼ cup minced parsley
Hot cooked brown rice
Garnish (optional): grape clusters

Place chicken quarters in shallow baking pan
skin side down. Blend white wine and lemon
juice with next 6 ingredients and pour over
chicken. Bake at 375° for 1 hour. Turn chicken

skin side up. Continue baking for 30 minutes. Then increase oven temperature to 450°; bake for 30 minutes or until drumstick twists easily out of thigh joint. Baste 2 or 3 times during baking time. Pour pan drippings over chicken for serving. Serve on brown rice; garnish with grape clusters, if desired. Makes 4 servings.

CHICKEN ROSEMARY

1 broiler-fryer chicken, quartered
Seasoned flour
⅓ cup vegetable oil
2 tablespoons butter or margarine
½ garlic clove, minced
1½ teaspoons salt
Pepper to taste
1 tablespoon rosemary
½ cup dry white wine
1 teaspoon white vinegar
½ cup giblet broth (page 107)

Dredge chicken with seasoned flour; cook slowly in oil and butter until lightly browned. Add garlic, salt, and pepper. Continue cooking until chicken is golden brown. Add rosemary, wine, vinegar, and broth from giblets. Cover; bake at 350° about 30 minutes or until chicken is tender. Makes 4 servings.

CHICKEN BURGUNDY

2 frying chickens, disjointed
½ cup seasoned flour
⅓ cup vegetable oil
1 bunch carrots
1 pound white onions
1 cup water
2 whole cloves
1 bay leaf
⅛ teaspoon marjoram
¼ teaspoon rosemary
Few grains mace
2 cans (3 ounces each) sliced broiled mushrooms
2 cups lima beans, cooked, canned, or quick-frozen
1 cup Burgundy

Dredge chicken with seasoned flour; brown on all sides in oil; remove to large casserole. Sprinkle with any remaining seasoned flour. Scrape carrots; slice crosswise or in thin strips; peel onions. Add carrots and onions to casserole. Pour water into pan in which chicken was browned; add cloves, bay leaf, marjoram, rosemary, and mace; boil 5 minutes; strain over chicken and vegetables. Cover casserole; bake at 325° for 1 hour. Add mushrooms, broth from can, lima beans, and wine. Raise oven temperature to 400°; continue baking 1 hour. Makes 8 servings.

BAKED CHICKEN ITALIAN

1 frying or roasting chicken, 3½ to 4 pounds, cut in pieces
Salt and pepper
2 tablespoons butter or margarine
2 tablespoons vegetable oil
1 can (10¾ ounces) condensed cream of mushroom soup
2 cans (8 ounces each) Italian-style spaghetti sauce with mushrooms
1 can (4 ounces) button mushrooms, drained
½ cup white wine
Hot cooked noodles

Dust pieces of chicken with salt and pepper. Heat butter and oil in large, heavy skillet; add chicken; fry until nicely browned, turning the pieces frequently. Transfer chicken to casserole. Combine next 4 ingredients in skillet; blend well; bring to boil; pour over chicken. Cover; bake at 350° about 1½ hours or until chicken is tender. Serve in ring of noodles. Makes 4 servings.

CHICKEN WITH SESAME RICE

¼ cup butter or margarine, divided
2 tablespoons sesame seeds
1 cup uncooked regular rice
2 cups chicken broth or stock, divided
1½ teaspoons salt, divided
1 frying chicken, 2½ pounds, cut up
⅓ cup flour
1 teaspoon paprika
½ cup dry white wine

Melt 1 tablespoon butter in skillet; add sesame seeds and rice; cook over moderate heat, stirring frequently, until lightly browned. Add 1½ cups chicken broth and ½ teaspoon salt; heat to boiling. Turn into 2-quart casserole; cover; bake at 300° while browning chicken. Combine flour, remaining salt, and paprika in a paper bag. Shake chicken pieces, one at a time, in flour mixture until well coated. Brown floured chicken slowly in remaining butter. Remove casserole from oven; place chicken on top. Heat remaining broth in skillet to loosen browned particles from pan; pour over all. Pour wine over chicken; cover; bake about 40 minutes longer or until chicken is tender. Makes 4 generous servings.

CHICKEN VIRGINIA

¼ cup butter or margarine
⅓ cup creamy peanut butter
⅔ cup milk
1 teaspoon salt
6 tablespoons flour
6 tablespoons corn meal
1 teaspoon paprika
6 broiler-fryer drumsticks
6 broiler-fryer wings

Put butter in foil-lined 15 x 10 x 1-inch baking pan. Set in 425° oven for 5 minutes until butter melts. Remove from oven. Blend peanut butter and milk until smooth; stir in salt. Combine flour, corn meal, and paprika. Dip chicken pieces in peanut butter mixture, then roll in flour mixture. Place coated chicken in melted butter. Bake at 425° for 20 minutes. Turn chicken; bake 15 to 20 minutes longer. Serve hot or cold. Makes 6 servings.

DEVILED DRUMSTICKS

1 cup packaged flavored fine dry bread
    crumbs
¼ teaspoon pepper
1 tablespoon prepared mustard
1 teaspoon Worcestershire sauce
½ cup light cream
16 broiler-fryer drumsticks
Zippy Dunking Sauce*

Combine bread crumbs and pepper; set aside. Blend mustard, Worcestershire sauce, and cream. Dip drumsticks in cream mixture; roll immediately in crumb mixture. Place in foil-lined shallow pans; do not crowd. Bake at 350° for 1½ hours or until tender. At end of 1 hour, exchange pans on shelves. Before serving, wrap ends in fringed double-thick strips of foil about 3 inches wide. Serve with Zippy Dunking Sauce. Makes 8 servings.
ACCOMPANIMENTS: Sesame crackers and relishes.

*ZIPPY DUNKING SAUCE

⅓ cup prepared mustard
⅓ cup pickle relish
⅔ cup catchup

Combine ingredients in bowl; mix thoroughly. Makes 1⅓ cups.

CURATE'S CHICKEN

2 broiler-fryer chickens, about 2½ pounds
    each, cut up
¼ pound butter or margarine
1 teaspoon tarragon
1 teaspoon thyme
1 cup chicken broth
1½ cups white wine, preferably sauterne
2 egg yolks, slightly beaten
1 cup dairy sour cream
1½ tablespoons Dijon mustard
Hot cooked wild rice (optional)

Sauté chicken in butter until browned on all sides. Remove chicken to another pan; reserve butter. Sprinkle chicken with herbs; add chicken broth and wine. Simmer for 20 minutes. Remove chicken; set aside. Let liquid stand until cool. Combine egg yolks, sour cream, mustard, and the butter used for sautéing. Stir in broth and wine. Return sauce and chicken to pan; heat to serving temperature. Serve at once with wild rice, if desired. Makes 6 servings.

CHICKEN AND HAM SOPHIA

⅓ cup vegetable oil
1 frying chicken, cut up
1 large onion, chopped
1 green pepper, chopped
1 cup slivered cooked ham
2 tablespoons flour
1 can (10½ ounces) chicken gravy
⅓ cup dry sherry
Salt and pepper to taste
Hot cooked rice

Heat oil in large, heavy skillet or Dutch oven; brown chicken on all sides; remove. Cook onion, green pepper, and ham gently in the drippings 5 minutes. Blend in flour; add gravy and sherry; cook, stirring, until mixture boils and thickens. Season with salt and pepper. Return chicken to pan. Cover; simmer gently 45 minutes to 1 hour or until chicken is tender, turning and basting chicken occasionally. Serve with rice. Makes 5 servings.

CHICKEN VALENCIA

6 tablespoons flour
1 teaspoon salt
2 frying chickens, cut up
¼ to ⅓ cup vegetable oil
Giblets
2 medium onions, sliced
1 cup diced cooked ham
2 garlic cloves, crushed
½ pound fresh mushrooms
2 cups apple cider
2 tablespoons minced parsley
½ teaspoon paprika
⅓ cup dry sherry
1 cup packaged croutons

Combine flour and salt in paper bag. Add 2 or 3 pieces of chicken at a time; shake until coated. Brown in oil. Cook giblets in 1 cup of water until done; drain; reserve ½ cup broth. Chop giblets. Remove chicken pieces as browned. Add onions, ham, and garlic to pan; cook over low heat until onion is soft but not brown. Push to one side. Add mushrooms; cook until golden brown. Combine cider, broth, chopped giblets, parsley, and paprika; stir to mix. Pour into pan. Return chicken to pan. Simmer, covered, 30 to 35 minutes or until chicken is done. Remove chicken to platter. Add sherry to pan; stir to mix; pour over chicken. Scatter croutons over all. Makes 8 to 12 servings.

VINEYARD FESTIVAL CHICKEN

1 frying chicken, 2½ to 3½ pounds, cut in
    serving pieces
3 tablespoons vegetable oil
1½ teaspoons seasoned salt
⅛ teaspoon seasoned pepper
⅛ teaspoon nutmeg
½ cup pineapple juice
2 tablespoons lemon juice
½ cup dry sherry
2 teaspoons cornstarch
1 tablespoon water
Garnish: pineapple chunks; lemon slices;
    small grape clusters

Brown chicken slowly in oil. Sprinkle with salt, pepper, and nutmeg. Combine pineapple juice, lemon juice, and sherry; pour over chicken. Cover tightly; simmer slowly on top of stove about ½ hour (or bake at 375° until tender). Remove chicken to hot serving dish. Skim off any excess fat from pan juices. Blend cornstarch with water; stir in. Cook and stir until thickened. Pour over chicken. Garnish with pineapple chunks, lemon slices, and small grape clusters. Makes 4 to 6 servings.

CHICKEN IN BEER

1 frying chicken, 3 to 3½ pounds, disjointed
4 tablespoons butter or margarine
16 small white onions, peeled*
1½ teaspoons salt
Few grains pepper
¼ teaspoon thyme
1½ teaspoons paprika
¾ cup beer
¼ cup tomato sauce
¼ cup heavy cream

Brown chicken pieces in butter; add onions; brown slightly. Add remaining ingredients except cream; bring to boil. Cover; simmer 30 minutes. Chill until fat rises to surface; skim off. Stir in cream; reheat. Makes 4 servings.

SPANISH CHICKEN FRICASSEE

1 stewing chicken, about 4 pounds, cut up
Salt and pepper
½ cup vegetable oil
Juice of 1 lemon
1 garlic clove, minced
⅔ cup finely chopped onions
3 tomatoes, peeled and diced
1½ cups giblet broth†
½ cup dry sherry
¼ cup whole small stuffed olives
⅓ cup light seedless raisins

Wash chicken; sprinkle with salt and pepper. Brown slowly on all sides in oil. Remove chicken. Add lemon juice, garlic, and onion to oil left in frying pan; cook until lightly browned. Return chicken to pan. Add tomatoes and giblet broth. Cover tightly; simmer over low heat about 1½ hours or until chicken is tender. Stir in

*Or use drained small white canned onions.
†To make giblet broth, simmer giblets, neck, and bony parts of chicken in about 2 cups water to make a rich broth.

sherry, olives, and raisins. Cover; simmer 15 minutes longer. Makes 6 servings.

COQ AU RHUM

1 chicken, 3½ to 4 pounds, cut in small
　sections
Salt and black pepper to taste
1 teaspoon Worcestershire sauce
1 teaspoon soy sauce
¼ cup rum
2 garlic cloves, minced
½ cup minced chives
6 tablespoons vegetable oil, divided
1 tablespoon brown sugar
1 cup minced onions
1 can (3 or 4 ounces) mushrooms, drained
1½ teaspoons sugar
½ cup water
2 teaspoons cornstarch
2 tablespoons water
2 pimientos, sliced

Season chicken pieces with mixture of salt, pepper, Worcestershire sauce, soy sauce, rum, garlic, and chives. Marinate for 1½ hours; remove chicken pieces from marinade; set both aside. Heat 4 tablespoons oil in heavy skillet. When oil is very hot, add brown sugar. When sugar has melted and turned dark brown, add chicken; cook about 8 minutes, turning occasionally until the chicken is fully browned. Add minced onion and marinade; cook 5 minutes on high heat. Add mushrooms, sugar, and ½ cup water. Cover; cook on medium to low heat for 30 minutes. Thicken sauce with cornstarch dissolved in 2 tablespoons water. Sauté pimientos in 2 tablespoons hot oil for 1 minute. Remove pimientos and use as garnish for chicken. Makes 4 servings.

CHICKEN CASTELLANA

1 stewing chicken, 4 to 5 pounds, disjointed
2 onions, sliced
1 green pepper, minced
1 garlic clove, minced
1 tablespoon minced parsley
2 tablespoons vegetable oil
1 cup dry red wine
½ cup tomato sauce
1½ teaspoons salt
Boiling water
¼ cup seedless raisins

4 cups hot cooked rice
Garnish (optional): salted almonds

Put chicken in kettle or Dutch oven. Cook onions, green peppper, garlic, and parsley in oil until soft but not brown. Add wine. Combine tomato sauce and salt; add to onion mixture; mix well. Pour over chicken. Add enough boiling water to half cover chicken. Cover kettle. Simmer until chicken is very tender. Remove bones from chicken and combine chicken meat and sauce. Add raisins; simmer 10 minutes. Make a rice ring on serving dish; fill center with chicken mixture. Garnish with salted almonds, if desired. Makes 6 servings.

BREAST OF CHICKEN JULIET

4 whole chicken breasts, about 3 pounds, split
¼ cup butter or margarine
1 can (6 ounces) sliced broiled mushrooms,
　drained
2 can (10¾ ounces each) condensed cream of
　chicken soup
1 large garlic clove, minced
Generous dash crushed thyme
⅛ teaspoon rosemary, crushed
⅔ cup light cream

Use large skillet or two 10-inch skillets, dividing the ingredients equally between them. Brown chicken in butter; remove. Brown mushrooms. Stir in soup, garlic, and seasonings. Add chicken. Cover; cook over low heat 45 minutes, stirring occasionally. Blend in cream; heat slowly to serving temperature. Makes 8 servings.

CHICKEN CACCIATORE

1 frying chicken, 3½ pounds, cut up
½ cup seasoned flour
⅓ cup vegetable oil
1 garlic clove, minced
2 medium onions, chopped
1 green pepper, diced
1 can (1 pound) tomatoes
1 can (6 ounces) tomato paste
½ pound mushrooms, sliced
1½ teaspoons salt
¼ teaspoon pepper
¾ teaspoon oregano

Dredge chicken in flour. Brown on all sides in oil. Add all remaining ingredients except oregano. Simmer for 30 minutes. Add oregano; simmer 15 minutes longer or until chicken is tender. Makes 6 servings.

SPANISH CHICKEN

¼ cup butter or margarine
2 broiler-fryer chickens, cut in serving pieces
2 garlic cloves, crushed
1 can (6 ounces) sliced broiled mushrooms
½ cup diced green pepper
3 cups chicken broth
4 oranges, divided
Salt to taste
4 tablespoons flour
Water
1 can (1 pound) whole tomatoes, drained

Heat butter in large skillet or Dutch oven; add chicken pieces; brown on both sides. Add garlic, mushrooms, and green pepper; cook a few minutes longer. Add chicken broth; reduce heat to simmer; add the shredded peel of 1 orange. Season with salt. Cover; cook gently 30 minutes or until chicken is tender. Remove chicken. Blend flour to a thin paste with a small amount of water; stir into skillet. Heat and stir until boiling. Peel remaining 3 oranges. Section all 4 oranges; add with tomatoes; stir until heated through. Return chicken to skillet. Heat to serving temperature. Makes 8 servings.

CALIFORNIA CHICKEN

3 tablespoons flour
1 teaspoon salt
¼ teaspoon pepper
1 frying chicken, 3 pounds, disjointed
3 tablespoons vegetable oil
1 can (1 pound) stewed tomatoes
1 tablespoon minced dried onion
½ cup chopped green pepper
2 tablespoons chopped parsley
¼ teaspoon garlic powder
½ teaspoon seasoned salt
¼ teaspoon oregano
1 cup canned pitted ripe olives

Combine flour, salt, and pepper. Coat chicken with seasoned flour. Heat oil; brown chicken on all sides. Add all remaining ingredients except ripe olives. Bring to boil; lower heat. Cover; simmer 25 minutes; add ripe olives. Cook 15 minutes longer or until chicken is fork-tender. Makes 4 servings.

DOCK JIM CHICKEN

1 fryer chicken, about 3½ pounds, cut up
3 cups water
1 teaspoon salt
¼ teaspoon dried ground chili peppers
½ cup soy sauce
2 tablespoons flour
½ cup chopped scallions
1 garlic clove, minced
3 tablespoons ground sesame seeds
Hot cooked rice (optional)

Add chicken pieces to water in cooking pot, along with salt and chili peppers. Simmer about 45 minutes or until chicken pieces are tender. Remove chicken. Bring stock to boil. Mix soy sauce and flour and stir into boiling stock. Reduce heat and cook over low heat, stirring steadily, until mixture boils. Return chicken; add scallions, garlic, and sesame seeds. Cook 10 minutes more. Serve on rice, if desired. Makes 4 to 6 servings.

CHICKEN JAMBALAYA

2 medium onions, minced
1 green pepper, minced
1 garlic clove, minced
2 tablespoons vegetable oil
1 stewing chicken, 4 to 5 pounds, cut up
1 can (8 ounces) tomato sauce
½ cup water
1½ teaspoons salt
Few grains pepper
1 teaspoon chili powder
Boiling water
1½ cups uncooked regular rice
⅓ cup seedless raisins
Garnish (optional): grated cheese; minced parsley

Cook onions, green pepper, and garlic in oil in large kettle or Dutch oven until soft but not brown. Add chicken. Combine tomato sauce, ½ cup water, salt, pepper, and chili powder; pour over chicken. Add enough boiling water to cover; cover kettle; simmer 45 minutes. Add rice; simmer 35 minutes longer or until chicken is tender, adding more water if necessary. Add raisins; simmer 10 minutes longer. Sprinkle with grated cheese and minced parsley, if desired. Makes 6 servings.

HAWAIIAN CHICKEN

1 broiler-fryer chicken, quartered
2 tablespoons vegetable oil
1 medium onion, chopped
1 garlic clove, minced
1 can (20 ounces) pineapple chunks
3 tablespoons soy sauce
1 bay leaf, crumbled
½ cup flaked coconut
1¼ cups water, divided
2 tablespoons cornstarch
1 cup diagonally sliced celery
2 medium tomatoes, peeled and cut in 8
    wedges each
1 green pepper, cut in 1-inch pieces
½ teaspoon salt
3 cups hot cooked rice
¼ cup toasted slivered almonds

Brown chicken on both sides in hot oil; remove. Add onion and garlic; cook until tender but not brown. Return chicken to skillet. Add syrup from pineapple, soy sauce, bay leaf, coconut, and 1 cup water. Cover; simmer 20 minutes. Blend cornstarch and ¼ cup water; add to skillet; stir constantly until thickened and clear. Add pineapple chunks, celery, tomatoes, and green pepper. Sprinkle with salt. Cover; simmer 10 minutes. Serve over hot cooked rice. Sprinkle with almonds. Makes 4 servings.

HARVEST CHICKEN

2 broiler-fryer chickens, quartered
1½ teaspoons salt
½ cup butter or margarine
1½ cups orange juice
2 tablespoons slivered orange peel*
2 teaspoons minced dried onion
½ teaspoon ginger
¼ teaspoon hot-pepper sauce
4 teaspoons cornstarch
2 oranges, peeled and sectioned
2 cups seedless grapes
½ cup toasted slivered almonds
Hot mashed potatoes
Garnish: parsley; orange sections; small grape
    clusters

Sprinkle chicken quarters on both sides with salt. Heat butter in large skillet. Add chicken

*To prepare slivered peel: Wash orange and remove peel (very thin) with vegetable peeler. Cut with scissors or knife into fine slivers.

quarters 4 at a time; brown on both sides, removing as browned. Return all of chicken to skillet; add orange juice and peel, onion, ginger, and hot-pepper sauce. Simmer, covered, 30 to 35 minutes or until chicken is tender. Arrange chicken on heated platter; keep warm. Blend cornstarch with a little cold water; stir into sauce in skillet. Cook, stirring constantly, until mixture thickens and comes to a boil. Add orange sections and grapes; heat gently. Add almonds. Pour a little sauce over chicken; serve remaining sauce separately. Surround chicken with hot mashed potatoes. Garnish with parsley, additional orange sections, and small grape clusters. Makes 8 servings.

MEXICAN CHICKEN

1 stewing chicken, about 5 pounds
Salt, few grains cayenne
¼ cup vegetable oil
¼ cup blanched almonds
⅓ cup seedless raisins
½ cup pineapple chunks
⅛ teaspoon cinnamon
⅛ teaspoon cloves
1½ cups orange juice
2 tablespoons flour
¼ cup water
Garnish: avocado wedges; orange sections;
    parsley

Season chicken with salt and cayenne; brown on all sides in oil. Add almonds, raisins, pineapple, cinnamon, cloves, and orange juice. Cover; simmer 1 hour or until chicken is tender. Remove chicken to platter. Make a smooth paste of flour and water; add to gravy. Cook, stirring constantly, until thickened. Pour over chicken. Garnish with avocado wedges, orange sections, and parsley. Makes 6 servings.

ISLAND CHICKEN

¼ cup butter or margarine
2 garlic cloves, chopped
2 pounds chicken wings and drumsticks
1 divider-pack can (42 ounces) chicken chow
    mein
1½ cups drained pineapple chunks
1 green pepper, cut in 1-inch squares
2 tablespoons soy sauce
1 teaspoon curry powder
Salt and pepper to taste

Melt butter in a large skillet. Add garlic and chicken pieces; brown on all sides. Drain liquid from vegetables in bottom can of divider-pack; pour liquid over chicken. Cover; simmer, stirring occasionally, until chicken is tender (about 35 minutes). Add vegetables and sauce from top can of divider-pack, pineapple, and green pepper. Stir in soy sauce and curry powder. Add salt and pepper to taste. Cover; simmer 5 minutes or until green pepper is tender, yet crisp. Makes 6 servings.

CHICKEN EUROPA

¼ cup flour
1 teaspoon salt
⅛ teaspoon pepper
1 broiler-fryer chicken, cut up
3 tablespoons vegetable oil
1 medium onion, chopped
1 garlic clove, minced
3 tablespoons lemon juice
1½ cups giblet broth (page 107)
2 cans (3 ounces each) sliced broiled
     mushrooms
½ package (4 ounces) noodles, cooked and
     drained
1 cup dairy sour cream
1 teaspoon paprika

Combine flour, salt, and pepper in large paper bag; shake chicken pieces in bag until well coated. Brown chicken in oil in large skillet. Add onion, garlic, lemon juice, broth, and mushrooms with liquid. Cover; simmer 20 minutes. Stir in noodles; cook 10 minutes longer. Top each serving with large spoonfuls of sour cream and a sprinkle of paprika. Makes 4 servings.

CHICKEN-NOODLE BARBECUE

1 frying chicken, about 3 pounds, disjointed
¼ cup butter or margarine
1 tablespoon chili powder
2 medium onions, sliced
1 garlic clove, minced
1 can (1 pound) tomatoes with juice
1 can (6 ounces) tomato paste
1 teaspoon dry mustard
2 teaspoons salt
1 teaspoon sugar
1 tablespoon vinegar
1 teaspoon Worcestershire sauce
¼ teaspoon hot-pepper sauce

2 tablespoons melted butter or margarine
1 package (8 ounces) medium egg noodles

Brown chicken in butter; sprinkle with chili powder when pieces are turned. Remove chicken; add onion slices and garlic; cook until tender. Add remaining ingredients except melted butter and noodles. Bring to a boil; add chicken; cover; simmer until tender (about 45 minutes). Add melted butter to drained cooked noodles; serve with chicken. Makes 4 servings.

QUICK BRAISED CHICKEN

1 broiler-fryer chicken, cut up
3½ cups water
2 teaspoons salt
⅛ teaspoon pepper
6 carrots, scraped and quartered
12 small whole onions
Herb Dumplings*

Wash and dry chicken; place in large skillet. Add water, salt, and pepper. Bring to boil; add carrots and onions. Cover; reduce heat to medium; cook 25 minutes. Bring to boil again. Drop Herb Dumplings by spoonfuls on top of chicken. Cook, uncovered, 10 minutes. Cook, covered, 10 minutes longer. Makes 4 to 6 servings.

*HERB DUMPLINGS

1½ cups biscuit mix
⅛ teaspoon oregano
2 tablespoons chopped parsley

Combine all ingredients. Add liquid as directed on package of biscuit mix. Mix just enough to combine all ingredients. Makes 8 small dumplings.

CHICKEN WITH EGGPLANT

2 broiler-fryer chickens, quartered
Salt and paprika
½ cup butter or margarine
½ pound fresh mushrooms
2 medium onions
2 celery stalks
1 medium eggplant, cut in ½-inch slices
1 can (1 pound) tomatoes with juice
1 can (10¾ ounces) tomato soup
¼ teaspoon hot-pepper sauce
¼ teaspoon dried leaf basil
¼ teaspoon dried leaf oregano

Shredded Parmesan cheese
2 tablespoons chopped parsley
Hot buttered noodles

Sprinkle chicken with salt and paprika. Melt butter in large skillet; brown chicken quarters on both sides. Remove chicken. Chop mushroom stems, onions, and celery stalks. Add to skillet with eggplant. When eggplant slices are lightly browned, add tomatoes, tomato soup, hot-pepper sauce, basil, and oregano. Return chicken to skillet; cover; simmer 45 minutes. Add mushroom caps; cook 5 minutes longer. To serve, sprinkle with Parmesan cheese and parsley. Serve with hot buttered noodles to which ½ cup slivered black olives have been added. Makes 8 servings.

CRANBERRY CHICKEN

¼ cup vegetable oil
2 tablespoons butter or margarine
1 frying chicken, about 3 pounds, disjointed
1 green pepper, minced
1 garlic clove, minced
2 tablespoons minced onion
2 tablespoons sweet vermouth
1 can (8 ounces) whole cranberry sauce
Salt and pepper to taste

Heat oil and butter in a 12-inch skillet. Add chicken; cook until golden brown on all sides. Pour off all but 2 tablespoons fat. Add green pepper, garlic, and onion; cook until soft. Add vermouth, cranberry sauce, salt, and pepper. Cover; simmer 25 minutes. Makes 4 to 6 servings.

CHICKEN WITH CRANBERRIES

¼ cup butter or margarine
4 whole chicken breasts, halved
½ cup chopped onion
2 cups apple cider, divided
1 teaspoon salt
¼ teaspoon pepper
1 teaspoon grated lemon peel
1 tablespoon cornstarch
⅓ cup sugar
2 cups fresh cranberries
4 bananas, sliced

Melt butter in large skillet; add chicken breasts; brown on all sides over medium heat. Add onion; cook until tender (about 5 minutes). Add 1½ cups cider, salt, pepper, and lemon peel. Cover; simmer 30 minutes. Remove chicken.

Combine cornstarch with remaining ½ cup cider; blend smooth. Add to skillet with sugar and cranberries. Add chicken and bananas. Heat to serving temperature. Transfer to heatproof serving dishes. Makes 8 servings.

COLD CHICKEN CATALAN

1 frying chicken, about 3 pounds
¼ cup vegetable oil
2 cups dry white wine
½ cup white vinegar
2 whole peeled garlic cloves
10 whole peppercorns
1 large onion, thinly sliced
1 orange, thinly sliced
1 lemon, thinly sliced
Salt
Juice of 1 lemon

Wipe chicken thoroughly inside and out. Heat oil; slowly brown whole chicken in a deep flameproof earthenware casserole, turning often for even browning. Chicken should be golden brown, but do not allow it to form a crust. Combine wine, vinegar, garlic cloves, peppercorns, onion, orange and lemon slices. Salt to taste; pour over chicken. Simmer 1 hour or until joints move easily. Keep covered with liquid at all times, adding wine and vinegar in the same proportions (4 to 1) if needed. When cooked, refrigerate in the same casserole overnight. Serve cold with the sauce, stirring in juice from remaining lemon. Makes 4 servings.

CHICKEN BREASTS EN GELÉE

6 whole chicken breasts
2 cups water
1 small onion, sliced
2 celery tops
2 bay leaves
1 teaspoon salt
¼ teaspoon pepper
1 envelope unflavored gelatin
½ teaspoon onion salt
1 cup dairy sour cream
½ teaspoon tarragon
Sliced raw carrots and radishes
Green scallion strips

Halve chicken breasts; bone; remove skin; put in large saucepan with water, onion, celery tops, bay leaves, salt, and pepper. Bring to boil; cover tightly; reduce heat; simmer 45 minutes or until tender. Remove from heat; strain broth. Refrigerate chicken and broth at once. When cool, skim any fat from broth. Measure ¾ cup broth into saucepan; sprinkle gelatin over broth. Place over low heat, stirring constantly, until gelatin is dissolved. Add another ¾ cup broth; stir in onion salt, sour cream, and tarragon. Chill until slightly thickened. Dip chicken breasts in chilled gelatin mixture; place on wire rack set on a pan or cookie sheet. Chill; collect drippings; soften if necessary. Decorate tops of chicken breasts with "flowers" of carrots and radish rings with green scallion strips as stems. Coat with remaining gelatin mixture. Chill until ready to serve. Makes 12 servings.

HONOLULU CHICKEN CURRY

6 tablespoons butter or margarine
1 small onion, grated
1 garlic clove
6 tablespoons flour
2 teaspoons chopped ginger root *or* 1 teaspoon powdered ginger
1½ teaspoons salt
2 to 3 tablespoons curry powder
2 cups milk
½ cup coconut milk*
1 cup chicken broth
3 cups diced cooked chicken
Hot cooked rice

Melt butter or margarine; add grated onion and garlic; simmer 5 minutes; remove garlic. Combine flour, ginger, salt, and curry powder; blend with butter. Combine milk, coconut milk, and chicken broth; add. Stir constantly over low heat until thickened. Add chicken; heat well. Serve with rice. Makes 6 servings.

ACCOMPANIMENTS: Chutney, flaked coconut, chopped peanuts or macadamia nuts, raisins.

CHICKEN AND PINEAPPLE CURRY

2 cups coconut milk
½ cup minced onion

*Coconut milk as used in Hawaii is extracted from grated fresh coconut and should not be confused with the watery liquid found in a mature coconut. When grated fresh coconut is not readily available, make coconut milk this way: Pour 2 cups milk over contents of 1 can or package of flaked coconut. Slowly bring to boil; remove from heat; let stand 20 minutes, stirring occasionally. Strain through double thickness of cheesecloth, pressing out all liquid.

⅓ cup butter or margarine
⅓ cup flour
1 tablespoon curry powder (or to taste)
1 teaspoon salt
¼ teaspoon ginger
2 cups chicken broth
3 cups diced cooked chicken
1½ cups canned pineapple chunks
Hot cooked rice

Prepare coconut milk. Cook onion in butter or margarine until soft but not brown. Blend in flour, curry powder, salt, and ginger. Add coconut milk and chicken broth. Cook over low heat, stirring constantly, until thickened. Add chicken and pineapple. Heat. Serve with fluffy rice. Makes 6 to 8 servings.

ACCOMPANIMENTS: Chutney, raisins, flaked coconut, macadamia nuts or peanuts.

CHICKEN CURRY I

2 broiler-fryer chickens, cut up
Vegetable oil
¾ cup finely chopped onion
1 garlic clove
4 tablespoons butter or margarine
1 teaspoon dried thyme
1 bay leaf
¼ cup tomato sauce
3 cups chicken broth
½ cup flaked coconut
1 teaspoon salt
¼ teaspoon sugar
6 tablespoons flour
2 tablespoons curry powder (or less, according to taste)
¾ cup nondairy powdered creamer
6 cups hot fluffy rice

Brown chicken pieces slowly in vegetable oil, turning to brown both sides, for about 35 minutes or until chicken is done. Keep warm. Cook bony parts of chicken in water to make 3 cups chicken broth. Meanwhile, make curry sauce: Cook onion and garlic in butter until soft but not brown. Add thyme, bay leaf, and tomato sauce; cook 3 minutes longer. Add chicken broth, coconut, salt, and sugar. Simmer 15 minutes. Remove from heat. Remove garlic and bay leaf. Combine flour, curry powder, and nondairy creamer; blend in about 1 cup of the hot mixture; return to remaining hot mixture. Cook and stir over low heat 5 minutes or until thickened. Remove browned chicken to serving platter; surround with rice. Pour some of the curry sauce over chicken; serve remainder separately. Makes 8 servings.

ACCOMPANIMENTS: Chutney, flaked coconut, golden raisins, and salted peanuts.

CHICKEN CURRY II

1 frying chicken, disjointed
1 onion, chopped fine
1 garlic clove, minced
1 tart apple, chopped
3 tablespoons vegetable oil
1 tablespoon curry powder
1 teaspoon paprika
½ teaspoon powdered ginger
¼ teaspoon sugar
¼ teaspoon chili powder
Few grains cayenne
1 can (6 ounces) tomato paste
Chicken broth or boiling water
Hot cooked rice

Bone the raw chicken, keeping pieces as large as possible. Boil bones to make broth. Cook onion, garlic, and apple in oil until golden brown. Add curry powder, paprika, ginger, sugar, chili powder, and cayenne; cook until quite brown; add chicken; brown lightly. Add tomato paste and enough chicken broth or boiling water to cover. Cover; simmer about 40 minutes or until chicken is tender. Serve in ring of rice. Makes 6 servings.

ACCOMPANIMENTS: Flaked coconut, peanuts, and chutney.

SIMPLE CHICKEN CURRY

½ cup butter or margarine
4 onions, chopped
2 or 3 garlic cloves, minced
2 bay leaves
1 teaspoon powdered cinnamon
6 whole cloves
1 roasting chicken, about 5 pounds, cut up and skinned
1½ teaspoons salt (or to taste)
2 to 3 tablespoons curry powder (or to taste)
1 tablespoon paprika
2 medium tomatoes, peeled and quartered

Melt butter in deep heavy skillet or Dutch oven. Add onions and garlic; cook over low heat until lightly browned. Add bay leaves, cinnamon, and cloves; cover; cook 5 minutes. Add chicken

pieces and about ½ cup water. Simmer, uncovered, until liquid has evaporated. Remove bay leaves and cloves. Combine salt, curry powder, and paprika; blend with about ½ cup water; add to skillet; mix well. Add tomatoes and enough water to cover chicken. Cover; simmer until chicken is tender (about 1½ hours). Makes 6 servings.

BRUNSWICK STEW

1 stewing chicken, about 4 pounds, cut up
Boiling water
1 teaspoon salt
¼ cup chopped onion
1 can (1 pound) tomatoes with juice
2 packages (10 ounces each) frozen lima beans
1 can (12 ounces) kernel corn
1 can (1 pound) cut okra
Few drops hot-pepper sauce
1 teaspoon Worcestershire sauce
¼ cup flour mixed with ½ cup cold water (optional)

Cover chicken with boiling water; cover; simmer ½ hour. Add salt, onion, and tomatoes; simmer ½ hour. Lift out chicken; cool enough to handle. Remove meat from bones in as large pieces as possible; return meat to kettle. Add lima beans, corn, and okra (including liquid). Add hot-pepper sauce and Worcestershire sauce. Cook ½ hour longer. (If desired, stew may be thickened slightly with ¼ cup flour mixed to a smooth paste with ½ cup cold water.) Makes 6 servings.

CAPTAIN'S CHICKEN STEW

½ cup flour
1 teaspoon salt
¼ teaspoon pepper
1 broiler-fryer chicken, cut in serving pieces
¼ cup butter or margarine
2 tablespoons minced dried onion
1 tablespoon dried parsley flakes
½ cup chopped green pepper
1 garlic clove, minced
1 teaspoon curry powder
½ teaspoon thyme
1 can (1 pound) tomatoes with juice
3 tablespoons seedless raisins
Hot cooked rice

Combine flour, salt, and pepper; roll chicken pieces in flour mixture. Brown chicken in butter in skillet 15 minutes on each side. Add onion, parsley flakes, green pepper, garlic, curry powder, and thyme to the skillet. Cook until green pepper is tender. Add tomatoes; bring to a boil. Cover; simmer 15 minutes. Uncover; add raisins; simmer 15 minutes longer. Serve with rice. Makes 4 servings.

MAINE CHICKEN AND OYSTER PIE

1 roasting chicken, about 5 pounds, disjointed
Boiling water
1 onion, sliced
Sprig of thyme
¼ pound salt pork
1 pint shucked oysters
Salt and pepper
Paprika
Flour
1 tablespoon chopped parsley
2 cups biscuit mix
1 egg, beaten
1 tablespoon cold water

Cover chicken with boiling water. Add onion and thyme. Simmer until chicken is tender. Dice salt pork; fry until crisp; drain. Drain oysters; add liquor to broth in which chicken was cooked. Arrange chicken, pork scraps, and oysters in layers in shallow casserole. Season with salt, pepper, and paprika. Measure broth; thicken with 1 tablespoon flour per cup broth. Add parsley. Pour into casserole. Make biscuit dough according to directions on package of biscuit mix. Roll out ¼ inch thick. Cut with doughnut cutter. Place circles on casserole. Brush tops with slightly beaten egg mixed with cold water. Bake at 450° until crust is golden brown. Makes 6 servings.

CREOLE CHICKEN PIE

1 stewing chicken, about 4 pounds, disjointed
Seasoned flour
⅓ cup vegetable oil
1 large can (27 to 29 ounces) tomatoes with juice
1 teaspoon salt
1 teaspoon Worcestershire sauce
2 teaspoons sugar
¼ cup chopped onion
2 tablespoons flour
¼ cup cold water
1 can (12 ounces) kernel corn
1 can (1 pound) okra
½ package piecrust mix

Dredge chicken in seasoned flour. Brown on all sides in oil. Add tomatoes, salt, Worcestershire sauce, sugar, and onion. Bring to boiling point; cover; simmer 1½ hours or until chicken is tender. Thicken sauce with 2 tablespoons flour blended with ¼ cup cold water. Place layer of chicken in sauce in casserole. Top with layer of drained corn and okra; repeat. Bake at 375° for 20 minutes. Prepare pastry dough according to package directions. Cut out pastry triangles with cardboard pattern. Bake at 425° for 10 to 12 minutes until golden brown. Place on casserole just before serving. Makes 6 servings.

HOT CHICKEN SALAD PIE

5 cups diced cooked chicken
1 teaspoon salt
1 cup mayonnaise
2 tablespoons lemon juice
1 teaspoon Worcestershire sauce
1 teaspoon dry mustard
⅟₁₆ teaspoon cayenne
10-inch baked pastry shell
3 tablespoons melted butter
2 cups tiny bread cubes
1 cup grated American cheese

Sprinkle chicken with salt. Combine mayonnaise, lemon juice, Worcestershire sauce, dry mustard, and cayenne; mix well. Add to chicken; toss to blend. Turn into prepared pastry shell. Combine butter and bread cubes; sprinkle over chicken. Sprinkle with cheese. Bake at 350° for 30 to 35 minutes or until heated through. Makes 8 servings.

CHICKEN ROLL

2 cans (10½ ounces each) chicken gravy, divided
1 egg, beaten
1 tablespoon minced dried onion
2 cups diced cooked chicken
Salt and pepper
3 cups biscuit mix

Heat 1 cup gravy; pour on egg; mix well; add onion and chicken. Season to taste with salt and pepper. Prepare biscuit mix as directed on package; roll out ¼ inch thick in rectangle about 14 x 10 inches. Spread chicken mixture on dough; roll up, starting at narrow end. Bake at 450° for 18 to 20 minutes. Heat remaining gravy; serve with chicken roll. Makes 6 servings.

CHICKEN CHILI BUNS

8 chicken thighs and drumsticks
¼ cup vegetable oil
½ teaspoon salt
½ cup chopped onion
1 can (1 pound) red kidney beans, drained
1 can (8 ounces) tomato sauce
1 can (1 pound) stewed tomatoes with juice
⅛ teaspoon pepper
2 teaspoons chili powder
8 split toasted hamburger buns
Garnish: onion rings; dill pickle slices

Brown thighs and drumsticks well in hot oil over high heat; sprinkle with salt. Remove browned chicken; lower heat; gently sauté onion until soft but not brown. Drain off oil. Turn beans, tomato sauce, and tomatoes into pan; add pepper and chili powder. Cook, stirring occasionally, until thickened (about 5 to 10 minutes). Return browned chicken pieces to chili. Reduce heat to low and cook 5 minutes longer or until chicken is tender. Serve on split toasted buns. Garnish with onion rings and dill pickle slices, if desired. Makes 8 servings.

CORN PANCAKES WITH CHICKEN FILLING

2 eggs, separated
1 can (1 pound) cream-style corn
½ cup pancake mix
2 teaspoons baking powder
⅛ teaspoon pepper
2 tablespoons butter or margarine, melted
1 cup diced cooked chicken
1 can (10¾ ounces) condensed cream of chicken soup, divided
½ cup milk

Beat egg yolks slightly; add corn; blend well. Add next 3 ingredients; mix until just blended. Stir in melted butter or margarine. Beat egg whites stiff; fold in. Bake on hot griddle, making twelve 4-inch pancakes. Turn once. Combine chicken and ½ can of undiluted soup. Put spoonful in center of each pancake; fold pancake over filling. Place in shallow baking dish with folded edges underneath. Blend remaining soup with milk; heat; pour over pancakes. Bake at 350° for 20 minutes. Makes 6 servings.

CHICKEN-POTATO CAKES

2 cups dry mashed potatoes
2 cups diced cooked chicken
2 tablespoons minced onion
1 tablespoon chopped parsley
¼ teaspoon each salt, leaf thyme, and hot-pepper sauce
3 tablespoons butter or margarine

Combine all ingredients except butter. Shape into 8 flat cakes. Melt butter in skillet; add chicken-potato cakes; brown well on both sides. Makes 4 servings.

CREAMED CHICKEN AND CORN

1 can (10¾ ounces) condensed cream of celery soup
½ cup light cream or milk
1 cup diced cooked chicken
1 can (12 ounces) kernel corn with juice
2 tablespoons diced pimientos (optional)
Hot cooked rice

Blend soup and cream; add chicken and corn. Add pimientos, if desired. Heat. Serve in rice ring. Makes 4 servings.

CHICKEN LIVERS SAVORY

4 slices bacon, quartered
½ pound pork sausage (bulk)
2 small green peppers, diced
1 garlic clove, crushed
2 small onions, sliced
1 teaspoon celery flakes
4 large mushrooms, sliced
2 pounds chicken livers
1 envelope instant chicken broth mix
⅔ cup boiling water
2 cans (5 ounces each) water chestnuts, drained
½ cup Marsala
½ cup whipping cream
3 cups hot parsley rice*

Cook bacon until crisp; remove from pan; set aside. In same pan cook sausage meat until golden brown, stirring with a fork and pouring off fat as it accumulates. Remove sausage; set aside. Pour all fat from pan. Measure 3 tablespoons; return to pan. Add green peppers, garlic,

*Rice to which minced parsley has been added to taste.

onions, and celery flakes; cook until soft and golden brown. Push to one side. Cook mushrooms until golden brown, adding more reserved fat if needed. Remove vegetables from pan. Add chicken livers. Cook until lightly browned. Dissolve broth mix in boiling water; add to chicken livers. Simmer 10 minutes. Return vegetables, sausage, and bacon to pan. Add water chestnuts and Marsala. Heat cream (do not boil); stir in slowly. Serve on hot parsley rice. Makes 6 servings.

CHICKEN LIVERS WITH ORANGE SAUCE

¼ cup butter or margarine
1 pound chicken livers, cut in half
1 cup diced cooked ham
½ cup chopped onion
1 teaspoon salt
¼ teaspoon each dried leaf thyme, basil, and tarragon
1 tablespoon cornstarch
1¼ cups orange juice
¼ teaspoon hot-pepper sauce
1 can (3 ounces) sliced broiled mushrooms
Halved orange slices (optional)
Hot cooked fine noodles
Sesame seeds

Melt butter in large skillet over high heat. Add chicken livers, ham, and onion. Sprinkle with salt and herbs. Cook over high heat, stirring often, until livers are browned and onion is tender (about 5 minutes). Blend cornstarch with a small amount of the orange juice; mix with remaining orange juice and hot-pepper sauce; stir into skillet. Cook, stirring constantly, until sauce is thickened and comes to a boil. Drain mushrooms; add with orange slices if used. Simmer 2 minutes. Serve over fine noodles mixed with toasted sesame seeds. Makes 4 servings.

ROCK CORNISH HENS NORMANDY

3 frozen Rock Cornish hens
1 teaspoon salt
½ teaspoon sage
½ teaspoon nutmeg
½ garlic clove, crushed
2 tablespoons lemon juice
½ cup butter or margarine
½ cup orange juice
3 thick slices unpeeled navel orange, halved
Butter
Powdered cloves

Thaw hens; split in half down the middle. Combine salt, sage, nutmeg, garlic, and lemon juice; rub over skin side of hens. Melt butter in shallow roasting pan in 350° oven. Place hens skin side down in melted butter. Roast 15 minutes. Turn skin side up. Roast 15 minutes longer. Pour orange juice over hens. Roast another 15 minutes or until hens are golden brown and fork-tender. Remove to platter; pour pan juice over all. Garnish with orange slices sautéed in a little butter to which a dash of powdered cloves has been added. Makes 6 servings.

ROCK CORNISH HENS GRENADINE

4 frozen Rock Cornish hens
Pineapple-Walnut Stuffing*
¼ cup lemon juice
½ cup honey
¼ cup grenadine syrup
½ cup soft butter or margarine

Thaw hens. Stuff. Combine lemon juice, honey, and grenadine syrup. Set aside ½ cup for basting; blend remainder with butter. Spread over surface of birds. Roast at 350° for about 1 hour or until done, brushing occasionally with honey mixture. Makes 4 servings.

*PINEAPPLE-WALNUT STUFFING

½ cup water
¼ cup butter or margarine
½ package (4 ounces) bread stuffing mix
1 egg, slightly beaten
½ cup crushed pineapple
¼ cup finely chopped walnuts

Heat water; add butter; heat until melted. Stir in remaining ingredients. Makes enough to stuff 4 hens.

ROCK CORNISH HENS CACCIATORE

3 frozen Rock Cornish hens, about 1 pound each
Salt
Pepper
⅓ cup melted butter or margarine
1 small onion, thinly sliced
½ pound fresh mushrooms, sliced
2 cans (15 ounces each) tomato-herb sauce
1 cup sauterne or other dry white wine
1 chicken bouillon cube
½ cup hot water

¼ teaspoon sugar
1 cup uncooked brown rice

Thaw hens. Wash and pat dry. Sprinkle cavities lightly with salt and pepper. Brush outside with melted butter; place breast side up in shallow baking pan. Bake at 400° for 30 minutes, brushing with butter every 10 minutes. Remove from oven; reduce oven temperature to 350°. Move partially baked hens to one end of baking dish; add onion slices and mushrooms to other end, stirring into drippings to coat. Stir in tomato-herb sauce, sauterne, bouillon cube dissolved in hot water, and sugar. When well mixed, arrange game hens in center of dish over sauce mixture; baste with sauce. Cover with foil. Return to oven; continue baking 30 to 45 minutes until done, basting frequently. Meanwhile, cook rice according to package directions. Serve hens, whole or halved, on bed of brown rice. Pour sauce over hens or serve separately. Makes 3 to 6 servings.

ROCK CORNISH HENS ROSÉ

4 Rock Cornish hens
1⅓ cups packaged precooked rice
¾ cup rosé wine
½ teaspoon salt
Few grains pepper
⅛ teaspoon nutmeg
⅛ teaspoon allspice
1 teaspoon sugar
¼ cup seedless golden raisins
¼ cup butter or margarine
¼ cup canned slivered blanched almonds

Preparing Hens:

Wash hens in cold water; pat dry with paper toweling. Prepare rice according to package directions. After removing from heat, add wine, seasonings, and raisins. Cover. Let stand 10 minutes. Melt butter; add almonds; stir over low heat until lightly browned; add to rice mixture. Stuff lightly into hens. Skewer legs to body. Preheat oven to 450° and prepare basting sauce. Hens will make 4 to 8 servings.

Basting Sauce:

¼ cup rosé wine
2 tablespoons melted butter or margarine
2 teaspoons lemon juice

Combine all ingredients. Brush hens with the mixture. Roast at 450° for 15 minutes. Lower heat

to 350°; roast ½ hour longer, basting once or twice with wine mixture. If necessary, place under broiler for a few minutes to finish browning.

Gravy:

1 tablespoon butter or margarine
½ cup red currant jelly
1 tablespoon lemon juice
3 whole cloves
Few grains cayenne pepper
½ cup water
½ cup rosé wine

Combine all ingredients except wine. Simmer 5 minutes; strain. Add wine and pan juices from hens. Thicken with cornstarch if desired, using 1 tablespoon cornstarch dissolved in 1 tablespoon cold water for each cup of gravy. Simmer until thickened and clear, stirring constantly.

ROCK CORNISH HENS STUFFED WITH HERB RICE

4 frozen Rock Cornish hens, about 1 pound each
2½ cups water
1 package (6 ounces) herb rice
½ cup butter or margarine
½ cup dry white wine
1 teaspoon rosemary

Thaw hens; remove giblets. Cook giblets until tender in 2½ cups water. Drain giblets, saving broth. Chop giblets. Cook rice according to package directions using giblet broth instead of water. Add chopped giblets to cooked rice; stuff hens with this mixture; truss with small skewers and white string. Heat butter, wine, and rosemary in saucepan until butter is melted. Arrange hens in shallow roasting pan; brush with butter mixture. Roast at 425° for about 1 hour or until done, basting several times with butter mixture. Makes 4 servings.

TURKEY JUBILEE

1 fryer-roaster turkey, 5 to 6 pounds, cut up
½ cup vegetable oil
1 can (6 ounces) broiled mushroom crowns
1 garlic clove, minced
2 teaspoons salt
¼ teaspoon pepper
¼ cup flour
½ cup water

1½ cups giblet broth (page 107)
2 tablespoons tomato paste
1 tablespoon grated orange peel
Hot cooked rice
Garnish: green pepper rings; half slices of
     orange

Brown turkey pieces in moderately hot oil, turn-ing to brown evenly. Remove turkey from pan. Drain mushrooms; measure liquid; add water to make ⅓ cup if necessary. Brown mushroom crowns in oil in which turkey was browned. Re-move. Add mushroom liquid, garlic, salt, and pepper. Heat to simmering. Blend flour and water until smooth; blend with broth; add tomato paste and orange peel. Pour into pan. Cook and stir until smooth and thickened. Return turkey and mushrooms. Cover; simmer about 1 hour. Arrange turkey pieces on fluffy rice; pour gravy over all. Garnish with green pepper rings and half slices of orange. Makes 6 servings.

TURKEY CHESTERFIELD

1 frozen boneless turkey roast
1 package piecrust mix
1 can (2½ ounces) deviled ham
1 egg yolk

Prepare and cook turkey roast as directed on package. Cool in refrigerator. Remove casing if there is one. Prepare piecrust as directed on package. Roll out on lightly floured pastry board or cloth into a rectangle large enough to enclose turkey roast. Place turkey roast along narrow edge of rectangle. Spread deviled ham on top and sides. Lift pastry up and over turkey roast, overlapping pastry under the roast. Tuck in both ends firmly. Place pastry-covered roast seam side down on jelly roll pan or cookie sheet. Roll out pastry scraps and cut out small decorative shapes. Brush pastry with slightly beaten egg yolk and arrange decorative cutouts on it. Brush cutouts with egg yolk. Bake at 425° for 10 min-utes. Lower heat to 350° for 50 minutes longer. Slice crosswise to serve. Yields 3 servings per pound.

FLAMING FRUIT GARNISH FOR TURKEY

For each serving you will need:
1 large canned pear half
1 large canned pineapple slice
1 small canned cling peach half
Melted butter

Parsley
Sugar cube
Lemon extract

Drain canned fruit thoroughly on paper towel-ing. Place cut side up on broiler rack; brush with melted butter. Broil with food surface 3 inches below source of heat for 6 to 8 minutes or until lightly browned. Place pear half on pineapple slice, peach half on pear, hollow side up. Place on platter around turkey; garnish with parsley. Just before serving, dip sugar cube in lemon ex-tract; place in peach. Ignite.

TURKEY SUPREME

4 cups cooked broccoli
Leftover turkey, sliced
Velvet Sauce*
Parmesan cheese, grated

Arrange hot cooked broccoli in ramekins or 1 large shallow baking dish; add layer of turkey. Fill dishes with hot Velvet Sauce; dust with grated cheese; place under broiler until top browns; serve at once. Makes 6 servings.

NOTE: Leftover gravy or part gravy and part soup (2⅔ cups in all) may be used in place of Velvet Sauce.

*VELVET SAUCE

2 tablespoons butter or margarine
2 tablespoons flour
1 teaspoon paprika
¾ teaspoon salt
⅛ teaspoon pepper
1 cup milk
2 cans (10¾ ounces each) condensed cream of
     chicken soup
½ pound process American cheese, cut in
     small pieces

Melt butter or margarine; blend in flour and sea-sonings; add milk gradually, stirring until thick-ened. Add soup; blend. Add cheese; stir over low heat until cheese melts.

TURKEY-PINEAPPLE CURRY

½ cup minced onion
⅓ cup butter or margarine
⅓ cup flour
1 tablespoon curry powder
1 teaspoon salt

4 chicken bouillon cubes
3 cups hot water
3 cups diced leftover turkey
1 can (8 ounces) pineapple tidbits, drained
Hot cooked rice

Cook onion in butter until soft but not brown. Blend in flour, curry powder, and salt. Crumble chicken bouillon cubes; add. Add water; cook over low heat, stirring constantly, until thickened. Add turkey and pineapple. Heat to serving temperature. Serve with rice. Makes 4 to 6 servings.

ACCOMPANIMENTS: Peanuts, chutney, golden raisins, and coconut.

TURKEY BUCKWHEAT CROQUETTES

1½ cups water
⅔ cup buckwheat groats (kasha)
¾ teaspoon salt
2 cups chopped leftover turkey or chicken
1 tablespoon finely chopped parsley
½ teaspoon hot-pepper sauce
1 teaspoon curry powder
¼ teaspoon oregano
1 tablespoon grated onion
Packaged fine dry bread crumbs
1 egg, slightly beaten
Fat for frying
Cranberry sauce

Bring water to full boil; gradually add buckwheat groats and salt; cook over low heat, stirring constantly, 5 minutes. Add turkey or chicken, parsley, hot-pepper sauce, curry powder, oregano, and onion. Dust pastry board with crumbs. Pat out croquette mixture ½ inch thick on board. Cut with doughnut cutter. Dip in beaten egg, then in crumbs. Fry in deep fat heated to 375° until golden brown. Drain on absorbent paper; fill centers with cranberry sauce. Makes 12 to 15 croquettes.

CREAMED TURKEY

⅓ cup butter or margarine
⅓ cup flour
6 chicken bouillon cubes
⅛ teaspoon pepper
1 teaspoon paprika
Leftover gravy (if available)
2 cups water
1 large can (1⅔ cups) evaporated milk

Leftover turkey, cubed
Farina Ring*

Melt butter or margarine. Blend in flour, crumbled chicken bouillon cubes, pepper, and paprika. If there is any leftover gravy, add it at this point; blend. Combine water and evaporated milk; add; cook, stirring constantly, until smooth and thickened. Add turkey; heat. Serve in Farina Ring. Makes 6 servings.

*FARINA RING

3 eggs, slightly beaten
1 cup cooked farina
1½ cups mashed cooked carrots
2 tablespoons melted butter or margarine
2 teaspoons finely chopped onion
2 teaspoons finely chopped parsley
¾ teaspoon salt
⅛ teaspoon nutmeg

Combine eggs and farina. (The farina may be left over or freshly cooked.) Mix thoroughly. Add remaining ingredients. Pour mixture into greased 8-inch ring mold. Bake at 350° for 45 to 50 minutes or until firm. Makes 6 servings.

TURKEY SEVILLE

¼ cup butter or margarine
1 tablespoon grated onion
½ cup flour
¼ teaspoon each white pepper and dry mustard
⅛ teaspoon nutmeg
2 cans (10½ ounces each) chicken gravy
1 can (6 ounces) broiled sliced mushrooms
¼ cup dry sherry
⅓ cup sliced stuffed olives
2 cups cubed cooked turkey
Savory Biscuits*

Melt butter; add onion; simmer 5 minutes; do not brown. Combine flour, pepper, mustard, and nutmeg; blend into butter mixture. Stir in chicken gravy, blending thoroughly over low heat. (Leftover turkey gravy may be used for some or all of the chicken gravy.) Add mushrooms with their broth, sherry, olives, and turkey; heat to serving temperature. Serve over hot split Savory Biscuits. Makes 4 servings.

*SAVORY BISCUITS

Add 1 teaspoon poultry seasoning for each cup of biscuit mix used; then prepare according to package directions. Roll out ½ inch thick. Cut with 3-inch biscuit cutter. Bake as directed.

TURKEY RAREBIT

½ cup dry sherry
2 tablespoons minced onion
½ cup diced green pepper
1 cup grated process American cheese
2 tablespoons flour
1 teaspoon salt
1 cup light cream
1 can (6 ounces) broiled sliced mushrooms
Leftover turkey, sliced or cubed

Combine all ingredients except mushrooms and turkey in top of double boiler. Add broth from mushrooms. Stir over hot water until cheese melts and mixture thickens. Add mushrooms. If there is enough turkey to slice, serve sauce separately. If not, cube and add to sauce. Serve on toast. Makes enough sauce for 6 servings.

TURKEY ROLL-UP

3 tablespoons butter or margarine
4 tablespoons flour
1 teaspoon minced dried onion
1 cup milk
1½ cups diced turkey
¼ cup chopped ripe olives
1 tablespoon finely diced pimiento
1 teaspoon salt
Few grains pepper
¼ teaspoon paprika
2 cups biscuit mix
1 egg yolk
Leftover turkey gravy *or* canned chicken
   gravy
Canned mushrooms, sliced

Melt butter or margarine; blend in flour and onion; add milk; stir over low heat until thick. Add turkey, olives, pimiento, salt, pepper, and paprika. Set aside to cool. Prepare biscuit dough as directed on package. Roll out in a square about ¼ inch thick; spread with turkey mixture, leaving a 1-inch margin. Roll up. Place on greased baking sheet seam side down. Prick top with fork. Brush with slightly beaten egg yolk mixed with a little water. Bake at 450° for 25 to 30 min-

utes. Serve with leftover turkey gravy or canned chicken gravy to which sliced canned mushrooms have been added. Makes 6 servings.

BRAISED DUCK CANTONESE

1 duck, 6 to 7 pounds
1 teaspoon salt
1 egg
1 tablespoon water
1 cup flour
2 cups vegetable oil
1 tablespoon minced scallions
Diced duck giblets
2 tablespoons cornstarch
¼ cup water
1 tablespoon soy sauce
1 tablespoon dry sherry
½ teaspoon cinnamon
Hot cooked rice

Have duck disjointed at market. Remove fat. Cover with cold water; bring to boil; cover; simmer 45 minutes or until tender. Remove from broth; reserve broth; cool duck. Remove bones and skin; cut meat into pieces about 2 inches by ½ inch. Sprinkle with salt. Beat egg slightly; add water. Dip duck first in flour, then in egg, then in flour again. Heat oil in deep frying pan or Dutch oven; add duck; cook over medium heat until golden brown, about 10 minutes; drain. Place on serving platter; sprinkle with scallions. Meanwhile, cook diced giblets in reserved broth about 10 minutes. Blend cornstarch and water; add to broth with remaining ingredients except rice. Cook, stirring, until thickened. Pour over duck. Serve with fluffy rice. Makes 4 servings.

PINEAPPLE DUCKLING

1 duckling, 4 to 5 pounds, quartered
2 teaspoons brown gravy seasoning sauce
2 tablespoons vegetable oil
1 teaspoon salt
½ teaspoon onion salt
½ teaspoon celery salt
½ teaspoon ginger
1 cup canned pineapple juice
2 cups raw carrots, diagonally sliced
1 can (9 ounces) sliced pineapple
2 medium-sized green peppers, cut in eighths
2 tablespoons cornstarch
2 tablespoons cold water

Skin duckling; brush lightly with seasoning sauce. Heat vegetable oil in large frying pan or Dutch oven; add duckling; brown on both sides. Combine seasonings; add. Add pineapple juice and carrots. Cover; cook over low heat until duckling is just tender (about 45 minutes). Cut pineapple slices in eighths; add with green pepper. Cook until green pepper is tender but still crisp (about 5 minutes). Combine cornstarch and cold water; stir in. Cook, stirring constantly, until sauce thickens and boils. Makes 4 servings.

DUCKLING MOUNTAIN STYLE

¼ cup vegetable oil
1 tablespoon paprika
1 duckling, 4 to 5 pounds, quartered
1 medium onion, thinly sliced
¼ cup flour
½ cup dry sherry
2 cups giblet stock or bouillon
1 medium tomato, sliced
¼ cup chopped stuffed olives
2 tablespoons minced parsley
Paprika

Combine oil and 1 tablespoon paprika in large skillet; mix well. Add duckling; cook until browned on all sides; remove duckling. Add onion to drippings; cook 5 minutes. Add flour; mix well. Gradually add sherry and stock or bouillon; stir over low heat until thickened. Add tomato, olives, parsley, and duckling. Cover; cook over low heat about 1 hour or until duckling is tender. Sprinkle with paprika. Makes 4 servings.

DUCKLING DELUXE

2 ducklings, 4 to 5 pounds each, quartered
¼ cup vegetable oil
1 medium onion, chopped
1 garlic clove, crushed
1 teaspoon salt
Few grains pepper
½ teaspoon oregano
⅓ cup dry sherry
1 cup dairy sour cream
Hot cooked wild rice

Simmer duckling livers in 2 cups water for 15 minutes. Drain; save broth. Chop livers; save. Brown ducklings slowly in vegetable oil until golden on all sides. Remove from pan. Pour off all but 2 tablespoons of oil. Brown onion and garlic in oil left in pan; add salt, pepper, oregano, and broth from livers. Return duckling to pan; cover; simmer 1½ hours or until done. Remove duckling to warm platter; strain liquid in pan. Add sherry, sour cream, and chopped livers to strained liquid. Heat to serving temperature but do not boil. Serve with duckling and wild rice. Makes 8 servings.

BRAISED DUCK WITH GRAPES

1 duck, about 4½ pounds, skinned and quartered
¼ cup brown gravy seasoning sauce
1 small onion, finely chopped
1 teaspoon butter or margarine
1 teaspoon ground ginger
Salt and pepper to taste
2 tablespoons red currant jelly
2 bay leaves
1 cup muscatel
1 cup chicken stock or broth
½ cup green or red grapes

Brush duck with seasoning sauce; refrigerate for about 2 hours. Sauté onion in butter in skillet. Add duck and all other ingredients except the grapes. Cover; simmer until duck is tender (approximately 1 hour). Remove duck; reduce sauce over high heat to ¾ cup. Strain sauce over duck; add grapes. Makes 4 servings.

OLD-FASHIONED BREAD STUFFING

2 large onions
½ cup butter or margarine
12 cups soft bread crumbs
½ cup water
1 cup sliced celery
2 teaspoons salt
⅛ teaspoon pepper
1 tablespoon poultry seasoning or sage

Chop onions fine; cook in butter or margarine until delicate brown. Add bread crumbs, water, celery, salt, pepper, and poultry seasoning; mix well. Makes enough stuffing for 12-pound turkey.

Oyster Stuffing: Drain 1 pint oysters; chop. Add to recipe above. Use oyster liquor instead of water.

Giblet Stuffing: Make giblet broth (p. 107); strain, reserving giblets and broth. Chop giblets;

add to recipe above. Use giblet broth instead of water.

Chestnut Stuffing: Cut amount of bread crumbs to 10 cups. Add 2 cups chopped cooked chestnuts.

MUSHROOM TURKEY STUFFING

1 cup butter or margarine
2 cans (4 ounces each) mushrooms, sliced or
    pieces
½ cup finely chopped onion
12 cups soft bread crumbs
1 cup finely diced celery
¼ cup chopped parsley
1½ teaspoons salt
¼ teaspoon pepper
1 tablespoon poultry seasoning
Chopped cooked giblets

Melt butter or margarine in deep kettle. Drain mushrooms; reserve liquid.* Add mushrooms and onion to melted butter; cook until onion is tender but not brown. Add bread crumbs, celery, parsley, seasonings, and giblets. Mix lightly. Stuff into bird lightly. Makes enough for 15-pound turkey.

NOTE: For small turkeys weighing 6 to 8 pounds, make half the recipe; for heavy birds weighing 20 pounds or more, increase measurements by one half.

*If a moist stuffing is desired, add mushroom liquid or giblet broth (page 107).

SAVORY CORN STUFFING

½ cup butter or margarine
½ cup chopped onion
1 cup chopped celery and leaves
1 can (1 pound) cream-style corn
1 package (8 ounces) prepared stuffing mix

Melt butter or margarine in large skillet. Add onion and celery; cook until onion is tender but not brown. Add corn. Prepare stuffing mix as directed on package; stir in; toss lightly. Makes about 6 cups, or enough for an 8-pound turkey.

QUICK MUSHROOM STUFFING

Drain 2 cans (6 ounces each) sliced broiled mushrooms, saving broth. Prepare 2 packages (8 ounces each) prepared bread stuffing according to package directions, using mushroom broth as part of the liquid and adding mushrooms. Makes enough stuffing for a 12-pound turkey.

PRINCESS STUFFING

2 loaves (1 pound each) unsliced bread
1 pound boned shoulder of pork
1 turkey liver
1 cup diced celery
1 medium onion, thinly sliced
2 tablespoons butter or margarine
2 eggs
Salt and pepper

Trim bread; let dry out completely. Soak bread in water; press out water thoroughly. Chill overnight in cloth bag with heavy weight on top to press out any remaining excess water. Put pork through food chopper, using medium blade; cook over low heat until no pink color shows. Clean chopper. Put turkey liver through chopper; cook with pork until lightly browned. In a separate small skillet, cook the celery and onion in butter or margarine until onion is transparent. Crumble bread in large mixing bowl; add pork and liver together with drippings. Add celery, onion, and eggs; mix well. Season to taste with salt and pepper. Makes enough stuffing for a 12-pound (dressed weight) turkey.

CORN BREAD PIMIENTO STUFFING

1 package (7 ounces) corn muffin mix
1 package (8 ounces) bread stuffing mix
1 cup sliced celery
½ cup chopped onion
1 jar or can (4 ounces) pimientos, chopped
1 teaspoon salt
Few grains pepper
1 cup giblet broth (page 107)
1 cup milk
2 eggs
½ cup melted butter or margarine

Prepare and bake corn muffin mix as directed for corn bread. When cool, crumble (makes about 4 cups crumbs). Combine with next 7 ingredients; toss well to mix. Beat milk and eggs together; stir in. Stir in melted butter. Makes enough to stuff 12-to-15-pound turkey.

CORN BREAD STUFFING

½ cup butter or margarine
6 cups crumbled corn bread

6 cups soft bread crumbs
½ cup drippings or shortening
1 cup diced celery
3 medium onions, minced
½ cup chopped green pepper
2 teaspoons salt
½ teaspoon pepper
1 tablespoon poultry seasoning
2 eggs, well beaten
1 to 1½ cups water

Cut butter or margarine in small pieces; mix with corn bread and bread crumbs. Melt drippings or shortening; add celery and onions; cook 5 minutes; add to crumb mixture. Add green pepper and seasonings; mix thoroughly. Add eggs; sprinkle water over surface, stirring lightly, until dressing is of desired moistness. Stuff lightly into neck region and body cavity of bird. Makes enough stuffing for 12-pound turkey.

Apple-Raisin Stuffing: Omit green pepper. Add 2 cups chopped apples, ½ cup raisins, and ⅓ cup sugar.

Sausage Stuffing: Omit poultry seasoning. Pan-fry 1 pound pork sausage. Use drippings to cook celery and onions; add meat to dressing.

Oyster Stuffing: Omit poultry seasoning. Add 1 pint oysters, chopped. Use oyster liquor for part of water.

THREE-FRUIT STUFFING

½ cup chopped onion
½ cup butter or margarine
12 cups soft bread crumbs
2 teaspoons salt
1 tablespoon poultry seasoning
Few grains pepper
1 cup drained canned crushed pineapple
1 cup raisins
1 cup canned pitted sour red cherries

Brown onion in butter or margarine; mix with crumbs, salt, poultry seasoning, and pepper. Add pineapple, raisins, and cherries; mix well. Makes enough stuffing for a 12-pound turkey.

WALNUT-RAISIN STUFFING

4 medium onions, coarsely grated
¾ cup butter or margarine
16 cups (4 quarts) whole wheat bread crumbs
2 cups chopped walnuts

1 cup golden raisins
2 cups finely diced celery
¼ teaspoon pepper
1 tablespoon salt
2 tablespoons poultry seasoning
Hot water

Cook onions in butter or margarine until soft but not brown; add to crumbs. Add remaining ingredients with enough hot water to make fairly moist. Makes enough stuffing for an 18-to-20-pound turkey. This recipe can be halved for a 9-to-10-pound turkey.

BRAZIL NUT APPLE STUFFING

½ package (4 ounces) prepared stuffing mix
½ teaspoon cinnamon
¼ teaspoon ginger
¼ teaspoon nutmeg
¼ cup butter or margarine
½ cup chopped Brazil nuts
½ cup water
¼ cup raisins
¾ cup diced peeled apple

Turn stuffing mix into bowl; add cinnamon, ginger, and nutmeg; toss to distribute seasonings. Melt butter in a skillet; add Brazil nuts and cook until light brown (about 5 minutes). Add water and raisins; bring to boil. Pour over stuffing; stir in diced apple. Makes enough stuffing for one chicken (about 4 pounds).

BROWNED RICE STUFFING

1 package (5½ ounces) precooked rice
3 tablespoons butter or margarine
3 tablespoons minced onion
1 cup diced celery
¼ cup finely chopped celery leaves
1 tablespoon chopped parsley
1 teaspoon salt
⅛ teaspoon pepper
1 teaspoon poultry seasoning
2 cups giblet broth (page 107), boiling hot

Fry precooked rice in butter until golden brown, stirring occasionally. Add onion and cook 1 minute longer. Add remaining ingredients. Mix just until all rice is moistened. Cover; remove from heat. Let stand 12 minutes. Makes enough stuffing for small roasting chicken (about 4 pounds).

ORIENTAL STUFFING FOR DUCKLING

3 packages (10 ounces each) frozen fried rice
    with pork, thawed
1 teaspoon salt
2½ cups finely sliced celery
1 cup chopped fresh or canned mushrooms
2 cans (5 ounces each) water chestnuts,
    drained and chopped
1 teaspoon thyme
½ teaspoon rosemary
2 eggs
¼ cup butter or margarine, melted

Combine ingredients; mix well. Makes enough
to stuff 2 large ducklings (4½ to 5 pounds each).
Stuff ducklings just before roasting. Place birds
on rack on open roaster pan. Do not add water,
and do not cover. Roast at 350° for about 2½
hours or until thoroughly done (25 to 30 minutes
per pound).

MUSHROOM-RICE STUFFING

2 cans (3 ounces each) broiled-in-butter
    mushroom crowns, chopped
1 package (7 ounces) precooked rice
2 tablespoons butter or margarine
½ cup chopped onion
½ teaspoon salt
1 teaspoon poultry seasoning

Drain mushrooms; measure mushroom broth.
Add enough water to make 2 cups. Cook rice
according to package directions, using mush-
room-water mixture instead of all water. Meanwhile, melt butter; add onion; cook until soft.
Add salt, poultry seasoning, and mushrooms; stir
into cooked rice; mix well. Makes enough for 5-
to-7-pound duck.

STUFFING RING

2 packages (8 ounces each) prepared bread
    stuffing mix
1 teaspoon oregano
1 teaspoon poultry seasoning
2 eggs, beaten
¼ cup minced onion
Meat in Sherry-Mushroom Sauce*

Prepare stuffing as directed in recipe on package; add next 4 ingredients. Pack into well-
greased 9- or 10-inch ring mold. Bake at 350° for
½ hour. Unmold on serving plate. Fill center
with Meat in Sherry-Mushroom Sauce. Makes 6
to 8 servings.

*MEAT IN SHERRY-MUSHROOM SAUCE

1 can (10¾ ounces) condensed cream of
    mushroom soup
⅓ cup cream
½ teaspoon Worcestershire sauce
1 egg, slightly beaten
2 cups diced meat
2 tablespoons dry sherry

Blend soup, cream, and Worcestershire sauce in
a saucepan; heat thoroughly but do not boil; pour
slowly on egg, stirring. Return to saucepan. Add
2 cups diced cooked ham or other meat or poultry; cook, stirring, until thoroughly heated. Remove from heat; add sherry. Serve in center of
Stuffing Ring.

CHAPTER 6
Fish

FISH IS fine food. Whenever someone says "I don't like fish" you can be fairly sure he or she has never tasted fish that was properly cooked. The general rule is "high temperature and brief cooking time," but, as with all cooking procedures, there are a few exceptions. However, we are willing to guarantee that you can win converts by following the recipes in this chapter!

BROOK TROUT
(Or Other Small Fish)

To Broil Small Fish: Line cookie sheet with foil (or grease well). Brush cleaned whole fish inside and out with melted butter or margarine. Sprinkle inside and out with salt and pepper. Place on foil. Broil with surface of fish 3 inches below source of heat 5 minutes. Turn; broil 4 to 5 minutes longer. Brush with melted butter or margarine several times during broiling. Trout and other small fish may be split and boned before or after broiling. If so, the head must be removed. Otherwise, trout are served whole.

To Pan-Fry: Put trout in skillet with a little butter or margarine; fry quickly on both sides.

GRILLED FISH CALIFORNIA

4 small whole fish
¼ cup lemon juice
½ teaspoon salt
Few grains pepper
Melted butter or margarine
California Sauce*
Garnish: lemon wedges; sprigs of fresh mint

Remove heads from fish and clean; do not split. Rub fish with lemon juice, salt, and pepper. Place on broiler rack; brush with melted butter. Broil with surface of fish 3 to 4 inches below source of heat 8 minutes; turn; brush with melted butter; broil 5 to 8 minutes longer, depending on size of fish, or until fish flakes easily with a fork. Serve with California Sauce; garnish with lemon wedges and fresh mint. Makes 4 servings.

*CALIFORNIA SAUCE

2 tablespoons butter or margarine
2 tablespoons flour
½ teaspoon salt
4 tablespoons brown sugar
½ cup lemon juice

½ cup water
½ cup golden raisins

Melt butter or margarine; blend in flour, salt, and brown sugar. Combine lemon juice and water; add; stir over low heat until smooth and thickened. Add raisins; simmer 5 minutes. Makes about 2 cups.

BARBECUED SWORDFISH

Barbecue Sauce*
1 swordfish steak

Prepare Barbecue Sauce. Marinate swordfish steak in this mixture for 2 hours before cooking. Drain fish; reserve marinade; place fish on rack in preheated broiler 2 inches below heat; broil about 15 minutes, turning only once, until fish is easily flaked with a fork, but moist. During broiling, brush occasionally with marinade.

*BARBECUE SAUCE

½ cup soy sauce
2 garlic cloves, chopped
4 tablespoons tomato sauce or catchup
2 tablespoons lemon juice
¼ cup chopped parsley
1 teaspoon powdered oregano
½ cup orange juice
1 teaspoon freshly ground pepper

Combine all ingredients and use as marinade for swordfish steak, above.

HERB-BROILED HALIBUT

2 pounds halibut* steak, fresh or frozen, cut 1
   inch thick
⅓ cup butter or margarine
2 tablespoons minced onion
½ teaspoon salt
1 garlic clove, minced
¼ teaspoon coarsely ground black pepper
¼ teaspoon thyme
⅛ teaspoon dried tarragon
¼ teaspoon dried basil
¼ teaspoon dried parsley
1 tablespoon lemon juice

If halibut is frozen, let stand 30 minutes at room temperature. Place halibut in broiler pan (without rack) lined with aluminum foil. Cream butter or margarine with onion, seasonings, and herbs. Add lemon juice, little by little, mixing thoroughly after each addition. Spread half the herb butter over fish. Broil in preheated broiler 2 inches below source of heat 3 minutes for fresh halibut, 5 minutes for partially thawed frozen halibut. With pancake turner, carefully turn fish; spread remaining herb butter over surface. Return to broiler; broil 3 to 5 minutes longer or until fish flakes easily when tested with a fork. (Do not overcook.) Remove to serving platter. Spoon sauce in broiler pan over fish. Makes 4 to 6 servings.

*Or cod or haddock.

CURRIED COD BAKE

2 pounds frozen cod steak, partly thawed
2 large onions, chopped
2 garlic cloves, minced
2 tablespoons water
2 medium apples, pared, cored, and sliced
1 can (8 ounces) tomato sauce
1 cup water
2 teaspoons salt
1 teaspoon curry powder
Dash pepper

Place cod steak or steaks in shallow baking dish. In saucepan, cook onions and garlic in 2 tablespoons water until soft. Stir in remaining ingredients. Stirring constantly, heat to boiling. Spoon over fish. Cover. Bake at 350° for 1 hour or until fish flakes easily with a fork. Makes 6 servings.

STUFFED FISH FILLETS

4 to 6 slices bacon, diced
¼ cup chopped onion
¼ cup chopped green pepper
1½ cups water
1 teaspoon salt
½ cup chopped celery
½ teaspoon thyme
Few grains pepper
1½ cups packaged precooked rice
1 cup finely crumbled corn bread or muffins
¼ cup chopped parsley
8 flounder fillets
2 tablespoons butter or margarine
4 lemon slices
Tomato-Lemon Sauce*

Fry bacon in saucepan until crisp. Remove bacon; set aside. Reserve 3 to 4 tablespoons bacon drippings in pan. Add onion and green pepper; cook until tender. Add water, salt, celery, thyme, and pepper. Bring quickly to boil over high heat. Add rice. Cover; remove from heat. Let stand 5 minutes. Add corn bread, parsley, and bacon; mix lightly with fork. Spread stuffing on 4 fillets. Top with remaining fillets. Place in shallow baking pan. Dot with butter or margarine; top with lemon slices. Add enough water to cover bottom of pan. Bake at 400° for 25 minutes. Serve with Tomato-Lemon Sauce. Makes 8 servings.

*TOMATO-LEMON SAUCE

¼ cup butter or margarine
1 teaspoon prepared mustard
1 teaspoon sugar
1 teaspoon Worcestershire sauce
Few grains pepper
1 tablespoon lemon juice
1 can (8 ounces) tomato sauce

Brown butter in skillet; add remaining ingredients. Heat to serving temperature.

SUNFLOWER SOLE

6 tablespoons raw shelled sunflower seeds
½ cup chicken broth
6 pieces fillet of sole,* about 1¾ pounds
6 tablespoons butter or margarine
¾ cup dry white wine
1½ tablespoons minced onion
¼ teaspoon thyme
1½ teaspoons savory salt
Juice of 1½ lemons
1 cup medium white sauce
⅔ cup half-and-half
Salt and pepper to taste
½ cup whipping cream
Chopped parsley

Simmer sunflower seeds in chicken broth 10 minutes. Fold each piece of sole lengthwise; place in shallow pan with butter, wine, and onion. Add thyme and savory salt. Cover pan with foil; bake at 325° for 10 minutes. Meanwhile, combine lemon juice, white sauce, and half-and-half. Stir in sunflower seeds and broth in which they were cooked. Heat; season to taste with salt and pepper. Whip cream; stir in. To serve, spoon sauce over sole; sprinkle with chopped parsley. Makes 6 servings.

*Or any filleted white fish.

FRIDAY FAVORITE

1 tablespoon mayonnaise
1 teaspoon mustard
6 flounder fillets
¼ pound process American cheese
1 can (8 ounces) tomato sauce
2 tablespoons butter or margarine
⅔ cup soft bread crumbs

Combine mayonnaise and mustard; spread on fish fillets. Cut cheese in 6 pieces; roll each fillet around a piece of cheese; fasten with wooden picks. Place on heatproof platter; pour tomato sauce over all. Dot with butter or margarine. Sprinkle with crumbs. Bake at 375° for 30 minutes. Makes 6 servings.

ORIENTAL STEAMED FISH

Sea bass, 1½ to 2 pounds
1 tablespoon chopped leek
1 teaspoon shredded ginger or powdered ginger
½ teaspoon salt
Dillweed
Soy sauce
1 garlic clove
1 tablespoon peanut oil or vegetable oil
2 teaspoons sesame oil *or* 1 tablespoon vegetable oil

Score and fillet the bass, or have this done at the fish market. Combine leek, ginger, and salt; rub into fish. Sprinkle lightly with dill; add a few drops soy sauce. Steam for about 15 minutes. Turn over and steam for another 5 minutes. Crush garlic clove into combined peanut oil and sesame oil; cook over high heat until garlic is slightly browned. Strain oils to remove garlic. Brush oils over fish just before removing from heat. Makes 4 to 5 servings.

SMORGASBORD SMELTS

1 pound fresh or frozen smelts
Fresh dill
½ cup white vinegar
1 cup water, divided
6 whole peppercorns
6 allspice berries
1 bay leaf
2 teaspoons salt
2 teaspoons sugar
2 envelopes unflavored gelatin

Rinse, drain, and split fish; remove backbone. Put sprig of dill on each fillet; roll tight, beginning at tail end. Fasten with wooden picks. Combine vinegar, ¾ cup water, peppercorns, allspice, bay leaf, salt, and sugar; bring to boiling point. Add fish; simmer 8 to 10 minutes. Remove picks; place fish in 8-inch square pan which has been rinsed in cold water; strain and reserve stock. Soften gelatin in remaining ¼ cup cold water; add to strained hot fish stock. Stir until gelatin is dissolved; pour over fish. Chill until firm. Unmold. Makes 12 servings.

FINNAN HADDIE LOCH LOMOND

    2 pounds finnan haddie (smoked haddock or cod)
    6 tablespoons butter or margarine
    2 tablespoons minced onion
    2 tablespoons minced green pepper
    2 tablespoons minced pimiento
    1 teaspoon paprika
    6 tablespoons flour
    1 large can (1⅔ cups) evaporated milk
    6 baked potatoes

Simmer finnan haddie in water to cover 10 to 15 minutes. Drain, saving stock. Melt butter or margarine; add onion, green pepper, and pimiento; cook until onion is soft but not brown. Blend in paprika and flour. Measure 1⅓ cups of the stock; blend with evaporated milk; add. Stir over low heat until thickened. Add finnan haddie, broken into large pieces. Serve on, or with, baked potatoes. Makes 6 servings.

SEAFOOD-VEGETABLE PIE

    Pastry for 2-crust 10-inch pie
    1 pound firm-fleshed white fish, cooked
    4 tablespoons butter or margarine
    5 tablespoons flour
    ½ teaspoon salt
    Few grains pepper
    1 teaspoon paprika
    1 teaspoon freeze-dried chives
    1 can (3 ounces) broiled sliced mushrooms
    Water
    1 cup evaporated milk
    1 cup cooked sliced carrots
    1 cup cooked lima beans
    ¼ cup dry sherry

Make and bake one 10-inch pie shell or 6 individual (6-inch) pastry shells. Roll out remaining pastry. Cut in 10-inch circle if 10-inch pie pan is being used or 6 small circles if individual pans are being used. Prick surfaces with fork. Bake at 425° for about 25 minutes or until golden brown. Flake fish, removing any bones. Melt butter; blend in flour, salt, pepper, paprika, and chives. Pour broth from mushrooms into measuring cup; add enough water to make 1 cup; combine with evaporated milk; add to butter mixture. Cook and stir over medium heat until smooth and thickened. Add fish, mushrooms, carrots, lima beans, and sherry. Heat to serving temperature; fill pie pan or pans; arrange top crusts. Makes 6 servings.

FISH TIMBALES IN TOMATO-OLIVE SAUCE

    3 eggs
    1½ cups milk
    2 cups flaked fish, cooked or canned
    2 teaspoons minced onion
    ½ teaspoon salt
    Few grains pepper
    ¼ cup chopped onion
    3 tablespoons vegetable oil
    4 tablespoons flour
    2 cans (11 ounces each) condensed tomato bisque
    ½ cup sliced stuffed olives

Beat eggs; add milk, fish, minced onion, salt, and pepper; mix well. Pour into greased custard cups; set in warm water. Bake at 350° for 1 hour. Unmold on serving platter. Meanwhile, cook chopped onion in oil until golden brown. Blend in flour. Add bisque; bring to boiling point. Add olives. Pour over timbales. Makes 6 servings.

FISH STICKS HAWAIIAN

    1 can (1 pound) sliced pineapple
    ½ cup butter or margarine, divided
    2 packages (10 ounces each) raw frozen breaded fish sticks
    1 tablespoon cornstarch
    ¼ teaspoon salt
    ½ teaspoon powdered rosemary
    1 tablespoon lemon juice
    3 cups hot cooked rice

Drain pineapple (save syrup); brown slices lightly on both sides in large skillet in 2 tablespoons butter or margarine; remove from skillet; keep warm. Heat remaining butter or margarine in same skillet; add fish sticks; cook 5 to 6 minutes over medium heat, turning to brown on all sides; remove from skillet; keep warm. Combine cornstarch, salt, and rosemary. Combine lemon juice, pineapple syrup, and enough water to make 1½ cups; blend into cornstarch mixture; pour into skillet; stir over low heat until thickened. Arrange pineapple slices around platter; add rice; top with fish sticks. Serve sauce separately. Makes 6 servings.

DEEP-SEA CASSEROLE

8 ounces medium egg noodles (about 4 cups)
¼ cup sweet pickle relish
¼ cup chopped stuffed olives
½ cup finely chopped onions
2 tablespoons chopped parsley
1 cup mayonnaise
¼ cup milk
2 tablespoons lemon juice
Salt and pepper to taste
1 package (10 ounces) frozen precooked fish sticks

Cook noodles according to package directions; drain. Combine noodles, pickle relish, olives, onions, parsley, mayonnaise, milk, and lemon juice. Season with salt and pepper. Turn into greased 2-quart casserole. Top with frozen fish sticks. Bake at 425° for 15 to 20 minutes. Makes 4 servings.

SALMON DUO

2 cups diced cooked potatoes
1 can (1 pound) red salmon, drained and flaked
2 tablespoons chopped onion
¼ cup chopped green pepper
1 hard-cooked egg, chopped
1 teaspoon salt
½ cup mayonnaise or salad dressing
2 teaspoons prepared mustard
2 teaspoons vinegar
⅛ teaspoon hot-pepper sauce
Salad greens
2 tomatoes

Salmon Salad: Combine potatoes, flaked salmon, onion, green pepper, and egg; sprinkle with salt. Mix together mayonnaise, mustard, vinegar, and hot-pepper sauce; add to potato mixture. Mix lightly with a fork, being careful not to break

potatoes; chill. Serve on salad greens; garnish with tomatoes, cut in wedges. Makes 4 servings.

Salmon Casserole: Prepare as for salad, but do not chill. Turn into a greased 9-inch pie plate or shallow casserole. Omit salad greens. Arrange tomatoes, cut in wedges or sliced, around edge. Bake at 375° for 25 minutes. Makes 4 servings.

BAKED SALMON CROQUETTES

1½ cups water
⅔ cup farina
¾ teaspoon salt
1 cup canned salmon
1 tablespoon lemon juice
1 tablespoon finely chopped parsley
Dash hot-pepper sauce
4 teaspoons grated onion
⅛ teaspoon pepper
1 egg, beaten
1 cup cornflake crumbs
2 hard-cooked eggs, sliced
1½ cups medium white sauce

Bring water to boil. Add farina and salt; stir until thickened. Cook 5 minutes. Flake salmon; add to farina mixture with lemon juice, parsley, hot-pepper sauce, grated onion, and pepper. Form into 8 cylinders. Dip croquettes in egg; coat with cornflake crumbs. Arrange on baking sheet. Bake at 350° for 20 minutes. Serve with sauce made by adding sliced hard-cooked eggs to medium white sauce. Makes 4 servings.

VARIATIONS

(In each case omit salmon, lemon juice, and egg sauce.)

Ham Croquettes: Add 1½ cups ground cooked ham or luncheon meat and 1 teaspoon dry mustard. Serve with green pea sauce made by adding 1 cup canned or cooked peas to 1½ cups medium white sauce.

Chicken Croquettes: Add 1½ cups finely cut chicken and ½ teaspoon curry powder. Serve with mushroom sauce made by adding ½ cup milk to 1 can (10¾ ounces) condensed cream of mushroom soup.

Cheese Croquettes: Decrease grated onion to 2 teaspoons. Add 1½ cups grated cheese and ½ teaspoon dry mustard. Serve with mustard sauce made by adding 2 teaspoons dry mustard to flour for 1½ cups medium white sauce.

SALMON MOUSSE I

1 envelope unflavored gelatin
½ cup cold water
½ cup mayonnaise
1 can (1 pound) salmon, drained
1¼ cups chopped celery
½ teaspoon salt
1 tablespoon lemon juice
1 tablespoon capers

Sprinkle gelatin on cold water; dissolve over boiling water; cool; add to mayonnaise. Combine flaked salmon with remaining ingredients; add to mayonnaise mixture. Turn into 1-quart mold; chill. Unmold. Makes 4 to 6 servings.

SALMON SHORTCAKE

2 cups sifted all-purpose flour
3 teaspoons baking powder
¾ teaspoon salt
6 tablespoons shortening
1 egg
½ cup milk
Melted butter
Milk
Salmon and Vegetables*

Mix and sift flour, baking powder, and salt. Cut in shortening with 2 knives or pastry blender. Beat together egg and milk; stir into flour mixture. Knead 10 strokes. Divide the dough in half. Pat half into a greased 8-inch cake pan; brush with melted butter. Pat out remaining dough; place on top of dough in pan; brush with milk. Bake at 425° for 20 minutes. Split shortcake; spoon Salmon and Vegetables between layers and on top. Makes 6 servings.

*SALMON AND VEGETABLES

1 can (1 pound) peas
1 can (4 ounces) mushrooms
Milk
4 tablespoons butter or margarine
4 tablespoons flour
½ teaspoon salt
1 can (1 pound) salmon, drained and flaked

Drain peas and mushrooms. Boil combined liquids rapidly until reduced to ½ cup; add enough milk to make 2 cups. Melt butter; add flour; stir to a smooth paste. Add liquid; cook, stirring constantly, until mixture thickens and comes to a boil. Add salt, peas, mushrooms, and salmon; heat to serving temperature.

BAKED POTATO SURPRISE

6 baking potatoes
Vegetable oil
Butter or margarine
¼ cup flour
1½ cups milk
½ teaspoon salt
Dash pepper
1 can (8 ounces) salmon
1½ cups cooked or canned peas
Hot milk
Salt and pepper
1 egg, slightly beaten

Scrub potatoes; brush with vegetable oil. Bake at 450° for 1 hour. Meanwhile, melt 3 tablespoons butter or margarine; blend in flour. Add milk. Cook over low heat, stirring, until smooth and thickened. Season with salt and pepper. Drain salmon; flake, removing bones. Add salmon and peas to milk mixture. Cut thin lengthwise slices from top of each baked potato; scoop out pulp and mash with a little hot milk, butter or margarine, and salt and pepper. Put an equal amount of salmon mixture in each potato shell; top with mashed potato. Brush tops with beaten egg. Return to oven to brown and glaze. Serve immediately. Makes 6 servings.

HOT SALMON-STUFFED GREEN PEPPERS

4 large green peppers
⅓ cup mayonnaise
2 tablespoons lemon juice
½ teaspoon hot-pepper sauce
2 tablespoons prepared mustard
1 egg, beaten
1½ cups soft bread crumbs, divided
¼ teaspoon salt
½ cup finely diced celery
1 can (1 pound) salmon, drained and flaked
½ cup hot water
2 tablespoons butter or margarine, melted

Cut slice from top of each pepper to make straight edge; dice tops. Remove seeds from peppers; parboil peppers 5 minutes; drain and set aside. Combine next 5 ingredients. Mix in 1 cup bread crumbs and salt; add celery, salmon, and diced green pepper. Fill green peppers with salmon mixture; stand upright in casserole. Add ½ cup hot water. Bake at 400° for 30 minutes. Combine remaining ½ cup bread crumbs and melted butter. Sprinkle on peppers last 15 minutes of baking time. Makes 4 servings.

SALMON MOUSSE II

1 envelope unflavored gelatin
½ cup cold water
½ cup mayonnaise
¾ cup dairy sour cream
1 can (1 pound) salmon, drained
1¼ cups chopped celery
½ teaspoon salt
1 tablespoon lemon juice
1 tablespoon capers
Salad greens
Bottled Italian salad dressing

Sprinkle gelatin over cold water; dissolve over boiling water; cool. Combine mayonnaise and sour cream; add dissolved gelatin. Flake salmon; remove skin and bones. Combine salmon, celery, salt, lemon juice, and capers. Fold in mayonnaise mixture. Turn into 5-cup mold that has been dipped into cold water. Chill until firm. Serve on salad greens with bottled Italian salad dressing. Makes 6 servings.

SALMON WIGGLE

1 cup well-seasoned thin white sauce (page 220)
1 egg yolk, beaten
1 can (1 pound) salmon
½ teaspoon Worcestershire sauce
1 cup cooked or canned peas
1 tablespoon lemon juice

Stir a little hot white sauce into beaten egg yolk; stir mixture into remaining sauce. Stir over low heat until thickened. Drain salmon; add liquid and Worcestershire sauce to white sauce. Flake salmon and add with drained peas to white sauce. Heat. Add lemon juice. Makes 4 servings.

SOUTHERN TUNA PIES

1 package (10 ounces) frozen mixed vegetables
1 can (6½ or 7 ounces) tuna, drained and flaked
1 can (10¾ ounces) condensed cream of celery soup
1½ cups sifted all-purpose flour
1 teaspoon salt
¼ cup creamy peanut butter
½ cup shortening
2 or 3 tablespoons cold water

Cook vegetables as directed on package; drain. Add tuna and soup; mix lightly. Combine flour and salt; add peanut butter and shortening; cut into mixture with 2 knives or pastry blender. Sprinkle mixture with cold water; blend in lightly (the pastry should hold together so that it may be gathered into a ball). Roll out half of the pastry on lightly floured surface. Line 4 small pie plates or ramekins with pastry. Fill with tuna-vegetable mixture. Roll remaining pastry; cut to fit for top crusts. Top pie plates or ramekins with pastry; trim; crimp edges together; cut slits in center. Bake at 425° for 12 minutes. Makes 4 servings.

TUNA-VEGETABLE CHOWDER

4 tablespoons butter or margarine
1 large onion, sliced
½ cup diced celery with leaves
1 can (1 pound) whole kernel corn
1 can (1 pound) peas
Boiling water
1 can (1 pound 13 ounces) tomatoes with juice
2 cups diced potatoes
2 teaspoons salt
½ teaspoon hot-pepper sauce
1 can (6½ or 7 ounces) tuna, drained and flaked

Melt butter in a large saucepan. Add onion and celery; cook until tender but not brown. Drain corn and peas; add enough boiling water to liquids to make 5 cups. Add to saucepan with tomatoes, potatoes, salt, and hot-pepper sauce. Simmer 40 minutes. Add corn, peas, and tuna; heat to serving temperature. Makes 12 servings.

TUNA RAREBIT

2 cans (6½ or 7 ounces each) tuna
Butter or margarine
4 tablespoons flour
1 teaspoon dry mustard
1 large can (1⅔ cups) evaporated milk
⅔ cup water
2 eggs, beaten
½ pound Cheddar cheese, grated
1 teaspoon salt
2 teaspoons Worcestershire sauce
Few drops hot-pepper sauce
6 Toast Cups*
Garnish: parsley; stuffed olives

Measure oil from tuna; add enough butter or margarine to make ¼ cup. Heat oil and butter; blend in flour and mustard. Add evaporated milk and water; cook over hot water, stirring constantly, until thickened. Stir hot milk mixture into eggs; return to double boiler. Add cheese, salt, Worcestershire sauce, and hot-pepper sauce; stir until cheese melts. Flake tuna; add. Heat thoroughly. Serve in Toast Cups. Garnish with parsley and stuffed olives. Makes 6 servings.

*TOAST CUPS

For each Toast Cup trim crusts from slice of bread. Press each slice in cup of muffin pan. Brush with butter or margarine. Bake at 500° until golden brown.

TUNA RABBIT

    2 tablespoons butter or margarine
    2 tablespoons flour
    1 teaspoon Dijon mustard
    2 cups milk
    2 eggs
    ½ pound sharp Cheddar cheese, grated
    1 teaspoon salt
    2 teaspoons Worcestershire sauce
    2 cans (6½ to 7 ounces each) tuna
    6 toasted English muffins

Melt butter or margarine; add flour and mustard; blend well. Add milk; cook, stirring constantly, until thickened. Beat eggs. Stir hot milk mixture into eggs. Return to pan; add cheese, salt, and Worcestershire sauce. Cook and stir until cheese melts. Drain tuna; flake; add. Heat thoroughly. Serve on toasted English muffins. Makes 6 servings.

TUNA CROUSTADES

Filling:
    2 cans (6½ or 7 ounces each) tuna
    2 tablespoons butter or margarine
    ⅓ cup flour
    1 teaspoon paprika
    Few grains pepper
    1 large can (1⅔ cups) evaporated milk
    1 can (6 ounces) broiled mushroom crowns
    1 cup water (about)
    6 hard-cooked eggs, quartered
    ¼ teaspoon each rosemary and savory

Pour oil from tuna into top of double boiler; add butter; melt. Blend in flour, paprika, and pepper. Combine evaporated milk, broth from mushrooms, and enough water to make 3 cups; add to double boiler. Cook, stirring, until thickened. Add tuna, mushrooms, eggs, and herbs. Cover; cook over hot water 15 minutes. Serve in croustades. Makes 6 servings.

Croustades:
    1 loaf of bread, unsliced
    Melted butter

Remove crusts from loaf of bread. Cut in six 2-inch slices. Hollow out. Brush with melted butter. Toast in hot oven or broiler. Makes 6.

TUNA TURNOVERS

    6 tablespoons butter or margarine
    6 tablespoons flour
    1½ cups milk
    1 cup canned chicken broth
    ½ cup sauterne
    Dash of mace
    Salt, celery salt, pepper to taste
    1 can (6½ or 7 ounces) tuna, flaked
    3 hard-cooked eggs, chopped
    ½ cup chopped ripe olives
    1 package piecrust mix
    2 tablespoons chopped parsley
    2 tablespoons chopped pimiento

Melt butter; blend in flour; add milk, broth, and sauterne. Cook, stirring, until thickened and smooth. Add mace, salt, celery salt, and pepper. To 1 cup of this sauce add tuna, eggs, and olives; chill. Prepare pastry from piecrust mix according to package directions; divide pastry in half; roll each half in an 11- or 12-inch square; with a sharp knife, cut each square in 4 equal-sized small squares. Place spoon of tuna mixture on each square; fold pastry to form triangle; crimp edges with wet fork; prick tops. Place on baking sheet; bake at 450° for 15 to 20 minutes. Add parsley and pimiento to remaining sauce; heat gently; serve with turnovers. Makes 8.

POTATO-TUNA BAKE

    2 packages (5½ ounces each) scalloped potato mix
    3 cans (6½ or 7 ounces each) tuna
    1 cup diced tart apples

Pour potatoes into 3-quart casserole. Drain and flake tuna; add to casserole with apples. Toss gently to mix. Prepare milk mixture as directed on potato package and pour into casserole. Bake as directed for scalloped potatoes. Makes 8 servings.

TUNA, EGGS, AND MUSHROOMS IN PATTY SHELLS

6 packaged frozen patty shells
⅔ cup butter or margarine, divided
6 tablespoons flour
1 teaspoon paprika
½ teaspoon salt
⅛ teaspoon pepper
2 cups milk
1 cup light cream
1 pound fresh mushrooms, sliced
¼ cup dry sherry
⅛ teaspoon rosemary
2 cans (6½ or 7 ounces each) tuna, flaked
6 eggs, hard-cooked and halved

Bake patty shells as directed on package. Melt ⅓ cup butter; blend in flour, paprika, salt, and pepper. Combine milk and cream; add all at once; cook and stir over medium heat until smooth and thickened; cover; cook over low heat 10 minutes. Meanwhile, sauté mushrooms in remaining butter until golden brown and tender; drain on absorbent paper; add to sauce with remaining ingredients. Heat to serving temperature; serve in patty shells. Makes 6 servings.

SKILLET TUNA

1 can (1 pound) potatoes, drained
3 tablespoons butter or margarine
1 can (1 pound) peas, drained
1 can (6½ or 7 ounces) tuna, drained
1 can (10¾ ounces) condensed cream of
    mushroom soup
⅓ cup pimiento strips

Brown potatoes in butter or margarine in skillet. Remove. Add peas, tuna, soup, and pimiento to skillet. Heat, stirring often. Just before serving add potatoes. Makes 6 servings.

TRIANGLE TUNA CASSEROLE

3 cans (8 ounces each) tomato sauce
1 can (3 or 4 ounces) sliced mushrooms
½ teaspoon dried leaf oregano
½ teaspoon salt
¼ teaspoon hot-pepper sauce
3 cans (6½ or 7 ounces each) tuna
1 package (8 ounces) medium noodles, cooked
2 packages (10 ounces each) frozen chopped
    spinach, cooked
1 package (8 ounces) sliced Old English
    cheese

Combine tomato sauce, mushrooms, oregano, salt, and hot-pepper sauce in saucepan. Bring to boil, stirring occasionally. Remove from heat. Drain tuna. Alternate layers of noodles, spinach, and tuna in 3-quart baking dish. Pour sauce over top. Cut each cheese slice in half crosswise. Stack the two halves together and cut in half diagonally to form two triangles. Continue with remaining slices. Overlap cheese triangles down center of baking dish. Bake at 400° for 20 to 25 minutes. Makes 8 servings.

TUNA-TOMATO RIBBON LOAF

Tuna Layer:

1 package (3 ounces) lemon-flavor gelatin
1 cup hot water
1 teaspoon salt
¼ cup vinegar
1 cup dairy sour cream
2 cans (6½ or 7 ounces each) tuna, drained
    and flaked
1 cup finely diced celery
¼ cup finely diced green peppers

Dissolve gelatin in hot water. Stir in salt, vinegar, sour cream, tuna, and vegetables. Turn half of mixture into loaf pan, 8 x 5 x 3 inches. Chill until almost firm. Reserve remaining mixture.

Tomato Layer:

1 package (3 ounces) lemon-flavor gelatin
½ teaspoon salt
⅛ teaspoon ground cloves
1¾ cups hot tomato juice
3 tablespoons vinegar
1 teaspoon Worcestershire sauce

Combine gelatin, salt, and cloves. Add hot tomato juice; stir until gelatin dissolves. Stir in vinegar and Worcestershire sauce. Chill until consistency of unbeaten egg white.

To Assemble:

Spoon tomato layer on top of almost-firm tuna

layer; chill until almost firm. Spoon remaining tuna mixture over tomato layer; chill until firm. Makes 8 servings.

TUNA-POTATO PIE

1 tablespoon minced dried onion
3 tablespoons cold water
2 eggs, slightly beaten
½ cup milk
2 cups soft bread crumbs
2 tablespoons minced parsley
½ teaspoon salt
½ teaspoon dry mustard
¼ teaspoon pepper
2 cans (6½ to 7 ounces each) tuna, flaked
Instant mashed potatoes for 4 servings
2 to 3 slices process American cheese

Combine onion and cold water; let stand until water is absorbed. Combine with eggs, milk, bread crumbs, parsley, and seasonings in large mixing bowl. Beat until blended. Mix in tuna. Turn into 9-inch pie pan. Bake at 350° for 40 minutes. Remove. Increase oven heat to 550°. Prepare mashed potatoes according to package directions; season to taste. Cut 2 large cheese slices into 3 triangles each or 3 small cheese slices into 2 triangles each. Spoon potatoes on top of tuna mixture; arrange cheese triangles over potatoes. Place under broiler heat just long enough to melt cheese. Makes 6 servings.

TUNA PUFF LOG

1 cup water
½ cup shortening
¼ teaspoon salt
1 cup sifted all-purpose flour
4 eggs
Tuna Filling*

Heat water, shortening, and salt in saucepan until shortening melts. Add flour and stir rapidly until mixture comes away from sides of pan and forms a ball. Add eggs one at a time and beat rapidly after each addition. Spoon onto greased cookie sheet, forming a "log" 12 inches long. Bake at 425° for 10 minutes. Reduce heat to 350°; bake 40 minutes longer. Remove from oven and puncture sides with paring knife to allow steam to escape. Replace in oven 5 minutes. Cool on cake rack. Cut off top and fill with hot Tuna Filling. Replace top. Slice to serve. Makes 8 servings.

*TUNA FILLING

½ cup butter or margarine
½ cup flour
2 teaspoons dry mustard
2 teaspoons Worcestershire sauce
1 quart milk
¼ cup grated Parmesan cheese
1 can (6 ounces) broiled sliced mushrooms
2 cups cooked lima beans
⅔ cup broken walnut meats
2 cans (6½ or 7 ounces each) tuna, drained and flaked

Melt butter; stir in flour. Blend in mustard and Worcestershire sauce. Add milk. Stir over low heat until thickened. Add cheese; stir until melted. Add drained mushrooms, lima beans, walnuts, and tuna. Heat to serving temperature. Fill Puff Log. Makes 8 servings.

TUNA-RICE CASSEROLE

1 can (4 ounces) pimientos, divided
1½ cups uncooked regular rice
2 tablespoons butter or margarine
1 tablespoon minced dried onion
⅛ teaspoon oregano
1 teaspoon seasoned salt
1½ cups dry white wine
2 cups chicken broth, divided
1 cup grated Cheddar cheese
2 cans (6½ or 7 ounces each) tuna

Dice pimientos. Combine half the pimientos with rice, butter, onion, oregano, and seasoned salt in 2-quart casserole. Combine wine and 1½ cups chicken broth; heat; pour over rice mixture. Cover; bake at 350° until rice is almost tender and liquid absorbed (about 40 minutes). Stir in remaining broth. Combine cheese, tuna, and remaining pimientos. Make a hollow in center of rice mixture; fill with tuna mixture. Bake, uncovered, 15 minutes longer. Makes 6 servings.

TUNA ROLL-UP

The Roll-up:

2 cans (6½ to 7 ounces each) tuna, flaked
½ teaspoon salt
¼ teaspoon pepper
1 pimiento, chopped
2 tablespoons minced onion
3 tablespoons minced parsley
½ lemon

½ cup water
2 cups biscuit mix
1 egg yolk
2 tablespoons milk

Drain tuna, reserving oil for use in sauce. Combine first 6 ingredients; heat gently. Grate peel from ½ lemon; add. Combine juice of ½ lemon with water. Make up biscuit mix according to package directions, using lemon-water mixture for liquid. Roll out in rectangle 8 x 13 inches. Spread with hot tuna mixture. Roll up. Dampen outside edge with egg yolk beaten with milk; press in firmly. Lay seam side down in floured shallow baking pan. Brush top and sides with more of egg mixture. Bake at 400° for 35 to 40 minutes. Slice crosswise to serve. Serve sauce separately. Makes 6 servings.

The Sauce:

1 tablespoon oil from tuna
1 tablespoon minced onion
2 tablespoons chopped pimiento
1 tablespoon flour
2 tablespoons pimiento brine
Leftover egg mixture (from above)
½ teaspoon salt
Dash pepper
1 cup water

Heat oil in saucepan; add onion and pimiento; heat until bubbling. Sprinkle with flour; mix well. Add pimiento brine, egg mixture, salt, and pepper. Stir over low heat until thickened. Add 1 cup water; continue stirring until smooth. Makes 6 servings.

TUNA TREAT RAMEKINS

2 cans (6½ or 7 ounces each) tuna
1 can (10¾ ounces) tomato soup
⅓ cup light cream
½ teaspoon prepared horseradish
½ teaspoon Worcestershire sauce
Few grains pepper
2 cups cooked or canned green beans, drained
1 can (12 ounces) kernel corn, drained
1 cup seasoned mashed potatoes
¼ cup canned diced roasted almonds

Drain tuna; break up in large pieces. Combine soup, cream, horseradish, Worcestershire sauce, and pepper; add green beans, corn, and tuna; spoon into 4 or 5 ramekins, depending on size. Top with large spoonful of mashed potatoes;

sprinkle with almonds. Bake at 350° for 15 to 20 minutes. Makes 4 or 5 servings.

SAUCY TUNA ROLL-UPS

2 cans (6½ or 7 ounces each) tuna
⅓ cup mayonnaise
½ teaspoon hot-pepper sauce
1 tablespoon lemon juice
6 ½-inch-thick slices very fresh bread
2 tablespoons butter or margarine, melted
½ cup evaporated milk
1 can (10¾ ounces) condensed cream of mushroom soup
1 can (1 pound) peas, drained
½ cup sliced pitted ripe olives (optional)

Drain and flake tuna. Combine mayonnaise, hot-pepper sauce, and lemon juice; add to tuna and mix well. Trim crusts from bread; roll bread thin with rolling pin. Brush one side with melted butter. Turn bread over and spread each slice on unbuttered side with ⅓ cup tuna mixture. Roll as for jelly roll; fasten with wooden picks. Bake at 400° for 15 minutes. To make sauce, combine evaporated milk with mushroom soup in saucepan. Add peas and olives. Heat to serving temperature. To serve, spoon sauce over hot tuna rolls. Makes 6 roll-ups.

TUNA TREATS

½ cup crisp pickle slices
1 package piecrust mix
Creamed Tuna*

Drain pickle slices on absorbent paper. Chop very fine. Add chopped pickles to piecrust mix; add water as directed on package. Wrap in waxed paper or foil; chill. Divide mixture into 4 equal portions. Roll each portion into 7-inch circle on lightly floured board. Fit circles into 4 individual pie pans 5 inches in diameter. Flute edges; prick shells with fork. Bake at 425° for 12 to 15 minutes. Fill with Creamed Tuna. Makes 4 servings.

*CREAMED TUNA

3 tablespoons butter or margarine
¼ cup minced onion
¼ cup minced green pepper
4 tablespoons flour
1 teaspoon salt
⅛ teaspoon pepper

2 cups milk
1 can (6½ or 7 ounces) tuna

Melt butter. Add onion and green pepper; cook until tender but not brown. Blend in flour, salt, and pepper. Add milk all at once. Cook and stir over low heat until thickened. Drain tuna; flake; add. Serve hot in pie shells. Makes filling for 4 individual pies.

TUNA LASAGNE

1 can (15½ ounces) spaghetti sauce with mushrooms
1 can (8 ounces) tomato sauce
1 teaspoon oregano
1 tablespoon minced dried onion
1 garlic clove, finely minced (optional)
2 cans (6½ or 7 ounces each) tuna, drained
1 package (8 ounces) lasagne noodles
½ pound ricotta or any fine-curd dry cottage cheese
½ pound mozzarella cheese, thinly sliced
3 ounces grated Parmesan cheese

Combine spaghetti sauce and tomato sauce; add oregano, minced onion, garlic, and tuna. Bring to boil; cover; simmer 15 minutes. While sauce is simmering, cook noodles according to package directions. Spoon about ⅓ tuna sauce into shallow 2-quart baking dish. Top with half the lasagne noodles, then layer with half the ricotta cheese and mozzarella cheese slices. Layer with half the remaining tuna sauce and remaining lasagne noodles, ricotta, and mozzarella slices. Top with tuna sauce; sprinkle with Parmesan cheese. Bake at 350° for 40 minutes. Makes 8 servings.

TUNA-STUFFED CABBAGE ROLLS

12 large cabbage leaves
2 cans (6½ or 7 ounces each) tuna, drained
1 cup cooked rice
½ cup finely chopped celery
½ cup chopped walnuts
½ cup finely chopped onion
1 egg, slightly beaten
1 tablespoon prepared mustard
2 teaspoons dill seed
¾ teaspoon salt, divided
¼ teaspoon pepper, divided
3 cups chicken stock
1 tablespoon brown sugar

½ cup light cream
3 tablespoons flour
¼ teaspoon nutmeg
3 tablespoons prepared horseradish
Garnish (optional): broken walnuts

Cook cabbage leaves in boiling salted water 2 minutes. Drain; cut lengthwise about 2 inches through heavy vein of each leaf. Combine tuna, rice, celery, walnuts, onion, egg, mustard, dill seed, ½ teaspoon salt, and ⅛ teaspoon pepper; mix well. Place ¼ cup of mixture on each cabbage leaf. Roll up, tucking in ends securely; fasten with wooden picks. Place rolls in large skillet with the chicken stock and brown sugar; cover and simmer 15 to 20 minutes or until rolls are tender. Turn after 10 minutes. Remove rolls to warm serving platter. Mix cream with flour to make smooth paste; gradually stir into hot liquid in skillet. Add remaining ¼ teaspoon salt, ⅛ teaspoon pepper, nutmeg, and horseradish; cook, stirring constantly, until sauce thickens and comes to a boil. Pour part of sauce over rolls. If desired, sprinkle with broken walnuts. Serve remaining sauce separately. Makes 6 servings.

SPANISH RICE AND TUNA

1 package (6 ounces) precooked Spanish rice mix
3 cans (6½ or 7 ounces each) tuna
¼ cup chopped parsley
¼ teaspoon garlic powder
½ teaspoon salt
2 tablespoons lemon juice
2 packages (10 ounces each) Brussels sprouts, cooked

Prepare Spanish rice mix as directed on package. Meanwhile, drain and flake tuna. Stir into rice; add remaining ingredients except Brussels sprouts. Cook, uncovered, 5 minutes longer, stirring frequently. Pack mixture into 6-cup ring mold. Unmold immediately onto heated platter. Fill center with hot well-seasoned Brussels sprouts. Makes 6 servings.

TUNA LOAF

½ pound wide noodles, broken up (4½ cups)
6 hard-cooked eggs, chopped
2 cans (6½ or 7 ounces each) tuna, flaked
1 can (6 ounces) broiled sliced mushrooms
½ cup minced onion
½ cup sweet pickle relish

⅓ cup butter or margarine
½ cup flour
2 teaspoons salt (or to taste)
Few drops hot-pepper sauce
2 teaspoons Worcestershire sauce
2 tablespoons lemon juice
2 cups chicken broth
2 cups milk or half-and-half
1 package (5 ounces) potato chips, finely
    crushed

Cook noodles as directed on package; drain. Combine with next 5 ingredients. Melt butter; blend in next 5 ingredients. Add chicken broth and milk; stir over low heat until thickened; add to tuna mixture; toss with a fork to blend. Grease a shallow baking dish (about 13 x 9 x 2 inches). Spread thin layer of crushed potato chips in bottom of dish. Spoon in half the tuna mixture; sprinkle with potato chips. Repeat, ending with potato chips. Chill overnight. Bake at 375° for 45 minutes. Makes 12 servings.

SPAGHETTI SAN FERNANDO

1 package (about 15 ounces) spaghetti sauce
    mix
1 can (27 to 29 ounces) tomatoes
½ teaspoon seasoned salt
1 teaspoon sugar
¼ cup dry white wine
2 cans (6½ to 7 ounces each) tuna, drained
1 package (8 ounces) thin spaghetti, cooked
    and drained

Combine spaghetti sauce mix, tomatoes, seasoned salt, and sugar in saucepan. Mix thoroughly. Bring to boil; cover; simmer 20 minutes. Add wine and tuna; simmer 5 minutes. Serve over cooked spaghetti. Makes 4 servings.

BAKED TUNA FONDUE

1 can (6½ to 7 ounces) tuna, flaked
1 cup finely diced celery
¼ cup mayonnaise
1 tablespoon prepared mustard
¼ teaspoon salt
12 thin slices whole wheat bread
1 package (8 slices) Old English cheese
3 eggs, beaten
2½ cups milk
2 teaspoons Worcestershire sauce

Combine tuna and celery. Blend mayonnaise, mustard, and salt; add to tuna; mix well. Spread between whole wheat bread slices. Cut sandwiches in half. Arrange sandwiches and cheese in casserole in alternate layers, ending with cheese. Combine eggs, milk, and Worcestershire sauce. Pour into casserole. Bake at 325° for 45 minutes. Makes 6 servings.

SEAMAN'S SUPPER CASSEROLE

3 tablespoons butter or margarine
⅔ cup coarsely chopped onion
½ cup flour
1 can (8 ounces) tomato sauce
2 cups milk
1 cup cooked rice
2 cans (6½ to 7 ounces each) tuna, drained
⅛ teaspoon oregano
1 teaspoon salt
Dash cayenne
Toast

Melt butter; add onion; cover; cook over low heat until onion is soft but not brown. Add flour; mix well. Add tomato sauce; blend. Add milk; cook, stirring constantly, until thickened. Add remaining ingredients; cook over moderate heat until thoroughly heated, stirring occasionally. Serve from a casserole garnished with half circles of toast. Makes 6 servings.

MOLDED MACARONI-TUNA LOAF

1 envelope unflavored gelatin
¼ cup cold water
½ cup hot water
8 ounces elbow macaroni (2 cups), cooked
1 can (6½ to 7½ ounces) chunk-style tuna
1 large can (1⅔ cups) evaporated milk
½ cup chopped pimientos
½ cup chopped parsley
1 tablespoon grated onion
1½ teaspoons salt
Garnish: crisp salad greens; cherry tomatoes

Soften gelatin in ¼ cup cold water for 5 minutes. Dissolve gelatin in hot water. Add cooked macaroni and remaining ingredients; mix lightly but thoroughly. Turn into lightly oiled 9 x 5 x 3-inch loaf pan. Chill several hours or until firm. Unmold; garnish with crisp salad greens and cherry tomatoes. Makes 6 to 8 servings.

CRUSTY TUNA TRIO

2 cans (6½ or 7 ounces each) tuna
1½ cups soft bread cubes
¼ cup chopped onion
½ teaspoon salt
⅛ teaspoon pepper
½ cup mayonnaise
1 teaspoon lemon juice
½ cup evaporated milk
Packaged cornflake crumbs

Drain oil from tuna into mixing bowl. Add bread cubes to oil; blend well. Mix in onion, salt, pepper, mayonnaise, and lemon juice. Flake tuna; add. For appetizers, shape into 1-inch balls; for croquettes, shape into 1½ x 4-inch ovals; for loaf, shape as desired or use small loaf pan. Dip balls or croquettes in evaporated milk; sprinkle with crumbs. Brush loaf with evaporated milk; sprinkle with crumbs. Place on foil-lined baking sheet. Bake at 375° for 10 minutes for appetizers, 20 minutes for croquettes, 30 minutes for loaf. Makes 5 dozen appetizers, 6 croquettes, or 1 loaf.

TUNA CARIBE WITH BANANAS SAUTÉ

2 cans (6½ or 7 ounces each) tuna
½ cup finely chopped onion
¼ cup finely chopped green pepper
1 garlic clove, minced
Flour
1 can (1 pound) tomatoes
1 can (8 ounces) tomato sauce
1 small bay leaf
¼ teaspoon dried leaf thyme
½ teaspoon salt
⅛ teaspoon pepper
6 small green-tipped bananas
3 tablespoons melted butter or margarine
Easy Rice and Beans*

Heat oil drained from tuna in large saucepan. Add onion, green pepper, and garlic. Cook 5 minutes or until tender. Add 1 tablespoon flour; cook 2 to 3 minutes, stirring constantly. Add tomatoes, tomato sauce, bay leaf, thyme, salt, and pepper. Bring to boil. Reduce heat; simmer, partially covered, 20 minutes. Add tuna; simmer 10 minutes. Discard bay leaf. Dust peeled bananas with flour; sauté in butter until lightly browned on all sides. Serve Tuna Caribe over hot Easy Rice and Beans garnished with bananas. Makes 6 servings.

*EASY RICE AND BEANS

2 cups cooked or canned dried pinto beans
3 cups cooked long-grain rice
1 tablespoon soy sauce
1 teaspoon Worcestershire sauce
2 tablespoons dry sherry

Drain beans before measuring. Combine all ingredients; heat gently to serving temperature. Makes 6 servings.

SARDINE RAREBIT

1 can (10¾ ounces) condensed tomato soup
½ cup water
¾ cup nonfat dry milk
¼ teaspoon salt
Few grains pepper
¼ pound American cheese, grated
4 hard-cooked eggs, halved
1 can sardines
4 toasted English muffins

Combine tomato soup and water in top of double boiler. Sprinkle dry milk, salt, and pepper over surface. Beat with rotary egg beater until blended; set over hot water. Add cheese; stir until melted. Arrange halved hard-cooked eggs and sardines on platter. Pour tomato-cheese sauce over all. Serve with toasted English muffins. Makes 4 servings.

SCALLOPED POTATOES AND SCALLOPS

2 pounds sea scallops, fresh or frozen
2 packages scalloped potato mix
2 tablespoons butter or margarine
Paprika

Defrost scallops if frozen. Prepare and bake scalloped potato mix as directed on package. About 15 minutes before end of baking time remove from oven. Arrange sea scallops on top; dot scallops with butter or margarine; sprinkle generously with paprika. Return to oven for remaining baking time. Makes 6 servings.

SPAGHETTI WITH SEA SCALLOPS

2 pounds sea scallops, fresh or frozen
4 strips bacon
1 large green pepper, cut in ½-inch pieces
½ pound sweet Italian sausage, sliced
   (optional)

1 medium onion, yellow or red, sliced
2 cans (14 or 15 ounces each) meatless
    spaghetti sauce
1 can (8 ounces) tomato sauce
8 ounces thin spaghetti, cooked

Defrost scallops if frozen. Cook bacon until crisp; reserve. Sauté green pepper, sausage, and onion in bacon drippings until lightly browned; remove from pan. Sauté scallops until golden brown. Crumble bacon; return to pan with green pepper, sausage, and onion. Combine spaghetti sauce and tomato sauce; pour over all. Simmer 5 minutes. Serve over spaghetti. Makes 6 to 8 servings.

NEW BEDFORD CASSEROLE

2 pounds sea scallops, fresh or frozen
2 cups biscuit mix
1 large can (1⅔ cups) evaporated milk
1 can (8 ounces) tomato sauce with tomato bits
1 can (1 pound) Italian peeled plum tomatoes,
    drained (save juice)
¼ teaspoon each rosemary and savory
⅓ cup flour
2 teaspoons salt
Dash of pepper
Dash of paprika
½ cup butter or margarine
1 can (12 ounces) Mexican-style kernel corn

Defrost scallops if frozen. Make and bake enough small baking powder biscuits to circle rim of casserole, using biscuit mix. Remove from oven when light brown. Simmer scallops 5 minutes in water to cover; drain, saving ½ cup broth. Combine reserved broth, evaporated milk, tomato sauce, juice from canned tomatoes, and herbs. Combine flour, salt, pepper, and paprika. Melt butter; blend in flour mixture. Add broth mixture all at once, stirring constantly. Cook, stirring, until thickened. Cover; cook 5 minutes over low heat. Add drained tomatoes, corn, and scallops. Pour into greased casserole. Place biscuits around edge. Bake at 350° for 15 minutes or until bubbly. Makes 6 servings.

SCALLOPED SCALLOPS

2 pounds sea scallops, fresh or frozen
8 slices bacon
2 tablespoons butter or margarine
2 tablespoons minced onion
3 tablespoons finely diced green pepper

¼ cup flour
1 envelope chicken broth mix
¾ cup hot water
1 cup light cream
1 can (3 ounces) sliced broiled mushrooms
½ teaspoon salt
Few grains pepper
3 tablespoons Marsala
2 tablespoons snipped parsley

Defrost scallops if frozen; cut in half, crosswise; cover with boiling water; simmer 5 to 7 minutes or until tender; drain. Dice bacon; cook until crisp; drain, reserving 2 tablespoons of drippings. Return 2 tablespoons bacon drippings to skillet; add butter, onion, and green pepper. Cook until soft but not brown. Blend in flour. Combine broth mix and hot water; add with cream and broth from mushrooms; stir until thickened. Add mushrooms, scallops, salt, pepper, and Marsala. Heat to serving temperature. Spoon into large scallop shells or ramekins. Sprinkle crisp bacon bits and parsley on top. Serve at once. Makes 6 servings.

SCALLOPS AU FROMAGE

1 pound sea scallops, fresh or frozen
2 tablespoons chopped onion
1 can (3 ounces) broiled sliced mushrooms,
    drained
2 tablespoons butter or margarine
1 can (11 ounces) condensed Cheddar cheese
    soup
2 tablespoons milk
2 teaspoons lemon juice
¼ teaspoon marjoram
2 tablespoons buttered soft bread crumbs

Defrost scallops if frozen. Cook onion and mushrooms in butter until lightly browned. Add scallops; cook 5 minutes. Divide scallop mixture among 4 shallow ramekins or large scallop shells. Combine soup, milk, lemon juice, and marjoram; blend well; pour into ramekins. Top with crumbs. Bake at 350° for 20 minutes. Makes 4 servings.

SEA SCALLOPS ORIENTAL

2 pounds sea scallops, fresh or frozen
¼ cup honey
¼ cup prepared mustard
2 teaspoons curry powder

1 teaspoon lemon juice
Garnish: lemon wedges

Defrost scallops if frozen. Line broiler pan with aluminum foil. Arrange scallops in bottom of pan. Combine honey, mustard, curry powder, lemon juice; mix well. Brush scallops generously with curry mixture. Place broiler pan in lowest position under source of heat. Broil slowly 10 minutes. Turn scallops; brush with curry mixture; broil 10 minutes longer or until nicely browned. Garnish with lemon wedges. Makes 4 to 6 servings.

SEA SCALLOP PLATTER

2 pounds sea scallops, fresh or frozen
⅓ cup melted butter or margarine
1 cup crushed wheat flakes
2 packages (10 ounces each) frozen broccoli
2 packages (10 ounces each) frozen French fried potatoes
Salt and pepper

Defrost scallops if frozen. Dip in melted butter; coat with crushed wheat flakes; arrange in single layer on baking sheet. Defrost broccoli; place in casserole; add boiling water to a depth of ½ inch; cover tightly. Bake scallops and broccoli at 550° for 5 minutes. Spread French fries on baking sheet; place in oven. Bake 10 minutes longer. Season broccoli (it will be crisp-tender) with melted butter and salt and pepper. Arrange all 3 foods on serving platter. Makes 4 to 6 servings.

CRAB CASSEROLE

1 cup grated sharp Cheddar cheese
2 cups medium white sauce (page 220)
2 egg yolks, beaten
2 cups crab meat, fresh or canned
2 tablespoons melted butter or margarine
½ cup soft bread crumbs

Add cheese to hot white sauce; stir until melted and remove from heat. Add to beaten egg yolks gradually. Add crab meat. Turn into 1-quart casserole. Mix butter and crumbs together. Scatter over top of casserole. Bake at 350° for 30 minutes. Makes 4 servings.

KING CRAB BENEDICT

2 cans (7½ ounces each) Alaska king crab *or* 2 packages (8 ounces each) frozen Alaska king crab

1 tablespoon lemon juice
2 jars (10½ ounces each) hollandaise sauce
2 packages (10 ounces each) frozen asparagus spears
12 slices toast
Garnish: 3 hard-cooked eggs, sliced

Drain canned crab or thaw and drain frozen crab. Slice into bite-size pieces; sprinkle with lemon juice. Heat hollandaise sauce; blend until smooth. Add crab. Stir over low heat until serving temperature. Cook asparagus according to package directions. Place spears on toast. Spoon crab mixture over asparagus. Garnish each serving with slices of hard-cooked egg. Makes 6 servings.

HOT-WEATHER RAMEKINS

2 medium cucumbers
1½ cups well-seasoned medium white sauce (page 220)
1 can (6½ ounces) crab meat,* drained
½ cup crushed potato chips

Pare cucumbers; dice. Simmer in salted water until transparent (about 10 minutes); drain well. Add to white sauce with flaked crab meat. Turn into ramekins; top with potato chips. Bake at 350° about 15 minutes. Makes 4 generous servings.

SHRIMP JAMBALAYA

1 cup sliced celery
2 cups diced green pepper
2 medium onions, thinly sliced
4 tablespoons butter or margarine, divided
1 or 2 garlic cloves, minced
1 pound cooked ham, ¾ inch thick, cubed
2 pounds peeled, deveined shrimp
1½ teaspoons salt
¼ teaspoon hot-pepper sauce
½ teaspoon chili powder
1 teaspoon sugar
2 cans (1 pound each) whole tomatoes
3 cups hot cooked rice

Cook celery, green pepper, and onions in half the butter or margarine until tender but not brown; add garlic and ham; cook 5 minutes longer. Add remaining butter, shrimp, salt, hot-pepper sauce, chili powder, and sugar. Cook, tossing often with fork, until shrimp are pink.

*Or 1 cup flaked cooked fish, shrimp, or canned salmon or tuna.

Add tomatoes; heat. Stir in rice. Makes 8 servings.

BANANA-SHRIMP CURRY

6 medium onions, sliced thin
6 tablespoons butter or margarine
2 or 3 teaspoons curry powder
1 cup milk
1 chicken bouillon cube
½ cup hot water
¼ teaspoon salt
2 medium bananas, sliced
3 cups cooked rice
1½ pounds cooked shrimp, peeled and
    deveined

Cook onions over low heat in butter until clear and golden. Add curry powder and milk. Dissolve bouillon cube in hot water; add with salt. Cook over medium heat 10 minutes. Add bananas. Cook 5 minutes longer, stirring occasionally. Serve over hot fluffy rice and hot shrimp. Makes 4 servings.

ACCOMPANIMENTS: Flaked coconut, chutney, and chopped peanuts.

SHRIMP SAUCE FOR SPAGHETTI

⅓ cup butter or margarine
1 large garlic clove, slashed
⅓ cup flour
1 envelope instant chicken broth mix
1 large can (1⅔ cups) evaporated milk
1⅔ cups water
1 jar (3 ounces) grated Romano cheese
1 teaspoon oregano
½ cup snipped parsley
2 pounds cooked shrimp, peeled and
    deveined

Melt butter; add garlic; cook over low heat 10 minutes; remove garlic. Blend in flour and broth mix. Combine evaporated milk and water; add. Stir over medium heat until thickened and smooth. Add cheese; stir until melted. Add oregano; cook 10 minutes longer. Stir in parsley. Serve on hot thin spaghetti. Top with hot shrimp. Makes 8 servings.

PEPPERED SHRIMP AND EGGS

2 strips bacon
2 tablespoons butter or margarine
1 medium green pepper, sliced thin
1 small onion, sliced
1 cup peeled, deveined shrimp, fresh, frozen,
    canned, or precooked
1 teaspoon salt
¼ teaspoon cayenne
4 eggs
3 teaspoons light cream
½ teaspoon Worcestershire sauce

Fry bacon crisp; drain; break into small pieces. Drain nearly all bacon fat from pan; add butter; cook green pepper and onion until nearly tender but not brown. Add shrimp. If fresh shrimp, cook mixture gently 5 to 6 minutes or until nearly moisture-free; season with salt and cayenne. If frozen shrimp, cook as directed on package, season with salt and cayenne. If canned or precooked shrimp, cook only 1 or 2 minutes, using less salt. Beat eggs slightly; add cream and Worcestershire sauce; stir in slowly. While mixture is cooking over low heat (about 5 minutes), add minced bacon. Makes 4 servings.

SHRIMP ROLLS WITH MUSHROOM SAUCE

18 slices very fresh bread, cut ½ inch thick
2 cans (about 5 ounces each) shrimp, rinsed
    and drained
¼ teaspoon Worcestershire sauce
Dash hot-pepper sauce
2 teaspoons prepared horseradish
½ cup mayonnaise
18 cooked asparagus spears
Melted butter or margarine
Paprika
Mushroom Sauce*

Trim crust from bread slices. Roll bread slices with rolling pin until very thin. Mash shrimp; add next 4 ingredients; mix well. Spread on bread slices. Place 1 spear asparagus at one end of each bread slice; roll up; secure with wooden picks. Brush lavishly with melted butter; sprinkle with paprika. Arrange on baking sheet. Bake at 450° for about 15 minutes or until deep golden brown. Remove picks. Serve with Mushroom Sauce. Makes 18.

*MUSHROOM SAUCE

1 can (10¾ ounces) condensed cream of
    mushroom soup
⅓ cup light cream
1 tablespoon cut chives, fresh or freeze-dried

Empty soup into saucepan. Add cream slowly, while stirring. Bring to boil. Stir in chives. Simmer 5 minutes.

SMOTHERED SHRIMP

3 cans (about 5 ounces each) shrimp *or* 1 pound frozen shrimp, cooked
1 cup finely chopped onion
½ cup finely chopped scallions
2 to 4 garlic cloves, minced (according to taste)
½ cup butter or margarine
2 tablespoons flour
2½ cups water
1 can (8 ounces) tomato sauce
1 tablespoon Worcestershire sauce
¼ teaspoon hot-pepper sauce
5 whole allspice, crushed
1 teaspoon salt
1 teaspoon sugar
½ teaspoon thyme
1 lemon slice
5 cups cooked rice
Garnish: 2 hard-cooked eggs, sliced

Drain shrimp; rinse. Cook onion, scallions, and garlic in butter until soft. Blend in flour. Add all remaining ingredients except shrimp, rice, and eggs. Cover; simmer about 10 minutes, stirring occasionally. Uncover; continue cooking over low heat until mixture is reduced by about half. Add shrimp; heat. Serve over fluffy rice garnished with sliced eggs. Makes 6 servings.

AVOCADOS AND SHRIMP

1 can (about 5 ounces) shrimp
½ cup diced celery
½ cup diced tomato
¼ cup French dressing
3 avocados
½ cup finely crushed cereal flakes
2 tablespoons melted butter or margarine
3 slices bacon, cut in half

Drain shrimp; combine with celery, tomato, and French dressing. Mix lightly. Cut avocados in half lengthwise; remove pits; pack shrimp mixture into cavities. Mix cereal flakes with melted butter; sprinkle over shrimp mixture; top with ½ slice of bacon. Place avocados in a shallow baking pan; bake at 350° for 15 minutes. Serve hot. Makes 6 servings.

CREAMED SHRIMP AND LIMA BEANS IN CHEESE TART SHELLS

⅓ cup butter or margarine
6 tablespoons flour
¼ teaspoon marjoram
1 teaspoon paprika
3 cups milk
2 cups cooked lima beans
2 cans (about 5 ounces each) shrimp, rinsed and drained
Salt and pepper
6 Cheese Tart Shells*

Melt butter or margarine; blend in flour, marjoram, and paprika. Add milk; stir until thickened. Cover; cook over hot water 10 minutes. Add lima beans and shrimp. Season to taste with salt and pepper. Serve in Cheese Tart Shells. Makes 6 servings.

*CHEESE TART SHELLS

Prepare 1 package pie crust mix as directed on package. Roll out in oblong. Sprinkle ½ cup grated Cheddar cheese over surface. Fold in thirds. Roll out ⅛ inch thick. Cut into 6 equal pieces. Press into 6 tart-shell pans. Prick surface with fork. Bake at 425° for 10 to 12 minutes. Remove from pans.

NEW ORLEANS SHRIMP AND SPAGHETTI

½ cup vegetable oil
½ cup chopped scallions
2 pounds cooked, peeled, deveined shrimp
2 teaspoons grated lemon peel
Salt and pepper
1 tablespoon lemon juice
½ cup sliced ripe olives
½ pound thin spaghetti, cooked

Heat oil in skillet, using medium heat; add scallions; cook about 5 minutes. Add shrimp, lemon peel, salt, and pepper. Cook until heated through. Stir in lemon juice. Add olives and spaghetti; mix well. Makes 4 to 6 servings.

PANTRY SHELF JAMBALAYA

¼ cup butter or margarine
¼ cup chopped onion
½ cup diced green pepper
½ cup chopped celery

1 large can (4½ ounces) deviled ham
2 cans (about 5 ounces each) shrimp, drained
2 cans (3 or 4 ounces) mushrooms
1 can (1 pound) tomatoes
1 can (10½ ounces) condensed bouillon
½ teaspoon each sugar and chili powder
½ teaspoon hot-pepper sauce
1 cup uncooked regular rice
1 cup cooked or canned peas

Melt butter in skillet; add onion, green pepper, and celery; cook until onion is tender but not brown. Add deviled ham and drained shrimp. Drain mushrooms and tomatoes, reserving liquids. Measure liquids and bouillon; add enough water to measure 2 cups. Add to skillet with sugar, chili powder, and hot-pepper sauce. Add rice; cover. Simmer 15 minutes. Uncover; top with drained tomatoes, mushrooms, and peas. Cover; simmer 15 minutes or until rice is tender. Toss lightly before serving. Makes 6 servings.

SHRIMP FIESTA

1 bottle or can (12 ounces) beer or ale
½ onion
1 sprig parsley
1 lemon wedge
1 bay leaf
1 teaspoon salt
2 pounds raw shrimp, peeled and deveined
2 tablespoons butter or margarine
2 tablespoons flour
1 can (8 ounces) tomato sauce
4 tablespoons chopped scallions
¼ teaspoon hot-pepper sauce
¼ teaspoon nutmeg
Pinch sugar
Hot buttered noodles

Bring beer, onion, parsley, lemon wedge, bay leaf, and salt to boil in kettle. Add shrimp. Bring to boil again; reduce heat; simmer 5 minutes. Remove shrimp. Strain liquid; reserve. Melt butter in skillet; add flour; stir to smooth paste. Add shrimp liquid, tomato sauce, scallions, hot-pepper sauce, nutmeg, and sugar. Cook, stirring constantly, until mixture thickens and comes to a boil. Add shrimp; reheat. Serve with hot buttered noodles. Makes 4 to 6 servings.

SHRIMP 'N' RICE

1 can (5 ounces) deveined jumbo shrimp
1 can (10¾ ounces) condensed tomato soup

2 teaspoons parsley flakes
¼ teaspoon garlic powder
½ teaspoon minced dried onion
⅛ teaspoon cayenne
¼ teaspoon salt
1 tablespoon butter or margarine
1½ cups packaged precooked rice

Drain shrimp; rinse. Measure soup; add enough water to make 1½ cups; heat. Add shrimp and all remaining ingredients except rice. Bring to boil. Add rice; cover; remove from heat; let stand 5 minutes. Fluff with fork. Makes 4 servings.

CHILI RICE WITH SHRIMP

3 tablespoons vegetable oil
1 cup uncooked regular rice
1 onion, chopped
1 garlic clove, minced
½ cup drained canned tomatoes
1 green pepper, chopped
1 teaspoon oregano
1 teaspoon chili powder
1 teaspoon salt
3 cups boiling water
1 cup cooked or canned cleaned shrimp

Heal oil in large frying pan; fry rice golden brown. Add onion and garlic; stir over low heat until onion is cooked; add remaining ingredients except shrimp. Cover. Boil rapidly until rice is tender. Remove cover; cook until rice is almost dry; stir in shrimp. Makes 4 servings.

LOBSTER ROLLS

4 frozen rock lobster tails, about ½ pound
    each
6 to 8 cups boiling water
2 envelopes instant chicken broth mix
1 tablespoon lemon juice
1 tablespoon parsley flakes
1½ teaspoons salt
6 frankfurter rolls, heated
Savory Sauce*

Place lobster tails in kettle; add just enough boiling water to cover; add broth mix, lemon juice, parsley flakes, and salt. When water reboils, lower heat and boil 10 to 12 minutes. Drain lobster tails; drench with cold water. Cut through undershell with kitchen shears. Insert fingers between shell and meat; pull firmly to remove meat in one piece. Cut crosswise into bite-size chunks; chill. To serve fill rolls with lobster chunks; top with a ribbon of Savory Sauce. Makes 6 servings.

*SAVORY SAUCE

½ cup mayonnaise
½ cup creamed cottage cheese
3 tablespoons minced celery
2 tablespoons snipped parsley
3 tablespoons minced sweet gherkins
3 tablespoons minced stuffed olives

Combine all ingredients. Makes about 1⅔ cups.

ROCK LOBSTER ALBERTO

4 frozen rock lobster tails, about ½ pound each
8 ounces medium noodles
1 egg yolk, beaten
¼ pound soft butter or margarine
Salt to taste
1 cup ricotta or farmer cheese (fine dry-curd cottage cheese)
½ cup grated or shredded Parmesan cheese
¼ cup light cream

Thaw lobster tails; prepare and cook in boiling salted water as directed on package. Cook noodles in boiling salted water, following directions on package; do not overcook; drain. Add remaining ingredients to noodles quickly; toss to mix thoroughly. Serve at once with drained lobster tails in their shells. Makes 4 servings.

LOBSTER SUPREME

8 frozen rock lobster tails, about ½ pound each
3 tablespoons butter or margarine
1 garlic clove, crushed
1 medium onion, sliced
1 small green pepper, sliced
3 sprigs parsley
1 cup grated sharp Cheddar cheese
½ cup whipping cream
½ cup dry sherry
3 tablespoons cornstarch
½ cup cold water
2 cups Duchess potatoes*

Cook lobster tails in water according to package directions. Remove and cool slightly. Measure

*To make Duchess potatoes, add 2 beaten egg yolks to 4 cups well-seasoned mashed potatoes. Beat well.

lobster stock; add water, if necessary, to make 3 cups. Remove lobster meat from shells; cut in crosswise slices. Melt butter or margarine. Add garlic, onion, green pepper, and parsley; cook until onion is soft but not brown. Add lobster stock; simmer 5 minutes. Strain stock; return to pan. Add cheese slowly, stirring constantly over low heat. When cheese is melted, stir in cream and sherry. Blend cornstarch with cold water and stir in. Cook and stir until sauce is thickened. Strain through fine sieve. Add lobster meat, then heat gently. Line sides of chafing dish with Duchess potatoes. Pour the lobster and sauce into center of dish. Makes 8 servings.

BROILED STUFFED LOBSTER TAILS

8 frozen rock lobster tails, about ½ pound each
⅓ cup butter or margarine
2 teaspoons dried green onion
⅓ cup flour
1 teaspoon salt
⅛ teaspoon pepper
Few grains turmeric (optional)
1½ cups milk
½ cup light cream
1 pound cooked shrimp, peeled and deveined
1 can (7 ounces) minced clams
¾ cup soft buttered crumbs

Cook lobster tails in water as directed on package. Cool; remove meat, leaving trimmed shells intact. Cut lobster meat in bite-size pieces. Melt butter; add dried green onion; cook 5 minutes over low heat. Blend in flour, salt, pepper, and turmeric. Combine milk and cream; add all at once. Cook and stir over medium heat until smooth and thick. Dice shrimp, reserving 8 for garnish; combine with lobster meat. Drain clams; add. Add diced shrimp, lobster, and clams to sauce. Refill shells. Sprinkle with buttered crumbs. Broil with surface of food about 4 inches below heat until golden brown. Decorate tops with whole shrimp; broil a few seconds longer. Makes 8 servings.

"OYSTER BAR" STEW

1 quart (4 cups) shucked oysters
¼ cup butter or margarine
1 teaspoon paprika
1 teaspoon Worcestershire sauce
1½ teaspoons salt

Few grains pepper
1½ quarts milk

Pick over oysters, removing bits of shell; strain oyster liquor. Melt butter or margarine in deep, heavy saucepan. Add paprika, Worcestershire sauce, salt, and pepper; stir until smooth. Add oysters and oyster liquor. Cook over low heat a few moments, until edges of oysters curl. Add milk. Heat slowly over low heat just to scalding point. Do not boil. Serve at once. Makes 6 generous servings.

SAUCY SEAFOOD ROLL

Filling:

1 can (7 ounces) crab meat, drained and flaked
1 can (4½ or 5 ounces) shrimp, drained and chopped
¼ cup dairy sour cream
2 tablespoons snipped fresh parsley

Combine crab meat, shrimp, sour cream, and parsley; set aside.

Dough:

2 cups buttermilk pancake mix
¼ cup soft shortening
⅔ cup milk

Place pancake mix in bowl. Cut in shortening until mixture resembles coarse crumbs. Add milk; stir lightly until mixture is dampened. (If necessary, add a little more milk to make a soft dough.) Turn out onto lightly floured board or canvas; knead gently a few seconds. Roll out to form a 15 x 12-inch rectangle.

Sauce:

1 can (10¾ ounces) condensed cream of celery soup
½ cup milk
1 package (10 ounces) frozen mixed vegetables, cooked and drained
⅛ teaspoon white pepper

Combine soup, milk, vegetables, and pepper; heat thoroughly.

To Assemble:

Spread dough with filling. Starting with short side, roll up as for jelly roll. Cut into 12 1-inch slices. Place on lightly greased cookie sheet cut side down. Bake at 400° for 15 to 20 minutes or until lightly browned. Serve with hot sauce. Makes 6 servings.

CASSEROLE ST. JACQUES

1 pound sea scallops
1 cup dry white wine
1 small onion, sliced thin
1 tablespoon minced parsley
1 teaspoon salt
1 can (3 ounces) broiled sliced mushrooms
¼ cup butter or margarine, divided
2 teaspoons lemon juice
4 tablespoons flour
1 cup light cream
⅓ cup grated Gruyère cheese
Few grains pepper
1 can (about 5 ounces) shrimp, drained
1 can (7 ounces) Alaska king crab meat, drained and flaked
1 cup buttered soft bread crumbs

Defrost scallops if frozen. Combine next 4 ingredients in saucepan; bring to boil; add scallops; simmer 5 minutes. Add mushrooms with their broth, 2 tablespoons butter or margarine, and lemon juice. Simmer until butter is melted. Drain scallops and mushrooms, saving liquid. Halve scallops. Measure liquid; add enough water to make 2 cups. Melt remaining butter or margarine; blend in flour; add scallop liquid and cream. Cook and stir over low heat until thickened and smooth. Add cheese and pepper; stir until cheese melts. Stir in scallops, mushrooms, shrimp, and crab meat; heat to serving temperature. Turn into shallow 2-quart casserole; sprinkle with buttered bread crumbs. Brown under broiler. Makes 6 to 8 servings.

SEAFOOD CHOWDER

2 tablespoons vegetable oil
1 tablespoon paprika
2 large onions, sliced
1 medium green pepper, cut in strips
1 pound tomatoes, sliced
2 garlic cloves, minced
¼ cup chopped parsley
1 pound shrimp, shelled and deveined
1 cup cooked flaked lobster meat or 1 can (6½ ounces) lobster meat, drained
½ cup chopped stuffed olives
2 cups water
2 cups tomato juice
Salt and pepper to taste
2 dozen raw oysters, shucked
½ cup dry sherry

Heat oil; add paprika and blend. Add onions, green pepper, tomatoes, garlic, and parsley. Cook over low heat until tender, stirring often. Add shrimp, lobster, olives, water, tomato juice, salt, and pepper. Cover; cook over low heat ½ hour, stirring occasionally. Add shucked oysters, with their liquid. Mix well. Cook until the edges of the oysters curl (about 4 or 5 minutes). Add sherry; mix well. Serve piping-hot. Makes 6 to 8 servings.

SEAFOOD CREPES

The Crepes:

1 cup milk
1 cup flour
8 eggs, slightly beaten
¼ teaspoon salt
Butter or margarine

Add milk to flour slowly while stirring until smooth and free from lumps. Stir in eggs, salt, and 2 tablespoons melted butter. Use a small skillet (7½ inches top diameter) heated and brushed with butter or margarine. For each crepe use scant ¼ cup batter, tilting the pan back and forth so that the batter spreads evenly. Cook until batter is set and lightly browned on underside (it is not necessary to turn and cook the other side). Continue until all batter is used. Makes 20 crepes, 6½ inches in diameter.

Seafood Sauce:

⅓ cup butter or margarine
⅓ cup flour
3 cups scalded milk or light cream
¾ teaspoon salt
Few grains pepper
3 egg yolks
⅓ cup sweet sherry
1½ pounds cooked flaked crab meat, lobster, or shrimp *or* a combination totaling 1½ pounds

Melt butter; blend in flour; stir over low heat until foaming. Add scalded milk slowly; stir vigorously (preferably with a wire whisk) until thickened and smooth. Add salt and pepper; simmer 5 minutes. Remove from heat. Add 1 egg yolk at a time, beating well after each addition. Add sherry. Cook and stir over low heat for about 2 minutes (do not boil). Add seafood; heat to serving temperature.

To Serve:

Spoon a strip of seafood sauce across unbrowned center of each crepe; fold edges over. If any sauce is left it may be spooned over the top of each serving. Makes 10 servings.

CHAPTER 7

Casseroles and One-Dish Meals

SOME OF the best casseroles ever made cannot be written up as recipes. They are really "flights of fancy" composed of the cook's imagination and ingenuity plus whatever leftovers happen to be in the refrigerator or freezer.

However, many good casseroles are planned in advance, and we have gathered together a collection of recipes for interesting and practical dishes that will be an invaluable help to any cook, especially those who must plan and prepare three meals a day. Many of these dishes can be prepared ahead of time and refrigerated until the dinner hour nears. All of them are fuel savers. And all of them are usually favorites with the family because of the delicious blend of flavors in one dish.

CHICKEN WILD RICE CASSEROLE

2 whole broiler-fryer chickens, about 3
    pounds each
1 cup water
1 cup dry sherry
1½ teaspoons salt
½ teaspoon curry powder
1 medium onion, sliced
½ cup sliced celery
1 pound fresh mushrooms
¼ cup butter or margarine
2 packages (6 ounces each) long-grain and
    wild rice with seasonings
1 cup dairy sour cream
1 can (10¾ ounces) cream of mushroom soup

Place chickens in deep kettle. Add water, sherry, salt, curry powder, onion, and celery. Bring to boil; cover tightly. Reduce heat; simmer 1 hour. Remove from heat; strain broth. Refrigerate chicken and broth at once. When chicken is cool, remove meat from bones; discard skin. Cut into bite-size pieces. Wash mushrooms, pat dry; sauté in butter or margarine until golden brown; reserve enough to circle top of casserole. Measure chicken broth; use as part of liquid for cooking rice, following package directions for firm rice. Combine chicken, rice, and mushrooms not reserved for top in 3½- or 4-quart casserole. Blend sour cream and undiluted mushroom soup. Toss together with chicken mixture. Arrange reserved mushrooms in circle on top of casserole. Cover; refrigerate. To serve, bake at 350° for 1 hour. Makes 8 to 10 servings.

CREOLE EGG-AND-NOODLE CASSEROLE

¼ cup butter or margarine
½ cup finely chopped onion
⅓ cup diced green pepper
¼ cup flour
1 cup milk
1 can (1 pound) tomatoes
¼ teaspoon oregano
2 teaspoons sugar
Salt and pepper to taste
1 package (8 ounces) medium egg noodles, cooked
8 hard-cooked eggs, coarsely chopped
2 tablespoons chopped parsley

Melt butter or margarine; add onion and green pepper; cook over low heat until tender. Blend in flour; add milk slowly, while stirring. Cook over low heat, stirring constantly, until thickened. Add undrained tomatoes, oregano, and sugar. Season to taste with salt and pepper. Arrange alternate layers of noodles, eggs, and tomato mixture in greased 2-quart casserole. Sprinkle with chopped parsley. Bake at 350° for 35 minutes. Makes 4 to 5 servings.

TAMALE CASSEROLE

¾ cup yellow corn meal
1 teaspoon salt
1 cup cold water
2 cups boiling water
½ pound pork sausage meat
1 cup chopped onion
1 pound ground beef
2 teaspoons seasoned salt
4 teaspoons chili powder
2 packages spaghetti sauce mix
3½ cups canned tomatoes
1 can (1 pound) whole kernel corn (2 cups)
1 cup pitted ripe olives
1 cup grated American cheese

Combine corn meal, salt, and cold water. Add slowly to boiling water. Cook slowly to a mush. (Keep mush warm while preparing meat filling.) Fry sausage meat in large skillet until crumbly. Add onion, ground beef, seasoned salt, chili powder, and spaghetti sauce mix. Blend well;

cook about 10 minutes or until ground beef is crumbly. Stir frequently. Blend in tomatoes and corn. Simmer 20 minutes. Spread meat mixture in baking dish (about 10 x 15 inches) which has been rubbed with garlic spread. Press olives into this layer. Top with corn meal mush; sprinkle with grated cheese. Bake at 350° for 45 minutes. Makes 8 servings.

ALL-WEATHER CASSEROLE

6 to 8 strips bacon, cut in 1-inch pieces
Vegetable oil
4 cups cubed smoked pork butt (1-inch cubes)
½ cup sliced fresh mushrooms
½ cup chopped onion
⅓ cup flour
½ teaspoon garlic powder
¼ teaspoon black pepper
½ cup dry white wine
1½ cups vegetable juice
2 cans or jars (1 pound 2 ounces each) brick-oven baked beans

Fry bacon until crisp in large skillet. Remove bacon; measure drippings. If necessary, add enough vegetable oil to measure ¼ cup; return to skillet. Sauté pork, mushrooms, and onion until lightly browned. Remove pork mixture to 2-quart shallow casserole; add bacon; mix lightly. Blend flour, garlic powder, and pepper into drippings in skillet. Slowly stir in wine and vegetable juice; blend well; cook and stir over medium heat until sauce thickens. Stir sauce and beans into casserole, mixing lightly. Cover; bake at 325° for about 45 minutes. Makes 6 to 8 servings.

CHILI-BEAN-RICE CASSEROLE

1 pound dried pinto or red kidney beans
1 cup chopped green pepper
1 cup sliced onion
6 tablespoons butter, margarine, or bacon drippings
¼ cup chopped parsley
½ teaspoon sugar
2 cans (1 pound 13 ounces each) tomatoes
2 teaspoons Worcestershire sauce
4 cups cooked rice
1 teaspoon chili powder (or more to taste)
2 teaspoons salt
¼ teaspoon freshly ground pepper

Wash beans; soak overnight in enough water to cover. Simmer slowly until skins burst. Cook green pepper and onion in butter or drippings until tender. Add cooked beans and remaining ingredients; mix lightly. Turn into 4-quart baking dish. Bake at 350° for 30 minutes. Makes 12 to 15 servings.

NOTE: This recipe may be halved if desired.

DEVILED EGG AND NOODLE CASSEROLE

1 package (8 ounces) medium egg noodles
Salt and pepper
1 cup grated American cheese, divided
2 packages (10 ounces each) frozen asparagus, cooked
6 hard-cooked eggs, deviled
1 tablespoon curry powder
1 can (10¾ ounces) condensed cream of celery soup, undiluted
½ cup milk

Cook noodles in boiling salted water until tender; drain. Season with salt and pepper to taste. Stir ¾ cup grated cheese into noodles. Place noodle mixture in buttered 1½-quart casserole, spreading noodles to cover bottom and sides. Arrange asparagus in center. Place eggs on top. Combine curry powder with a little of the soup; add remaining soup and milk; pour over ingredients in casserole. Sprinkle center with remaining cheese. Bake at 350° for 25 to 30 minutes. Makes 4 servings.

COUNTRY KITCHEN CASSEROLE

1 pound dried lima beans
2 medium onions, sliced
1 can (6 ounces) broiled sliced mushrooms
4 slices bacon, cooked and crumbled
Salt and pepper
½ cup chili sauce or catchup
1 tablespoon Worcestershire sauce
1 teaspoon sugar
½ cup dry red wine
2 tablespoons cornstarch
2 tablespoons cold water
1 cup soft bread crumbs
Garnish: cooked bacon strips (optional)

Soak beans overnight in cold water to cover; drain. Cover with boiling water. Add onions; cook slowly until beans are tender, according to package directions. Drain mushrooms; save

broth. Add mushrooms and crumbled bacon to beans (reserve drippings); season with salt and pepper; mix well. Combine mushroom broth, chili sauce, Worcestershire sauce, sugar, and wine. Add enough water to make 2 cups. Mix cornstarch and cold water; add to wine mixture. Cook and stir over low heat until thickened and clear; add to bean mixture; mix well. Turn into 2-quart casserole. Combine crumbs and reserved bacon drippings; sprinkle on top. Bake at 400° for about 30 minutes. Garnish with a "wheel" of cooked halved bacon strips if desired. Makes 8 servings.

FRANKFURTER CASSEROLE

1 pound frankfurters
2 tablespoons butter or margarine
1 cup sliced onion
1 package (9 ounces) frozen Italian green beans
1 can (10¾ ounces) condensed cream of mushroom soup
1 cup milk
½ teaspoon salt
¼ teaspoon marjoram
1 package (9½ ounces) refrigerated biscuits
½ cup shredded sharp Cheddar cheese

Cut frankfurters in half lengthwise, then crosswise; set aside. Melt butter in heavy skillet (be sure handle is ovenproof). Add onion; cook slowly until soft. Separate green beans (do not defrost); add to onion. Stir in soup, milk, salt, and marjoram; mix well. Set over low heat until mixture begins to simmer. Fold in frankfurters; heat until bubbling. Remove biscuits from package; separate; cut each into fourths. Arrange in a border around skillet. Bake at 375° until biscuits are browned. (See package directions.) Remove from oven; sprinkle cheese over biscuits. Serve as soon as cheese has melted. Makes 4 servings.

POLLY BERGEN'S CHILI

3 garlic cloves, minced
2 tablespoons vegetable oil
4 pounds round steak, ground
6 large onions, sliced
4 large green peppers, seeded and sliced
3 cans (1 pound each) tomatoes with juice
4 cans (1 pound each) red kidney beans, drained
2 cans (6 ounces each) tomato paste

¼ cup chili powder
1 teaspoon white vinegar
3 dashes cayenne
3 whole cloves
1 bay leaf
Salt and pepper to taste
Hot cooked rice

Cook garlic in oil until golden. Add crumbled ground round and cook 10 minutes, being careful to brown evenly. Pour off some of the oil and drippings into another skillet; add sliced onions and green peppers; cook until tender. Add to cooked ground round with tomatoes, kidney beans, tomato paste, chili powder, vinegar, cayenne, cloves, bay leaf, salt and pepper. Cover; cook over low heat 1 hour, stirring several times. If too dry, add additional tomatoes. If too much liquid, uncover and simmer longer. Serve with rice. Makes 12 servings.

CASSEROLE DINNER

1 cup uncooked regular rice
¼ cup minced onion
¼ cup minced green pepper
½ cup shredded blanched almonds
1 can (4 ounces) mushroom stems and pieces (including broth)
4 instant chicken bouillon cubes
2 cups water
2 tablespoons butter or margarine
Salt and pepper to taste
1 cup grated Cheddar cheese

Combine all ingredients except cheese in a saucepan. Stir well; bring to boil. Pour into greased 1½-quart casserole; cover. Bake at 375° for 30 minutes. Uncover; gently stir in cheese with fork. Cover; continue baking 10 minutes. Makes 4 to 5 servings.

SAUERKRAUT SUPPER CASSEROLE

3 tart apples
⅓ cup brown sugar, divided
3 cups mashed yams
3 cups sauerkraut
Bacon strips

Pare and core apples; slice thin. Arrange a layer of apple slices in 1½-quart casserole; sprinkle with some of the brown sugar. Next add a layer of yams and one of sauerkraut. Repeat until casserole is filled, ending with kraut. Arrange bacon

strips in a lattice pattern on top. Bake at 375° for 40 minutes. Makes 4 to 6 servings.

BEEF-AND-VEGETABLE CASSEROLE

6 slices bacon
1 pound lean beef chuck, about ½ inch thick
½ cup flour
1 teaspoon salt
1 cup dry red wine
2 tablespoons parsley
½ garlic clove
½ teaspoon thyme
1 can (10½ ounces) condensed beef broth
6 medium potatoes, peeled and halved
12 small white onions, peeled
3 carrots, sliced lengthwise
1 can (4 ounces) mushroom stems and pieces, finely chopped

Cook bacon until crisp; drain on paper towels; reserve drippings. Cut beef into cubes. Shake a few cubes at a time in paper bag containing flour and salt. Brown cubes on all sides in bacon drippings; remove to 2-quart casserole. Pour wine into electric blender; add parsley, garlic, thyme, and beef broth; blend until solid ingredients are puréed. Pour over meat in casserole. Cover casserole; bake at 350° for 1 hour. Stir potatoes, onions, and carrots into casserole. Replace cover. Bake 1 hour longer or until vegetables are done. Stir in mushrooms. Crumble bacon; scatter on top with additional parsley. Makes 4 to 5 servings.

DEVILED CORN CASSEROLE

2 cans (1 pound each) whole kernel corn
1 medium green pepper, diced
Salt
1 cup grated American cheese
3 slices white bread
1 large can (4½ ounces) deviled ham
2 medium tomatoes, sliced
1 medium onion, sliced
Pepper, butter

Drain corn; add green pepper to liquid; boil rapidly until reduced to ¾ cup. Add corn and ¼ teaspoon salt; heat to serving temperature. Remove from heat; add cheese; stir until melted. Toast bread; spread with deviled ham; cut into cubes. Put half the cubes in a 2½-quart greased casserole; spoon over half the corn mixture; repeat. Alternate tomato and onion slices in center of casserole; sprinkle with salt and pepper; dot with butter. Broil 6 to 8 minutes. Makes 6 servings.

SAVORY NOODLE CASSEROLE

1 package (8 ounces) medium egg noodles
¼ cup butter or margarine
½ cup finely chopped onion
⅓ cup diced green pepper
¼ cup flour
1 cup milk
1 can (1 pound) tomatoes
2 cups grated sharp cheese
¼ teaspoon oregano
2 teaspoons sugar
Salt and pepper
2 tablespoons chopped parsley
Deviled Eggs*

Cook noodles as directed on package; drain. Melt butter; add onion and green pepper; cook over low heat until tender but not brown. Blend in flour. Add milk; stir over low heat until thickened. Add undrained tomatoes, cheese, oregano, and sugar. Stir until cheese is melted. Season to taste with salt and pepper. Arrange alternate layers of noodles and tomato mixture in greased 1½-quart casserole. Bake at 350° for 35 minutes. Remove from oven; sprinkle with parsley; top with Deviled Eggs; return to oven for 5 minutes. Makes 4 servings.

*DEVILED EGGS

6 hard-cooked eggs
Deviled ham
Mayonnaise

Peel and chill eggs. Halve lengthwise; remove yolks carefully. Mash yolks; add deviled ham and mayonnaise to taste. Mound yolk mixture in whites. Place on top of casserole. Makes 12.

FISH-AND-VEGETABLE CASSEROLE

2 pounds fish fillets, fresh or frozen (any white
    fish such as cod, haddock, whiting, etc.)
1 small onion, sliced
1 bay leaf
2 cups cooked or canned green beans, drained
1 cup sliced cooked carrots, drained
¼ cup butter or margarine
¼ cup flour

1 teaspoon salt
Few grains pepper
1 can (10¾ ounces) condensed tomato soup
⅔ cup evaporated milk
½ teaspoon rosemary
3 cups hot well-seasoned mashed potatoes
Melted butter or margarine

Cover fillets (defrosted if frozen) with cold water; add onion and bay leaf. Bring to boil; lower heat; simmer about 10 minutes or until fish flakes easily with fork. Cool in pan; drain, saving stock; break into fairly large pieces; place in 2½-quart casserole with green beans and carrots. Meanwhile, melt butter or margarine in top of double boiler; blend in flour, salt, and pepper. Combine soup, evaporated milk, and 1 cup of the fish stock; add all at once; stir over low heat until smooth and thickened. Add rosemary. Cover; set over hot water; cook 10 minutes; pour into casserole. Top with ring of mashed potatoes; brush with melted butter or margarine. Bake at 425° for about 15 minutes or until golden brown. Makes 6 servings.

MARINE MEDLEY CASSEROLE

3 to 4 slices bread
2 tablespoons butter or margarine, melted
1 can (1 pound) green beans
1 can (10¾ ounces) condensed cream of
    mushroom soup
1 can (6½ or 7 ounces) tuna, flaked

Cut bread slices with small fish cookie cutter or cut into cubes; toss in melted butter. Drain beans; add liquid to pan in which butter was melted; cook until liquid is reduced to ¼ cup. Add soup, beans, and undrained tuna; heat. Turn into shallow baking dish. Arrange "fish" or cubes on top. Bake at 400° for 15 minutes. Makes 4 servings.

BAKED TUNA-CHEESE FONDUE

12 slices buttered bread, divided
2 cans (6½ or 7 ounces each) tuna
Mayonnaise
12 slices (¾ pound) packaged square-cut Old
    English cheese, divided
Salt and pepper
6 eggs, beaten
5 cups milk
1 teaspoon Worcestershire sauce
Dash hot-pepper sauce

Place 6 slices bread buttered side up in greased baking dish, 13 x 9 x 2 inches. Drain and flake tuna; mix to spreading consistency with mayonnaise. Spread half this mixture on bread slices. Top with 6 slices cheese. Sprinkle with salt and pepper. Repeat, using remaining bread, tuna mixture, cheese, and seasonings. Combine remaining 4 ingredients. Pour slowly into baking dish. Let stand ½ hour. Bake at 350° for about 40 minutes or until top is golden brown, puffed, and shiny. Serve at once. Makes 6 generous servings.

PANTRY SHELF CASSEROLE

1 can (12 ounces) boned chicken
1 can (1 pound) green peas, drained
1 can (1 pound) baby carrots, drained
1 can (1 pound) small white onions, drained
2 cans (10½ ounces each) chicken gravy
Instant mashed potatoes to make 4 servings
Melted butter or margarine

Cut chicken in bite-size pieces. Arrange half on bottom of shallow baking dish. Add half the vegetables and pour 1 can gravy over all. Repeat. Prepare instant mashed potatoes as directed on package; spoon around rim of baking dish. Brush potatoes with melted butter. Bake at 400° for about 15 minutes or until potatoes are gold-tipped and mixture heated through. Makes 6 servings.

RAVIOLI MEAT LOAF CASSEROLE

1½ pounds ground beef
1 egg
½ cup finely chopped onion
1½ teaspoons salt
½ cup soft bread crumbs
6 tablespoons milk
¼ cup minced parsley
1 tablespoon Worcestershire sauce
Few drops hot-pepper sauce
2 cans (15 ounces each) beef ravioli

Combine all ingredients except ravioli; mix thoroughly. Arrange contents of 1 can ravioli on bottom of greased 1½-quart casserole. Top with meat mixture, pressing down firmly. Arrange contents of second can of ravioli on top. Cover casserole (use heavy foil if the casserole has no cover). Bake at 350° for 1 hour 15 minutes. Remove cover during last 15 minutes. Makes 6 servings.

CASSOULET AMÉRICAINE

2 cups cubed leftover meat*
Salt and pepper
3 tablespoons vegetable oil
1 medium onion, chopped
1 to 1½ cups boiling water
1 garlic clove
1 herb bouquet
2 cans (1 pound each) pork and beans in tomato sauce
½ pound small sausage links or cakes, browned
½ cup chili sauce, strained
3 tablespoons buttered soft bread crumbs

Cut meat into 1½-inch cubes. Season with salt and pepper; sauté in very hot oil until browned on all sides. Drain off excess oil; add chopped onion; cook until onion is golden brown. Cover meat and onion with boiling water; add garlic and herb bouquet; simmer 15 minutes. Remove herbs and garlic. Rub inside of casserole with garlic. Place layer of beans in casserole; then a layer of browned sausage and pieces of meat. Cover with layer of baked beans. Add strained chili sauce to liquid in which meat was cooked; pour over beans and meat. Top with buttered crumbs. Bake at 350° for 45 minutes. Makes 6 servings.

PATIO CASSOULET

1 medium onion, finely diced
½ pound sweet Italian link sausage, cut into chunks
2 tablespoons vegetable oil
1 frying chicken (3½ to 4 pounds), cut up
½ teaspoon salt
1 can (1 pound) Italian plum tomatoes
1 green pepper, cut into rings
1 can (1 pound 4 ounces) white kidney beans (cannellini)
¼ teaspoon hot-pepper sauce
1 teaspoon Worcestershire sauce

Cook onion and sausage in oil in large skillet until sausage is brown; push to one side. Brown chicken pieces in same skillet; remove. Add salt, tomatoes, and green pepper to skillet; mix with onion and sausage; cook 5 minutes. Turn into 3-quart casserole. Add beans, hot-pepper sauce, and Worcestershire sauce; stir to mix well. Add

*Instead of leftover meat, 1 can (12 ounces) cubed luncheon meat may be used.

chicken pieces. Cover; bake at 350° for 45 to 60 minutes or until chicken is done. Makes 4 servings.

SPIRAL LOAF

¼ cup sugar
1 tablespoon salt
⅓ cup shortening
1 cup milk
1 package active dry yeast
¼ cup warm water (105° to 115°)
4 cups sifted all-purpose flour
    (approximately), divided
⅔ cup enriched corn meal
2 eggs, beaten
Melted butter or margarine
3 hard-cooked eggs, finely chopped
1½ cups finely chopped cooked chicken
1 can (6 ounces) mushroom stems and pieces,
    drained and chopped fine
Seasoned salt

Mix sugar, salt, and shortening. Scald milk; pour over sugar mixture; stir until shortening melts; cool to lukewarm. Dissolve yeast in warm water; stir into milk mixture. Stir in 2 cups of the flour and the corn meal. Add eggs one at a time, beating well after each addition. Stir in enough more flour to make a soft dough. Knead on lightly floured board until satiny, about 10 minutes. Round dough into a ball; place in greased bowl; brush with melted butter. Cover; let rise in warm place until double in bulk, about 1 hour. Punch down; let rest 10 minutes. Roll out to form a rectangle about 12 inches wide and 20 inches long. Brush with melted butter or margarine. Spoon half the chopped eggs across the width of the dough in a strip about 3 inches wide. Make another strip with half the chicken, and another with half the mushrooms. Repeat with 3 more strips in same order. Sprinkle generously with seasoned salt. Roll up as for jelly roll, starting with narrow end. Seal edges; place seam side down on greased baking sheet. Cut 3 gashes in center of roll, about 1 inch apart. Cover; let rise until double in bulk, about 1 hour. Bake at 350° for 35 to 40 minutes. Brush immediately with melted butter. To serve, slice crosswise in 1-inch slices. Serve with hot tomato sauce or canned chicken gravy. Makes 8 servings.

MYSTERY SUPPER RING

4 tablespoons butter or margarine
4 tablespoons flour
2 cups milk
3 instant chicken bouillon cubes
2 eggs, well beaten
1 cup mayonnaise
1 to 2 cups diced turkey
½ cup slivered blanched almonds
1 can Chinese fried noodles
Mushroom Sauce*

Melt butter; blend in flour; add milk and bouillon cubes; stir over low heat until smooth and thickened. Cool slightly. Add to eggs. Stir in mayonnaise. Fold in turkey, almonds, and noodles. Bake in well-greased 8-cup ring mold at 350° for 50 to 60 minutes or until set. Let stand 5 minutes. Unmold. Fill center with Mushroom Sauce. Makes 6 servings.

*MUSHROOM SAUCE

½ pound fresh mushrooms
3 tablespoons butter or margarine
3 tablespoons flour
½ teaspoon salt
1 can (10¾ ounces) condensed cream of
    celery soup
⅓ cup cream

Slice mushrooms; cook in butter or margarine until golden brown. Blend in flour and salt. Combine soup and cream; add to mushrooms; stir smooth over low heat. Makes 6 servings.

SAVORY MACARONI AND CHEESE

8 ounces elbow macaroni
2 cups Tomato-Cheese Sauce*
2 strips bacon, cooked
½ cup ready-to-serve cereal flakes
1 tablespoon bacon fat

Cook macaroni as directed on package; drain; pour into shallow baking dish; add sauce. Crumble crisp bacon; combine with cereal flakes and bacon fat; sprinkle on top. Bake at 375° for about 20 minutes. Makes 4 servings.

*TOMATO-CHEESE SAUCE

Make 2 cups medium white sauce using 1 cup tomato juice and 1 cup evaporated milk as the liquid. Add 1½ cups grated sharp Cheddar cheese. Stir over low heat until cheese melts. Makes 4 servings.

MONEY BAGS

Filling:

1½ tablespoons butter or margarine
¼ cup chopped onion
¼ cup chopped celery
¼ cup chopped canned mushrooms
2 tablespoons chopped olives
½ teaspoon salt
Dash pepper
1 to 2 cups diced cooked meat or poultry

Melt butter in frying pan; add onion and celery. Cook until barely tender; add mushrooms, olives, salt, pepper, and meat or poultry. Cook over very low heat until thoroughly heated, stirring occasionally.

Pastry:

¼ cup enriched corn meal
¾ cup sifted all-purpose flour
¼ teaspoon salt
¼ teaspoon marjoram
¼ cup shortening
3 to 4 tablespoons water
Leftover gravy or canned beef gravy

Mix and sift corn meal, flour, salt, and marjoram. Cut in shortening until mixture resembles coarse crumbs. Add water a little at a time, mixing with a fork, until pastry can be formed into a ball. Roll out on lightly floured board or canvas to form a rectangle 12 x 14 inches. Cut into 4 pieces 6 x 7 inches. In center of each piece, place about ½ cup filling. Pinch 4 corners together at top to resemble drawstring "money bag." Bake at 400° for 45 minutes. Serve with gravy. Makes 4 servings.

CHILI CORN BAKE

2 cans (1 pound each) cream-style yellow corn
Milk or light cream
2 tablespoons butter or margarine
2 tablespoons flour
½ teaspoon salt
2 eggs, beaten
3 medium green peppers
1 can chili con carne with beans
2 medium tomatoes

Drain liquid from corn; measure; add enough milk or cream to make 1 cup. Melt butter or mar-garine; blend in flour and salt; add liquid; cook, stirring constantly, until thickened. Remove from heat; add drained corn. Stir in eggs. Turn into greased shallow baking dish. Cut peppers in half crosswise; scoop out seeds, being careful not to cut through the pepper. Push down into corn, open end up. Fill with chili. Cut tomatoes in sixths. Place around and on top of peppers. Bake at 350° for 50 to 60 minutes or until mixture is firm. Makes 6 servings.

NEW ORLEANS JAMBALAYA

1 pound smoked sausage or ham, cut in ½-inch cubes
½ cup vegetable oil
2 medium onions, chopped
1 bunch scallions (bulbs plus 3 inches green tops), chopped
1 large green pepper, chopped
½ cup celery, sliced or diced
¼ teaspoon leaf thyme
2 bay leaves
2 to 6 garlic cloves, minced (according to taste)
½ teaspoon salt
1 pinch cayenne
2 pounds raw shrimp,* peeled and deveined
2 cans (1 pound each) tomatoes
1 can (6 ounces) tomato paste
½ lemon, quartered
3 cups cooked long-grain rice

Cook sausage or ham in hot oil until light brown. Add onions, scallions, green pepper, celery, thyme, bay leaves, garlic, salt, and cayenne. Cook 3 minutes longer. Add shrimp, tomatoes with liquid, tomato paste, and lemon quarters. Simmer slowly, uncovered, tossing often with fork until shrimp are pink. Remove bay leaves and lemon. Stir in rice. Makes 8 servings.

SOUTHERN VEGETABLE SHORTCAKE

½ cup grated American Cheddar cheese
3 cups well-seasoned medium white sauce
1 cup cooked lima beans
1 cup cooked sliced carrots
½ cup cooked sliced or diced celery
6 squares hot corn bread (made with corn muffin mix)

*Recipe may be made with 2 pounds cooked diced chicken or chicken livers instead of shrimp.

Butter
Garnish: paprika; parsley

Add cheese to white sauce; stir over hot water until cheese melts. Add vegetables; heat thoroughly. Split squares of corn bread; butter lightly. Place hot vegetable mixture between layers and on top. Sprinkle with paprika; garnish with parsley. Makes 6 generous servings.

STUFFED CABBAGE ROLLS

1 head cabbage
1 pound lean beef, ground
2 green peppers, chopped fine
2 medium onions, chopped fine
2 tablespoons vegetable oil
1 cup soft bread crumbs
⅓ cup chili sauce
2 teaspoons Worcestershire sauce
½ teaspoon salt
½ teaspoon marjoram
Few grains pepper
1 can (8 ounces) tomato sauce
2 tablespoons butter or margarine
½ cup dairy sour cream

Core cabbage; cook 7 minutes in boiling salted water to cover. Drain; cool; remove 12 large outer leaves.* Meanwhile, cook ground beef, green peppers, and onions in oil until meat is browned. Add bread crumbs, chili sauce, Worcestershire sauce, and seasonings; mix well. Place equal amount of meat mixture on each cabbage leaf; roll up; secure with wooden picks; place in large skillet; pour in tomato sauce; dot with butter or margarine; cover; simmer about 1 hour. Remove cabbage rolls to platter. Stir sour cream into tomato sauce in skillet. Pour some of this mixture over cabbage rolls; serve remainder separately. Makes 6 servings.

SWEET-AND-SOUR CABBAGE ROLLS

1 medium head cabbage
1 tablespoon flour
1 cup raisins, divided
1 pound ground beef
1½ cups cooked rice
2 tablespoons grated onion
1 teaspoon salt
¼ teaspoon pepper

*Cook remaining cabbage until tender; serve another day, chopped and creamed or in a cheese sauce.

1 medium onion, sliced
1 can (1 pound) Italian-style tomatoes with juice
1 bay leaf
2 tablespoons vegetable oil
½ cup water
2 tablespoons lemon juice
2 tablespoons brown sugar
¼ cup crushed gingersnaps

Plunge cabbage into large kettle of boiling water; cook 10 minutes. Drain. Carefully separate 12 outer leaves, trimming away cores. Shred remaining cabbage. Use wide foil to line a large kettle or deep roasting pan, leaving enough for 3-inch overlap. Dust lightly with flour. Combine half the raisins with beef, rice, grated onion, salt, and pepper. Roll up about ¼ cup mixture in each cabbage leaf, tucking in ends to secure. Layer shredded cabbage and sliced onion on foil; place cabbage rolls on top. Sprinkle with remaining raisins. Add tomatoes and bay leaf. Combine remaining ingredients and pour over all.

To Cook on Top of Range: Double-fold foil to make a secure package. Add boiling water to reach halfway up package. Cover; boil slowly 2 hours. Add more water as needed to maintain level.

To Bake: Double-fold foil to make a secure package. Bake at 400° for about 1½ hours. Let package stand for a few minutes before opening. Makes 4 to 6 servings.

TAMALE PIE

3 tablespoons vegetable oil
1 medium green pepper, diced
1 large onion, chopped
2 pounds lean beef, ground
2 teaspoons salt
¼ teaspoon pepper
1 can (1 pound) tomatoes with juice
1 tablespoon chili powder
1 package (12 ounces) corn muffin mix
1 cup evaporated milk
¾ cup grated sharp Cheddar cheese

Heat oil in a 3-quart flameproof casserole on top of range. Add green pepper and onion; cook until onion is tender but not brown. Sprinkle beef with salt and pepper; brown in casserole, breaking up meat with fork. Add tomatoes and chili powder. Let simmer while preparing topping.

Follow package directions for preparing corn muffin mix, omitting egg and substituting 1 cup evaporated milk for liquid called for in directions. Remove casserole from heat; pour corn muffin mixture over top. Sprinkle with grated cheese. Bake at 400° for 20 minutes. Makes 8 servings.

PARTY LUNCHEON PIE

2 cups mashed sweet potatoes
2 eggs
5 tablespoons butter or margarine, divided
2 tablespoons brown sugar
1 tablespoon grated orange peel
1½ teaspoons salt
½ teaspoon powdered ginger
½ cup packaged fine dry bread crumbs
2 tablespoons minced onion
3 tablespoons flour
1 can (3 ounces) chopped broiled mushrooms
1 chicken bouillon cube
½ teaspoon brown gravy seasoning sauce
2 cups diced cooked meat or chicken

Put cooked or canned sweet potatoes through a food mill or sieve; measure 2 cups. Add eggs; whip with large kitchen fork until thoroughly blended. Add 2 tablespoons butter or margarine, melted, brown sugar, orange peel, salt, ginger, and crumbs; mix well. Melt remaining butter or margarine; add onion; cook over low heat about 3 minutes. Blend in flour. Drain mushrooms; measure liquid; add enough water to make 1 cup; stir into flour mixture with bouillon cube and seasoning sauce. Cook, stirring constantly, until sauce thickens and boils. Add mushrooms and diced meat or chicken. Line bottom and sides of greased shallow baking dish with potato mixture. Fill center with meat mixture. Bake at 350° until potato is lightly browned (about 45 minutes). Makes 4 servings.

"ALL IN ONE" DINNER

¾ pound ground veal
½ pound ground pork
¾ cup rolled oats, quick or old-fashioned, uncooked
¾ teaspoon salt
½ teaspoon oregano
⅛ teaspoon pepper
½ cup milk
1 egg

1 package (10 ounces) frozen mixed vegetables, cooked
Hot mashed potatoes

Combine veal and pork with next 6 ingredients. Line bottom and sides of 10-inch ungreased pie plate with meat mixture. Bake at 350° for 40 minutes. While meat is baking, cook mixed vegetables according to package directions; season to taste with salt, pepper, and butter or margarine. Fill center of meat "crust" with drained vegetables and return to oven for 5 minutes. Garnish with mashed potato ring, made quickly with instant mashed potatoes. Makes 4 servings.

HAM-YAM PIE

¼ cup chopped green pepper
4 tablespoons butter or margarine, divided
1 can (10¾ ounces) condensed mushroom soup
Milk
½ teaspoon onion salt
¼ teaspoon pepper, divided
1 tablespoon Dijon-style mustard
3 tablespoons flour
¼ cup cold water
2 to 3 cups diced cooked ham
2 cups mashed yams
½ teaspoon salt

Sauté green pepper in 2 tablespoons butter or margarine for 2 to 3 minutes. Combine soup and ⅔ cup milk. Add onion salt, ⅛ teaspoon pepper, and mustard. Make thin paste of flour and water. Add to soup; heat until thickened, stirring constantly. Add green pepper and ham. Turn into greased 2-quart casserole. Mash yams. Add remaining butter or margarine, melted, salt, remaining pepper, and ¼ cup warm milk. Beat until fluffy. Spoon on ham mixture. Bake at 350° for 30 minutes or until heated through and lightly browned. Makes 6 to 8 servings.

MOLASSES-APPLE BEAN BAKE

2 cans (1 pound each) baked beans with tomato sauce
¼ cup molasses
1 tablespoon vinegar
1 tablespoon prepared mustard
1 can (20 ounces) pie-sliced apples

Turn beans into 1½-quart casserole. Combine molasses, vinegar, mustard; add. Stir in half the apple slices; arrange remaining slices on top. Cover. Bake at 375° for ½ hour. Makes 4 to 6 servings.

BAKED BEANS SUPREME

2 cups dried pea beans
6 cups cold water
1 medium onion, chopped
2 cups tomato pulp*
½ cup vegetable oil
2 small sweet pickles
½ cup stuffed olives
1 small stalk celery
½ cup grated sharp cheese

Rinse beans; drain; add cold water; bring to boil; boil 1 hour (add water if necessary); drain. Combine onion, tomato pulp, and oil; simmer until thick. Chop pickles, olives, and celery; add to beans; pour into small bean pot or casserole. Pour tomato mixture over bean mixture. Cover; bake at 350° about 1½ hours or until beans are fork-tender. Remove cover; sprinkle cheese over beans; return to oven; bake until cheese melts and browns. Makes 8 servings.

GOLDEN GATE BAKED BEANS

1 pound (2½ cups) dried navy or pea beans
¾ cup firmly packed brown sugar
2 teaspoons salt
1 teaspoon dry mustard
¼ teaspoon ground cloves
¼ cup finely chopped onion
3 dashes hot-pepper sauce
1½ cups quartered seedless green grapes
¼ pound salt pork

Put beans in Dutch oven; cover with cold water; soak overnight. Simmer 1 hour, adding more water if necessary. Combine sugar, salt, mustard, cloves, and onion; stir into beans. Add hot-pepper sauce and grapes; mix well. Transfer to 2½-quart bean pot or casserole. Slash rind of salt pork; bury to top of rind in beans. Liquid should reach surface of beans. If not enough, add boiling water. Cover; bake at 300° for 6 hours. If necessary, add more boiling water during baking. Remove cover for last hour to brown beans. Makes 8 to 10 servings.

*Or 2 cans (8 ounces each) tomato sauce.

COLA BAKED BEANS

¼ pound fat salt pork
1 medium onion
2 cans (18 ounces each) brick-oven baked beans
¼ cup molasses
1 teaspoon dry mustard
1 tablespoon vinegar
2 teaspoons Worcestershire sauce
¼ cup chili sauce
Cola beverage

Scrape rind off salt pork; score deeply with sharp knife. Place onion in deep casserole; add beans. Bury pork in beans so only rind shows. Combine molasses, mustard, vinegar, Worcestershire sauce, and chili sauce. Add enough cola-type beverage to make 1½ cups. Pour over beans. Bake at 300° for 1½ hours. Makes 8 servings.

QUICK BAKED BEANS

4 cans (18 ounces each) brick-oven baked beans
2 medium onions, sliced
⅓ cup light molasses
⅓ cup chili sauce
3 tablespoons vinegar
1 tablespoon Worcestershire sauce
1 teaspoon dry mustard
¼ teaspoon hot-pepper sauce

Alternate baked beans and sliced onion in heavy casserole or bean pot. Combine molasses and chili sauce; stir in remaining ingredients. Pour over beans. Bake at 350° for 1 hour. Makes 12 servings.

SPANISH BEAN POT

2 cans (1 pound each) red kidney beans
2 tablespoons bacon fat
¼ teaspoon thyme
2 whole cloves
¼ teaspoon cayenne
1 teaspoon salt
1 large garlic clove, minced
1 small bay leaf
2 teaspoons dry mustard
2 tablespoons vinegar
½ cup syrup from canned peaches or pears

1 onion, sliced thin
¼ cup strong coffee
2 teaspoons brandy flavoring

Combine all ingredients in bean pot or casserole; mix well. Bake, uncovered, at 350° about 2 hours or until liquid is reduced to level of beans. Makes 6 servings.

SAVORY BEAN BAKE

½ cup molasses
3 tablespoons vinegar
3 tablespoons prepared mustard
½ teaspoon hot-pepper sauce
3 cans (18 ounces each) brick-oven baked
  beans
1 can (1 pound) kidney beans
1 medium onion, chopped

Combine molasses, vinegar, mustard, and hot-pepper sauce. Add to baked beans, kidney beans, and onion in 2½-quart casserole. (Reserve pork from baked beans and place on top, if desired.) Bake at 375° for 1 hour. Stir before serving. Makes 8 servings.

EMPIRE STATE BAKED BEANS

2 cups dried navy or pea beans
3 cups lukewarm water
4 cups cold water (about)
2 onions, sliced
¼ to ½ pound salt pork, sliced
⅓ cup sugar
¼ teaspoon pepper
1 teaspoon salt
1 teaspoon dry mustard
1 teaspoon paprika

Wash beans; place in large saucepan with luke-warm water; cover. Let stand 12 hours. Do not drain. Add enough cold water to cover the beans well. Slowly bring to a boil; reduce heat; simmer 2 hours. Add water as needed. Add onions and salt pork; cover; simmer until tender (about 2 hours). Transfer to greased shallow 1½-quart baking dish, covering pork with beans. (There should be enough liquid to cover.) Combine remaining ingredients; sprinkle over beans. Bake, uncovered, at 300° until beans are soft and a brown crust forms on top and along sides (3 to 3½ hours). As the beans dry out, moisten with hot water. Beans can be reheated successfully. Makes 6 to 8 servings.

CHAPTER 8
Eggs and Cheese

EGGS

EGGS ARE temperamental. They don't like high temperatures or prolonged low temperatures, and they show it by becoming tough and rubbery, with hard, discolored yolks. Give them gentle heat, for the correct time, and the whites will be tender and the yolks a clear yellow-to-gold.

To cook eggs in the shell, puncture the large ends with a pin and immerse them in water. Avoid overcrowding and be sure the water covers them by at least an inch. Over high heat, bring water to a full boil. Remove from heat *at once*; cover tightly. For hard-cooked eggs let stand 15 minutes; for medium soft-cooked eggs, 1 minute. Pour off hot water and run cold water over eggs to stop cooking.

To shell hard-cooked eggs, tap each one gently against a flat surface until entire surface of egg is cracked. Peel off shell under cold running water, starting at large end.

Fried eggs need a moderate temperature, a minimum of fat, and as short a cooking time as possible.

For poaching, eggs must be cold and the liquid into which they are dropped about 2 inches deep. Break each egg into a saucer and slip into simmering liquid. Cook 3 to 5 minutes. Remove with slotted spoon.

Don't overcook scrambled eggs or stir them constantly. Beat eggs slightly with 2 tablespoons milk or water for every 2 eggs. Melt 1 tablespoon butter or margarine in skillet over medium heat. Pour in egg mixture. As mixture starts to set, stir cooked portion slightly, so that uncooked portion flows to bottom. Cook 3 to 5 minutes. Eggs will be soft and creamy.

Remember that even a speck of fat—a bit of the yolk, for example—will prevent egg whites from beating to their fullest volume. Be sure they are at room temperature before beginning to beat. When overbeaten, egg whites become dry and liquid settles out.

The size of eggs does not affect grade or nutritive quality, just the price. Most standard recipes are tested with Large eggs. Other sizes are Jumbo, Extra Large, Medium, and Small.

The color of the shell has nothing to do with quality. Different breeds of hens lay different color eggs. Nevertheless, regional preferences for brown or white eggs do exist!

Eggs may be stored in their carton, large ends up, for about 5 weeks.

You will find recipes for omelets, shirred eggs, and baked eggs among those that follow.

Caution: When preparing dishes that require a final baking or broiling, be sure to *use an oven-proof pan.* Pans with wood or plastic handles are not suitable.

FLUFFY OMELET

3 tablespoons quick-cooking tapioca
1 teaspoon salt
⅛ teaspoon pepper
1 cup milk
Butter
6 egg yolks, beaten thick
6 egg whites, stiffly beaten
Green Pea Sauce*

Combine tapioca, salt, pepper, and milk in saucepan. Cook over medium heat until mixture comes to a full boil, stirring constantly. Add 1½ tablespoons butter; remove from heat; let cool slightly. Add egg yolks; mix well. Fold egg yolk mixture into egg whites. Turn into hot buttered 10-inch skillet or omelet pan; cook over low heat 3 minutes. Bake at 350° for 15 minutes. If skillet is used, run spatula quickly around edge; cut across at right angles to handle of pan, being careful not to cut all the way through. Pour about half of Green Pea Sauce on omelet; fold carefully from handle to opposite side. Serve on hot platter with remaining sauce. Makes 4 servings.

*GREEN PEA SAUCE

Cook 1 box (10 ounces) frozen green peas as directed. Drain. Prepare 1½ cups well-seasoned medium white sauce. Add peas; heat thoroughly. Makes 3 cups sauce.

FLUFFY OMELET WITH VEGETABLE-CHEESE SAUCE

3 tablespoons quick-cooking tapioca
1 teaspoon salt
⅛ teaspoon pepper
1 cup milk
1½ tablespoons butter or margarine
6 eggs, separated
Vegetable-Cheese Sauce*

Combine tapioca, salt, pepper, and milk in saucepan. Bring to full boil over medium heat, stirring constantly. Add butter or margarine. Remove from heat; let cool slightly. Beat egg whites stiff but not dry; beat yolks until thick and lemon-colored. Add beaten yolks to tapioca mixture; mix well; fold into beaten egg whites. Turn into hot well-greased 10-inch skillet or omelet pan. Cook over low heat 3 minutes. Bake at 350° for 15 minutes. Make Vegetable-Cheese Sauce while omelet is baking. Pour some of the sauce over half of the omelet; fold. Top with remaining sauce. Makes 6 servings.

*VEGETABLE-CHEESE SAUCE

1 can (8 ounces) tomato sauce
½ teaspoon salt
1 teaspoon sugar
Few grains pepper
Pinch oregano or marjoram
1 cup grated sharp Cheddar cheese
2 cups canned or quick-frozen (cooked) mixed vegetables

Combine tomato sauce, salt, sugar, pepper, oregano. Add cheese; stir over low heat until cheese melts; add vegetables; heat thoroughly. Makes about 4 cups.

ROLLED OMELET LOUISIANA

2 tablespoons butter or margarine
6 eggs
6 tablespoons water
½ teaspoon salt
Few grains pepper
Shrimp Sauce*

Melt butter or margarine in 10-inch frying pan. Beat eggs slightly; add water, salt, and pepper. Pour into frying pan. Cook over low heat until eggs set on bottom of pan. Lift edge and tilt pan so that some of the uncooked egg mixture flows under cooked eggs. Repeat until omelet is cooked through and brown on bottom. Spread with Shrimp Sauce; loosen with spatula; roll. Turn out onto hot platter. Makes 4 to 6 servings.

*SHRIMP SAUCE

4 tablespoons butter or margarine
3 tablespoons flour
1 cup milk or light cream
Salt and pepper to taste
1 can (5½ ounces) small shrimp, drained

Combine first 5 ingredients to make cream sauce. Stir in shrimp. Heat thoroughly. Makes about 1½ cups sauce.

HERB OMELET

¾ cup cheese wafer crumbs
¾ cup milk
6 eggs, separated
3 tablespoons melted butter or margarine, divided
¾ teaspoon salt
Dash of pepper
¼ teaspoon savory
¼ teaspoon marjoram
Tomato sauce

Soak crumbs in milk. Beat egg yolks light; combine with crumb mixture. Add 1½ tablespoons butter, seasonings, and herbs. Beat egg whites stiff; fold into yolk mixture. Spoon into skillet or omelet pan coated with remaining butter. Cook over low heat until golden brown on bottom. Place in 350° oven for 5 minutes to "set." Crease in middle; fold over. Serve at once with hot tomato sauce. Makes 4 servings.

MACARONI-AND-CHEESE OMELET

Creole Sauce*
1¼ cups elbow macaroni
4 eggs, separated
2 tablespoons minced green pepper
2 tablespoons minced pimiento
½ teaspoon salt
½ cup diced Cheddar cheese

Prepare Creole Sauce; set aside. Cook macaroni as directed on package; drain; rinse with hot water. Beat egg yolks until thick and lemon-colored. Add macaroni with remaining ingredients except egg whites and sauce. Beat egg whites stiff; fold in. Pour into moderately hot well-greased frying pan. Cook over very low heat about 20 minutes or until underside is deep golden brown. Set under low broiler heat until top is dry but not brown. Cut omelet partway through center; fold over. Turn out onto hot platter. Serve at once with hot Creole Sauce. Makes 4 servings.

*CREOLE SAUCE

1 can (3 ounces) broiled sliced mushrooms
2 tablespoons minced green pepper
2 tablespoons minced onion
2 tablespoons vegetable oil
1 can (1 pound) tomatoes with juice
1½ teaspoons salt
Few grains pepper

Cook mushrooms, green pepper, and onion in oil about 5 minutes. Add remaining ingredients. Simmer ½ hour or until sauce is rather thick. Makes about 1½ cups.

POET'S OMELET

2 eggs
Few grains salt
Few grains pepper
Dash garlic powder
1 tablespoon butter or margarine
2 tablespoons grated (or diced) Bonbel, Cheddar, Gruyère, or Parmesan cheese
Melted butter
Garnish (optional): paprika; parsley sprig or flakes

Combine first 4 ingredients in mixing bowl; stir briskly with fork. Using any no-stick-surface pan (preferably 10-inch skillet), melt butter over medium heat. When the butter stops bubbling or sizzling, pour egg mixture into the skillet, making sure to tilt the skillet so that egg covers bottom completely and evenly. Immediately begin to shake the pan in a circular motion. When eggs start to set, sprinkle cheese in a strip down the middle. Shake pan sideways or tilt forward and backward with a quick motion to fold half of omelet mixture over the other half. Slide omelet out of pan onto plate; brush with melted butter. If desired, garnish with lots of paprika and a sprig of parsley or parsley flakes. Serve omelet immediately. Serves one.

TWO-TONE SCRAMBLED EGGS

Drop eggs into buttered frying pan. Add 1 tablespoon milk for each egg. Season with salt and pepper. Set over low heat. When egg whites begin to cook, break yolks. Continue to cook slowly, stirring occasionally, until eggs are cooked through.

CHILI SCRAMBLED EGGS

¼ pound dried beef
2 tablespoons butter or margarine
1 teaspoon chili powder
¼ pound American Cheddar cheese, grated
1 cup drained canned tomatoes
4 eggs, slightly beaten
4 slices toast
Garnish (optional): avocado slices; stuffed
   olives

Shred dried beef; cook crisp in butter or margarine. Stir in chili powder, cheese, and tomatoes.
When mixture simmers, stir in eggs; stir until
eggs are cooked. Serve at once on toast, garnished with avocado slices and stuffed olives, if
desired. Makes 4 servings.

HAM AND EGGS IN SNAPPY ASPARAGUS
SAUCE

2 cups cubed baked ham
3 hard-cooked eggs, sliced
Snappy Asparagus Sauce*
Poppy Seed Squares†

Combine first 3 ingredients; heat over hot water.
Serve on hot Poppy Seed Squares. Makes 4 servings.

*SNAPPY ASPARAGUS SAUCE

Blend 2 tablespoons prepared mustard with 3
cups medium white sauce. Add 2 cups diced
cooked well-drained asparagus.

†POPPY SEED SQUARES

Trim crusts from small loaf unsliced bread. Cut
in half lengthwise almost through to bottom; cut
crosswise in fourths in same way. Brush outside
and all cut surfaces with melted butter or margarine; sprinkle with poppy seeds. Bake at 450°
for 15 minutes or until hot and golden brown.
Break into squares to serve. Makes 8 squares.

EGGS MARGUERITE

8 slices bread
Prepared mustard
8 slices cooked ham
½-pound package (8 square slices) American
   cheese
8 eggs, separated

Toast bread slices on one side. Spread untoasted
side with prepared mustard; top with 1 slice of
ham, then with 1 slice of cheese. Beat egg whites
stiff; mound on cheese, making a hollow in center. Slip 1 whole egg yolk into each hollow. Place
on greased cookie sheet. Bake at 350° until yolks
are set and whites lightly browned. Serve at
once. Makes 8 servings.

EGGS BENEDICT, NEW STYLE

4 English muffins
1 large can (4½ ounces) deviled ham
8 poached eggs
Mock Hollandaise Sauce (page 222)
Garnish: cut chives, fresh or freeze-dried

Split and toast English muffins; spread with
deviled ham. Top each muffin half with a
poached egg and Mock Hollandaise Sauce.
Sprinkle with cut chives. Makes 4 servings.

CREAMED EGGS AND SAUSAGES

4 tablespoons butter or margarine
4 tablespoons flour
½ teaspoon salt
Few grains pepper
1 teaspoon paprika
2 cups milk
6 hard-cooked eggs, quartered
2 cans (4 ounces each) Vienna sausages
4 to 6 waffles
Garnish: minced parsley

Melt butter or margarine; blend in flour, salt,
pepper, and paprika. Add milk; stir over low heat
until smooth and thickened. Cover; cook over
hot water 10 minutes. Add eggs and sausages.
Heat. Serve on waffles. Sprinkle with minced
parsley. Makes 4 to 6 servings.

CREAMED EGGS DIABLO

6 tablespoons butter or margarine
6 tablespoons flour
½ teaspoon salt
1 teaspoon chili powder
1 teaspoon Worcestershire sauce
1 tablespoon cut chives, fresh or freeze-dried
3 cups milk
9 hard-cooked eggs, quartered

Melt butter or margarine; blend in flour, salt,
chili powder, and Worcestershire sauce. Add

chives. Add cold milk all at once. Cook over low heat, stirring constantly, until smooth and thickened. Add eggs. Keep hot over hot water. Serve on toast, toasted English muffins, or baked potatoes. Makes 6 servings.

EGGS CONTINENTAL

½ cup fine soft bread crumbs
4 hard-cooked eggs, sliced
3 slices bacon, diced
1 cup (½ pint) dairy sour cream
2 tablespoons minced parsley or chives
¼ teaspoon salt
Few grains pepper
Paprika
½ cup (⅛ pound) grated sharp Cheddar
   cheese

Line 4 individual ramekins with bread crumbs. Place sliced eggs in layer over crumbs. Meanwhile, fry bacon until crisp; drain off fat; add bacon to sour cream, parsley or chives, salt, pepper, and ¼ teaspoon paprika; mix thoroughly; spoon over eggs. Top with grated cheese; sprinkle with additional paprika. Bake at 375° for 15 to 20 minutes or until the cheese is melted and bubbly. Serve at once. Makes 4 servings.

HAM AND EGGS FLORENTINE

2 cups cooked chopped spinach
Thinly sliced baked ham
4 hard-cooked eggs, deviled
2 cups Cheese Sauce*

Place spinach in greased shallow baking dish. Top with ham slices and deviled eggs. Pour Cheese Sauce over all. Bake at 350° for 20 minutes. Makes 4 servings.

*CHEESE SAUCE

Add 1 cup grated sharp Cheddar cheese to 2 cups medium white sauce. Stir over hot water until cheese melts.

CHEESE

The infinite variety of cheeses and their many uses make them a menu planner's delight. Just to wander through a shop that specializes in cheese is a delightful and enlightening experience, stimulating to the imagination of a creative hostess.

For example, a tray of assorted cheeses accompanied by crisp crackers and colorful fruits is a sophisticated way to climax a dinner party. For simpler pleasures, nibble on crackers and cheese for an evening snack. Add brisk-flavored crumbly cheese to salad dressings. Cube firmer varieties and toss with the salad itself. Use types that lend themselves to cooking in sauces, casseroles, lasagne and other pasta specialties. You'll find recipes for all types of dishes that call for cheese both in this chapter and throughout the book.

But remember—cheese resents high temperatures and reacts by becoming stringy and tough. Use just enough heat to melt it and allow it to blend with the other ingredients. For oven-baked dishes, shred, grate, or dice the cheese. Add it to a sauce or use it to top a casserole toward the end of the cooking time. Cheese grates or shreds more easily when it is thoroughly chilled.

TWO-STEP CHEESE SOUFFLÉ

1⅓ cups evaporated milk
4 tablespoons flour
½ teaspoon salt
¼ teaspoon dry mustard
¼ teaspoon hot-pepper sauce
½ pound process sharp Cheddar cheese
4 eggs, separated

Pour evaporated milk into top of double boiler. Add flour, salt, dry mustard, and hot-pepper sauce; beat with rotary beater until smooth. Place over boiling water; beat until slightly thickened (about 5 minutes). Slice cheese into milk mixture and stir occasionally with rotary beater until cheese has melted and mixture has thickened (about 10 minutes). Beat until smooth. Remove from heat. Add egg yolks one at a time, beating after each addition. (Now wash beater thoroughly. Any trace of fat will prevent egg whites from whipping.) Beat egg whites in an ungreased 2-quart casserole until very stiff but not dry. Gradually fold in cheese mixture. Bake at 300° for 1 hour. Serve immediately. Makes 4 generous servings.

CHEESE FONDUE

1½ pounds Emmentaler cheese, shredded
4 tablespoons flour
3 cups dry white wine
2 garlic cloves, peeled and split

½ teaspoon salt
Pinch white pepper
Dash nutmeg
2 tablespoons kirsch, brandy, or cognac
Bite-size pieces of French bread

Dredge cheese with flour. Set wine over low heat. When air bubbles rise to surface (never let wine reach the boiling point), stir with silver fork. Add cheese little by little; keep stirring. Be sure each lot is melted before adding more. Keep stirring until mixture is bubbling lightly. Set a round earthenware 2-quart casserole on fondue heating unit. Rub bottom and sides with garlic cloves. Remove garlic. Add seasonings and kirsch to cheese mixture; blend well; pour into casserole. Spear bread on fondue forks, securing points of fork in crust. Dunk with stirring motion. Keep mixture bubbling lightly. Keep stirring as bread is speared and dunked. Makes 6 to 8 servings.

CLASSIC WELSH RABBIT

1 pound aged Cheddar cheese
1 teaspoon butter or margarine
1 cup beer at room temperature
2 teaspoons dry mustard
1 teaspoon Worcestershire sauce
1 teaspoon paprika
Hot toast triangles

Shred cheese coarsely. Melt butter; tip pan to coat bottom. Add cheese; as it begins to melt, gradually add beer. Stir constantly with wooden spoon. Add seasonings; stir until cheese mixture follows spoon around pan. If too thick, add a little more beer. Spoon over hot toast. Makes 6 to 8 servings.

QUICK PINK RABBIT

1 can (10¾ ounces) condensed tomato soup
2 jars (5 ounces each) Old English cheese spread
1 tablespoon prepared mustard
1 cup pitted ripe olives
Buttered toast

Combine soup, cheese, and mustard. Stir over hot water until blended. Add olives. Serve on crisp buttered toast. Makes 3 to 4 servings.

MONTEREY RABBIT

2 tablespoons butter or margarine
¼ cup minced onion
2 tablespoons flour
1 teaspoon salt
⅛ teaspoon pepper
1 cup milk
1½ cups grated sharp Cheddar cheese
1 can (1 pound) red kidney beans
Toast

Melt butter or margarine in saucepan. Add onion; cook over low heat until tender. Blend in flour, salt, and pepper. Add milk; stir over low heat until thick and smooth. Add cheese; stir until melted. Add kidney beans; heat thoroughly. Serve on toast. Makes 6 servings.

DUTCH CHEESE TAART

10-ounce Holland Edam or Gouda cheese, divided
¼ cup plus 1 tablespoon melted butter or margarine
1 cup soft bread crumbs
3 medium tomatoes, sliced
6 to 8 small mushroom caps

Shred 4 ounces Edam or Gouda (should yield 1 cup). With a sharp knife, cut remaining cheese in thin slices. Blend shredded cheese, ¼ cup melted butter, and bread crumbs. Press firmly on bottom and sides of well-greased 9-inch pie pan. Cover with a layer of sliced cheese and then a layer of tomato slices. Top with mushroom caps. Brush with remaining 1 tablespoon melted butter. Bake at 350° for 20 minutes. Makes 6 servings.
NOTE: The crumb crust may be made ahead of time, if desired.

COTTAGE CHEESE PATTIES

2 cups cottage cheese, sieved
⅔ cup plus ½ cup packaged fine dry bread crumbs
½ cup sliced scallions
2 tablespoons chopped parsley
1 teaspoon salt
4 eggs, divided
Butter or margarine
Spanish Sauce*

Combine cottage cheese, ⅔ cup dry bread crumbs, scallions, parsley, salt, and 2 slightly beaten eggs; blend thoroughly. Shape into 12 patties. Roll patties in ½ cup bread crumbs; dip in 2 more slightly beaten eggs, then again in bread crumbs. Let stand 15 minutes. Sauté in butter until brown; turn and brown other side. Allow 2 patties to a serving. Top with Spanish Sauce. Makes 6 servings.

*SPANISH SAUCE

2 tablespoons butter or margarine
¼ cup chopped green pepper
1 can (3 ounces) sliced broiled mushrooms, drained
1 can (8 ounces) tomato sauce

Melt butter; add green pepper and mushrooms; cook until green pepper is tender. Add tomato sauce gradually; heat to serving temperature. Makes about 1½ cups.

CHEESE LASAGNE

Tomato Sauce*
1 package (1 pound) lasagne noodles
1 pound ricotta or farmer's cheese
½ cup grated Parmesan cheese
½ pound sliced mozzarella cheese

Prepare Tomato Sauce. Cook noodles in boiling salted water as directed on package. Drain. Spread half the drained noodles over bottom of lightly oiled 13 x 9 x 2-inch baking dish. Pour about ⅓ of the sauce over noodles. Add alternating layers of half the ricotta, Parmesan, and mozzarella cheeses. Add remaining noodles, another ⅓ of the sauce, and remaining cheeses. End with sauce. Bake at 350° for 30 minutes or until bubbling and hot. Makes 6 to 8 servings.

*TOMATO SAUCE

½ cup chopped onion
1 garlic clove, minced
¼ cup minced celery
2 tablespoons vegetable oil
2 teaspoons salt
2 cans (1 pound each) tomatoes with juice
1 can (6 ounces) tomato paste
¼ cup water
1 teaspoon sugar
½ teaspoon oregano

Cook onion, garlic, and celery in oil over low heat until soft but not brown. Stir in remaining ingredients except oregano. Cover; bring mixture to boil. Reduce heat; simmer, stirring frequently, 3 hours or until thick. Chill; skim off fat. When ready to use, add oregano; simmer 10 minutes. Makes about 5 cups.

CHAPTER 9

Rice and Pasta

SCATTERED THROUGHOUT this book are other recipes that use rice or one of the many forms of pasta as an ingredient, but the recipes that follow call for these products as the basis of the recipes in which they are used. Both products are popular throughout the world, and rice in particular is the main article of diet in many Eastern and Near Eastern countries.

The recipes that follow offer new ways as well as variations on familiar ways to serve these two products.

BROWNED RICE

    3 tablespoons vegetable oil
    ¾ cup uncooked regular rice
    3 cups boiling water
    1 teaspoon salt

Heat vegetable oil in deep, heavy saucepan. Add rice; stir over low heat until each kernel is deep golden brown. Slowly and carefully add 3 cups boiling water. (Much steam will rise.) Add salt. Cover tightly. Simmer 25 minutes. (Do not lift cover or stir.) At the end of this time the rice will have absorbed all the water. Makes 4 servings.

RICE WITH PEAS AND PIMIENTO

    2 cups packaged precooked rice
    1 cup cooked peas, drained
    2 tablespoons diced pimiento

Prepare rice as directed on package. Add peas and pimiento; mix lightly with fork. Makes 4 to 5 servings.

PILAF

    1 medium onion, chopped
    ½ cup diced celery
    3 tablespoons butter or margarine
    2 cups chicken broth
    2 tablespoons raisins
    1 cup uncooked regular rice
    ¼ cup toasted slivered almonds

Cook onion and celery in butter until tender but not brown. Add chicken broth, raisins, and rice. Bring to boil; cover tightly; reduce heat; cook about 15 minutes or until liquid is absorbed and rice is tender. Stir in almonds. Makes 6 servings.

PINEAPPLE PILAU

½ cup uncooked regular rice
Boiling water
3 tablespoons butter or margarine, melted
1 can (18 ounces) pineapple juice
¼ cup firmly packed brown sugar
⅓ cup raisins
½ cup broken walnut meats
⅛ teaspoon salt
Few grains mace
½ cup whipping cream

Cover rice with boiling water; cover; let stand 10 minutes; drain thoroughly. Add drained rice to melted butter in large saucepan; stir until every grain is coated with butter. Add pineapple juice; cover; cook over low heat 50 minutes or until juice is absorbed and rice is tender. Combine brown sugar, raisins, walnuts, salt, and mace; stir in. Chill. Whip cream; fold in. Makes 6 servings.

RISOTTO ROMANO

1 quart Freeze-Ahead Meat Sauce (page 222), thawed
2 cups packaged precooked rice, cooked according to package directions
8 ounces mozzarella cheese, sliced

Heat Freeze-Ahead Meat Sauce in saucepan. Place cooked rice around sides of shallow casserole; turn hot sauce into center. Place sliced cheese on sauce. Place in 400° oven for 5 minutes, until cheese melts. Makes 6 servings.

OR

Arrange layers of cooked elbow macaroni, grated sharp Cheddar cheese, and Freeze-Ahead Meat Sauce in casserole. Bake at 350° until hot and bubbly.

QUICK SPANISH RICE AVOCADO

¼ cup vegetable oil
1 medium onion, chopped fine
⅓ cup diced green pepper
1 package (7 ounces) precooked rice
1¾ cups hot water
2 cans (8 ounces each) tomato sauce
1 teaspoon salt
Few grains pepper
1 can (6 ounces) lobster*
4 ripe avocados

*Or 1 cup diced cooked ham, chicken, or other meat.

Heat oil in saucepan or skillet. Add onion, green pepper, and rice; cook and stir over high heat until lightly browned. Add hot water, tomato sauce, salt, and pepper. Mix well. Bring quickly to boil. Cover tightly; simmer 10 minutes. Cut lobster into bite-size pieces; add to rice. Heat well. Cut avocados in half lengthwise; remove seeds. (Do not peel.) Fill avocados with rice mixture; place in shallow baking pan. Bake at 350° for 5 minutes. Makes 4 servings.

ORANGE RICE I

¼ cup butter or margarine
1 cup diced celery
3 tablespoons chopped onion
1 package (7 ounces) precooked rice
½ teaspoon sugar
1½ teaspoons salt
¾ cup water
¾ cup orange juice
2 teaspoons grated orange peel

Melt butter or margarine in saucepan. Add celery and onion; cook until tender but not brown. Add rice, sugar, salt, water, and orange juice. Bring to a full boil; cover; remove from heat; let stand 10 minutes. Add orange peel; fluff rice with fork. Makes 4 to 6 servings.

ORANGE RICE II

4 tablespoons butter or margarine
1 tablespoon minced dried onion
3 tablespoons slivered orange peel*
1⅓ cups orange juice
2 cups water
¼ teaspoon savory
1½ teaspoons salt
1⅓ cups uncooked regular rice

Melt butter or margarine in heavy saucepan; add onion; cook over low heat 3 to 4 minutes. Add orange peel, orange juice, water, savory, and salt. Bring to a boil; add rice slowly. Cover tightly; cook over low heat until all liquid is absorbed (about 25 minutes). Makes 6 to 8 servings.

*Using vegetable peeler, remove very thin outer peel from 1 orange. Cut in ⅛-inch slivers with scissors or knife.

ORANGE-ALMOND RICE

1 package (7 ounces) precooked rice
1 cup peeled diced orange
2 tablespoons sugar
⅓ cup canned toasted slivered almonds

Cook rice as directed on package. Fold in remaining ingredients. Makes 6 servings.

MUSHROOM RICE

Prepare precooked rice as directed on 7-ounce package for number of servings desired. Drain 1 can (3 ounces) broiled sliced mushrooms; heat with ¼ cup butter until butter melts; pour over rice; toss with a fork until well mixed. Season to taste.

MEXICAN RICE

½ cup uncooked regular rice
¼ cup vegetable oil
1 medium onion, chopped
1 garlic clove, minced
1 pound lean ground beef
2 teaspoons salt
1 tablespoon chili powder
1 can (1 pound) tomatoes
¾ cup seedless raisins

Cook rice in oil in frying pan, stirring frequently until each kernel is golden brown. Add onion, garlic, and beef. Stir until meat is lightly browned. Add remaining ingredients; cook and stir 5 minutes longer. Pour into casserole; cover. Bake at 350° for 45 minutes. Remove cover; bake 15 minutes longer. Makes 4 servings.

COTTAGE CHEESE RICE LOAF

1 package (7 ounces) precooked rice
2 cups (1 pound) cottage cheese
3 eggs, slightly beaten
1½ cups milk
2 tablespoons butter, melted
1½ teaspoons salt
Dash of pepper
Olive-Mushroom Sauce*

Prepare rice as directed on package. Press cheese through food mill or sieve; add eggs, milk, butter, salt, and pepper; stir to blend well. Add rice; mix. Turn into greased loaf pan. Place in pan of hot water; bake at 350° for 1 hour. Re-move loaf pan from hot water; let stand 10 minutes; unmold onto platter. Serve with Olive-Mushroom Sauce. Makes 6 servings.

*OLIVE-MUSHROOM SAUCE

Combine 1 can (10¾ ounces) condensed cream of mushroom soup, ½ cup sliced stuffed olives, ½ cup milk, 2 teaspoons Worcestershire sauce, and a few drops hot-pepper sauce in saucepan. Mix well; heat.

NOODLES WITH PORK SAUCE

¼ cup flour
1 tablespoon curry powder
2 teaspoons salt
¼ teaspoon pepper
3 pounds lean pork shoulder, cut in 1½-inch cubes
2 tablespoons butter or margarine
3 cups chicken bouillon
1 large onion, sliced
1 pound medium egg noodles
1 cup diagonally sliced celery
2 medium carrots, sliced
1 can (6 ounces) broiled sliced mushrooms, undrained
1 can (5 ounces) water chestnuts, drained and sliced
½ cup seedless raisins

Combine flour, curry powder, salt, and pepper. Coat pork cubes with flour mixture; brown lightly in butter. Stir in bouillon and half the onion slices. Bring to boil. Reduce heat; cover; simmer 45 to 60 minutes or until tender, stirring occasionally. Cook noodles as directed on package; drain; set aside, keeping warm. Add remaining onion slices and other remaining ingredients to pork. Cover; cook about 15 minutes or until carrots are just tender. Serve with prepared noodles. Makes 8 servings.

NOODLE CASSEROLE

1 package (8 ounces) medium egg noodles, cooked and drained
¼ cup butter or margarine, melted
½ cup grated Swiss cheese
2 tablespoons lemon juice
3 cups pared and thinly sliced tart apples (4 to 5 apples)

½ teaspoon salt
¼ teaspoon each ground cloves and cinnamon
½ pound sliced Canadian bacon
Snipped parsley

Combine noodles with butter; add cheese, lemon juice, apples, salt, and spices. Turn half the noodle mixture into greased 2-quart casserole. Top with half the sliced Canadian bacon. Repeat. Cover and bake at 350° for 30 minutes; uncover; bake 15 minutes longer. Sprinkle with parsley. Makes 6 to 8 servings.

NOODLES NAPOLI

1 medium onion, finely chopped
1 garlic clove, minced
2 tablespoons vegetable oil, divided
1 pound ground beef
1 can (3 or 4 ounces) sliced mushrooms
1 can (8 ounces) tomato sauce
1 can (6 ounces) tomato paste
2 teaspoons salt, divided
1 teaspoon oregano
2 eggs
1 package (8 ounces) wide noodles, cooked and drained
1 package frozen chopped spinach, thawed and drained
1 cup creamed cottage cheese
⅓ cup grated Parmesan cheese
Sliced mozzarella cheese

Brown onion and garlic lightly in 1 tablespoon oil; add beef; cook and stir until brown. Stir in mushrooms and liquid, tomato sauce, tomato paste, 1 teaspoon salt, and oregano; simmer 15 minutes. Beat 1 egg slightly; pour over noodles; mix well. Beat second egg; add spinach, 1 tablespoon oil, cottage cheese, Parmesan cheese, and 1 teaspoon salt; mix well. Pour half the tomato mixture into shallow oblong baking dish; layer half the noodles on top; spread with all the spinach mixture; repeat noodle layer; top with remaining tomato mixture. Cover with foil. Bake at 350° for 45 minutes. Remove foil; arrange slices of mozzarella cheese on top. Bake 5 minutes longer. Makes 6 servings.

NOODLES WITH POPPY SEEDS AND CROUTONS

1 package (8 ounces) medium noodles
1 cup packaged croutons
2 tablespoons melted butter or margarine

1 tablespoon poppy seeds
Salt and pepper

Cook noodles as directed on package; drain. Meanwhile, heat croutons in butter or margarine; add to noodles with poppy seeds. Toss to mix well. Season with salt and pepper. Makes 6 servings.

SEEDED NOODLES

8 ounces medium egg noodles
¼ cup butter or margarine
2 tablespoons sesame seeds
2 tablespoons poppy seeds
1 tablespoon dill seeds
½ cup chopped stuffed olives
½ teaspoon salt
¼ teaspoon coarsely ground black pepper

Cook noodles as directed on package; drain. Stir in remaining ingredients. Toss to mix thoroughly. Makes 6 servings.

MACARONI WITH WALNUT SAUCE

3 tablespoons butter or margarine
1 cup sliced onions
3 tablespoons flour
1 can (1 pound) tomatoes
1½ cups tomato juice
1 tablespoon soy sauce
Pepper to taste
1 cup broken walnut meats
1 package (8 ounces) shell macaroni

Melt butter or margarine; add onions; cook slowly until onions are tender. Stir in flour; cook until flour is lightly browned. Add next 4 ingredients; cover; simmer 20 minutes. Add walnuts; heat. Meanwhile, cook macaroni shells according to package directions; drain. Serve macaroni with the walnut sauce. Makes 4 servings.

MACARONI-TUNA PIE

1 package (8 ounces) elbow macaroni
1 can (14½ ounces) evaporated milk
2 cups grated process American cheese (½ pound), divided
1 can (6½ or 7 ounces) tuna, drained
1 teaspoon salt
Few grains pepper
2 tomatoes

Cook macaroni according to package directions; drain. Combine milk, 1¾ cups grated cheese, tuna, salt, pepper, and cooked macaroni; mix thoroughly. Turn into greased 10-inch pie plate. Cut tomatoes in wedges. Arrange tomato wedges in a ring on top of macaroni mixture. Sprinkle with remaining ¼ cup cheese. Bake at 325° for 30 to 35 minutes. Serve piping-hot. Makes 4 to 6 servings.

CHEESE AND PASTA IN A POT

2 pounds lean beef, ground
Vegetable oil
2 medium onions, chopped
1 garlic clove, crushed
1 jar (14 ounces) spaghetti sauce
1 can (1 pound) stewed tomatoes
1 can (3 ounces) broiled sliced mushrooms
1 package (8 ounces) shell macaroni
1½ pints dairy sour cream
1 package (½ pound) sliced provolone cheese
1 package (½ pound) mozzarella cheese, sliced thin

Cook ground beef in a little vegetable oil in large, deep frying pan until brown, stirring often with a fork. Drain off any excess fat. Add onions, garlic, spaghetti sauce, stewed tomatoes, and un-drained mushrooms; mix well. Simmer 20 minutes or until onions are soft. Meanwhile, cook macaroni shells according to package directions; drain and rinse with cold water. Pour half the shells into a deep casserole. Cover with half the tomato-meat sauce. Spread half the sour cream over sauce. Top with slices of provolone cheese. Repeat, ending with slices of mozzarella cheese. Cover casserole. Bake at 350° for 35 to 40 minutes. Remove cover; continue baking until mozzarella melts and browns slightly. Makes 8 servings.

MACARONI-AND-CHEESE CUTLETS

1 package (8 ounces) elbow macaroni
1 tablespoon chopped parsley
1½ cups grated sharp Cheddar cheese
1 tablespoon grated onion
1 cup thick well-seasoned white sauce
Flour
Fat for frying

Cook macaroni as directed on package; drain; cool slightly; put through food chopper using medium blade. Add parsley. Combine cheese, onion, and white sauce; add to macaroni. Shape to resemble cutlets; dust with flour. Fry in shallow fat (1½ inches deep) heated to 375° about 4 minutes. Drain on absorbent paper. Makes 4 large or 6 small cutlets.

SPAGHETTI WITH MEAT SAUCE

¼ cup minced onion
¼ cup minced green pepper
1 garlic clove, minced
½ pound hamburger
¼ cup vegetable oil
Few grains pepper
1 teaspoon sugar
1 teaspoon Worcestershire sauce
1 can (10¾ ounces) condensed tomato soup
1 package (8 ounces) spaghetti
Grated Parmesan cheese

Sauté onion, green pepper, garlic, and hamburger in oil. Add pepper, sugar, Worcestershire sauce, and soup. Bring to boiling point; lower heat; cover and simmer ½ hour. Cook spaghetti in boiling salted water until tender; drain; rinse in hot water. Pour sauce over spaghetti; sprinkle with cheese. Makes 4 servings.

SPAGHETTI WITH ZUCCHINI-BEEF SAUCE

2 tablespoons vegetable oil
1 pound ground beef chuck
1 garlic clove, crushed
1 pound small zucchini, sliced
1 cup diced green pepper
2 medium tomatoes, quartered
1 teaspoon salt
¼ teaspoon pepper
2 tablespoons all-purpose flour
2 tablespoons water
8 ounces spaghetti, cooked and drained

Heat oil. Add beef and garlic. Cook over medium heat, stirring occasionally, 5 minutes. Add zucchini, green pepper, tomatoes, salt, and pepper. Cover; cook over low heat, stirring occasionally, 30 minutes or until zucchini is tender. Blend flour and water. Add flour mixture to zucchini mixture; mix well. Cook, stirring constantly, until thickened. Serve sauce over spaghetti. Makes 4 servings.

TUNA-ANCHOVY SPAGHETTI

1 jar (14 ounces) spaghetti sauce
1 can (6 ounces) tomato paste
Garlic powder
1 can (2 ounces) rolled anchovy fillets, drained
1 small green pepper, slivered or diced
2 cans (6½ or 7 ounces each) tuna
1 package (8 ounces) thin spaghetti, cooked
Grated Parmesan cheese

Combine spaghetti sauce, tomato paste, and garlic powder to taste; mix well. Simmer 15 minutes. Add anchovies, green pepper, and tuna (drained and broken in chunks). Heat to serving temperature. Pour over cooked spaghetti; sprinkle with Parmesan cheese. Makes 4 servings.

SPAGHETTI AND STEAK

2 medium onions, sliced
1 green pepper, sliced
1 garlic clove, crushed
3 tablespoons vegetable oil
2 cans (8 ounces each) tomato sauce
¼ cup catchup
½ teaspoon salt
¼ teaspoon pepper
¼ teaspoon oregano
¼ teaspoon basil
1 package (8 ounces) thin spaghetti
1 flank steak, 1½ to 2 pounds
Unseasoned natural meat tenderizer

Cook onions, green pepper, and garlic in oil until onions are crisp-tender. Stir in tomato sauce, catchup, salt, and pepper. Cover; simmer 30 minutes. During last 10 minutes, add oregano and basil. Meanwhile, cook spaghetti according to package directions. Treat steak with tenderizer as directed on label; broil 3 to 5 minutes on each side, according to degree of rareness desired. Slice steak in thin slices, on the diagonal. Drain spaghetti; heap on platter; arrange steak slices on top; garnish with a ribbon of sauce. Serve remaining sauce separately. Makes 6 servings.

SPAGHETTI NEW ORLEANS

1 package (8 ounces) thin spaghetti
¼ cup butter or margarine
¼ cup flour
1 cup chicken broth
1 cup whipping cream
⅓ cup shredded Gruyère or Swiss cheese
2 tablespoons dry sherry
Dash white pepper
1 can (6 ounces) broiled sliced mushrooms, drained
1½ pounds shrimp, cooked, peeled, and deveined
⅓ cup grated Parmesan cheese
Slivered toasted almonds (optional)

Cook spaghetti as directed on package; drain. Melt butter in large saucepan; blend in flour. Gradually add broth and cream; cook over low heat, stirring constantly, until sauce thickens. Blend in Gruyère cheese, sherry, and pepper; heat and stir until cheese melts; add mushrooms. Remove from heat; stir in shrimp. Add spaghetti to the sauce. Turn into 1½-quart shallow flameproof casserole. Sprinkle Parmesan cheese on top. Sprinkle with slivered toasted almonds, if desired. Broil in preheated broiler 3 to 4 inches from source of heat for 5 to 7 minutes or until lightly brown. Serve immediately. Makes 6 servings.

CHAPTER 10

Vegetables

VEGETABLES CAN be dull or they can be delightful—it's all up to you. In any supermarket you can find a bountiful variety of fresh, frozen, and canned vegetables, the latter two packed separately or in delicious combinations such as mixed vegetables, green beans with mushrooms, green peas with tiny white onions, foreign specialties, and many others.

In this chapter you will find a bouquet of vegetable recipes, many of which are based on a product from a can or package, but with added flavor touches that make them uniquely your own.

HOW TO COOK ASPARAGUS

2 pounds asparagus

Wash asparagus; break off each stalk as far down as it snaps easily. Cook, covered, in boiling salted water in a large skillet 8 to 10 minutes, just until crisp-tender. Drain. Serve topped with any of the following sauces. Makes 4 servings.

LEMON-SESAME SAUCE

2 teaspoons sesame seed
4 tablespoons butter or margarine, divided
1 tablespoon lemon juice
¼ teaspoon salt

Brown sesame seed in 1 tablespoon butter in saucepan. Add remaining 3 tablespoons butter, lemon juice, and salt. Heat to serving temperature. Makes about ⅓ cup.

FRESH TOMATO SAUCE

¼ cup butter or margarine
¼ teaspoon dried leaf oregano
½ teaspoon lemon juice
¼ teaspoon salt
1 small tomato, finely chopped (½ cup)

Combine all ingredients in saucepan; heat to serving temperature. Makes about ⅔ cup.

HERB SAUCE

¼ cup butter or margarine
¼ teaspoon each dried leaf basil, thyme, and
    tarragon
1 tablespoon finely chopped parsley
½ teaspoon lemon juice
¼ teaspoon salt

Combine all ingredients in saucepan; heat to serving temperature. Makes about ⅓ cup.

VINAIGRETTE SAUCE

½ cup vegetable oil
¼ cup vinegar
1 teaspoon salt
1½ teaspoons paprika
Few grains pepper
1½ teaspoons dry mustard
½ teaspoon sugar
1½ teaspoons grated onion
1 hard-cooked egg, minced

Combine all ingredients; shake well. Serve on chilled asparagus. Makes about 1 cup.

ASPARAGUS PIE

3 tablespoons butter or margarine
1 tablespoon cornstarch
¾ teaspoon salt, divided
⅛ teaspoon pepper
1 cup milk
¼ cup mayonnaise
2 cups diced cooked ham
1 pound hot cooked asparagus
1 tablespoon lemon juice
9-inch baked pie shell
¼ cup grated Parmesan cheese

Melt butter or margarine in a 2-quart saucepan over medium heat. Stir in cornstarch, ¼ teaspoon salt, and pepper. Remove from heat. Gradually stir in milk, mixing until smooth. Cook over medium heat, stirring constantly, until sauce comes to a boil and boils 1 minute. Stir small amount of cornstarch mixture into mayonnaise, then stir into mixture in saucepan. Add ham; cook over low heat about 5 minutes or until ham is heated. Cut all but 6 asparagus spears into halves or thirds; toss with lemon juice and ½ teaspoon salt. Line pie shell with asparagus pieces. Cover with the ham mixture. Arrange remaining whole spears of asparagus on top. Sprinkle with grated cheese. Broil about 4 inches from heat 2 to 3 minutes or until lightly browned. Makes 6 servings.

BEETS ORLANDO

This is an unusual and flavorful vegetable dish.

¼ cup butter or margarine
2 tablespoons sugar

1 thin-skinned grapefruit
2½ cups hot, seasoned sliced beets

Melt butter in saucepan. Add sugar. Remove sections from grapefruit; add to butter mixture. Cook slowly until grapefruit is heated. Pour contents of saucepan over beets. Makes 6 servings.

PICKLED BEETS AND EGGS

Pickled Beets*
6 hard-cooked eggs, shelled

Drain Pickled Beets, saving liquor; arrange beets and eggs in a glass jar or bowl; strain beet liquor; pour over all; cover; let stand 24 to 48 hours in refrigerator (the longer they stand, the more deeply the beet color will penetrate the white of the eggs).

*PICKLED BEETS

1 can (1 pound) sliced beets
½ cup wine vinegar
1 tablespoon sugar
1 bay leaf
6 whole cloves
6 allspice berries
1 tablespoon broken stick cinnamon

Drain beets, saving liquid. Combine beet liquid with remaining ingredients; bring to boil; boil 5 minutes; pour over beets; chill overnight.

BEETS WITH SOUR CREAM

1 can (1 pound) beets, drained
1 teaspoon sugar
¼ teaspoon salt
3 tablespoons prepared horseradish
½ cup dairy sour cream
3 cups coleslaw

Chop beets very fine. Add next 4 ingredients; mix well; chill. Press coleslaw into ring mold; unmold. Place beets in center of coleslaw ring. Makes 6 servings.

HARVARD BEETS

1 can (1 pound) sliced beets
2 tablespoons butter or margarine
2 tablespoons flour
¼ cup beet liquid from can
⅓ cup firmly packed brown sugar
¼ cup vinegar

½ teaspoon salt
Few grains pepper
⅛ teaspoon cloves

Drain beets; save ¼ cup of the liquid. Melt butter or margarine; blend in flour. Add ¼ cup beet liquid; cook, stirring constantly, until thickened. Add remaining ingredients; stir until sugar dissolves. Add drained beets. Heat to serving temperature. Makes 6 servings.

BROCCOLI MOLD

3 envelopes unflavored gelatin
¾ cup cold water
1½ cups boiling water
6 chicken bouillon cubes
1½ cups bottled green goddess salad dressing
2 packages (10 ounces each) frozen chopped
    broccoli, cooked, drained
⅓ cup grated Parmesan cheese
Garnish: deviled eggs

Sprinkle gelatin over cold water in blender; allow to stand while assembling remaining ingredients. Add boiling water and bouillon cubes; cover; blend at low speed until gelatin dissolves. If gelatin granules cling to sides of container, use a rubber spatula to push them into the mixture. When gelatin is dissolved, add salad dressing; cover; blend until smooth. Chill until slightly thickened. Stir in broccoli and cheese. Turn into 6-cup mold. Chill until firm. Unmold; garnish with deviled eggs. Makes 6 to 8 servings.

BRUSSELS SPROUTS IN CELERY SAUCE

1 can (10¾ ounces) condensed cream of
    celery soup
¼ cup cream
1 can (6 ounces) broiled sliced mushrooms
3 cups cooked Brussels sprouts

Combine soup and cream; heat. Add mushrooms and Brussels sprouts. Heat over hot water. Makes 4 to 6 servings.

BRUSSELS SPROUTS WITH WALNUT BUTTER

4 packages (10 ounces each) frozen Brussels
    sprouts
¼ pound butter or margarine
½ cup finely chopped walnuts

Cook Brussels sprouts as directed on package; drain. Melt butter; stir in walnuts; pour over sprouts. Makes 8 to 10 servings.

DEVILED BRUSSELS SPROUTS

⅓ cup butter or margarine
2 teaspoons prepared mustard
1 teaspoon Worcestershire sauce
¼ teaspoon salt
Dash cayenne
2 packages (10 ounces each) frozen Brussels
    sprouts, cooked

Melt butter; blend in mustard, Worcestershire sauce, salt, and cayenne. Pour over hot drained sprouts. Makes 6 servings.

RED CABBAGE FLORIDA

Shred 1 head of red cabbage. Cook in small amount of water and ⅓ cup grapefruit juice about 10 minutes or until tender. Add sections from 1 carefully cored thin-skinned grapefruit; heat thoroughly. Makes 6 servings.

SAUCEPAN CABBAGE

This sauce is also good with cauliflower or lima beans.

2 tablespoons butter or margarine
4 cups finely shredded cabbage
1 cup thinly sliced celery
2 tablespoons minced dried onion
1 can (8 ounces) tomato sauce
½ cup sauterne
½ teaspoon salt

Melt butter in large saucepan. Add remaining ingredients; toss to mix well. Cover; cook over low heat about 10 minutes or until cabbage is crisp-tender. Makes 4 servings.

GLAZED CARROT CIRCLES

Cook thinly sliced carrots in a small amount of salted water until almost tender; boil off any remaining water. Drain and dry on absorbent paper. Coat with granulated sugar. Simmer in melted butter or margarine, stirring often, until tender and glazed. Sprinkle with chopped parsley, or fresh mint when available.

CAULIFLOWER POLONAISE

2 heads cauliflower
2 hard-cooked eggs
2 tablespoons minced parsley
½ cup bread crumbs
⅓ cup melted butter or margarine

Separate cauliflower into flowerets; add boiling salted water to cover; cook until tender; drain. Chop eggs; sprinkle over cauliflower with parsley. Brown bread crumbs in butter or margarine; pour over all. Makes 6 to 8 servings.

CELERY SAUTERNE

3 cups sliced outer stalks green celery, ½ inch thick
2 tablespoons butter or margarine
½ cup whipping cream
⅓ cup sauterne
1½ teaspoons minced dried onion
Salt and nutmeg to taste

Cook celery in boiling salted water until tender; drain. Add remaining ingredients; heat slowly to just below boiling point. Makes 4 servings.

CORN PUDDING

2 tablespoons flour
1 can (1 pound) cream-style corn
1 tablespoon sugar
1 cup milk
½ teaspoon salt
3 tablespoons butter or margarine, melted
3 eggs, beaten

Mix flour and corn. Add sugar, milk, salt, and butter. Stir in eggs. Grease 1-quart casserole; pour in pudding. Place in pan of hot water; bake at 325° for about 1½ hours or until firm. Makes 4 to 6 servings.

DEVILED CUCUMBERS AND MUSHROOMS

1 medium onion
2 tablespoons butter or margarine
1 pound fresh mushrooms
2 medium cucumbers, diced
3 tablespoons vinegar
2 teaspoons deviled ham
¾ cup whipping cream

Slice onion very thin; cook in butter or margarine over low heat about 5 minutes. (Do not brown.) Slice mushrooms; add to onion; cook slowly 10 minutes, stirring often. Add cucumbers and vinegar; cook 5 to 7 minutes longer. Stir in deviled ham and cream. Heat to serving temperature. Makes 6 to 8 servings.

STUFFED EGGPLANT

4 small or 2 medium eggplants
6 tablespoons vegetable oil, divided
3 garlic cloves, peeled
8 anchovies
6 sprigs parsley, preferably Italian
1 tablespoon capers
2 tablespoons coarsely chopped pitted ripe olives
1 teaspoon oregano
1½ cups fresh bread crumbs
½ teaspoon chopped hot green or red pepper (optional)
8 to 12 thin slices tomato
Salt and freshly ground pepper to taste

Cut eggplants in half lengthwise; scoop out pulp, leaving a ½-inch shell. Chop the pulp fine. Heat 2 tablespoons oil; add eggplant pulp. Cook, stirring, about 1 minute. Chop garlic, anchovies, and parsley together; add this mixture to eggplant pulp. Add capers, olives, oregano, bread crumbs, hot pepper, and 3 tablespoons oil; stir to blend. Fill eggplant shells with mixture. Top each filled shell with thin, slightly overlapping tomato slices; sprinkle with salt and pepper to taste. Dribble remaining oil over tomatoes; place stuffed eggplant on baking sheet. Bake 30 minutes or until piping-hot and bubbling. Makes 8 servings.

EGGPLANT PATRICE

1 small eggplant
4 medium tomatoes, sliced
2 medium green peppers, chopped
2 medium onions, chopped
Seasoning (salt, pepper, garlic salt, sugar)
¾ pound sharp Cheddar cheese, sliced ⅛ inch thick, *or* 12 prepackaged slices

Slice unpeeled eggplant about ¼ inch thick. Parboil until partially tender. Place layer of eggplant slices in large casserole. Add a layer of sliced tomatoes. Fill spaces with a mixture of chopped green peppers and onions. Sprinkle lightly with each of the seasonings. Add a layer of cheese. Repeat until casserole is filled, ending with cheese. Cover; bake at 400° until steaming (about ½ hour). Remove cover; reduce heat to 350°; cook until eggplant is tender and sauce thick and golden (about ½ hour). Makes 6 servings.

EGGPLANT STUFFED WITH KRAUT

1 medium eggplant
3 tablespoons minced onion
3 tablespoons diced green pepper
1½ tablespoons vegetable oil
2 cups drained sauerkraut
Grated American cheese

Parboil eggplant 10 minutes. Sauté onion and green pepper in oil; add sauerkraut. Halve eggplant lengthwise; scoop out pulp; dice; combine with the sauerkraut mixture. Fill eggplant shells with sauerkraut mixture. Top with grated cheese. Bake in shallow pan in a little water at 375° for 35 minutes. Makes 4 servings.

HERB-FLAVORED GREEN BEANS

1 can (1 pound) green beans
2 tablespoons butter or margarine
¼ teaspoon each rosemary, basil, and curry
Salt and pepper to taste

Drain liquid from beans into saucepan. Boil liquid, uncovered, until reduced to half. Add beans; cook about 8 minutes. Melt butter with seasonings; pour over heated beans. Add salt and pepper to taste. Makes 4 servings.

GREEN BEANS AND CELERY VINAIGRETTE

3 cups cold cooked green beans
2 cups sliced celery
1 teaspoon salt
¼ teaspoon paprika
Few grains pepper
2 tablespoons vinegar
1 tablespoon tarragon vinegar
6 tablespoons vegetable oil
2 tablespoons drained sweet pickle relish
1 tablespoon chopped parsley
1 tablespoon chopped chives, fresh or freeze-dried
1 teaspoon sugar

Combine green beans and celery; set aside. Mix remaining ingredients in order given; beat until well blended. Pour over vegetables; toss to mix

well. Chill until ready to serve. Makes 6 servings.

GREEN BEANS CALIFORNIA

Prepare 2 packages (10 ounces each) frozen Italian green beans as directed on packages. Season with butter, salt, and pepper. Stir in ½ cup canned slivered toasted almonds. Makes 6 servings.

GREEN BEANS PIMIENTO

1 tablespoon minced dried onion
3 to 4 tablespoons butter or margarine
1 can (4 ounces) pimientos, drained
1 tablespoon vinegar
1 cup water
Salt and pepper to taste
1 tablespoon cornstarch
4 cups cooked green beans

Cook onion in butter about 5 minutes (do not brown). Chop pimientos; stir into onion with vinegar and water; season with salt and pepper to taste. Dissolve cornstarch in a little cold water; stir into hot sauce; cook, stirring, until thickened. Add beans; heat through. Makes 6 servings.

GREEN BEANS VINAIGRETTE

3 tablespoons cider vinegar
1½ tablespoons tarragon vinegar
½ teaspoon salt
¼ cup pickle relish
½ cup vegetable oil
4 cups cold cooked green beans

Combine first 5 ingredients. Mix well. Pour over beans. Toss to mix. Makes 6 servings.

GREEN BEANS WITH CHESTNUTS

1 can (1 pound) green beans
¼ teaspoon mace
2 tablespoons butter or margarine
½ cup thinly sliced roasted chestnuts
Salt

Drain liquid from beans into saucepan. Reduce liquid by boiling to about half. Add beans and remaining ingredients, seasoning to taste with salt. Heat. Makes 4 servings.

GREEN BEANS AMANDINE

2 cans (1 pound each) green beans
2 tablespoons finely chopped onion
1 can (10¾ ounces) condensed cream of
    mushroom soup
½ cup canned toasted slivered almonds,
    divided
2 tablespoons grated Parmesan cheese

Drain bean liquid into saucepan. Add onion and boil rapidly until reduced to ½ cup. Gradually stir in soup. Add beans and ¼ cup almonds. Heat. Turn into baking dish, 10 x 6 x 2 inches. Sprinkle with remaining ¼ cup almonds and the Parmesan cheese. Bake at 400° for 15 minutes. Makes 8 servings.

MUSHROOM CUTLETS

2 tablespoons butter or margarine, divided
2 medium onions, chopped
1 pound fresh mushrooms, chopped
1 cup diced cooked potato (1 medium)
2 eggs
1 cup whole wheat bread crumbs
¼ cup wheat germ
1 teaspoon salt
¼ teaspoon hot-pepper sauce
2 tablespoons chopped parsley
½ teaspoon dried leaf thyme
Mushroom Cream Sauce*
Garnish: olives

Melt 1 tablespoon butter in large skillet. Add onions; cook until tender but not brown. Add mushrooms and remaining 1 tablespoon butter. Cover; cook over low heat until mushrooms are tender (10 to 15 minutes). Reserve 1 cup onion-mushroom mixture, draining any liquid back into skillet. Place remaining onion-mushroom mixture, liquid, diced potato, and eggs in container of electric blender; process at high speed until smooth (if blender is not available, purée vegetables in food mill). Turn into large bowl and add bread crumbs, wheat germ, salt, hot-pepper sauce, parsley, thyme, and ½ cup reserved onion-mushroom mixture (set aside remaining ½ cup for Mushroom Cream Sauce); mix well. Spoon mixture in mounds, ⅓ cup each, on well-greased baking sheet. Bake at 350° for 20 minutes. Serve hot with Mushroom Cream Sauce. Garnish with olives. Makes 8 cutlets (4 main dish or 8 accompaniment servings).

*MUSHROOM CREAM SAUCE

1 cup dairy sour cream
½ cup reserved onion-mushroom mixture
1 tablespoon lemon juice
½ teaspoon salt
¼ teaspoon hot-pepper sauce

Mix all ingredients in small saucepan. Heat gently to serving temperature. Do not boil. Makes about 1½ cups.

BAKED STUFFED ONIONS

6 large onions
1 cup ground cooked meat
1 tablespoon Worcestershire sauce
Salt and pepper
2 tablespoons packaged fine dry bread crumbs
1 tablespoon butter or margarine
1 can (1 pound) tomatoes
Sugar

Peel onions; parboil 10 minutes. Drain; remove centers, leaving shells ½ inch thick. Chop onion centers; combine ½ of chopped onions with meat and Worcestershire sauce. Season with salt and pepper. Fill onion shells. Combine crumbs and butter or margarine; sprinkle on filling. Arrange onions on heatproof platter. Bake at 450° for 20 minutes. Combine remaining chopped onion and tomatoes; season with salt, pepper, and sugar. Pour around onions; bake 10 minutes longer. Serve from same platter. Makes 6 servings.

GREEN PEAS, COUNTRY STYLE

5 strips bacon
1 cup chopped onion
2 tablespoons flour
2 cups cooked or canned peas
⅛ teaspoon pepper
1 cup condensed consommé

Cut bacon in small pieces; fry until crisp. Remove bacon. Pour off all but 2 tablespoons fat. Add onion; cook until soft. Sprinkle with flour; cook until flour browns, stirring constantly. Add drained peas, bacon, pepper, and consommé; simmer 5 minutes, stirring constantly. Makes 4 generous servings.

PEAS AND ONIONS IN CREAM

2 cans (1 pound each) tiny green peas (*petits pois*)
1 can (1 pound) small white onions
2 tablespoons butter or margarine, melted
Salt and pepper to taste
½ cup whipping cream

Drain liquid from peas; boil rapidly until reduced to ½ cup. Drain onions; combine with peas and reduced liquid. Add butter, salt, and pepper. Stir in cream. Heat to serving temperature. Makes 8 servings.

PEPPERS PARMIGIANA

4 medium green peppers
1 can (1 pound) corned-beef hash
¼ cup grated process American cheese
¼ cup catchup
1 garlic clove, minced
1 teaspoon oregano
2 teaspoons grated Parmesan cheese

Wash peppers; cut slice from stem ends; scoop out cores and seeds. Parboil in salted water 5 minutes; drain. Combine corned-beef hash, grated American cheese, catchup, garlic, and oregano. Fill peppers. Sprinkle with grated Parmesan cheese. Bake at 375° for 30 minutes. Makes 4 servings.

STUFFED PEPPERS

4 medium green peppers
2 egg whites
½ cup cornflakes
1 teaspoon grated onion
¼ teaspoon paprika
1½ cups cottage cheese
1 can (8 ounces) tomato sauce

Cut tops off peppers; remove seed sections. Whip egg whites stiff. Crush cornflakes to crumbs. Combine onion, paprika, cornflakes, egg whites, and cottage cheese. Fill peppers. Pour tomato sauce into deep baking dish; set peppers in sauce; cover. Bake at 350° for ½ hour. Makes 4 servings.

BUFFET POTATOES

8 large potatoes
¼ cup butter or margarine
¼ cup finely chopped onion
¼ cup flour
4 cups light cream
1 teaspoon salt
¼ teaspoon hot-pepper sauce
¼ teaspoon dried leaf marjoram
½ pound Swiss cheese, shredded
½ pound bacon, cooked and crumbled
Garnish: bacon curls

Cover potatoes (not peeled) with water in large saucepan. Cover pan; bring to boil; cook 30 minutes until tender but not soft. Drain, cool, and peel. Cut into cubes. While potatoes are cooking, melt butter in large saucepan. Add onion; cook until tender but not brown (about 5 minutes). Blend in flour. Remove from heat; stir in cream. Return to heat; stir constantly until mixture thickens and comes to a boil. Stir in salt, hot-pepper sauce, marjoram, and cheese. Add potatoes and bacon; heat. Spoon into serving dish. Garnish with bacon curls. Makes 8 servings.

CREAMED POTATO LOAF

4 tablespoons butter or margarine
4 tablespoons flour
½ teaspoon salt
Few grains pepper
1¼ cups milk
7 medium potatoes, cooked
2 tablespoons minced parsley
1 cup grated sharp Cheddar cheese, divided

Melt butter or margarine; blend in flour, salt, and pepper. Add milk; stir over low heat until thick. Slice potatoes thin; add to sauce with parsley; mix well. Spoon half the creamed potatoes into well-greased loaf pan, 8 x 5 x 3 inches. Pack down firmly. Sprinkle with half the cheese. Add remaining potatoes. Press down firmly. Chill several hours or overnight. Unmold on heatproof platter. Sprinkle with remaining cheese. Bake at 375° until heated through, about ½ hour. Makes 6 servings.

MINT POTATOES

4 large potatoes, peeled and quartered
1 cup chicken stock
1 bay leaf
Water
½ cup butter or margarine
⅓ cup whipping cream
½ cup milk (optional)
⅛ teaspoon nutmeg

1 tablespoon finely chopped fresh mint
Salt and white pepper

Cook potatoes in chicken stock with bay leaf, adding enough water to barely cover potatoes. When done, drain; remove bay leaf. Mash; beat in butter and cream. If not fluffy, add some or all of the milk. Stir in nutmeg and mint. Season to taste with salt and pepper. Heat in double boiler until piping-hot. Makes 4 to 6 servings.

OLIVE CREAMED POTATOES

9 medium potatoes, cooked
3 cups dairy sour cream
4 tablespoons minced onion
3 tablespoons minced stuffed olives
Salt and pepper to taste
Garnish: chopped parsley; paprika

Dice potatoes. Pour sour cream into large skillet; add potatoes. Heat slowly until cream bubbles over potatoes. Stir in onion and olives. Just before serving season with salt and pepper to taste. Garnish with chopped parsley and paprika. Makes 8 generous servings.

PAPRIKA POTATOES

4 tablespoons butter or margarine
2 cans (1 pound each) whole potatoes
Paprika

Melt butter in skillet. Drain potatoes. Add potatoes to skillet; sprinkle generously with paprika. Cook over medium heat, turning occasionally, until browned on all sides. Remove. Use to garnish roast. Makes 6 to 8 servings.

POTATO PYRAMIDS

4 cups mashed potatoes
Butter
Salt and pepper to taste
2 eggs
Milk
Melted butter

Season potatoes with butter, salt, and pepper. Beat in eggs. Add just enough milk to make the mixture stiff enough to put through a pastry bag. Use a large rosette tip to form 6 pyramids. Brush with melted butter. Run under broiler until tipped with brown. Makes 6 servings.

25-MINUTE DELMONICO POTATOES

¼ cup butter or margarine, divided
1 cup cornflakes, slightly crushed
3 tablespoons flour
½ teaspoon salt
Dash pepper
1½ cups milk
1 large package (1 pound) frozen French fries
1 package (8 ounces) process sharp cheese, thinly sliced or shredded

Melt butter or margarine. Blend 1 tablespoon with cornflakes; set aside. Stir flour and seasonings into remaining butter; add milk. Cook over low heat, stirring until mixture is smooth and thick. Spread half the French fries over bottom of 1½-quart baking dish. Pour half the sauce over potatoes; cover with half the cheese. Repeat. Sprinkle cornflakes over top. Bake at 375° for about 25 minutes or until heated through. Makes 4 servings.

SWEET-POTATO PUFFS

Shape well-seasoned mashed sweet potatoes around pineapple chunks to form balls about 1½ inches in diameter. Chill. Roll in packaged cornflake crumbs. Just before serving, heat at 425° until brown.

COCONUT YAM BALLS

6 medium yams, cooked and peeled
Grated peel of 1 lemon
1 egg, beaten
1 tablespoon whipping cream
Flaked coconut
Vegetable oil for frying

Mash yams while hot; add lemon peel. Shape into balls. Combine egg and cream; dip yam balls in egg mixture; roll in coconut. Fry in deep oil heated to 375° until golden brown. Drain on absorbent paper. Makes 12.

LOUISIANA YAM RING

8 medium yams, cooked and peeled
½ cup milk
1 teaspoon salt
Dash of pepper
½ cup butter or margarine, softened
¾ cup firmly packed dark brown sugar
⅓ cup chopped pecans

Mash hot yams in large bowl with milk, salt, and pepper. Spread some of the butter (about 5 tablespoons) over bottom and sides of 6½-cup ring mold; blend remaining butter with yams. Spread sugar over bottom and sides of buttered mold, pressing lightly. Sprinkle nuts over bottom. Spoon mashed yams into mold; spread evenly. Bake, uncovered, at 350° for 15 minutes. Cover with foil; bake 10 minutes longer. Unmold onto serving plate. Fill center with creamed ham or chicken. Makes 8 servings.

SPINACH FLORIDA

Melt 3 tablespoons butter or margarine. Add sections from 1 grapefruit; heat thoroughly. Use to top 3 cups hot chopped spinach. Makes 6 servings.

SPINACH RING

2 cups cooked chopped spinach
Few grains nutmeg
Salt and pepper
2 cups rich medium white sauce
½ cup soft bread crumbs
2 eggs, separated

Season spinach to taste with nutmeg, salt, and pepper. Stir in white sauce and bread crumbs. Beat egg yolks; add to spinach. Beat egg whites stiff; fold in. Pour into well-greased 6-cup ring mold. Set mold in pan of hot water. Bake at 325° for 1 hour or until set. Unmold. Fill center with creamed leftover meat, chicken, or fish, and vegetables. Makes 6 servings.

SAVORY ACORN SQUASH

2 medium acorn squash
1 can (1 pound) corned-beef hash
½ cup chili sauce
1 tablespoon minced onion
1 teaspoon dry mustard
2 tablespoons molasses

Wash squash. Halve lengthwise; remove seeds and stringy portions. Place cut side down in greased shallow baking pan. Bake at 375° for 30 minutes. Combine corned-beef hash, chili sauce, minced onion, and dry mustard. Turn squash cut side up; brush inside with molasses. Fill with hash mixture. Bake 30 minutes longer or until hash is lightly browned and squash is tender. Makes 4 servings.

CHOW MEIN IN SQUASH ROUNDS

3 acorn squash
½ cup bottled sweet-and-sour sauce
1 divider-pack can (48 ounces) chicken chow mein
⅓ cup canned slivered toasted almonds
Chow mein noodles

Slice top and bottom from each acorn squash and discard; cut each squash into two crosswise rings; remove seeds. Cover rings with salted water; simmer 15 minutes or until almost tender. Put rings in greased shallow pan and brush with sweet-and-sour sauce. Bake at 350° for 15 minutes or until tender, brushing rings with sweet-and-sour sauce several times during baking. Meanwhile, separate cans of divider-pack. Heat sauce; drain vegetables and discard liquid; stir vegetables into sauce, heating only until mixture bubbles. Stir in almonds. To serve, fill centers of squash rings with hot chow mein. Sprinkle each serving with crisp chow mein noodles. Makes 6 servings.

GRAPEFRUIT-STUFFED ACORN SQUASH

3 acorn squash
Grapefruit sections
Brown sugar
Butter or margarine

Wash squash and bake, whole, at 375° for about 50 minutes or until tender when pierced with a fork. Remove from oven; cool enough to handle. Slice lengthwise; scoop out seeds. Fill centers with grapefruit sections; sprinkle generously with brown sugar; dot with butter or margarine. Set in shallow baking dish containing ½ inch of water. Return to oven for 15 minutes. Serve hot. Makes 6 servings.

BAKED SQUASH CASSEROLE

2 pounds zucchini or yellow summer squash
3 tablespoons chopped onion
3 eggs, beaten
½ teaspoon hot-pepper sauce
2 teaspoons parsley flakes
Salt and pepper to taste
½ cup butter or margarine, melted
2 cups cracker crumbs

Slice squash in ½-inch pieces. Boil 3 minutes or until tender. Drain; add onion, eggs, and seasonings. Mix until well blended. Pour into 1-quart buttered casserole. Mix butter and crumbs; sprinkle over squash. Bake at 350° for 35 to 40 minutes or until browned. Makes 6 servings.

SHERRIED SQUASH

2 acorn squash
Salt
4 tablespoons brown sugar
2 teaspoons grated orange peel
4 tablespoons dry sherry
2 tablespoons butter or margarine

Cut squash in halves; scoop out seeds and stringy portions. Sprinkle lightly with salt. Bake cut side down on greased baking sheet at 350° for 40 minutes. Turn cut side up; prick inside surfaces with fork. Sprinkle each half with 1 tablespoon brown sugar, ½ teaspoon orange peel, and 1 tablespoon sherry. Dot each with ½ tablespoon butter. Bake 10 minutes longer. Makes 4 servings.

MARINATED SLICED TOMATOES

½ cup vegetable oil
3 tablespoons cider vinegar
½ teaspoon sugar
⅛ teaspoon pepper
1 tablespoon cut chives, fresh or freeze-dried
¼ teaspoon celery salt
⅛ teaspoon oregano
Sliced tomatoes

Combine all ingredients except tomatoes; stir or shake until well mixed. Pour over sliced tomatoes. Refrigerate until ready to serve.

OLD-FASHIONED FRIED TOMATOES IN MILK GRAVY

4 medium or 3 large tomatoes
¼ cup packaged fine dry bread crumbs or flour
½ teaspoon salt
Dash of pepper
Bacon fat for frying*
2 tablespoons flour
1½ cups milk
½ teaspoon Worcestershire sauce

*Bacon fat adds flavor, but other fat or oil may be used.

Cut tomatoes in thick slices, about 4 to each tomato. Combine bread crumbs, salt, and pepper. Coat tomato slices on both sides in bread crumb mixture. Fry in hot fat, about ¼ inch deep, turning carefully to brown on both sides. Remove to hot platter. Pour off all but 2 tablespoons fat. Blend in flour. Add milk gradually, stirring constantly until thickened. Add Worcestershire sauce. Pour gravy over tomatoes. Makes 6 servings.

SAVORY ZUCCHINI

2 pounds zucchini
2 teaspoons minced dried onion
⅓ cup barbecue sauce

Slice zucchini in 1-inch circles; cook in boiling salted water with minced onion until tender (about 15 minutes). Drain. Add favorite barbecue sauce; heat gently to serving temperature. Makes 4 servings.

GRATED ZUCCHINI

Wash and grate zucchini squash, using a coarse grater. Cook in a heavy saucepan, covered, and without added water until just tender. Season with butter or margarine, salt, and pepper.

VEGETABLE SOUFFLÉ

Follow any favorite recipe for cheese soufflé. Place 3 tablespoons hot mixed cooked vegetables in each of 5 individual baking dishes (approximately 8 to 10 ounces). Pour soufflé mixture over vegetables. Bake at 300° for 35 minutes. Serve immediately. Makes 5 servings.

OVEN-COOKED VEGETABLE DINNER

4 medium baking potatoes
1 medium head cauliflower
1 can (1 pound) whole kernel corn
1 can (3 or 4 ounces) mushrooms
1 package (10 ounces) frozen asparagus
Salt and pepper
Butter or margarine
1 tablespoon lemon juice

Baking directions: Preheat oven to 425°. Bake potatoes 1 hour; vegetables 45 minutes. Makes 4 servings.

Potatoes: Place each potato in center of oblong heavy-duty aluminum foil. Bring sides of foil over potatoes and seal; fold ends tightly. Bake. To serve: Slit potatoes and force open. Sprinkle with salt and pepper; add 1 tablespoon butter or margarine to each.

Cauliflower: Break up cauliflower into buds. Place in center of oblong heavy-duty foil. Partially bring up sides of foil; add 1 tablespoon lemon juice, ½ teaspoon salt, and few grains pepper. Dot with 1 tablespoon butter or margarine. Bring sides of foil over cauliflower and seal; fold ends tightly. Bake.

Corn and Mushrooms: Drain corn and mushrooms. Combine and place in center of oblong heavy-duty foil. Sprinkle with ½ teaspoon salt and few grains pepper. Dot with 1 tablespoon butter or margarine. Bring sides of foil over corn and mushrooms and seal, with foil close to ingredients. Secure ends tightly. Bake.

Asparagus: Place frozen block of asparagus in center of oblong heavy-duty aluminum foil. Use same seasoning and wrapping methods as for corn and mushrooms. Bake.

MIDWEST VEGETABLE MEDLEY

2 cans (1 pound each) peas
1 can (3 or 4 ounces) sliced mushrooms
1 can (1 pound) tiny onions
3 tablespoons butter or margarine
¼ teaspoon salt
¼ teaspoon rosemary

Drain liquid from vegetables into saucepan; boil rapidly until reduced to about half. Add butter, salt, rosemary, and drained vegetables. Heat to serving temperature. Makes 8 servings.

MARINATED VEGETABLES

Vegetables:

1 cauliflower, cut in flowerets, cooked and chilled
1 pound fresh mushrooms, lightly sautéed and chilled
2 packages (9 ounces each) frozen artichoke hearts, cooked and chilled
2 packages (9 ounces each) frozen regular-cut green beans, cooked and chilled
2 packages (10 ounces each) frozen asparagus spears, cooked and chilled
2 packages (10 ounces each) frozen green limas, cooked and chilled
1 can (1 pound) sliced beets, chilled

Combine all ingredients in large bowl.

Marinade:

½ cup tarragon vinegar
2 teaspoons salt
2 teaspoons sugar
2 tablespoons dried fines herbes
¼ teaspoon cayenne
1 cup vegetable oil
½ cup chopped fresh parsley

Measure vinegar into small bowl. Add salt, sugar, fines herbes, and cayenne; stir until dissolved. Add oil and parsley. Beat or stir vigorously until blended. Pour over vegetables; cover; refrigerate several hours or overnight. Drain off excess marinade. Arrange attractively on large chop plate or platter. Makes 8 to 10 generous servings.

CHAPTER 11

Salads and Salad Dressings

In a relatively short time, salads have raced ahead in popularity. Now we rarely plan a meal that does not include one, either as a first course, an accompaniment to the main course, a course by itself, or as dessert.

We like the West Coast custom of serving a tossed green salad for the first course. It begins the meal on a fresh, zestful note that seems to stimulate appetite.

Among the recipes that follow, you will find salads of all types for your family's enjoyment.

Don't forget the stunning array of salad dressings—from French and Italian to Russian and Green Goddess—available at your supermarket. Some come in attractive bottles, some in packages, needing only the addition of liquid. Keep a few varieties on hand to lend distinctive flavor to the salads you create.

MARINATED MUSHROOM SALAD

1 package French salad dressing mix
1⅓ cups (2 cans, 4 ounces each) sliced or button mushrooms
Rings from 2 small onions
½ cup diced green pepper
2 tablespoons diced pimiento

Prepare salad dressing mix as directed on package. Measure ⅔ cup of dressing. Drain mushrooms; combine with remaining ingredients and measured dressing. Chill several hours. Serve over lettuce wedges. Makes 4 to 6 servings.

BACON-AND-RICE SALAD

8 slices bacon, cooked and crumbled
3 cups cooked rice
1 cup cooked green peas (fresh, canned, or frozen)
¼ cup snipped chives
1 cup thinly sliced celery
¼ cup diced pimientos
½ teaspoon salt
¼ teaspoon pepper
½ cup mayonnaise
Crisp salad greens
Garnish: green and ripe olives

Combine first 9 ingredients; toss slightly. Serve on crisp greens. Garnish with green and ripe olives. Makes 4 to 6 servings.

CHEF'S SALAD

1 head romaine lettuce
1 bunch watercress
1 cucumber
1 bunch radishes
¼ pound cooked ham
¼ pound Swiss cheese
6 small tomatoes
8 large stuffed olives
Onion French Dressing*

Wash romaine and watercress; drain; put in covered vegetable crisper in refrigerator. Pare cucumber; score lengthwise with tines of fork; slice into ice water. Make radish roses; drop into ice water. Cut ham and cheese in thin strips. Cut tomatoes in wedges. Slice olives. Put greens in salad bowl. Arrange remaining ingredients in attractive pattern on greens. Just before serving, toss with Onion French Dressing. Makes 6 to 8 servings.

*ONION FRENCH DRESSING

½ cup vegetable oil
3 tablespoons vinegar
¾ teaspoon salt
2 teaspoons sugar
¾ teaspoon dry mustard
½ teaspoon paprika
Few grains pepper
2 tablespoons minced onion

Combine all ingredients. Let stand ½ hour. Shake well before using. Makes about ¾ cup dressing.

TAVERN SALAD

2 cans (1 pound each) red kidney beans, well drained
1 can (1 pound) cut green beans, well drained
1 can (1 pound) whole kernel corn, well drained
1 can (4 ounces) pimiento, well drained and coarsely cut
1½ cups diagonally sliced celery
¼ cup snipped parsley
2 tablespoons capers
¼ cup minced onion
¾ teaspoon salt
⅔ cup bottled blue cheese dressing
Salad greens

Combine kidney beans, green beans, corn, pimiento, and celery. Sprinkle with parsley, capers, onion, and salt. Add salad dressing; toss to mix well. Chill. Serve with salad greens. Makes 6 servings.

ACCOMPANIMENT: Cold sliced meat.

ALL-GREEN SALAD

1 can (1 pound) green beans
French dressing, bottled or homemade
1 small head lettuce
2 cups shredded uncooked spinach
½ teaspoon curry powder (optional)
1 peeled avocado, diced or sliced
Crushed dry-roasted peanuts *or* chopped hard-cooked egg *or* grated Swiss cheese (optional)

Drain liquid from can of green beans and fill can with French dressing. Put can of green beans in the refrigerator to marinate 2 hours. Wash greens well; drain; refrigerate. When chilled and crisp, tear lettuce and spinach into salad bowl. Drain green beans, saving the dressing. Shake curry powder into dressing at this point if you're fond of that flavor. Add green beans and avocado to the salad and toss, using only enough of the dressing to moisten. If desired, sprinkle with crushed dry-roasted peanuts or chopped hard-cooked egg or grated Swiss cheese for 3 different accents. Makes 4 to 6 servings.

CALIFORNIA GREEN GODDESS SALAD

1 garlic clove, grated
1 can (2 ounces) anchovy fillets, finely chopped
¼ cup cut chives
1 tablespoon lemon juice
3 tablespoons tarragon wine vinegar
½ cup dairy sour cream
1 cup mayonnaise
¼ cup minced parsley
Salt and coarse black pepper to taste
Mixed greens, coarsely torn

Combine all ingredients except greens in order given. Pour over coarsely torn mixed greens. Toss well. Makes about 2 cups.

COTTAGE CHEESE AND RAISIN SALAD

1 pound cottage cheese
½ cup dairy sour cream
½ cup seedless raisins

Boiling water
½ cup broken walnut meats
Watercress

Combine cottage cheese and sour cream. Cover raisins with boiling water; let stand 5 minutes; drain on absorbent paper; add to cheese mixture with ½ cup broken walnut meats. Serve on watercress. Makes 4 to 6 servings.

CALIFORNIA SALAD BOWL

2 heads iceberg lettuce, cut into small chunks
¼ cup Garlic-Flavored Vegetable Oil*
½ cup plain vegetable oil
1 tablespoon Worcestershire sauce
Salt and pepper to taste
½ cup grated hard cheese, such as Romanelle
¼ cup crumbled blue cheese
½ teaspoon dry mustard
⅓ cup lemon juice
1 egg
Toast Croutons†

Combine all ingredients except croutons in large salad bowl. Toss until lettuce is coated with oils, egg, seasonings, and cheese. Dip Toast Croutons in additional Garlic-Flavored Vegetable Oil; drain; add to salad just before serving. Makes 8 large servings.

*GARLIC-FLAVORED VEGETABLE OIL

Cut 4 garlic cloves into 1 cup vegetable oil; let stand for several hours until oil is well flavored. Remove garlic. Save any unused oil for another time.

†TOAST CROUTONS

Cut trimmed bread slices in ½-inch cubes; measure 2 cups. Toast at 350° until golden brown and crisp, stirring often to make sure that all cubes are evenly browned.

PATIO SALAD

1 large head lettuce, chopped
4 hard-cooked eggs, sliced
1 cup chopped dill pickles
4 medium-sized tomatoes, sliced and
    quartered
Rings from 1 large sweet onion
⅔ cup vegetable oil
⅓ cup vinegar

2 tablespoons lemon juice
2 garlic cloves, crushed
2 teaspoons seasoned salt
2 eggs, raw

Combine lettuce, hard-cooked eggs, pickles, tomatoes, and onion rings. Combine oil, vinegar, lemon juice, garlic, and seasoned salt; mix well. Pour oil mixture over lettuce mixture; toss lightly but thoroughly. Break raw eggs into lettuce mixture; toss until all traces of egg disappear. Makes 8 to 12 servings.

OLD-FASHIONED COLESLAW

⅓ cup sugar
½ teaspoon dry mustard
¼ teaspoon salt
Few grains of pepper
1 egg
⅓ cup milk
⅓ cup vinegar
1 tablespoon butter or margarine
3 cups shredded cabbage
Paprika

Combine sugar, mustard, salt, and pepper. Beat egg; add to sugar mixture with milk; mix well. Add vinegar slowly. Cook, stirring constantly, until mixture boils. Add butter or margarine; stir until melted. Chill. Toss dressing with shredded cabbage; sprinkle with paprika. Makes 6 servings.

SAUERKRAUT SLAW

1 can (1 pound) sauerkraut
1 cucumber, sliced thin
1 cup dairy sour cream
½ cup mayonnaise
1 tablespoon celery seed
Garnish: tomato wedges

Drain sauerkraut; rinse thoroughly; drain again. Add sliced cucumber to sauerkraut. Combine sour cream, mayonnaise, and celery seed; add. Garnish with tomato wedges. Makes about 6 servings.

VEGETABLE COLESLAW

1 envelope French salad dressing mix
Vinegar
Water
Oil

8 cups shredded cabbage
2 cups grated carrots
2 green peppers, minced
Garnish (optional): radish roses

Combine salad dressing mix, vinegar, water, and oil as directed on package. Combine vegetables; mix well. Toss with 1 cup of the prepared dressing. Garnish with radish roses if desired. Makes 18 small servings.

TUNA SALAD MOLDS

6 tablespoons cornstarch
¼ teaspoon salt
1 tablespoon sugar
1 cup orange juice
1 cup grapefruit juice
1 cup finely shredded cabbage
1 tablespoon chopped pimiento
1 can (6½ or 7 ounces) tuna
½ cup diced celery
1 tablespoon chopped green pepper
Salad greens
Garnish: stuffed olives
Mayonnaise or salad dressing

Blend cornstarch, salt, sugar, orange and grapefruit juices; cook, stirring constantly, until thickened and clear. Cool slightly. Halve mixture; to one half add cabbage and pimiento. To remaining half add tuna, celery, and green pepper. Place tuna mixture in bottom of 6 to 8 individual molds that have been oiled; add cabbage mixture. Chill. Unmold. Serve on salad greens garnished with stuffed olives. Serve mayonnaise or salad dressing separately. Makes 6 to 8 salads.

TURKEY SALAD IN A MOLD

2 envelopes unflavored gelatin
1 cup cold water
1 can (10¾ ounces) condensed chicken broth
1 cup mayonnaise
1 teaspoon curry powder
2 tablespoons lemon juice
1 teaspoon salt
⅛ teaspoon pepper
2½ cups diced cooked turkey
½ cup thinly sliced celery
¼ cup finely chopped onion
¼ cup chopped pitted ripe olives
¼ cup finely diced pimiento
Garnish: chicory; canned cranberry sauce

Sprinkle gelatin on cold water; stir over low heat until gelatin dissolves (about 5 minutes). Remove from heat. Combine next 11 ingredients; mix well. Stir in dissolved gelatin; mix thoroughly. Turn into 6-cup mold. Chill until firm. Unmold onto serving plate. Garnish with chicory and half slices of canned cranberry sauce. Makes 6 to 8 servings.

TWO-TONE SALAD LOAF

2 packages (3 ounces each) lemon-flavor gelatin
2½ cups hot water, divided
2 cans (8 ounces each) tomato sauce
3 tablespoons vinegar, divided
2 cups potato salad
2 cups diced bologna sausage
Salad greens
Mayonnaise

Dissolve each package of gelatin in separate bowl in 1¼ cups hot water. Add 1 can tomato sauce and half the vinegar to each. Chill 1 bowl until mixture begins to thicken; add potato salad; fold in; turn into oiled loaf pan, 8 x 5 x 3 inches. Chill until set. Chill remaining gelatin until it begins to thicken; fold in bologna sausage; pour on top of potato salad layer; chill until set. Unmold onto salad greens. Serve with mayonnaise. Makes 8 servings.

MOLDED GARDEN SALAD

1 envelope unflavored gelatin
½ cup cold water
¾ cup hot water
¼ cup sugar
½ teaspoon salt
¼ cup mild vinegar
2 tablespoons lime juice
12 thin slices unpeeled cucumber
¾ cup thinly sliced radishes
¼ cup thinly sliced scallions
½ cup diced celery
Lettuce
Mayonnaise

Soften gelatin in cold water. Add hot water, sugar, and salt; stir until gelatin and sugar dissolve. Add vinegar and lime juice. Chill until consistency of unbeaten egg whites. Stir in cucumber, radishes, scallions, and celery. Spoon into 1 large or 6 individual molds; chill. Unmold; serve on lettuce with mayonnaise. Makes 6 servings.

TWIN-STAR BUFFET SALAD

First Star:

1½ envelopes unflavored gelatin
⅓ cup cold water
4 instant chicken bouillon cubes
2 cups boiling water
1 teaspoon crumbled rosemary
1 teaspoon onion salt
⅛ teaspoon pepper
2 cups diced canned or cooked chicken
2 hard-cooked eggs, diced
¼ cup minced celery
2 tablespoons minced pimiento
2 tablespoons minced green pepper

Sprinkle gelatin on cold water; dissolve in hot chicken bouillon made with cubes and boiling water. Add rosemary, onion salt, and pepper; chill until consistency of unbeaten egg white. Combine remaining ingredients; fold in. Turn into rinsed star-shaped 5-cup mold; chill.

Second Star:

1½ envelopes unflavored gelatin
⅓ cup cold water
2 cups tomato juice
1 small bay leaf
1 teaspoon onion salt
¾ teaspoon celery salt
Few grains pepper
2 tablespoons lemon juice
2 tablespoons sweet pickle relish
2 cups potato salad

Sprinkle gelatin on cold water. Combine tomato juice, bay leaf, onion salt, celery salt, and pepper; bring to boil; simmer 5 minutes; remove bay leaf. Add gelatin; stir until dissolved. Add lemon juice; chill until consistency of unbeaten egg white. Fold in remaining ingredients. Turn into rinsed star-shaped 5-cup mold. Chill.

To Serve:

Garnish: lettuce; radish roses
Mayonnaise
Crumbled rosemary

Unmold both stars onto large platter or tray. Garnish with lettuce and radish roses. Serve with mayonnaise flavored with crumbled rosemary. Makes 10 servings.

GALA GRAPEFRUIT RING

2 envelopes (2 tablespoons) unflavored
  gelatin
2 cups grapefruit juice
2 cups cold water
2 cups shredded cabbage
⅔ cup finely diced green pepper
Salad greens
Florida Filling*
French dressing

Combine gelatin, grapefruit juice, and water in a saucepan. Heat and stir 2 to 3 minutes. Chill until syrupy; fold in cabbage and green pepper. Pour into 7-cup ring mold that has been rinsed in cold water; chill until firm. Unmold onto salad greens. Fill center with Florida Filling and serve with French dressing. Makes 6 servings.

*FLORIDA FILLING

Combine 2 grapefruit, sectioned; 1 avocado, pared and sliced; 12 radishes, sliced. Mix lightly. Fill center of ring mold. Serve at once.

QUICK TOMATO ASPIC

2 envelopes unflavored gelatin
½ cup cold water
2 teaspoons sugar
½ teaspoon salt
2 cans (8 ounces each) tomato sauce
2 cups water
Dash hot-pepper sauce
1 teaspoon Worcestershire sauce

Sprinkle gelatin on cold water in top of small double boiler; dissolve over hot water. Combine remaining ingredients. Add gelatin; mix well. Pour into 8 to 10 individual molds; chill until set. Unmold to serve.

SHRIMP-AND-TOMATO SALAD

Tomato Aspic:

2 envelopes unflavored gelatin
3½ cups tomato juice, divided
1 tablespoon lemon juice
½ teaspoon sugar
½ teaspoon Worcestershire sauce

Sprinkle gelatin over 1 cup tomato juice in saucepan. Place over low heat; stir constantly until gelatin dissolves (about 4 or 5 minutes). Remove from heat; stir in remaining tomato juice, lemon juice, sugar, and Worcestershire sauce. Pour half this mixture into 10-cup mold. Chill until almost firm.

Shrimp Layer:

    2 envelopes unflavored gelatin
    2 cups cold water, divided
    2 containers (8 ounces each) plain yogurt
    1 tablespoon dried dillweed
    2 teaspoons salt
    2 tablespoons lemon juice
    ¼ teaspoon hot-pepper sauce
    2 cups diced shrimp (about ¾ pound cooked,
        cleaned shrimp)
    1 cup sliced celery
    ½ cup diced green pepper
    ¼ cup chopped gherkins

Sprinkle gelatin over 1 cup cold water in saucepan. Place over low heat; stir constantly until gelatin dissolves (about 4 or 5 minutes). Remove from heat; stir in remaining 1 cup cold water, yogurt, dillweed, salt, lemon juice, and hot-pepper sauce. Chill, stirring occasionally, until mixture is consistency of unbeaten egg white. Fold in shrimp and remaining ingredients. Turn into mold over almost-firm aspic layer. Chill until almost firm. Top with remaining tomato aspic. Chill until firm.

To Serve:

Unmold; garnish with salad greens and additional whole shrimp, if desired. Makes 8 servings.

RELISH SALAD

    2 envelopes unflavored gelatin
    1 cup cold water
    1 teaspoon salt
    1 cup creamed cottage cheese
    1 cup mayonnaise
    2 tablespoons prepared mustard
    ¼ teaspoon hot-pepper sauce
    1 tablespoon grated onion
    1 cup pickle relish
    ½ cup diced green pepper
    1 cup chopped cucumber
    1½ cups diced celery
    ¼ cup chopped stuffed olives
    Garnish: sprigs of parsley

Sprinkle gelatin on cold water to soften. Place over boiling water; stir until gelatin is dissolved.

Add salt; cool. Put cottage cheese through strainer or beat on high speed of electric mixer until smooth; add mayonnaise, prepared mustard, and hot-pepper sauce; gradually add gelatin mixture, stirring until well blended. Mix in remaining ingredients except parsley. Turn into 8 or more individual molds; chill until firm. Unmold; garnish with sprigs of parsley.

ACCOMPANIMENT: Assorted cold cuts.

CUCUMBER-LIME MOUSSE

    1 package (3 ounces) lime-flavor gelatin
    1 cup hot water
    2 large cucumbers
    1 tablespoon lime juice
    1 teaspoon Worcestershire sauce
    1 teaspoon salt
    ½ teaspoon pepper
    ¼ teaspoon hot-pepper sauce
    1 tablespoon prepared horseradish
    ½ cup mayonnaise
    2 cups dairy sour cream
    Salad greens
    1 small cucumber
    French dressing

Dissolve gelatin in hot water; chill until consistency of unbeaten egg white. Meanwhile, peel 2 large cucumbers; discard seeds; chop fine (makes about 1½ cups); sprinkle with lime juice. Let stand 5 minutes. Drain thoroughly; add next 7 ingredients; blend well. Fold into chilled gelatin. Turn into 5-cup mold. Chill until set. Unmold onto salad greens. Decorate top with thin slices of unpeeled cucumber marinated in French dressing. Makes 6 servings.

COTTAGE CHEESE RING WITH FRUIT

    2 envelopes unflavored gelatin
    ½ cup cold water
    3 cups creamed cottage cheese
    1½ cups mayonnaise
    2 tablespoons lemon juice
    2 tablespoons sugar
    Salt to taste
    Mixed fresh fruit
    Banana Dressing*

Sprinkle gelatin on cold water; dissolve over hot water; cool slightly. Mix cottage cheese and mayonnaise; stir in dissolved gelatin; mix thoroughly. Add lemon juice, sugar, and salt; blend gently but thoroughly. Turn into an oiled 5-cup ring mold; chill until firm. Unmold. Fill center of ring with mixed fresh fruit. Serve with Banana Dressing. Makes 8 servings.

*BANANA DRESSING

2 large fully ripe bananas
¼ cup mayonnaise
¼ cup whipping cream

Peel bananas; mash; combine with mayonnaise. Whip cream; fold in. Or put cut-up bananas, mayonnaise, and whipping cream in an electric blender; blend smooth. Makes about 2 cups.

EASY TOMATO ASPIC

1 envelope unflavored gelatin
2 cups tomato juice, divided
½ teaspoon salt
Few drops hot-pepper sauce
1 tablespoon grated onion
1 tablespoon lemon juice
1 tablespoon sugar

Soften gelatin in ½ cup of cold tomato juice. Combine 1½ cups tomato juice with salt, hot-pepper sauce, and onion. Bring to boiling point; add lemon juice and sugar. Add to gelatin mixture; stir until gelatin fully dissolves. Pour into 4 to 6 individual molds. Chill until set. Unmold to serve.

JELLIED FRUIT SALAD IN GRAPEFRUIT HALVES

3 medium grapefruit, halved
Grapefruit juice
1 large package (6 ounces) lime-flavor gelatin
¼ teaspoon salt
2 cups boiling water
½ cup halved seeded red grapes
½ cup diced unpeeled red apple
⅓ cup broken walnuts
Quince Whipped Cream Topping*

Remove grapefruit pieces carefully from halves; drain; reserve juice. Squeeze grapefruit halves carefully to remove remaining juice. Add additional grapefruit juice to make 1¾ cups. Remove white membrane with scissors, being careful not to puncture shell. Dissolve gelatin and salt in boiling water. Add grapefruit juice. Chill until consistency of unbeaten egg whites; stir in grapefruit pieces, grapes, apples, and walnuts.

Spoon into prepared shells. Chill until firm. Serve with Quince Whipped Cream Topping or your favorite dressing. Makes 6 servings.

*QUINCE WHIPPED CREAM TOPPING

½ cup whipping cream, whipped
¼ cup quince (or apple) jelly

Whip cream until it just holds its shape. Do not overbeat. Break up jelly with fork; blend into whipped cream. Makes about 1 cup.

SWISS CHEESE RING

2 envelopes unflavored gelatin
1 cup cold water
1½ cups milk
¼ teaspoon salt
⅛ teaspoon nutmeg
2 packages (3 ounces each) cream cheese at room temperature
2 cups (8 ounces) grated Swiss cheese
1 cup whipping cream, whipped
Mixed summer fruits *or* 2 packages (10 ounces each) frozen fruit, thawed

Sprinkle gelatin over cold water in saucepan. Stir over low heat until gelatin dissolves (4 or 5 minutes). Remove from heat; stir in milk, salt, and nutmeg. Soften cream cheese; gradually beat in about ½ cup of the gelatin mixture. Stir in remaining gelatin mixture and Swiss cheese. Fold in whipped cream. Turn into 6-cup ring mold. Chill until firm. Unmold. Fill center with fruit. Serve on lettuce with French dressing, if desired. Makes 8 servings.

STRAWBERRY DESSERT SALAD

1½ cups lightly sweetened sliced fresh strawberries
1 package (3 ounces) lemon-flavor gelatin
1 cup hot water
½ cup mayonnaise
⅛ teaspoon salt
½ cup drained pineapple tidbits
½ cup chopped pecans
Garnish: whole fresh strawberries; watercress

Drain juice from berries; reserve ¼ cup. Dissolve gelatin in hot water. Add strawberry juice, mayonnaise, and salt. Blend with rotary beater. Pour into refrigerator tray. Quick-chill in freezing unit (without changing control) 15 to 20 minutes or until firm about 1 inch from edge but soft in center. Turn mixture into bowl and whip with rotary beater until fluffy. Fold in drained strawberries, pineapple, and pecans. Spoon into 5-cup mold. Chill in refrigerator (not freezing unit) until firm (30 to 60 minutes). Unmold; garnish with whole strawberries and watercress. Makes 6 servings.

SEAFOOD MOUSSE

2 envelopes unflavored gelatin
½ cup cold water
1½ cups mayonnaise
⅓ cup lemon juice
2 teaspoons dry mustard
2 teaspoons sugar
¼ teaspoon hot-pepper sauce
1 cup sliced celery
2 pounds sea scallops, cooked and quartered
1 pound shrimp, cooked or canned, diced*
1 cup whipping cream
Garnish: salad greens; cucumber slices, unpeeled and scored; stuffed olives

Sprinkle gelatin on cold water; dissolve over boiling water. Combine mayonnaise, lemon juice, mustard, sugar, and hot-pepper sauce. Add dissolved gelatin; mix well. Stir in celery, scallops, and shrimp. Whip cream; fold in. Spoon into 8-cup mold. Chill until set. Unmold onto serving dish. Garnish with salad greens, scored unpeeled cucumber slices, and stuffed olives. Makes 12 servings.

JELLIED CHICKEN-AND-TOMATO SALAD

Layer I:

1 envelope unflavored gelatin
1 cup cold water, divided
1 can (10¾ ounces) condensed cream of chicken soup
¼ teaspoon salt
½ teaspoon Worcestershire sauce
¼ teaspoon hot-pepper sauce
1 tablespoon lemon juice
1 can (5 ounces) boned chicken, diced
½ cup chopped celery
¼ cup chopped green pepper
2 tablespoons chopped pimiento
2 teaspoons grated onion

*Reserve a few whole shrimp for garnish, if desired.

Sprinkle gelatin on ½ cup of the cold water to soften. Place over boiling water and stir until gelatin is thoroughly dissolved. Blend remaining ½ cup cold water into soup. Stir in dissolved gelatin, salt, Worcestershire sauce, hot-pepper sauce, and lemon juice. Chill until mixture is consistency of unbeaten egg white. Fold in remaining ingredients. Turn into 5-cup mold; chill until almost firm.

Layer II:

1 envelope unflavored gelatin
1¾ cups tomato juice, divided
½ teaspoon Worcestershire sauce
½ teaspoon sugar
¼ teaspoon salt
2 tablespoons lemon juice

Sprinkle gelatin on ½ cup of tomato juice to soften. Place over boiling water and stir until gelatin is dissolved. Stir in rest of tomato juice and remaining ingredients. Chill until mixture is consistency of unbeaten egg white. Spoon on top of almost-firm first layer. Chill until firm.

To Serve:

Unmold on salad greens and serve with mayonnaise or salad dressing. Makes 8 servings.

POTATO SALAD IN TOMATO ASPIC

4 cups tomato juice
1 small bay leaf
½ teaspoon salt
Few drops hot-pepper sauce
1 tablespoon grated onion
½ teaspoon celery salt
1 teaspoon sugar
2 envelopes unflavored gelatin
½ cup cold water
1 tablespoon lemon juice
3 cups potato salad, homemade or delicatessen
Salad greens
Garnish: 3 hard-cooked eggs, sliced
Salad dressing

Combine tomato juice, bay leaf, salt, hot-pepper sauce, onion, celery salt, and sugar. Simmer 10 minutes. Remove bay leaf. Sprinkle gelatin on cold water; dissolve in hot tomato juice. Stir in lemon juice. Chill until consistency of unbeaten egg white. Fold in potato salad. Spoon into 6-cup mold. Chill until set. Unmold onto salad greens; garnish with slices of hard-cooked eggs. Serve with any desired salad dressing. Makes 6 servings.

JELLIED VEGETABLE SALAD

2 envelopes unflavored gelatin
¼ cup cold water
1 cup boiling water
4 tablespoons sugar
1 teaspoon salt
2 tablespoons lemon juice
¼ cup vinegar
½ cup grated raw carrots
1 cup shredded cabbage
1 cup cooked green peas
Salad greens
Mayonnaise or salad dressing

Sprinkle gelatin on cold water. Add boiling water; stir until dissolved. Add sugar, salt, lemon juice, and vinegar. Chill until syrupy. Combine carrots, cabbage, and peas. Fold into gelatin mixture. Pour into individual molds that have been rinsed in cold water. Chill until firm. Unmold onto crisp salad greens. Serve with mayonnaise or salad dressing. Makes 6 servings.

GARDEN RELISH SALAD

1 package (3 ounces) lemon-flavor gelatin
2 cups water
1 teaspoon salt
1 teaspoon vinegar
1 cup diced cucumber
1 cup sliced radishes
½ cup sliced scallions
Garnish: watercress

Dissolve gelatin in water as directed on package. Add salt and vinegar. Chill until slightly thicker than unbeaten egg white. Fold in cucumber, radishes, and scallions. Spoon into 1-quart mold. Chill until set. Unmold. Garnish with watercress. Makes 6 servings.

RELISH MOLDS

1 envelope unflavored gelatin
¼ cup cold water
¾ cup sugar
2 teaspoons dry mustard
¾ teaspoon salt
1 cup cider vinegar
3 eggs, slightly beaten

⅓ cup finely diced cucumber
⅓ cup finely diced green pepper

Soften gelatin in cold water. Combine next 5 ingredients in saucepan. Stir over low heat until thickened (do not boil). Add gelatin; stir to dissolve. Chill until slightly thickened. Fold in cucumber and green pepper. Spoon into individual molds. Chill until set. Makes 4 to 6 molds, depending on size.

JELLIED MACARONI RING

1 can (14½ ounces) chicken broth
1 can water
2 envelopes unflavored gelatin
1 teaspoon minced dried onion
2 teaspoons parsley flakes
⅛ teaspoon pepper
1 teaspoon celery salt
2 cups cooked elbow macaroni
1 large can (4½ ounces) deviled ham
½ cup diced green pepper
½ cup diced cucumber
⅓ cup mayonnaise
2 packages (10 ounces each) frozen mixed vegetables
⅓ cup bottled Italian dressing
Deviled eggs
Garnish: watercress; olives

Combine chicken broth and water, using soup can to measure water. Add ½ cup broth mixture to gelatin to soften. Heat remaining broth mixture; add to gelatin. Stir until dissolved. Pour some of this mixture into 8-inch ring mold to a depth of ½ inch; chill until firm. Add onion, parsley, pepper, and celery salt to remaining hot gelatin mixture. Let stand 10 minutes. Chill to consistency of unbeaten egg white. Meanwhile, combine macaroni, ham, green pepper, cucumber, and mayonnaise; fold into thickened gelatin; spoon into mold on top of clear layer. Chill until firm. Unmold onto serving plate. Fill center with frozen mixed vegetables that have been cooked, chilled, and mixed with bottled Italian dressing. Surround with deviled eggs. Garnish with watercress and olives. Makes 6 servings.

SALAD TWINS
(To serve at 2 different meals.)

Basic Gelatin:

2 envelopes unflavored gelatin
1 cup cold water

1½ cups hot water
½ cup sugar
½ teaspoon salt
½ cup lemon juice

Soften gelatin in cold water; add hot water, sugar, and salt; stir until dissolved. Add lemon juice. Chill until mixture is consistency of unbeaten egg white. Divide into 2 batches (1¾ cups to each).

Dinner Salad:

½ Basic Gelatin recipe (above)
½ cup diced cucumber
¾ cup sliced radishes
¼ cup sliced scallions
½ cup diced celery

Fold into gelatin mixture all remaining ingredients. Spoon into 1-quart mold. Chill until set. Makes 4 servings.

Dessert Salad:

½ Basic Gelatin recipe (above)
½ cup diced peaches
½ cup diced bananas
½ cup red raspberries

Fold into gelatin mixture all remaining ingredients. Turn into 4 individual 1-cup molds. Chill until firm.

SALAD DRESSING DUET

½ teaspoon salt
⅛ teaspoon dry mustard
¼ teaspoon paprika
2 tablespoons sugar
3 tablespoons mayonnaise
1 tablespoon vinegar
½ cup lemon juice
1 small can (⅔ cup) evaporated milk, chilled

To Serve with Dinner Salad: Combine ingredients this way: Mix salt, mustard, paprika, and sugar. Add mayonnaise. Stir in vinegar and lemon juice, then evaporated milk. Beat smooth with egg beater.

To Serve with Dessert Salad: Mix dry ingredients. Add vinegar and lemon juice. Whip chilled milk stiff; add first mixture slowly, beating. Fold in mayonnaise.

SUMMER SALAD-ON-THE-SQUARE

1 package (3 ounces) lime-flavor gelatin
¼ teaspoon salt
1 cup hot water
¾ cup cold water
1 cup diced fresh peaches
½ cup cultivated blueberries
⅔ cup diced honeydew melon or cantaloupe
1 envelope French salad dressing mix
2 tablespoons frozen concentrated orange juice, undiluted
Crisp salad greens

Dissolve gelatin and salt in hot water. Add cold water. Chill until consistency of unbeaten egg white; fold in fruits. Spoon into 9-inch square pan. Chill until firm. Cut in 1-inch squares. Prepare salad dressing mix as directed on package; add orange juice; mix well. Just before serving, add dressing to crisp salad greens. Toss lightly. Arrange fruited squares on top. Makes 6 generous salads.

CRANBERRY CROWN BUFFET SALAD

3 envelopes unflavored gelatin
1 cup cold water
4 cups cranberry juice cocktail, divided
¼ cup sugar
1 tablespoon lemon juice
Turkey Salad*
¼ cup canned toasted slivered almonds

Sprinkle gelatin over water and ½ cup cranberry juice cocktail in saucepan. Stir over medium heat until gelatin dissolves (3 to 4 minutes). Remove from heat. Add sugar. Stir until dissolved. Add lemon juice and remaining 3½ cups cranberry juice cocktail. Pour into 5-cup ring mold. Chill until firm. Unmold onto serving platter. Fill center with Turkey Salad. Sprinkle with almonds. Makes 6 servings.

*TURKEY SALAD

3 cups diced cooked turkey
½ cup chopped celery
1 cup halved seeded Tokay grapes
⅔ cup mayonnaise
1 tablespoon lemon juice
¼ teaspoon powdered ginger

Combine turkey, celery, and grapes. Blend mayonnaise, lemon juice, and ginger. Add to turkey mixture and toss lightly. Chill.

THREE ASPIC SALADS

Basic Aspic:

2 envelopes unflavored gelatin
½ cup cold water
2 cups tomato juice
Few drops hot-pepper sauce
2 tablespoons grated onion
2 tablespoons lemon juice
2 tablespoons sugar
1 teaspoon Worcestershire sauce
2 envelopes instant chicken broth mix
1½ cups cold water

Sprinkle gelatin on cold water. Combine tomato juice, hot-pepper sauce, and onion; bring to boiling point. Add lemon juice, sugar, Worcestershire sauce, and instant broth mix; add to softened gelatin; stir until gelatin and broth mix dissolve. Add cold water. Chill until consistency of unbeaten egg white. Fold in any one of the combinations that follow.

Combination I:

1 package (8 ounces) cream cheese
16 walnut meats
24 cooked or canned shrimp, cleaned, divided
½ cup cooked or canned green peas
1 cup halved cucumber slices
½ cup sliced stuffed olives
Salad greens

Divide cream cheese in 16 portions; roll each portion into a ball; press walnut meat into each ball. Arrange 8 cheese balls and 8 shrimp in bottom of 8-cup mold. Dice 8 more shrimp; combine with next 3 ingredients; fold into aspic. Spoon into mold. Arrange remaining cheese balls and remaining 8 shrimp on top, pressing down into gelatin. Chill until set. Unmold onto salad greens. Makes 8 servings.

Combination II:

2 cans (5½ ounces each) crab meat
1½ cups cooked or canned green lima beans
⅓ cup thinly sliced sweet gherkins

Drain and flake crab meat, removing all bits of cartilage. Combine crab meat with remaining ingredients. Fold mixture into aspic. Spoon into 8-cup mold. Chill until set. Makes 8 servings.

Combination III:

1 cup diced cooked chicken
1 cup cooked mixed vegetables
1 cup diced or slivered ham
¼ cup drained pickle relish

Combine all ingredients; fold into aspic. Spoon into 8-cup mold. Chill until set. Makes 8 servings.

ROCKY MOUNTAIN SALAD

1 can (1 pound) sweet cherries, light or dark
½ orange, grated peel and juice
1 package (3 ounces) orange-flavor gelatin
1 cup hot water
1 can (9 ounces) crushed pineapple, drained
1 pint (2 cups) creamed cottage cheese
Salad greens
Dressing of choice (see below)

Drain syrup from cherries; reserve syrup; chill cherries. Combine orange juice and peel with enough syrup from cherries to make 1 cup. Dissolve gelatin in hot water. Add orange juice mixture. Chill until syrupy. Fold in drained pineapple. Pour into pan to depth of ½ inch. Chill until firm and cut in cubes. Make a ring of cottage cheese on salad greens on 4 individual salad plates. Fill centers with gelatin cubes. Circle with sweet cherries. Serve with any favorite dressing, such as cream mayonnaise (½ mayonnaise, ½ dairy sour cream or whipped cream). Makes 4 servings.

TUNA-TOMATO ASPIC

1 envelope unflavored gelatin
¼ cup cold water
2 cups tomato juice
1 teaspoon Worcestershire sauce
¼ teaspoon salt
2 teaspoons lemon juice
1 can (6½ or 7 ounces) tuna
½ cup finely diced cucumber
½ teaspoon capers

Sprinkle gelatin on cold water; dissolve in hot tomato juice. Add Worcestershire sauce, salt, and lemon juice. Brush 6 to 8 individual molds lightly with oil from tuna. Fill molds about ¼ full with gelatin mixture. Chill until almost firm. Chill remaining gelatin mixture until consistency of unbeaten egg white. Flake tuna; fold in with cucumber and capers. Spoon on top of clear gelatin in molds. Chill until firm. Unmold. Makes 6 to 8 servings.

TUNA PERFECTION SALAD

2 envelopes unflavored gelatin
1 cup cold water
3 tablespoons sugar
1 teaspoon salt
1½ cups ice water
⅓ cup white vinegar
2 tablespoons lemon juice
1 cup shredded cabbage
1 pimiento, diced
1 medium unpeeled red apple, diced
2 cans (6½ or 7 ounces each) tuna, drained
Salad greens
Garnish: cherry tomatoes; cucumber slices
Bottled Italian dressing

Sprinkle gelatin over 1 cup cold water in saucepan to soften. Place over low heat, stirring constantly until gelatin dissolves (about 3 minutes). Remove from heat. Add sugar and salt; stir until dissolved. Add ice water, vinegar, and lemon juice. Chill until mixture mounds when dropped from spoon. Add next 4 ingredients. Spoon into 6-cup mold. Chill until set. Unmold onto salad greens. Garnish with cherry tomatoes and cucumber slices. Serve with bottled Italian dressing. Makes 6 servings.

CREAMY POTATO SALAD

4 cups sliced hot cooked potatoes
Bottled Italian dressing
1 cup dairy sour cream
¼ cup sliced green onion
2 tablespoons snipped parsley
2 tablespoons chopped dill pickle
2 tablespoons diced pimiento
2 tablespoons vinegar
1 tablespoon prepared mustard
1 teaspoon salt
⅛ teaspoon pepper
1 cup sliced celery
3 hard-cooked eggs, chopped
Garnish: sliced stuffed olives

Cook potatoes in jackets. Peel and slice while hot. Add a small amount of Italian dressing to coat the warm sliced potatoes. Refrigerate. Combine sour cream with onion, parsley, dill pickle, pimiento, vinegar, mustard, salt, and pepper. Add to potatoes, with celery and chopped eggs. Toss gently; chill. Garnish with sliced stuffed olives. Makes 6 servings.

SALMON POTATO SALAD

1 cup pitted ripe olives
1 can (8 ounces) red salmon
2 cups diced cooked potatoes
½ cup diced cucumber
1 small onion, thinly sliced
½ cup dairy sour cream
1 teaspoon salt
2 tablespoons cider vinegar
Freshly ground black pepper
Salad greens

Slice olives. Drain salmon; remove skin and bones; break into large pieces. Combine olives, salmon, potatoes, cucumber, and onion. Chill. Blend sour cream, salt, vinegar, and pepper. Add to salmon mixture; mix lightly. Serve on crisp salad greens. Makes 4 to 6 servings.

BAKED POTATO SALAD

3 tablespoons butter or margarine
3 tablespoons flour
1 teaspoon salt
¾ teaspoon dry mustard
¼ teaspoon pepper
1½ cups milk
¾ cup mayonnaise or salad dressing
6 medium potatoes, cooked, peeled, and
    diced
1 package (10 ounces) frozen cut green beans,
    cooked
1 medium onion, chopped
6 frankfurters, cut in ¼-inch diagonal slices
¼ cup buttered soft bread crumbs

Melt butter in small saucepan; blend in flour, salt, mustard, and pepper. Add milk all at once. Stir over medium heat until mixture thickens and boils 1 minute. Remove from heat; blend in mayonnaise; reserve ¼ cup for topping. Fold potatoes, green beans, onion, and all but 6 frankfurter slices into remaining sauce; spoon into 2-quart casserole. Arrange 6 frankfurter slices to make a flower in center. Spoon reserved sauce over slices; sprinkle crumbs over top. Bake at 350° for 30 to 40 minutes or until bubbly hot. Makes 6 servings.

HOT POTATO SALAD

¼ cup vinegar
¼ cup vegetable oil
1 teaspoon salt

⅛ teaspoon pepper
2 teaspoons sugar
1 egg yolk
3 beef bouillon cubes
1 quart hot water
2 packages (9 ounces each) frozen French
    fried potatoes
½ cup chopped onion
2 tablespoons chopped pimiento
2 tablespoons sliced sweet gherkins
1 tablespoon capers
¼ cup chopped parsley

Combine vinegar, oil, salt, pepper, sugar, and egg yolk. Dissolve bouillon cubes in hot water; bring to a boil. Add frozen French fried potatoes to bouillon. Remove from heat; cover; let stand 4 minutes; drain. Return potatoes to pan or turn into a large frying pan. Pour vinegar mixture over potatoes. Add onion, pimiento, gherkins, and capers; heat slowly, stirring gently with fork to blend. Sprinkle with parsley just before serving. Makes 6 servings.

POTATO-APPLE SALAD

4 cups sliced cooked potatoes
1½ tablespoons cut chives, fresh or freeze-
    dried
1⅓ cups thinly sliced celery
¼ teaspoon salt
Few grains pepper
1 green pepper, cut in thin strips, 1 inch long
¼ cup minced onion
2 hard-cooked eggs, chopped
2 red apples, unpeeled, cored, and diced
1 cup salad dressing
Salad greens (optional)

Combine all ingredients except greens in order given. Toss to mix well. Chill. Carry to picnic in covered container, either packed in ice or in a portable icebox. Carry salad greens separately, if desired. Makes 8 servings.

SAVORY POTATO SALAD

6 medium potatoes, cooked and peeled
1 cup sliced celery
2 tablespoons minced parsley
Salt and pepper to taste
6 strips bacon
¼ cup cider vinegar
1 tablespoon sugar

Cut potatoes in thin slices. Add celery, parsley, salt, and pepper. Cut bacon in 1-inch pieces; fry until crisp; add vinegar and sugar to bacon and drippings; heat; pour over potato mixture; toss gently to mix. Cover; let stand over low heat until warm. Makes 6 servings.

BLUE CHEESE POTATO SALAD

5 medium-sized potatoes, cooked, peeled, and
    diced
¾ cup crumbled blue cheese (about ¼ pound)
1 cup diced celery
2 tablespoons cut chives, fresh or freeze-dried
¾ cup dairy sour cream
¾ cup mayonnaise
3 tablespoons vinegar
1 tablespoon sugar
Salt and pepper to taste
Crisp salad greens (optional)

Combine potatoes, cheese, celery, and chives; mix well. Combine sour cream, mayonnaise, vinegar, and sugar; stir until sugar is dissolved. Add potato mixture; season to taste with salt and pepper. Mix well; chill. Serve with crisp salad greens, if desired. Makes 4 servings.

Potato-Shrimp Salad: Dice 2 cups cooked shrimp (about 1 pound) and add to recipe, or use whole shrimp as garnish. Makes 6 servings.

Chicken-Cheese Salad: Add 2 cups diced cooked or canned chicken to recipe; garnish with slices of hard-cooked eggs, if desired. Makes 6 servings.

Down-East Salad: Add 2 cups diced cooked or canned lobster meat to recipe. Garnish with lobster claws or strips of canned pimiento. Makes 6 servings.

Deep-Sea Salad: Drain 1 can (6½ or 7 ounces) tuna; break up into medium-sized pieces; add to recipe; garnish with fluted cucumber slices. Makes 6 servings.

CURRIED POTATO SALAD

3 cups water
1½ teaspoons curry powder
Salt
4 cups diced raw potatoes
3 tablespoons French dressing
2 tablespoons lemon juice
2 tablespoons grated onion

¼ teaspoon pepper
¼ teaspoon garlic powder
1½ cups diced celery
½ cup diced green pepper
3 hard-cooked eggs, diced
¾ cup mayonnaise

Combine water, curry powder, and 1 teaspoon salt. Add potatoes; cook, covered, until tender. Drain. Combine French dressing, lemon juice, onion, 1½ teaspoons salt, pepper, and garlic powder. Mix lightly with potatoes; let stand 30 minutes. Add celery, green pepper, and eggs. Mix. Blend in mayonnaise. Chill well. Serve on crisp, young spinach leaves. Makes 6 servings.

POTATO-CUCUMBER SALAD

½ teaspoon salt
¼ teaspoon coarsely ground black pepper
⅓ cup vegetable oil
2 tablespoons wine vinegar
3 cups sliced cooked potatoes
½ teaspoon dried basil
1 large cucumber, thinly sliced
½ cup mayonnaise
3 tablespoons whipping cream
¼ cup minced onion
1 teaspoon dill seed
1 teaspoon lemon juice
Romaine

Combine salt and pepper in small mixing bowl. Add oil. Add vinegar, little by little, stirring. Add potatoes, basil, and cucumber; let stand in refrigerator 1 or 2 hours; drain. Combine mayonnaise with next 4 ingredients; add to potato mixture; mix well. Chill until ready to serve. Serve on romaine. Makes 6 servings.

POTATO CORNED-BEEF SALAD

2 cups sliced cooked potatoes
2 cups cubed canned corned beef
3 hard-cooked eggs, sliced
½ cup diced cooked carrots
¼ cup diced green pepper
2 tablespoons minced onion
2 tablespoons chopped pimiento
½ cup mayonnaise or salad dressing
2 tablespoons vinegar
1 tablespoon prepared mustard
1 teaspoon prepared horseradish
Dash hot-pepper sauce

Salt and pepper to taste
Romaine

Combine potatoes, corned beef, eggs, carrots, green pepper, onion, and pimiento. Combine mayonnaise, vinegar, and seasonings. Toss with potato mixture. Serve on romaine. Makes 6 servings.

POTATO-AND-VEGETABLE SALAD

6 medium potatoes
1 cup cooked peas
1 cup cooked diced carrots
1 small onion, minced
1 cup diced celery
Mayonnaise or salad dressing

Cook potatoes until just tender. Peel and dice while warm; combine with peas, carrots, onion, and celery. Add enough mayonnaise or salad dressing to hold ingredients together. Chill overnight. Makes 6 generous servings.

NEAPOLITAN POTATO SALAD

8 medium potatoes
⅓ cup sliced scallions with tops
1 cup sliced celery
¼ cup diced green pepper
¼ cup sliced pitted ripe olives
1 teaspoon oregano
¼ cup vegetable oil
1 teaspoon salt
¼ teaspoon freshly ground pepper
3 tablespoons red wine vinegar
Tomato shells
Lettuce

Cook, peel, and dice potatoes. Combine with scallions, celery, green pepper, and olives. Combine oregano with next 4 ingredients. Pour over potato mixture; toss lightly. Serve in tomato shells set in lettuce cups. Save the tomato pulp for use in soups or sauces. Makes 6 servings.

MACARONI-VEGETABLE SALAD

8 ounces elbow macaroni, cooked and chilled
1 package frozen mixed vegetables, cooked and chilled
½ cup thinly sliced celery
1 cup cubed sharp Cheddar cheese
½ cup mayonnaise
¼ cup dairy sour cream

¼ cup chili sauce
¼ teaspoon Worcestershire sauce
¼ teaspoon coarsely ground black pepper
⅛ teaspoon salt
Salad greens
Garnish: tomato wedges; sliced cucumber

Combine macaroni, mixed vegetables, celery, and cheese; mix well. Combine mayonnaise with next 5 ingredients; blend well; pour over macaroni mixture. Toss to mix. Serve on crisp salad greens garnished with tomato wedges and sliced cucumber. Makes 6 to 8 servings.

MACARONI-HAM SALAD

2 cups (8 ounces) elbow macaroni
1 pound cooked ham, ½ inch thick
1 cup sliced celery
1 medium green pepper, chopped
¾ cup sliced pitted black olives
⅓ cup prepared mustard
½ cup whipping cream
⅓ cup minced onion
1 tablespoon prepared horseradish
1 teaspoon salt
½ teaspoon garlic salt
½ teaspoon pepper
Crisp salad greens
Garnish: 2 cups cherry tomatoes

Cook macaroni according to package directions. Drain in colander. Rinse with cold water; drain. Cut ham in ½-inch cubes; combine with macaroni, celery, green pepper, and olives; toss to mix. Combine mustard, cream, onion, horseradish, salt, garlic salt, and pepper; mix well. Add dressing to macaroni mixture; toss well. Chill. Serve on salad greens; garnish with cherry tomatoes. Makes 6 to 8 servings.

MAYTIME SALAD BOWL

4 cups cooked elbow macaroni
½ cup diced green pepper
1 cup diced celery
3 sweet gherkins, sliced
½ cup mayonnaise
½ teaspoon salt
½ cup flat beer
½ teaspoon celery seed
Salad greens
½ cup bologna sausage, cubed
Garnish: tomato wedges

Combine macaroni, green pepper, celery, and gherkins; mix well. Combine mayonnaise, salt, beer, and celery seed; add to macaroni mixture; mix well. Serve on salad greens, topped with bologna cubes; garnish with tomato wedges. Makes 6 servings.

PICNIC SALAD

3 cups elbow macaroni, uncooked
½ cup minced onion
3 cups sliced celery
⅓ cup chopped pimiento
2 teaspoons salt
¾ cup chopped sweet pickles
1 cup mayonnaise
½ cup dairy sour cream
2 teaspoons chopped fresh dill (optional)

Cook macaroni in boiling salted water until just tender. Drain. Chill. Add onion, celery, pimiento, salt, and pickles. Combine mayonnaise, sour cream, and dill; add to macaroni mixture; mix carefully but thoroughly. Chill. Makes 12 servings.

MACARONI SALAD

6 cups cooked elbow macaroni
1 medium green pepper, diced
1 cup sliced celery
12 large stuffed olives, sliced
1 small Bermuda onion, cut into rings
¼ cup snipped dill
1 tablespoon snipped parsley
¾ cup mayonnaise
½ cup chili sauce
Salt and pepper to taste
Salad greens

Combine all ingredients except greens; mix thoroughly. Serve on crisp salad greens. Makes 6 to 8 servings.

SPRINGTIME MACARONI SALAD

2 cups elbow macaroni
1 can (9 ounces) Vienna sausage, drained
1 can (8¾ ounces) pineapple tidbits, drained
¼ cup chopped pimientos
½ cup chopped celery
1 tablespoon prepared mustard
1 cup dairy sour cream
1½ teaspoons salt
½ teaspoon paprika

3 medium cantaloupes, cut in halves
Garnish (optional): watercress

Cook macaroni according to package directions. Drain in colander. Rinse with cold water; drain again. Cut each Vienna sausage in quarters; combine with macaroni, pineapple tidbits, pimientos, and celery. Combine mustard, sour cream, salt, and paprika; toss with macaroni mixture; chill. Scoop seeds from cantaloupes. Fill with macaroni salad. Garnish with watercress, if desired. Makes 6 servings.

TUNA IN WATERMELON BASKET

⅓ cup vegetable oil
¼ teaspoon lemon peel
3 tablespoons lemon juice
1 teaspoon sugar
¼ teaspoon salt
2 teaspoons honey
Dash paprika
2 cans (6½ or 7 ounces each) tuna
1 cup sliced celery
1 small round watermelon, chilled*
Salad greens

Blend oil, lemon peel, lemon juice, sugar, salt, honey, and paprika. Beat well. Drain tuna; flake; combine with celery in bowl. Add half the dressing; toss lightly. Refrigerate several hours or overnight. When ready to serve, cut melon in half crosswise. Scoop out 2 cups small watermelon balls from one half, using melon-ball cutter. (Refrigerate second half for later use.) With a spoon, remove enough remaining watermelon pulp to make a hollow to hold salad. Remove seeds; invert watermelon to drain. Add watermelon balls to tuna salad. Line watermelon "basket" with salad greens; pile tuna mixture in center. Serve with remaining dressing. Makes 4 servings. Recipe is easily doubled to use both halves of melon and will then make 8 servings.

TUNA, RICE, AND PINEAPPLE SALAD

⅔ cup packaged precooked rice
½ teaspoon salt
⅔ cup boiling water
1 can (6½ or 7 ounces) tuna, drained
½ cup diced celery

*Round end of large melon may be substituted for small melon if latter is not available.

1 package (12 ounces) quick-frozen pineapple chunks, defrosted, *or* 1 can (1 pound) pineapple chunks
¾ cup mayonnaise or salad dressing
1 tablespoon lemon juice
Salad greens

Add rice and salt to rapidly boiling water. Cover; remove from heat. Let stand 5 minutes; fluff with fork. Cool. Break tuna into fairly large pieces; add to rice with celery. Add well-drained pineapple and next 2 ingredients. Toss lightly to mix. Chill 1 hour. Serve on salad greens. Makes 4 servings.

PARTY TUNA SALAD

½ cup dairy sour cream or mayonnaise
¼ cup chutney, coarsely chopped
2 teaspoons curry powder
½ teaspoon salt
1 cup sliced celery
2 cups cooked rice
1 can (20 ounces) pineapple tidbits, drained
3 cans (6½ or 7 ounces each) tuna, drained
Salad greens
Garnish: slivered almonds

Combine sour cream or mayonnaise, chutney, curry powder, and salt. Toss with celery, rice, pineapple, and tuna. Chill. To serve, arrange on salad greens; garnish with slivered almonds. Makes 6 servings.

TUNA BANANA-SPLIT SALAD

1 cup mayonnaise
Lemon juice
1 teaspoon curry powder
¼ cup finely chopped chutney
1 cup diced unpared apple
2 cans (6½ or 7 ounces each) tuna, drained
2 bananas
Salad greens

Combine mayonnaise, 2 tablespoons lemon juice, curry powder, and chutney; blend well. Add apple and tuna; mix lightly. Chill several hours. When ready to serve, peel bananas. Cut each in half lengthwise. Brush with additional lemon juice to prevent discoloration. Place greens in individual boat-shaped dishes; place half banana on greens. Top with 2 small scoops of tuna mixture. Makes 4 servings.

SEATTLE SALAD

½ large honeydew melon
1 can (8 ounces) red salmon
½ green pepper, minced
½ cup sliced celery
½ cup vegetable oil
2½ tablespoons lime juice
¼ teaspoon salt
Few grains pepper
½ teaspoon sugar
Few grains paprika
1 tablespoon snipped parsley
Salad greens
Salad dressing (optional, see below)

Remove seeds and stringy center from melon half. Scoop out pulp with melon-ball cutter, making scalloped edge. Drain salmon; remove skin and bones; separate into chunks; add to melon balls with green pepper and celery. Combine oil, lime juice, salt, pepper, sugar, and paprika. Beat with rotary beater until well blended. Add parsley and toss with melon-ball mixture. Fill melon shell with mixture. Serve salad greens separately. If additional dressing is desired, serve ½ mayonnaise and ½ dairy sour cream, blended. Makes 3 servings. This recipe is easily doubled to use both halves of melon and will then serve 6.

FLOWER-PETAL SALAD

1 can (5½ ounces) shrimp
¾ cup diced celery
3 hard-cooked eggs, chopped
¼ cup chopped nuts
⅓ cup mayonnaise
1 tablespoon lemon juice
¼ teaspoon salt
½ teaspoon curry powder
6 large tomatoes
Salad greens

Drain shrimp; combine with celery, eggs, and nuts. Mix together mayonnaise, lemon juice, salt, and curry powder; add to shrimp mixture; mix lightly. Cut tomatoes into sixths, halfway through (do not cut through to the bottom), and fill centers with shrimp mixture. Serve on salad greens. Makes 6 servings.

CRAB MEAT SUPREME

1 can (7 ounces) Alaska king crab meat,
    drained

½ cup minced celery
2 tablespoons minced onion
⅛ teaspoon curry powder
Few grains pepper
¼ teaspoon salt
1 can (3 or 4 ounces) sliced mushrooms,
    drained
½ cup coarsely chopped cashew nuts
3 tablespoons mayonnaise
Salad greens

Save large pieces of crab meat for garnish; flake remainder, removing any bits of shell or cartilage; toss with celery, onion, curry powder, pepper, and salt. Reserve a few mushroom slices for garnish; toss remaining mushroom slices and cashew nuts with crab meat mixture and mayonnaise. Mound on serving platter; surround with crisp salad greens; garnish with reserved crab meat and mushrooms. Makes 4 servings.

SCALLOP SALAD

1 pound sea scallops, fresh or frozen
½ pound macaroni shells, cooked and chilled
2 cups cherry tomatoes, sliced
½ cup diced green peppers
½ cup sliced radishes
⅓ cup sliced stuffed olives
⅓ cup sliced gherkins
1 medium onion, sliced thin
1 bottle green goddess salad dressing
Salad greens

Thaw scallops if frozen. Simmer 5 to 7 minutes; drain; chill; slice. Combine all ingredients except salad greens; toss until well mixed. Heap on salad greens. Makes 6 servings.

CHICKEN-AND-VEGETABLE SALAD

1 package (6 ounces) yellow rice (saffron)
2 tablespoons tarragon vinegar
⅓ cup vegetable oil
1⅛ teaspoons salt, divided
⅛ teaspoon dry mustard
2½ cups diced cooked chicken (from
    Simmered Chicken*)
1 tomato, peeled and chopped
1 green pepper, chopped
½ cup cooked green peas
¼ cup minced onion
⅓ cup finely sliced celery
1 tablespoon chopped pimiento
Salad greens

Cook rice according to package directions. Mix together vinegar, oil, ⅛ teaspoon salt, and dry mustard. Immediately pour over cooked rice. Let stand at room temperature until cool. Add chicken, remaining 1 teaspoon salt, and other remaining ingredients except salad greens; toss lightly to mix well. Refrigerate for 2 or 3 hours. Serve on crisp salad greens. Makes 6 servings.

*SIMMERED CHICKEN

1 broiler-fryer chicken, whole or cut in
    serving pieces
2 cups water
1 small onion, sliced
2 celery tops
1 bay leaf
1 teaspoon salt
¼ teaspoon pepper

Put chicken in kettle; add water and remaining ingredients. Bring to boil; cover tightly. Reduce heat; simmer 1 hour or until tender. Remove from heat; strain broth. Refrigerate chicken and broth at once. When chicken is cool, remove meat from bones; cut into bite-size pieces. Reserve broth for another use.

NOTE: A 3-pound broiler-fryer chicken yields about 2½ cups diced cooked chicken and approximately 2 to 2½ cups broth.

SUMMER SUPPER SALAD

1 head romaine
4 cups shredded cabbage
1 large onion
2 small green peppers
1 can (1 pound) red kidney beans
2 to 3 cups cubed cooked ham
Tomato Aspic Cubes*
Chili-Cream Dressing†

Line salad bowl with leaves of romaine. Break remaining romaine into bite-size pieces and place in bowl. Add shredded cabbage. Slice onion thin; separate slices into rings. Core and seed green peppers; slice into rings. Drain beans. Arrange a border of ham cubes around bowl; top with onion and green pepper rings. Inside this border spoon a circle of drained kidney beans. Fill center with Tomato Aspic Cubes. Just before serving, toss with Chili-Cream Dressing. Makes 6 servings.

*TOMATO ASPIC CUBES

1 package (3 ounces) lemon-flavor gelatin
1 cup hot tomato juice
2 teaspoons prepared horseradish
1 cup cold tomato juice
2 teaspoons grated onion
1½ teaspoons salt
Dash cayenne

Dissolve gelatin in hot tomato juice. Add remaining ingredients. Pour into shallow pan to a depth of ½ inch. Chill until firm. Cut into ½-inch cubes.

†CHILI-CREAM DRESSING

Combine ¾ cup mayonnaise, ½ cup dairy sour cream, and ¼ cup chili sauce; chill. Makes 6 servings.

SNAPPY DRESSING

1½ cups mayonnaise or salad dressing
½ cup chili sauce
⅓ cup pickle relish
¼ teaspoon hot-pepper sauce
½ teaspoon Worcestershire sauce
1 tablespoon grated onion *or* 2 tablespoons
    chopped anchovies

Combine all ingredients; mix well. Makes about 2½ cups.

FRUIT SALAD DRESSING

1 cup vegetable oil
⅓ cup cider vinegar
2 tablespoons sugar
1½ teaspoons salt
½ teaspoon paprika
¼ cup maraschino cherry juice
1 egg white, unbeaten

Combine all ingredients in a bowl. Beat with rotary egg beater until thoroughly blended. Serve at once or beat again just before serving. Makes 6 servings.

CUCUMBER CREAM DRESSING

1 can (10¾ ounces) condensed cream of
    celery soup
½ cup dairy sour cream
½ cup diced cucumber
½ teaspoon dried dill
⅛ teaspoon pepper

Blend soup and sour cream. Add remaining ingredients. Chill. Thin to desired consistency with milk. Serve with fish salad such as tuna, shrimp, or crab; or on lettuce wedges. Makes about 2½ cups.

GREEN GODDESS SALAD DRESSING

¼ bunch watercress
¼ bell pepper
12 sprigs parsley
3 to 4 scallions
1 garlic clove
1 can (2 ounces) anchovy fillets, drained
1 quart mayonnaise

Put watercress, pepper, parsley, scallions, garlic, and anchovies through food chopper, using fine blade. Combine with mayonnaise. Serve over mixed salad greens. Dressing may be refrigerated for later use.

QUICK GREEN GODDESS DRESSING

1 can (10¾ ounces) condensed cream of
    celery soup
¼ cup mayonnaise
2 tablespoons chopped parsley
4 anchovies, chopped
1 teaspoon lemon juice

Chill unopened can of soup in refrigerator 3 to 4 hours. Blend soup and mayonnaise; stir in remaining ingredients. Serve with green salads. Makes about 1½ cups dressing.

FRENCH DRESSING

1 cup vegetable oil
⅓ cup cider vinegar
1 to 3 teaspoons sugar
1½ teaspoons salt
½ teaspoon paprika
½ teaspoon dry mustard
1 garlic clove

Measure all ingredients into a bottle or jar. Cover tightly and shake well. Chill several hours. Shake well before serving. Makes 1⅓ cups.

CAROLYN'S SALAD DRESSING

1 large garlic clove
¾ cup vegetable oil
1 egg
2 tablespoons lemon juice
½ teaspoon salt
1 teaspoon sugar
¼ teaspoon black pepper
1 teaspoon Worcestershire sauce
¼ cup grated Parmesan cheese
1 tablespoon cut chives, fresh or freeze-dried

Slash garlic clove; drop into oil; let stand at least 1 hour. Remove garlic. Submerge egg in boiling water for 1 minute. Break into bowl; beat until fluffy. Continue beating at high speed, slowly adding oil. Reduce speed; add remaining ingredients. Makes about 1 cup.

MARINADE FOR SLICED TOMATOES

½ cup vegetable oil
3 tablespoons cider vinegar
½ teaspoon sugar
⅛ teaspoon pepper
1 tablespoon cut chives, fresh or freeze-dried
¼ teaspoon celery salt
⅛ teaspoon oregano

Combine all ingredients; stir or shake until well mixed. Pour over sliced tomatoes. Refrigerate until ready to serve.

CHAPTER 12

Sandwiches

PLAIN OR fancy, hearty or light, as a snack or as a meal—no matter what kind of sandwich you are looking for, you'll find it in this chapter.

PEPBURGERS

1 pound lean beef, ground
¾ teaspoon salt
¼ teaspoon pepper
4 hamburger buns
4 tablespoons peanut butter
4 slices cooked crisp bacon, crumbled
4 pineapple slices

Break up beef with fork in mixing bowl. Sprinkle salt and pepper over entire surface of meat. Toss gently with fork to distribute seasonings. Shape into 4 patties. Pan-broil or grill to desired doneness. Spread half of each bun with peanut butter; top with bacon, hamburger, and pineapple slice. Cover with other half bun. Makes 4 sandwiches.

VARIATIONS

1. Substitute deviled ham for peanut butter, onion slice for pineapple, and pickle relish for bacon.

2. Substitute cheese spread for peanut butter, tomato slice for pineapple, and sliced or chopped stuffed olives for bacon.

HOT CORNED-BEEF BUNWICHES

4 hamburger buns
2 tablespoons melted butter
½ teaspoon dry mustard
1 can (1 pound) corned-beef hash
½ cup finely diced celery
⅓ cup mayonnaise
1 tablespoon horseradish
½ teaspoon salt

Split hamburger buns; cut small circle from center of each top half; reserve. Combine melted butter and mustard; brush over cut sides of buns and circles. Toast under broiler heat until golden brown. Mix together corned-beef hash, celery, mayonnaise, horseradish, and salt. Heat. Spread bottom half of each bun with hash mixture; cover with top half of bun. Fill the hole in top half of each bun with additional hash mixture and top with toasted circles. Makes 4 sandwiches.

SWISS TURKEY-AND-HAM SANDWICHES

8 slices buttered freshly made toast
4 portions sliced cooked turkey
4 portions sliced boiled or baked ham
1 package (8 ounces) sliced process Swiss
    cheese
⅓ cup white wine
1 tablespoon prepared mustard
1 tablespoon grated onion
Paprika

Using the toast, turkey, and ham, make 4 turkey and ham sandwiches. Arrange sandwiches in a single layer in baking pan; cover; keep warm at 300° while preparing the following sauce: Melt cheese in double boiler; gradually stir in wine; add mustard and onion; heat piping-hot. Halve heated sandwiches; place 2 halves on each of 4 heated plates; pour hot sauce over each sandwich. Dust with paprika; serve at once. Makes 4 sandwiches.

GRILLED BACON SANDWICHES

Cook bacon strips on table grill or in electric skillet until crisp; drain on absorbent paper. Press off excess fat. Put bacon between slices of white or whole wheat bread. Brush both sides of sandwiches with hot bacon fat. Grill until golden brown on both sides. Serve with hot maple syrup. For a variation, spread one slice of the bread lightly with peanut butter before adding bacon and second bread slice.

TOASTED BACON ROLLS

Split frankfurther rolls partway through. Toast. Spread one side with butter or margarine, the other side with marmalade. Fill with 2 slices of crisp bacon. Keep hot at 250° until ready to serve.

HOT TUNA WAFFLE-WICHES

1 can (1 pound) green peas
1 can (10¾ ounces) cream of mushroom soup
2 cans (6½ or 7 ounces each) tuna, drained
¼ teaspoon hot-pepper sauce
1 package (10 ounces) frozen waffles
Cheese Sauce*

Stir ¼ cup liquid from peas into soup in saucepan. Add drained peas, tuna, and hot-pepper sauce. Heat, stirring occasionally, to serving temperature. Heat waffles according to package directions. Put waffles together with hot tuna filling; serve topped with Cheese Sauce. Makes 3 sandwiches.

*CHEESE SAUCE

1 can (11 ounces) condensed cheese soup
¼ cup milk
1 teaspoon prepared mustard

Combine cheese soup and milk in small saucepan; stir in mustard until smooth. Heat to serving temperature. Makes 1½ cups.

HUSH PUPPY SANDWICHES

⅔ cup corn meal
⅔ cup cold water
1 teaspoon salt
1¾ cups boiling water
1 can (6½ or 7 ounces) tuna, drained
¼ cup chopped celery
½ cup grated sharp cheese
¼ cup sweet pickle relish
¼ cup mayonnaise
1 egg, well beaten
Packaged fine dry bread crumbs
Vegetable oil for frying

Combine corn meal and cold water. Add corn meal mixture and salt to rapidly boiling water. Cook over medium heat until corn meal is done (about 30 minutes). Turn into small loaf pan or a 2-cup square dish. Cool; chill until corn meal is firm. Flake tuna; add celery, cheese, pickle relish, and mayonnaise; mix well. When corn meal is solid, cut in 12 equal slices. Spread tuna mixture on 6 slices; cover with remaining slices to form sandwiches. Dip sandwiches first in egg, then in crumbs. Heat oil to depth of ½ inch in skillet. Fry sandwiches in hot oil until browned on both sides. Serve with tomato sauce, if desired. Makes 6 sandwiches.

GRILLED DEVILED SANDWICHES

1 large can (4½ ounces) deviled ham
⅓ cup grated sharp Cheddar cheese
Mayonnaise
8 slices white or whole wheat bread
Melted butter or margarine

Combine deviled ham and cheese with enough mayonnaise for easy spreading. Spread between bread slices. Brush sandwiches generously on both sides with melted butter. Grill until golden brown and crisp. Serve at once. Makes 4 sandwiches.

FRENCH TOAST SANDWICHES

   1 large can (4½ ounces) deviled ham
   2 tablespoons mayonnaise or salad dressing
   2 tablespoons chopped stuffed olives
   12 thin slices bread
   2 eggs
   1⅓ cups milk
   Few grains salt
   Butter or margarine

Combine deviled ham, mayonnaise or salad dressing, and chopped olives; mix thoroughly. Spread on 6 bread slices; top with remaining bread slices. Beat eggs; add milk and salt. Dip sandwiches in egg-and-milk mixture. Sauté in butter or margarine, turning once, until golden brown. Makes 6 sandwiches.

DEVILED SKILLET SANDWICHES

   1 large can (4½ ounces) deviled ham
   ½ cup finely diced celery
   ½ cup well-drained sweet pickle relish
   ¼ cup mayonnaise
   12 slices white bread
   2 eggs
   1 cup milk
   Butter or margarine

Mix together deviled ham, celery, relish, and mayonnaise. Spread on bread to make 6 closed sandwiches. Beat eggs slightly with milk. Dip each sandwich in egg mixture; brown on both sides in butter or margarine. Serve at once. Makes 6 sandwiches.

QUICK MEATWICHES

   Canned deviled ham or other meat spread
   8 slices bread
   1 egg
   ½ cup milk
   ⅛ teaspoon salt
   3 tablespoons butter or margarine

Allow about 2 tablespoons meat spread per sandwich. Spread 4 slices bread with desired meat spread; top each with second slice. Beat egg with fork in shallow dish; mix in milk and salt. Dip sandwiches in mixture; fry in butter on heavy griddle or skillet. Brown evenly on both sides. Makes 4 sandwiches.

DIPWICHES

   ¾ cup evaporated milk
   3 eggs, slightly beaten
   1 tablespoon prepared mustard
   1 tablespoon grated onion
   1½ teaspoons poppy seeds
   1 teaspoon salt
   1 can (12 ounces) luncheon meat
   1 package (8 ounces) sliced process Swiss
      cheese
   16 slices bread
   Butter or margarine

Combine first 6 ingredients. Cut luncheon meat in 16 crosswise slices. Place 1 slice cheese and 2 slices meat on each of 8 bread slices; top with remaining slices. Dip each sandwich in egg mixture. Brown on both sides in small amount butter or margarine. Makes 8 sandwiches.

GRILLED APPLE-CHEESE SANDWICHES

   1 cup grated sharp Cheddar cheese
   1 cup finely chopped apples
   ⅓ cup minced stuffed olives
   Mayonnaise
   8 thin slices white bread
   Melted butter or margarine

Combine cheese, apples, and olives with enough mayonnaise to hold ingredients together. Spread between slices of bread. Brush outside of sandwiches generously with melted butter; grill until golden brown on both sides. Serve hot. Makes 4 sandwiches.

GRILLED PEANUT BUTTER SANDWICHES

Spread 6 slices bread generously with peanut butter. Crumble crisp bacon over peanut butter; top with 6 slices of bread. Brush sandwiches on both sides with melted butter or margarine. Grill until golden brown on electric table grill or hot griddle. (Crunch-style peanut butter may be used, if desired.) Makes 6 sandwiches.

PICKLE 'N' HAM SALAD SANDWICHES

   1 cup ground or finely minced ham
   ¼ cup mayonnaise
   ¼ cup chopped sweet gherkins

½ cup minced celery
Pinch salt
Freshly ground pepper
8 slices buttered bread *or* 4 buttered
    frankfurter rolls

Combine ham, mayonnaise, gherkins, celery, salt, and pepper; stir until evenly blended. Spread on 4 slices of bread; top with remaining 4 slices. Or spread between halves of sliced frankfurter rolls. Makes 4 sandwiches.

TUNA NIÇOISE ROLLS

2 cans (6½ or 7 ounces each) tuna
1 cup diced cooked potatoes
1 cup drained cooked green beans
2 hard-cooked eggs, chopped
1 tomato, diced
¼ cup chopped green pepper
¼ cup chopped red onion
¼ cup chopped pitted ripe olives
6 anchovy fillets, chopped
Basil Vinaigrette Dressing*
10 large club rolls

Drain tuna; turn into large mixing bowl; break in small chunks. Add potatoes, green beans, eggs, tomato, green pepper, onion, olives, and anchovies. Mix gently but thoroughly. Pour Basil Vinaigrette Dressing over mixture; chill 1 hour. Cut a ¼-inch slice off the end of each roll. Scoop out inside. (Use crumbs in bread pudding, for stuffing, or for crumb topping.) Fill with tuna mixture, draining off any excess dressing. Pack mixture tightly into roll. Replace cut slice on end of each roll and secure with wooden picks. Makes 10 stuffed rolls.

*BASIL VINAIGRETTE DRESSING

¼ cup white wine vinegar
½ cup vegetable oil
½ teaspoon salt
¼ teaspoon hot-pepper sauce
½ teaspoon dried leaf basil

Combine all ingredients; beat until thoroughly blended. Makes ¾ cup.

ZESTWICHES

1 can (12 ounces) luncheon meat
3 tablespoons mayonnaise
2 tablespoons drained pickle relish
1 tablespoon prepared mustard
½ cup minced celery
6 slices each white and whole wheat bread,
    trimmed
Garnish: dill pickle strips

Chop luncheon meat fine; combine with remaining ingredients except bread. Make 3 sandwiches from each kind of bread. Cut in quarters diagonally. Arrange 4 triangles pinwheel-fashion on each plate; garnish with dill pickle strips. Makes 6 sandwiches.

DEVILED-SWISS ROLLS

4 frankfurter rolls
½-pound package (8 slices) Swiss cheese at
    room temperature
1 can (2¼ ounces) deviled ham
Dill pickles, cut in 8 narrow strips
Prepared mustard
Butter or margarine

Split frankfurter rolls, but do not cut all the way through. Cut rolls in half crosswise to make 8 half rolls. Spread cheese slices with deviled ham. Place pickle strip at one end of slice; roll up as firmly as possible. Spread inner cut surfaces of halved frankfurter rolls with mustard and butter or margarine; press a cheese-ham roll in each. Makes 8 sandwiches.

SAVORY BROWN BREAD SANDWICHES

2 jars (5 ounces each) pimiento-cheese spread
1 tablespoon prepared horseradish
Few drops hot-pepper sauce
⅓ cup finely chopped stuffed olives
3 cans Boston brown bread with raisins

Combine first 4 ingredients. Spread between slices of brown bread. Makes about 16 sandwiches.

PEANUT-BUTTER-RAISIN SANDWICHES

¼ cup raisins or currants
1 package (3 ounces) cream cheese
¼ cup chunky peanut butter
1 tablespoon honey
12 slices bread
Butter or margarine

Soak raisins in hot water 15 minutes; drain; chop fine. Combine cream cheese, peanut butter, and honey; add raisins; mix thoroughly. Spread mixture on 6 slices buttered bread; top with remaining 6 slices. Trim crusts; cut in triangles or fingers.

PICNIC CHIVE-MAYONNAISE SANDWICHES

Add a generous amount of chopped chives, fresh or freeze-dried, to mayonnaise. Spread between thin slices of white and whole wheat bread. Picnickers can add slices of ham or tomatoes if they wish.

MR. MAC TAVISH SANDWICH

¼ pound ground beef
2 slices white sandwich bread
2 teaspoons softened butter or margarine
1 teaspoon grated Parmesan cheese
½ cup Welsh rabbit
1 strip crisp bacon
Garnish: parsley

Shape ground beef into a square patty; grill to desired degree of doneness. Toast bread. Mix butter and Parmesan cheese. Spread on toast. Place patty on one slice of toast; cut remaining slice in half on the diagonal and place on either side of patty. Top with hot Welsh rabbit and bacon. Garnish with parsley. Makes 1 open-face sandwich.

ACCOMPANIMENTS: French fried onion rings and tomato slices.

HOT HASH SANDWICHES

¼ cup minced onion
2 tablespoons butter or margarine
2 cans (15½ ounces each) corned-beef hash
¼ cup tomato catchup
12 slices bread
1 cup shredded sharp Cheddar cheese

Sauté onion in skillet in melted butter or margarine until lightly browned. Add corned-beef hash and catchup. Cook 5 minutes. Toast bread lightly. Heap bread slices with hash mixture. Top with shredded cheese; broil until cheese melts. Makes 12 open-face sandwiches.

OPEN-FACE APPLE SANDWICHES

6 slices white sandwich bread
Mayonnaise
Mustard

6 slices cooked ham
3 to 4 apples
12 slices (1 ounce each) process American cheese

Spread bread slices with mayonnaise, then with mustard. Top with ham slices. Core apples; do not peel; slice crosswise about ⅛ inch thick to make 18 slices. Place 3 apple slices on each sandwich. Top each sandwich with 2 cheese slices. Broil under medium heat until cheese melts and browns slightly. Serve at once. Makes 6 open-face sandwiches.

BROILED LUNCHEON SANDWICHES

4 thin slices baked ham
4 slices white bread
24 to 32 stalks cooked green asparagus
Salt and pepper
4 slices process Cheddar cheese
4 poached or fried eggs

Place 1 slice ham on each slice bread. Top with 6 to 8 short asparagus spears; sprinkle with salt and pepper. Cover with cheese slices. Broil 3 to 4 inches from source of heat about 3 to 5 minutes or until cheese is melted and golden brown. Top each with poached or fried egg. Makes 4 open-face sandwiches.

OL' NUMBER 7

4 slices bread
4 generous slices white meat of chicken or turkey
4 slices packaged natural Swiss cheese
8 slices tomato
Crisp shredded lettuce
2 hard-cooked eggs, sliced
1 cup mayonnaise
2 tablespoons chili sauce
1 jar or can (4 ounces) pimientos, chopped fine
4 rolled anchovy fillets

On each slice of bread, place a slice of chicken or turkey, then a slice of cheese and 2 slices of tomato. Heap the lettuce high over surface; add the egg slices. Combine mayonnaise, chili sauce, and pimientos; pour lavishly over all. Top with anchovy. Makes 4 open-face sandwiches.

SNACKS FOR EVENING

8 English muffins
Mustard Butter*
½ pound sliced Canadian bacon (16 slices)
½ pound mozzarella cheese (16 slices)
Pickles
Olives

Split muffins crosswise; spread each half with Mustard Butter; top each with 1 slice bacon and 1 slice cheese. Broil with surface of food 5 inches below source of heat about 5 minutes or until cheese melts and browns lightly. Garnish with pickles and olives. Makes 16 open-face Snacks.
ACCOMPANIMENT: Hot tomato soup.

FOR A LUNCHEON OR SUPPER MAIN DISH

1 can (6 ounces) broiled sliced mushrooms
2 tablespoons butter or margarine
1 tablespoon catchup
¼ cup cream

Drain mushrooms; reserve broth. Heat mushrooms in butter or margarine. Add 2 tablespoons reserved broth and remaining ingredients; mix well. Spoon over 8 Snacks.

OR

¼ cup butter or margarine
¼ cup flour
1 can (1 pound) tiny peas
1 large can (1⅔ cups) evaporated milk

Melt butter; blend in flour. Drain peas, reserving liquid. Combine ⅓ cup reserved liquid with evaporated milk; add to butter-flour mixture. Stir over low heat until thickened. Add peas; heat. Serve over 8 Snacks.

*MUSTARD BUTTER

Cream together ½ cup butter or margarine and ¼ cup prepared mustard.

HOT TUNA SANDWICHES

8 strips of bacon
2 cans (6½ or 7 ounces each) tuna, drained
½ cup chopped ripe olives
Mayonnaise
2 packages corn bread rounds (12 in all)
6 tablespoons grated sharp Cheddar cheese

Cook bacon crisp; crumble. Flake tuna and combine with bacon and olives. Add enough mayonnaise to hold ingredients together. Toast 6 rounds of corn bread. Heap tuna mixture on the toasted rounds; sprinkle with cheese. Broil until cheese melts. Toast remaining rounds and cut in half. Place on plate with tuna-topped round, to be used as "cover" or eaten separately. Makes 6 hearty open-face sandwiches.

OPEN-FACE CURRIED SHRIMP SANDWICHES

2 cans (5 ounces each) peeled, deveined shrimp
½ teaspoon curry powder
⅛ teaspoon powdered ginger
½ cup mayonnaise
2 tablespoons drained minced chutney
Pumpernickel rounds, 2 inches diameter
Garnish: sliced small stuffed olives

Drain shrimp; mash with fork; blend in spices, mayonnaise, and chutney. Spread on pumpernickel rounds. Garnish with sliced stuffed olives. Makes about 1⅔ cups shrimp mixture, enough for 8 open-face sandwiches.

SNOWCAP CIRCLES

2 hamburger buns
1 can (2¼ ounces) deviled ham
2 small tomatoes
½ cup dairy sour cream
Garnish: chopped parsley or cut chives, fresh or freeze-dried

Split buns; spread cut surfaces with deviled ham. Slice tomatoes thin; arrange on ham. Top with sour cream. Broil until cream "crackles." Sprinkle with parsley or chives. Makes 2 open-face servings.

BOSTON SPECIALS

3 slices white bread
1 can (2¼ ounces) deviled ham
1 small can (13 ounces) brick-oven baked beans
3 slices process American cheese

Spread bread slices generously with deviled ham. Drain beans; spread beans over deviled ham. Top with cheese slices. Broil until cheese bubbles and browns. Makes 3 open-face sandwiches.

HAM SAVORIES

10 slices fresh white bread
1 can (12 ounces) luncheon meat
6 tablespoons mayonnaise
4 tablespoons pickle relish

Trim crusts from bread slices. Press each slice into greased muffin pan section to form a cup. Chop luncheon meat coarsely; combine with mayonnaise and drained pickle relish. Mix well. Fill bread cups with pickle mixture. Bake at 400° for 10 to 15 minutes or until toasted. Serve hot. Makes 10 servings.

PATIO SANDWICHES

8 slices white bread
8 slices American Cheddar cheese
1 can or jar (1 pound) applesauce, heated
16 strips (about 1 pound) crisply cooked bacon

Toast bread on one side. Place cheese slices on untoasted side. Broil until cheese melts and browns. Top with hot applesauce and bacon strips. Serve at once. Makes 8 open-face sandwiches.

HAM 'N' CHEESE BURGERS

Hamburger buns
Mustard
Ham salad
Sliced American Cheddar cheese
Chopped walnut meats

Halve hamburger buns; spread with mustard. Top with ham salad; add slice of cheese. Sprinkle with walnuts. Broil until cheese is golden brown and bubbly. Serve at once.

CHEESE SOUFFLÉ SANDWICHES

1 package (10 ounces) corn bread mix
3 eggs, separated
1 tablespoon minced pimiento
1 cup grated sharp Cheddar cheese

Prepare corn bread mix as directed on package. Bake in 8-inch square pan. While still warm cut in 6 oblong pieces. Split each oblong in half. Beat egg whites until stiff but not dry. Beat egg yolks until thick and lemon-colored. Fold yolks into whites. Combine pimiento and cheese; fold into egg mixture. Top each piece of corn bread with soufflé mixture. Broil with surface of food about 3 inches from heat for 3 to 4 minutes or until topping is puffed and delicately browned. Serve at once. Makes 12 open-face sandwiches, or 6 servings.

BOSTON PÂTÉ SANDWICHES

1 can (1 pound) pork and beans with tomato sauce
1 tablespoon each minced onion, chili sauce, and mayonnaise
¼ teaspoon hot-pepper sauce
½ teaspoon seasoned salt
Dash bitters
Canned brown bread

Drain beans; put through food mill or sieve or mash in electric blender. Add remaining ingredients except brown bread; mix well. Heat. Heap on rounds of toasted brown bread. Makes 4 open-face sandwiches.

DOUBLE-DECKERS

Butter or margarine (optional)
6 slices whole wheat bread
6 slices white bread
Chicken Filling*
Ham Filling**

Lightly butter bread slices, if desired. Use 3 bread slices and 2 fillings for each sandwich. Cut each sandwich in half diagonally. For 2 of the sandwiches, start with brown bread and end with brown. For remaining 2, reverse procedure. Place halves together to make a brown-and-white-topped sandwich. Makes 4 sandwiches.

*CHICKEN FILLING

1 tablespoon lemon juice
¼ teaspoon salt
⅛ teaspoon hot-pepper sauce
¼ cup mayonnaise
1 cup ground cooked chicken
½ cup finely diced celery

Add lemon juice, salt, and hot-pepper sauce to mayonnaise; mix well. Put chicken and celery in mixing bowl; add mayonnaise mixture and toss lightly.

**HAM FILLING

2 cans (4½ ounces each) ham or tongue spread
1 package (3 ounces) cream cheese
2 teaspoons prepared mustard
2 tablespoons finely diced pickle

Combine all ingredients; beat until blended.

CLUB SANDWICH

2 tablespoons mayonnaise, divided
3 slices toast
Heart leaves of lettuce
Sliced chicken
Salt and pepper
Tomato slices
2 crisp bacon strips

Spread 1 tablespoon mayonnaise on 1 slice toast; top with lettuce and chicken; sprinkle with salt and pepper; add second slice of toast, tomato, salt and pepper, bacon, and lettuce. Spread remaining slice of toast with remaining mayonnaise; place on top, mayonnaise side down. Serve at once. Makes 1 sandwich.

CLUBWICHES

1 can (6 ounces) boned chicken
Mayonnaise or salad dressing
12 slices bread, toasted
6 slices bacon, cooked and crumbled
1 can (12 ounces) luncheon meat
2 large ripe tomatoes, sliced
Garnish: small stuffed olives; sweet gherkins

Chop chicken; combine with enough mayonnaise to hold together. Spread on 4 slices toast; sprinkle with crumbled bacon; top with 4 slices toast spread with mayonnaise. Cut luncheon meat into 8 crosswise slices; place 2 on each sandwich; top with tomato slices. Spread remaining toast with mayonnaise; place mayonnaise side down on tomatoes. Cut each sandwich in half on diagonal. Garnish with small stuffed olives and sweet gherkins on wooden picks. Makes 4 sandwiches.

SKYSCRAPER SANDWICHES

⅓ cup butter or margarine
1 tablespoon chopped parsley
1 tablespoon chopped chives, fresh or freeze-dried

1 teaspoon prepared mustard
¼ teaspoon hot-pepper sauce
9 slices sandwich bread
1 large can (4½ ounces) deviled ham
2 slices Cheddar cheese, size of bread
1 can (4¾ ounces) liverwurst spread
1 can (4 ounces) sardines
1 tablespoon lemon juice

Cream together butter, parsley, chives, mustard, and hot-pepper sauce. Remove crusts from bread. Spread 1 slice bread with about 1 teaspoon of the creamed mixture; spread evenly with half of deviled ham. Spread second slice with teaspoon of creamed mixture; place creamed side down on deviled ham. Spread top of bread slice with creamed mixture; top with slice of cheese. Repeat with half of liverwurst spread, then half the sardines mashed with lemon juice. Then repeat fillings and bread slices spread with 1 teaspoon of creamed mixture. Put 4 skewers through corners of stacked bread slices. Chill. Cut through stack from top to bottom in two directions to make 4 sections, each held together with skewer. Makes 4 servings.

LITTLE HEROES

18 club rolls
Mustard
1 pound thinly sliced Canadian-style bacon
3 packages (6 ounces each) sliced process American cheese (18 slices in all)
2 cans (about 1 pound each) kidney beans, drained
1 large dill pickle, chopped
1 or 2 Spanish or Bermuda onions, thinly sliced
Melted butter or margarine

Cut each roll into 3 lengthwise slices. Spread bottom slice with mustard; top with 1 slice Canadian-style bacon, 1 slice cheese. (Fold or cut bacon and cheese slices in half, to fit roll.) Add middle slice of roll. Top with slightly mashed beans; sprinkle with chopped pickle; add sliced onion. Add top slice of roll. Brush with melted butter or margarine. Repeat for each roll. Heat at 425° for a few minutes, until cheese begins to melt. Makes 18 sandwiches.

HEROINE SANDWICHES

Use thin-sliced square-cut loaves of bread. Do not remove crusts. Make stacks, using 9 slices of bread and alternating fillings (3 of Avocado,* 3 of Walnut-Cheese,** and 2 of Crab Meat*** per stack). Wrap firmly in foil; chill thoroughly. Cut stack from corner to corner twice, to make 4 portions.

*AVOCADO FILLING

1 large ripe avocado, mashed
½ teaspoon lemon juice
Few drops hot-pepper sauce
2 tablespoons finely diced seeded cucumber
2 tablespoons finely chopped well-drained chutney

Combine all ingredients. Makes about 1¼ cups, or enough for 2 "stacks."

**WALNUT-CHEESE SPREAD

2 jars (5 ounces each) relish-cheese spread
2 tablespoons minced parsley
2 tablespoons finely chopped walnuts

Combine all ingredients. Makes about 1¼ cups, or enough for 2 "stacks."

***CRAB MEAT FILLING

1 can (6½ ounces) crab meat, drained
3 tablespoons minced celery
2 teaspoons cut chives, fresh or freeze-dried
Mayonnaise or salad dressing

Combine all ingredients, using enough mayonnaise to hold ingredients together. Makes about 1 cup, or enough for 2 "stacks."

A "YARD" OF TUNA HEROES

3 cans (6½ or 7 ounces each) tuna, drained
¾ cup minced celery
1½ teaspoons minced onion
¾ teaspoon salt
¼ teaspoon pepper
¾ cup mayonnaise
1 tablespoon lemon juice
3 12-inch loaves French bread
3 hard-cooked eggs, sliced
Catchup
Sliced stuffed olives
Gherkins
Radish slices

Combine tuna, celery, onion, salt, pepper, mayonnaise, and lemon juice; blend thoroughly. Cut

off both ends from 1 loaf of the bread and 1 end from remaining 2 loaves. Place cut ends together lengthwise to make a yard-long loaf. Split loaves. Spread bottom half with tuna mixture. Arrange egg slices over tuna. Spoon on catchup; top with olive slices. Cover with top half of bread. Cut in 6 or 9 pieces. Secure with wooden picks topped with gherkins and radish slices. Makes 6 to 9 sandwiches.

HOT HEROES

2 loaves brown 'n' serve French bread
3 cans (4 ounces each) sardines
½ pound packaged sliced American cheese
Prepared mustard
Garlic butter

Before browning in oven, cut loaves in half lengthwise. On cut surface of bottom halves, arrange a layer of sardines. Top with sliced cheese cut to fit. Spread generously with prepared mustard. Replace top halves. Brush with garlic butter. Bake as directed. Cut each loaf in thirds to serve. Makes 6 sandwiches.

BABY HEROES

12 soft dinner rolls
Sharp prepared mustard
12 slices liverwurst, ¼ inch thick
½ pound sliced Muenster cheese
2 cans (4 ounces each) pimientos

Cut dinner rolls in half lengthwise; spread cut surfaces with mustard. Top 12 halves with 1 slice liverwurst, slices of cheese cut to fit, and ½ pimiento. Top with remaining roll halves. Makes 12 sandwiches.

HOMEMADE HEROES

1 package (8 ounces) refrigerated buttermilk biscuits
Egg white
Sesame seed
Soft butter or margarine
¼ cup chili sauce
1 can (4¾ ounces) liverwurst spread
Green pepper slices
Bermuda onion slices

Separate package of biscuits in half. To form each loaf, stand 5 biscuits on edge on cookie sheet, press together lightly, flatten slightly, and taper ends. Brush tops and sides with egg white; sprinkle with sesame seeds. Bake at 375° for 15 to 20 minutes or until brown; cool. Slice each loaf in half lengthwise; spread with butter. For each loaf, spread both halves generously with chili sauce. Spread bottom half with liverwurst spread; top with green pepper and onion slices. Close with top half; slice each loaf in half crosswise. Makes 4 sandwiches.

KING-SIZE SANDWICH LOAF

1 loaf French bread
1 cup milk, scalded
1 pound ground beef
1 egg, slightly beaten
1 medium onion, minced
1½ teaspoons salt
¼ teaspoon hot-pepper sauce
1 tablespoon prepared mustard
2 teaspoons prepared horseradish
¼ cup catchup
1 teaspoon Worcestershire sauce
2 tablespoons each finely chopped green pepper and celery

Cut thin slice from top of French bread. Scoop out inside of loaf, leaving a firm shell. Soak 2 cups of scooped-out crumbs in hot milk 5 minutes. Add remaining ingredients to crumbs; mix well. Fill bread shell with this mixture, making top level with shell. Bake at 350° for 1 hour. Heat top slice and replace just before serving. Makes 6 servings.

ACCOMPANIMENT: Canned beef gravy or canned tomato sauce.

SAUCY SANDWICH LOAF

1 large unsliced loaf white bread
Soft butter or margarine
Ripe-Olive–Ham Filling*
Chopped Egg Filling**
Cheese Sauce***
Garnish: whole pitted ripe olives

Trim crusts from bread; cut loaf in 4 lengthwise slices. Spread 2 slices with butter and Ripe-Olive–Ham Filling. Spread third slice with butter and Chopped Egg Filling. Assemble spread slices alternating olive-ham and egg layers. Top with unspread slice of bread. Place on baking sheet; lightly brush top and sides of loaf with soft butter. Toast at 400° for about 10 minutes. Slice

crosswise in 6 pieces. Serve with Cheese Sauce. Garnish with whole pitted ripe olives. Makes 6 servings.

*RIPE-OLIVE–HAM FILLING

2 cups ground cooked ham
½ cup mayonnaise
⅔ cup canned pitted ripe olives, coarsely chopped

Combine all ingredients; mix well. Makes about 3 cups.

**CHOPPED EGG FILLING

3 hard-cooked eggs, chopped
1 teaspoon prepared mustard
¼ teaspoon salt
3 tablespoons mayonnaise

Combine all ingredients; mix well. Makes about 1 cup.

***CHEESE SAUCE

¼ cup butter or margarine
¼ cup flour
¾ teaspoon salt
1½ cups milk
½ teaspoon prepared mustard
1¼ cups grated sharp Cheddar cheese
2 tablespoons white wine

Melt butter or margarine; blend in flour and salt. Add milk. Cook, stirring, until mixture boils and thickens. Add remaining ingredients. Stir over low heat until cheese melts. Makes about 2½ cups, enough for 6 servings.

SUMPTUOUS SANDWICH LOAF

1 loaf (1 pound) sliced white bread (not thin sliced)
Deviled Ham Filling*
Tuna Filling**
Liverwurst Spread Filling***
2 large packages (8 ounces each) cream cheese
Pimiento strips
Parsley
Pitted ripe olives

Trim crusts from bread slices. Place 4 slices side by side on flat serving platter. Spread with Deviled Ham Filling. Place 4 more bread slices over ham filling; spread with Tuna Filling. Place 4 more bread slices over tuna; spread with Liverwurst Spread Filling. Top with remaining 4 bread slices. Place stacks close together on platter. Beat cream cheese until smooth and fluffy. Frost top and sides of loaf. Decorate with pimiento strips, parsley, and ripe olive slices. Chill. To serve, cut into 1½-inch slices. Makes 8 servings.

*DEVILED HAM FILLING

1 large can (4½ ounces) deviled ham
1 teaspoon prepared mustard
2 tablespoons finely chopped green pepper *or* drained pickle relish

Combine all ingredients; mix well. Makes about ¾ cup.

**TUNA FILLING

¼ cup mayonnaise
1 teaspoon minced onion
¼ teaspoon salt
1 can (6½ or 7 ounces) tuna, drained and chopped fine
¼ cup minced celery
2 tablespoons snipped parsley

Blend mayonnaise, onion, and salt. Add remaining ingredients; mix well. Makes about 1½ cups.

***LIVERWURST SPREAD FILLING

1 can (4¾ ounces) liverwurst spread
¼ cup mayonnaise
¼ cup finely chopped ripe olives

Combine liverwurst spread and mayonnaise; mix well. Stir in olives. Makes about ¾ cup.

SALAD-SANDWICH LOAF

Remove crusts from unsliced loaf of bread. Cut lengthwise in 5 slices. Put layers together with following fillings. Frost as directed. Chill. Slice crosswise to serve.

First Layer:

½ cup flaked salmon
2 tablespoons drained pickle relish
2 tablespoons minced celery
2 tablespoons mayonnaise

Combine all ingredients; mix well.

Second Layer:

½ cup creamed cottage cheese
1 tablespoon cut chives
2 tablespoons chopped stuffed olives
2 tablespoons cream

Combine all ingredients; mix well.

Third Layer:

2 hard-cooked eggs, chopped
¼ cup minced green pepper
¼ cup chili sauce

Combine all ingredients; mix well.

Fourth Layer:

1 large can (4½ ounces) deviled ham
2 tablespoons mayonnaise
¼ cup minced cucumber
1 tablespoon minced pimiento

Combine all ingredients; mix well.

Frosting:

¾ pound (12 ounces) cream cheese
1½ tablespoons mayonnaise
1½ tablespoons cream
Garnish: black olives; stuffed green olives; green pepper

Mash cream cheese; add mayonnaise and cream. Whip until fluffy. Spread on top and sides of loaf. Garnish with "flowers" made of black olive petals, stuffed olive centers, and green pepper stems. Makes 6 servings.

SANDWICH LOAF I

1 sandwich loaf unsliced white bread
King Crab Spread*
Egg Salad Spread**
Cheese-Olive Spread***
¾ pound (12 ounces) cream cheese
Cream
Garnish: sliced stuffed olives, pitted ripe olives, green pepper, cut in strips

Trim crusts from loaf unsliced bread. Cut loaf lengthwise in fourths. Cover with damp towel while preparing spreads. To assemble, spread King Crab Spread over one slice of bread; spread Egg Salad Spread over another slice of bread; spread Cheese-Olive Spread over a third slice of bread; stack the slices; top with fourth slice of bread. Soften cream cheese with cream to spreading consistency. Spread over sides and top of loaf. Garnish with sliced stuffed olives, pitted ripe olives, and strips of green pepper. Chill before serving. Slice crosswise to serve.

*KING CRAB SPREAD

1 can (7½ ounces) Alaska king crab *or* ½
    pound frozen Alaska king crab
4 ounces cream cheese
½ teaspoon celery salt

Drain and chop crab. Blend with cream cheese and celery salt. Chill.

**EGG SALAD SPREAD

4 hard-cooked eggs
¼ cup mayonnaise
1 tablespoon prepared mustard
¼ teaspoon salt
1 tablespoon snipped parsley

Sieve or chop eggs. Blend well with remaining ingredients. Chill.

***CHEESE-OLIVE SPREAD

1 jar (5 ounces) sharp Cheddar cheese spread
¼ cup chopped ripe olives
¼ cup diced pimiento

Combine all ingredients; blend well. Chill.

SANDWICH LOAF II

1 large loaf unsliced white bread
Egg-Celery-Anchovy Filling*
Tongue-and-Pickle Filling**
Chicken Filling***
1 pound cream cheese
½ cup whipping cream (about)
Garnish: sliced stuffed olives

Trim crusts from loaf; cut in fourths lengthwise. Form loaf with bread slice, then Egg-Celery-Anchovy Filling, bread, Tongue-and-Pickle Filling, bread, Chicken Filling, bread. Beat cream cheese until smooth. Add cream slowly while beating until mixture is fluffy and easy to spread. Frost loaf with cheese mixture. Garnish top with rosettes of cheese mixture and sliced stuffed olives. Makes 8 to 10 servings.

*EGG-CELERY-ANCHOVY FILLING

¾ cup finely chopped hard-cooked eggs (3)
¼ cup minced celery
1 tablespoon cut chives
3 anchovies, minced
2 tablespoons minced watercress
⅓ cup mayonnaise

Combine all ingredients; mix well.

**TONGUE-AND-PICKLE FILLING

¾ cup finely chopped cooked tongue
2 tablespoons minced sweet gherkins
1 tablespoon capers
1 tablespoon prepared mustard
⅓ cup mayonnaise

Combine all ingredients; mix well.

***CHICKEN FILLING

¾ cup finely chopped cooked chicken
2 tablespoons chopped toasted almonds
½ cup well-drained grated pineapple
1 tablespoon minced pimiento
½ cup mayonnaise

Combine all ingredients; mix well.

LUNCHEON SANDWICH LOAF

1 round loaf Italian bread (or homemade loaf
    casserole bread)
2 large packages (8 ounces each) cream
    cheese, divided
1 package (3 ounces) cream cheese
½ cup dairy sour cream
2 tablespoons chopped pitted ripe olives
2 tablespoons chopped stuffed olives
1 pound medium shrimp, cooked, shelled,
    and deveined
2 tablespoons finely chopped fresh dill
Mayonnaise
4 hard-cooked eggs, finely chopped
1 tablespoon anchovy paste
½ cup chopped watercress
Cream or milk
Garnish: sprays of fresh dill

Cut bread crosswise in 4 slices. Mash 1 package (8 ounces) cream cheese; combine with sour cream; beat until fluffy. Blend in ripe and stuffed olives. Set aside. Chop shrimp (save several whole shrimp for garnish); add dill and enough mayonnaise to make spreadable. Set aside. Combine eggs, anchovy paste, and watercress with enough mayonnaise to make spreadable. Assemble loaf, with shrimp spread on bottom slice, olive spread on second slice, egg spread on third slice. Top with fourth slice. Whip remaining cream cheese with enough cream or milk to make it fluffy. Spread over entire surface of loaf. Garnish with reserved whole shrimp and sprays of fresh dill. Cut in wedges to serve. Makes 10 servings.

RAINBOW SANDWICH LOAVES

Cut crusts from 30 thin slices of bread. Put 5 slices together with 4 fillings (below). Cut each stack in half. Continue until bread and fillings are used. Frost as directed. Makes 12 "loaves."

Filling I:

1 cup flaked crab meat
⅓ cup minced celery
¼ cup mayonnaise
1 teaspoon prepared mustard
Salt and pepper to taste

Combine all ingredients; mix well.

Filling II:

1 can (4½ ounces) deviled ham
¼ cup mayonnaise
¼ cup pickle relish, drained

Combine all ingredients; mix well.

Filling III:

3 hard-cooked eggs, chopped
2 tablespoons chopped ripe olives
1 teaspoon curry powder
Mayonnaise

Combine first 3 ingredients with enough mayonnaise to make of spreading consistency.

Filling IV:

1 jar (5 ounces) pimiento-cheese spread
1 small onion, grated
Few drops hot-pepper sauce

Combine all ingredients; mix well.

Frosting:

½ pound (8 ounces) cream cheese
1 tablespoon mayonnaise
1 tablespoon light cream
Garnish: ripe and stuffed olives; green pepper

Combine cream cheese with mayonnaise and cream; whip until fluffy. Frost top and sides of each "loaf." Garnish with olive and green pepper "flowers."

SPIEDANO ROMANO

1 loaf unsliced white bread
½ cup butter or margarine
¼ cup finely minced or grated onion
¼ cup prepared mustard
1 tablespoon poppy seeds
½ pound sliced process Swiss cheese
2 or 3 slices bacon, cut in half

Remove all crusts from bread. Make regularly spaced diagonal cuts about 1½ inches apart, but do not cut completely through loaf. Soften butter; blend in onion, mustard, and poppy seeds. Spread all but 2 tablespoons of mixture between cuts. Fill cuts with slices of cheese. Press loaf together. Spread outside and over top with reserved butter mixture. Arrange bacon on top. Place in greased shallow baking dish. Bake at 350° until cheese is melted and loaf is browned (about 15 minutes). Serve at once. Makes 4 to 6 servings.

RIBBON SANDWICHES

Spread softened butter or cream cheese between 1 whole wheat and 1 white bread slice, sandwich-fashion. Spread softened butter or cream cheese between 2 of these sandwiches, alternating white and whole wheat bread; press firmly together; trim off crusts; cut each block in half; wrap in waxed paper; chill. To serve, slice crosswise.

CHECKERBOARD SANDWICHES

Follow directions for Ribbon Sandwiches. After trimming the crusts, cut each block in 4 lengthwise strips. Stack 3 strips together with softened butter between so that light and dark breads alternate to form a checkerboard design. Wrap each block in waxed paper. Chill thoroughly. To serve, slice each block crosswise.

ASPARAGUS ROLLS

Use very thin sliced fresh bread; remove crusts. Spread slices with mustard or mayonnaise; roll each slice around an asparagus tip. Fasten with wooden picks. Place in shallow pan; cover with damp towel; chill. Remove picks before serving.

PINWHEELS

Cut thin, lengthwise slices from loaf of unsliced bread; trim off crusts. Tint softened cream cheese with pink or green food coloring. Spread cheese on bread slices. Roll up like a jelly roll. Wrap each roll in waxed paper. Chill. To serve, slice roll crosswise.

CORNUCOPIAS

Trim crusts from thin bread slices to form perfect squares. Spread with soft butter. Fold edges to form a cornucopia. Fasten with wooden picks. Place in shallow pan; cover with a damp towel. Chill. To serve, remove picks; insert spray of watercress.

"FINGER" SANDWICHES

Use thin-sliced bread, white and whole wheat, putting together one slice of each with any of the following fillings. Cut in small fancy shapes easy to eat with the fingers.

SARDINE FILLING

2 cans boneless sardines, undrained
4 tablespoons softened butter or margarine
2 tablespoons lemon juice
1 teaspoon Worcestershire sauce
2 teaspoons prepared mustard

Mash sardines; add remaining ingredients; mix thoroughly.

HAM FILLING

¼ pound cooked ham, ground
2 tablespoons mayonnaise
1½ teaspoons minced onion
1 tablespoon minced green pepper

Combine all ingredients; mix thoroughly.

EGG FILLING

2 hard-cooked eggs, minced
2 teaspoons minced pimiento
2 teaspoons minced green olives
1 tablespoon mayonnaise

Combine all ingredients; mix thoroughly.

FRANKFURTER FILLING

4 skinless frankfurters
1 tablespoon prepared mustard
1 tablespoon drained pickle relish

Put frankfurters through food chopper, using fine blade. Add remaining ingredients; mix thoroughly.

CHICKEN-CURRY SANDWICHES

1 can (13 ounces) boned chicken with broth, drained and diced
½ cup finely chopped peanuts
½ cup chopped fresh or canned peaches
¼ cup minced celery
½ teaspoon salt
¼ teaspoon pepper
2 teaspoons curry powder
2 tablespoons minced chutney
½ teaspoon lemon juice
½ cup mayonnaise
2 tablespoons dairy sour cream
Thin-sliced white bread
Garnish (optional): watercress; peach slices

Combine all ingredients except bread and garnish in a bowl. Chill in refrigerator about 1 hour to allow flavors to mingle. Trim crusts from 12 slices bread; spread with chicken mixture. Cut 12 circles from additional bread slices; place circles on chicken mixture. Garnish with watercress and peach slices, if desired. Makes 12 sandwiches.

ROLLED SANDWICHES

35 thin slices very fresh white bread
Curried Lobster Filling*
Pineapple Cream Filling**

Trim crusts from bread; flatten each slice with rolling pin. Spread 16 slices with Curried Lobster Filling; roll up tightly; place close together seam side down in tightly covered refrigerator dish; chill several hours. Spread remaining 19 slices with Pineapple Cream Filling; roll up and chill as above. Makes 35 sandwiches.

*CURRIED LOBSTER FILLING

1 can (5 ounces) lobster meat
⅓ cup finely minced celery
¼ teaspoon curry powder
Mayonnaise

Drain lobster meat; pick over, removing any bits of shell or cartilage; chop fine; combine with celery and curry powder. Add just enough mayonnaise to hold ingredients together.

°°PINEAPPLE CREAM FILLING

1 large package (8 ounces) cream cheese
⅓ cup drained crushed pineapple
2 teaspoons pineapple juice from can
1 teaspoon grated lemon peel

Mash cream cheese; beat until fluffy; beat in crushed pineapple, pineapple juice, and grated lemon peel.

RAINBOW SLICES

4 tablespoons drained sweet pickle relish
1 package (3 ounces) cream cheese
4 hard-cooked eggs, chopped
1 cup grated raw carrot
¼ teaspoon salt
6 club rolls

Combine pickle relish and cream cheese; blend well. Add eggs, carrot, and salt. Cut 6 club rolls in half lengthwise; hollow out center of half of each roll; fill hollows with pickle mixture. Put halves together firmly. Wrap each roll in waxed paper; chill 1 hour. Slice crosswise. Makes about 36.

STRAWBERRY PINWHEEL SANDWICHES

1 package (8 ounces) cream cheese
2 tablespoons whipping cream
¼ cup crushed sweetened strawberries
1 small loaf very fresh unsliced white bread

Mash cream cheese; add cream; beat until fluffy. Beat in strawberries. Trim crusts from bread; cut in 6 lengthwise slices. Run rolling pin over each slice to flatten. Spread each slice with cheese mixture. Roll up like jelly roll, from narrow end. Wrap each roll in foil; chill several hours. Slice crosswise about ½ inch thick. Makes about 48 sandwiches.

CHUTNEY PINWHEELS

1 large package (8 ounces) cream cheese
1 tablespoon chutney syrup
⅓ cup finely chopped chutney
1 loaf unsliced white bread

Mash cheese until soft; add syrup; beat until creamy; stir in chutney. Remove crusts from loaf of bread. Cut in 6 thin lengthwise slices. Spread each slice with cheese mixture; roll up like jelly roll. Wrap each roll in foil; chill thoroughly. Slice crosswise ¼ inch thick. Makes 3 to 4 dozen.

HOOTENANNY SANDWICHES

1 jar (12 ounces) peanut butter
½ pound cream cheese
1 large can (4½ ounces) deviled ham
½ cup well-drained sweet pickle relish
Sliced whole wheat and white bread

Combine first 4 ingredients; beat until well blended. Spread between bread slices. Makes enough filling for 15 sandwiches.

BUTTER-CRESS SANDWICHES

Watercress
1 cup butter or margarine
1 loaf fresh very thin sliced bread

Snip enough watercress with scissors to fill 1 cup (do not pack). Cream butter until soft and fluffy; add snipped cress. Trim crusts from bread slices; spread each slice with butter mixture. Roll up around a spray of watercress. Cover with foil; chill. Makes 2 dozen.

SNACK SANDWICHES

A loaf of sliced "party rye" bread makes up into tiny sandwiches just right for a snack. Try some of the fillings below.

CHEESE-WALNUT FILLING

1 jar (5 ounces) sharp cheese spread
2 tablespoons cream
⅓ cup chopped walnuts

Combine cheese spread and cream; beat smooth; stir in walnuts.

DEVILED HAM 'N' EGG FILLING

1 can (4½ ounces) deviled ham
1 hard-cooked egg, finely chopped
⅓ cup mayonnaise

Combine all ingredients; mix well.

PLANTATION RELISH FILLING

⅔ cup peanut butter
⅓ cup drained sweet pickle relish

Combine and mix thoroughly.

SUGGESTED SANDWICH FILLINGS

I

1 can (2¼ ounces) deviled ham
1 jar (5 ounces) pineapple-cheese spread

Combine deviled ham and cheese spread; mix well. Makes about ¾ cup.

II

1 can (3¾ ounces) salmon
2 tablespoons chopped celery
½ teaspoon Worcestershire sauce
2 tablespoons mayonnaise

Combine ingredients; mix well. Makes ½ cup.

III

1 package (3 ounces) cream cheese
2 tablespoons snipped dates
1 tablespoon chopped pecans
1 tablespoon honey

Combine all ingredients; mix well. Makes about ½ cup.

SHRIMP SAVORY FILLING

1 jar (5 ounces) pimiento-cheese spread
1 tablespoon chili sauce
1 can (5 ounces) shrimp

Combine pimiento-cheese spread and chili sauce. Drain shrimp; mash; add to first mixture; blend well. Makes about 1¼ cups.

CHICKEN BENGAL FILLING

1 cup minced cooked or canned chicken
3 tablespoons minced chutney
1 teaspoon curry powder
1 tablespoon mayonnaise

Combine all ingredients; blend thoroughly. Makes about 1¼ cups.

CHICKEN-CURRY SANDWICH FILLING

1½ cups chopped cooked or canned chicken
2 tablespoons finely chopped onion
½ cup chopped sweet mixed pickles
1 teaspoon curry powder
¼ cup mayonnaise
Salt and pepper to taste

Combine chicken, onion, and pickles; mix lightly. Blend curry powder and mayonnaise; add to chicken mixture; mix thoroughly. Season to taste with salt and pepper. Makes about 2 cups.

CORNED-BEEF-AND-CABBAGE SANDWICH FILLING

1 cup chopped cooked or canned corned beef
1 cup finely shredded cabbage
½ cup chopped dill pickles
2 tablespoons mayonnaise
2 teaspoons prepared horseradish
⅛ teaspoon pepper

Combine all ingredients; mix well. Makes about 2½ cups.

AFTERNOON TEA SANDWICH FILLINGS

Try any of the fillings that follow to perk up an afternoon teatime, or to perk up any time, for that matter!

DEVILED HAM FILLING

1 can (2¼ ounces) deviled ham
2 tablespoons dairy sour cream
1 tablespoon drained sweet pickle relish
¼ teaspoon Worcestershire sauce
Dash hot-pepper sauce

Combine all ingredients; mix well.

CALIFORNIA FILLING

1 package (3 ounces) cream cheese
2 tablespoons chopped ripe olives
2 teaspoons prepared horseradish
1 tablespoon catchup

Combine all ingredients; mix well.

SNAPPY FILLING

1 roll (3 ounces) snappy cheese
1 tablespoon mayonnaise
2 tablespoons finely chopped stuffed olives

Mash cheese; blend with mayonnaise; add olives; mix well.

APPLE-CHEESE SANDWICH FILLING

1 tablespoon butter or margarine
½ cup canned slivered roasted almonds
1 cup coarsely chopped apple
1 cup grated sharp Cheddar cheese
½ cup raisins
Mayonnaise

Melt butter or margarine; add almonds. Stir over low heat until golden brown; drain almonds on absorbent paper. Combine almonds, apple, cheese, and raisins with enough mayonnaise to hold ingredients together. Use as a filling for canned brown bread sandwiches. Makes about 2½ cups.

PIMIENTO-CHEESE FILLING

2 packages (3 ounces each) cream cheese
¼ cup minced pimientos
2 tablespoons minced ripe olives
Whipping cream

Mash cheese; add pimientos and olives; beat until fluffy, adding enough cream to make an easy spreading consistency. Makes about 1 cup.

CHAPTER 13

Sauces

PRESENTED IN this chapter is an exciting array of sauces to go with many different meals or desserts. There are some familiar old favorites, such as a Basic Cheese Sauce, and some new flavors to dress up a dish. Have fun with your imagination—try something new on tonight's dinner, or something wickedly sweet and gooey on the ice cream, and have yourself a special treat.

WHITE SAUCE

THIN:	2 tablespoons butter or margarine
	2 tablespoons all-purpose flour
	½ teaspoon salt
	⅛ teaspoon pepper
	2 cups milk

MEDIUM:	¼ cup butter or margarine
	¼ cup all-purpose flour
	½ teaspoon salt
	⅛ teaspoon pepper
	2 cups milk

THICK:	6 tablespoons butter or margarine
	6 tablespoons all-purpose flour
	½ teaspoon salt
	⅛ teaspoon pepper
	2 cups milk

Melt butter or margarine over low heat in medium-size, heavy saucepan. It should just melt—not bubble or turn brown. Stir flour, salt, and pepper quickly into melted butter. Cook, stirring constantly, just till it bubbles. Stir in milk slowly. (This helps to keep sauce from lumping.) Continue cooking and stirring until sauce thickens and bubbles, about 3 minutes. Makes 2 cups.

CUMBERLAND SAUCE

1 cup currant or other red jelly
1 tablespoon prepared mustard
1 teaspoon grated onion
⅛ teaspoon powdered ginger
Grated peel of 1 orange
Grated peel of 1 lemon
½ cup orange juice
2 tablespoons lemon juice
½ cup port
1½ tablespoons cornstarch

Combine jelly, mustard, onion, ginger, orange peel, lemon peel, orange juice, and lemon juice in a saucepan. Place over low heat, stirring, until jelly melts. Mix port with cornstarch and stir into jelly mixture. Cook over low heat, stirring constantly, until sauce bubbles and thickens. Serve warm or cold with sliced leftover ham or other meats. Makes 2 cups.

CRANBERRY GLAZE FOR HAM

Soften 1 envelope unflavored gelatin in ¼ cup cold water. Heat 1 can strained cranberry sauce; add to gelatin; stir until gelatin dissolves. Makes about 2 cups.

PEANUT-CURRY SAUCE

½ cup apple jelly
½ cup peanut butter
1 cup water
1 teaspoon brown-gravy seasoning sauce
1 teaspoon curry powder (or to taste)

Combine ingredients in saucepan; blend well. Bring to a boil. Simmer 5 minutes; serve hot. Serve with ham slice, baked or picnic ham, or smoked pork butt. Makes about 1 cup.

EAST INDIA CURRY SAUCE

¼ cup butter or margarine
¼ cup flour
2 to 3 teaspoons curry powder
1 teaspoon salt
Few grains pepper
1 cup milk
1 cup light cream

Melt butter or margarine. Combine flour, curry powder, salt, and pepper; blend into butter or margarine. Add milk and cream all at once. Cook over hot water, stirring constantly, until smooth and thickened. Cover; cook 5 minutes longer, stirring occasionally. Add ingredients for desired variation. Makes 4 servings.

Shrimp and Mushroom Curry Sauce: Combine 3 cups cooked or canned shrimp and 1 cup sliced sautéed mushrooms with curry sauce. Heat thoroughly.

Lamb Curry Sauce: Substitute lamb stock or thin lamb gravy for milk in recipe for curry sauce. Combine 3 cups cubed cooked lamb and 1 cup cooked or canned peas with sauce. Heat thoroughly.

Chicken Curry Sauce: Substitute chicken broth or thin chicken gravy for milk in recipe for curry sauce. Combine 3 cups cubed cooked chicken and ½ cup sliced salted almonds with sauce. Heat well.

BASIC CHEESE SAUCE

1 cup evaporated milk
½ teaspoon salt
1 tablespoon prepared mustard
2 cups (8 ounces) grated process American cheese

Heat evaporated milk in saucepan over low heat. Add salt, mustard, and grated cheese; heat, stirring until cheese is melted. Makes 2 cups.

Spring Special: Add 1 can (4 ounces) pimiento, diced, to Basic Cheese Sauce. Serve with cooked asparagus spears.

Olive Spectacular: Add ½ cup chopped stuffed olives to Basic Cheese Sauce. Serve with deviled eggs.

All-American Special: Add 1 can (3 or 4 ounces) sliced mushrooms, drained, to Basic Cheese Sauce. Serve with grilled tomatoes and bacon on toast.

ITALIAN MUSHROOM SAUCE
(For frozen cooked breaded sea scallops, thawed and heated.)

1 can (8 ounces) tomato sauce
3 tablespoons wine vinegar
½ teaspoon oregano
1 garlic clove, minced
⅛ teaspoon pepper
¼ teaspoon salt
2 cans (3 or 4 ounces each) sliced or button mushrooms, drained

Combine tomato sauce with rest of the ingredients. Marinate 1 hour. Makes about 2 cups.

CRANBERRY-LEMON SAUCE

2 cups sugar
1 cup water
4 cups fresh cranberries
1 lemon, juice and grated peel

Combine sugar and water in saucepan; stir over low heat until sugar dissolves. Add cranberries; cook over medium heat until skins pop; remove from heat; add lemon juice and grated peel. Chill. Makes about 1 quart.

NEVER-FAIL HOLLANDAISE SAUCE

3 egg yolks
2 tablespoons lemon juice

¼ teaspoon each salt, sugar, dry mustard, and
hot-pepper sauce
½ cup very cold butter or margarine

Beat together egg yolks, lemon juice, and seasonings in top of double boiler. Divide butter in 3 equal portions. Add one portion of butter to the egg mixture. Cook over hot water, stirring constantly, until butter is melted. Add second portion of butter, and when this is melted, repeat with third portion, stirring constantly as butter melts and sauce thickens. Remove from heat. Serve hot or at room temperature. Leftover sauce may be kept in refrigerator. Makes 4 servings.

MOCK HOLLANDAISE SAUCE

2 tablespoons butter or margarine
4 tablespoons flour
1 cup water
¾ teaspoon salt
⅛ teaspoon white pepper
2 eggs, beaten
2½ tablespoons strained lemon juice
Dash cayenne

Melt butter or margarine; blend well with flour; add water gradually, stirring constantly until mixture thickens. Add salt and pepper. Remove from heat. Pour slowly on beaten eggs; beat well. Cook 1 minute. Stir in lemon juice and cayenne. Makes 6 servings.

PEPPERY ONION BUTTER

1 tablespoon finely chopped green pepper
1 tablespoon finely chopped parsley
1 tablespoon finely chopped onion
½ cup butter or margarine

Blend all ingredients together. Makes ½ cup.

MUSHROOM-MEAT SAUCE

2 medium onions, chopped
3 tablespoons vegetable oil
1 can (6 ounces) broiled sliced mushrooms
1 pound lean beef, ground
2 cups bouillon
1 can (8 ounces) tomato sauce
3 tablespoons flour
6 tablespoons water
1 teaspoon salt
⅛ teaspoon pepper
Dash cayenne

Cook onions in oil until soft. Add drained mushrooms; cook 5 minutes; push to one side of frying pan. Form meat into small balls; brown in frying pan. Add bouillon and tomato sauce. Blend flour and water; add; stir until slightly thickened. Season sauce well with salt, pepper, and cayenne. Makes 4 to 6 servings.

TOMATO-CELERY SAUCE

½ cup sliced onion
1 cup sliced celery
2 tablespoons vegetable oil
¼ teaspoon marjoram
½ teaspoon chili powder
Few grains pepper
1 can (8 ounces) tomato sauce

Cook onion and celery in oil until onion is soft. Add remaining ingredients; heat thoroughly. Makes about 2 cups.

FREEZE-AHEAD MEAT SAUCE

3 pounds ground beef
3 medium onions, chopped
2 garlic cloves, minced
2½ teaspoons salt
3 cans (1 pound each) tomatoes
3 cans (6 ounces each) tomato paste
1 can (6 ounces) broiled sliced mushrooms
1½ cups water
2 bay leaves
1 tablespoon oregano
1 tablespoon basil
½ teaspoon thyme
¼ teaspoon cinnamon
½ teaspoon hot-pepper sauce
⅓ cup chopped parsley

Break up ground beef in large kettle. Cook over medium heat, stirring frequently, until some fat collects. Add onion and garlic. Sprinkle with salt. Cook until meat is browned and onion and garlic are tender but not brown. Add remaining ingredients. Simmer 45 minutes to 1 hour, until sauce is thickened and flavors are blended. Remove bay leaves. Pack in pint or quart freezer containers, leaving ½- to 1-inch head space; store in freezer. Recipe makes 3 quarts.

QUICK MEAT SAUCE

1 garlic clove, minced
1 medium onion, chopped

2 tablespoons vegetable oil
1 pound lean beef, ground
1 can (8 ounces) tomato sauce
2 cans (6 ounces each) tomato paste
1 cup water
½ teaspoon sugar
1 can (3 ounces) chopped broiled mushrooms, drained
¼ teaspoon oregano

Brown garlic and onion lightly in oil. Add meat; stir with fork until brown. Add tomato sauce, tomato paste, water, and sugar. Simmer ½ hour. Add mushrooms and oregano; simmer 5 to 10 minutes longer. Makes 6 to 8 servings.

SAUSAGE-AND-CHEESE SPAGHETTI SAUCE

½ pound pork sausage meat
½ cup chopped onion
1 garlic clove, minced
½ cup chopped green pepper
½ cup sliced mushrooms, fresh or canned
2 cans (8 ounces each) tomato sauce
2 cups shredded sharp Cheddar cheese

Cook sausage, onion, garlic, green pepper, and mushrooms in a skillet until green pepper is tender. Drain off excess drippings. Add tomato sauce; simmer 15 minutes. Add cheese; stir until melted. Serve over hot spaghetti, sprinkled with shredded Parmesan cheese, if desired. Makes 6 servings.

WHITE CLAM SPAGHETTI SAUCE

¼ cup vegetable oil
¼ cup butter or margarine
1 or 2 garlic cloves, minced
½ cup water
½ cup chopped parsley
1 teaspoon salt
¼ teaspoon pepper
½ teaspoon oregano
1½ tablespoons flour
2 cans (8 ounces each) whole clams *or* 1 can (7 ounces) minced clams

Heat oil and butter in skillet. Add garlic; cook until lightly browned. Cool slightly. Add water slowly. Stir in parsley, salt, pepper, and oregano. Blend flour with enough clam broth to make a smooth paste; stir in. Add clams and clam broth; cook and stir over medium heat until slightly thickened. Makes about 3 cups.

Red Clam Spaghetti Sauce: Before adding flour and clams, stir in 2 cans (8 ounces each) tomato sauce; simmer 10 minutes. Continue as above.

HOT FUDGE SAUCE I

1 package (6 ounces) semisweet chocolate pieces
½ cup light corn syrup
¼ cup sugar
¼ cup milk
2 teaspoons butter or margarine
¼ teaspoon vanilla

Combine chocolate and corn syrup in top of double boiler. Cook over hot, not boiling, water, stirring occasionally, until chocolate is melted. Stir in remaining ingredients; mix until smooth. Serve warm or cold. Makes 1½ cups.

HOT FUDGE SAUCE II

1 small can (⅔ cup) evaporated milk
1 package (6 ounces) semisweet chocolate pieces

Combine evaporated milk and chocolate pieces in top of double boiler. Cook over hot water until chocolate is melted. Serve hot. Makes about 1 cup.

QUICK CARAMEL SAUCE

1 small can (⅔ cup) evaporated milk
½ pound vanilla caramels (about 30)

Combine evaporated milk and caramels in top of double boiler. Cook over hot water until caramels are melted. Serve warm or cold. Makes 1¼ cups.

PEANUT BUTTER SAUCE

1 small can (⅔ cup) evaporated milk
½ cup peanut butter
¼ cup light corn syrup

Add evaporated milk to peanut butter, a small amount at a time, blending until smooth. Stir in corn syrup. Makes 1⅓ cups.

CHOCOLATE SAUCE

1 package (6 ounces) semisweet chocolate pieces
¼ cup shortening

1 cup evaporated milk
⅛ teaspoon salt
1 teaspoon vanilla

Melt semisweet chocolate pieces and shortening over hot, not boiling, water. Gradually add evaporated milk, stirring until smooth. Remove from heat. Stir in salt and vanilla. Serve warm or cool over cake or ice cream. Makes 1⅔ cups.

Chocolate Marshmallow Sauce: Stir in 8 large marshmallows with evaporated milk. Stir until marshmallows dissolve.

Chocolate Mint Sauce: Substitute ⅛ teaspoon peppermint extract for vanilla.

Mocha Sauce: Blend 1 tablespoon instant coffee into melted chocolate mixture before adding evaporated milk.

CHOCOLATE SUNDAE SAUCE

1 package instant chocolate pudding
1 cup light corn syrup
¼ cup water

Stir pudding into corn syrup. Stir in water. Makes 1¼ cups.

COFFEE SUNDAE SAUCE

1 package instant vanilla pudding
1 cup light corn syrup
2 tablespoons instant coffee
3 tablespoons cream or evaporated milk

Stir pudding into corn syrup. Thoroughly dissolve coffee in cream or evaporated milk. Stir into syrup mixture. Makes 1¼ cups.

BUTTERNUT SUNDAE SAUCE

1 package instant butterscotch pudding
1 cup light corn syrup
¼ cup cream
½ cup broken walnut meats

Stir pudding into corn syrup. Stir in cream and walnut meats. Makes 1¼ cups.

COFFEE CARAMEL SAUCE

¾ cup firmly packed brown sugar
1 cup sugar
⅔ cup light corn syrup
4 tablespoons butter or margarine

⅛ teaspoon salt
⅓ cup cream
½ teaspoon vanilla
½ cup double-strength coffee

Combine sugars, corn syrup, butter or margarine, and salt in saucepan; cook, stirring, until sugar dissolves; cook without stirring to 236° or until a little syrup forms a soft ball when dropped in cold water. Cool slightly. Stir in cream and vanilla. Add coffee; mix well. Makes about 2 cups.
NOTE: This sauce thickens when chilled.

TAFFY SAUCE

½ cup butter or margarine
½ cup sugar
½ cup light molasses
½ cup evaporated milk
1 teaspoon vanilla

Melt butter in saucepan; add sugar and molasses. Bring to a full rolling boil; reduce heat; boil 2 minutes, stirring constantly. Remove from heat; stir in evaporated milk and vanilla. Serve warm or cool over cake or ice cream. Makes 1⅔ cups.

Taffy Peanut Sauce: Stir in ½ cup salted peanuts with evaporated milk and vanilla.

Taffy Sauce Hawaiian: Omit vanilla; add one 9-ounce can (1 cup) crushed pineapple, thoroughly drained. Sprinkle with flaked coconut, if desired.

Taffy Rum Sauce: Add 1 teaspoon rum flavoring (or to taste) instead of vanilla.

MARSHMALLOW SAUCE

½ cup light corn syrup
½ cup sugar
¼ cup water
⅛ teaspoon salt
1 egg white
1 teaspoon vanilla

Combine first 3 ingredients in saucepan. Cook and stir over low heat until sugar is dissolved. Cook over medium heat to 234° or until a small amount dropped in cold water forms a soft ball. Add salt to egg white; beat until stiff but not dry. Pour sugar syrup slowly into egg white, beating constantly, until thick and glossy. Beat in vanilla. Serve warm or cold. Makes 2 cups.

MARSHMALLOW-MINT SAUCE

½ cup sugar
¼ cup water
8 marshmallows, cut in small pieces
1 egg white, stiffly beaten
⅛ to ¼ teaspoon peppermint extract

Boil sugar and water until they make a thin syrup, or to temperature of 230° (syrup will not be thick enough to spin a thread). Remove from heat; add marshmallows; let stand 2 minutes or until marshmallows are melted, pressing them under syrup. Pour syrup slowly over egg white, beating constantly, until mixture is cool. Add peppermint extract to taste. Makes 1 cup.

CREAMY CINNAMON SAUCE

½ cup light corn syrup
1 cup sugar
¼ cup water
1 teaspoon cinnamon
½ cup evaporated milk

Combine corn syrup, sugar, water, and cinnamon in saucepan. Bring to full boil over medium heat, stirring constantly. Stir and boil 2 minutes. Cool 5 minutes. Stir in evaporated milk. Serve warm or chilled. Makes about 1⅔ cups.

Ginger Sauce: Use 1½ teaspoons powdered ginger in place of cinnamon.

Nutmeg Sauce: Use 1 teaspoon nutmeg in place of cinnamon.

MARMALADE SAUCE

2 tablespoons lemon juice
1 cup orange marmalade
1½ tablespoons cornstarch
1 cup cold water
1 banana, thinly sliced

Combine lemon juice and marmalade. Dissolve cornstarch in cold water; add. Cook over low heat, stirring constantly, until thickened and clear. Simmer 10 minutes longer. Remove from heat; add banana slices; cool. Makes about 2 cups.

CHERRY SAUCE I

1 can (1 pound) pitted sour red cherries
Water

½ cup sugar
¼ teaspoon salt
4 teaspoons cornstarch
2 teaspoons butter or margarine
½ teaspoon almond extract
Red food coloring (optional)

Drain cherries; measure liquid; add enough water to make 1½ cups. Combine sugar, salt, and cornstarch; blend in liquid gradually. Cook and stir over low heat until mixture comes to a boil. Add cherries, butter, and almond extract. If desired, add a few drops red food coloring. Serve warm or cold. Makes about 2 cups.

CHERRY SAUCE II

1 can (1 pound) pitted sour red cherries
    (packed in water)
½ cup sugar
1 tablespoon cornstarch
¼ teaspoon salt
Red food coloring
1½ teaspoons lemon juice
¼ teaspoon almond extract

Drain cherries; measure liquid; add enough water to make 1⅓ cups. Mix together sugar, cornstarch, and salt in saucepan; gradually stir in cherry liquid. Cook over low heat, stirring constantly, until mixture comes to a boil; boil 1 minute. Remove from heat. Stir in a few drops red food coloring. Add cherries, lemon juice, and almond extract. Mix well. Makes about 2½ cups.

PINEAPPLE-COCONUT SAUCE

½ cup sugar
⅛ teaspoon salt
1 tablespoon cornstarch
1 can (8 ounces) crushed pineapple
2 tablespoons butter or margarine
½ teaspoon nutmeg
½ cup flaked coconut

Combine sugar, salt, and cornstarch in saucepan. Blend pineapple into dry ingredients slowly. Bring to boil, stirring constantly; simmer, stirring often, until slightly thickened and clear (about 10 minutes). Add butter and nutmeg. Serve warm, topped with coconut. Makes about 2 cups.

CHAPTER 14

Breads

YEAST BREADS

Bread is more than just another form of food. Down through the ages it has come to symbolize security, hospitality, warmth, friendship, comfort, pleasure—even life itself.

Today bread takes its place, along with cereals, in one of the four basic food groups needed every day for sound nutrition and good health. The market abounds with breads of all kinds—good, healthful enriched breads that are flavorful and nutritious.

When there is time, and you are in the mood for baking, there is great fun and satisfaction in baking bread yourself. Turning out a handsome loaf of bread is not difficult if a few basic rules are followed.

Be sure the *yeast* you use is fresh, whether it is active dry yeast or compressed (fresh) yeast. Look for the expiration date on the back of the package of dry yeast. Keep compressed yeast in the refrigerator and use it soon after purchase. It will keep for several months if placed in the freezer, but after defrosting at room temperature it must be used immediately. Dry yeast does not need refrigeration—just store it on any cool, dry shelf.

Use all-purpose *flour*. Select a brand that is known from coast to coast for its quality—a standardized quality that never varies. The gluten in wheat flour forms an elastic framework that holds the gas bubbles formed by the yeast. Flours with the highest gluten content produce breads with the biggest volume. Whole wheat flour has less gluten than white flour; therefore, loaves made entirely with whole wheat flour are heavier and smaller. Rice and soy flour do not contain any gluten and must be combined with wheat flour in making bread.

Liquids must be at the proper temperature (see recipes).

Use *standard level measures* and *pans* of correct size.

Strong *beating* makes gluten form faster. This is especially important for batter breads that are not kneaded. These breads call for a step called "stirring down"—the raised dough is stirred until it is almost back to its original size.

Kneading: This is an important technique. Use a board or flat surface dusted with a little flour and rub some flour on your hands. Form the dough into a round ball. Fold it toward you. Push dough away with a rolling motion, using the heels of your hands. Turn dough one quarter turn. Repeat until dough is smooth and elastic (8 to 10 minutes). If necessary, sprinkle more flour under dough and on your hands.

Rising: Shape kneaded dough into a ball; place in greased bowl; turn over so greased side is up. Cover bowl. Set in a warm place (80° to 85°) until dough doubles in size. To test, press tips of two fingers lightly ½ inch into dough. If dent remains, dough has doubled.

Punching down: Push fist into center of dough. Pull edges of dough to center and turn dough over.

Shaping loaves: For each loaf, roll dough into a rectangle. Beginning with upper short side, roll toward you. Seal with thumbs. Seal ends and fold under. Place seam side down in greased pan.

Second rising: Cover pan; let dough rise in warm place (80° to 85°) until doubled (see test, above, pressing near edge of loaf).

Test for doneness: When baking time is up, tap top of loaf. If it sounds hollow, the bread is done.

To cool: Remove from pan to rack. If desired, brush top with melted butter.

STREAMLINED WHITE BATTER BREAD

1 package active dry yeast
1¼ cups warm water (105° to 115°)
2 tablespoons soft shortening
2 teaspoons salt
2 tablespoons sugar
3 cups sifted all-purpose flour
Melted butter

Dissolve yeast in warm water. Add shortening, salt, sugar, and half the flour. Beat 2 minutes at medium speed on mixer or 300 vigorous strokes by hand. Scrape sides and bottom of bowl frequently. Add remaining flour; blend with spoon until smooth. Scrape batter from sides of bowl. Cover with cloth; let rise in warm place (85°) until double (about 30 minutes). Stir down batter by beating about 25 strokes. Spread batter evenly in greased 9 x 5 x 3-inch loaf pan. Batter will be sticky. Smooth out top of loaf by flouring hand and patting into shape. Let rise in warm place (85°) until batter reaches 1 inch from top of pan (about 40 minutes). Bake at 375° for 45 to 50 minutes or until brown. To test loaf, tap the top crust; it should sound hollow. Remove from pan to rack. Brush top with melted butter. Do not place in draft. Makes 1 loaf.

FRENCH BREAD

2½ cups warm water (105° to 115°)
1 tablespoon sugar
1 tablespoon salt
1 package active dry yeast
8½ cups sifted all-purpose flour
2 tablespoons soft shortening
Corn meal
½ cup water
½ teaspoon salt
1½ teaspoons cornstarch
Sesame seeds

Combine first 4 ingredients; stir to dissolve yeast; let stand 5 minutes. Stir in flour and shortening; then work flour in with hands. Knead until smooth and elastic. Cover; let rise in warm place (85°) until doubled. Shape into 3 balls. Let rest 15 minutes. Shape each ball into a roll 15 inches long, tapered at each end. Place on baking sheet liberally sprinkled with corn meal. Cover with towel; let rise until light. Meanwhile, combine water, ½ teaspoon salt, and cornstarch. Cook and stir until thickened and clear. Brush over loaves; sprinkle tops with sesame seeds. Make several diagonal gashes ½ inch deep in top of each loaf. Heat oven to 450°. Place a large pan of hot water on lower shelf. Place bread on upper shelf; bake 10 minutes. Reduce heat to 350°; bake 50 to 60 minutes longer. Cool on racks. Makes 3 loaves.

SOURDOUGH FRENCH BREAD

½ cup milk
1 cup water
1½ tablespoons vegetable oil
1 package active dry yeast
¼ cup warm water (105° to 115°)
4½ teaspoons sugar
2½ teaspoons salt
4¾ cups sifted all-purpose flour
2 tablespoons Starter Dough*
1 egg white
1 tablespoon cold water

Combine milk, water, and oil; bring to a boil; cool to lukewarm (95° to 100°). Sprinkle yeast on warm water; stir until dissolved; add with sugar and salt to cooled milk mixture. Place flour in large bowl; make a well in the center; pour milk mixture into well; add starter; stir until well blended. *Do not knead.* Dough will be soft. Place dough in greased bowl; cover; let stand in warm place (85°) until doubled in size. Turn onto lightly floured board. *Do not knead.* Divide into 2 even portions. Flatten each portion with palms of hands. For each portion, fold opposite sides toward center until they meet; fold in half lengthwise; press outward from center to make a tapered loaf 15 inches long and about 1¼ inches high. Place on baking sheet covered with heavy foil. (Pleat foil between loaves.) Make gashes about ⅛ inch deep diagonally along loaves, about 2 inches apart. Let rise, uncovered, in warm place (85°) until a little more than double in size. Bake at 425° for 15 minutes. Reduce heat to 350°; bake 15 to 20 minutes longer. Brush tops and sides with 1 egg white mixed with 1 tablespoon cold water. Bake 5 minutes longer. Cool on racks in a draft or in front of open window for a crackly-crisp crust. Makes 2 loaves.

*STARTER DOUGH

¼ cup milk
½ cup water
2 teaspoons vegetable oil
1 package active dry yeast
¼ cup warm water (105° to 115°)
2 teaspoons sugar
1¼ teaspoons salt
2⅓ cups sifted all-purpose flour

Combine milk, water, and oil; bring to a boil; cool to lukewarm (95° to 100°). Sprinkle yeast on warm water; stir until dissolved; add with sugar and salt to cooled mixture. Stir liquid into flour just enough to blend thoroughly. Cover; let stand in warm place 12 to 18 hours to sour.

NOTE: Remaining starter can be stored, covered, in refrigerator for several days, or, properly packaged, in a freezer for several weeks to be used as needed. Bring measured amount to room temperature before adding.

OLIVE-NUT FRENCH BREAD

2 packages active dry yeast
1¼ cups warm water (105° to 115°)
3 tablespoons soft shortening
2 tablespoons sugar
1½ teaspoons salt
1 cup chopped stuffed olives
¾ cup coarsely chopped walnuts
3½ cups all-purpose flour (about)
1 egg white
2 tablespoons water

Dissolve yeast in warm water. Stir in shortening, sugar, salt, olives, and walnuts. Mix in enough flour to make a dough that is easy to handle. Turn onto lightly floured board; knead until smooth. Round up; place in greased bowl; cover with cloth. Let rise in warm place (85°) until double (1½ to 2 hours). Punch down; let rise again until double (45 minutes). Punch down; cover; let rest 15 minutes. Divide dough in half. Shape each half into a long loaf with tapered ends. Place on lightly greased baking sheet. Make slashes 2 inches apart on tops of loaves. Let rise, uncovered, about 1 hour. Heat oven at 375°. Put pan of water in oven on top shelf 30 minutes before baking; leave the pan of water in oven during baking. Brush bread with cold water. Bake 20 minutes. Brush with mixture of 1 egg white and 2 tablespoons water. Return to oven and bake 25 minutes longer. Cool on racks. Makes 2 loaves.

WHEATEN HERB BREAD

2 packages active dry yeast
½ cup warm water (105° to 115°)
1¾ cups warm milk (105° to 115°)
2 tablespoons sugar
1 tablespoon salt
3 tablespoons butter or margarine, melted
5 to 5½ cups all-purpose flour
⅔ cup wheat germ
2 tablespoons minced parsley
1 tablespoon cut chives, fresh or freeze-dried
1 teaspoon sage
1 teaspoon basil
Vegetable oil
Melted butter or margarine

Rinse large mixing bowl in hot water. Dissolve yeast in warm water. Add milk, sugar, salt, and butter or margarine. Beat in 2 cups flour with rotary beater. Add 1 cup flour; beat vigorously with spoon 150 strokes. Stir in wheat germ, parsley, chives, and herbs. Add enough remaining flour gradually to make soft dough that leaves sides of bowl. Knead on lightly floured surface until smooth and springy (5 to 10 minutes). Cover; let dough rest 20 minutes. Punch down. Divide in half. Roll each half to uniform thickness. Shape each half into 8 x 12-inch rectangle. Beginning with upper 8-inch side, roll toward you; seal. Seal ends; fold under. Place seam side down in greased 8 x 4 x 3-inch loaf pans. Brush with oil. Cover loosely with oiled waxed paper and plastic wrap. Do not tuck paper under pans.

Refrigerate 2 to 24 hours (bread will rise well above top of pans). Remove. Uncover; let stand at room temperature 10 minutes. Prick any gas bubbles with oiled wooden pick. Bake at 400° for 30 to 40 minutes, until crust is deep brown and loaves sound hollow when tapped lightly. Remove from pans immediately. Brush with butter or margarine. Cool on racks before slicing. Makes 2 loaves.

FREEZER WHOLE WHEAT BREAD

1 cup milk
½ cup firmly packed light brown sugar
¼ cup sugar
2 tablespoons salt
½ cup butter or margarine
2¼ cups warm water (105° to 115°)
3 packages active dry yeast
3 cups unsifted whole wheat flour
7 to 8 cups unsifted white flour
Melted butter or margarine

Scald milk; stir in sugars, salt, and ½ cup butter. Stir until butter melts. Cool to lukewarm. Measure warm water into large bowl. Sprinkle in yeast; stir until dissolved. Add lukewarm milk mixture, whole wheat flour, and 1 cup white flour; beat until smooth. Stir in enough additional white flour to make a stiff dough. Turn out onto lightly floured surface; knead until smooth and elastic (about 12 minutes). Cover; let rest on board 15 minutes. Roll dough out into 18 x 12-inch rectangle. Cut in 3 equal pieces 6 x 12 inches each. Brush with melted butter. Stack dough on greased baking sheet brushed side up, placing plastic wrap between the pieces. Cover sheet tightly with plastic wrap; place in freezer. When frozen, separate pieces of dough and wrap each with plastic wrap. Keep frozen up to 4 weeks. Remove from freezer. Unwrap and place on ungreased baking sheets brushed side up. Cover; let stand at room temperature until fully thawed (about 2½ hours). Roll each piece to an 8 x 12-inch rectangle. Beginning at an 8-inch end, roll dough as for jelly roll. Pinch seam to seal. With seam side down, press down ends with heel of hand. Fold underneath. Place each, seam side down, in a greased loaf pan, 8 x 4 x 3 inches. Cover; let rise in warm place, free from draft, until doubled in bulk, about 2 hours and 15 minutes. Bake on lowest rack position at 375° for about 35 minutes or until done. Remove from pans; cool on racks. Makes 3 loaves.

WHOLE WHEAT BATTER BREAD

1 package active dry yeast
1¼ cups warm water (105° to 115°)
2 tablespoons honey, brown sugar, or molasses
1 cup unsifted whole wheat flour, divided
2 cups sifted all-purpose flour, divided
2 teaspoons salt
2 tablespoons soft shortening
Melted butter or margarine

In mixer bowl, dissolve yeast in warm water. Add honey, half of each kind of flour, salt, and shortening. Beat 2 minutes at medium speed on mixer or 300 vigorous strokes by hand. Scrape sides and bottom of bowl frequently. With spoon, blend in remaining flours until smooth. Cover; let rise in warm place (85°) until double (about 30 minutes). Stir down batter by beating about 25 strokes. Spread batter evenly in greased loaf pan, 9 x 5 x 3 inches. Batter will be sticky. Smooth out top of loaf by flouring hand and patting into shape. Let rise in warm place (85°) until batter reaches 1 inch from top of pan (about 40 minutes). Bake at 375° for 45 to 50 minutes or until brown. To test loaf, tap the top crust. It should sound hollow. Remove from pan immediately. Place on cooling rack or across bread pan. Brush top with melted butter or margarine. Do not place in direct draft. Cool before slicing. Makes 1 loaf.

3-WAY MOLASSES-OATMEAL BREAD

⅔ cup milk
1 cup rolled oats, quick or old-fashioned, uncooked
1¼ teaspoons salt
6 tablespoons shortening
½ cup light molasses
2 packages active dry yeast
⅔ cup warm water (105° to 115°)
2 tablespoons brown sugar
3 eggs, beaten
7 cups sifted all-purpose flour, divided

Scald milk and pour over oats in large mixing bowl. Add salt and shortening; stir until shortening is melted. Blend in molasses. Sprinkle yeast on warm water; add sugar and let stand 5 minutes. Stir and add to molasses-milk mixture. Add beaten eggs; mix well. Stir in 3 cups flour and beat until smooth. Stir in another 3 cups flour to make a smooth dough. Work in remaining flour, kneading dough until smooth and elastic. Place in oiled bowl. Turn once to bring oiled side up. Cover; let rise in a warm place (85°) until double in bulk (about 1½ hours). Divide dough in half. Use to make any desired combination of bread, pecan sticky buns, or pan rolls. Proceed as follows.

For a Loaf:

Roll half of basic recipe dough into a rectangle 9 x 7 inches. Fold each 7-inch end of the oblong into the center and overlap slightly. Seal dough by pinching center seam and ends. Place dough seam side down in a greased loaf pan, 9 x 5 x 3 inches. Let rise in a warm place until center is slightly higher than edge of pan. Bake at 350° for 45 minutes. Remove from pan; cool on rack. Makes 1 loaf.

For Pecan Sticky Buns:

5 tablespoons melted butter or margarine, divided
½ cup sugar, divided
1 teaspoon cinnamon
½ cup raisins
4 tablespoons light molasses
½ cup pecans

Roll half of basic recipe dough into a rectangle 11 x 16 inches. Brush top of dough with 1 tablespoon butter. Combine ¼ cup sugar, cinnamon, and raisins; sprinkle over dough. Roll up dough as for jelly roll, rolling from 16-inch side. Cut in 16 slices. Combine remaining butter and sugar; add molasses and pecans and divide between two 9-inch round pans. Place 8 slices cut side down in each pan. Let rise about 1½ hours or until double in bulk. Bake at 350° for 30 minutes. Remove from pans; cool on racks. Makes 16 buns.

For Pan Rolls:

Roll half of basic recipe dough about ½ inch thick. Cut with 2-inch round cutter into 32 rounds. Place in 2 greased 9-inch square pans. Let rise about 1½ hours, or until double in bulk. Bake at 350° for 25 minutes. Remove from pans; cool on racks. Makes 32 rolls.

OATMEAL BATTER BREAD

1 package active dry yeast
1¼ cups warm water (105° to 115°)
3 tablespoons sugar
1½ teaspoons salt
2 tablespoons soft shortening
2½ cups sifted all-purpose flour, divided
1 cup rolled oats, quick or old-fashioned, uncooked
½ cup golden seedless raisins

Dissolve yeast in warm water in mixing bowl. Add sugar, salt, and shortening; stir. Add 1 cup flour and oats. Beat 2 minutes with electric mixer at medium speed or 300 vigorous strokes by hand. Stir in remaining flour and raisins. Cover; let rise in warm place (85°) until double in size. Stir hard about ½ minute. Spread batter in greased loaf pan, 9 x 5 x 3 inches. Smooth top of loaf and pat into shape with floured hand. Cover; let rise until batter is 1 inch from top of pan. Bake at 375° for 45 minutes. Remove from pan. Brush with soft shortening. Cool on rack. Makes 1 loaf.

MOLASSES-BRAN BREAD

½ cup soft shortening
2 tablespoons sugar
⅓ cup light molasses
2 teaspoons salt
½ cup boiling water
½ cup whole bran
1 package active dry yeast
½ cup warm water (105° to 115°)
1 egg, beaten
4½ cups sifted all-purpose flour (about)

Combine shortening, sugar, molasses, salt, and boiling water; stir in bran; cool to lukewarm (90°). Sprinkle yeast on warm water; stir until dissolved; add with egg to bran mixture. Stir in enough flour to make a soft dough; mix well. Knead on well-floured board until smooth and elastic. Place in greased bowl; cover; let rise in warm place (85°) until double. Shape into loaf and place in greased loaf pan, 9 x 5 x 3 inches. Let rise again until double. Bake at 375° for 45 to 50 minutes. Remove from pan; cool on rack. Makes 1 loaf.

COTTAGE-STYLE ONION BREAD

¾ cup milk
1 envelope (1⅜ ounces) onion soup mix
½ cup sugar
½ cup soft butter or margarine
2 packages active dry yeast
½ cup warm water (105° to 115°)
1 egg, beaten

4 cups unsifted all-purpose flour
Melted butter or margarine

Scald milk. Stir in onion soup mix; blend well. Stir in sugar and butter, mixing until butter melts. Cool to lukewarm. Sprinkle yeast over warm water; stir to dissolve. Add lukewarm milk mixture, egg, and half the flour. Beat until smooth. Add remaining flour to make a stiff batter. Cover tightly; chill at least 2 hours. Cut dough in half. Flatten and press one portion evenly into well-greased 1½-quart casserole. Repeat with remaining dough. Brush with melted butter or margarine. Cover with clean towel. Let rise in warm place (85°), free from drafts, until doubled in size. Bake at 375° for about 35 minutes or until done (bread should sound hollow when tapped). Remove from casseroles to rack. Brush again with melted butter or margarine. Makes 2 loaves.

CORN MEAL BATTER BREAD

¾ cup boiling water
½ cup yellow corn meal
3 tablespoons soft shortening
¼ cup light molasses
2 teaspoons salt
1 package active dry yeast
¼ cup warm water (105° to 115°)
1 egg
2¾ cups sifted all-purpose flour

Combine first 5 ingredients in mixing bowl; mix well. Cool to lukewarm. Dissolve yeast in warm water. Add yeast, egg, and half the flour to lukewarm mixture. Beat 2 minutes with electric mixer at medium speed or 300 vigorous strokes by hand. Scrape sides and bottom of bowl frequently. Add rest of flour; mix with spoon until flour is thoroughly blended into dough. Cover; let rise in warm place (85°) until double in size (about 30 minutes). Stir hard about ½ minute. Spread batter evenly in greased loaf pan, 9 x 5 x 3 inches. Flour hands and smooth top of loaf. Cover; let rise until dough reaches to 1 inch from top of pan. Sprinkle top with a little corn meal and salt. Bake at 375° for 50 minutes. Remove from pan. Brush top with soft shortening. Makes 1 loaf.

ANADAMA BATTER BREAD

1½ cups boiling water
1 cup yellow corn meal

6 tablespoons shortening
½ cup light molasses
3 teaspoons salt
2 packages active dry yeast
½ cup warm water (105° to 115°)
2 eggs, beaten
5½ cups sifted all-purpose flour
½ teaspoon salt
2 teaspoons yellow corn meal
2 teaspoons soft butter or margarine

Pour boiling water over 1 cup corn meal. Stir in shortening, molasses, and 3 teaspoons salt. Cool to lukewarm. Sprinkle yeast over warm water; stir until dissolved. Stir into corn meal mixture. Add eggs and half the flour. Beat 2 minutes at medium speed. Add remaining flour; beat 1 minute longer. Divide batter evenly between 2 greased 9 x 5 x 3-inch loaf pans; spread evenly, smoothing tops with buttered spatula. Cover; let rise in warm place (85°) until double in bulk (about 1½ hours). Sprinkle tops with remaining salt and corn meal. Bake at 375° for 50 to 55 minutes or until loaves sound hollow when tapped. Remove from pans to rack. Brush tops with butter. Cool. Makes 2 loaves.

CORN MEAL YEAST BREAD

2 packages active dry yeast
1⅓ cups warm water (105° to 115°)
1⅓ cups milk, scalded
½ cup shortening
¼ tablespoon sugar
1 tablespoon salt
1⅓ cups enriched corn meal
6 cups sifted all-purpose flour (about)
Melted shortening

Soften yeast in warm water. Pour scalded milk over shortening, sugar, and salt; stir occasionally until shortening melts. Cool to lukewarm. Stir in corn meal and 1 cup flour. Add softened yeast. Stir in enough more flour to make a soft dough. Turn out onto lightly floured surface; knead until satiny (about 10 minutes). Round dough into ball; place in greased bowl; brush lightly with melted shortening. Cover; let rise in warm place (85°) until double in size (about 1 hour). Punch dough down; cover; let rest 10 minutes. Divide dough into 3 equal parts.

For a Loaf:

Shape ⅓ of dough into a loaf. Place in well-greased loaf pan, 8 x 4 x 3 inches. Grease top of loaf lightly. Cover; let dough rise until double in size (about 45 minutes). Bake at 400° for 35 to 40 minutes. Remove from pan; cool on rack. Makes 1 loaf.

For Cheese Rolls:

Knead 1 cup grated sharp Cheddar cheese into ⅓ of dough. Shape into about 1½ dozen rolls. Place on greased cookie sheets or in pans; lightly brush tops of rolls with melted butter; sprinkle with sesame seeds. Let rise until double in size (about 45 minutes). Bake at 400° for 15 to 18 minutes. Cool on racks. Makes about 18 rolls.

For Swedish Tea Ring:

Roll out ⅓ of dough to form a rectangle, 9 x 18 inches. Brush with melted butter. Sprinkle with Brown Sugar Mixture.* Roll up tightly, starting with long edge; seal edge. With sealed edge down, shape into ring. With scissors make cuts every inch ⅔ of the way through the ring. Turn each section on its side. Place in 9-inch layer-cake pan. Brush top with melted butter. Cover; let rise until double in size (about 45 minutes). Bake at 400° for 30 to 35 minutes. Remove from pan; cool on rack. Drizzle top with thin Confectioners' Sugar Icing (page 240), if desired. Makes 1 tea ring.

*BROWN SUGAR MIXTURE

¼ cup firmly packed brown sugar
¼ teaspoon cinnamon
¼ teaspoon nutmeg
¼ cup raisins
¼ cup canned slivered blanched almonds

Combine all ingredients; mix thoroughly. Makes about ¾ cup.

RYE BATTER BREAD

1 package active dry yeast
1¼ cups warm water (105° to 115°)
2 tablespoons brown sugar
1 cup rye flour
2½ cups sifted all-purpose flour
2 teaspoons salt
1 teaspoon caraway seeds, if desired
2 tablespoons soft shortening

Dissolve yeast in water in mixing bowl. Add brown sugar, half the flours, salt, caraway seeds, and shortening. Beat 2 minutes at medium speed on mixer or 300 vigorous strokes by hand. Stir in remaining flour. Scrape batter from sides of bowl. Cover; let rise in warm place (85°) until double in size (about 30 minutes). Stir hard ½ minute. Spread batter evenly in greased loaf pan, 9 x 5 x 3 inches. Smooth top of loaf by flouring hand and patting into shape. Cover; let rise again until batter reaches about 1 inch from top of pan. Bake at 375° for 45 minutes or until brown. Remove from pan. Brush with shortening. Cool on rack. Makes 1 loaf.

CHEESE BATTER BREAD

1 package active dry yeast
¾ cup warm water (105° to 115°)
¾ cup evaporated milk
1 tablespoon sugar
1 teaspoon salt
½ teaspoon paprika
3½ cups sifted all-purpose flour
1 cup grated sharp Cheddar cheese
Soft shortening

Dissolve yeast in water in mixing bowl. Stir in evaporated milk, sugar, salt, paprika, and about half the sifted flour. Beat 2 minutes with electric mixer at medium speed or 300 vigorous strokes by hand. Stir in grated cheese and remaining flour. Scrape batter from sides of bowl; cover. Let rise in warm place (85°) until double in size, about 30 minutes. Stir hard ½ minute. Spread batter evenly in greased loaf pan, 9 x 5 x 3 inches. Let rise in warm place until center of batter reaches top of pan, about 30 minutes. Bake at 375° for 50 minutes. Remove from pan; brush top with soft shortening; cool on rack. Makes 1 loaf.

Cinnamon-Raisin Batter Bread: Increase sugar to 2 tablespoons; omit paprika; add 1 teaspoon cinnamon to sugar; substitute 1 cup seedless raisins for the grated Cheddar cheese. If desired, frost the top with thin Confectioners' Sugar Icing (page 240). Makes 1 loaf.

COTTAGE LOAF

1 package active dry yeast
½ cup warm water (105° to 115°)
½ cup well-drained creamed cottage cheese
1 tablespoon butter or margarine
1 egg, beaten

⅓ cup finely chopped onion
1 tablespoon sugar
1 tablespoon dill seed
1 teaspoon salt
¼ tablespoon baking soda
½ cup wheat germ
1¾ to 2 cups unsifted all-purpose flour

Soften yeast in warm water. Heat cottage cheese and butter or margarine until lukewarm. Combine cottage cheese mixture, egg, onion, sugar, dill seed, salt, and baking soda; mix well. Stir in softened yeast. Add wheat germ and flour gradually to make stiff dough, beating well. Cover; let rise in warm place until double in size. Stir down. Knead on lightly floured board about 1 minute. Pat evenly in well-greased 9-inch layer-cake pan at least 2 inches deep. Let rise until double in size. Bake at 350° until done and well browned (about 40 minutes). Remove from pan; cool on wire rack. Serve warm. Makes 1 loaf.

COFFEE CAN BREAD

4 cups unsifted all-purpose flour, divided
1 package active dry yeast
½ cup water
½ cup milk
½ cup butter or margarine
¼ cup sugar
1 teaspoon salt
½ cup ground almonds
½ cup chopped raisins
2 eggs, slightly beaten
2 one-pound coffee cans
Vegetable oil

Mix 2 cups flour with yeast. Stir water, milk, butter, sugar, and salt over low heat until butter melts. Cool for about 5 minutes; add to flour and yeast. Add remaining flour, nuts, raisins, and eggs. Dough will be stiff. Knead on a floured board until dough is smooth and elastic and raisins are well distributed throughout. Coat the inside of each coffee can, using a small amount of oil. Divide dough in half; place one half in each can; cover cans with plastic tops. Let rise in warm place (85°) until dough reaches to approximately 1 inch from top. Remove plastic tops; bake at 375° for about 35 minutes or until top sounds hollow when tapped and cake tester comes out clean. Remove from cans; cool on rack. Makes 2 loaves.

POTATO-CINNAMON BREAD

2 packages active dry yeast
1 tablespoon honey
1 cup warm water (105° to 115°)
⅓ cup butter or margarine
½ cup sugar
1 teaspoon salt
1 cup scalded milk
1 cup mashed potatoes (made from packaged instant potatoes)
3 eggs, slightly beaten
8 cups sifted all-purpose flour (about)
⅓ cup butter or margarine, melted
1½ cups firmly packed brown sugar
1 teaspoon cinnamon
1 cup golden raisins

Combine yeast, honey, and warm water; stir until yeast dissolves. Add butter or margarine, sugar, and salt to scalded milk; stir until melted; cool to lukewarm. Add potatoes, yeast mixture, and eggs to milk mixture; beat until smooth. Stir in enough flour to make a soft dough. Turn dough onto lightly floured surface. Knead until smooth and elastic. Place in large greased bowl; cover with damp cloth; let rise until doubled. Turn out onto lightly floured surface. Divide dough into 3 equal portions. Roll each piece into rectangle, 12 x 8 x ¼ inches. Brush each oblong with ⅓ of the melted butter, sprinkle with ⅓ of the brown sugar, ⅓ of the cinnamon, and ⅓ of the raisins. Roll up lengthwise; cut crosswise into 2-inch slices. Flatten each slice to 1-inch thickness; stand slices from each oblong upright in a greased loaf pan, 9 x 5 x 3 inches. Cover; let rise until double in size. Bake at 350° for 40 to 50 minutes or until done and golden brown. Remove from pans; cool on racks. Makes 3 loaves.

HOT CROSS BREAD

1 package active dry yeast
¼ cup warm water (105° to 115°)
½ cup soft butter or margarine
⅓ cup sugar
2 eggs
½ teaspoon salt
⅓ cup milk
3 to 3¼ cups unsifted all-purpose flour, divided
1 teaspoon cinnamon
¼ cup raisins
¼ cup chopped mixed candied fruits
Frosting*

Dissolve yeast in warm water. Blend butter, sugar, eggs, and salt. Add milk. Sift 1½ cups flour with cinnamon; add to milk mixture and beat until smooth. Stir in dissolved yeast. Add raisins and candied fruits. Blend in enough additional flour to make a soft dough. Turn out onto lightly floured surface. Knead until smooth and elastic (about 8 minutes). Form into ball and place in greased bowl. Turn dough greased side up. Cover; let rise in warm place (85°) until double in bulk (about 1½ to 2 hours). Punch down and form into smooth oval. Place in greased loaf pan, 9 x 5 x 3 inches, and press dough into corners of pan. Use scissors to cut bread through center lengthwise. Make 6 crosswise cuts. Let rise until double in bulk (about 45 minutes). Bake at 350° for 30 minutes. Cover with foil; bake 15 minutes longer. Remove from pan; cool on rack. Make crosses on each section of the bread with Frosting. To serve, pull sections apart. Makes 1 loaf.

*FROSTING

½ cup confectioners' (powdered) sugar
1 tablespoon butter or margarine, softened
1 teaspoon milk
½ teaspoon vanilla

Blend all ingredients until smooth. To frost Hot Cross Bread, force frosting through pastry tube with plain tip or waxed paper cone. Makes about ½ cup.

SWISS BATTER BREAD

1 package active dry yeast
1¼ cups warm water (105° to 115°)
2 tablespoons soft shortening
2 teaspoons salt
2 tablespoons sugar
3 cups sifted all-purpose flour
¼ teaspoon nutmeg
¼ teaspoon mace
⅛ teaspoon cloves
¼ cup golden raisins
½ cup chopped walnuts

Sprinkle yeast on warm water; stir until dissolved. Add shortening, salt, sugar, and half the flour. Beat 2 minutes using medium speed on electric mixer or 300 vigorous strokes with spoon. Add remaining flour, spices, raisins, and nuts; blend in with spoon. Cover; let rise in warm place (85°) until double. Stir down by beating about 25 strokes. Spread evenly in greased

loaf pan, 9 x 5 x 3 inches. Batter will be sticky. Smooth top with floured hand. Cover; let rise again until batter reaches about 1 inch from top of pan. Bake at 375° for 45 to 50 minutes. Remove from pan; cool on rack. Makes 1 loaf.

CHALLAH

1 package active dry yeast
¼ cup warm water (105° to 115°)
2 teaspoons sugar
4½ cups sifted all-purpose flour
2 teaspoons salt
⅛ teaspoon saffron (optional)
2 eggs
2 tablespoons vegetable oil
1 cup warm water
1 egg yolk, slightly beaten

Sprinkle yeast on ¼ cup warm water; stir to dissolve; add sugar; mix well; let stand 5 minutes. Sift flour with salt and saffron. Make a "well" in center of flour; drop in 2 eggs, oil, 1 cup warm water, and yeast mixture; work into the flour. Knead on floured surface until smooth and elastic. Shape into a ball; place in greased bowl; turn over to bring greased surface to top. Cover; set in warm place (85°), free from drafts; let rise 1 hour. Punch down; cover; let rise until double in size. Divide dough into 3 equal portions. With floured hands, roll each portion in strips of equal length. Braid strips together; seal ends. Place in greased bread pan, 9 x 5 x 3 inches. Cover; let rise again until double in size. Brush with egg yolk. Bake at 350° about 50 minutes or until deep golden brown. Remove from pan; cool on rack. Makes 1 loaf.

BUILT-IN-SANDWICH BREAD

1 envelope active dry yeast
1¼ cups warm water (105° to 115°)
1 tablespoon sugar
1½ teaspoons salt
3½ cups sifted all-purpose flour
1½ cups thinly sliced frankfurters (4 average size)
1½ cups finely diced Cheddar cheese
1 cup raisins
¼ cup well-drained pickle relish

Stir yeast into warm water; let stand 5 minutes; stir well. Add sugar and salt. Beat in flour. Knead on floured surface until dough is elastic (about 5 minutes). Cover with a towel; let rise in warm place until double in bulk. With fingers, knead in rest of ingredients until evenly distributed and covered with dough. (This takes time and patience!) Shape into 2 loaves; put in greased loaf pans, 8 x 4 x 3 inches. Cover; let rise until double in size. Bake at 350° for 50 minutes, until crusty and brown. Remove from pans; cool on racks. Makes 2 loaves.

CASSEROLE BREAD

½ cup boiling water
3 tablespoons shortening
1½ teaspoons salt
¼ cup sugar
½ cup evaporated milk
¼ cup warm water (105° to 115°)
1 package active dry yeast
2 eggs, beaten
½ cup chopped walnuts
½ cup raisins
3½ cups sifted all-purpose flour

Pour boiling water over shortening; stir until shortening is melted. Stir in salt, sugar, and evaporated milk. Measure warm water into small bowl. Sprinkle in yeast; stir until dissolved. Stir into first mixture. Stir in eggs, nuts, and raisins. Stir in half the flour; beat until smooth. Stir in remaining flour. Cover; let rise in a warm place until doubled in bulk (about 1½ hours). Punch down and turn into lightly greased 2-quart casserole. Cover; let rise until nearly doubled in bulk (about 1 hour). Bake at 375° for 1 hour. Remove from casserole; cool on rack. Makes 1 loaf.

To Frost if Desired: Combine ⅔ cup sifted confectioners' (powdered) sugar, 1 tablespoon evaporated milk, and ½ teaspoon vanilla. Spread lightly on top of bread. Sprinkle with chopped walnuts.

ORANGE-CARROT BREAD

2 packages active dry yeast
1 cup warm water (105° to 115°)
2 tablespoons sugar
2 teaspoons salt
½ teaspoon cinnamon
¼ teaspoon nutmeg
¼ teaspoon allspice
1 egg, beaten
3 tablespoons butter or margarine
⅔ cup lukewarm orange juice
2 tablespoons grated orange peel

6 to 6½ cups sifted all-purpose flour, divided
1 cup seedless raisins
1½ cups grated raw carrots, at room temperature

Sprinkle yeast on warm water; stir until dissolved. Add sugar, salt, spices, egg, butter, orange juice and peel. Stir in 3 cups of the flour. Beat until smooth. Add raisins and carrots; blend well. Gradually add enough remaining flour to make a soft dough. Turn out onto lightly floured board; knead until smooth (about 5 to 8 minutes). Place in greased bowl, turning to grease top. Cover; let rise in warm place (85°), free from draft, until double in bulk (about 1 hour). Divide in half; shape each half into a loaf. Place each loaf in greased 9 x 5 x 3-inch loaf pan. Cover; let rise in warm place until doubled (about 1 hour). Bake at 400° about 35 to 40 minutes or until done. Remove from pan; cool on rack. Makes 2 loaves.

CRUNCHY MUFFIN-ROLLS

1 package active dry yeast
¼ cup warm water (105° to 115°)
¾ cup lukewarm milk
1 egg, beaten
1 teaspoon salt
1 tablespoon sugar
½ cup melted butter or margarine
2 cups all-purpose flour
½ cup wheat germ
Melted butter
Wheat germ

Dissolve yeast in warm water; add to lukewarm milk; stir in next 4 ingredients. Mix in flour and wheat germ; stir smooth. Turn batter into greased bowl; brush with additional butter; cover; let rise until almost doubled. Stir down. Spread additional wheat germ in shallow bowl. Drop spoonfuls of batter into wheat germ; lift into well-greased muffin cups. Let rise about 40 minutes or until doubled and very light. Bake at 400° about 15 minutes. Remove from muffin cups; cool on rack. Makes 12 rolls.

MOLASSES WHOLE WHEAT ROLLS

2 packages active dry yeast
½ cup warm water (105° to 115°)
1½ cups scalded milk
⅔ cup molasses
2 teaspoons salt
2 eggs, unbeaten

3¾ cups sifted all-purpose flour
3 cups unsifted whole wheat flour
⅓ cup shortening, melted
Soft shortening

Dissolve yeast in warm water as directed on package. Cool milk to lukewarm; add to yeast. Stir in molasses, salt, and eggs. Combine all-purpose flour and whole wheat flour; add 4 cups of this mixture to yeast mixture. Beat until smooth (batter will fall in sheets from spoon). Beat in shortening. Add remaining flour mixture gradually, working it in well. Knead on lightly floured surface until dough is smooth and elastic. Place in well-greased bowl; brush with soft shortening. Cover bowl; place in refrigerator until ready to use (will keep 4 or 5 days). When ready to bake, knead dough for a few seconds; shape into rolls; arrange on greased cookie sheet, brush with melted shortening. Let rise in warm place (85°) until double in bulk. Bake at 400° for 12 to 15 minutes. Cool on racks. Makes about 5 dozen.

WHEAT FLAKE ROLLS

1½ cups milk, scalded
2 packages active dry yeast
½ cup warm water (105° to 115°)
2 teaspoons salt
¼ cup sugar
2 egg yolks, slightly beaten
4 tablespoons melted shortening
3 cups crisp whole wheat cereal flakes
4½ cups sifted all-purpose flour (about)
Melted butter

Cool milk to lukewarm. Meanwhile, dissolve yeast in warm water; add to lukewarm milk. Add salt, sugar, egg yolks, and shortening; mix well. Add cereal and part of flour; beat thoroughly; add enough remaining flour to make a soft dough; mix well. Turn out on well-floured board; knead lightly 3 or 4 minutes. Place dough in well-greased bowl; cover; let rise in warm place (85°) until doubled in size. Punch down. Shape into rolls; place on greased baking sheet; brush with melted butter; cover; let rise until double. Bake at 400° for 12 to 15 minutes. Cool on racks. Makes about 3 dozen.

ONION BATTER ROLLS

1 package active dry yeast
1¼ cups warm water (105° to 115°)
2 tablespoons soft shortening

2 teaspoons salt
2 tablespoons sugar
2 to 3 tablespoons minced dried onion
3 cups sifted all-purpose flour
Melted butter or shortening

Dissolve yeast in warm water. Add shortening, salt, sugar, onion, and half the flour. Beat 2 minutes at medium speed on mixer or 300 vigorous strokes by hand. Scrape sides and bottom of bowl frequently. Add remaining flour; blend in with spoon until smooth. Scrape batter from sides of bowl. Cover; let rise in warm place (85°) until double in bulk (about 30 minutes). If kitchen is cool, place dough on rack over bowl of hot water; cover completely with towel. Stir down batter by beating about 25 strokes. Spoon batter evenly into greased muffin cups, filling cups half full. Let rise in warm place (85°) until batter reaches ½ inch from top of cups (about 40 minutes). Bake at 375° for 20 to 25 minutes, depending on size of cups, or until brown. To test, tap top crust; it should sound hollow. Immediately remove from cups to rack. Brush tops with melted butter or shortening. Do not place in direct draft. Makes 9 to 12 rolls.

HOT-ROLL MIX VARIATIONS

With hot-roll mix it's so easy to dress up a menu with piping-hot raised rolls! Easy, too, to vary the product. Here's how.

BUTTERFLAKES

Roll dough in 4 oblong pieces ⅛ inch thick. Spread each oblong with melted butter or margarine; stack in 4 layers. Roll up. Cut crosswise in slices 1½ inches thick. Place each slice in cup of greased muffin pan cut side up. Let rise and bake as directed on package.

POPPY SEED BRAIDS

Roll out dough; cut in strips 8 x ½ inch. Braid 3 strips together and pinch ends. Brush with egg yolk; sprinkle with poppy seed. Let rise and bake on greased cookie sheet as directed on package.

CARAWAY CRESCENTS

Roll out dough about ¼ inch thick; shape in a circle. Cut circle in pie-shaped wedges; roll up from wide end; shape into crescents. Brush with egg white. For the final touch, sprinkle with caraway seeds. Let rise and bake on greased cookie sheet as directed on package.

CLOVERLEAVES

Form dough in small balls by folding edges under. Place 3 balls in each muffin cup. Let rise and bake on greased cookie sheet as directed on package.

TEA RING

Roll dough in oblong. Spread with melted butter or margarine. Sprinkle with brown sugar, raisins, and cinnamon. Roll up. Form into ring. Slash ring at 1-inch intervals almost to center. Turn each slice partway over. Let rise and bake on greased cookie sheet as directed on package.

CORN MEAL BAGELS

2¼ cups sifted all-purpose flour
¾ cup enriched corn meal
1½ teaspoons salt
4 tablespoons sugar, divided
1 package active dry yeast
1 cup warm water (105° to 115°)
2 tablespoons vegetable oil
1 egg
1 egg yolk *or* 1 egg white

Mix and sift flour, corn meal, salt, and 2 tablespoons of the sugar. Dissolve yeast in ½ cup of the warm water. Add to flour mixture. Add oil to remaining ½ cup water; stir into flour mixture. Add whole egg; stir until dough forms a ball. Turn out onto well-floured board and knead 5 minutes. Place dough in greased bowl; cover; let rise in warm place (85°) until double in size (about 1 hour). Punch dough down; let rise a second time, until double in size (about 1 hour). Punch dough down; turn out onto lightly floured surface; knead until smooth and satiny (about 10 minutes). Divide dough into 12 equal portions. Form into ropes 6 inches long. Pinch ends together to form rings. Drop into rapidly boiling water in deep kettle to which the remaining 2 tablespoons sugar have been added. Cook over moderate heat until rings rise to the surface. Reduce heat; simmer 5 to 6 minutes. Remove bagels with slotted spoon; place on lightly greased cookie sheet; cool 5 minutes. Brush tops with

slightly beaten egg yolk or egg white. Bake at 375° for 25 to 30 minutes or until crust is golden brown and crisp. Cool on racks. Makes 1 dozen.

Variations: Sprinkle tops with poppy seeds, sesame seeds, or finely minced sautéed onion before baking.

CHERRY CLOVERLEAF BUNS

1 package active dry yeast
1 cup warm water (105° to 115°)
2 tablespoons sugar
1 teaspoon salt
¼ cup butter or margarine, melted and cooled
1 egg, slightly beaten
3½ cups sifted all-purpose flour
¾ cup sugar
2 teaspoons cinnamon
1 jar (8 ounces) maraschino cherries
¼ cup chopped walnuts
⅓ cup butter or margarine, melted

Dissolve yeast in warm water. Stir in 2 tablespoons sugar, salt, ¼ cup butter, and egg. Add 2 cups flour; beat until smooth. Gradually add remaining flour. Knead on lightly floured surface until smooth and elastic. Place dough in greased bowl; cover with damp towel. Let rise in warm place (85°) until double in bulk. Meanwhile, mix ¾ cup sugar with cinnamon. Drain cherries; cut in fourths. Combine with walnuts. Punch dough down; pinch off pieces and shape into 1-inch balls. Dip in remaining melted butter, then in cinnamon-sugar mixture. Place 3 balls in each of 18 greased 3-inch muffin cups. Sprinkle with cherry-walnut mixture. Cover; let rise until doubled. Bake at 350° for 30 minutes. Serve warm. Makes 18 large buns.

BUTTERSCOTCH-OATMEAL BUNS

1 package active dry yeast
½ cup warm water (105° to 115°)
½ cup scalded milk
¼ cup shortening
¼ cup sugar
1½ teaspoons salt
2½ to 3 cups sifted all-purpose flour
1 egg
¾ cup quick-cooking rolled oats, uncooked
Melted shortening
Butterscotch Glaze*

Dissolve yeast in warm water as directed on package. Pour scalded milk over shortening, sugar, and salt. Stir. Stir in 1 cup flour. Add egg and yeast; beat with a rotary beater 2 minutes. Add oats and enough more flour to make a soft dough. Knead until satiny (10 minutes) on lightly floured surface. Round dough into ball; place in greased bowl; brush lightly with melted shortening. Let rise in warm place (85°) until double in bulk (about 1 hour). Punch down; cover; let rest 10 minutes. Divide dough in 12 parts. Shape each part in a long roll about ½ inch in diameter. On greased baking sheet, coil each long roll into a circular bun. Brush lightly with melted shortening; cover; let rise until double in bulk. Bake at 375° for 20 to 25 minutes. Spoon glaze over hot buns. Cool on racks. Makes 12 buns.

*BUTTERSCOTCH GLAZE

    2 tablespoons butter or margarine, melted
    ¼ cup firmly packed brown sugar
    1 teaspoon cream
    ¼ teaspoon vanilla

Combine all ingredients.

SUGAR BUNS

    1 package active dry yeast
    ¼ cup warm water (105° to 115°)
    ¾ cup scalded milk
    ⅓ cup sugar
    ½ cup butter or margarine
    2 teaspoons salt
    3½ to 4 cups all-purpose flour
    1 cup rolled oats, quick or old-fashioned, uncooked
    3 eggs
    1 teaspoon grated lemon peel
    Melted shortening
    ½ cup apricot preserves
    2 tablespoons butter or margarine, melted
    1 tablespoon sugar

Dissolve yeast in warm water. Pour milk over sugar, butter, and salt; cool to lukewarm. Stir in 1 cup flour, then softened yeast and oats. Beat in eggs one at a time. Add lemon peel and enough flour to make a soft dough. Turn out onto lightly floured board or canvas; knead until satiny (about 10 minutes). Round dough into ball; place in greased bowl; brush lightly with melted shortening. Cover; let rise in warm place until double in size (about 1 hour). Punch dough down; turn out onto lightly floured board or canvas. Cover; let rise 10 minutes. Divide dough in 2 equal parts. Roll each to form a 12-inch square. Cut each square into strips 4 x 12 inches, then crosswise to make 4 x 6-inch pieces. Spread center of each with preserves. Roll up, starting with 4-inch side. Cut in ¾-inch slices. Place in shallow greased baking pans; cover; let rise in warm place until nearly double in size (about 45 minutes). Brush with melted butter. Bake at 400° about 15 minutes. Sprinkle with sugar. Makes about 6 dozen.

CINNAMON-NUT COFFEE RINGS

    1 package active dry yeast
    ¼ cup warm water (105° to 115°)
    1 cup milk, scalded
    ½ cup sugar
    ⅓ cup butter or margarine
    1 teaspoon salt
    1 egg, well beaten
    3¾ cups sifted all-purpose flour
    1¼ cups rolled oats, quick or old-fashioned, uncooked
    ½ cup chopped pecans
    ¾ cup sugar
    1½ teaspoons cinnamon
    ¼ cup butter or margarine, melted

Sprinkle yeast on warm water. Pour scalded milk over ½ cup sugar, butter, and salt; stir occasionally until butter melts. Cool to lukewarm. Beat in softened yeast, egg, and 2 cups flour until batter is smooth. Add oats and remaining flour. Beat thoroughly. Place in large greased bowl. Cover and let rise in warm place (85°) until double in size (about 1½ hours). Punch down; cover and let rest 10 minutes. Place ⅓ of the nuts in the bottom of greased 8-inch ring mold. Repeat with second ring mold. Combine sugar and cinnamon. Pinch off small pieces of dough; shape to form 1½-inch balls. Roll each ball in melted butter, then in cinnamon-sugar. Arrange balls of dough in ring molds. Sprinkle with remaining cinnamon-sugar and remaining ⅓ of nuts. Cover; let rise in warm place until nearly double in size (about 40 minutes). Bake at 350° for 20 to 25 minutes or until brown. Loosen rings; invert immediately on serving plates. Serve warm. Makes 2 rings.

FILBERT BUBBLE RING

1 cup firmly packed brown sugar
2 teaspoons cinnamon
Sweet Dough*
½ cup butter or margarine, melted
1 cup toasted chopped filberts
¼ cup golden raisins

Mix sugar and cinnamon. Shape dough into 1-inch balls; dip in butter; coat with sugar-cinnamon mixture. Place half the balls in well-greased 9-inch tube pan; scatter with half the filberts and raisins. Repeat. Cover; let rise in warm place (85°) until double in bulk (about 1 hour). Bake at 375° for 1 hour or until cake tests done. Cool in pan 10 minutes. Invert pan on serving dish; let stand several minutes before removing pan. Serve ring warm or cooled. Makes 1 ring.

*SWEET DOUGH

½ cup milk
½ cup sugar
1 teaspoon salt
½ cup butter or margarine, softened
2 packages active dry yeast
½ cup warm water (105° to 115°)
2 eggs, slightly beaten
1 tablespoon grated lemon peel
4½ cups sifted all-purpose flour

Scald milk; stir in sugar, salt, and butter. Cool to lukewarm. Sprinkle yeast over warm water in large bowl; let stand 5 minutes, then stir until blended. Stir in milk mixture, eggs, lemon peel, and 2 cups flour. Beat until smooth. Stir in remaining flour to make soft dough. Cover with damp towel. Chill at least 2 to 3 hours or overnight. Knead dough on lightly floured surface until smooth and elastic. Shape into 1-inch balls.

TWIN BRUNCH COFFEECAKES

1 package active dry yeast
¼ cup warm water (105° to 115°)
⅔ cup milk, scalded
¼ cup sugar
1 teaspoon salt
¼ cup butter or margarine
2½ cups sifted all-purpose flour (about)
1 egg, beaten
1 tablespoon grated orange peel
1 cup rolled oats, quick or old-fashioned, uncooked

Melted butter
⅓ cup peach preserves
⅓ cup red raspberry jam

Sprinkle yeast on warm water; stir to dissolve. Pour scalded milk over sugar, salt, and butter. Cool to lukewarm. Stir in 1 cup flour and egg. Add softened yeast, orange peel, and oats. Stir in enough more flour to make soft dough. Turn out on lightly floured surface; knead until smooth and satiny (about 10 minutes). Round dough into ball; place in greased bowl; turn to bring greased side up. Cover; let rise in warm place (85°) until double (about 1 hour). Punch down; cover; let rest 10 minutes. Divide dough in half. Roll out half the dough to form a 9 x 12-inch rectangle. Brush with melted butter; spread with peach preserves. Roll up as for jelly roll. Seal edge; place on greased cookie sheet with sealed edge down. Slice halfway through roll at 1-inch intervals. Brush with melted butter. Repeat with other half of dough, using raspberry jam. Cover; let rise in warm place until double in size (about 1 hour). Bake at 350° for 30 to 35 minutes. Cool on racks. Frost if desired. Makes 2 coffeecakes.

CHOCOLATE FRENCH COFFEECAKE

1 small can (⅔ cup) evaporated milk, divided
¾ cup sugar
½ teaspoon salt
4 egg yolks
½ cup soft butter or margarine
4½ cups sifted all-purpose flour, divided
2 packages active dry yeast
½ cup warm water (105° to 115°)
1 package (6 ounces) semisweet chocolate pieces
½ teaspoon cinnamon
Crumb Topping*

Reserve ¼ cup evaporated milk. Add water to remaining milk to make ½ cup; combine with sugar, salt, and egg yolks in large bowl of electric mixer. Beat well. Add butter and 2 cups flour; beat until smooth. Sprinkle yeast on warm water; stir until dissolved. Add yeast and 1 more cup of flour to first mixture; beat at medium speed 3 minutes. Blend in remaining 1½ cups flour. Cover; let rise in warm place (85°) until double in bulk (about 1½ hours). Heat reserved ¼ cup evaporated milk in small saucepan just to boiling; remove from heat. Add chocolate pieces and cinnamon; stir until mixture is smooth. Cool to room temperature. Punch down dough; turn out onto well-floured surface; let rest a few minutes. Knead lightly a few times; roll into 10 x 15-inch rectangle. Spread with chocolate mixture; roll up from long side like jelly roll. Place roll seam side down in greased 10-inch tube pan (preferably with removable bottom). Press ends together to seal. If necessary, stretch roll to fit pan. Sprinkle with Crumb Topping. Cover; let rise in warm place until double in bulk (about 1 hour). Bake at 350° for 45 minutes or until cake tests done. Carefully remove from pan; cool on rack, topping side up. Makes 1 coffeecake.

*CRUMB TOPPING

½ cup all-purpose flour
⅓ cup sugar
½ cup semisweet chocolate pieces
½ cup chopped walnuts
¼ cup soft butter or margarine
1½ teaspoons cinnamon

Mix all ingredients with fork until well blended and crumbly.

CHRISTMAS TREE COFFEECAKE

2 packages active dry yeast
¼ cup warm water (105° to 115°)
1¼ cups milk
½ cup butter or margarine
½ cup sugar
1 teaspoon salt
2 eggs, beaten
1 teaspoon grated lemon peel
5½ cups sifted all-purpose flour
1 cup wheat germ
Confectioners' Sugar Icing*
Sliced almonds

Soften yeast in warm water. Scald milk; add butter or margarine, sugar, and salt. Cool to lukewarm. Stir in eggs, lemon peel, and softened yeast. Add enough flour to make a batter. Beat well (by hand or on low speed of electric mixer). Add wheat germ and enough remaining flour to make a soft dough. Turn out onto floured board; knead about 20 times. Place in greased bowl; turn to bring greased side up; cover; let rise until double in bulk. Punch down. Divide in 2 portions. Divide 1 portion into 5 parts. Reserve 1 part. Roll remaining 4 parts into long, smooth rolls about ¾ inch thick. Swirl back and forth on greased cookie sheet to make branches of tree.

Make trunk and ornaments with remaining part. Repeat with other half of dough. Let rise again until double in bulk. Bake at 375° for 25 to 30 minutes. When cake cools drizzle with Confectioners' Sugar Icing and sprinkle with sliced almonds. Makes two 12-inch trees.

*CONFECTIONERS' SUGAR ICING

Mix enough egg white into sifted confectioners' (powdered) sugar to make a frosting of spreading consistency.

OLD-FASHIONED JELLY DOUGHNUTS

1 cup milk
1 package active dry yeast
¼ cup warm water (105° to 115°)
1 tablespoon sugar
1½ cups sifted all-purpose flour
3 tablespoons butter or margarine
¾ cup granulated sugar
1 egg
1½ teaspoons nutmeg
1 teaspoon salt
3 cups sifted all-purpose flour
Vegetable oil
Currant jelly
Vegetable oil for frying
Confectioners' (powdered) sugar

Scald milk; cool till lukewarm. Sprinkle yeast on warm water; stir until dissolved. Stir into milk with 1 tablespoon sugar. Add 1½ cups flour; beat well. Cover; let rise in warm place about 1 hour. Cream butter with ¾ cup sugar until light and fluffy. Add egg, nutmeg, and salt. Beat into yeast mixture. Beat in 3 cups flour; place in well-greased bowl. Brush dough with vegetable oil. Cover; let rise in warm place until doubled in bulk. Turn out onto lightly floured surface; roll out ¼ inch thick. With floured cookie cutter, cut in 2½-inch rounds. Place ½ teaspoon jelly in center of half the rounds. Moisten the edges with cold water; top with remaining rounds, pinching edges together firmly. Cover; let rise. Fry in vegetable oil 1½ inches deep heated to 370°. Turn often until golden brown. Remove with slotted spoon. Drain on paper toweling. Dust with confectioners' sugar. Makes about 24.

RAISED ORANGE DOUGHNUTS

1 package active dry yeast
1 tablespoon sugar
1¼ cups warm orange juice (105° to 115°)
2 tablespoons grated orange peel
4½ cups sifted all-purpose flour
¾ cup sugar
1 egg, beaten
½ teaspoon salt
3 tablespoons butter or margarine, melted and
    cooled
Fat for frying

Add yeast and sugar to warm orange juice; let
stand 5 minutes; stir until yeast is thoroughly
dissolved. Add grated orange peel and 1½ cups
of the flour; beat well. Cover and let rise in a
warm place (85°) about 1 hour. Add sugar gradually to beaten egg and beat until light; stir in salt
and melted butter. Add to yeast mixture; beat
until smooth. Add enough of the remaining flour
to make a soft dough. Turn dough onto lightly
floured surface; knead until smooth and elastic.
Place in oiled bowl; turn once to bring greased
side up. Cover and let rise in warm place (85°)
until double in bulk (about 1½ hours). Roll
dough on lightly floured surface to ¼-inch thickness. Cut with 3-inch floured doughnut cutter.
Let rise again until double in bulk (about 1 hour).
Fry in deep fat heated to 350° until golden
brown, turning once. Drain on absorbent paper.
Frost if desired. Makes about 36 doughnuts.

CHOCOLATE-NUT DOUGHNUTS

2 cups sifted all-purpose flour
1½ teaspoons baking powder
¼ teaspoon baking soda
½ teaspoon salt
1 teaspoon cinnamon
2 packages (3¾ ounces each) chocolate fudge
    pudding and pie mix, not instant
¼ cup finely chopped walnuts
2 eggs
2 tablespoons vegetable oil
½ cup milk
Fat or vegetable oil for frying

Mix and sift flour, baking powder, baking soda,
salt, cinnamon, pudding mix, and walnuts. Add
eggs, oil, and milk. Stir until dough cleans the
bowl. Place dough on a heavily floured board
and knead gently until dough is smooth. Roll out
to ¼-inch thickness. Cut with floured doughnut

cutter. Fry in deep fat or vegetable oil heated to
360° for 2 to 3 minutes on each side. Drain on
absorbent paper. Cool. Makes about 18 doughnuts.

QUICK BREADS

Quick breads have always been popular, and
how they do dress up an ordinary meal! Some
are quicker than quick when a packaged mix is
used as a base. Some are ready-to-serve after a
brief stay in the oven. So there is really no excuse
not to serve them often!

One thing to remember, when making muffins
or loaves, be careful not to overstir. Just use the
spoon until all the dry ingredients are moistened. The batter will look lumpy, and this is the
way it should be. Overmixing results in poor tex-
ture—tunnels, holes, etc.

So look these recipes over, and start soon to
enjoy making and serving them.

SAVORY BUTTERFLAKE LOAF

¼ cup softened butter or margarine
½ cup grated Parmesan cheese
½ teaspoon minced dried onion
¼ teaspoon caraway seed
1 teaspoon minced parsley
2 packages refrigerated quick butterflake
    dinner rolls

Combine first 5 ingredients. Spread each butterflake roll with seasoned butter. Stand on edge in
9 x 5 x 3-inch loaf pan, making 2 rows. Bake at
375° for 30 to 35 minutes, until deep golden
brown. Loosen edges; turn out immediately.
Serve warm. Makes 1 loaf.

BARBECUE FRENCH LOAF

2 packages refrigerated buttermilk biscuits (10
    biscuits in each)
3 tablespoons bottled barbecue sauce
Sesame seeds

Open packages and place unseparated biscuits
on ungreased cookie sheet; lightly press rolls together and shape ends to form a long loaf. Brush
with barbecue sauce. Sprinkle with sesame
seeds. Bake at 350° for 30 to 35 minutes, until
golden brown. Serve warm. Makes 1 loaf.

BUNKER HILL BROWN BREAD

1½ cups sifted all-purpose flour
2 teaspoons baking soda
1½ teaspoons salt
1 cup wheat germ
1 cup graham cracker crumbs
2 eggs
⅓ cup vegetable oil
1 cup light molasses
2 cups buttermilk

Mix and sift flour, baking soda, and salt. Stir in wheat germ and graham cracker crumbs. Combine eggs, oil, molasses, and buttermilk. Beat to blend. Add to dry ingredients; stir until well blended. Spoon into 4 clean, well-greased 1-pound cans that have held fruit or vegetables; set in pan (for ease of handling); do not cover. Bake at 350° for 50 to 55 minutes or until cake tester inserted in center comes out clean. Cool in cans on rack 10 minutes. Run knife carefully around loaves to base of cans to loosen. Turn out of cans. Cool on rack. Makes 4 loaves.

HEIRLOOM BOSTON BROWN BREAD

2 cups graham or whole wheat flour
½ cup all-purpose flour
2 teaspoons baking soda
1 teaspoon salt
2 cups buttermilk
½ cup molasses
1 cup seedless raisins

Combine all ingredients; mix well. Spoon into 3 well-greased 1-pound tin cans. Let stand ½ hour. Bake at 350° for 45 to 50 minutes or until cake tester comes out clean. Run knife carefully around loaves to base of cans to loosen. Turn loaves out of cans. Cool on rack. Makes 3 loaves.

SERVING HINTS

1. A loaf of this brown bread, decoratively wrapped, makes a nice hostess gift, or a gift for neighbor or friend.
2. Use the bread for lunch-box sandwiches, filled with a mixture of peanut butter and sweet pickle relish.
3. If you like the New England custom of serving baked beans on Saturday night, be sure to make hot brown bread to go along with them.
4. Slice and serve, well buttered, with hearty soup or salad for luncheon or supper.

ONION-CHEESE BREAD

3 tablespoons soft butter or margarine
1½ cups chopped onion
2 cups unsifted all-purpose flour
3 teaspoons baking powder
1 teaspoon salt
2 tablespoons parsley flakes
⅓ cup soft butter or margarine
1 egg
1 cup milk
½ cup grated sharp Cheddar cheese

Heat 3 tablespoons butter or margarine in small skillet. Add onion; cook over low heat, stirring occasionally, for 10 minutes or until tender. Mix flour, baking powder, salt, parsley, and 2 tablespoons of the sautéed onions in mixing bowl. Cut in ⅓ cup butter or margarine until mixture is like coarse meal. Make depression in center. Beat egg and milk together; add to flour mixture. Stir until moistened. Spread in 8 x 8 x 2-inch or 9 x 9 x 2-inch greased baking pan. Spoon remaining onions over top; sprinkle with grated cheese. Bake at 425° for 30 minutes for 8-inch pan or 20 minutes for 9-inch pan until top is golden brown. Turn out of pan and quickly turn right side up. Cut in squares and serve hot. Makes 9 to 12 squares.

CHEDDAR BRAN LOAF

1½ cups sifted all-purpose flour
1½ teaspoons baking powder
¼ teaspoon baking soda
½ teaspoon salt
3 tablespoons butter or margarine
⅓ cup sugar
1 egg, well beaten
1 cup buttermilk
1 cup shredded Cheddar cheese
1 cup all bran cereal, crushed fine

Mix and sift flour, baking powder, baking soda, and salt. Cream butter or margarine and sugar; blend in egg. Add flour mixture alternately with buttermilk, beginning and ending with flour mixture. Fold in cheese and bran. Spoon into well-greased loaf pan, 8 x 4 x 3 inches. Bake at 350° about 1 hour. Remove from pan; cool on wire rack. Bread slices more easily when cold. Makes 1 loaf.

IRISH SODA BREAD I

4 cups sifted all-purpose flour
¼ cup sugar
1 teaspoon salt
1 teaspoon baking powder
¼ cup butter or margarine
2 cups seedless raisins
1⅓ cups buttermilk
1 egg
1 teaspoon baking soda

Mix and sift flour, sugar, salt, and baking powder. Cut in butter or margarine with pastry blender or 2 knives until mixture resembles coarse corn meal. Stir in raisins. Combine buttermilk, egg, and baking soda. Stir buttermilk mixture into flour mixture until just moistened. Bake in greased 1-quart pudding pan or casserole at 375° for 45 to 50 minutes or until golden brown. Remove from pan; cool on wire rack. Makes 1 loaf.

IRISH SODA BREAD II

2 cups sifted all-purpose flour
¾ teaspoon baking soda
½ teaspoon salt
1 tablespoon sugar
¼ cup plus 2 tablespoons shortening
½ cup raisins
1 tablespoon caraway seeds (optional)
¼ cup vinegar
½ cup sweet milk

Mix and sift flour, baking soda, salt, and sugar into large mixing bowl. Cut in shortening with pastry blender or 2 knives. Stir in raisins and caraway seeds. Mix together vinegar and milk. Add to flour mixture; blend with a fork. Turn into greased 8-inch layer-cake pan 1½ inches deep; spread or pat smooth. Bake at 375° for 30 minutes or until done. Serve hot, in wedges. Makes 1 loaf.

DOUBLE-DUTY QUICK BREAD

½ cup shortening
⅔ cup firmly packed brown sugar
2 eggs, lightly beaten
1 cup chopped nutmeats
2 cups drained diced cooked pitted prunes
2 cups rolled oats, quick or old-fashioned, uncooked
4 cups sifted all-purpose flour
4 teaspoons baking powder
1½ teaspoons baking soda

3 teaspoons salt
2½ cups buttermilk

Cream shortening; add sugar gradually. Add eggs; mix well. Stir in nuts, prunes, and rolled oats. Mix and sift flour, baking powder, baking soda, and salt. Add alternately with buttermilk to first mixture. Fill greased loaf pan 9 x 5 x 3 inches ¾ full; set in refrigerator. Fill 18 greased muffin cups ⅔ full; bake at 400° about 25 minutes. Remove from oven; lower heat to 375°. Remove muffins from pans; cool on racks. After 10 minutes put loaf in oven. Bake about 1¼ hours. Remove from pan; cool on rack. Makes 1 loaf and 18 medium-sized muffins (or 12 muffins, 7 sticks).

NOTE: For a large supper, make up the whole recipe and have a big loaf and 18 muffins, or cut the recipe in half and bake either bread or muffins. If you have cornstick pans, you may wish to use them instead of muffin pans, or bake a pan of each.

NUT BREAD

3 cups biscuit mix
½ cup sugar
⅓ cup flour
1 egg
1 cup milk
1½ cups chopped nuts

Mix together biscuit mix, sugar, flour, egg, and milk. Beat vigorously with spoon ½ minute. Stir in nuts. Pour into well-greased 9 x 5 x 3-inch loaf pan. Bake at 350° for 55 to 60 minutes. Cool slightly before removing from pan to rack. Cool thoroughly before slicing. Makes 1 loaf.

Banana Walnut Bread: Follow directions for Nut Bread but use ⅔ cup sugar and only ½ cup milk; use only ¾ cup chopped walnuts and add 1 cup mashed bananas (2 to 3 fully ripe bananas).

DATE BREAD

1¾ cups sifted all-purpose flour
2 teaspoons baking powder
1¼ teaspoons salt
½ teaspoon baking soda
1 cup finely cut pitted dates
¾ cup firmly packed brown sugar
¾ cup rolled oats, quick or old-fashioned, uncooked
1 teaspoon grated lemon peel

1¼ cups buttermilk
2 eggs, beaten
¼ cup vegetable oil

Mix and sift flour, baking powder, salt, and baking soda. Coat dates with 2 tablespoons of flour mixture. Add dates, brown sugar, oats, and lemon peel to remaining flour mixture. Combine buttermilk, eggs, and oil. Add all at once to flour mixture. Stir just until dry ingredients are thoroughly moistened. Pour batter into greased loaf pan 8 x 4 x 3 inches. Bake at 375° for 55 to 60 minutes. Let stand 10 minutes before removing from pan; cool. Wrap cooled bread in foil or transparent plastic wrap and store one day before slicing. Makes 1 loaf.

ORANGE-DATE BREAD

2 tablespoons butter or margarine, melted
¾ cup orange juice
2 tablespoons grated orange peel
½ cup finely cut dates
1 cup sugar
1 egg, slightly beaten
½ cup coarsely chopped pecans
2 cups sifted all-purpose flour
½ teaspoon baking soda
1 teaspoon baking powder
½ teaspoon salt

Combine first 7 ingredients. Mix and sift remaining ingredients; stir in. Mix well. Turn into greased loaf pan, 8 x 4 x 3 inches. Bake at 350° for 50 minutes or until done. Remove from pan; cool on rack. Makes 1 loaf.

MOLASSES-BRAN TEA LOAVES

3 cups sifted all-purpose flour
1 teaspoon baking soda
2½ teaspoons baking powder
½ teaspoon salt
1 cup whole bran
1 cup chopped pitted dates
1 cup chopped nuts
1 egg, beaten
1 cup milk
½ cup molasses
¼ cup boiling water

Mix and sift flour, baking soda, baking powder, and salt. Stir in bran, dates, and nuts. Combine egg, milk, molasses, and boiling water. Add milk mixture to flour mixture all at once; stir only until flour disappears. Spoon into 6 oiled condensed soup cans. Set in shallow pan for ease in handling. Bake at 350° for 1 hour. Remove from cans while hot. When cool, slice thin. Makes 6 small loaves.

PINEAPPLE BRAN BREAD

⅔ cup pineapple syrup (from can of crushed pineapple)
⅔ cup whole bran
2 cups sifted all-purpose flour
½ cup sugar
2 teaspoons baking powder
¼ teaspoon baking soda
1 teaspoon salt
½ cup chopped walnuts
½ cup drained canned crushed pineapple
1 egg, well beaten
2 tablespoons melted shortening

Measure pineapple syrup from can of crushed pineapple; add water if necessary to make ⅔ cup; pour over bran; let stand 15 minutes. Sift together flour, sugar, baking powder, baking soda, and salt. Add walnuts, crushed pineapple, egg, and melted shortening to bran mixture; add to sifted dry ingredients. Mix until just blended. Turn into greased loaf pan, 9 x 5 x 3 inches. Bake at 325° for 1 hour 15 minutes. Remove from pan; cool on rack. Makes 1 loaf.

CRANBERRY WHEAT GERM BREAD

2 cups sifted all-purpose flour
1 cup sugar
2 teaspoons baking powder
½ teaspoon baking soda
1½ teaspoons salt
1 cup halved raw cranberries
½ cup chopped pecans
½ cup wheat germ
3 tablespoons grated orange peel
1 egg, slightly beaten
½ cup orange juice
¼ cup warm water
2 tablespoons vegetable oil

Mix and sift flour, sugar, baking powder, baking soda, and salt. Stir in cranberry halves, pecans, wheat germ, and orange peel. Combine egg, orange juice, water, and oil. Add to flour mixture; stir just enough to moisten ingredients. Spoon into greased loaf pan, 9 x 5 x 3 inches. Bake at 350° for 50 to 60 minutes or until done. Cool in pan 5 minutes; remove from pan; finish cooling on rack. Makes 1 loaf.

CRANBERRY FRUIT LOAF

½ teaspoon ground cinnamon
½ teaspoon ground mace
1 package (about 1 pound) pound cake mix
1 cup fresh cranberries, coarsely chopped
½ cup mixed diced candied fruits
1 teaspoon grated orange peel

Add spices to cake mix, then proceed according to package directions. Fold in cranberries, candied fruits, and orange peel. Pour mixture into greased and floured 8-inch tube pan. Bake at 325° for 1½ hours or until cake springs back when lightly touched. Let stand for 10 minutes; turn out on rack to cool before slicing. Makes 1 loaf.

TEA PARTY LOAF

Loaf:

2 cups sifted all-purpose flour
½ teaspoon salt
½ cup sugar
2 teaspoons baking powder
¾ cup quick-cooking rolled oats, uncooked
½ cup chopped walnuts
½ cup prepared mincemeat
1 teaspoon molasses
2 tablespoons vegetable oil
1 egg, slightly beaten
¾ cup milk

Mix and sift flour, salt, sugar, and baking powder. Stir in oats, walnuts, and mincemeat. Add molasses, oil, egg, and milk. Stir just until well blended. Pour batter into greased loaf pan, 8 x 5 x 3 inches. Bake at 350° for 50 to 60 minutes. Remove from pan; cool thoroughly. Makes 1 loaf.

Filling:

1 large package (8 ounces) cream cheese
1 tablespoon milk
½ teaspoon lemon juice

Blend all ingredients.

To Assemble:

Make 2 diagonal slices in loaf from corner to corner. Spread cut surfaces with cream cheese filling; rebuild loaf to its original shape. Chill thoroughly in refrigerator. To serve, slice loaf in ¼-inch slices.

MOLASSES PEANUT BREAD

½ cup sugar
3 cups sifted all-purpose flour
1 teaspoon baking soda
1 teaspoon baking powder
½ teaspoon salt
1 cup coarsely chopped peanuts
¾ cup evaporated milk
2 tablespoons grated orange peel
½ cup orange juice
2 tablespoons melted shortening
½ cup light molasses
Chopped peanuts (optional)

Mix and sift sugar, flour, baking soda, baking powder, and salt; stir in 1 cup nuts. Combine evaporated milk, orange peel, orange juice, melted shortening, and molasses. Add to flour mixture all at once; stir just enough to blend. Turn into a well-greased loaf pan, 9 x 5 x 3 inches. If desired, sprinkle with additional chopped peanuts. Bake at 325° for 1 hour 15 minutes. Remove from pan; cool on rack. Makes 1 loaf.

FILBERT CALICO LOAF

¾ cup chopped toasted filberts
1 cup sugar, divided
2 cups fresh cranberries, coarsely ground
Grated peel of 1 orange
2 cups sifted all-purpose flour
4 teaspoons baking powder
1 teaspoon salt
1 cup quick-cooking rolled oats, uncooked
2 eggs, beaten
⅔ cup milk
3 tablespoons vegetable oil

Toast filberts at 350° for 8 to 10 minutes. Rub off skins; chop. Sprinkle ¼ cup of the sugar over ground cranberries and grated orange peel. Set filberts and cranberry mixture aside. Mix and sift flour, baking powder, salt, and remaining sugar. Mix in rolled oats and filberts. Combine eggs, milk, oil, and cranberry mixture. Add to dry ingredients. Mix just enough to thoroughly dampen flour. Turn into greased loaf pan, 8 x 4 x 3 inches. Let stand 10 minutes. Bake at 350° for 1 hour. Remove from pan; cool on rack. Makes 1 loaf.

HONEY PECAN LOAF

1 loaf unsliced bread
⅓ cup butter or margarine, melted
⅓ cup honey
¼ cup firmly packed brown sugar
¼ cup chopped pecans
10 pecan halves

Cut loaf of bread in half lengthwise, cutting almost through to bottom; slice bread crosswise 4 times. Place loaf in well-greased bread pan, 9 x 5 x 3 inches. Combine melted butter or margarine, honey, and brown sugar. Pour over bread. Sprinkle chopped pecans between cuts. Arrange pecan halves on top. Bake at 350° for 25 minutes. Serve warm. Makes 1 loaf.

BEEHIVE OVEN APRICOT NUT BREAD

¾ cup boiling water
1 cup dried apricots, chopped
3 cups unsifted all-purpose flour
1 tablespoon baking powder
½ teaspoon salt
⅓ cup butter or margarine, softened
1 cup sugar
2 eggs
½ cup light corn syrup
1 cup chopped nuts

Grease and lightly flour 9 x 5 x 3-inch loaf pan. Pour boiling water over apricots; let stand 15 minutes. Mix together flour, baking powder, and salt. Blend butter, sugar, eggs, and corn syrup; mix until smooth and well blended. Stir in apricots with water in which they were soaked; stir in nuts. Add dry ingredients gradually. Turn into prepared pan. Bake at 350° about 1¼ hours or until cake tester inserted in center of loaf comes out clean. Cool in pan 10 minutes. Remove from pan; cool on rack.

HOLIDAY CONFETTI BREAD

2½ cups sifted all-purpose flour
4 teaspoons baking powder
¾ teaspoon salt
¾ cup chopped nuts
1½ cups mixed diced candied fruits
⅓ cup raisins
½ cup shortening
¾ cup sugar

3 eggs
½ cup mashed bananas
½ cup orange juice

Mix and sift flour, baking powder, and salt. Stir in chopped nuts, candied fruits, and raisins. Cream shortening; add sugar; beat until light and fluffy. Add eggs one at a time, beating after each addition. Combine mashed bananas and orange juice; add to creamed mixture alternately with flour mixture, beginning and ending with dry ingredients. Turn into waxed-paper-lined and greased 9 x 5 x 3-inch loaf pan. Bake at 350° for 1 hour. Let bread cool in pan ½ hour before turning out onto cake rack. Makes 1 loaf.

ORANGE BREAD

2 tablespoons butter or margarine, melted
¾ cup orange juice
2 tablespoons grated orange peel
½ cup finely cut pitted dates
1 cup sugar
1 egg, slightly beaten
½ cup coarsely chopped pecans
2 cups sifted all-purpose flour
½ teaspoon baking soda
1 teaspoon baking powder
½ teaspoon salt

Combine melted butter or margarine, orange juice, orange peel, dates, sugar, beaten egg, and pecans. Mix and sift flour, baking soda, baking powder, and salt; stir in. Mix well. Turn into greased loaf pan, 9 x 5 x 3 inches. Bake at 350° for 50 to 60 minutes or until done. Remove from pan; cool on rack. Makes 1 loaf.

BANANA MOLASSES BREAD

3 ripe bananas
1 egg, unbeaten
⅔ cup sugar
2 tablespoons light molasses
2 tablespoons melted butter or margarine
2 cups sifted all-purpose flour
1 teaspoon baking powder
1 teaspoon baking soda
½ teaspoon salt
1 cup chopped walnuts

Mash bananas until smooth. Add unbeaten egg; mix well. Beat in sugar, molasses, and butter. Mix and sift flour, baking powder, baking soda, and salt; stir in. Stir in walnuts. Bake in greased loaf pan, 9 x 5 x 3 inches, at 325° for about 1 hour. Remove from pan; cool on rack. Makes 1 loaf.

ZUCCHINI WALNUT BREAD

1 cup walnuts
4 eggs
2 cups granulated sugar
1 cup vegetable oil
3½ cups unsifted all-purpose flour
1½ teaspoons baking soda
1½ teaspoons salt
1 teaspoon cinnamon
¾ teaspoon baking powder
2 cups grated zucchini (not pared)
1 cup raisins
1 teaspoon vanilla

Chop walnuts into medium-sized pieces. Beat eggs; gradually beat in sugar, then oil. Combine dry ingredients; add to first mixture alternately with zucchini. Stir in raisins, walnuts, and vanilla. Turn into 2 greased and lightly floured loaf pans, 9 x 5 x 3 inches. Bake on lowest rack at 350° for about 55 minutes, until loaves test done. Let stand about 10 minutes; turn out onto wire racks to cool. This bread freezes well. Makes 2 loaves.

NOTE: If desired, loaves may be lightly glazed with confectioners' (powdered) sugar mixed to spreading consistency with a little cream.

SPOON BREAD

1 cup enriched corn meal
1 teaspoon salt
1 cup cold milk
1½ cups milk, scalded
2 tablespoons butter or margarine
4 egg yolks
4 egg whites, stiffly beaten

Combine corn meal, salt, and cold milk. Add to scalded milk, stirring constantly. Cook until thickened, about 5 minutes, stirring frequently. Remove from heat. Stir in butter. Beat egg yolks until thick and lemon-colored. Stir a small amount of corn meal mixture into egg yolks; add egg mixture to corn meal, mixing well. Fold in beaten egg whites. Pour into greased 1½-quart soufflé dish or casserole. Bake, uncovered, at 350° for about 50 minutes without opening oven door. Serve immediately. Makes 6 servings.

CRUNCHY PEACH COFFEECAKE

Topping:

½ cup all-purpose flour
½ cup firmly packed brown sugar
¼ cup wheat germ
1 teaspoon cinnamon
¼ cup butter or margarine
1 can (1 pound 13 ounces) sliced cling
    peaches

Combine ½ cup flour, brown sugar, ¼ cup wheat germ, and cinnamon in bowl; mix well. Cut in ¼ cup butter or margarine until mixture is crumbly, using a pastry blender or 2 knives. Set aside. Drain sliced peaches.

Batter:

1½ cups all-purpose flour
¼ cup wheat germ
¼ cup sugar
2 teaspoons baking powder
½ teaspoon salt
¼ cup butter or margarine
2 eggs, beaten
½ cup milk

Combine 1½ cups flour, ¼ cup wheat germ, sugar, baking powder, and salt in bowl; mix well. Cut in ¼ cup butter or margarine until mixture is crumbly, using a pastry blender or 2 knives. Add eggs and milk; stir just until dry ingredients are moistened.

To Assemble:

Spread batter over bottom of greased 13 x 9 x 2-inch baking pan. Sprinkle with ½ the reserved topping mixture. Arrange peach slices in rows on top. Sprinkle with remaining topping mixture. Bake at 350° for about 25 minutes or until done. Remove from pan; cool on rack, topping side up. Makes 1 coffeecake.

TWIN MOUNTAIN BLUEBERRY COFFEECAKE

2 cups all-purpose flour
1 cup sugar
3 teaspoons baking powder
¼ teaspoon salt
½ cup shortening
2 eggs, beaten
1 cup milk
1½ cups fresh blueberries
1 can (1⅓ cups) flaked coconut

Mix and sift flour, sugar, baking powder, and salt. Cut in shortening with 2 knives or pastry blender. Combine eggs and milk; stir into dry ingredients. Fold in blueberries. Divide batter between 2 greased 9-inch layer-cake pans. Sprinkle coconut evenly over tops. Bake at 375° for 25 minutes. Remove from pans; cool on racks. Makes 2 coffeecakes.

MAPLE-WALNUT COFFEECAKE

¼ cup maple syrup
2 tablespoons brown sugar
3 tablespoons chopped walnuts
3 tablespoons butter or margarine, melted
1 package (8 ounces; 12 biscuits) refrigerated tender flaky biscuits

Combine maple syrup, brown sugar, walnuts, and butter or margarine in lightly greased 8- or 9-inch pie pan. Arrange biscuits over mixture. Bake at 425° for 12 to 15 minutes. Turn upside down on serving plate. Cool 1 minute; remove from pan. Makes 1 coffeecake.

MINCEMEAT BRAID

Prepare hot-roll mix as directed on package. Let rise. Roll into an oblong 16 x 8 inches. Spread drained mincemeat down center third of oblong. Cut 15 slits in dough along each side of mincemeat, spaced about 1 inch apart. Braid strips at an angle across filling. Bake at 350° for 30 to 35 minutes. Brush top with melted butter or margarine while hot. Slice crosswise to serve. Makes 1 loaf.

HOLIDAY PINWHEEL

1 package hot-roll mix
½ cup diced candied fruits and peels
¾ cup warm water (105° to 115°)
1 egg
¾ cup sugar
¼ cup firmly packed brown sugar
2 teaspoons cinnamon
¾ cup chopped walnuts
½ cup melted butter or margarine

Empty dry mix into bowl; stir in candied fruits. Dissolve yeast from package in warm, not hot, water. Blend egg with dissolved yeast. Add dry mixture; mix well. Cover; let rise in warm place (85°) until doubled. Punch down; knead until elastic. Combine sugar, brown sugar, cinnamon, and nuts. Set aside. Place a 14-inch sheet of heavy-duty foil on baking sheet. Grease; turn up edges to form a 12-inch round pan (or use a 12-inch pizza pan). Pinch off a small piece of dough; roll into a 6-inch strip ½ inch thick. Dip in butter, then in sugar-nut mixture. Wind a coil in center of pan. Continue making strips, placing them close together to make a round, flat coffeecake. Sprinkle any remaining sugar-nut mixture over top. Cover. Let rise again until doubled (30 to 60 minutes). Bake at 350° until golden brown. Cool on rack. Makes 1 loaf.

NOTE: If desired, drizzle with glaze, using ½ cup sifted confectioners' (powdered) sugar combined with 1 to 2 teaspoons milk.

GLAZED CINNAMON BUNS

¾ cup dark corn syrup
¼ cup butter or margarine
¼ cup firmly packed brown sugar
3 cups biscuit mix
Raisin-Nut Filling*

Combine corn syrup, butter or margarine, and brown sugar in a saucepan; bring to boil over medium heat; boil 1 minute. Pour into ungreased 9-inch layer-cake pan. Prepare biscuit mix as directed on package. Roll out into rectangle ¼ inch thick. Spread with Raisin-Nut Filling. Roll up like jelly roll. Cut in 1-inch slices; place cut side up in syrup. Bake at 375° for 45 minutes. Let stand in pan 5 minutes; invert on serving plate. Makes about 12 buns.

*RAISIN-NUT FILLING

¼ cup dark corn syrup
2 tablespoons butter or margarine, melted
¼ cup firmly packed brown sugar
2 teaspoons cinnamon
½ cup seedless raisins
½ cup chopped walnut meats

Combine corn syrup with melted butter or margarine; spread over surface of dough. Combine brown sugar with remaining ingredients; sprinkle over surface.

UPSIDE-DOWN APRICOT BUNS

¼ cup butter or margarine, melted
¼ cup firmly packed brown sugar
10 cooked dried apricots
1 package (8 ounces) refrigerated country-style biscuits (10)

Combine butter and brown sugar. Divide among 10 ungreased muffin cups. Drain apricots. Place 1 apricot cut side up in each muffin cup; place 1 biscuit over each apricot. Bake at 425° for 12 to 15 minutes. Turn upside down; let cool 1 minute; remove from pan. Makes 10 buns.

BUTTERMILK CORN BREAD SQUARES

Prepare corn muffin mix as directed on package, using buttermilk plus ¼ teaspoon baking soda instead of milk. Bake as directed for corn bread. Serve hot. Two packages of the mix baked in a greased 9 x 13 x 2-inch pan can be cut into 24 squares.

ORANGE CORN MUFFINS

Muffins:

1 cup enriched corn meal
1 cup sifted all-purpose flour
⅓ cup sugar
4 teaspoons baking powder
½ teaspoon salt
1 egg, beaten
1 cup milk
¼ cup soft shortening
½ cup chopped pecans
1 teaspoon grated orange peel

Sift together corn meal, flour, sugar, baking powder, and salt into bowl. Add egg, milk, and shortening. Beat with rotary beater until smooth, about 1 minute. Lightly stir in pecans and orange peel. Fill greased medium-sized muffin cups ¾ full. Bake at 425° for 15 to 18 minutes or until lightly browned. While muffins are baking, prepare topping. Makes 1 dozen muffins.

Topping:

1 teaspoon grated orange peel
¼ cup sugar
¼ cup butter or margarine, melted

Combine orange peel and sugar. Remove baked muffins from muffin cups immediately. Dip tops into melted butter, then into orange-sugar mixture. Serve piping-hot.

FOUR WAYS WITH CORN MUFFIN MIX

Four interesting ways to vary corn muffin mix follow. Take your choice, or even better, try all four.

RAISIN-CHEESE CORNSTICKS

1 package corn muffin mix
½ cup seedless raisins
½ cup grated sharp Cheddar cheese

Prepare corn muffin mix as directed on package. Stir in raisins and cheese. Spoon into well-greased cornstick pans, filling ⅔ full. Bake as directed on package. Makes about 14 sticks.

CORN DIXIES

1 package corn muffin mix
½ cup peanut butter
½ cup dairy sour cream
¼ cup brown sugar
½ cup chopped peanuts

Prepare corn muffin mix as directed on package. Spoon batter into well-greased tart shell pans or large muffin pans, filling ⅔ full. Bake as directed for 15 minutes. Combine remaining ingredients. Spread thickly on partly baked Dixies. Bake 10 minutes longer. Makes 8 to 10.

BACON SQUARES

1 package corn muffin mix
½ to 1 cup drained whole kernel corn
6 crisply cooked bacon strips

Prepare corn muffin mix as directed on package. Stir corn into batter. Spoon into well-greased 8- or 9-inch square pan. Crumble bacon; scatter on top. Bake as directed on package. Makes 9 to 12 squares.

APPLE-CORN GRIDDLE CAKES

1 package corn muffin mix
1½ cups finely chopped apples
2 tablespoons sugar
¼ teaspoon baking soda
1½ cups buttermilk
1 egg, beaten
2 tablespoons vegetable oil

Combine corn muffin mix, apples, and sugar. Add baking soda to buttermilk; add with beaten egg and vegetable oil to apple mixture. Let stand 10 minutes. Bake on hot greased griddle. Makes about 18 griddle cakes 4 inches in diameter.

BRANBERRY MUFFINS

¾ cup cranberries, fresh or frozen
⅓ cup sugar
1½ cups sifted all-purpose flour
3 teaspoons baking powder
1 teaspoon salt
½ cup sugar
1½ cups whole bran cereal
1 cup milk
1 egg
⅓ cup soft shortening

Thaw cranberries if frozen; chop coarsely; combine with ⅓ cup sugar; mix well; let stand until sugar is thoroughly dissolved; drain well; set aside. Mix and sift flour, baking powder, salt, and ½ cup sugar. Set aside. Combine bran and milk; let stand until most of the moisture is absorbed. Add egg and shortening; mix well. Add sifted dry ingredients to bran mixture, stirring only until combined. (Batter will be stiff.) Stir in drained cranberries. Fill greased 2½-inch muffin cups ¾ full. Bake at 400° for about 25 minutes or until muffins are golden brown. Serve hot. Makes 12 muffins.

LEMON-GLAZED BLUEBERRY MUFFINS

1 cup fresh blueberries
2 cups sifted all-purpose flour
⅓ cup sugar
3 teaspoons baking powder
1 teaspoon salt
1 egg, well beaten
1 cup milk
¼ cup melted shortening
1 tablespoon sugar
1 teaspoon grated lemon peel

Pick over berries; wash; drain; spread on paper toweling; shake gently to dry. Mix and sift flour, sugar, baking powder, and salt. Combine egg, milk, and melted shortening; add all at once to flour mixture; stir just until liquid is absorbed. (Batter will be lumpy.) Gently fold in berries. Fill greased muffin cups ⅔ full. Mix 1 tablespoon sugar and the grated lemon peel; sprinkle over tops. Bake at 425° for 20 minutes or until golden brown. Makes 12 medium-sized muffins.

DOUGHNUT MUFFINS

⅓ cup soft shortening
1 cup sugar, divided
1 egg
1½ cups sifted all-purpose flour
1½ teaspoons baking powder
½ teaspoon salt
¼ teaspoon nutmeg
½ cup milk
6 tablespoons melted butter or margarine
1 teaspoon cinnamon

Cream shortening and ½ cup sugar; add egg; beat well. Mix and sift flour, baking powder, salt, and nutmeg. Add alternately with milk to egg mixture. Fill greased muffin cups ⅔ full. Bake at 350° for 20 to 30 minutes or until golden brown. Remove from pans at once and roll muffins in melted butter, then in mixture of remaining ½ cup sugar and cinnamon. Makes 12 medium-sized muffins or 18 small muffins.

BISCUITS

4 cups sifted all-purpose flour
2 tablespoons baking powder
1 tablespoon sugar
1 teaspoon salt
6 tablespoons shortening
1½ cups milk

Sift flour, baking powder, sugar, and salt together in large bowl. Work in shortening with pastry blender or 2 knives until mixture is crumbly. Make well in center of flour mixture; add milk, all at once, stirring until well blended. Divide dough in half; turn out one portion at a time onto lightly floured pastry cloth or board; knead gently for ½ minute. Roll out dough to ½-inch thickness; cut in 3-inch rounds. Place biscuits on greased cookie sheets; bake at 450° for 18 to 20 minutes. Makes about 2 dozen.

VARIATIONS WITH REFRIGERATED BUTTERMILK BISCUITS
(10 biscuits in package.)

Try one of the recipes below to transform refrigerated buttermilk biscuits into special treats.

BLACK-EYED SUSANS

1 slice process American cheese
10 pitted ripe olives

1 package refrigerated buttermilk biscuits
Melted butter

Cut 10 strips of cheese to fit into pitted ripe olives, making them long enough to extend about ¼ inch over top. Stuff olives with cheese. Lightly pat biscuits into even shape. Cut biscuits with scissors or knife 4 times, from outer edge to about ½ inch from center, to form 4 petals. Place biscuits on baking sheet; set cheese-stuffed olive in center of each biscuit; brush with melted butter. Bake at 450° for about 10 to 12 minutes. Makes 10.

POPPY-SEED TWISTS

¼ cup butter or margarine
1 package refrigerated buttermilk biscuits
Poppy seeds

Melt butter or margarine; pour half into 8-inch square pan. Shape each refrigerated biscuit into an 8-inch strip by rolling between hands and twisting. Place strips in pan. Pour remaining butter over strips; sprinkle with poppy seeds. Bake at 450° for about 8 to 10 minutes. After removing from oven let stand about 2 minutes so that sticks will absorb the butter. Makes 10.

SESAME-SEED FOLDOVERS

1 package refrigerated buttermilk biscuits
Melted butter
Grated American cheese
Sesame seeds

Pat out each refrigerated biscuit until it is ¼ inch thick. Brush lightly with melted butter; sprinkle with cheese. Fold each biscuit in half. Brush tops with melted butter; sprinkle with sesame seeds. Place close together in greased 8-inch square pan. Bake at 450° for about 15 to 18 minutes. Makes 10.

VERSATILE PANCAKE MIX

One package, even half a cup, of pancake mix when used in the following recipes becomes a special treat.

COFFEECAKE

1 cup sugar
1 egg, beaten
1 cup pancake mix
½ cup milk

3 tablespoons melted shortening
¼ cup brown sugar
1 teaspoon cinnamon
1 tablespoon flour
1 tablespoon melted butter
⅓ cup chopped nutmeats

Beat sugar into beaten egg. Add, alternately, pancake mix and milk. Add melted shortening. Spread in greased 8-inch square pan. Combine remaining ingredients; sprinkle on batter. Bake at 375° for 25 to 30 minutes. Makes about 12 servings.

CREPES SUZETTE

3 eggs, beaten
½ cup milk
½ cup pancake mix
1 teaspoon grated lemon peel
Butter
Fruit sauce

Combine beaten eggs and milk. Add pancake mix and lemon peel. Heat 1 teaspoon butter in small frying pan. Coat bottom of pan with a thin layer of batter. When underside is browned, turn. Cook each crepe in this way. Roll up; serve with fruit sauce. Makes 18 to 24 crepes.

DOUGHNUTS

3 cups buckwheat pancake mix
⅔ cup sugar
1½ teaspoons cinnamon
½ teaspoon nutmeg
2 eggs, beaten
¾ cup milk
2 tablespoons melted shortening
Vegetable oil for frying

Mix first 4 ingredients. Combine beaten eggs and milk; add to pancake mixture. Add melted shortening. Roll out ½ inch thick. Cut with doughnut cutter. Fry in vegetable oil, 2 inches deep, heated to 375°. Drain on absorbent paper. Makes about 1 dozen doughnuts and holes.

CORN PANCAKES

1 cup drained kernel corn
1 package buckwheat pancake mix

Add corn to package recipe for buckwheat pancake batter. Bake on hot greased griddle.

ACCOMPANIMENT: Pork sausage in a creamy pan gravy.

CHEESE PANCAKES

⅔ cup grated American Cheddar cheese
1 package pancake mix

Add cheese to package recipe for pancake batter. Bake on hot greased griddle.

ACCOMPANIMENTS: Hot applesauce and crisp bacon.

GOTHAM PANCAKES

3 eggs
1 teaspoon salt
3 tablespoons sugar
1½ cups sifted all-purpose flour
1½ cups cold water
¾ cup light cream
Soft Maple Butter*

Beat eggs lightly. Add salt and sugar; beat a few seconds longer. Sift flour. Add water alternately with flour to egg mixture, beating constantly. Add cream slowly, beating constantly. Let batter stand at least 30 minutes, then beat again before baking the cakes. Use about ¼ cup batter for each pancake. Bake on hot, lightly greased griddle, turning to brown delicately on both sides. Put about 1 teaspoon Soft Maple Butter in center of each cake and roll up. Place rolls on baking sheet. Spread remaining maple butter over tops of cakes; run under broiler a minute. Makes about 14 pancakes.

ACCOMPANIMENT: Crisp bacon strips.

*SOFT MAPLE BUTTER

Blend 2 tablespoons maple syrup into ½ cup softened butter or margarine.

CORN MEAL GRIDDLE CAKES

1 cup enriched white corn meal
1 teaspoon salt
1 cup boiling water
2 tablespoons melted butter or margarine
1 cup buttermilk
1 egg, slightly beaten
¼ cup all-purpose flour
¼ teaspoon baking soda

Combine corn meal and salt. Stir in boiling water and melted butter slowly. Cover; let stand 10 minutes. Stir in buttermilk and egg. Combine flour and baking soda; stir in quickly (batter will be very thin, like a crepe batter). Bake on well-greased griddle over medium heat, using a measuring tablespoon of batter for each griddle cake. Stir batter often and keep griddle well greased. When golden brown underneath, turn griddle cakes to brown other side. Serve at once. Makes about 4 dozen small, thin griddle cakes.

COTTAGE CHEESE PANCAKES WITH ORANGE SAUCE

1 cup pancake mix
½ cup sugar
1 tablespoon cornstarch
¼ teaspoon salt
1 cup orange juice
2 teaspoons grated orange peel
2 tablespoons butter or margarine
2 oranges, sectioned
2 cups (1 pound) creamed cottage cheese

Prepare pancake batter according to package directions. Make 4 large pancakes using ½ cup batter for each, baking one at a time. Keep warm while preparing sauce. Combine sugar, cornstarch, and salt in saucepan. Gradually stir in orange juice. Cook over medium heat, stirring constantly, until mixture thickens and comes to a boil. Stir in orange peel and butter; add orange sections; heat. Stack pancakes with about ½ cup cottage cheese and a little orange sauce between cakes. Pile remaining cottage cheese on top. Add some orange sauce. Cut in wedges; serve with remaining sauce. Makes 4 to 6 servings.

GINGERBREAD-RAISIN PANCAKES

2½ cups sifted all-purpose flour
5 teaspoons baking powder
1½ teaspoons salt
1 teaspoon baking soda
1 teaspoon cinnamon
½ teaspoon ginger
¼ cup molasses
2 cups milk
2 eggs, slightly beaten
6 tablespoons butter or margarine, melted
1 cup raisins

Mix and sift flour, baking powder, salt, baking soda, and spices. Combine molasses and milk; add to eggs; stir in melted butter. Add molasses mixture to flour mixture; stir only until moistened. Stir in raisins. Bake on a hot griddle, using ¼ cup batter for each pancake. Serve with any desired syrup. Makes 20 pancakes.

TROPICAL DESSERT PANCAKES

1 can (1 pound 13 ounces) fruit cocktail
2 packages (3 ounces each) cream cheese
1 egg, beaten
2 cups milk
2 cups pancake mix
2 tablespoons melted shortening
1 ripe banana, finely diced

Drain syrup from fruit cocktail; reserve. Cream the cheese until light and fluffy; slowly add 2 tablespoons syrup while beating. Fold fruit lightly into cheese. Combine egg and milk; add to pancake mix all at once, stirring lightly. (The batter should be somewhat lumpy.) Fold in melted shortening and banana. Pour ¼ cup batter for each pancake onto hot griddle. Bake golden brown, turning once. Serve with the cheese-fruit sauce. Makes 6 to 8 servings.

BEST-EVER WAFFLES

2 cups sifted cake flour
3 teaspoons baking powder
¼ teaspoon salt
2 egg yolks
1¼ cups milk
⅓ cup melted butter or margarine
2 egg whites

Mix and sift flour, baking powder, and salt. Beat egg yolks until light. Combine with milk. Add milk mixture slowly to dry ingredients, stirring until batter is smooth. Add melted butter. Beat egg whites stiff but not dry; fold in. Bake in hot waffle baker. (Follow manufacturer's directions for using baker.) Makes 6 to 8 waffles.

ORANGE FRY-CAKES

1 cup sugar
3 cups sifted all-purpose flour
3 teaspoons baking powder
½ teaspoon baking soda
½ teaspoon salt
3 eggs
1 tablespoon vegetable oil
1 cup orange juice
1 tablespoon grated orange peel
Fat for frying
Sugar

Sift together sugar, flour, baking powder, baking soda, and salt. Beat eggs until very light; add oil, orange juice, and grated peel. Add to sifted dry ingredients; mix only until blended. Drop by teaspoonfuls into deep fat heated to 365°. Fry until golden brown on both sides, turning once. Drain on absorbent paper. Coat with sugar. Makes 3 dozen.

CHAPTER 15

Cakes

WHEN YOU are not baking bread most likely you are baking cakes. Cakes are the most exciting and rewarding treats for any cook to create. Mothers teach their children the art of cooking by first starting with a simple and basic layer cake, letting the little ones' imaginations run wild in deciding what flavor to use in the frosting.

Cakes have been the traditional ending for all types of parties—birthdays, anniversaries, weddings, and so forth—and they can be decorated to express any emotion or tell any story.

In this chapter you will find cakes for every occasion. There are simple ones and elaborate ones; ones to whip up quickly for guests and ones that take more time and patience. All are delicious and easy to prepare, and you, your family, and your friends will enjoy every mouthful.

PICNIC CAKE

1 package cake mix (any favorite flavor)
⅓ cup butter or margarine
⅔ cup firmly packed light brown sugar
¼ cup evaporated milk
1½ cups flaked coconut
1 teaspoon vanilla

Prepare cake mix as directed on package; turn into well-greased and floured oblong pan, 9 x 13 x 2 inches. Bake as directed. Cool slightly in pan. Cream butter or margarine until fluffy. Add sugar gradually, while creaming. Add remaining ingredients; mix well. Spread over top of cake. Broil with surface of frosting about 4 inches below source of heat until coconut is delicately browned. Cool in pan; cut in squares to serve.

EASY BOSTON CREAM "PIE"

Cake Layers:

2 eggs
¼ teaspoon salt
1 cup sugar
1 teaspoon vanilla
½ cup milk
1 tablespoon butter or margarine
1 cup sifted all-purpose flour
1 teaspoon baking powder

Beat eggs until thick and light. Beat in salt, sugar, and vanilla. Heat milk and butter to boiling point; beat in. Mix and sift flour and baking powder; beat in. Turn into 2 greased and floured 8-inch layer-cake pans. Bake at 350° for 25 to 30 minutes. Remove from pans to rack to cool.

To Assemble:

1 container (17½ ounces) frozen vanilla-flavor pudding,* thawed
1 package (6 ounces) semisweet chocolate pieces
½ cup evaporated milk

Put one cake layer on serving plate; spread with pudding to within ½ inch of outer edge. Top with second cake layer, pressing down firmly. Combine semisweet chocolate pieces and evaporated milk in small saucepan. Stir over medium heat until chocolate is melted and mixture is smooth. Spread chocolate mixture on top layer. Keep at room temperature until ready to serve.

*Extra pudding may be served at another meal.

To make a Washington "Pie":

Spread raspberry jam between cake layers; dust top with confectioners' (powdered) sugar.

MYSTERY MOCHA CAKE I

¾ cup sugar
1 cup sifted all-purpose flour
2 teaspoons baking powder
⅛ teaspoon salt
1 square unsweetened chocolate
2 tablespoons butter or margarine
½ cup milk
1 teaspoon vanilla
½ cup firmly packed brown sugar
½ cup sugar
4 tablespoons cocoa (not instant)
1 cup cold double-strength coffee

Mix and sift first 4 ingredients. Melt chocolate and butter together over hot water; add to first mixture; blend well. Combine milk and vanilla; add; mix well. Pour into greased 8-inch square cake pan. Combine brown sugar, ½ cup sugar, and cocoa. Sprinkle evenly over batter. Pour coffee over top. Bake at 350° for 40 minutes. Serve warm.

MYSTERY MOCHA CAKE II

1 package cake mix (white, yellow, spice, or chocolate)
½ cup firmly packed brown sugar
½ cup sugar
4 tablespoons cocoa (not instant)
1 cup cold strong coffee

Prepare cake mix as directed on package. Pour into greased 9-inch square cake pan. Combine sugars and cocoa. Sprinkle evenly over batter. Pour coffee over top. Bake at 350° for 40 minutes. Serve warm.

EASY FUDGE CAKE

2 squares unsweetened chocolate
1 cup boiling water, divided
1 cup sugar
2 tablespoons vegetable oil
1 egg
1½ cups sifted all-purpose flour
1 teaspoon baking soda
1 teaspoon baking powder
½ teaspoon salt
1 teaspoon vanilla
Mocha Frosting (optional; page 279)

Melt chocolate over hot water. Add ½ cup boiling water; stir until custardlike in consistency. Remove from heat. Add sugar and oil; mix well. Beat egg; add. Mix and sift dry ingredients; stir in. Add vanilla. Add remaining boiling water. Bake in greased 8-inch square cake pan at 350° for 45 to 50 minutes. Cool on cake rack. Split in 2 layers. Fill and top with Mocha Frosting, if desired.

COLLINS' CAKE

⅓ cup shortening
3½ cups sugar, divided
3 squares unsweetened chocolate, divided
2¼ cups sifted all-purpose flour
2 teaspoons baking powder
¾ teaspoon baking soda
1½ teaspoons cinnamon
¾ teaspoon salt
1½ cups buttermilk
½ cup milk
1 teaspoon vanilla

Cream shortening and 1½ cups sugar. Melt 1½ squares chocolate over hot water; blend in. Mix and sift flour, baking powder, baking soda, cinnamon, and salt. Add alternately with buttermilk to chocolate mixture. Bake in well-greased and floured 9-inch square cake pan at 350° for about

50 minutes or until cake tests done. Cool 10 minutes in pan. Remove carefully to cake rack. Combine milk and remaining 2 cups sugar in deep saucepan. Stir over low heat until sugar dissolves. Cook without stirring to 234°, or soft ball stage. Add vanilla. Beat just until spreadable; spread over surface of cake. Melt remaining chocolate; spread over icing.

CHOCOLATE SWIRL CAKE

1¾ cups sifted cake flour
1½ cups sugar
2 teaspoons baking powder
¼ teaspoon baking soda
1 teaspoon salt
½ cup shortening (at room temperature)
1 cup evaporated milk, undiluted
2 eggs
1 teaspoon vanilla
2 squares unsweetened chocolate, melted
Fluffy Brandy Filling*

Measure flour, sugar, baking powder, baking soda, and salt into flour sifter. Place shortening in mixing bowl; stir to soften. Sift in dry ingredients. Add ¾ cup milk; mix until all flour is dampened. Beat 2 minutes at low speed of electric mixer or 300 vigorous strokes by hand. Add eggs, remaining ¼ cup milk, and vanilla. Beat 1 minute longer in mixer or 150 strokes by hand. Pour batter into greased and floured 13 x 9 x 2-inch pan. Pour melted chocolate in 4 even rows across batter. With a table knife, cut through batter along these rows, in continuous circles, to make swirled pattern. Bake at 350° for 35 to 40 minutes or until done. Remove from pan; cool on rack. Cut cake in half crosswise; split each half, making 4 layers. Spread Fluffy Brandy Filling between the layers and around the sides of the cake. Chill well before serving.

*FLUFFY BRANDY FILLING

1½ cups vegetable shortening
1 cup sugar
½ teaspoon salt
¼ cup water
1 teaspoon brandy flavoring
2 eggs

Combine all ingredients in small mixing bowl. Beat at high speed of electric beater (or with sturdy rotary beater) about 10 minutes or until smooth and fluffy.

CHOCOLATE MARBLE TORTE

Cake:

¼ teaspoon salt
3 eggs
¾ cup sugar
½ teaspoon vanilla
¾ cup pancake mix
1 square unsweetened chocolate, melted and cooled
Confectioners' (powdered) sugar

Grease bottom and sides of 10 x 15 x 1-inch jelly roll pan; line with waxed paper; grease again and flour. Add salt to eggs; beat until thick and lemon-colored. Add sugar, a little at a time, beating well after each addition. Add vanilla. Fold in pancake mix gently but thoroughly. Spread evenly in pan. Drizzle chocolate over batter; swirl into batter. Bake about 10 minutes. Remove from oven; loosen edges; remove cake from pan to towel sprinkled with confectioners' sugar. Peel off waxed paper. Cut cake crosswise into three 5 x 10-inch sections. Cool.

Filling:

2 cups whipping cream
½ cup sifted confectioners' (powdered) sugar
⅓ cup cocoa (not instant)

Beat whipping cream until soft peaks form. Combine confectioners' sugar and cocoa; add to cream; beat until stiff.

To Assemble:

Place one layer of cake on serving plate; spread with filling. Repeat with second layer of cake and filling. Top with remaining layer of cake. Decorate with border of filling. Refrigerate until ready to serve. Makes 8 servings.

CHOCOLATE MAYONNAISE CAKE

2 cups unsifted all-purpose flour
1 cup sugar
½ cup unsweetened cocoa
1½ teaspoons baking powder

1 teaspoon baking soda
1 cup mayonnaise
1 cup water
1 teaspoon vanilla

Grease 9-inch square baking pan; line bottom with waxed paper. Grease waxed paper. Mix and sift flour, sugar, cocoa, baking powder, and baking soda. Stir in mayonnaise. Gradually stir in water and vanilla until smooth and blended. Pour into prepared pan. Bake at 350° for 40 to 45 minutes or until cake tester inserted in center comes out clean. Cool completely. Remove from pan. Remove waxed paper. Frost as desired.

PICNIC MARBLE CAKE

1 package white cake mix
1 package devil's food cake mix
Cinnamon
Sugar
Broken walnut meats

Prepare cake mixes according to package directions. Spoon batters alternately into well-greased oblong pan, 13 x 9 x 2 inches. Run table knife through batters in circular motion to obtain marbled effect. Combine cinnamon and sugar; scatter mixture over top of batter. Sprinkle with broken walnut meats. Bake at 350° for 50 to 60 minutes. Cool in pan. Carry to picnic without removing from pan.

CHOCOLATE SCOTCH MERINGUE CAKE

1 package white cake mix
2 tablespoons sugar
1¼ cups milk, divided
2 egg yolks, unbeaten
Chocolate Glaze*
Brown Sugar Meringue**
¼ cup chopped walnuts

Empty cake mix into bowl. Add sugar and ⅓ cup milk. Blend; beat 1 minute. Add ¼ cup more milk. Blend; beat 1 minute. Add egg yolks and remaining milk; beat 1 minute longer. Bake in 9-inch square cake pan at 375° for 35 to 40 minutes or until done. Cool in pan 5 minutes. Spread Chocolate Glaze over top of warm cake in pan. Swirl Brown Sugar Meringue over glaze, covering completely. Sprinkle walnuts over meringue.

Return to oven; bake 15 minutes longer or until meringue is lightly browned.

*CHOCOLATE GLAZE

1 square unsweetened chocolate
1 tablespoon butter or margarine
1½ tablespoons hot milk
½ cup sifted confectioners' (powdered) sugar
Dash of salt

Melt together unsweetened chocolate and butter or margarine. Combine remaining ingredients; stir in melted chocolate mixture gradually, blending well.

**BROWN SUGAR MERINGUE

Beat 2 egg whites with dash of salt until foamy. Add 1 cup firmly packed brown sugar, 2 tablespoons at a time, beating after each addition until sugar is blended. After all sugar has been added, continue beating until meringue will stand in peaks.

THREE-LAYER RAISIN CAKE

4 eggs, separated
2 cups sugar, divided
1 cup shortening (half butter or margarine)
3 cups sifted all-purpose flour
3 teaspoons baking powder
1¼ teaspoons salt
¾ cup milk
¼ cup brandy
1 teaspoon cinnamon
¾ cup dark raisins
¾ cup golden raisins
½ cup chopped pecans
Raisin Brandy Filling*
Butter Cream Frosting**
Garnish (optional): whole pecan meats

Beat egg whites until soft peaks form. Beat in ½ cup sugar gradually, beating until stiff. Set aside. Cream shortening with remaining 1½ cups sugar. Beat in egg yolks. Mix and sift flour, baking powder, and salt. Add to egg yolk mixture alternately with milk and brandy. Fold in beaten egg whites. Grease and flour three 9-inch layer-cake pans. Turn approximately ⅓ batter into one pan. Add cinnamon, raisins, and pecans to remaining batter, mixing well. Divide between remaining 2 pans. Bake at 350° for about 50 minutes or until layers test done. Let stand 5 minutes. Turn out on racks to cool. Put layers together with Raisin Brandy Filling. Spread Butter Cream Frosting over top of cake. Garnish with whole pecan meats, if desired.

*RAISIN BRANDY FILLING

½ cup sugar
4 tablespoons cornstarch
⅛ teaspoon salt
1 cup water
1 egg, beaten
2 tablespoons brandy
¾ cup chopped seedless raisins

Blend sugar with cornstarch and salt. Stir in 1 cup water. Cook over moderate heat, stirring constantly, until sauce boils and clears. Stir into beaten egg. Return to very low heat; cook 1 minute longer, stirring briskly. Remove from heat; blend in brandy and raisins. Cool thoroughly.

**BUTTER CREAM FROSTING

2½ tablespoons butter or margarine, softened
2 cups sifted confectioners' (powdered) sugar
1 tablespoon brandy
1 to 2 teaspoons milk

Blend butter or margarine with sifted confectioners' sugar and brandy. Add enough milk to make frosting of good spreading consistency.

SHERRY CAKE

1½ cups raisins
2 cups sweet sherry
½ cup shortening
¾ cup sugar
1 egg, slightly beaten
1½ cups sifted all-purpose flour
1 teaspoon baking powder
½ teaspoon each cinnamon, nutmeg, and salt
1 cup finely chopped walnuts
Eggnog Hard Sauce*

Rinse raisins; add sherry; simmer about 10 minutes or until raisins are plump. Drain off liquid; measure ¾ cup plus 2 tablespoons (add more wine if necessary). Cool. Chop raisins. Cream shortening and sugar; add raisins. Blend in egg. Mix and sift flour, baking powder, spices, and salt; add to egg mixture alternately with measured liquid. Stir in walnuts. Spoon into greased and floured 9-inch square cake pan. Bake at 350° for 1 hour. Cool in pan 10 minutes. Remove to cake rack. When thoroughly cool, frost with Eggnog Hard Sauce. Cut in small squares to serve.

*EGGNOG HARD SAUCE

¼ cup butter or margarine
1 pound sifted confectioners' (powdered) sugar
1 egg, slightly beaten
4 tablespoons sweet sherry

Cream butter or margarine. Add alternately the sifted confectioners' sugar, slightly beaten egg, and sweet sherry, beating well after each addition.

SAUCY SURPRISE CAKE

1½ cups sifted all-purpose flour
2 teaspoons baking powder
1 teaspoon salt
½ cup butter or margarine, divided
⅔ cup sugar
1 cup milk
½ cup seedless raisins
1 lemon, grated peel and juice
½ cup light molasses
1¼ cups water

Mix and sift flour, baking powder, and salt. Cream 4 tablespoons butter or margarine. Gradually add sugar; cream until light and fluffy. Add milk alternately with flour mixture, beating smooth after each addition. Stir in raisins and lemon peel. Spoon into well-greased 8-inch square cake pan. Combine lemon juice, remaining butter, molasses, and water in saucepan. Bring to boil. Remove from heat; pour gently and evenly over batter. Bake at 350° for 45 to 50 minutes. Serve warm. Makes 9 servings.

CARROT-WALNUT-RAISIN CAKE

2½ cups walnuts, divided
1¼ cups sifted all-purpose flour
1 teaspoon salt
1 teaspoon baking soda
1 teaspoon baking powder
3 eggs
1 cup granulated sugar
1 cup vegetable oil
3 cups grated carrots
1½ cups raisins
Cream Cheese Frosting*

Drop walnuts into boiling water; boil 5 minutes. Drain well; spread in shallow pan. Toast at 350° for 15 to 20 minutes, until golden brown, stirring often. Set aside ½ cup of halves and large pieces for decoration. Chop remainder coarsely. Resift flour with salt, baking soda, and baking powder. Beat eggs; beat in sugar and oil. Add flour mixture; mix to smooth batter. Stir in carrots, raisins, and chopped walnuts. Turn into greased 10-inch tube pan. Set pan on sheet of aluminum foil, cupping edges up around pan slightly if pan has a removable bottom. Bake at 350° for 60 to 65 minutes or until cake tests done. Cool in pan. When cake is cold, remove from pan; spread with Cream Cheese Frosting. Decorate with walnut pieces. Cake may be frozen, if desired.

*CREAM CHEESE FROSTING

1 package (3 ounces) cream cheese, at room temperature
½ cup soft butter or margarine
3 cups sifted confectioners' (powdered) sugar
1 teaspoon vanilla, brandy, or lemon extract

Cream the cheese together with soft butter. Gradually beat in sifted confectioners' sugar. Blend in vanilla, brandy, or lemon extract.

HIDDEN GOLD CAKE

2 cups sugar
2 cups sifted all-purpose flour
2 teaspoons baking soda
1 teaspoon salt
1 cup vegetable oil
4 eggs
3 cups grated raw carrots
Lemon frosting*
Garnish: chopped nuts

Mix and sift sugar, flour, baking soda, and salt. Add oil; mix well. Add eggs one at a time, beating well after each addition. Stir in carrots. Divide batter equally among 3 greased and floured 8-inch layer-cake pans. Bake at 350° for 35 minutes or until cake tests done. Do not open oven door for first 25 to 30 minutes of baking time. Let cool in pans 10 minutes. Remove to cake racks. When thoroughly cool, fill and top with lemon frosting. Garnish with nuts.

*Use canned ready-to-spread lemon frosting or packaged lemon frosting mix. Both are available at groceries and supermarkets.

FALL FESTIVAL CAKE

1 package spice cake mix
Sunshine Filling*
Festival Frosting**

Prepare 1 package spice cake mix according to package directions. Pour batter into 2 greased and floured 8-inch round cake pans. Bake as directed. Cool. Meanwhile, prepare Sunshine Filling. When cake is thoroughly cooled, slice each layer in half crosswise. Spread Sunshine Filling between layers. Frost top and sides with Festival Frosting. Let stand 1 hour before slicing.

*SUNSHINE FILLING

¾ cup sugar
3 tablespoons flour
½ teaspoon salt
1½ cups orange juice
1 tablespoon grated orange peel
1 egg yolk
3 tablespoons butter or margarine

Mix sugar, flour, and salt in saucepan. Add orange juice, orange peel, and egg yolk. Bring to boil over medium heat, stirring constantly. Cook 1 minute. Add butter; stir well. Cool. Reserve ⅔ cup for Festival Frosting.

**FESTIVAL FROSTING

1 package (6 ounces) butterscotch pieces (1 cup)
⅓ cup milk
2 tablespoons butter or margarine
⅛ teaspoon salt
⅔ cup reserved Sunshine Filling
3 cups sifted confectioners' (powdered) sugar
½ cup chopped nuts

Melt butterscotch pieces over hot, not boiling, water. Add milk, butter, and salt; stir until smooth. Blend in reserved Sunshine Filling. Gradually beat in confectioners' sugar. Cool to spreading consistency. Frost sides and top of cake. Sprinkle chopped nuts around cake to make a border.

MOLASSES POUND CAKE

3 cups sifted all-purpose flour
1 teaspoon baking soda
1 teaspoon salt
1½ teaspoons ground cinnamon
½ teaspoon ground nutmeg
½ teaspoon ground cloves
¾ cup sugar
1 cup light molasses
1 cup soft shortening
1 cup buttermilk
5 eggs

Mix and sift flour, baking soda, salt, spices, and sugar. Stir to blend well. Add molasses, shortening, and buttermilk. Beat for 2 minutes with an electric beater until batter is smooth and thick. Add eggs one at a time, beating well after each addition. Pour into greased and floured 2½-quart Kugelhupf mold or tube pan. Bake at 350° for 1 hour and 15 minutes or until cake springs back when touched lightly. (Cake may crack on top but this will do no harm.) Cool in pan 5 minutes. Loosen edges with sharp knife; tap mold to loosen cake. Place rack on top of pan and invert to unmold cake. Cool thoroughly before slicing.

SUGGESTION: If desired, serve with whipped cream, whipped topping, ice cream, lemon sauce, or orange sauce.

NOTE: Cake may be frozen. After cooling, wrap tightly in foil or plastic wrap. Before serving, let stand at room temperature, without unwrapping, for 1 hour to thaw.

MUSTER DAY GINGERBREAD

⅓ cup butter or margarine
⅓ cup firmly packed brown sugar
1 egg, slightly beaten
½ cup light molasses
2½ cups sifted all-purpose flour
1 teaspoon baking soda
1½ teaspoons powdered ginger
¼ teaspoon cinnamon
¼ teaspoon salt
Sugar

Cream butter or margarine and sugar; add egg and molasses; mix well. Mix and sift flour, baking soda, spices, and salt. Stir in. Roll out ¼ inch thick on lightly floured board or canvas to fit in greased, floured jelly roll pan, 15 x 10 x 1 inch. Pat even with floured fingertips. Mark deeply into squares. Sprinkle lightly with sugar. Bake at 375° for about 20 minutes or until cake tester comes out clean. Makes 15 squares.

HIGH-HAT GINGERBREAD

1 package (14½ ounces) gingerbread mix
½ pound marshmallows
2 squares unsweetened chocolate

Make and bake gingerbread according to package directions. Split hot gingerbread. Cut marshmallows in quarters; grate chocolate. Spread cut surface of half of gingerbread with half the marshmallows; sprinkle with half the chocolate. Place remaining half of gingerbread on top; cover surface with remaining marshmallows; top with remaining chocolate. Place in 350° oven long enough to melt marshmallows slightly. Makes 8 servings.

OLD-TIME BUTTERMILK GINGERBREAD

⅓ cup shortening
½ cup sugar
1 egg, beaten
½ cup light molasses
1¾ cups sifted all-purpose flour
1 teaspoon ginger
1 teaspoon cinnamon
¼ teaspoon salt
1 teaspoon baking soda
½ cup buttermilk

Cream shortening and sugar; add egg and molasses; mix well. Mix and sift flour, spices, and salt. Dissolve baking soda in buttermilk; add alternately with flour mixture to molasses mixture. Pour into a greased and floured 8-inch square cake pan. Bake at 350° for 45 minutes or until cake tester comes out clean.

SPUD-AND-SPICE CAKE

1¾ cups sugar
1 cup cold mashed potatoes*
¾ cup soft shortening
1 teaspoon cinnamon
½ teaspoon nutmeg

½ teaspoon salt
3 eggs, unbeaten
1 teaspoon baking soda
1 cup buttermilk
2 cups sifted all-purpose flour
¾ cup walnuts, chopped
2 tablespoons all-purpose flour
Quick Caramel Frosting**

Combine sugar, potatoes, shortening, spices, and salt. Cream well. Add eggs, beating until blended. Combine baking soda and buttermilk. Add alternately with 2 cups flour to creamed mixture, beginning and ending with flour. Coat walnuts with 2 additional tablespoons flour; stir into batter. Turn into greased and floured 13 x 9 x 2-inch pan. Bake at 350° for 50 to 60 minutes. Cool and frost with Quick Caramel Frosting.

*Or reconstitute instant mashed potatoes as directed on package and let cool before measuring.

**QUICK CARAMEL FROSTING

¼ cup butter or margarine
¾ cup firmly packed brown sugar
3 tablespoons milk
2 cups sifted confectioners' (powdered) sugar

Melt butter or margarine in saucepan; stir in brown sugar. Continue cooking over low heat 2 minutes. Add milk. Bring to a full boil; cool to lukewarm without stirring. Add sifted confectioners' sugar; beat until smooth and of spreading consistency.

BUTTERCRUNCH CAKE RING

¼ cup butter or margarine
⅓ cup firmly packed brown sugar
½ cup broken walnut meats
1 package white cake mix
1 cup whipping cream
1½ teaspoons vanilla
3 tablespoons sugar
1½ cups pitted Bing cherries, fresh, canned, or frozen
1 cup pineapple chunks, fresh, canned, or frozen

Grease 10-inch ring mold. Cut butter or margarine in small pieces; place in bottom of mold. Sprinkle brown sugar and walnuts over butter. Prepare cake mix batter as directed on package; pour evenly into mold. Bake at 350° for 45 to 50 minutes; remove from pan at once; cool. Whip cream; whip in vanilla and sugar; fold in fruits. Fill center of cake with cream mixture. Makes 8 to 10 servings.

BURNT ALMOND CAKE

Layers:

½ cup white shortening
1 cup sugar
3 egg whites
½ teaspoon almond extract
2 cups sifted all-purpose flour
3 teaspoons baking powder
¼ teaspoon salt
⅔ cup milk

Cream shortening to consistency of mayonnaise; add sugar while continuing to cream. Add unbeaten egg whites one at a time, beating well after each addition. Add almond extract. Mix and sift flour, baking powder, and salt. Add alternately with milk to first mixture. Bake in 2 greased 9-inch cake pans at 375° for 25 to 30 minutes. Cool on cake rack.

Frosting:

1½ cups blanched almonds
2 tablespoons vegetable oil (about)
1 cup butter or margarine
2⅔ cups confectioners' (powdered) sugar
Hot milk or cream
½ teaspoon almond extract

Put almonds in shallow pan with about 2 tablespoons vegetable oil. Bake at 450°, stirring often, until almonds are deep golden brown. Drain on absorbent paper. Crush quite fine with rolling pin. Cream butter or margarine. Add sugar gradually, with enough hot milk to make good spreading consistency. Add flavoring.

To Assemble:

Put cake layers together with frosting. Frost top and sides. Cover entire cake with crushed almonds, pressing into frosting.

POPPY SEED CAKE

1 package white cake mix
1 tablespoon soft butter or margarine
⅓ cup poppy seeds, soaked overnight in water and well drained in small sieve
Topping*
Choice of frosting (see below)

Make cake according to package directions, adding the butter. During the last minute of beating the ingredients, add the poppy seeds. Bake according to directions in a 9 x 13-inch pan, until cake tests done and is golden brown on top. Cool in pan for 10 minutes. Remove cake to cake rack to finish cooling. Spread cold cake with Topping. Top with any favorite cooked white frosting.

*TOPPING

1 can (20 ounces) crushed pineapple
½ cup sugar
2 tablespoons cornstarch
Juice of ½ lemon

Combine all ingredients. Cook over hot water, stirring often, until thickened. Cool to room temperature; spread on cold cake.

GOLDEN SPICE RING CAKE

3 eggs
1¼ cups sugar
1 cup canned pumpkin
½ cup vegetable oil
⅓ cup water
1¾ cups sifted all-purpose flour
1 teaspoon salt
¾ teaspoon baking soda
2 teaspoons cinnamon
1 teaspoon nutmeg
1 cup quick-cooking rolled oats, uncooked
Orange Butter Frosting*

Beat eggs until frothy; add sugar gradually; beat until thick and lemon-colored. Stir in pumpkin, oil, and water; blend well. Mix and sift flour, salt, baking soda, cinnamon, and nutmeg. Add gradually to pumpkin mixture, blending well. Stir in oats. Pour into well-greased and floured 1½-quart ring mold. Bake at 350° for about 30 minutes. Loosen edges with knife or spatula; cool 10 minutes, then invert on serving plate. Cool. Ice top with Orange Butter Frosting.

*ORANGE BUTTER FROSTING

2 tablespoons butter or margarine
2½ cups confectioners' (powdered) sugar
3 tablespoons orange juice (approximately)
1 teaspoon grated orange peel
Few grains salt

Cream butter or margarine. Add confectioners' sugar gradually, alternating with enough orange juice to make frosting right consistency for spreading. Stir in orange peel and salt.

DELLA ROBBIA CAKE

1 cup chopped filberts
1 teaspoon ground mace
¼ teaspoon salt
1 cup butter or margarine
1½ teaspoons vanilla
1¾ cups sugar
5 large eggs
2 cups sifted all-purpose flour
Confectioners' Sugar Icing (page 240)
Marzipan (page 381)

Toast filberts at 325° for 10 to 15 minutes. Combine mace, salt, butter, and vanilla in large mixing bowl. Beat until consistency of mayonnaise. Beat in sugar gradually. Beat in 4 eggs, one at a time, beating well after each addition. Stir in flour, mixing well after each addition. Beat in remaining egg. Fold in toasted filberts. Spoon into greased and floured 3-quart ring mold. Bake at 325° for 1 hour. Cool 20 minutes. Turn out on wire rack to finish cooling. Store in tightly closed cake box. Flavor of cake will improve with age. Before serving, drizzle with Confectioners' Sugar Icing and wreathe rim of top with tiny Marzipan candies.

SOUR CREAM BLUEBERRY CAKE

½ cup soft butter or margarine
1 cup sugar
3 eggs
2 cups sifted all-purpose flour
1 teaspoon baking powder
1 teaspoon baking soda
½ teaspoon salt
1 cup dairy sour cream
1 teaspoon vanilla
1 teaspoon ground cardamom (optional)
2 cups fresh blueberries
½ cup firmly packed brown sugar

Cream butter and sugar; add eggs one at a time, beating well after each addition. Sift dry ingredients together; add gradually to the egg mixture, alternating with sour cream, ending with flour mixture. Stir in vanilla and cardamom. Fold in 1 cup blueberries. Pour half the batter into well-greased and floured pan, 9 x 13 x 2 inches.

Cover with remaining blueberries. Sprinkle with brown sugar. Top with remaining batter. Bake at 325° for 45 to 50 minutes or until cake tests done. Cool in pan 10 minutes. Remove to rack to finish cooling. To serve, cut in 12 pieces.

CHERRY-WALNUT CAKE

½ cup shortening
1 cup sugar
1 egg
1 square unsweetened chocolate, melted
1½ cups sifted all-purpose flour
1 teaspoon baking soda
⅛ teaspoon salt
⅓ cup chopped maraschino cherries, drained
½ cup chopped walnuts
1 cup buttermilk
Maraschino Cherry Frosting*

Cream shortening, sugar, and egg until fluffy. Add melted chocolate; blend well. Mix and sift dry ingredients; add maraschino cherries and nutmeats, dredging thoroughly. Add fruit-nut mixture alternately with buttermilk to egg mixture; beat well after each addition. Turn into greased 8-inch square cake pan. Bake at 350° for 55 to 60 minutes. Cool; frost with Maraschino Cherry Frosting.

*MARASCHINO CHERRY FROSTING

Soften ¼ cup butter or margarine. Add gradually 1 pound sifted confectioners' (powdered) sugar and enough maraschino cherry juice to make a spreading consistency. Beat until frosting is smooth and creamy.

FOUR-LAYER LEMON CAKE

Thaw one frozen pound cake. Cut lengthwise into 4 slices. Spread 3 layers with English Lemon Curd.* Replace top slice. Frost with whipped topping. Slice crosswise to serve.

*ENGLISH LEMON CURD (OR BUTTER)

½ pound butter or margarine
1½ cups sugar
½ cup lemon juice
5 eggs, well beaten

Melt butter in double boiler; add sugar; blend well. Stir until sugar dissolves. Stir in lemon juice. Add eggs gradually, stirring constantly, until well blended. Continue to cook and stir until mixture thickens. Cover; continue cooking 15 minutes. Remove from heat; pour into jelly glasses. Makes about 3 cups. (Can be stored in refrigerator for at least 2 weeks.)

PINEAPPLE ANGEL CAKE

1 package angel food mix
1 envelope unflavored gelatin
1 tablespoon cold water
1 can (about 13 ounces) crushed pineapple
3 tablespoons confectioners' (powdered) sugar
½ teaspoon vanilla
1½ cups whipping cream

Make and bake angel food cake as directed on package. Cool; split into 2 layers. Meanwhile, soften gelatin in cold water. Place in top part of double boiler. Drain pineapple, reserving syrup. Add ⅓ cup syrup and drained pineapple to gelatin. Add confectioners' sugar and vanilla. Cook, stirring constantly, over hot water until thickened. Whip cream until stiff; fold into pineapple mixture. Spread between layers and on sides and top of cake. Chill. Makes 10 servings.

TUTTI-FRUTTI CAKE

¼ cup orange juice
1 tablespoon lemon juice
1¼ cups sugar, divided
½ cup butter or margarine
3 tablespoons finely grated orange peel
1 tablespoon finely grated lemon peel
½ cup raisins, chopped
1 egg, beaten
1⅓ cups sifted cake flour
½ teaspoon baking powder
1 teaspoon baking soda
½ teaspoon salt
1 cup buttermilk
Whipped cream *or* whipped cream topping

Combine fruit juices and ½ cup sugar. Stir until sugar dissolves. Let stand. Cream butter to consistency of mayonnaise. Add remaining sugar gradually while creaming. Beat in grated peels and raisins. Add egg; beat well. Mix and sift flour, baking powder, baking soda, and salt. Sift into butter mixture alternately with buttermilk. Bake in 9-inch well-greased and floured square cake pan at 350° for about 40 minutes or until cake tests done. Remove from oven. Spoon juice-sugar mixture evenly over top. Cool in pan.

Cut in squares to serve, with whipped cream or whipped topping. Makes 9 servings.

CHERRY-PINEAPPLE CAKE DESSERT

1 can (8 ounces) crushed pineapple
1¼ cups sifted all-purpose flour
1 teaspoon baking powder
¼ teaspoon salt
¼ cup butter or margarine
½ cup sugar
½ cup milk
¼ cup chopped maraschino cherries
¾ cup firmly packed brown sugar
Sweetened whipped cream

Drain pineapple, reserving juice. Sift flour with baking powder and salt. Cream butter; gradually add sugar, creaming well. Add dry ingredients alternately with milk, beginning and ending with dry ingredients. Blend thoroughly with each addition. (With electric mixer use low speed.) Spread in 9-inch square pan, well greased on the bottom. Top with cherries, drained pineapple, and brown sugar. Combine pineapple juice with enough water to measure ¾ cup. Bring to boil; pour over batter. Bake at 350° for 35 to 40 minutes or until cake springs back when touched lightly in center. Serve warm with sweetened whipped cream. Makes 6 to 8 servings.

RUBY-RED CRANBERRY CAKE

2 cups sifted all-purpose flour
3 tablespoons sugar
3 teaspoons baking powder
½ teaspoon salt
1 cup whipping cream
1 egg, slightly beaten
Canned jellied cranberry sauce (about ½ of 1-pound can)
3 apples, pared, cored, and quartered
¼ cup sugar
½ teaspoon cinnamon
2 tablespoons melted butter or margarine
Cream *or* whipped cream (optional)

Mix and sift flour, sugar, baking powder, and salt. Whip cream; blend in egg. Add to dry ingredients; stir until dough clings together. Spread in well-greased 9-inch square pan. Cut cranberry sauce in nine ¼-inch slices. Place on dough. Cut each apple quarter in 3 slices; arrange in rows on cranberry sauce, pressing cut edges through

sauce to dough. Sprinkle with combined sugar and cinnamon. Drizzle with butter. Bake at 400° for 30 to 35 minutes. Serve warm, with plain or whipped cream, if desired.

GOLDEN LOAF CAKE

1 package yellow cake mix
¾ cup apricot nectar
1 package (3 ounces) orange-flavor gelatin
4 eggs, separated
1 teaspoon lemon extract

Combine first 3 ingredients. Mix well. Add egg yolks one at a time, beating after each addition. Add lemon extract. Beat egg whites stiff but not dry; fold in. Spoon into 2 greased and floured loaf pans, 9 x 5 x 3 inches. Bake at 325° for 40 minutes or until cake tests done. Cool.

FRESH LIME CAKE

1 package white cake mix
2 tablespoons grated lime peel, divided
6 tablespoons butter or margarine
¼ teaspoon salt
1 teaspoon vanilla
1 egg white, unbeaten
3½ cups sifted confectioners' (powdered) sugar
2½ tablespoons lime juice

Prepare cake mix as directed on package; stir in 1 tablespoon lime peel. Pour into 2 greased 8-inch layer-cake pans. Bake as directed on package. Cool. Cream butter with salt and vanilla. Add egg white; mix well. Add confectioners' sugar alternately with lime juice, beating well after each addition. Fill and frost cake. Sprinkle top with remaining lime peel.

GLAZED PEAR CAKE

2 squares unsweetened chocolate, divided
1 tablespoon butter or margarine
½ cup sugar
1 cup whipping cream, divided
1 teaspoon vanilla
1 chocolate cake, 9 inches square
8 canned pear halves

Melt 1 square chocolate in butter. Remove from heat; add sugar slowly, then ¼ cup of the cream. Beat smooth; bring slowly to a boil. Remove from heat; add remaining chocolate; stir until melted;

add vanilla. Cool. Whip remaining cream. Cut cake in quarters, then diagonally to make 8 pieces. Separate. On each piece of cake, place a mound of whipped cream. Cover pear halves with chocolate mixture; place on mounds of cream. Reassemble cake. Decorate between pear halves and around edges with remaining whipped cream.

INDIVIDUAL JELLY ROLL LAYER CAKES

> 4 eggs
> ½ teaspoon salt
> ¾ cup sugar
> 1 teaspoon vanilla
> ¾ cup pancake mix
> Confectioners' (powdered) sugar
> Choice of filling (see below)
> Choice of topping (see below)

Combine eggs and salt; beat until thick and lemon-colored. Add sugar a little at a time, beating after each addition. Add vanilla. Add pancake mix; beat until smooth. Grease jelly roll pan, 10 x 15 x 1 inch. Line with waxed paper; grease again. Spread batter evenly in pan. Bake at 400° for 10 to 12 minutes. Sprinkle dry towel with confectioners' (powdered) sugar. As soon as cake is done, loosen edges; turn out on towel; peel waxed paper carefully from cake. When cool, cut in 12 pieces. Put 2 pieces of cake together, sandwich-fashion, with any filling; top as desired. Makes 6 servings.

SERVING SUGGESTIONS

1. Raspberry jam filling; sprinkle top with confectioners' (powdered) sugar.
2. Coffee ice cream between cake layers; top with warm butterscotch sauce.
3. Chocolate filling, made with pudding mix, between layers; top with whipped cream.

GOLDEN JAM CAKE

> 2 baked 9-inch cake layers
> 1½ cups apricot, peach, or pineapple jam
> ⅔ cup firmly packed brown sugar
> ½ cup canned blanched slivered almonds
> ¼ cup water
> 1 teaspoon rum flavoring
> Whipped topping

Spread each cake layer generously with jam. Sprinkle with brown sugar and almonds. Combine water and flavoring; pour over layers; bake at 400° until sugar melts. Top with whipped topping just before serving. Makes 12 servings.

APPLE-LIME CHIFFON CAKE

> 2 cups sifted all-purpose flour
> 1½ cups sugar
> 3 teaspoons baking powder
> 1 teaspoon salt
> ½ cup vegetable oil
> 7 egg yolks, unbeaten
> ¾ cup bottled apple juice
> 1 teaspoon almond extract
> 2 teaspoons grated lime peel
> 1 cup egg whites (7 or 8)
> ½ teaspoon cream of tartar
> Confectioners' (powdered) sugar

Sift together into mixing bowl flour, sugar, baking powder, and salt. Make a well in flour mixture and add, in order, oil, unbeaten egg yolks, apple juice, almond extract, and lime peel. Beat with a spoon until smooth. Whip egg whites with cream of tartar until they form very stiff peaks—much stiffer than for angel food or meringue. Pour first mixture gradually over egg whites, gently folding in with rubber spatula, until just blended. Pour into ungreased 10-inch tube pan 4 inches deep. Bake at 325° for 55 minutes, then increase heat to 350° and bake 10 to 15 minutes longer or until top springs back when lightly touched. At once, turn pan upside down with extreme outer edges of pan resting on 2 other pans. Let hang, free of table, until cold. Loosen from sides and tube with spatula. Turn pan over and hit edge sharply on table to loosen. Dust top with confectioners' sugar.

PEACH GOLD CHIFFON CAKE

> 2 to 3 canned peach halves
> 1⅛ cups (1 cup plus 2 tablespoons) sifted cake flour
> ¾ cup sugar
> 1½ teaspoons baking powder
> ½ teaspoon salt
> ¼ cup vegetable oil
> 3 egg yolks
> 1½ teaspoons grated lemon peel
> ½ cup egg whites (about 4)
> ¼ teaspoon cream of tartar
> Frosting of choice
> Peach halves

Force well-drained peaches through sieve or food mill, or mash thoroughly, to make ⅜ cup (¼ cup plus 2 tablespoons). Sift flour, sugar, baking powder, and salt together. Make a well in dry ingredients; add oil, unbeaten egg yolks, lemon peel, and peach pulp. Beat until smooth. Beat egg whites and cream of tartar with rotary beater until they form very stiff peaks. Pour first mixture slowly over egg whites, folding together until blended. Pour into ungreased 9-inch tube pan. Bake at 350° for 30 to 35 minutes. Immediately turn pan upside down, resting edges on 2 other pans to allow for circulation of air under cake. When pan is cold, loosen sides of cake with spatula; turn pan over and hit edge sharply on table. Frost as desired. Serve with remaining peach halves.

GRAPEFRUIT CHIFFON CAKE

2¼ cups sifted cake flour
1½ cups sugar
3 teaspoons baking powder
1 teaspoon salt
8 eggs, separated
½ cup vegetable oil
¾ cup fresh grapefruit juice
2 teaspoons grated fresh orange peel
½ teaspoon cream of tartar
Whipped Cream Frosting*
4 grapefruits, sectioned

Mix and sift flour, sugar, baking powder, and salt. In another bowl mix egg yolks, oil, grapefruit juice, and orange peel. Make a well in the dry ingredients; add liquid mixture all at once; stir until batter is smooth. Beat egg whites and cream of tartar in large mixing bowl until stiff peaks form. Pour batter over egg whites; fold in gently but thoroughly. Turn into ungreased 10-inch tube pan. Bake at 325° for 60 to 65 minutes or until cake tester inserted in cake comes out clean. Remove from oven; invert; cool completely. Turn cake out of pan; frost with Whipped Cream Frosting. Serve with grapefruit sections. Makes 12 servings.

*WHIPPED CREAM FROSTING

2 cups whipping cream
2 tablespoons sugar
2 teaspoons vanilla

Whip cream until soft peaks form; beat in sugar and vanilla; whip until stiff.

MOLASSES-CUSTARD CHIFFON CAKE

7 eggs, separated
½ cup light molasses
½ cup milk, scalded
2 cups sifted all-purpose flour
1 cup sugar
3 teaspoons baking powder
½ teaspoon baking soda
1 teaspoon salt
¼ teaspoon nutmeg
½ cup vegetable oil
2 teaspoons vanilla
½ teaspoon cream of tartar
Confectioners' (powdered) sugar
Peaches and Cream*

Beat egg yolks until very thick and light in color. Beat in molasses. Pour in hot milk slowly, beating constantly; cool. Mix and sift flour, sugar, baking powder, baking soda, salt, and nutmeg. Make a well in dry ingredients and add, in order, oil, vanilla, and cooled egg yolk mixture. Beat until smooth. Add cream of tartar to egg whites. Beat in large bowl until stiff enough to form sharp points. Fold molasses batter into egg whites. Turn into ungreased 10-inch tube pan. Bake at 325° for 50 minutes. Increase oven temperature to 350°; bake an additional 10 minutes. Invert cake to cool. When completely cooled, remove from pan. Dust lightly with sifted confectioners' sugar. Serve with Peaches and Cream.

*PEACHES AND CREAM

2 tablespoons light molasses
2 cups whipping cream
1 can (1 pound) sliced cling peaches, drained

Add molasses to cream; beat until soft peaks form. Spoon over cake slices; top with sliced peaches.

CHOCOLATE CHERRY FRUITCAKE

3 eggs, well beaten
1 cup sugar
1½ cups sifted all-purpose flour
1½ teaspoons baking powder
¼ teaspoon salt
1 package (6 ounces) semisweet chocolate pieces, divided
2 cups coarsely chopped pecans or walnuts
1 cup coarsely cut dates
1 cup halved candied cherries

Beat eggs and sugar together. Sift dry ingredients. Add ¾ cup chocolate pieces, nuts, dates, and cherries to flour mixture; fold in egg-sugar mixture. Spoon into oiled, waxed-paper-lined loaf pan, 9 x 5 x 3 inches. Scatter remaining chocolate pieces on top. Bake at 325° for 1¼ hours or until crusty brown; remove; cool on rack.

REFRIGERATOR FRUITCAKE I

6 cups fine graham cracker crumbs
1 cup diced candied pineapple (mixture of red, green, and yellow)*
1 cup candied red cherries
1 box (15 ounces) golden raisins
1 cup dark raisins
1 cup chopped dates
1 cup chopped pecans
1½ cups chopped walnuts
1 can (3½ ounces) flaked coconut
1 teaspoon ground cinnamon
½ teaspoon ground nutmeg
1 cup plus 2 tablespoons undiluted evaporated milk
½ cup light molasses
2 tablespoons frozen orange juice concentrate, undiluted
2 teaspoons rum flavoring

Combine first 11 ingredients in a large bowl. Heat milk to lukewarm. Combine milk and molasses. Add to first mixture with orange juice concentrate and rum flavoring. Mix well. Be very sure no dry crumbs remain. Line a greased 9 x 5 x 2¾-inch loaf pan with waxed paper or plastic wrap. Grease paper. Pack cake mixture firmly into cake pan. (It may seem as if pan is too small, but it will hold all of the mixture if it is packed firmly and evenly.) Store in refrigerator at least 2 days before cutting. Cake mixture will be sticky before storage, but the moisture will be absorbed.

*Or use diced candied fruits and peels.

REFRIGERATOR FRUITCAKE II

1½ cups seedless raisins
1 cup pitted prunes
1 cup sliced pitted dates
1½ cups mixed diced candied fruits and peels
½ cup butter or margarine
½ cup confectioners' (powdered) sugar
¼ cup light corn syrup
½ cup orange marmalade
1 teaspoon cinnamon
¼ teaspoon cloves
½ teaspoon salt
½ cup chopped walnuts
5 cups fine graham cracker crumbs

Rinse and drain raisins and prunes. Pour boiling water over prunes; let stand 5 minutes; drain; cool; slice. Combine all fruits and peels. Cream butter and confectioners' sugar together. Blend in syrup, marmalade, spices, and salt. Mix lightly with fruits. Let stand 2 hours or longer. Blend in walnuts and crumbs. Pack into loaf pan, 9 x 5 x 3 inches, which has been lined with waxed paper. Chill 48 hours or longer.

FAVORITE FRUITCAKE

1 cup vegetable oil
1½ cups firmly packed brown sugar
4 eggs
3 cups sifted all-purpose flour, divided
1 teaspoon baking powder
2 teaspoons salt
2 teaspoons cinnamon
2 teaspoons allspice
1 teaspoon cloves
1 cup pineapple juice
1 cup chopped candied pineapple
1½ cups whole candied cherries
1 cup raisins
1 cup chopped figs or dates
3 cups coarsely chopped walnuts
1 cup diced citron

Combine oil, sugar, and eggs; beat vigorously with spoon or electric mixer for 2 minutes. Sift 2 cups flour with baking powder, salt, and spices. Stir into oil mixture alternately with pineapple juice. Mix remaining cup of flour with fruits and nuts. Pour batter over this mixture, blending well. Turn into well-oiled 10-inch tube pan. Set pan of water on lower oven rack. Bake at 275° for 2½ to 3 hours. Let stand 15 minutes before removing from pan, then cool on rack. Wrap in aluminum foil; store to ripen. Glaze before using. (See p. 272). An hour or two before slicing, chill cake in refrigerator.

FROZEN FRUITCAKE

2 cups milk
2 eggs
¾ cup sugar
1 teaspoon salt

5 shredded-wheat biscuits
½ cup raisins
½ cup dried currants
½ cup broken pecan meats
1 cup candied cherries, halved
1 teaspoon rum flavoring
1 teaspoon vanilla
1 cup whipping cream

Line 9 x 5 x 3-inch loaf pan with waxed paper. Scald milk in top of double boiler. Beat eggs until foamy. Add sugar and salt to eggs; beat until sugar dissolves. Add a little hot milk to eggs. Return to remaining hot milk. Cook over hot water, stirring constantly, until mixture coats spoon. Cool. Roll shredded wheat into fine crumbs (about 1½ cups). Stir crumbs, raisins, currants, pecans, cherries, rum flavoring, and vanilla into egg mixture. Whip cream stiff; fold in. Turn into prepared pan. Freeze 12 hours or overnight. Let stand in refrigerator 1 hour before serving.

FRUITCAKE CARIBE

2¾ cups sifted all-purpose flour
3 teaspoons baking powder
½ teaspoon baking soda
¾ teaspoon salt
½ cup butter or margarine
1 cup sugar
3 eggs
1½ cups mashed ripe bananas
¾ cup broken walnut meats
1¼ cups diced candied fruits and peels
6 tablespoons raisins

Mix and sift flour, baking powder, baking soda, and salt. Cream butter to consistency of mayonnaise; add sugar gradually while continuing to cream. Add eggs to sugar one at a time, beating well after each addition. Add dry ingredients and mashed bananas alternately. Stir in nuts, fruits, and raisins. Spoon evenly into well-greased bundt pan or 9- or 10-inch tube pan. Bake at 350° for about 1 hour and 10 minutes or until cake is deep golden brown and tests done.

HOLIDAY FRUITCAKE

¾ cup butter or margarine
½ cup sugar
¾ teaspoon salt
½ teaspoon baking soda
½ teaspoon cinnamon
½ teaspoon nutmeg

¾ cup molasses
3 small eggs
2 cups sifted all-purpose flour
3 cups (1½ pounds) diced candied fruits and peels
¾ cup coarsely chopped walnuts
Candied pineapple slices and cherries (optional)

Cream together first 6 ingredients. Add molasses; mix well. Beat in eggs one at a time. Gradually stir in flour. Add fruits and nuts; mix thoroughly. Line bottom of large tube pan with waxed paper. Grease paper and sides of pan and tube. Spoon in batter. Decorate top with candied pineapple slices and cherries, if desired. Bake at 300° for 3 hours. Keep a large shallow pan of hot water on rack underneath cake while baking.

EASY FRUITCAKE

3 cups sifted all-purpose flour
1 teaspoon baking soda
1 teaspoon salt
1 teaspoon cinnamon
1 teaspoon nutmeg
¾ cup shortening
½ cup sugar
½ cup honey
2 eggs
½ cup applesauce
2 jars (1 pound each) diced candied fruits and peels

Mix and sift first 5 ingredients. Cream shortening; add sugar and honey gradually; continue to cream until light and fluffy. Add eggs one at a time, beating well after each addition. Stir in applesauce; stir in mixed fruits and peels. Add dry ingredients gradually, beating well with a spoon until blended. Pour into greased and floured 9-inch tube pan. Bake at 300° for 2 hours and 15 minutes.

WHITE FRUITCAKE

1 cup butter or margarine
1 cup extra-fine (instant) granulated sugar
5 eggs, separated
2½ cups sifted all-purpose flour
1 teaspoon mace
¼ teaspoon nutmeg
1 cup diced candied fruits
½ cup golden raisins
2 tablespoons red wine

2 teaspoons brandy flavoring
Confectioners' Sugar Icing (page 240)
Garnish: leaf-shaped green gumdrops; tiny
    red gumdrops

Cream butter or margarine until consistency of mayonnaise. Add sugar gradually, then egg yolks; cream until light and fluffy. Mix and sift flour and spices; combine with fruits; add wine and brandy flavoring. Gradually add dry ingredients to creamed mixture. Mix well. Beat egg whites stiff; fold in. Spoon into greased and floured 9-inch tube cake pan. Bake at 325° for 1 hour and 15 minutes or until golden brown and done. Cool on rack. Frost with Confectioners' Sugar Icing, letting the icing slide down the side of the cake. When icing is set, garnish with a holly wreath made with leaf-shaped green gumdrops and tiny red gumdrops for berries.

CANDIED ORANGE CUPS FILLED WITH FRUITCAKE

Candied Orange Cups:

6 oranges
Sugar
1 cup water
1 teaspoon powdered ginger

Slice oranges in half, making scalloped edges if desired; ream juice. Gently remove pulp without tearing skin. Cover orange halves with cold water; bring to boil. Boil 10 minutes; drain. Repeat 3 times. Combine 2 cups sugar, water, and ginger in heavy 3-quart saucepan; stir over low heat until sugar dissolves. Boil gently, uncovered, to 238°. Add orange halves. Cook gently 10 minutes or until most of syrup is absorbed. Roll orange halves in sugar. Let dry thoroughly.
halves in sugar. Let dry thoroughly.

Fruitcake:

2 cups graham cracker crumbs
2 cups raisins
1 cup (8 ounces) diced candied fruits and
    peels
½ cup chopped walnuts
½ pound marshmallows
⅓ cup frozen orange juice concentrate,
    thawed, undiluted
½ teaspoon vanilla
1 tablespoon grated orange peel
½ teaspoon each nutmeg and ginger
¼ teaspoon each cinnamon and cloves

Combine crumbs, raisins, candied fruits, and nuts. Quarter marshmallows; place in top of double boiler. Add undiluted orange juice concentrate and vanilla. When melted, stir in grated peel and spices. Stir marshmallow mixture into crumb mixture until well blended.

To Assemble:

Pack fruitcake in candied orange shells. Chill 6 to 8 hours. Garnish tops with halved candied cherries and strips of angelica, if desired. Makes 12.

NO-BAKE FRUITCAKE

1½ cups golden seedless raisins
2 cups mixed diced candied fruit and peel
2 containers (about 1 cup each) junior prunes
2 containers (about 1 cup each) junior
    applesauce
1 cup sugar
1 teaspoon each cinnamon, allspice, nutmeg
½ cup orange juice
1 tablespoon brandy flavoring
4 envelopes unflavored gelatin
⅓ cup cold water
1½ pints (3 cups) whipping cream
1 cup chopped walnut meats
Garnish (optional): whole walnut meats;
    candied cherries

Combine first 4 ingredients. Mix sugar and spices; add; mix well. Combine orange juice and brandy flavoring; add; let stand 1½ hours. Heat to boiling point, stirring occasionally; remove from heat. Soften gelatin in cold water; dissolve over hot water; add to hot fruit mixture; mix thoroughly. Chill until mixture begins to thicken. Whip cream to thick custard consistency; fold in with chopped walnuts. Spoon carefully into lightly oiled 10-inch tube cake pan. Chill until firm. Loosen sides and unmold on serving plate. Garnish top with whole walnut meats and candied cherries, if desired. Makes 24 servings.

BIRTHDAY CAKE

2 packages white cake mix
Butter Frosting*

Prepare cake mix as directed on package; bake one 9-inch layer and 18 large cupcakes. Cool. Frost top and sides of cake layer with Butter Frosting. Frost cupcakes upside down. Arrange 7 cupcakes on cake layer; surround with a circle of remaining cupcakes. Top each cupcake with a birthday candle.

*BUTTER FROSTING

1 cup butter or margarine
2 pounds confectioners' (powdered) sugar, sifted
⅔ cup milk or cream (about)
1 teaspoon vanilla
Food coloring

Cream butter or margarine until consistency of mayonnaise. Add confectioners' sugar alternately with milk or cream, beating in each addition until frosting is of good spreading consistency. Add vanilla. Tint with food coloring to any desired pastel shade.

FOUR-LAYER PARTY CAKE

1 package yellow cake mix
1 package (6 ounces) semisweet chocolate pieces
2 packages (3 ounces each) cream cheese
4 tablespoons milk (about), divided
4½ cups sifted confectioners' (powdered) sugar
Dash of salt
1 teaspoon vanilla
⅓ cup raspberry preserves
½ cup apricot preserves
Garnish (optional): chopped nuts

Prepare cake batter according to package directions. Bake in greased 15 x 10-inch pan 20 to 25 minutes. Cool; cut crosswise into fourths to make four 10 x 3½-inch layers. Melt semisweet chocolate over hot, not boiling, water. Blend cream cheese with 3 tablespoons milk; slowly stir in confectioners' sugar, then salt and vanilla; blend well. Stir in melted chocolate and about 1 tablespoon additional milk until mixture is of good spreading consistency. Spread one cake layer with raspberry preserves. Top with second layer and spread with ½ cup of the chocolate mixture. Top with third layer and spread with apricot preserves. Top with fourth layer and frost with remaining chocolate mixture. Garnish with chopped nuts, if desired. Makes 10 to 12 generous servings.

PERSONALIZED PARTY CAKE

1 package chocolate cake mix
1 package (6 ounces) semisweet chocolate pieces
2 tablespoons butter or margarine
¼ cup milk
1 cup sifted confectioners' (powdered) sugar
1 teaspoon vanilla

Prepare cake mix as directed on package. Bake in well-greased oblong pan, 13 x 9 x 2 inches, according to package directions until cake tests done. Cool. Combine semisweet chocolate pieces, butter, and milk in saucepan. Stir over low heat until chocolate is melted and mixture smooth. Beat in confectioners' sugar and vanilla. Frost cake. Mark into squares; write name of guest in each square with canned ready-to-spread pink frosting put through pastry tube or with pressurized cake and cookie decorator.

PINK PARTY CAKE

1 package white cake mix
1 package (3 ounces) strawberry-flavor gelatin
¾ cup water
½ cup vegetable oil
4 eggs
1 can (16½ ounces) ready-to-spread strawberry frosting
Flaked coconut

Empty cake mix into the large bowl of electric mixer. Add remaining ingredients except frosting and coconut. Blend at low speed just to moisten. Beat 3 minutes at medium speed of mixer or with a spoon until creamy. Pour batter into greased 9-inch tube pan. Bake at 350° for 60 to 65 minutes or until cake tester inserted in center comes out clean. Cool in pan 15 minutes. Then loosen from sides of pan and tube. Turn out and finish cooling on cake rack. Frost top and sides with frosting. Scatter coconut on top.

BIG-TOP CAKE

Make and bake any favorite cake in 3 layers or in a large tube pan. Frost with white icing. Cut circle from slightly stiff white paper, making it 2 inches larger in diameter than the pan that was used to bake the cake; i.e., if an 8-inch pan was used, make the paper circle 10 inches in diameter. At one side of paper, cut from edge to center of circle. Lap one edge of cut surface over the other about ¼ inch to make conical shape of tent top. Fasten edges with transparent tape. To make scalloped edging around tent, cut strip from red paper that is 1¼ inches wide and 1 inch longer than circumference of tent top. To make scalloped edge, use a 25-cent coin. Trace scallop around coin edge, then cut out. Place scalloped edging on tent top; fasten at 6 or 8 places from the inside with tape. Cut a pennant about 4 inches long; insert wooden pick and stick in tent top. Place tent on top of cake.

FESTIVE HOLIDAY CAKE

1 package lemon cake mix
Cranberry Filling*
1 package fluffy white frosting mix

Prepare cake mix as directed on package. Bake in oblong pan, 13 x 9 x 2 inches, as directed on package. Cool. Cut cake in half crosswise to make 2 pieces 9 x 6½ inches. Place one layer topside down on serving plate; split this layer in half. Fill split layers with 1 cup Cranberry Filling; spread another 1 cup filling on top. Split other half of cake; repeat, making 4 layers, each topped with 1 cup filling. Frost top and sides with fluffy white frosting. Makes 12 to 18 servings.

*CRANBERRY FILLING

2 cans (1 pound each) whole cranberry sauce
⅓ cup cornstarch
1 tablespoon lemon juice
1 cup finely chopped blanched almonds

Break up cranberry sauce in saucepan. Add cornstarch; mix well. Cook and stir over medium heat until mixture thickens; boil 2 minutes, stirring constantly. Remove from heat; add lemon juice and almonds. Cool thoroughly before using.

CHRISTMAS CAKE CENTERPIECE

1¾ cups sifted all-purpose flour
1¾ cups sugar
1¼ teaspoons baking soda
1 teaspoon salt
¼ teaspoon baking powder
⅔ cup soft butter or margarine
1¼ cups water
1 teaspoon vanilla
4 squares unsweetened chocolate, melted
3 eggs

1 package (about 7 ounces) fluffy white frosting mix
1 can (3½ ounces) flaked coconut
Garnish: candied cherries and angelica
Pistachio ice cream

Measure flour, sugar, baking soda, salt, baking powder, butter or margarine, water, and vanilla into large mixer bowl. Add melted chocolate. Beat at low speed to blend. Then beat 2 minutes at medium speed, scraping sides and bottom of bowl frequently. Add eggs. Beat 2 minutes longer. Turn into greased 12-cup ring mold. Bake at 350° for 35 to 40 minutes. Cool 5 to 10 minutes; turn out of pan and finish cooling on rack. Prepare frosting mix and frost cake. Sprinkle with coconut. Garnish with candied cherries and angelica. Use as a centerpiece for the Christmas dinner table. At dessert time, fill center with pistachio ice cream. Makes 8 to 10 servings.

CHRISTMAS SPICE CAKE

3 packages spice cake mix
Snowdrift Icing*

To make this cake you will need a set of tier cake pans 10, 8, 6, and 4 inches in diameter and 2 inches deep. For the cake itself, make up 3 packages of spice cake mix, one at a time, as directed by manufacturer. Divide 2 packages to equal depths in greased 10- and 8-inch pans. Use third package to fill greased 6- and 4-inch pans to same depth as larger pans. (There will be some batter left over, which can be made into cupcakes, if desired.) Bake at 350° for about 1 hour for 10- and 8-inch pans, 35 to 40 minutes for smaller ones, or until cake tester comes out clean. Cool in pans 10 minutes. Remove from pans; finish cooling on racks. Cut the smallest layer with a star-shaped cutter. Frost with Snowdrift Icing. Decorate as suggested below.

*SNOWDRIFT ICING

1½ cups light corn syrup
2 egg whites
⅛ teaspoon salt
1 teaspoon vanilla
Silver or gold dragées (optional)

Bring corn syrup to a boil; beat egg whites to soft peaks; add salt. Pour hot syrup slowly on egg whites, beating constantly until peaks form when beaters are lifted. Stir in vanilla. Spread on bottom layer. Center next-largest layer on frosted layer; spread with icing. Continue, ending with star-shaped layer. Sprinkle with silver or gold dragées, if desired.

TWELFTH NIGHT CAKE

In Mexico, where Twelfth Night (Epiphany or Little Christmas) is a time for fun and festivity, a special cake is often served. Inside the cake is a tiny porcelain figurine of a child, and the one who finds this figurine in his portion of cake is proclaimed ruler of the festivities.

In some parts of England a cake is also baked, to accompany the Lamb's Wool (page 24). In this cake, slits are cut in opposite sides of the cake, near the bottom. A dried pea is inserted in one slit, a dried bean in the other. The one who finds the bean becomes king of the festivities, while the one who finds the pea becomes queen. A mock court is set up and each guest is given an office and title of importance.

1 cup molasses
½ cup water
1 package (15 ounces) raisins
1 package (16 ounces) pitted prunes, cut fine
1 package (6 ounces) semisweet chocolate pieces
2 jars (1 pound each) diced candied fruits and peels
1 cup butter or margarine
1¼ cups sugar
6 eggs
2¼ cups sifted all-purpose flour
¼ teaspoon baking soda
1½ teaspoons cinnamon
1 teaspoon nutmeg
¾ teaspoon allspice
½ teaspoon ground cloves
½ cup frozen orange juice concentrate, thawed
3 cups coarsely chopped walnuts
White Glaze*
Garnish: cherries, citron, walnut halves

Blend molasses and water in large, deep saucepan. Stir over low heat until mixture comes to a boil. Add raisins and prunes; bring to a boil again. Reduce heat; simmer 5 minutes. Remove from heat; add chocolate pieces; stir until melted. Stir in candied fruit; set aside. Cream butter and sugar. Beat in eggs one at a time. Mix and sift flour, baking soda, and spices. Add to creamed mixture alternately with undiluted concentrate. Stir in molasses-fruit mixture. Stir in

nuts. Turn into greased and floured 10-inch tube pan (preferably with removable bottom). Bake at 275° for 3 hours. Cool. Turn right side up; spread top with White Glaze; garnish with cherries, citron, and walnuts.

*WHITE GLAZE

Mix 1 cup confectioners' (powdered) sugar with 2 to 3 tablespoons cream or milk.

KILLARNEY CAKE

2 eggs, separated
1½ cups sugar, divided
1¾ cups sifted cake flour
¾ teaspoon baking soda
¾ teaspoon salt
⅓ cup vegetable oil
1 cup buttermilk, divided
2 squares unsweetened chocolate, melted
1 teaspoon vanilla
7-minute frosting, tinted green
Garnish: chocolate-covered almonds

Beat egg whites until frothy. Beat in ½ cup of the sugar gradually. Continue beating until very stiff and glossy. Mix and sift remaining 1 cup sugar, flour, baking soda, and salt. Add oil and ½ cup buttermilk. Beat at medium speed on mixer for 1 minute or 150 vigorous strokes by hand. Scrape sides and bottom of bowl constantly. Add remaining ½ cup buttermilk, egg yolks, melted chocolate, and flavoring. Beat 1 minute more. Fold egg white mixture gently but thoroughly into batter. Spoon into 2 deep 8-inch greased and floured layer-cake pans. Bake at 350° for 30 to 35 minutes. Cool. Split both layers crosswise, making 4 layers. Fill and frost with green-tinted 7-minute frosting. Garnish with shamrocks made of chocolate-covered almonds.

EASTER EGG CAKE

½ cup butter or margarine
1¼ cups sugar
2 eggs
2 squares unsweetened chocolate, melted
2 teaspoons vanilla
2 cups sifted cake flour
1¼ teaspoons baking soda
¼ teaspoon salt
¾ cup dairy sour cream
¼ cup boiling water

1 cup broken walnut meats
Chocolate Frosting*

Cream butter to consistency of mayonnaise; add sugar gradually while continuing to cream until light and fluffy. Add eggs one at a time, beating well after each. Blend in cooled chocolate and vanilla. Mix and sift flour, baking soda, and salt; add to creamed mixture alternately with sour cream, beginning and ending with dry ingredients. Blend in boiling water. Stir in walnuts. Spoon into well-greased 2½-quart melon mold. Bake at 350° for 1½ hours or until cake tests done. Cool in mold 10 minutes; remove to rack to finish cooling. Frost with Chocolate Frosting, smoothing the surface as much as possible. When frosting is firm, decorate with stalks of pink hyacinths and green leaves, made with a cake decorator.

NOTE: This cake may be baked at the same temperature in an oblong pan, 13 x 9 x 2 inches, for 40 to 45 minutes or in 2 deep 9-inch layer-cake pans for about 40 minutes.

*CHOCOLATE FROSTING

2½ cups sifted confectioners' (powdered)
    sugar (about)
¼ cup soft butter or margarine
1 tablespoon milk
1 teaspoon vanilla
⅛ teaspoon salt
1 egg
3 squares unsweetened chocolate, melted and
    cooled

Combine confectioners' sugar, butter, milk, vanilla, and salt; beat until blended. Beat in egg. Blend in chocolate. If frosting is too soft, add a little more confectioners' sugar.

SWEETHEART CAKE

1 package white cake mix
½ teaspoon almond extract
Snowdrift Frosting*
½ can (21 ounces) cherry pie filling**

Prepare white cake mix as directed on package, adding almond extract with liquid called for in directions. Bake in 2 greased and floured 9-inch layer-cake pans (heart-shaped, if available) as directed on package. Cool. Put layers together with Snowdrift Frosting between. Frost sides of cake,

making a high rim; let set. Top cake with cherry pie filling.

**This is a prepared pie filling, not to be confused with pitted sour red cherries. The remaining half of the pie filling may be spread between the cake layers, if desired, or saved for a future dessert.

*SNOWDRIFT FROSTING

1⅓ cups light corn syrup
2 egg whites
⅛ teaspoon salt
½ teaspoon almond extract

Bring corn syrup to boiling point. Beat egg whites until soft peaks form. Add syrup very slowly while continuing to beat until stiff peaks form. Stir in salt and almond extract.

BRIDE'S CAKE I

3 cups sifted cake flour
3 teaspoons baking powder
1½ cups sugar
1 teaspoon salt
¾ cup soft shortening
1¼ cups milk, divided
7 egg yolks*
2 teaspoons vanilla extract
Fluffy White Frosting**

Mix and sift flour, baking powder, sugar, and salt; add to shortening. Add ½ the milk with egg yolks and vanilla extract. Mix until flour is dampened. Beat 1 minute. Add remaining milk; blend in. Beat 2 minutes. (Count actual beating time.) Scrape bowl and spoon often. Bake in greased 10-inch tube pan at 325° for 75 minutes or until done. Cool on rack 10 minutes. Remove from pan. Cool. Swirl Fluffy White Frosting on top and sides of cake. Fill center with sweetheart roses or tiny bouquet garden flowers, if desired.

*Reserve enough egg whites for frosting in separate container. Store any remaining in covered dish in refrigerator for other cooking purposes.

**FLUFFY WHITE FROSTING

1¼ cups light corn syrup
2 egg whites
Pinch salt
½ teaspoon almond extract

Heat corn syrup to a boil. With electric mixer, beat egg whites until they form *soft* peaks when beater is raised. Add salt. With beater on medium speed, slowly pour in hot syrup, beating all the time. Increase speed and continue to beat until mixture is very fluffy and forms stiff peaks. Fold in almond extract. Makes enough to fill and frost two 9-inch layers or 10-inch tube cake.

BRIDE'S CAKE II

½ cup vegetable shortening
2 cups extra-fine (instant) sugar
2⅔ cups sifted cake flour
3 teaspoons baking powder
½ teaspoon salt
1 cup milk
2 teaspoons vanilla
6 egg whites*
Any white icing
Tinted frosting (pressure-canned)

Cream shortening to consistency of mayonnaise; add sugar gradually, continuing to cream. Mix and sift flour, baking powder, and salt; combine milk and vanilla. Add dry ingredients and milk alternately to creamed mixture, stirring in gently but thoroughly. Beat egg whites stiff but not dry. Fold in. Spoon into 4 greased and floured tier-cake pans. Bake at 375° for about 30 minutes or until cake tests done. Cool in pans 10 minutes; remove from pans to cake racks; finish cooling. Frost all 4 layers, tops and sides, with any favorite white icing, keeping surfaces as smooth as possible. Decorate with pressure-canned tinted frosting.

*Save egg yolks to use later in baked custard or gold cake.

How to Cut a Four-Tiered Cake

Number layers (mentally) 1 through 4 from bottom to top:
1. With point of sharp knife, cut through layer 1 around base of layer 2, cutting through to bottom of cake; serve this freed portion of first layer in modified wedges.
2. Repeat, cutting through layer 2 only around base of layer 3; serve this freed portion of layer 2.
3. Repeat with layer 3 and serve as before.
4. Remove top layer, which is usually given to the bride.
5. Cut layer 3 in wedges and serve.
6. Cut layer 2 in wedges and serve.
7. Cut layer 1 (base) in wedges and serve.

BABY SHOWER CAKE

1 package white or yellow cake mix
3 cups sifted confectioners' (powdered) sugar, divided
⅓ cup soft butter or margarine
⅛ teaspoon salt
3 tablespoons milk, divided
Few drops blue food coloring
2 tablespoons quick strawberry-flavor beverage mix

Prepare cake mix according to package directions. Bake in 2 layer-cake pans according to package directions. Combine 1 cup of the confectioners' sugar, butter, and salt; beat until creamy. Gradually add 1 more cup confectioners' sugar alternately with 2 tablespoons milk, beating until creamy. Take out ¼ cup frosting; tint to desired shade of blue. Dissolve strawberry-flavor beverage mix in remaining 1 tablespoon milk; add to remaining frosting with remaining 1 cup confectioners' sugar; beat until blended. Put cake layers together with pink frosting. Frost sides and top of cake with pink frosting. On top of cake, outline booties with blue frosting, using pastry tube with writing tip.

NEW NEIGHBOR CAKE

1 package yellow cake mix
1 package (6 ounces) semisweet chocolate pieces
⅔ cup dairy sour cream
1 teaspoon vanilla
¼ teaspoon salt
3 cups sifted confectioners' (powdered) sugar
Garnish: miniature marshmallows

Prepare cake mix as package directs, turning batter into a 13 x 9 x 2-inch pan. Bake as directed. Cool in pan. Loosen edges. Melt semisweet chocolate pieces over hot, not boiling, water. Remove from heat. Add sour cream, vanilla, and salt; mix until well blended. Beat in sugar gradually. Spread over top of cake. Form the word "Hi!" with miniature marshmallows.

WELCOME CAKE

1 package yellow or chocolate cake mix
1 package (6 ounces) butterscotch pieces
1 large package (8 ounces) cream cheese
⅛ teaspoon salt
2¼ cups sifted confectioners' (powdered) sugar

½ package (½ cup) semisweet chocolate
pieces

Prepare cake mix as directed on package. Bake in greased 10 x 15 x 1-inch jelly roll pan at 350° for 20 to 25 minutes. Melt butterscotch pieces over hot, not boiling, water. Blend cream cheese and salt. Stir in melted butterscotch; stir until smooth. Beat in sugar gradually until of spreading consistency. Frost top of cooled cake. Melt semisweet chocolate pieces over hot, not boiling, water. Force melted chocolate through cake decorator or paper cone to write "WELCOME" in center of cake and make border of X's around top of cake.

CHOCOLATE REFRIGERATOR CAKE I

6 squares (6 ounces) sweet chocolate
3 eggs, separated
½ teaspoon vanilla
⅓ cup ground walnuts
Graham crackers
½ pint whipping cream

Melt chocolate over boiling water; remove from heat; add egg yolks one at a time, beating vigorously after each addition. Beat egg whites stiff; add to chocolate mixture; beat smooth. Add vanilla and walnuts. Spread on graham crackers; pack together upright in oblong pan lined with waxed paper; top with remaining chocolate mixture. Fold waxed paper over top. Chill overnight. Whip cream; spread on top. Slice on diagonal. Makes 6 servings.

CHOCOLATE REFRIGERATOR CAKE II

20 ladyfingers
½ pound sweet cooking chocolate
3 eggs, separated
1 teaspoon vanilla
1 cup whipping cream, divided

Line straight-sided loaf pan, 11 x 4 x 2½ inches, with waxed paper, leaving overhang. Separate ladyfingers. Place 8 halves in a row in bottom of pan. Melt chocolate over hot water; remove from heat; add egg yolks one at a time, beating vigorously after each addition. Beat egg whites stiff; fold in. Add vanilla. Whip ½ cup cream; fold in. Spread ¼ chocolate mixture on ladyfingers in pan. Add another row of ladyfinger halves. Repeat until there are 4 layers of chocolate. Top with remaining ladyfingers. Chill several hours

or overnight. Lift cake from pan, using waxed paper overhang. Remove waxed paper. Place cake on serving dish. Whip remaining cream. Frost sides of cake. Makes 8 servings.

TOFFEE REFRIGERATOR BOWL CAKE

1 package baker's sponge cake (2 layers)
1 package butterscotch or chocolate pudding
    mix (not instant)
2 cups milk
1 cup whipping cream, whipped
Garnish: melted chocolate; salted almonds

Cut sponge layers in half crosswise to make 4 layers. Prepare pudding mix as directed on package, using the 2 cups milk. Press one of the cake layers into a medium-sized mixing bowl, shaping to sides of bowl. Spread with ⅓ of the cooked pudding. Add second cake layer; spread with pudding; repeat, ending with fourth cake layer placed straight across top of bowl. Chill several hours or overnight. Unmold on serving plate. Swirl whipped cream on top and sides. Decorate with chocolate-tipped salted almonds. (Dip wide ends of almonds in melted chocolate.) Makes 8 servings.

ORANGE REFRIGERATOR CAKE

1 package (18½ ounces) orange chiffon cake
    mix
4 cups rhubarb, cut in 1-inch pieces (about 9
    stalks)
⅔ cup sugar
½ cup water
1 quart fresh strawberries
1 pint whipping cream

Make and bake the orange chiffon cake according to package directions. Cool completely in pan. Remove from pan; cut crosswise to make 3 equal layers. Meanwhile, cook rhubarb, sugar, and water until rhubarb is tender but has not lost its shape; cool; drain.* Wash and hull strawberries. Save enough whole berries for garnish; cut remaining berries in quarters; sweeten to taste. Whip cream; fold in rhubarb and drained strawberries.* Spread between layers and on top of cake. Chill several hours in refrigerator. Garnish with whole strawberries. Serves 12.

*Save syrup for use in fruit cups, cold drinks, etc.

BLUEBERRY ROLL

Cake Roll:

3 eggs
½ teaspoon salt
¾ cup sugar
¾ teaspoon rum or vanilla extract
¾ cup pancake mix
Confectioners' (powdered) sugar

Heat oven to 400°. Grease bottom of 15 x 10 x 1-inch jelly roll pan. Line with waxed paper; grease again and flour. Beat eggs and salt until thick and lemon-colored. Add sugar gradually, beating constantly. Stir in extract and pancake mix. Spread evenly in pan. Bake at 400° for 8 to 10 minutes. Immediately loosen edges and turn out on towel sprinkled with confectioners' sugar. Carefully peel paper from cake. Roll cake in towel, starting at narrow end. Cool about 30 minutes; unroll. Spread with blueberry filling. Roll up.

Blueberry Filling:

4 cups fresh blueberries, divided
2 tablespoons cornstarch
4 tablespoons sugar
2 tablespoons grated lemon peel
2 tablespoons lemon juice

Pour 2 cups blueberries into saucepan. Combine cornstarch, sugar, grated lemon peel and juice. Add to berries. Cook over low heat, mashing and stirring, until mixture thickens and is clear. Remove from heat. Add remaining 2 cups blueberries. Cool slightly.

Cream Cheese Frosting:

1 package (8 ounces) cream cheese, soft
2 tablespoons milk

Beat cream cheese and milk together until creamy. Spread evenly on cake roll. Refrigerate at least 2 hours before cutting and serving. Makes 8 servings.

CAKE ROLL CAPRI

Cake:

4 eggs
½ teaspoon salt
¾ cup sugar
½ teaspoon almond flavoring
¾ cup pancake mix
Confectioners' (powdered) sugar

Combine eggs and salt; beat until thick and lemon-colored. Add sugar a little at a time, beating after each addition. Add flavoring. Add pancake mix; beat until smooth. Grease jelly roll pan, 10 x 15 x 1 inch. Line with waxed paper; grease again. Spread batter evenly in pan. Bake at 400° for 10 to 12 minutes. Sprinkle dry towel with confectioners' sugar. As soon as cake is done, loosen edges and turn out on towel; peel waxed paper carefully from cake. Roll up quickly in towel. Let stand 20 minutes. Unroll. Spread with filling; reroll; frost with Lemon Icing.

Filling:

1 pound ricotta (Italian cream cheese)
½ cup sugar
2 squares unsweetened chocolate
Few drops almond extract

Combine ricotta and sugar. Grate chocolate; add to ricotta mixture with few drops almond extract.

Lemon Icing:

1 egg white
2 cups confectioners' (powdered) sugar
½ teaspoon lemon extract
2 teaspoons grated lemon peel

Beat egg white slightly; gradually beat in confectioners' sugar until of spreading consistency. Add lemon extract and grated lemon peel.

CHERRY ICE CREAM ROLL

4 eggs, at room temperature
1 teaspoon baking powder
¼ teaspoon salt
¾ cup sugar
1 teaspoon vanilla
¾ cup sifted cake flour
Confectioners' (powdered) sugar
2 pints cherry-vanilla ice cream

Grease bottom of a 15 x 10 x 1-inch pan; line with waxed paper and grease lightly. Beat eggs until foamy. Add baking powder and salt; beat until very light. Add sugar, about 1 tablespoon at a time; continue beating until very thick. Fold in vanilla and sifted flour a little at a time. Pour batter into prepared pan. Bake at 400° for 13 minutes. While cake is baking, sift confectioners' sugar lightly over towel. Loosen cake from pan with point of paring knife; invert onto towel. Remove pan; quickly remove waxed paper and trim off crisp edges. Roll up cake from narrow side. Wrap towel tightly around roll to hold it in shape. Cool. Unroll cake carefully. Spread with slightly softened ice cream. Reroll. Freeze until firm. Dust with confectioners' sugar. Makes 10 to 12 servings.

For Individual Jelly Rolls: Pour half the batter into prepared pan. Bake at 400° for 9 minutes. While cake is baking, sift confectioners' (powdered) sugar lightly over towel. Beat ½ cup jelly with fork until smooth. Invert pan onto towel. Remove pan; remove waxed paper. Trim crisp edges. Spread with jelly. Cut in half lengthwise and 4 times crosswise to make 10 small rectangles. Roll each rectangle as for jelly roll. Bake remaining batter; repeat. Serve with ice cream. Makes 20 rolls.

MOCHA ICE CREAM CAKE ROLL

½ teaspoon salt
4 eggs
¾ cup sugar
¾ cup pancake mix
1 teaspoon vanilla
Confectioners' (powdered) sugar
1 quart vanilla* ice cream, softened
Icing**

Grease bottom and sides of a 15 x 10 x 1-inch jelly roll pan. Line with waxed paper; grease again and dust with flour. Add salt to eggs; beat until thick and lemon-colored. Add sugar, a little at a time, beating well after each addition. Add pancake mix and vanilla; stir until smooth. Spread evenly in prepared pan. Bake at 400° for 8 to 10 minutes. While cake is baking, sprinkle a towel with confectioners' sugar. Immediately on taking cake from oven, loosen edges and turn out on towel. Peel off waxed paper. Roll cake in towel. Let stand 20 minutes, then unroll. Spread softened ice cream over cake. Roll up quickly. Wrap cake in foil; place in freezer for several hours or until firm. Ice as directed below. Makes 8 servings.

*Or use chocolate, coffee, or peach ice cream if you prefer.

**ICING

1 cup whipping cream
½ cup confectioners' (powdered) sugar
3 tablespoons powdered cocoa (not instant)

2 teaspoons instant coffee
¼ cup canned toasted slivered almonds

Beat whipping cream until foamy. Add sugar, cocoa, and coffee; continue beating until soft peaks form. Remove ice cream roll from freezer and unwrap. Place on baking sheet. Spread icing on top and sides of cake roll; sprinkle with almonds. Return to freezer until firm. Slice to serve.

CHOCOLATE CAKE LOG

½ teaspoon salt
4 eggs
¾ cup sugar
2 squares (1 ounce each) unsweetened chocolate, melted
1 teaspoon vanilla
¾ cup pancake mix
Confectioners' (powdered) sugar
Softened ice cream *or* whipped cream *or* whipped topping
Mocha Butter Frosting*

Add salt to eggs; beat until thick and lemon-colored. Add sugar a little at a time, beating well after each addition. Add melted chocolate, vanilla, and pancake mix; stir lightly until batter is smooth. Spread batter evenly in greased, waxed-paper-lined jelly roll pan, 10 x 15 x 1 inch. Bake at 400° for 10 to 12 minutes. While cake is baking, sprinkle a dry towel with confectioners' sugar. When cake is done, loosen edges at once; turn out on towel. Peel waxed paper carefully from cake. Roll cake quickly in towel. Let stand 20 minutes; unroll. Spread with softened ice cream or whipped cream or whipped topping. Roll up quickly. Wrap cake in aluminum foil; chill. If ice cream is used as filling, place in freezer for several hours. (May be made a day or two in advance.) Frost with Mocha Butter Frosting put through a pastry tube to resemble bark. Make snowdrifts with confectioners' sugar. Makes 8 to 10 servings.

*MOCHA BUTTER FROSTING

½ pound unsalted butter
½ cup sugar
1 teaspoon Dutch-process cocoa
1 tablespoon instant coffee (dry)

Cream butter to consistency of mayonnaise. Combine sugar, cocoa, and coffee; sift through fine sieve. Add sugar mixture, 1 tablespoon at a time, to butter; be sure to cream thoroughly after each addition is made.

GINGER CREAM GEMS

1¼ cups sifted all-purpose flour
¾ teaspoon baking soda
½ teaspoon salt
1 teaspoon cinnamon
½ teaspoon powdered ginger
¼ teaspoon nutmeg
⅓ cup shortening
½ cup sugar
⅓ cup light molasses
1 egg
½ cup boiling water
Orange Fluff Cream*

Mix and sift first 6 ingredients. Cream shortening; add sugar gradually, creaming well; add molasses and egg; mix well. Blend in dry ingredients. Add boiling water; stir smooth. Divide batter into 12 well-greased muffin cups, filling ½ full. Bake at 350° for 15 to 20 minutes. Cool on racks. Cut cone-shaped piece from center of each cupcake; fill hollow with Orange Fluff Cream. Top with cutouts. Makes 12.

*ORANGE FLUFF CREAM

Whip ½ cup whipping cream until stiff. Fold in ¼ cup orange marmalade.

FRUITCAKE CUPCAKES

½ cup light molasses
¼ cup water
1 teaspoon brandy flavoring
1 package (15 ounces) raisins
1 jar (1 pound) mixed diced candied fruits
½ cup butter or margarine
⅔ cup sugar
3 eggs
1 cup plus 2 tablespoons sifted all-purpose flour
¼ teaspoon baking soda
1 teaspoon cinnamon
1 teaspoon nutmeg
¼ teaspoon allspice
¼ teaspoon cloves
¼ cup milk
1 cup chopped nuts

Blend molasses, water, and brandy flavoring in saucepan. Stir over low heat until mixture comes to a boil. Add raisins; bring to a boil again. Reduce heat; simmer 5 minutes. Remove from heat; stir in candied fruit. Reserve; cool. Cream butter and sugar. Blend in eggs one at a time. Mix and sift flour, baking soda, and spices; add to butter mixture alternately with milk. Add molasses-fruit mixture and chopped nuts; blend. Line 1¾-inch cupcake pans with fluted bonbon papers. Spoon in fruitcake mixture. Bake at 325° for 25 minutes. Cool before storing. Makes 60 cupcakes.

CHOCOLATE APPLESAUCE CUPCAKES

½ cup shortening
1 cup sugar
1 egg, unbeaten
1 cup applesauce
1½ cups sifted all-purpose flour
⅓ cup cocoa (not instant)
1 teaspoon cinnamon
1 teaspoon baking soda
1 teaspoon water
Choice of frosting

Cream shortening and sugar; add egg; beat well. Put applesauce through fine sieve; add. Sift flour, cocoa, and cinnamon 3 times; add. Dissolve baking soda in water; add; mix well. Bake in 12 greased muffin cups at 350° for 25 to 30 minutes. Frost as desired. Makes 12 cupcakes.

CHOCOLATE GLAZE

⅓ cup sugar
4 teaspoons cornstarch
⅛ teaspoon salt
½ cup boiling water
1 package (6 ounces) semisweet chocolate pieces

Combine sugar, cornstarch, and salt in saucepan. Add ½ cup boiling water; cook, stirring constantly, until mixture comes to a boil. Boil, stirring, 1 minute. Remove from heat. Stir in chocolate pieces until smooth. Spread glaze on 9 x 13-inch cake while warm for a glossy frosting that remains soft and smooth.

DAISY WREATH

To make daisy, arrange almond halves like petals around a piece of semisweet chocolate. Repeat daisies around top of cake.

SUNDAE FROSTING FOR CUPCAKES

Melt 1 package (6 ounces) semisweet chocolate pieces or butterscotch pieces over hot, not boiling, water. Prepare 1 package fluffy frosting mix according to package directions; swirl on cakes. Top with melted chocolate or butterscotch. Decorate with walnut halves, flaked coconut, maraschino cherry, or candied fruit. Recipe makes enough frosting to top 2 dozen cupcakes.

MOCHA FROSTING

⅓ cup butter or margarine
3 cups confectioners' (powdered) sugar,
    divided
1½ squares unsweetened chocolate
Strong cold coffee

Cream butter or margarine; add 1½ cups confectioners' sugar while continuing to cream. Melt unsweetened chocolate over hot water; add. Add remaining confectioners' sugar and enough coffee to make frosting fluffy and easy to spread. Makes enough to fill and frost 8-inch layer cake.

PINEAPPLE-COCONUT FILLING

1 can (8¼ ounces) crushed pineapple
½ cup firmly packed brown sugar
3 tablespoons cornstarch
¼ teaspoon salt
2 teaspoons lemon juice
2 teaspoons butter or margarine
1 cup flaked coconut
8 maraschino cherries, sliced thin

Drain pineapple; add water to pineapple syrup from can to make 1 cup. Combine sugar, cornstarch, salt, and pineapple syrup mixture in saucepan. Cook and stir over medium heat until mixture comes to a boil. Remove from heat; add pineapple and remaining ingredients. Mix well; chill. Makes 2¼ cups, or enough filling to spread between four 9-inch cake layers.

FLUFFY PINK FROSTING

2 egg whites
1¼ cups sugar
1 package (3 ounces) strawberry-flavor gelatin
Dash of salt
⅓ cup water
2 teaspoons light corn syrup

Combine all ingredients in top of double boiler. Beat about 1 minute or until thoroughly mixed, then place over rapidly boiling water and beat constantly at high speed of electric hand mixer (or with rotary beater) for 7 minutes, until frosting will stand in stiff peaks. Use rubber scraper, spatula, or spoon to stir frosting up from bottom and sides of pan occasionally. Remove from boiling water. For very smooth and satiny frosting, pour at once into a large bowl for final beating. Beat 1 minute, until thick enough to spread. Fills and frosts two 8- or 9-inch layers; or frosts 13 x 9 x 2-inch cake or 2 dozen cupcakes.

STRAWBERRY-GLAZED CHEESECAKE

12 graham crackers, crushed
½ cup ground walnut meats
1 tablespoon sugar
¼ cup butter or margarine, melted
5 large eggs
1½ cups sugar
1 teaspoon vanilla
1 teaspoon lemon juice
1½ pounds cream cheese, softened
2 cups dairy sour cream
¾ cup crushed strawberries*
1 cup sugar
1 envelope unflavored gelatin
¼ cup cold water
Garnish: whole strawberries

Combine first 4 ingredients. Press on bottom and sides of 9-inch springform pan. Chill. Beat eggs until light and thick; add 1½ cups sugar, vanilla, and lemon juice while beating. Beat in cream cheese and sour cream, a little at a time. Beat until smooth and without lumps. Pour into springform pan. Bake at 350° for 75 to 80 minutes. Turn off heat; leave cake in closed oven for 90 minutes. Remove from oven; let cool in pan to room temperature. Meanwhile, combine crushed strawberries and 1 cup sugar. Heat to boiling. Soften gelatin in cold water; stir in. Cook and stir for 2 minutes. Chill until very thick. Spread over top and sides of cheesecake. Garnish top with whole strawberries. Chill until ready to serve. Makes 12 to 16 servings.

*Frozen strawberries may be used when fresh ones are not available.

UNBAKED STRAWBERRY-GLAZED CHEESECAKE

2 envelopes unflavored gelatin
1 cup sugar, divided
¼ teaspoon salt
2 eggs, separated
1 cup milk
1 teaspoon grated lemon peel
3 cups (24 ounces) creamed cottage cheese
1 tablespoon lemon juice
1 teaspoon vanilla
1 cup whipping cream, whipped
Strawberry Glaze*

Line sides of 8-inch springform pan with waxed paper; set aside. Combine gelatin, ¾ cup of the sugar, and salt in top of double boiler. Beat egg yolks and milk; add to gelatin mixture. Stir over boiling water until gelatin is dissolved (about 6 minutes). Remove from heat; add lemon peel. Chill until mixture mounds slightly when dropped from a spoon. Beat cottage cheese on high speed of electric mixer 3 minutes. Stir in lemon juice and vanilla; stir into gelatin mixture. Beat egg whites until stiff but not dry. Beat in remaining ¼ cup sugar gradually; beat until very stiff. Fold into gelatin mixture. Fold in whipped cream. Turn into prepared pan; chill until firm. Remove from pan. Top with Strawberry Glaze. Makes 8 servings.

*STRAWBERRY GLAZE

1 quart strawberries, divided
¾ cup water, divided
⅔ cup sugar
2 tablespoons cornstarch

Wash and hull strawberries. Combine 1 cup berries with ½ cup water and sugar in saucepan. Bring to boil; lower heat; simmer 15 minutes. Blend cornstarch with remaining water. Gradually add to hot mixture, stirring constantly. Cook, stirring, until thickened and clear. Remove from heat; strain through sieve. Cool. Put remaining berries on top of cheesecake; spoon glaze over top. Chill several hours.

VELVET CHEESECAKE

½ cup butter or margarine, softened
1 package (6 ounces) zwieback, crushed
½ cup extra-fine (instant) sugar
1 tablespoon grated lemon peel, divided

2½ pounds cream cheese
1¾ cups granulated sugar
3 tablespoons flour
1½ teaspoons grated orange peel
½ teaspoon vanilla
5 eggs, unbeaten
2 egg yolks
¼ cup heavy cream

Grease bottom and sides of 9-inch springform pan with a little of the butter or margarine. Combine remaining butter or margarine, zwieback crumbs, extra-fine sugar, and ½ tablespoon grated lemon peel. Mix well; press on bottom and sides of springform pan, reserving about ⅓ cup for top. Combine cream cheese, granulated sugar, flour, remaining lemon peel, orange peel, and vanilla; beat until smooth and fluffy. Add 1 egg at a time, stirring in lightly. Add egg yolks one at a time. Stir in heavy cream. Spoon into springform pan, spreading evenly. Sprinkle remaining crumb mixture on top. Bake at 250° for 1 hour. Turn off heat; leave in closed oven 1 hour longer. Remove from oven. Let cool slowly to room temperature. Chill. Makes 12 servings.

CRUNCHY CHEESECAKE

Crust:

⅔ cup canned slivered blanched almonds
1 teaspoon vegetable oil
1 cup fine zwieback crumbs
2 tablespoons sugar
2 tablespoons soft butter or margarine

Toss almonds with oil in small frying pan until coated with oil. Stir over low heat until golden brown. Reserve ⅓ cup for garnish; chop remainder finely. Blend crumbs, sugar, and butter. Mix in chopped almonds. Press firmly onto bottom and sides of well-greased 9-inch springform pan. Bake at 325° for 10 minutes. Remove from oven; carefully spoon in filling. Bake 1 hour. Turn off heat; open oven door; let stand ½ hour. Remove from oven; cool completely. Spread with topping; sprinkle with reserved slivered almonds. Bake at 500° for 5 minutes. Cool completely before removing sides of pan. Makes 8 to 10 servings.

Filling:

1 pound cream cheese
1 cup light cream
¾ cup sugar

2 tablespoons flour
¼ teaspoon salt
1 teaspoon vanilla
1 teaspoon grated lemon peel
1 tablespoon lemon juice
4 eggs

Let cheese stand at room temperature until soft. Gradually blend in cream, beating until very smooth. Blend in sugar, flour, salt, vanilla, lemon peel and juice. Separate eggs; beat whites until stiff. Beat yolks lightly; blend into cheese mixture. Fold in egg whites.

Topping:

1 cup dairy sour cream
2 tablespoons sugar
½ teaspoon vanilla

Blend all ingredients.

SWIRL-TOP CHEESECAKE

Crust:

2 cups fine graham cracker crumbs
½ cup sugar
¼ teaspoon cinnamon
⅛ teaspoon nutmeg
½ cup butter or margarine

Combine crumbs, sugar, and spices; cut in butter or margarine until completely blended. Press mixture evenly on bottom and sides of heavily buttered 9- or 10-inch springform pan. Chill.

Filling:

1 square unsweetened chocolate
2 large packages (8 ounces each) cream cheese
1 cup sugar
6 eggs, separated
1 teaspoon vanilla
1 tablespoon grated orange peel
1 tablespoon orange juice
1 cup whipping cream

Melt chocolate over hot water. Meanwhile, blend cream cheese and sugar until creamy and light. Add egg yolks one at a time, beating well after each addition; stir in vanilla, orange peel and juice. Beat egg whites until stiff but not dry; spoon onto cheese mixture. Whip cream; fold with egg whites into cheese mixture until well blended. Spoon ⅓ of the filling into crumb-lined pan; trickle a little of the melted chocolate over

surface; swirl lightly into filling with tip of knife. Repeat twice more, ending with chocolate. Bake at 300° for 1 hour. Turn heat off; leave cheesecake in oven with door closed 1 hour longer. Remove from oven; cool at room temperature; then chill. (Center will sink somewhat during cooling.) When cold, loosen crust around sides with knife, release spring, and remove pan. Serves 12 to 16.

THRIFTY CHEESECAKE

Cookie Crust:

1 egg
¼ cup vegetable oil
2 cups sifted all-purpose flour
1 teaspoon baking powder
¼ cup sugar
½ teaspoon salt
6 tablespoons milk

Beat egg; beat in oil. Mix and sift dry ingredients; add alternately with milk to egg mixture. Using a rubber spatula, spread evenly in thin layer on bottom and sides of 8-inch springform pan.

Filling:

1 cup fine-curd cottage cheese
1 cup dairy sour cream
¾ cup sugar, divided
4 eggs, separated
2 tablespoons flour
1 teaspoon grated lemon peel
1 tablespoon lemon juice
Cinnamon

Blend cheese, sour cream, and ½ cup sugar. Beat egg yolks slightly; blend into cheese mixture with flour, lemon peel and juice. Beat egg whites until soft peaks form; beat in remaining sugar, 1 tablespoon at a time; fold into cheese mixture gently but thoroughly. Spoon into springform pan. Sprinkle with cinnamon. Bake at 350° for 10 minutes. Lower heat to 325°; bake 1 hour longer. Turn oven off; open door. Let cake cool to room temperature in open oven; chill. Makes 8 servings.

REFRIGERATOR LEMON CHEESECAKE

Crust:

1 cup quick or old-fashioned oats, uncooked
¼ cup firmly packed brown sugar
¼ cup butter or margarine, melted

Toast oats in shallow baking pan at 350° about 10 minutes. Pour into bowl. Add brown sugar; mix well. Add melted butter; mix thoroughly. Pat into bottom of 9-inch springform pan. Refrigerate until ready to use.

Filling:

1 package (3 ounces) lemon-flavor gelatin
½ cup boiling water
1 large package (8 ounces) cream cheese
1 cup sugar
1 teaspoon vanilla
1 can (13 ounces) evaporated milk, whipped*
Garnish: whipped topping; grated lemon peel

Place gelatin in 2-cup liquid measuring cup. Add boiling water; stir until dissolved. Add ice cubes to make 1 cup liquid; stir until ice is melted. Set aside until ready to use. Place cream cheese, sugar, and vanilla in small mixer bowl; beat until creamy. Add gelatin mixture. Fold in whipped evaporated milk. Pour into crust; refrigerate several hours or overnight. Decorate with whipped topping and grated lemon peel, if desired. Makes 8 servings.

*To whip evaporated milk, pour milk into freezer tray; place in freezing compartment until ice crystals form around edges, then whip.

POPPY SEED CHEESECAKE

2 cups fine zwieback crumbs
½ cup sugar
1½ tablespoons poppy seeds
½ cup softened butter or margarine
4 eggs
1 cup sugar
¼ teaspoon salt
2 tablespoons lemon juice
1 cup light cream
1½ pounds cottage cheese
¼ cup flour

Combine crumbs, ½ cup sugar, and poppy seeds. Blend with butter or margarine. Set aside ¾ cup crumbs for top. Press remaining crumbs on bottom and sides of 8- or 9-inch springform pan. Beat eggs until thick and lemon-colored. Add remaining 1 cup sugar; beat well. Add salt, lemon juice, cream, cheese, and flour. Force through fine sieve; beat well. Turn into pan; sprinkle top with remaining crumbs. Bake at 325° for 1¼ to 1½ hours or until center is well set. Turn off heat; leave cake in oven for 1 hour. Cool; remove from pan; serve cold. Makes 10 servings.

"JEWEL" CHEESECAKE

½ cup soft butter or margarine
1 package (6 ounces) zwieback, crushed into fine crumbs
½ cup extra-fine (instant) sugar
1 tablespoon grated lemon peel
1 cup granulated sugar
2 tablespoons flour
½ teaspoon salt
3 large packages (8 ounces each) cream cheese
4 eggs
6 tablespoons whipping cream
½ teaspoon almond extract (optional)
½ cup dairy sour cream
Halved seedless green grapes

Grease bottom and sides of 9-inch springform pan with a little of the butter. Combine remaining butter, zwieback crumbs, extra-fine sugar, and grated lemon peel. Mix well. Press firmly on bottom and sides of springform pan. Combine granulated sugar, flour, and salt; blend gradually into cream cheese. Beat until smooth and light. Add eggs one at a time, beating well after each addition. Blend in cream (do not whip) and flavoring. Spoon into crumb-lined pan. Bake at 250° for 1 hour. Turn off heat. Leave in closed oven for 1 hour longer. Remove from oven. Spread sour cream on top. Cover top with halved seedless green grapes. Let cool slowly to room temperature. Chill. Garnish with additional grapes, if desired. Makes 10 to 12 servings.

MINCEMEAT CHEESECAKE

Mincemeat Layer:

1 package (9 ounces) condensed mincemeat
¾ cup strong coffee
3 tablespoons sugar
1 envelope unflavored gelatin
¼ cup cold water

Break mincemeat in small pieces; add coffee and sugar. Stir over medium heat until well blended. Boil briskly 1 minute. Soften gelatin in cold water; add hot mincemeat mixture; stir until gelatin dissolves. Lightly grease 9-inch square pan (or rinse with cold water). Line with waxed paper cut to fit; let ends extend a little above sides of pan. Spread mincemeat mixture in pan; chill.

Cheesecake:

2 envelopes unflavored gelatin
1 cup sugar, divided
¼ teaspoon salt
2 eggs, separated
1 cup milk
1 teaspoon grated lemon peel
3 cups (3 cartons, 8 ounces each) creamed
    cottage cheese, sieved
1 tablespoon lemon juice
1 teaspoon vanilla
1 cup whipping cream
Garnish: whole walnut meats

Combine gelatin, ¾ cup sugar, and salt in top of double boiler. Beat together egg yolks and milk; add to gelatin mixture. Cook over boiling water, stirring constantly, until gelatin dissolves and mixture thickens (about 10 minutes). Remove from heat; add lemon peel; cool. Stir in sieved cottage cheese, lemon juice, and vanilla. Chill, stirring occasionally, until mixture mounds slightly when dropped from a spoon. Beat egg whites until stiff but not dry. Gradually add remaining ¼ cup sugar; beat until very stiff. Whip cream; fold into gelatin-cheese mixture with egg whites. Spoon on top of mincemeat layer. Chill until firm. Invert on serving plate; remove waxed paper. Garnish with whole walnut meats. Makes 9 to 12 servings.

PEACH CHEESECAKE

1 cup finely chopped canned peaches,
    drained
2 cups (1 pound) creamed cottage cheese
1 teaspoon salt
½ cup peach syrup from can
1 tablespoon lemon juice
1 package (3 ounces) lemon-flavor gelatin
1 cup whipping cream
¼ cup sugar
½ cup finely crushed graham cracker crumbs
3 tablespoons melted butter or margarine
3 tablespoons finely chopped walnuts

Combine chopped peaches, cheese, and salt. Heat peach syrup to boiling; add lemon juice; pour on lemon gelatin; stir until dissolved; cool to room temperature. Beat cheese mixture into cooled gelatin. Whip cream; blend in sugar lightly; fold into cheese mixture. Spoon into very lightly oiled 6-cup mold. Chill until firm. Unmold. Combine crumbs, melted butter, and walnuts. Sprinkle evenly over top and sides of cheesecake. Makes 8 servings.
ACCOMPANIMENT: Sliced peaches.

NO-BAKE CHEESECAKE

Crumb Mixture:

¾ cup chocolate cookie crumbs
3 tablespoons sugar
3 tablespoons butter or margarine, melted

Combine all ingredients. Press ½ cup of this mixture in bottom of 8- or 9-inch springform pan.* Reserve remaining crumbs for top.

*If springform pan is not available, use loaf or square pan that holds 8 cups. Grease pan lightly so waxed paper cut to fit will cling to pan. To unmold, invert on serving plate; remove waxed paper.

Filling:

3 envelopes unflavored gelatin
1 cup milk
2 eggs, separated
¾ cup sugar, divided
3 cups (24 ounces) creamed cottage cheese
1 can (6 ounces) frozen orange juice
    concentrate, unthawed
1 cup whipping cream, whipped
1 tablespoon grated orange peel (optional)

Sprinkle gelatin over milk in 2½-quart saucepan to soften. Stir in egg yolks. Place over low heat; stir until gelatin dissolves and mixture thickens slightly (about 3 minutes). Remove from heat; stir in ½ cup sugar. Sieve or beat cottage cheese on high speed of electric mixer until smooth (3 to 4 minutes). Stir cottage cheese and unthawed concentrate into gelatin mixture. Beat egg whites until stiff; add remaining ¼ cup sugar gradually; beat until very stiff. Fold into gelatin mixture; fold in whipped cream. Turn into prepared pan; sprinkle with remaining crumbs and grated orange peel. Chill until firm (2 to 3 hours). Loosen cake from sides of pan with knife; release springform. Makes 10 to 12 servings.

CHAPTER 16
Pies and Pastries

IT IS a skill to be able to make good pastry. Some are born with it; some, with time and patience, acquire it; and then some never quite get the hang of it.

There are three things that can be bothersome about making pastry: cutting in the shortening until the flour/fat mixture is exactly right; adding just the right amount of water—no more, no less; and rolling out the pastry to fit the pan.

Today there is an answer to all these problems. If the first step bothers you, begin with a mix in which flour and shortening are already combined. If the second step is troublesome, work with a mix that is already combined and shaped into sticks—1 stick per crust. Or if you just can't roll out pastry, buy ready-to-bake frozen pie shells or pie crust circles and avoid everything!

As for fillings, try the delicious variety in the recipes that follow. But don't forget the ready-to-use fillings such as apple and cherry available in cans; the ready-to-serve puddings; or the mixes for cream fillings and whipped fillings. You'll discover all of these, and more, in your supermarket.

DEEP-DISH APPLE-RAISIN PIE

3 tablespoons quick-cooking tapioca
¾ cup granulated sugar
⅓ cup firmly packed brown sugar
¼ teaspoon salt
1 teaspoon cinnamon
½ teaspoon nutmeg
10 cups thinly sliced tart apples
⅓ cup raisins
½ cup water
2 tablespoons butter or margarine
Cream Pastry for 1-crust pie

Combine tapioca, sugars, salt, cinnamon, nutmeg, apples, raisins, and water. Turn mixture into deep 8-inch square baking dish. Dot with butter or margarine. Roll pastry ⅛ inch thick; cut several slits near center. Fold pastry in half or roll loosely on rolling pan. Center on filling. Open slits with a knife. (Well-opened slits are important to permit escape of steam during baking.) Trim pastry, allowing it to extend ½ inch over rim. Fold pastry and flute. Bake at 425° for 45 minutes. Serve warm with plain cream.

DEEP-DISH APPLE CRUMB PIE

7 cups peeled, sliced apples (about 3 pounds)
⅓ cup orange juice
½ cup firmly packed brown sugar
½ cup sugar
2 teaspoons grated orange peel

½ teaspoon nutmeg
½ teaspoon cinnamon
¼ teaspoon salt
¾ cup sifted all-purpose flour
½ cup butter or margarine
Ice cream (optional)

Place apples in deep pie pan; add orange juice. Mix together sugars, orange peel, nutmeg, cinnamon, salt, and flour. Cut in butter or margarine. Sprinkle evenly over apples. Bake at 350° for 1 hour. Serve warm or cold, with a topping of ice cream, if desired. Makes 8 servings.

CHEESE APPLE PIE

Crumb Crust and Topping:

1 box (8 ounces) cheese crackers, rolled into
 fine crumbs
6 tablespoons softened butter or margarine
2 tablespoons sugar
1 teaspoon cinnamon
2 tablespoons water

Blend cheese cracker crumbs and butter or margarine thoroughly. Measure ½ cup of this mixture; to this, add sugar and cinnamon; reserve for topping. To remainder of crumbs, add water; blend well; turn into 9-inch pie pan; firmly press into even layer against bottom and sides of pan. Bake at 375° for 15 minutes. Cool.

Filling:

½ cup sugar
3 tablespoons cornstarch
Dash of salt
¼ teaspoon cinnamon
1 cup water
2 pounds tart apples, peeled, cored, and
 sliced thin
1 tablespoon lemon juice

Blend sugar, cornstarch, salt, and cinnamon in saucepan. Stir in water gradually. Add apples; cook over medium heat until mixture is thickened, stirring constantly. Continue cooking until apple slices are tender. Remove from heat; add lemon juice. Cool. Pour into cheese cracker crumb crust. Sprinkle with topping.

CRANBERRY-APPLE-CHEESE PIE

1 package piecrust mix
1½ cups sugar
⅓ cup flour

½ teaspoon nutmeg
1 cup shredded sharp Cheddar cheese
3 cups peeled, cubed apples
3 cups fresh cranberries

Prepare pastry according to package directions. Roll out half the pastry; line 9-inch pie pan. Combine remaining ingredients; toss lightly; pour into pastry-lined pan. Roll out remaining pastry; place over filling. Moisten edges of pastry; seal and flute edge. Cut a few slits in top crust to allow steam to escape. Bake at 425° for 35 to 40 minutes or until crust is browned. Cool thoroughly before cutting.

ENGLISH APPLE FLAN

1 package piecrust mix
3 cups well-drained homemade applesauce,
 spiced and sweetened
3 to 5 large tart apples
⅔ cup apricot jam
⅓ cup cold water
Whipped cream

Roll pastry ⅛ inch thick; place in 12-inch pizza pan; flute edge. Spoon applesauce into pastry-lined pan. Pare and core apples; slice thin. Place on applesauce in concentric circles. Combine apricot jam and water; heat and stir until well blended. Spread over apple slices. Bake at 425° about 30 minutes or until apple slices are tender. Serve warm with whipped cream. Makes 12 servings.

GLAZED APPLE-CRANBERRY PIE

½ cup sugar
2 tablespoons quick-cooking tapioca
¼ teaspoon cinnamon
¼ teaspoon salt
1 teaspoon grated orange peel
½ cup honey
1 tablespoon butter or margarine
3 cups raw cranberries
2 cups pared, diced apples
¼ cup water
Pastry for 2-crust pie
Lemon Glaze*
Garnish: coarsely grated orange peel

Combine sugar, tapioca, cinnamon, salt, orange peel, honey, and butter. Cook 2 minutes, stirring, until sugar dissolves. Add cranberries, apples, and water; boil 5 minutes or until cranberries burst. Cool. Roll out pastry for bottom crust; line 9-inch pie pan. Pour cranberry mixture into pastry-lined pie pan. Roll out top crust; cut slits to permit escape of steam and adjust over fruit, opening slits with knife. Flute edge. Bake at 425° for 35 to 40 minutes. Cool. Spread top with thin layer of Lemon Glaze. Sprinkle with coarsely grated orange peel.

*LEMON GLAZE

Combine ¾ cup sifted confectioners' (powdered) sugar with 2 teaspoons lemon juice. Add enough water (about 2 teaspoons) to make a thin, smooth spreading consistency.

ORANGE-APPLE PIE

     4 to 5 tart apples
     3 navel oranges
     ½ cup sugar
     ¼ cup flour
     ¾ cup firmly packed brown sugar
     ½ teaspoon nutmeg
     ½ teaspoon cinnamon
     ¼ teaspoon allspice
     Grated peel of 1 orange
     Grated peel of 1 lemon
     Pastry for 2-crust 10-inch pie
     3 tablespoons butter or margarine

Pare and core apples; slice crosswise in thin slices. Peel oranges, removing all white membrane; slice thin, crosswise. Combine sugar, flour, brown sugar, spices, and grated peels. Line 10-inch pie pan with pastry. Arrange alternate layers of apple and orange slices in pan, sprinkling each layer with sugar mixture. Dot with butter or margarine. Adjust lattice-weave top crust. Bake at 425° for 15 minutes. Reduce to 400°. Bake 30 minutes longer.

FRENCH APPLE PIE

     2 teaspoons flour
     ¾ cup firmly packed brown sugar
     ¾ teaspoon cinnamon
     ⅛ teaspoon salt
     ¼ teaspoon nutmeg
     1 tablespoon grated orange peel
     5 cups thinly sliced raw apples
     Pastry for 2-crust 8-inch pie
     2 tablespoons butter or margarine
     Sugar Glaze*
     Garnish: grated orange peel

Mix flour, sugar, cinnamon, salt, nutmeg, orange peel, and apples. Line pie pan with pastry rolled ⅛ inch thick. Fill with apple mixture; dot with butter. Moisten edge of pastry. Cut slits in top crust to permit escape of steam and adjust, opening slits with knife. Bake at 425° for 40 to 50 minutes or until apples are tender. Frost top with Sugar Glaze. Sprinkle with additional grated orange peel.

*SUGAR GLAZE

Combine ¾ cup confectioners' (powdered) sugar with 3 to 4 teaspoons milk to make a thin, smooth frosting.

VERMONT APPLE PIE

     6 to 8 large tart apples
     9-inch unbaked pastry shell
     ½ cup sugar
     ¾ cup gingersnap crumbs
     1 tablespoon flour
     ½ teaspoon cinnamon
     Few grains salt
     ½ cup chopped walnuts
     ¼ cup melted butter or margarine
     ⅓ cup maple syrup

Core and pare apples; slice thin. Spread about half the slices in pastry shell. Combine all remaining ingredients except maple syrup; mix well; spread half of this mixture over apples in pastry shell. Add remaining apple slices; spread remaining crumb mixture evenly over top. Bake at 350° for about 40 minutes. Heat maple syrup to boiling point; pour evenly over pie; bake 15 minutes longer.

JOHNNY APPLESEED PIE

     5 to 7 tart cooking apples
     ⅔ cup sugar, divided
     1 teaspoon cinnamon
     9-inch unbaked pastry shell
     1 package (6 ounces) semisweet chocolate
          pieces, divided
     1 tablespoon lemon juice, divided (optional)
     1 cup biscuit mix
     ¼ cup butter or margarine

Pare and core apples; slice thin. Combine ⅓ cup sugar and cinnamon. Arrange half the apples in unbaked pastry shell and sprinkle with half the sugar mixture and ½ cup semisweet chocolate pieces. Repeat except for chocolate pieces. (If apples are not tart, sprinkle each layer with ½ tablespoon lemon juice.) Combine remaining ⅓ cup sugar with biscuit mix; cut in butter until mixture is crumbly; spread over top of pie. Bake at 400° for about 40 minutes or until apples are tender. Sprinkle remaining chocolate pieces evenly over top of pie; bake 5 minutes longer.

CHRISTMAS TREE PIE

½ cup sugar
2 tablespoons flour
¼ teaspoon cinnamon
¼ teaspoon salt
1 teaspoon grated orange peel
½ cup honey
1 tablespoon butter or margarine
3 cups fresh cranberries
2 cups peeled, diced apples
Pastry for 2-crust 9-inch pie

Combine sugar, flour, cinnamon, salt, orange peel, honey, and butter or margarine. Cook 2 minutes, stirring, until sugar dissolves. Add cranberries and apples; boil 5 minutes or until cranberries burst. Cool. Pour into pastry-lined 9-inch pie pan. Cut a large Christmas tree from remaining pastry. Place over filling. Bake at 425° for 35 to 40 minutes.

GRAPEFRUIT PIE

Pastry for 2-crust 9-inch pie
2 cans (1 pound each) grapefruit sections
¼ cup firmly packed brown sugar
2½ tablespoons flour
1 teaspoon cinnamon
½ teaspoon nutmeg
2 tablespoons butter or margarine

Line 9-inch pie pan with pastry. Drain grapefruit sections. Mix brown sugar, flour, cinnamon, and nutmeg. Place half the grapefruit sections in pie pan. Sprinkle with half the brown sugar mixture. Repeat. Dot with butter or margarine. Top with pastry, pricked in a design. Press edges together with tines of fork or make fluted edge. Bake at 450° for 25 minutes.

NOTE: Fresh grapefruit sections may be used. Increase amount of brown sugar by ¼ cup or more, depending on tartness of fruit.

SPICED BLUEBERRY PIE

1 quart cultivated blueberries
1 package piecrust mix
1 teaspoon vinegar
1 cup sugar
3 tablespoons flour
½ teaspoon cinnamon
¼ teaspoon nutmeg
¼ teaspoon allspice
2 tablespoons butter or margarine

Wash and pick over blueberries. Prepare piecrust mix as directed on package; divide pastry in half. Roll out one half; line 9-inch pie pan; trim edge. Pour blueberries into pie pan; sprinkle with vinegar. Mix and sift sugar, flour, and spices; pour over berries; mix lightly with fork; dot with butter or margarine. Roll out remaining pastry; cut in strips about 1 inch wide, using pastry wheel. Arrange, lattice-fashion, over blueberries; trim edges; press with tines of fork. Bake at 425° for 15 minutes. Reduce heat to 375°; bake 25 minutes longer.

CHEDDAR PEAR PIE

¾ cup sugar
¼ cup flour
Few grains salt
¼ teaspoon nutmeg
¼ teaspoon ginger
4 cups sliced fresh winter pears
1 lemon, juice and grated peel
Pastry for 2-crust 9-inch pie
1 tablespoon butter or margarine
½ cup grated sharp Cheddar cheese

Combine sugar, flour, salt, and spices. Add pear slices. Add lemon juice and peel. Turn into pastry-lined pie pan. Dot with butter or margarine. Cut remaining pastry in strips; arrange on pie lattice-fashion; seal. Bake at 425° for 35 to 40 minutes. Sprinkle immediately with grated cheese; serve warm.

PEACH PIE

4 cups sliced fresh peaches
1½ tablespoons quick-cooking tapioca
⅔ to ¾ cup sugar
1 teaspoon lemon juice
Pastry for 2-crust 9-inch pie

Combine peaches, tapioca, sugar, and lemon juice. Line 9-inch pie plate with pastry. Fill with peach mixture. Cut remaining pastry in long strips, 1 inch wide, and arrange lattice-fashion over peaches. Fold ends of strips under lower crust. Bake at 425° for 40 to 45 minutes.

PEACH-BLUEBERRY PIE

1 package piecrust mix
4 cups sliced fresh peaches
2 cups cultivated blueberries
⅔ to ¾ cup sugar
2 tablespoons flour
½ teaspoon cinnamon
¼ teaspoon mace
⅛ teaspoon salt
1 tablespoon lemon juice
Pastry for 2-crust 9-inch pie
1 tablespoon butter or margarine

Prepare piecrust as directed on package. Line 9-inch pie pan with pastry. Combine peaches and blueberries. Combine sugar, flour, cinnamon, mace, salt, lemon peel and juice; add to fruits; toss with fork; pour into pie pan, heaping slightly in center. Dot with butter or margarine. Roll out remaining pastry. Cut into 10 strips about 11 inches long and ½ inch wide; arrange lattice-fashion over fruit. Trim and flute edges. Bake at 425° for 45 minutes.

BLUEBERRY PIE

3 tablespoons quick-cooking tapioca
1 cup sugar
¼ teaspoon salt
4 cups fresh blueberries
1 tablespoon lemon juice
Pastry for 2-crust 9-inch pie
1 tablespoon butter or margarine
Lemon Freeze*

Combine first 5 ingredients; let stand 15 minutes. Line 9-inch pie pan with pastry; fill pan with berry mixture; dot with butter or margarine. Cover with top crust; press edges together. Cut slits or holes in top crust to allow steam to escape. Bake at 425° about 55 minutes. Serve warm, with Lemon Freeze.

°LEMON FREEZE

¾ cup evaporated milk
6 tablespoons (½ can) frozen lemonade
    concentrate, thawed
¼ cup sugar
⅛ teaspoon salt

Chill evaporated milk in freezer tray until ice crystals form around edges. Whip in chilled bowl with beater until stiff. Combine remaining ingredients; add to evaporated milk, 1 tablespoon at a time, continuing to whip. Freeze firm. Makes 1 quart.

DOUBLE FRUIT PIE

½ cup sugar
2 tablespoons cornstarch
⅛ teaspoon salt
2 cups sliced fresh peaches
2 cups cultivated blueberries
1-2-3 Pastry*
1 tablespoon butter or margarine, divided
Melted butter or margarine
Sugar

Combine sugar, cornstarch, and salt. Sprinkle half over peaches and half over blueberries. Toss each to mix well. Divide pastry in half. Flatten one portion slightly; roll out into 12-inch circle between 2 pieces of waxed paper. (Wipe table with damp cloth to keep paper from slipping.) Peel off top paper; place pastry circle in 9-inch pie pan, paper side up. Peel off paper. Fit pastry loosely into pan, extending about ½ inch beyond rim. Arrange blueberry mixture in half the pan. Dot with ½ tablespoon butter or margarine. Flip uncovered half of pastry lining over blueberry filling, leaving half the pie pan empty. Roll out remaining pastry to 12-inch circle as directed above. Fit into empty half of pie pan, with pastry around rim extending ½ inch and other half resting on top of blueberry pie. Fill half pan with peach mixture; dot with remaining ½ tablespoon butter or margarine. Flip uncovered half of pastry over peach filling. Trim pastry, if necessary. Seal; flute all around rim. Cut slits in top of pastry to permit steam to escape during baking. Brush with melted butter or margarine. Sprinkle with sugar. Bake at 425° until fruit is tender and crust is browned (about 35 minutes). Makes about 6 servings.

°1-2-3 PASTRY

2 cups sifted all-purpose flour
1 teaspoon salt
½ cup vegetable oil
3 tablespoons cold water

Combine flour and salt in mixing bowl. Blend in oil, mixing thoroughly with fork. Sprinkle all water on top; mix well. Press firmly into ball with hands. (If slightly dry, mix in an additional 1 to 2 tablespoons oil.)

LATTICE-TOP CRANBERRY-PEAR PIE

1 package piecrust mix
1 cup sugar
2 tablespoons cornstarch
¼ teaspoon salt
½ teaspoon cinnamon
½ teaspoon nutmeg
3 cups peeled, sliced fresh pears
3 cups fresh cranberries
2 tablespoons butter or margarine

Prepare piecrust mix according to package directions. Roll out half the pastry; line 9-inch pie pan. Combine sugar, cornstarch, salt, spices, pears, and cranberries; toss lightly. Pour into pastry-lined pan. Dot with butter. Roll out remaining pastry; cut in ½-inch strips. Arrange strips lattice-fashion over filling; flute rim. Bake at 425° for 35 to 40 minutes or until crust is browned. Cool thoroughly before cutting.

ONE-CRUST RHUBARB PIE

2 eggs, well beaten
2 tablespoons butter or margarine, melted
3½ cups finely diced rhubarb (approximately 1½ pounds)
1¾ cups sugar
½ teaspoon cinnamon
½ teaspoon salt
7 tablespoons flour
9-inch unbaked pie shell

Combine eggs, butter, and rhubarb. Mix and sift sugar, cinnamon, salt, and flour. Add to rhubarb mixture; blend well. Spoon into pie shell. Bake at 375° for 50 to 60 minutes or until set.

ORANGE-STRAWBERRY PIE

1 package piecrust mix
1 cup sugar
2 tablespoons grated orange peel
¼ teaspoon salt
3 tablespoons quick-cooking tapioca
2 cups orange sections
2 cups washed and hulled strawberries
2 tablespoons butter or margarine

Prepare piecrust mix as directed on package. Roll out ⅔ of pastry on lightly floured board or pastry cloth; fit into 9-inch pie pan. Combine sugar, orange peel, salt, and tapioca. Arrange half the fruits in pie pan; sprinkle with half the sugar mixture. Repeat; dot with butter. Roll out remaining pastry; cut in strips. Arrange lattice-fashion on top of pie; secure ends. Flute edges. Bake at 425° for 30 minutes. Cool before cutting.

VIENNESE PIE

1 can (1 pound) pitted sour red cherries (water pack)
½ cup sugar
2 tablespoons cornstarch
9-inch baked pie shell
1 package chocolate pudding mix (not instant)
Frozen whipped topping

Drain cherries; reserve ¾ cup liquid. Combine sugar and cornstarch in saucepan; gradually blend in liquid. Cook over low heat, stirring constantly, until mixture comes to a boil. Add cherries (reserving ¼ cup for garnish); cool. Turn into baked pie shell; chill. Prepare pudding according to package directions for pie filling. Spoon over cherry mixture. Chill. Garnish with whipped topping and cherries.

TWENTY-MINUTE CHERRY PIE

½ cup sugar
2 tablespoons cornstarch
⅛ teaspoon salt
1 can (1 pound) pitted sour red cherries (water pack)
⅛ teaspoon red food coloring
8-inch baked pie shell

Combine sugar, cornstarch, and salt in saucepan. Drain liquid from cherries into saucepan with sugar mixture; stir until blended. Cook over moderate heat, stirring constantly, until mixture comes to a boil; boil ½ minute. Stir in red food coloring. Turn drained cherries into baked pie shell; spoon hot thickened sauce over the fruit. Top with baked pastry cutouts, if desired.

TAKE-YOUR-CHOICE PIE

Apple Filling:

¾ tablespoon quick-cooking tapioca
6 tablespoons sugar
Few grains salt
½ teaspoon cinnamon
⅛ teaspoon nutmeg
2½ cups thinly sliced peeled fresh apples

Combine all ingredients.

Cranberry Filling:

2 tablespoons quick-cooking tapioca
¾ cup sugar
¼ teaspoon salt
⅓ cup raisins
1½ cups fresh cranberries
½ cup plus 2 tablespoons water
1 teaspoon grated orange peel

Combine all ingredients except orange peel in saucepan. Cover; bring to boil. Cool, stirring occasionally. Add orange peel.

To Make the Pie:

Prepare pastry for 2-crust 9-inch pie. Roll out pastry for one crust; line pie pan. Cover half of pastry with Apple Filling; dot with butter or margarine. Fold unfilled half of crust over filling toward rim; seal edges and flute. Roll out remaining pastry; put in unfilled half of pie pan. Fill with Cranberry Filling; fold pastry over filling toward rim; seal edges; flute. Make well-opened slits in top of each half to allow steam to escape. Bake at 425° for 50 to 55 minutes or until apples are tender.

GOLDEN RAISIN RHUBARB PIE

Pastry for 2-crust 9-inch pie
Melted butter or margarine
6 tablespoons flour, divided
1¼ cups sugar, divided
3 cups unpeeled rhubarb, cut in 1-inch pieces
1 cup golden raisins
2 tablespoons butter or margarine

Line 9-inch pie pan with pastry. Brush with a little melted butter or margarine; chill. Combine 2 tablespoons each of the measured flour and sugar; sprinkle over chilled pastry. Combine rhubarb and raisins; pour into pie pan. Combine remaining flour and sugar; sprinkle over rhubarb mixture. Dot with butter or margarine. Cut re-

maining pastry into strips for lattice topping. Bake at 450° for 15 minutes. Lower heat to 350°; bake 40 to 45 minutes longer.

CRANBERRY CLARET PIE

2¼ cups sugar
1 tablespoon flour
¼ teaspoon salt
½ teaspoon mace
¼ cup water
¼ cup claret
4 cups fresh cranberries
1 tablespoon grated lemon peel
Pastry for 2-crust 9-inch pie
2 tablespoons butter or margarine

Combine first 4 ingredients. Add water and claret. Stir over low heat until sugar dissolves. Add cranberries; cook slowly until all skins pop open. Stir in lemon peel. Pour into pastry-lined pie pan. Dot with butter. Top with crisscross strips of pastry, lattice-fashion, or with pastry cutouts. Bake at 425° for 30 minutes.

PEACH CHEESE PIE

Crumb Crust:

16 graham crackers
3 tablespoons sugar
⅓ cup melted butter or margarine

Roll graham crackers into crumbs; add sugar and melted butter or margarine; blend well. Pack into 9-inch pie pan to cover bottom and sides. Bake at 350° for 10 minutes. Cool.

Filling:

3 packages (3 ounces each) cream cheese, softened
⅓ cup milk
⅓ cup sugar
2 eggs
¼ teaspoon vanilla
1 can (1 pound) sliced cling peaches, drained
Garnish (optional): peach slices; nutmeg

Blend cream cheese and milk. Add sugar, eggs, and vanilla; beat with rotary beater until smooth. Arrange peach slices in pie shell; pour cheese mixture over peaches. Bake at 350° for 30 minutes. If desired, garnish top with additional peach slices and dust with nutmeg.

CREAM-TOP STRAWBERRY PIE

Pastry for 2-crust pie
4 cups whole strawberries
3 tablespoons quick-cooking tapioca
1 cup sugar
¼ teaspoon salt
1 tablespoon lemon juice
½ cup whipping cream

Line 9-inch pie pan with pastry. Combine strawberries, tapioca, sugar, salt, and lemon juice; mix gently but thoroughly with fork; pour into pie pan. Arrange strips of pastry over filling, lattice-fashion; trim; flute edge. Bake at 425° for 45 to 50 minutes. Remove from oven. Carefully and slowly pour ½ cup cream into openings in lattice top. Let stand 15 minutes. Serve warm.

STRAWBERRY CREAM PIE

1 quart strawberries
1 cup sugar
1⅓ cups water, divided
3 tablespoons cornstarch
½ pint whipping cream
1 teaspoon vanilla
9-inch baked pie shell

Wash strawberries; hull. Simmer 1 cup strawberries, 1 cup sugar, and 1 cup water 15 minutes. Mix remaining ⅓ cup water with cornstarch; add to cooked strawberries. Cook until thick, stirring constantly; cool. Add uncooked strawberries. Cool. Whip cream; add vanilla. Spread cream in baked pie shell; top with strawberry mixture. Chill 3 to 4 hours.

BANANA CREAM PIE

2 cups milk, divided
¼ cup light corn syrup
4 tablespoons cornstarch
½ cup sugar
¼ teaspoon salt
3 eggs, separated
1 teaspoon vanilla
9-inch baked pie shell (made with piecrust mix)
3 to 4 ripe bananas (depending on size)
6 tablespoons sugar

Scald 1¾ cups milk with corn syrup in top of double boiler. Blend cornstarch with remaining ¼ cup milk; add ½ cup sugar and salt. Add egg yolks to cornstarch mixture; beat until well blended. Add a little hot milk mixture to egg mixture, then add to remaining hot milk mixture. Stir over hot water until thickened; cover; cook 7 minutes. Remove from heat; add vanilla; cool. Cover bottom of pie shell with thinly sliced bananas. Add cornstarch filling; top with another layer of bananas. Top with meringue made by whipping 3 egg whites and 6 tablespoons sugar until firm. Run under broiler just long enough to brown tips of meringue.

SPICY BANANA CREAM PIE

2 packages vanilla pudding and pie filling mix (not instant)
¼ teaspoon nutmeg
1 teaspoon cinnamon
1 teaspoon rum flavoring
2 medium bananas
Crumb Crust*
Garnish: whipped cream or whipped topping; sliced bananas

Prepare pudding and pie filling mix as directed for pie filling, combining spices with dry mix. After cooking, stir in flavoring. Cool slightly. Slice 2 bananas into Crumb Crust. Spoon filling over bananas, mounding higher in center. Chill until firm. Garnish as desired with whipped cream or whipped topping and sliced bananas.

*CRUMB CRUST

¾ cup graham cracker crumbs
¾ cup wheat germ
⅓ cup sugar
¼ teaspoon nutmeg
⅓ cup butter or margarine, melted

Combine crumbs, wheat germ, sugar, nutmeg, and melted butter; mix well. Pack evenly over bottom and up sides of 9-inch pie pan, making a firm rim. Bake at 350° for 5 minutes. Chill.

FLUFFY CHERRY PIE

24 sugar wafers (vanilla flavor)
2 tablespoons melted butter or margarine
1 can (1 pound) pitted sour red cherries (water pack)
1 package cherry-flavor gelatin
1 small can evaporated milk (⅔ cup)
¼ teaspoon almond extract
2 egg whites
3 tablespoons sugar
Garnish (optional): crushed sugar wafers

Crush 24 sugar wafers to fine crumbs; combine with melted butter or margarine. Pat crumbs onto well-buttered 9-inch pie pan. Chill thoroughly. Drain juice from cherries. Add enough water to juice to make 1 cup; bring to boil; pour over gelatin in bowl; stir until gelatin dissolves; cool slightly. Combine gelatin mixture and evaporated milk (mixture may curdle slightly but final beating will restore smoothness); add extract. Chill mixture until it will mound slightly when dropped from a spoon. Meanwhile, beat egg whites until foamy; add sugar slowly while continuing to beat until mixture forms soft peaks. Beat gelatin mixture until it is thick and fluffy. Fold egg whites and cherries into gelatin, reserving a few cherries for garnish. Spoon into pie shell, mounding higher in center; sprinkle with additional crushed sugar wafers, if desired. Chill until firm.

QUICK AMBROSIA PIE

1 package (3¾ ounces) coconut-cream pudding mix
1½ cups orange juice
1 tablespoon grated orange peel
1 cup whipping cream, whipped
9-inch baked pie shell
1 large grapefruit, sectioned
2 oranges, sectioned
Garnish (optional): whipped cream

Prepare pudding mix according to package directions, substituting orange juice for milk. Remove from heat; stir in orange peel. When cold, fold in the whipped cream. Spread evenly in pie shell. Chill in refrigerator several hours or overnight. When ready to serve, mark pie into 6 wedges. Place 2 grapefruit sections lengthwise on each serving. Place 1 or 2 orange sections on top of grapefruit. Garnish with more whipped cream, if desired.

HEAVENLY PIE

3 egg whites
¼ teaspoon salt
¼ teaspoon cream of tartar
¾ cup sugar
½ cup finely chopped walnuts
½ teaspoon vanilla
2 packages vanilla pudding mix (not instant)
3½ cups milk
Blueberries
Sliced peaches

Beat egg whites until foamy; add salt and cream of tartar; beat until mixture stands in soft peaks. Add sugar gradually, while beating, until mixture is very stiff. Fold in nuts and vanilla. Spoon into lightly greased 9-inch pie pan and make a nestlike shell, building up sides to form rim. Bake at 300° for 50 to 55 minutes. Cool. Meanwhile, prepare pudding according to directions on package, using 3½ cups milk instead of 4. Cool. Pour into meringue shell; chill. Top with fruits.

LEMON ANGEL PIE

Meringue Shell:

4 egg whites
¼ teaspoon cream of tartar
1 cup sugar

Beat egg whites until foamy; sprinkle with cream of tartar; beat until meringue starts to hold its shape. Add sugar gradually, beating until meringue is stiff. Spread in greased 10-inch pie pan, making a shell. Bake at 275° for 1 hour. Cool.

Filling:

1 package lemon pudding and pie filling mix (not instant)
½ cup sherry
1 can (1 pound) sliced cling peaches *or* 2 cups sliced, sweetened fresh peaches
Garnish: 1 cup whipping cream; candy decorettes

Prepare mix as directed on package for pie filling, substituting sherry for ½ cup of the liquid. Cool, stirring several times. Place drained peaches in meringue shell. Add lemon mixture. Chill. Garnish with whipped cream and decorettes.

FLUFFY LEMON PIE

6 eggs, separated
1½ cups sugar, divided
¼ cup flour
3 tablespoons grated lemon peel
6 tablespoons lemon juice
4 tablespoons water
1 baked pie shell (9- or 10-inch size)

Beat egg yolks until thick and fluffy. Combine ¾ cup sugar and the flour thoroughly and add gradually to egg yolks while continuing to beat. Gradually stir in lemon peel, lemon juice, and water. Stir over hot, not boiling, water until thick (about 5 to 7 minutes). Remove from heat. Beat egg whites to soft peaks and add remaining ¾ cup sugar, 1 tablespoon at a time, beating until stiff and glossy. Fold half this meringue into warm lemon mixture gently but thoroughly. Pour into baked pie shell. Make a frill of remaining meringue around rim of pie. Bake at 325° for about 15 minutes or until meringue is golden brown. Cool, then chill.

HAWAIIAN PINEAPPLE MERINGUE PIE

6 tablespoons cornstarch
1 cup sugar, divided
½ teaspoon salt
2 cans (20 ounces each) crushed pineapple
4 eggs, separated
2 tablespoons lemon juice
10-inch baked pie shell

Combine cornstarch, ½ cup sugar, salt, and pineapple (undrained) in saucepan. Cook over low heat, stirring constantly, until clear and thickened. Beat egg yolks; add a little of the hot mixture to yolks; return to saucepan with lemon juice. Cook 1 minute. Cool thoroughly. Pour into pie shell. Beat egg whites until stiff but not dry; add remaining ½ cup sugar slowly while beating until meringue stands in stiff peaks. Swirl on pie, covering entire surface to edge of pastry rim. Bake at 425° for 4 minutes.

STRAWBERRY-PINEAPPLE PIE

½ cup sugar
½ cup flour
¼ teaspoon salt
1 can (1 pound) crushed pineapple
Hot water
3 egg yolks
2 tablespoons butter or margarine
9-inch baked pie shell
1 pint strawberries
Strawberry Glaze*

Combine sugar, flour, and salt. Drain syrup from pineapple; measure syrup; add enough hot water to make 1⅔ cups; add to sugar mixture. Cook over boiling water until thick, stirring constantly. Cover; cook 15 minutes. Beat egg yolks; add hot custard slowly. Cook over hot water 5 minutes. Add pineapple and butter; stir until butter melts. Cool; pour into baked pie shell. Wash strawberries; hull; halve largest berries; arrange on pie; reserve smaller berries (½ to ⅔ cup) for Strawberry Glaze. Pour cooled Strawberry Glaze on pie. Chill.

*STRAWBERRY GLAZE

½ to ⅔ cup strawberries (reserved from above)
½ to ⅔ cup strawberries
½ cup light corn syrup
1½ tablespoons cornstarch
1 tablespoon water
1 teaspoon lemon juice

Mash strawberries; add light corn syrup. Cook until berries are soft. Press through sieve or food mill. Mix cornstarch with water; add to strawberry syrup. Cook until thickened, stirring constantly. Add lemon juice. Cool slightly before pouring on pie.

CHOCOLATE CHIFFON PIE

1 envelope unflavored gelatin
1¼ cups cold milk, divided
1 package (6 ounces) semisweet chocolate pieces
½ cup sugar
¼ teaspoon salt
1 teaspoon vanilla
1 tablespoon lemon juice
1 small can (⅔ cup) evaporated milk
9-inch baked pie shell

Soften gelatin in ½ cup of the cold milk. Combine remaining milk, chocolate, sugar, and salt. Cook over hot water, stirring occasionally, until chocolate is melted. Beat with rotary beater until smooth. Remove from heat; add gelatin and vanilla; stir until gelatin dissolves. Chill until consistency of unbeaten egg white. Add lemon juice to ice-cold evaporated milk; whip until stiff. Fold in gelatin mixture. Turn into pie shell; chill until firm.

CHIFFON CUSTARD PIE

1 envelope unflavored gelatin
½ cup sauterne or other white wine, divided
½ cup sugar
½ teaspoon salt
1 cup milk
3 eggs, separated
½ teaspoon vanilla
1 cup whipping cream, divided

2 tablespoons sugar
9-inch baked pie shell
Garnish (optional): toasted flaked coconut *or*
  berries or fruit in season

Soften gelatin in ¼ cup sauterne. Combine sugar, salt, milk, and slightly beaten egg yolks in top of double boiler. Cook over hot water until mixture thickens and coats spoon. Add gelatin and vanilla, stirring until gelatin dissolves. Remove from heat; add remaining wine. Chill until mixture begins to stiffen. Meanwhile, whip ½ cup cream. Beat egg whites until foamy; add 2 tablespoons sugar slowly; beat until a soft meringue is formed. Fold whipped cream and meringue into gelatin mixture. Spoon into pie shell. Chill until firm. Whip remaining cream; spread on surface of pie. If desired, garnish with toasted flaked coconut or berries or fruit in season.

NESSELRODE CLOUD PIE

Chocolate Meringue Shell:

3 egg whites
¼ teaspoon cream of tartar
¼ teaspoon salt
¾ cup sugar
1 square unsweetened chocolate, grated

Beat egg whites with cream of tartar and salt until stiff but not dry. Gradually add sugar, about 1 tablespoon at a time; beat until very stiff. Fold in grated chocolate. Spread over bottom and sides of well-greased 9-inch pie plate. Bake at 275° for 1 hour. Cool.

Filling:

1 envelope unflavored gelatin
½ cup sugar, divided
¼ teaspoon salt
2 eggs, separated
1 cup milk
⅓ cup cognac or light rum
1 cup heavy cream, whipped
Garnish: candied cherries; candied
  pineapple, diced; candied orange peel

Mix gelatin, ¼ cup sugar, and salt in saucepan. Beat egg yolks with milk; stir into gelatin mixture. Stir over low heat until gelatin dissolves and mixture thickens slightly (8 to 10 minutes). Remove from heat; stir in cognac. Chill, stirring occasionally, until mixture mounds slightly when dropped from spoon. Beat egg whites until stiff but not dry; add remaining ¼ cup sugar

gradually; beat until very stiff. Fold into gelatin mixture; fold in whipped cream. Spoon into Chocolate Meringue Shell. Chill overnight. Garnish with wreath of candied cherries, pineapple, and orange peel.

QUICK NESSELRODE PIE

1 package (3 ounces) lemon-flavor gelatin
1 cup whipping cream
½ cup broken pecan meats
½ cup chopped maraschino cherries
1 teaspoon rum flavoring
Cereal Crumb Crust*

Prepare gelatin as directed on package. Chill until syrupy. Whip with rotary egg beater until light and fluffy. Whip cream; fold into gelatin with pecans, cherries, and rum flavoring. Spoon lightly into Cereal Crumb Crust. Chill until set.

*CEREAL CRUMB CRUST

1¼ cups fine cereal flake crumbs
⅓ cup melted butter or margarine
¼ cup sugar

Combine all ingredients; mix well. Press firmly on bottom and sides of 9-inch pie pan. Bake at 325° for 8 minutes. Cool.

FRUITED CHIFFON PIE

1 envelope unflavored gelatin
½ cup cold water
½ cup sugar
½ cup lemon juice
2 drops green food coloring
¼ teaspoon salt
3 egg whites
½ cup light corn syrup
1 cup cultivated blueberries
1 cup thinly sliced ripe bananas
9-inch baked pie shell
Whipped cream (optional)

Sprinkle gelatin over water in small saucepan. Let stand a few minutes to soften gelatin. Add sugar; stir over hot water or very low heat until gelatin and sugar are completely dissolved. Remove from heat; stir in lemon juice and food coloring. Chill to unbeaten egg white consistency. Add salt to egg whites; beat until stiff but not dry. Slowly add light corn syrup, beating until smooth and glossy. Fold chilled gelatin mixture into beaten egg whites; chill until thick enough to mound in a spoon (about ½ hour). Stir mixture occasionally while chilling. Fold in blueberries and bananas. Pile lightly into baked pie shell; chill until ready to serve. Top with whipped cream, if desired.

PUMPKIN CHIFFON PIE

3 eggs, separated
⅔ cup sugar, divided
1½ cups canned pumpkin
⅓ cup milk
½ teaspoon each salt, ginger, cinnamon, and
    nutmeg
1 envelope unflavored gelatin
¼ cup cold water
9-inch baked pie shell

Beat egg yolks; add ⅓ cup sugar, pumpkin, milk, salt, and spices. Heat in double boiler, stirring. Sprinkle gelatin on cold water. Dissolve in hot mixture. Chill until slightly thickened. Beat egg whites stiff; add remaining sugar gradually. Fold in pumpkin mixture. Pour into pie shell. Chill.

PUMPKIN BONBON CHIFFON PIE

1 envelope unflavored gelatin
¾ cup firmly packed light brown sugar
½ teaspoon salt
1 teaspoon each cinnamon and ginger
½ teaspoon each nutmeg and allspice
1 large can (1⅔ cups) evaporated milk,
    divided
1½ cups canned pumpkin
1 tablespoon lemon juice
Bonbon Pie Shell*

Mix unflavored gelatin, sugar, salt, and spices in saucepan. Stir in 1 cup of the evaporated milk. Cook over low heat, stirring constantly, until gelatin dissolves (about 5 minutes). Remove from heat; stir in pumpkin. Chill until mixture mounds slightly when dropped from a spoon (about 1 hour). Meanwhile, chill remaining ⅔ cup of the evaporated milk in freezer tray of refrigerator until ice crystals form around edges. Turn chilled evaporated milk into bowl; whip with rotary beater or on high speed of electric mixer until stiff. Add lemon juice; beat until blended. Fold in pumpkin mixture. Turn into Bonbon Pie Shell. Chill until firm.

*BONBON PIE SHELL

Line a 9-inch pie pan by pressing 12-inch square of aluminum foil on bottom, sides and over rim to assume shape of pan. Gently remove foil from pan, being careful to keep foil in shape. Place on ungreased cookie sheet. Place in foil 1 package (6 ounces) semisweet chocolate pieces and 2 tablespoons shortening. Place in 350° oven 2 to 3 minutes. Remove from oven. Replace foil in pan, crimping edge over rim. With back of teaspoon, gently blend chocolate with shortening. Spread over bottom of pan. Refrigerate 4 to 5 minutes or until chocolate mixture is cooled enough to spread on sides. With back of spoon, spread chocolate mixture upward to edge (not top) of rim, being careful to coat entire pan evenly. Refrigerate 25 minutes. Carefully remove from pan and remove foil. Replace shell in pan.

PRALINE PUMPKIN PIE

1 envelope unflavored gelatin
½ cup cold water
¾ cup firmly packed light brown sugar
1 can (1 pound) pumpkin
¼ cup milk
½ teaspoon salt
1 teaspoon cinnamon
¾ teaspoon nutmeg
1 cup heavy cream, whipped
Praline Crunch*
9-inch baked pie shell
Garnish: whipped cream; Praline Crunch

Sprinkle gelatin over water in saucepan. Place over low heat; stir constantly until gelatin dissolves (2 or 3 minutes). Remove from heat; add brown sugar; stir until dissolved. In mixing bowl, combine pumpkin, milk, salt, cinnamon, and nutmeg. Gradually blend in gelatin mixture; stir until smooth. Fold in whipped cream. Sprinkle 1 cup Praline Crunch over bottom of baked pie shell. Turn pumpkin mixture into pie shell. Chill until firm. At serving time, garnish with ring of additional whipped cream and remaining Praline Crunch.

*PRALINE CRUNCH

¼ cup butter or margarine
½ cup sugar
1 cup coarsely chopped pecan meats

Melt butter in small skillet. Stir in sugar. Add pecan meats. Cook over moderate heat, stirring constantly, until sugar mixture begins to turn golden (about 3 minutes). Remove from heat; turn out onto piece of foil. Cool. Crumble into small pieces. Makes 1½ cups.

ALMOND PUMPKIN PIE

Almond Mixture:

1 cup sugar
¼ cup water
1 cup canned toasted slivered almonds
3 tablespoons soft butter or margarine

Combine sugar and water in heavy saucepan. Bring to boil over medium heat, stirring occasionally. Boil 4 minutes, without stirring, until a light golden brown. Remove from heat; stir in almonds; pour onto greased baking sheet. Cool completely. Crush with rolling pin or pulverize in electric blender. Mix 1¼ cups almond powder with soft butter and press over bottom and sides of 9-inch pie pan. Bake at 350° for 5 to 7 minutes. Cool. Reserve remaining almond mixture.

Pumpkin Filling:

1 envelope unflavored gelatin
½ cup firmly packed brown sugar
½ teaspoon salt
1 teaspoon cinnamon
¾ teaspoon nutmeg
¼ teaspoon ginger
2 eggs, separated
½ cup milk
1 can (1 pound) pumpkin
¼ cup sugar
Reserved almond powder (about ¾ cup)
1 cup whipping cream
Garnish (optional): chocolate curls

Combine gelatin, brown sugar, salt, cinnamon, nutmeg, and ginger in large saucepan. Beat egg yolks and milk together; stir into gelatin mixture. Stir over very low heat until gelatin dissolves and mixture thickens slightly (about 5 minutes). Remove from heat; blend in pumpkin. Chill, stirring occasionally, until mixture mounds slightly when dropped from a spoon. Beat egg whites until soft peaks form; gradually add sugar and continue to beat until stiff peaks form. Fold into pumpkin mixture. Fold in reserved almond powder. Whip cream; fold in. Spoon into prepared almond pie shell; chill until set. Garnish with chocolate curls, if desired.

SKY-HIGH LEMON CHIFFON PIE

1 package lemon-flavor gelatin
¾ cup boiling water
½ cup sugar
1 lemon, juice and grated peel
1 large can (1⅔ cups) evaporated milk,
    whipped (page 288)
9-inch baked pie shell

Dissolve gelatin in boiling water; add sugar, lemon juice and grated peel; chill until syrupy. Fold in whipped evaporated milk; spoon into pie shell. Chill.

LEMON CHIFFON PIE

1 envelope unflavored gelatin
¼ cup cold water
½ cup lemon juice
¼ teaspoon salt
1 teaspoon grated lemon peel
⅔ cup sugar, divided
4 eggs, separated
9-inch baked pie shell

Soften gelatin in cold water and lemon juice. Add salt, lemon peel, and ⅓ cup sugar. Place over boiling water; stir until gelatin dissolves. Beat egg yolks slightly. Add hot mixture slowly. Cook over hot water, stirring, until slightly thickened. Chill until consistency of unbeaten egg white. Beat egg whites stiff; gradually beat in remaining sugar. Beat lemon gelatin mixture; fold into egg whites. Turn into baked pie shell; chill until firm.

LEMON FLUFF PIE

Crust:

1⅓ cups quick-cooking rolled oats, uncooked
½ cup firmly packed brown sugar
¼ cup butter or margarine, melted

Combine all ingredients; mix thoroughly. Press firmly on bottom and sides of 9-inch pie pan. Set 8-inch pie pan inside to hold crumbs in place. Bake at 375° about 8 minutes. Remove inside pie pan; cool.

Filling:

1 envelope unflavored gelatin
⅓ cup cold water
4 eggs, separated
⅔ cup sugar, divided

Grated peel of 1 lemon
⅓ cup lemon juice
⅛ teaspoon salt

Soften gelatin in cold water. Beat egg yolks slightly; combine with ⅓ cup of the sugar, lemon peel and lemon juice in top of double boiler. Cook over hot water, stirring constantly, until thickened. Stir in softened gelatin. Beat egg whites and salt until soft peaks form. Add remaining ⅓ cup sugar, 1 tablespoon at a time, beating well after each addition. Beat until stiff and glossy; fold into gelatin mixture. Pour into crust; chill thoroughly. Let stand at room temperature about 10 minutes before cutting.

ORANGE CHIFFON PIE

¾ cup orange juice
1 package (3 ounces) orange-flavor gelatin
½ cup sugar
Juice of 1 lemon
Grated peel of 1 orange
1 large can (1⅔ cups) evaporated milk,
    whipped (page 288)
Chocolate Wafer Crust*
Garnish: orange sections

Heat orange juice; dissolve gelatin in orange juice; add sugar; stir until dissolved. Add lemon juice and grated orange peel. Chill until consistency of unbeaten egg white. Fold in whipped evaporated milk. Spoon into Chocolate Wafer Crust. Chill until firm. Garnish with orange sections.

°CHOCOLATE WAFER CRUST

Place chocolate wafers in 9-inch pie pan. Fill spaces between wafers with wafer crumbs. Place halves of wafers in rim around edge, rounded side up.

EGGNOG PIE

1 envelope unflavored gelatin
½ cup sugar, divided
⅛ teaspoon salt
1¾ cups milk
3 eggs, separated
¼ teaspoon nutmeg
1 tablespoon rum flavoring
9-inch baked pie shell
Garnish: whipped topping; diced candied
    fruits and peels

Combine gelatin, ¼ cup of the sugar, and salt in top of double boiler. Stir in milk. Let stand 5 minutes. Place over boiling water; stir until gelatin and sugar are dissolved. Beat egg yolks slightly; gradually stir in small amount of the hot mixture; return to double boiler; cook until mixture is slightly thickened. Remove from heat; add nutmeg and flavoring. Chill mixture until slightly thicker than the consistency of unbeaten egg white. Whip egg whites until stiff but not dry; gradually beat in remaining ¼ cup sugar. Fold in gelatin mixture. Turn into pie shell; chill until firm. Garnish with whipped topping and diced candied fruits and peels.

HOLIDAY EGGNOG PIE

1 envelope unflavored gelatin
2 tablespoons sugar
2¼ cups bottled nonalcoholic eggnog, divided
¼ teaspoon nutmeg
2 teaspoons rum flavoring
½ cup whipping cream, whipped
9-inch baked pie shell
Garnish: whipped cream; chocolate curls;
    diced candied fruits and peels

Combine gelatin and sugar in top of double boiler. Stir in 1 cup cold eggnog. Stir over boiling water until gelatin and sugar are dissolved. Remove from heat; add remaining eggnog, nutmeg, and flavoring. Chill until slightly thicker than consistency of unbeaten egg white. Whip until light and fluffy; fold in whipped cream. Turn into pie shell; chill until firm. Garnish with additional whipped cream, shaved unsweetened chocolate curls, and diced candied fruits and peels.

PEPPERMINT PIE

1 envelope unflavored gelatin
1 cup cold water
½ cup sugar, divided
⅛ teaspoon salt
3 eggs, separated
½ teaspoon peppermint extract
⅛ teaspoon red food coloring
1 cup whipping cream, whipped
Double Chocolate Pie Shell*
Garnish: chocolate cookie crumbs (from
    Double Chocolate Pie Shell)

Sprinkle gelatin over water in medium saucepan. Add ¼ cup sugar, salt, and egg yolks; stir until thoroughly blended. Place over low heat; stir constantly until gelatin dissolves and mixture thickens slightly (about 5 minutes). Remove from heat; stir in extract and food coloring. Chill, stirring occasionally, until mixture mounds slightly when dropped from spoon. Beat egg whites until stiff but not dry; gradually add remaining ¼ cup sugar and beat until very stiff and glossy. Fold in gelatin mixture. Fold in whipped cream. Turn into prepared 9-inch Double Chocolate Pie Shell. Chill until firm. Garnish with chocolate cookie crumbs.

*DOUBLE CHOCOLATE PIE SHELL

> 1 package (6 ounces) semisweet chocolate pieces
> 1 teaspoon vegetable shortening
> About 2 dozen thin chocolate cookie wafers

Melt semisweet chocolate pieces and vegetable shortening over hot, not boiling, water. Spread the tops of 11 wafers with melted chocolate; place on waxed-paper-lined cookie sheet; chill. Spread chocolate halfway down back of same wafers; chill again. Spread tops of 7 additional wafers with melted chocolate and set in bottom of 9-inch pie plate. Crush some wafers to fill up spaces on bottom of pie plate; chill. When chocolate is firm, line up the 11 cookies around edge of pie plate so that the frosted backs stick up over the rim of the plate. Fill pie shell with peppermint filling.

GRENADINE-ALMOND BAVARIAN PIE

> 1 envelope unflavored gelatin
> ¼ cup cold water
> ¼ teaspoon salt
> ¾ cup grenadine syrup, divided
> 4 eggs, separated
> 1 cup ground blanched almonds (not toasted)
> 1½ teaspoons grated lemon peel
> 1 tablespoon lemon juice
> Chocolate cookie "snaps"
> 1 cup whipping cream
> Garnish (optional): chocolate cookie crumbs

Sprinkle gelatin over cold water in saucepan or top of double boiler. Add salt. Add ¼ cup grenadine syrup; mix well. Add egg yolks; mix well. Place over very low heat or simmering water; stir constantly until gelatin dissolves and mixture thickens slightly (about 5 minutes). Remove from heat; add almonds, lemon peel and lemon juice.

Cool, stirring occasionally, at room temperature; do not refrigerate. While gelatin mixture is cooling, prepare pie shell. Place chocolate cookies over bottom and stand around inside edge of 9-inch pie plate. Use small pieces of cookies to fill in space on the bottom. When gelatin mixture is cool, beat egg whites until stiff but not dry; gradually add remaining ½ cup grenadine syrup and beat until very stiff. Fold into gelatin mixture. Whip cream; fold in. Turn into prepared cookie pie shell, piling high in center. Chill until firm. If desired, garnish with chocolate cookie crumbs.

FRUITED CREAM PIE

> 1½ envelopes (1½ tablespoons) unflavored gelatin
> 2 cups milk
> 6 tablespoons sugar
> ⅛ teaspoon salt
> 2 egg yolks
> ½ teaspoon vanilla
> 2 egg whites
> 1 cup sliced strawberries
> 1 cup diced canned pineapple
> 1 tablespoon extra-fine (instant) granulated sugar
> Sweet Coconut Pie Shell*
> Garnish: ½ pint whipping cream, whipped; strawberries

Sprinkle gelatin on milk; heat over hot water. Add sugar and salt; dissolve. Beat egg yolks. Add hot milk to beaten yolks; cook over hot water, stirring, until mixture coats spoon. Add vanilla. Chill until mixture begins to stiffen. Beat egg whites stiff; fold in. Combine fruits; add fine granulated sugar; pour into Sweet Coconut Pie Shell. Spoon custard mix over fruit. Chill until firm. Garnish with whipped cream and whole strawberries.

*SWEET COCONUT PIE SHELL

Spread 9-inch pie pan with 1 tablespoon softened butter. Combine 1 can flaked coconut with just enough sweetened condensed milk to hold it together (about 2 tablespoons). Press into pie pan. Bake at 325° for 15 minutes or until golden brown. Cool.

MARGARITA PIE

Crumb Crust:

¾ cup pretzel crumbs
⅓ cup butter or margarine
3 tablespoons sugar

Combine all ingredients; mix well. Press against the bottom and sides of a greased 9-inch pie pan. Chill.

Filling:

½ cup lemon juice
1 envelope unflavored gelatin
4 eggs, separated
1 cup sugar, divided
¼ teaspoon salt
1 teaspoon grated lemon peel
⅓ cup tequila
3 tablespoons triple sec

Sprinkle lemon juice with unflavored gelatin; let stand until softened. Beat egg yolks in top half of double boiler; blend in ½ cup sugar, salt, and grated lemon peel. Add softened gelatin. Cook over boiling water, stirring constantly, until slightly thickened and gelatin is completely dissolved. Transfer to a bowl; blend in tequila and triple sec. Chill until mixture is cold, but not further thickened. Beat egg whites until foamy; gradually beat in remaining ½ cup sugar until whites hold soft peaks. Pour cooked mixture slowly on egg white, about ⅓ at a time, folding carefully after each addition. Let stand until mixture mounds in spoon. Swirl into pie shell. Chill until set.

MILE-HIGH CHOCOLATE CHESTNUT PIE

2 envelopes unflavored gelatin
1¼ cups milk, divided
4 eggs, separated
⅛ teaspoon salt
1 package (6 ounces) semisweet chocolate
    pieces
¼ cup syrup of marrons in vanilla syrup
½ teaspoon vanilla
½ teaspoon cream of tartar
¼ cup sugar
1 cup chopped marrons
1 cup whipping cream
9-inch baked pie shell
Garnish (optional): whipped cream; sliced
    marrons

Sprinkle gelatin over ½ cup milk in top of double boiler. Combine egg yolks and remaining ¾ cup milk. Add to gelatin and cook, stirring constantly, over boiling water until gelatin dissolves and mixture thickens slightly (about 5 minutes). Remove from heat; add salt, chocolate pieces, syrup, and vanilla; stir until chocolate is melted and smooth. Chill, stirring occasionally, until mixture mounds slightly when dropped from spoon. Beat egg whites in large bowl with cream of tartar until soft peaks form. Gradually beat in ¼ cup sugar; continue to beat until stiff peaks form. Fold into chocolate mixture; fold in chopped marrons. Whip cream; fold in. Chill, stirring frequently, until mixture mounds when dropped from a spoon, about 10 minutes. Spoon into prepared pie shell, heaping higher in center. Chill several hours. Garnish with additional whipped cream and sliced marrons, if desired. Makes 8 to 10 servings.

PEANUT-BRITTLE CHIFFON PIE

1 envelope unflavored gelatin
¼ cup cold water
½ cup evaporated milk
½ cup water
2 eggs, separated
2 tablespoons brown sugar
2 tablespoons sugar
¾ cup crushed peanut brittle, divided
1 teaspoon vanilla
⅔ cup evaporated milk, chilled icy cold
9-inch baked pie shell

Soften gelatin in ¼ cup cold water. Mix ½ cup evaporated milk and ½ cup water. Heat gently to scalding. Beat egg yolks slightly; add brown sugar, 1 tablespoon at a time; continue beating until fluffy; stir in a little scalded milk; add to remaining scalded milk. Cook over very low heat, stirring constantly, until mixture thickens slightly (about 2 to 3 minutes). Remove from heat. Pour over softened gelatin; stir until gelatin dissolves. Chill until mixture is slightly thicker than unbeaten egg white, stirring frequently. Beat egg whites until foamy. Add sugar, 1 tablespoon at a time; continue beating until whites are stiff. Fold into egg yolk mixture with ½ cup peanut brittle and vanilla. Whip chilled milk until stiff. Fold into peanut-brittle mixture. Turn into pie shell. Sprinkle with remaining peanut brittle. Chill until set.

PERSIAN LIME PIE

12 ladyfingers
⅓ cup semisweet chocolate pieces
1 teaspoon shortening
1 envelope unflavored gelatin
¼ cup cold water
4 eggs, separated
1 cup sugar, divided
¼ teaspoon salt
½ cup lime juice
2 teaspoons grated lime peel
½ cup whipping cream, whipped

For ladyfinger pie shell, split ladyfingers; cut ½ inch off one end; stand, cut side down, around edge of 9-inch pie plate. Put remaining ladyfingers and pieces evenly in bottom of pie plate. Melt semisweet chocolate pieces and shortening over hot water. Remove ladyfingers from edge of pie plate one at a time. Dip rounded ends into melted chocolate; put back into place. Soften gelatin in cold water. Beat egg yolks in top of double boiler; stir in ½ cup sugar, salt, and lime juice. Cook over hot water, stirring constantly, until mixture thickens. Remove from heat; add softened gelatin; stir until gelatin dissolves. Stir in lime peel; cool. Beat egg whites until stiff; gradually add remaining ½ cup sugar; beat very stiff. Fold gelatin mixture into beaten egg whites. Fold in whipped cream. Turn into prepared pie shell; chill until firm.

COOKIE-CRUST PEACH PIE

⅓ cup butter or margarine
1 cup quick-cooking rolled oats, uncooked
¼ cup sugar
¼ teaspoon cinnamon
1 can (29 ounces) sliced cling peaches
1 envelope unflavored gelatin
½ cup frozen lemonade concentrate
Few grains salt
1 small can (⅔ cup) evaporated milk, whipped

Place butter in 9-inch pie pan and set in oven to melt. While oven is heating to 350°, combine oats, sugar, and cinnamon; mix with melted butter in pie pan. Bake 15 minutes. Remove from oven; shape into shell by pressing mixture against sides and bottom of pie pan with back of spoon. Cool shell thoroughly; drain peaches. Combine ¾ cup syrup from peaches with gelatin in small saucepan. Stir over low heat until gela-

tin is dissolved. Remove from heat; stir in frozen lemonade concentrate and salt. Chill until slightly thickened. Fold into whipped evaporated milk. Dice enough peach slices to make 1 cup; fold in. Spoon into pie shell. Top with remaining peach slices. Chill until firm.

CRANBERRY STAR PIE

1 cup sugar
1 cup water
3 cups cranberries
1 package (3 ounces) lemon-flavor gelatin
1 cup hot water
10-inch baked pie shell
Garnish: 1 cup whipping cream; canned
cranberry jelly

Combine sugar and water in saucepan. Stir over medium heat until sugar dissolves. Add cranberries; cook just until berries pop. Remove from heat. Drain cranberries thoroughly; measure 1 cup syrup. Chill. Chill cranberries. Dissolve lemon gelatin in 1 cup hot water; add chilled syrup; chill until consistency of unbeaten egg white. Beat until light and fluffy; chill, stirring occasionally, until mixture mounds slightly when dropped from a spoon. Fold in cranberries. Spoon into baked pie shell; chill until set. Garnish with whipped cream and stars cut from slices of canned cranberry jelly with tiny cutter.

FROZEN LIME PIE

1 package (5½ ounces) chocolate-covered
graham crackers
3 tablespoons softened butter or margarine
2 eggs, separated
1 can (15 ounces) sweetened condensed milk
1 tablespoon grated lime peel
⅔ cup lime juice
Green food coloring
¼ cup sugar
Garnish (optional): whipped cream;
unsweetened chocolate, grated

Roll graham crackers between 2 pieces of waxed paper to make 1½ cups fine crumbs. Combine crumbs with softened butter or margarine; mix thoroughly. Press mixture evenly on bottom and sides of 9-inch pie pan with back of spoon. Beat egg yolks until thick; combine with condensed milk. Stir in lime peel and lime juice; mix well; tint pale green with a few drops green food coloring. Beat egg whites until stiff but not dry. Gradually add sugar and beat until very stiff. Fold into lime-milk mixture. Turn into prepared pie pan. Place in freezer or freezing compartment of refrigerator and freeze until firm (about 6 hours). If desired, garnish with a frill of whipped cream and grated unsweetened chocolate.

PEACH ALASKA PIE

Walnut Pastry:

Add ½ cup finely chopped walnuts to the dry ingredients for pastry for 1-crust pie. Line 9-inch pie pan with pastry; trim edges; press to rim of pan with tines of fork. Prick surface with fork. Bake at 450° for 12 to 15 minutes. Cool thoroughly.

To Assemble Pie:

    1 quart peach ice cream, slightly softened
    2 egg whites
    ¼ cup sugar
    Satin Fudge Sauce*

Fill baked pie shell with ice cream; freeze until ice cream is firm. Beat egg whites until foamy; add sugar slowly; beat until stiff peaks form. Beat 5 minutes longer. Swirl over ice cream, making sure that all ice cream is thickly covered. Bake at 400° for 3 to 5 minutes or until golden brown. Serve at once with Satin Fudge Sauce.

*SATIN FUDGE SAUCE

    1 package (¼ pound) sweet cooking chocolate
    2 tablespoons water
    3 tablespoons cream

Combine chocolate and water in small saucepan. Stir constantly over low heat until chocolate is melted (about 3 to 5 minutes). Remove from heat. Add cream; stir until smooth.

ICE-CREAM NESSELRODE PIE

    ¾ cup fine vanilla wafer crumbs
    ½ cup wheat germ
    2 tablespoons sugar
    ½ teaspoon nutmeg
    ¼ cup butter or margarine, melted
    ½ cup diced candied fruits and peels
    2 tablespoons rum
    2 to 3 pints vanilla ice cream, softened

Combine crumbs, wheat germ, sugar, nutmeg, and butter. Mix well. Press evenly over bottom and sides of 9-inch pie pan. Bake at 350° for 5 minutes. Cool. Combine fruit and rum; fold into softened ice cream; spoon into pie shell. Freeze until firm (3 to 4 hours). Makes 8 servings.

FROZEN RASPBERRY PIE

    1 package (10 ounces) frozen raspberries
    1 cup sugar
    2 egg whites, at room temperature
    1 tablespoon lemon juice
    Dash salt
    1 cup whipping cream, whipped
    ¼ cup chopped roasted almonds
    9-inch baked almond pie shell*
    Garnish: raspberries; sprigs of mint

Thaw raspberries. Reserve a few for garnish. Combine raspberries, sugar, egg whites, lemon juice, and salt. Beat for 15 minutes or until stiff. Fold in whipped cream and almonds. Mound in baked pie shell. Freeze until firm. Garnish with reserved raspberries and sprigs of mint.

    *Add ½ teaspoon almond extract to pastry for 1 pie shell.

FROZEN GALA PUMPKIN PIE

    1½ cups crushed sugar-coated cereal flakes
    ⅓ cup firmly packed brown sugar
    ⅓ cup butter or margarine, melted
    1 quart butter pecan ice cream
    1 cup canned pumpkin
    ½ cup sugar
    1 teaspoon cinnamon
    ¼ teaspoon ginger
    ¼ teaspoon nutmeg
    Garnish: whipped cream or whipped topping;
        halved candied cherries; pineapple
        tidbits; pecan meats; halved seeded
        Tokay grapes

Combine crushed cereal flakes, brown sugar, and melted butter; press firmly on bottom and sides of 9-inch pie pan. Chill about ½ hour. Meanwhile, soften ice cream; combine with remaining ingredients; mix well. Spoon into chilled cereal crust. Freeze several hours or overnight. Just before serving, decorate rim of pie with frill of whipped cream or whipped topping and a garland of halved candied cherries, pineapple tidbits, pecan meats, and halved seeded Tokay grapes.

A CHOCOLATE TREAT

Crust:

6 tablespoons butter or margarine
1½ cups chocolate wafer crumbs

Melt butter or margarine. Stir into wafer crumbs. Press evenly onto bottom and sides of 8-inch pie pan.

Filling:

24 marshmallows
½ cup milk
8 squares (8 ounces) semisweet chocolate
2 tablespoons crème de cacao *or* 4
    tablespoons strong coffee
2 tablespoons coffee liqueur
1 cup whipping cream
Garnish (optional): semisweet chocolate,
    grated

Melt marshmallows in milk over low heat; cool. Melt chocolate over hot water. Add liqueurs to chocolate. Pour chocolate mixture into marshmallow mixture. Whip cream; fold chocolate mixture into the cream. Pour into pie shell. Garnish with grated semisweet chocolate, if desired. Freeze. Remove from freezer 5 to 10 minutes before serving.

CREAMY PECAN PIE

⅓ cup butter or margarine
¾ cup sugar
2 eggs, slightly beaten
½ cup dark corn syrup
¼ teaspoon salt
1 teaspoon vanilla
1¼ cups chopped pecans
1 cup dairy sour cream
9-inch unbaked pastry shell
Whole pecan meats

Cream butter and sugar until light and fluffy. Add eggs, corn syrup, salt, and vanilla; mix well. Stir in chopped pecans and sour cream. Pour into pastry shell. Garnish surface with whole pecan meats. Bake at 375° for 40 to 45 minutes.

GEORGIA PECAN PIE

3 eggs, lightly beaten with fork or whisk
¾ cup dark corn syrup
¾ cup sugar
¼ teaspoon salt

2½ teaspoons vanilla
1 cup pecan halves
9-inch unbaked pastry shell
3 tablespoons melted butter or margarine

Combine eggs and corn syrup; mix well. Add sugar; mix thoroughly. Stir in salt and vanilla. Let stand about 5 minutes. Meanwhile, spread pecans evenly on bottom of pastry shell. Stir melted butter into syrup mixture; pour over pecans. Be sure all the pecans rise to the top. Bake at 375° for 40 to 45 minutes or until center is firm.

COLONIAL INNKEEPER'S PIE

1½ squares unsweetened chocolate
½ cup water
⅔ cup sugar
¼ cup butter or margarine
2 teaspoons vanilla, divided
1 cup sifted all-purpose flour
¾ cup sugar
1 teaspoon baking powder
½ teaspoon salt
¼ cup soft shortening
½ cup milk
1 egg
9-inch unbaked pastry shell with high rim
½ cup chopped walnuts

Melt chocolate in water; add ⅔ cup sugar. Bring to boil, stirring constantly. Remove from heat. Stir in butter and 1½ teaspoons vanilla. Set aside. Mix and sift flour, ¾ cup sugar, baking powder, and salt. Add shortening, milk, and ½ teaspoon vanilla. Beat 2 minutes. Add egg; beat 2 minutes. Pour batter into unbaked pastry shell. Stir chocolate sauce and pour carefully over batter. Sprinkle top with nuts. Bake at 350° for 55 to 60 minutes or until cake tester inserted in center comes out clean.

CREAMY RAISIN PIE

¾ cup sugar
1 teaspoon cinnamon
½ teaspoon cloves
½ teaspoon nutmeg
½ teaspoon salt
⅓ cup cornstarch
1 large can (1⅔ cups) evaporated milk
1 cup water
2 tablespoons vinegar
3 egg yolks, slightly beaten
1 cup raisins

1 teaspoon vanilla
9-inch baked pie shell
Lemon-Apple Meringue*

Combine sugar, spices, salt, and cornstarch with evaporated milk, water, and vinegar over low heat or in double boiler. Cook until slightly thickened (about 5 to 10 minutes), stirring constantly. Add small amount of cooked mixture to egg yolks, stirring constantly; mix and pour into remaining mixture. Add raisins and vanilla. Stir over low heat 2 to 3 minutes longer or until thickened. Pour into cooled pie shell; cool. Top with Lemon-Apple Meringue; brown at 350° for 12 to 15 minutes.

*LEMON-APPLE MERINGUE

3 egg whites
½ cup sugar
¼ cup grated raw apple
1 tablespoon grated lemon peel

Beat egg whites until frothy; gradually add sugar. Continue beating until egg whites will hold in soft peaks. Add grated raw apple and grated lemon peel. Continue beating until egg whites stand in slightly firmer peaks. Swirl meringue on pie, sealing to edge of pie crust.

RAISIN-WINE PIE

2 cups golden raisins
1½ cups boiling water
½ cup port wine
½ cup sugar
3 tablespoons flour
1 tablespoon grated lemon peel
3 tablespoons lemon juice
Few drops red food coloring
Pastry for 2-crust 8-inch pie
1 egg white
Sugar
Cinnamon

Rinse raisins; add water; boil 5 minutes. Stir in wine. Blend sugar and flour; stir in; boil 1 minute longer, stirring constantly. Remove from heat; stir in lemon peel, lemon juice, and coloring. Turn into pastry-lined pie pan. Cover with top crust. Flute edges; prick surface with fork. To glaze, brush with slightly beaten egg white. Sprinkle lightly with sugar and cinnamon. Bake at 425° for 30 minutes.

SWEET-POTATO–PECAN PIE

2 cups mashed sweet potatoes
5 tablespoons melted butter or margarine
¾ cup firmly packed brown sugar
4 eggs, slightly beaten
¼ teaspoon salt
1 teaspoon cinnamon
¼ teaspoon mace
⅓ cup broken pecan meats
2 cups milk
1 deep 10-inch unbaked pastry shell

Combine first 7 ingredients; mix well. Add pecans. Blend in milk. Pour into unbaked pastry shell. Bake at 425° for 15 minutes. Reduce heat to 375°; bake for 25 to 30 minutes longer or until firm.

CANDIED MINCE PIE

3 cups prepared mincemeat
1 cup diced candied fruits and peels
2 teaspoons brandy flavoring
Pastry for 2-crust 9-inch pie

Combine prepared mincemeat and candied fruits and peels; stir in flavoring. Spoon into pastry-lined 9-inch pie pan. Arrange pastry strips, lattice-fashion, over filling. Bake at 425° for 40 to 45 minutes.

BROWN-SUGAR PEANUT CUSTARD PIE

½ cup firmly packed brown sugar
¼ cup sugar
¼ teaspoon salt
4 eggs, slightly beaten
½ teaspoon vanilla
2½ cups milk, scalded
1 cup chopped salted peanuts
9-inch unbaked pastry shell
Garnish (optional): whipped topping;
    chopped salted peanuts

Combine brown sugar, sugar, salt, eggs, and vanilla in large mixing bowl. Beat with a rotary beater until thoroughly blended. Stir in scalded milk gradually. Stir in 1 cup peanuts. Pour into pastry shell. Bake at 425° for 30 minutes or until silver knife inserted in center of filling comes out clean. Cool on wire rack 30 minutes. Chill until ready to serve. Garnish with whipped topping and additional chopped salted peanuts, if desired.

SOUTHERN PEANUT BUTTER PIE

1 cup light or dark corn syrup
1 cup sugar
3 eggs, slightly beaten
½ teaspoon vanilla
⅓ cup chunky peanut butter
9-inch unbaked pastry shell
1 cup whipping cream, whipped

Combine first 5 ingredients, mixing until thoroughly blended. Pour into prepared pastry shell. Bake at 400° for 15 minutes. Reduce heat to 350°; bake 30 to 35 minutes longer. Filling should appear slightly less set in center. Chill. Top with whipped cream.

PEANUT BUTTER CREAM PIE

¾ cup confectioners' (powdered) sugar
½ cup creamy peanut butter
9-inch baked pie shell
½ cup sugar
¼ cup cornstarch
½ teaspoon salt
3 eggs, separated
2½ cups milk
1 teaspoon vanilla
6 tablespoons sugar

Mix confectioners' sugar and peanut butter together until crumbs form. Cover bottom of pie shell with crumbs, reserving about 3 tablespoons for top. Mix together ½ cup sugar, cornstarch, and salt in medium saucepan. Beat egg yolks slightly; add milk; stir into sugar mixture until well blended. Cook over medium heat, stirring constantly, until mixture comes to boil and boils 1 minute. Remove from heat. Stir in vanilla. Cool to room temperature. Spoon into prepared pie shell. Beat egg whites until foamy. Add sugar, 1 tablespoon at a time, beating well after each addition. Continue beating until stiff peaks form. Spread meringue over filling, touching pastry on all sides. Top with remaining crumb mixture. Bake at 425° about 5 minutes or until lightly browned. Cool at room temperature, away from drafts.

MOCHA MERINGUE PIE

3 cups water
½ cup nonfat dry milk
3 squares (3 ounces) unsweetened chocolate
3 tablespoons instant coffee (dry)

3 tablespoons cornstarch
1½ cups sugar, divided
½ teaspoon salt
2 eggs, separated
1½ teaspoons vanilla
9-inch baked pie shell

Pour water into top of double boiler. Add nonfat dry milk; beat with rotary beater until blended. Add chocolate and instant coffee. Cook over hot water until chocolate melts, stirring frequently. Combine cornstarch, 1¼ cups sugar, and salt; add a little hot mixture; stir smooth; blend with remaining hot mixture. Cook over hot water, stirring constantly, until thickened. Cover; cook 25 minutes. Beat egg yolks slightly; add a little hot mixture; blend into remaining hot mixture; cook 2 minutes longer, stirring. Cool slightly; add vanilla; pour into baked pie shell. Top with meringue made with egg whites and remaining ¼ cup sugar. Bake at 325° about 15 minutes or until meringue is tipped with brown.

CHOCOLATE COCONUT PIE

¼ cup soft butter or margarine
¾ cup sugar, divided
2 squares unsweetened chocolate, melted and cooled
3 eggs, separated
⅓ cup milk
1 teaspoon vanilla
2 cups flaked coconut
9-inch unbaked pastry shell
Garnish (optional): whipped cream; flaked coconut

Cream together soft butter and ½ cup sugar; blend in chocolate. Beat in egg yolks one at a time. Blend in milk, vanilla, and 2 cups coconut. Beat egg whites until stiff but not dry; gradually add remaining ¼ cup sugar; beat until very stiff; fold into chocolate-coconut mixture. Turn into prepared pastry shell. Bake at 425° for 10 minutes. Reduce temperature to 350° and bake 30 minutes longer. Cool. Garnish with whipped cream and additional flaked coconut, if desired.

CHOCOLATE PRETZEL PIE

1¼ cups fine pretzel crumbs
1 teaspoon sugar
½ cup melted butter or margarine
⅔ cup sugar
4 tablespoons cornstarch

2½ cups milk
3 squares unsweetened chocolate, cut in small
   pieces
3 egg yolks, slightly beaten
1 teaspoon vanilla
Pretzel thin sticks and bowknots
1 tablespoon crushed toasted almonds

Combine first 3 ingredients; press evenly into 9-inch pie pan, covering bottom and sides completely; press down firmly. Bake about 8 minutes at 325°. Cool thoroughly. Combine next 4 ingredients in top of double boiler. Cook over boiling water until thickened, stirring constantly. Cover; cook 15 minutes longer. Stir a little of the hot mixture into egg yolks; add to remaining mixture in double boiler. Cook and stir 2 minutes over hot, not boiling, water. Cool. Add vanilla. Pour into pretzel crust. Decorate with pretzels. Sprinkle with almonds. Chill.

MOCHA PLUM PIE

1 package vanilla pudding and pie filling mix
1 tablespoon instant coffee
2 tablespoons sugar
4 cups milk, divided
1 package chocolate pudding and pie filling
   mix
9-inch baked pie shell
Whipped cream
9 canned purple plums
Sugar and cinnamon, combined

Combine vanilla pudding mix, instant coffee, sugar, and 2 cups milk. Cook, stirring, over medium heat until mixture comes to a full boil and is thickened slightly. Let cool 5 minutes. Meanwhile, combine chocolate pudding mix and remaining 2 cups milk. Cook, stirring, over medium heat until mixture comes to a full boil and is slightly thickened. Let cool about 2 minutes. Stir each filling just to mix. Then alternately spoon fillings into pie shell. (For a marbled effect, use a small spatula to mark circles in filling from center of pie to rim.) Chill. Garnish with a border of whipped cream. Drain plums; roll in a mixture of sugar and cinnamon; arrange on whipped cream.

CHOCOLATE-CRESTED COCONUT PIE

4 eggs, slightly beaten
½ cup sugar
¼ teaspoon salt

3 cups milk
1 teaspoon vanilla
1 cup flaked coconut
9-inch unbaked pastry shell
2 tablespoons sugar
1 square unsweetened chocolate, melted
2 tablespoons hot water
Garnish: flaked coconut

Combine eggs, ½ cup sugar, salt, milk, vanilla, and 1 cup coconut; mix well. Pour into pastry shell. Bake at 425° for 30 minutes or until custard is set. Combine remaining 2 tablespoons sugar and chocolate. Add hot water gradually, blending well. Pour chocolate mixture evenly on top of baked pie. Reduce heat to 300°; bake 7 to 10 minutes longer or until chocolate is set. Cool. Garnish with additional flaked coconut.

GRANDMA'S PUMPKIN PIE

1 large can (1 pound 13 ounces) pumpkin
1 cup firmly packed brown sugar
1 cup sugar
¼ teaspoon cloves
3 teaspoons cinnamon
2 teaspoons ginger
1 teaspoon salt
4 eggs, beaten
1 cup evaporated milk
1 cup whipping cream
2 unbaked 9-inch pastry shells

Combine first 8 ingredients; mix well. Combine evaporated milk and cream; heat to scalding point; add; mix well. Pour into unbaked pastry shells. Bake at 350° for about 1 hour. Pies are done when knife inserted near rim comes out clean. Makes 2 pies.

PUMPKIN CHEESECAKE PIE

15 graham crackers
2 tablespoons brown sugar
¼ cup butter or margarine, melted
½ pound cottage cheese
½ cup canned pumpkin
2 egg yolks
¾ cup sugar
½ teaspoon nutmeg
3 teaspoons cornstarch
¾ cup top milk
1 tablespoon grated lemon peel
2 tablespoons lemon juice
1 teaspoon lemon extract
2 egg whites

Roll graham crackers into fine crumbs; combine with brown sugar and melted butter or margarine. Set aside ¼ cup. Press remaining mixture firmly into deep 9-inch pie pan. Bake at 350° for 8 minutes. Cool. Press cottage cheese through a fine sieve; combine with pumpkin, unbeaten egg yolks, sugar, and nutmeg; mix well. Blend cornstarch to thin paste with some of the milk; add remaining milk; combine with cheese mixture. Add lemon peel, juice, and extract. Beat egg whites stiff; fold in. Spoon into pie pan. Sprinkle top with reserved crumbs. Bake at 350° for ½ hour or until inserted knife comes out clean. Cool before serving.

PUMPKIN CREAM PIE

1¾ cups cold milk
1 cup canned pumpkin
2 tablespoons sugar
½ teaspoon cinnamon
¼ teaspoon cloves
⅛ teaspoon nutmeg
1 package instant vanilla pudding mix
9-inch baked pie shell

Pour milk into large bowl; add pumpkin, sugar, cinnamon, cloves, nutmeg, and instant vanilla pudding; whip rapidly with rotary beater 30 seconds, until smooth. Turn into baked pie shell; chill.

ORANGE-PUMPKIN-PECAN PIE

2 eggs, beaten
¾ cup sugar
1½ teaspoons cinnamon
½ teaspoon nutmeg
½ teaspoon ginger
¼ teaspoon allspice
¼ teaspoon cloves
½ teaspoon salt
1½ cups canned pumpkin
3 tablespoons molasses
1 cup evaporated milk, undiluted
1 can (6 ounces) frozen orange juice
    concentrate, undiluted, thawed
9-inch unbaked pastry shell
¾ cup pecan meats
Garnish: whipped cream *or* whipped
    evaporated milk

Combine beaten eggs, sugar, spices, salt, pumpkin, and molasses. Add evaporated milk and thawed orange juice; stir until smooth. Pour into pastry shell. Sprinkle with broken pecan meats or make a border of whole pecan meats. Bake at 450° for 15 minutes. Reduce heat to 350°; bake 40 minutes longer. Cool; garnish with whipped cream or whipped evaporated milk.

COCONUT MACAROON PIE

Pastry for 9-inch pie shell
¼ teaspoon salt
3 eggs, separated
1½ cups sugar
¼ cup milk
2 tablespoons butter or margarine, melted and
    cooled
1 teaspoon lemon juice
¼ teaspoon almond extract
1½ cups flaked coconut
Garnish: whipped cream

Line 9-inch pie pan with pastry; flute edges. Add salt to egg yolks; beat until thick and lemon-colored. Add sugar, ½ cup at a time, beating well after each addition. Add milk, butter, lemon juice, and almond extract; blend well. Fold in coconut and stiffly beaten egg whites; turn into pie shell. Bake at 375° for 50 minutes or until inserted knife comes out clean. Cool. Garnish with whipped cream.

PARFAIT PIE

½ package piecrust mix
1¼ cups water
1 package (3 ounces) lemon-flavor gelatin
1 pint vanilla ice cream
1 cup crushed fresh strawberries, sweetened;
    or quick-frozen, thawed
Garnish (optional): whole strawberries

Prepare and bake 9-inch pastry shell as directed on package of piecrust mix; cool. Heat water to boiling in 2-quart saucepan. Remove from heat. Add gelatin; stir until dissolved. Add ice cream, cut in pieces, to hot liquid; stir in immediately until melted. Chill until mixture is thickened but not set (15 to 20 minutes). Fold in crushed strawberries. Turn into cooled baked pie shell. Chill until firm (30 to 35 minutes). Garnish with whole berries, if desired.

VARIATIONS

1. Lemon-flavor gelatin, pistachio ice cream, raspberries.

2. Orange-flavor gelatin, peach ice cream, peaches.
3. Cherry-flavor gelatin, vanilla ice cream, crushed pineapple.

LEMON CAKE PIE

1 cup sugar
¼ cup flour
¼ cup butter or margarine, melted
⅛ teaspoon salt
2 eggs, separated
2 lemons, juice and grated peel (about ¼ cup juice)
1 cup milk
9-inch unbaked pastry shell

Combine sugar, flour, melted butter or margarine, salt, and egg yolks. Beat until smooth. Beat in lemon juice and peel. Add milk slowly while beating. Beat egg whites stiff but not dry; fold in. Bake pie shell at 350° for 5 minutes. Pour in filling. Bake 40 minutes longer or until filling is firm. When served, there will be a layer of delicate cake on top of the pie filling.

CHERRY-GLAZED CHEESE PIE

2 large packages (8 ounces each) cream cheese
3 tablespoons lemon juice, divided
⅓ cup light cream
4 eggs, well beaten
1 teaspoon grated lemon peel
¾ cup sugar
1 tablespoon all-purpose flour
Graham Cracker Crumb Crust*
⅓ cup currant jelly
30 well-drained maraschino cherries, cut in half

Beat cream cheese and 2 tablespoons lemon juice together until smooth; add cream, eggs, and lemon peel. Combine sugar and flour; add to cream cheese mixture; beat until all ingredients are well blended. Turn into Graham Cracker Crumb Crust; bake at 350° for 40 minutes or until firm. Combine currant jelly and remaining 1 tablespoon lemon juice; cook over low heat, stirring until jelly is melted. Dip cherries in jelly mixture; arrange cut side down on cheese filling. Cool thoroughly before serving.

*GRAHAM CRACKER CRUMB CRUST

2 cups graham cracker crumbs (about 25 crackers)
⅓ cup sugar
1 teaspoon cinnamon
⅓ cup melted butter or margarine

Combine all ingredients; mix well. Press crumb mixture firmly against sides and bottom of 10-inch pie pan. Chill thoroughly.

FROSTED BROWNIE PIE

2 squares unsweetened chocolate
⅓ cup shortening
⅔ cup sifted all-purpose flour
½ teaspoon baking powder
¼ teaspoon salt
2 eggs, unbeaten
1 cup sugar
1 teaspoon vanilla
1 cup coarsely chopped walnuts
Coffee Walnut Frosting*
Garnish: whole walnut meats

Melt chocolate and shortening together over hot water. Mix and sift flour, baking powder, and salt. Beat eggs; gradually beat in sugar; add vanilla and melted chocolate and shortening; blend. Stir in flour and chopped walnuts. Spread in greased 9-inch pie pan. Bake at 350° for 25 minutes. Remove from pan. Cool. Frost with Coffee Walnut Frosting. Garnish with whole walnut meats.

*COFFEE WALNUT FROSTING

¼ cup butter or margarine
2 cups confectioners' (powdered) sugar
3 tablespoons strong cold coffee
¼ teaspoon brandy flavoring

Cream butter or margarine until consistency of mayonnaise. Add confectioners' sugar alternately with coffee, beating well after each addition. Add flavoring. Spread on Brownie Pie.

LEMON CHESS PIE

2 cups sugar
2 tablespoons flour
1 tablespoon corn meal
¼ cup butter or margarine, melted
4 eggs, well beaten

2 lemons, grated peel and strained juice
9-inch unbaked pastry shell with high, fluted
rim

Combine sugar, flour, and corn meal. Add with melted butter to eggs. Beat well. Stir in grated lemon peel and strained lemon juice. Pour carefully into pastry shell. Bake at 375° for 40 minutes or until knife inserted near rim comes out clean. Chill until center is firm enough to cut.

SHOOFLY PIE

1½ cups sifted all-purpose flour
½ cup sugar
⅛ teaspoon salt
½ teaspoon cinnamon
¼ teaspoon ginger
¼ teaspoon nutmeg
¼ cup butter or margarine
½ teaspoon baking soda
½ cup molasses
¾ cup boiling water
8-inch unbaked pastry shell

Mix together flour, sugar, salt, cinnamon, ginger, and nutmeg. Cut in butter until mixture resembles coarse meal. Mix together baking soda and molasses and immediately stir in boiling water. Stir in 1⅓ cups of the crumb mixture. Turn into pastry shell. Sprinkle remaining ⅔ cup crumb mixture over top. Bake at 375° for 30 to 40 minutes, until crust is lightly browned.

BAKED APPLE TARTS

1 package piecrust mix
4 cooking apples
2 tablespoons grenadine syrup
Light corn syrup
1 large package (8 ounces) cream cheese
1 tablespoon light cream or milk
2 tablespoons finely chopped packaged diced
    dates
2 tablespoons chopped walnuts
1 tablespoon chopped maraschino cherries

Prepare piecrust mix as directed. Line 8 shallow tart pans with pastry. Bake at 425° for 12 to 15 minutes. Cool in pans. Peel and core apples; cut in half crosswise; arrange in shallow baking dish. Pour grenadine into measuring cup; fill to ¾ mark with corn syrup; blend well. Pour syrup over apples. Bake at 350° for 25 to 30 minutes or until tender, basting occasionally with syrup in

pan. Chill. Combine remaining ingredients. Chill. Just before serving remove tart shells from pans and arrange baked apple halves in shells. Pour any remaining syrup over apples. Divide cream cheese mixture into 8 portions; place 1 portion on each apple. Makes 8 tarts.

LEMON-RAISIN TARTS

2 teaspoons cornstarch
½ cup sugar
¼ teaspoon salt
1 egg, well beaten
½ cup light corn syrup
2 teaspoons grated lemon peel
⅓ cup melted butter or margarine
1 tablespoon lemon juice
⅔ cup raisins
8 unbaked tart shells

Mix cornstarch, sugar, and salt. Add egg; blend well. Add remaining ingredients except shells, mixing well. Chill. Turn into unbaked tart shells. Bake at 400° for 15 minutes. Reduce heat to 350°; bake 10 minutes longer. Cool in pans. Makes eight 3-inch tarts.

FROSTED CRANBERRY TARTS

1 package piecrust mix
4 tablespoons cream cheese
8 marshmallows
1 cup whipping cream, whipped
3 tablespoons confectioners' (powdered) sugar
½ cup broken walnut meats
1 can whole cranberry sauce, chilled
Garnish (optional): whole walnut meats

Prepare piecrust mix as directed on package; roll out thin; cut in 6 rounds; fit over outside of 6 fluted tart shell pans, pressing firmly; trim edges; prick pastry with fork; bake upside down at 450° for 10 to 12 minutes. Cool. Mash cream cheese; cut marshmallows fine; fold both into whipped cream with sugar and walnuts. Fill tart shells with cranberry sauce. Top with whipped cream mixture. Garnish with whole walnut meats, if desired. Makes 6 servings.

MOCHA BANANA TARTS

1 envelope unflavored gelatin
¼ cup cold water
½ cup milk
1 tablespoon instant coffee

2 eggs, separated
½ cup sugar, divided
⅛ teaspoon salt
1 teaspoon vanilla
6 to 8 baked tart shells
Banana slices

Soften gelatin in cold water. Scald milk; add instant coffee; stir until dissolved. Beat egg yolks; beat in ¼ cup sugar and ⅛ teaspoon salt. Add scalded milk mixture slowly. Cook over hot water, stirring constantly, until mixture coats spoon. Remove from heat; add softened gelatin and vanilla; stir until gelatin dissolves. Chill until just beginning to set. Beat egg whites until stiff but not dry; add remaining sugar slowly, beating constantly; fold into gelatin mixture. Line bottom of each baked tart shell with banana slices. Cover with gelatin mixture. Chill until set. Just before serving, top with fluted banana slices. Makes 6 to 8 tarts, depending on size of tart shell pans or individual pie pans.

BANANA-COCONUT BANBURY TARTS

1 package (10 ounces) refrigerated buttermilk
    biscuits (10)
1 cup diced banana
¼ cup seedless raisins
¼ cup flaked coconut
1 lemon, grated peel
1 teaspoon lemon juice
¼ cup sugar
½ teaspoon cinnamon

Roll biscuits to 4- or 5-inch circles. Combine remaining ingredients; place rounded tablespoon on half of each circle. Fold over to form half-moon. Seal edges with fork; prick top. Place on greased baking sheets. Bake at 425° for 12 to 15 minutes. Makes 10 tarts.

VIENNESE PEACH TART

½ cup butter or margarine
¼ cup confectioners' (powdered) sugar
1 cup sifted all-purpose flour
1 tablespoon cornstarch
2 tablespoons sugar
¼ teaspoon mace
½ cup orange juice
½ cup red currant jelly, melted
8 large fresh peaches (about)
Garnish: whipped cream

Cream butter until soft. Add confectioners' sugar gradually, continuing to cream. Blend in flour to make a soft dough. Pat evenly into 12-inch pizza pan, covering bottom and sides. Bake at 350° for 20 minutes. Combine cornstarch, 2 tablespoons sugar, and mace. Add orange juice. Cook over hot water, stirring, until thick and clear. Stir in melted currant jelly. Cool slightly. Peel and slice peaches. Arrange in single layer in baked shell. Spoon glaze evenly over peaches. Chill. Garnish with whipped cream. Makes 8 to 10 servings.

PUMPKIN ICE CREAM TARTS

1 pint soft coffee ice cream
1 cup canned pumpkin
1 package vanilla instant pudding mix
6 baked tart shells
Garnish (optional): whipped cream *or*
    whipped topping; whole walnut meats

Blend ice cream and pumpkin. Add pudding mix; beat 1 minute. Spoon at once into baked tart shells. Chill. If desired, garnish each tart with a swirl of whipped cream or whipped topping and a whole walnut meat. Makes 6 tarts.

MOCHA COCONUT TARTS

Coconut Shortbread Tart Shells:

⅔ cup butter or margarine
6 tablespoons sugar
2 eggs, separated
2 cups sifted all-purpose flour
2 cups flaked coconut, finely chopped

Cream butter or margarine; add sugar gradually, while creaming. Beat in egg yolks. (Save whites for filling.) Stir in flour and coconut; mix until well blended. Divide mixture among sixteen ungreased 2¾-inch muffin cups, pressing mixture with fingers to line bottom and sides of each cup. Prick with tines of fork. Bake at 350° for 20 to 25 minutes. Cool 3 minutes; remove from cups. Makes 16 shells.

Mocha Filling:

1 envelope unflavored gelatin
1 teaspoon instant coffee
⅔ cup sugar, divided
¼ teaspoon salt
¾ cup evaporated milk
¾ cup water
1 square unsweetened chocolate

1 egg yolk, slightly beaten
1 teaspoon vanilla
3 egg whites
Garnish: whipped cream; flaked coconut

Mix together gelatin, coffee, ⅓ cup of the sugar, and salt in saucepan. Add evaporated milk, water, and chocolate. Stir over medium heat until chocolate is melted and gelatin is dissolved. (Do not boil.) Blend with rotary beater. Pour slowly over beaten egg yolk, stirring constantly. Return to saucepan; cook 1 minute longer, stirring constantly. Remove from heat; stir in vanilla. Chill until mixture mounds slightly when dropped from a spoon. Beat 3 egg whites until stiff but not dry. Gradually add remaining ⅓ cup sugar; beat until very stiff. Fold in chocolate mixture. Spoon into prepared tart shells. Garnish each tart with whipped cream and flaked coconut. Makes 16 servings.

CHEESE TART SHELLS

Add 1 cup grated Cheddar cheese to 1 package piecrust mix; toss lightly with a fork. Follow package directions for making pastry. Roll out ⅛ inch thick; cut out twelve 5-inch rounds to fit tart pans or large muffin cups. Cut out remaining dough with a 2-inch scalloped cookie cutter. Bake at 400° for 8 to 10 minutes for tarts, 5 minutes for rounds. When tarts are filled, top with rounds.

FRUIT-CHEESE PASTRY

1 package piecrust mix *or* 1 pastry recipe
  calling for 2 cups flour
2 cans (1 pound each) sliced peaches,*
  drained
2 teaspoons lemon juice
⅔ cup firmly packed brown sugar
1 teaspoon cinnamon
½ teaspoon nutmeg
⅛ teaspoon salt
2 tablespoons butter or margarine
Packaged slices Cheddar cheese cut in strips

Prepare piecrust mix according to package directions. Roll into 2 rectangles, 6½ x 5½ x 1 inch. Place on ungreased baking sheet. Fold edges under and flute. Prick pastry well with tines of fork. Bake at 425° for 12 minutes. Arrange fruit in rows on each rectangle. Sprinkle each with 1 teaspoon lemon juice. Combine sugar, spices, and salt; cut in butter. Top each with half of sugar

mixture. Place cheese strips over topping. Bake at 425° for 8 minutes. Cut each rectangle in 3 pieces. Makes 6 servings.

*Or Bing cherries, apple slices, berries, pears, pitted plums, pineapple chunks, fruit cocktail, etc.

CHEESE-DATE PASTRIES

1 package (7¼ ounces) pitted dates, chopped
½ cup firmly packed brown sugar
¼ cup water
½ cup butter or margarine
¼ pound Cheddar cheese, grated
1 cup all-purpose flour

Cook dates, brown sugar, and water over low heat, stirring constantly, until soft. Cool. Cream butter and cheese together. Blend in flour. Chill for at least 1 hour. Roll ⅛ inch thick on lightly floured board. Cut in rounds. On half of rounds place 1 heaping teaspoon date filling. Cover each with another round of pastry. Press edges together with fork. Prick tops. Bake at 350° for 15 minutes. Makes about 18 pastries.

APPLESAUCE TURNOVERS

Make pastry with piecrust mix. Roll out ⅛ inch thick. Cut in 4-inch squares. Place spoonful of applesauce in center of each square; fold over to form triangle; press edges together with tines of fork. Prick top of each with fork. Bake at 450° for 15 to 18 minutes or until golden brown.

APPLE-CHEESE TURNOVERS

2 packages piecrust mix
2½ cups finely chopped tart apples
½ cup raisins
¾ cup grated sharp Cheddar cheese
⅓ to ½ cup sugar (depending on tartness of
  apples)
1 teaspoon cinnamon
¼ teaspoon nutmeg

Make pastry according to package directions. Roll out half the pastry on lightly floured board. Cut into 9 or 10 four-inch squares. Repeat, making total of 18 to 20 squares. Combine remaining ingredients. Place about 1 tablespoon apple mixture in center of each square. Fold over to make triangles. Press edges together with tines of fork. Prick tops. Bake at 425° for 20 minutes. Makes 18 to 20.

SWISS CRISPS

Roll pie pastry into rectangle ¼ inch thick. Divide dough in half. Sprinkle half the dough with finely shaved Swiss cheese and caraway seeds. Cover with other half of dough. With sharp knife, cut squares or strips about 3 inches long and ¼ inch wide. Lay strips 1 inch apart on greased baking sheet. Bake at 425° about 5 minutes or until golden brown. May be stored in covered container and reheated in slow oven before serving. Serve as soup or salad accompaniment.

CHEESE STICKS

⅓ cup shortening
⅓ cup butter or margarine
1 cup grated Cheddar cheese
1 egg
3 tablespoons water
1⅓ cups sifted all-purpose flour
⅔ cup enriched corn meal
1 teaspoon salt
1 teaspoon paprika
Dash cayenne

Beat shortening and butter together until creamy. Stir in cheese, egg, and water, mixing well. Mix and sift dry ingredients; add to creamed mixture, blending well. Chill thoroughly. Roll out ⅛ inch thick on lightly floured board or pastry cloth. With a fluted pastry wheel cut into strips ¾ inch wide and 3 inches long. Place on ungreased cookie sheet. Bake at 375° for about 12 minutes. Cool a few minutes before removing to racks to finish cooling. Makes about 4½ dozen.

CHAPTER 17

Cookies

IT'S A comfortable feeling to know that there is a good supply of cookies in the house. Then when a bevy of hungry kids comes trooping in, or friends drop in for tea, or hunger pangs beckon you to the kitchen late in the evening, a beverage, hot or cold, and a plate heaped with cookies will fill the bill.

Nowadays there are packaged cookies in keep-crisp boxes or bags, rolls of refrigerated cookie dough ready to slice and bake, and all sorts of mixes for brownies, bar cookies, drop or rolled cookies.

But sometimes it's fun to fill a fat cookie jar with cookies that you've baked yourself, and there are still many types that can't be found on the supermarket shelf. The sweet, spicy fragrance of cookies turning to a golden hue in the oven is so enticing that you may have trouble getting them in the cookie jar before they are all eaten!

On the pages that follow are recipes for cookies of every kind—delicate meringues, sturdy bars, soft sugar cookies, filled cookies, crisp, brown-edged lemon wafers, and many more. Treat your eyes first by just flipping through the recipes; then get out the mixing bowl!

FILBERT OATMEALIES

1 cup shortening
½ cup honey
1 teaspoon vanilla
½ cup chopped toasted filberts
½ cup semisweet chocolate pieces
¼ cup minced maraschino cherries
2 cups sifted all-purpose flour
½ teaspoon salt
1 cup quick-cooking rolled oats

Cream shortening and honey. Blend in vanilla, filberts, chocolate pieces, and cherries. Stir in flour, salt, and rolled oats. Mix well. Drop by teaspoons onto ungreased cookie sheets. Bake at 400° for 10 to 12 minutes. Makes about 5 dozen.

MINCEMEAT OATMEAL COOKIES

1¼ cups sifted all-purpose flour
¾ teaspoon baking soda
½ teaspoon salt
½ cup shortening
1 cup firmly packed brown sugar
1 egg, slightly beaten

1⅓ cups mincemeat
1½ cups quick-cooking rolled oats, uncooked

Sift together flour, baking soda, and salt. Cream shortening; gradually add sugar, beating until fluffy. Beat in egg. Stir in mincemeat. Add flour mixture in 3 parts, blending well after each addition. Stir in rolled oats. Drop by teaspoons onto greased cookie sheet, about 2 inches apart. Flatten cookies slightly with back of spoon. Bake at 350° until lightly browned (about 15 minutes). Makes about 4 dozen.

OATMEAL GINGER DROPS

2 cups sifted all-purpose flour
1 teaspoon baking powder
½ teaspoon salt
¼ teaspoon baking soda
¾ teaspoon cinnamon
¾ teaspoon powdered ginger
½ teaspoon cloves
½ cup soft shortening
½ cup firmly packed brown sugar
1 egg
½ cup light molasses
⅓ cup water
1 cup rolled oats, quick or old-fashioned, uncooked

Mix and sift flour, baking powder, salt, baking soda, and spices. Add shortening, sugar, egg, molasses, and water. Beat until smooth (about 2 minutes). Stir in oats. Drop by tablespoons onto greased cookie sheets. Bake at 375° for 10 to 12 minutes. Makes 3 dozen.

TWO-WAY DATE-OATMEAL COOKIES

1 cup sifted all-purpose flour
½ teaspoon baking powder
½ teaspoon baking soda
½ teaspoon salt
½ cup shortening
½ cup granulated sugar
½ cup firmly packed brown sugar
1 egg
1 tablespoon grated orange peel
2 tablespoons orange juice
1½ cups rolled oats, quick or old-fashioned, uncooked
½ cup chopped pitted dates

Mix and sift first 4 ingredients. Add shortening (at room temperature), sugars, egg, orange peel

and juice. Beat 2 minutes. Fold in rolled oats and dates. Drop half the batter by teaspoons onto greased baking sheet; place remaining batter in thin layer in greased 7 x 11-inch pan. Bake drop cookies 12 to 15 minutes; bake layer cookies 15 to 20 minutes at 350°. Makes about 2½ dozen drop cookies and about 1½ dozen 2-inch squares.

RAISIN ENERGY COOKIES

1 cup raisins, light or dark
1 cup dried apricots
½ cup nonfat dry milk
¼ teaspoon baking powder
¾ teaspoon salt
¼ teaspoon baking soda
¾ cup whole wheat flour
⅓ cup wheat germ
½ cup butter or margarine
½ cup peanut butter
1 cup firmly packed brown sugar
1 egg
1 teaspoon vanilla
3 tablespoons liquid milk
⅓ cup unsalted sunflower seeds
1 cup quick-cooking oats, uncooked

Chop or cut raisins and apricots coarsely; set aside. Mix and sift dry milk, baking powder, salt, and baking soda. Stir in whole wheat flour and wheat germ. Cream butter until consistency of mayonnaise; cream in peanut butter. Add brown sugar while continuing to cream until mixture is fluffy. Add egg; beat well. Add vanilla; mix well. Add flour mixture slowly, alternating with liquid milk. Stir in sunflower seeds and oats. (Dough will be very stiff.) Work in fruits until they are well distributed. For jumbo cookies, place heaping (serving) tablespoon of dough on greased baking sheet and spread to a 4½-inch circle for each cookie. Allow ample room between cookies for spreading, baking only 4 on a large baking sheet. Bake at 375° for about 12 minutes. Let cookies remain on baking sheets about 5 minutes, then remove to wire racks to cool. Makes 9 to 12 large cookies.

To make smaller cookies, use a heaping (measuring) tablespoon of dough for each cookie, spreading to a 3-inch circle. Bake 10 minutes. Makes about 2 dozen.

ROSY RAISIN-NUT COOKIES

1 cup butter or margarine
½ cup sugar
½ cup firmly packed light brown sugar
2 eggs
1 teaspoon vanilla
2¾ cups sifted all-purpose flour
½ teaspoon baking soda
¼ teaspoon salt
¼ cup tomato catchup
½ cup raisins
½ cup broken walnuts
Orange Glaze*

Cream butter or margarine until consistency of mayonnaise. Beat in sugars gradually. Beat in eggs one at a time. Add vanilla. Mix and sift flour, baking soda, and salt; add to creamed mixture alternately with catchup. Stir in raisins and nuts. Drop batter by rounded measuring teaspoonfuls onto greased baking sheet, spacing 2 inches apart. Bake at 375° for 10 to 12 minutes or until edges are browned and cookies spring back when touched with a finger. Remove to racks. Spread with Orange Glaze while hot. Makes about 5 dozen.

*ORANGE GLAZE

1½ cups sifted confectioners' (powdered)
    sugar
2 tablespoons strained orange juice

Combine and beat until smooth. If not thin enough for transparent glaze, add a little more orange juice.

PLUMP MOLASSES COOKIES

½ cup shortening
½ cup sugar
1 egg
1 cup dark molasses
1 tablespoon lemon juice
3½ cups sifted all-purpose flour
1 teaspoon cinnamon
¾ teaspoon ground cloves
½ teaspoon ground ginger
2 teaspoons baking soda
½ teaspoon salt
⅓ cup boiling water
Sugar

Cream shortening and ½ cup sugar together; beat in egg. Add molasses and lemon juice;

blend well. Mix and sift dry ingredients; add to creamed mixture. Add boiling water; mix well. Chill thoroughly. Drop by teaspoons onto greased cookie sheets. Sprinkle with sugar. Bake at 350° for 8 to 10 minutes. Makes 4 dozen small cookies.

For large cookies, drop by tablespoons. Bake 10 to 15 minutes. Makes about 2 dozen.

MOLASSES CIRCLES

1 cup shortening
1 cup sugar
1 egg
½ cup light molasses
¾ teaspoon vinegar
¾ cup rich milk or light cream
3 cups sifted all-purpose flour
1 teaspoon cinnamon
1 teaspoon powdered ginger
½ teaspoon mace
2 teaspoons baking soda
1 teaspoon salt

Cream shortening and sugar. Add egg; beat well. Add molasses; beat well. Combine vinegar and milk or cream. Sift flour, spices, baking soda, and salt. Add to molasses mixture alternately with milk mixture. Drop by tablespoons about 2 inches apart onto greased cookie sheets. Bake at 350° for 8 to 10 minutes. Makes about 6 dozen.

MOLASSES-POTATO COOKIES

½ cup shortening
¾ cup firmly packed brown sugar
1 cup warm mashed potatoes
½ cup molasses
2 cups sifted all-purpose flour
1 teaspoon baking soda
1 teaspoon ginger
1 teaspoon cinnamon
¼ teaspoon nutmeg
½ teaspoon allspice
½ teaspoon salt

Cream shortening and brown sugar. Add potatoes while continuing to cream. Mix in molasses. Mix and sift flour, baking soda, spices, and salt. Add. Drop by tablespoons onto greased cookie sheets. Flatten by pressing with floured tines of fork in two directions. Bake at 350° for 20 minutes. Makes 5 dozen.

BACK-TO-SCHOOL COOKIES

1 cup shortening
1 cup sugar
1 egg
½ cup molasses
¾ teaspoon vinegar
¾ cup undiluted evaporated milk *or* 1 cup dairy sour cream
3 cups sifted all-purpose flour
2 teaspoons baking soda
1 teaspoon salt
1 teaspoon cinnamon

Cream shortening and sugar. Add egg and molasses; beat well; stir in vinegar and evaporated milk or sour cream. Mix and sift dry ingredients. Add to molasses mixture. Drop from tablespoon onto greased baking sheets. Bake at 350° for about 15 minutes. Makes about 6 dozen.

JUMBO COOKIES

1¼ cups sifted all-purpose flour
¾ teaspoon baking soda
½ teaspoon baking powder
½ teaspoon salt
1 teaspoon cinnamon
½ teaspoon powdered ginger
½ cup soft butter or margarine
½ cup sugar
½ cup molasses
2 eggs
1½ cups rolled oats, quick or old-fashioned, uncooked
1 cup raisins
1 cup chopped walnuts
1 package (6 ounces) semisweet chocolate pieces

Sift flour, baking soda, baking powder, salt, and spices together into mixing bowl. Add remaining ingredients. Mix at low speed of electric mixer or by hand until blended. To make king-size cookies, use ¼ cup dough for each cookie; place well apart on ungreased cookie sheets and bake at 350° for 15 minutes. For smaller cookies, drop by heaping teaspoons onto ungreased cookie sheets; bake 10 to 12 minutes. Makes approximately 1½ dozen large cookies or 3 dozen smaller cookies.

PEANUT COOKIES

1 cup shortening
1½ cups firmly packed brown sugar

¼ cup light molasses
3 eggs, unbeaten
3½ cups sifted all-purpose flour
½ teaspoon salt
1 teaspoon baking soda
3 teaspoons cinnamon
½ teaspoon cloves
½ teaspoon nutmeg
1 package (6 ounces) semisweet chocolate pieces
1 cup finely chopped raw apples
1 cup chopped peanuts

Cream shortening with brown sugar until light and fluffy; add molasses. Add unbeaten eggs one at a time, beating after each addition. Mix and sift flour, salt, baking soda, and spices; add. Mix lightly. Stir in chocolate pieces, chopped apples, and peanuts. Mix well. Drop by spoonfuls onto greased baking sheets. Bake at 350° for 12 to 15 minutes. Makes 5 to 6 dozen.

PEANUT LACE COOKIES

½ cup sifted all-purpose flour
½ to 1 cup finely chopped peanuts
¼ cup light or dark corn syrup
¼ cup butter or margarine
¼ cup firmly packed brown sugar
½ teaspoon vanilla

Combine flour and peanuts. Combine corn syrup, butter, and brown sugar in heavy saucepan. Cook over medium heat, stirring constantly, until mixture comes to a boil. Remove from heat. Gradually blend in peanut-flour mixture. Stir in vanilla. Drop by small teaspoons about 3 inches apart onto ungreased cookie sheet. Bake at 325° for 8 to 10 minutes. Let stand 3 to 5 minutes before removing from cookie sheet. Cool on wire racks covered with absorbent paper. If cookies are hard to remove from pan, return to warm oven for a few minutes to soften. Makes about 2 dozen.

PEANUT MACAROONS

1 egg white
⅔ cup sugar
⅛ teaspoon salt
½ cup chopped peanuts
¼ teaspoon almond extract

Beat egg white stiff; add sugar and salt while beating. Fold in peanuts and almond extract.

Drop by teaspoons onto greased baking sheet. Bake at 325° for 15 minutes. Makes 2 dozen.

PEANUT BUTTER CHEWS

16 large marshmallows
1 cup crunchy peanut butter
3 tablespoons butter or margarine
2 tablespoons milk
1 teaspoon vanilla
1 cup flaked coconut
1 cup quick-cooking rolled oats, uncooked
Whole peanuts

Melt marshmallows, peanut butter, and butter over very low heat or over hot water. Add milk and vanilla; stir well. Remove from heat; stir in coconut and oats. (Mixture will be very stiff.) Drop from teaspoon onto waxed paper. Decorate with whole peanuts. Chill thoroughly. Makes 3½ dozen.

PEANUT BUTTER MOUNTAINS

1 package (6 ounces) chocolate pieces
⅓ cup crunchy peanut butter
2 boxes (1⅜ ounces each) Cracker Jack

In 3-quart saucepan, combine chocolate pieces and peanut butter. Stir over medium heat until chocolate is melted and well combined with peanut butter. Remove from heat. Quickly stir in Cracker Jack. Stir until all Cracker Jack is coated with chocolate mixture. Drop by spoonfuls onto waxed paper. Let stand until firm (about 4 hours). Or chill in refrigerator until firm (about 30 minutes). Makes about 2½ dozen.

MAPLE-CHOCOLATE MOUNDS

1 package (6 ounces) semisweet chocolate
    pieces
3 tablespoons butter or margarine
1 tablespoon water
⅓ cup light corn syrup
2 teaspoons maple extract
2½ cups ready-to-eat cereal flakes
½ cup coarsely chopped nuts
½ cup raisins

Melt semisweet chocolate pieces and butter in double boiler over hot, not boiling, water. Remove from heat. Add water, syrup, and maple extract; stir until smooth. Fold in cereal flakes, nuts, and raisins. Drop by heaping teaspoons

onto waxed-paper-lined baking sheet. Chill several hours until firm. Makes approximately 2½ dozen.

CHOCOLATE WALNUT WAFERS

2 squares (1 ounce each) unsweetened
    chocolate
1 can (15 ounces) sweetened condensed milk
1 cup chopped walnuts

Melt chocolate over hot water. Add sweetened condensed milk; stir until well blended. Add walnuts. Drop mixture by teaspoons onto greased baking sheet. Bake at 350° for 12 to 15 minutes. Remove from sheet at once. Cool on wire cake rack. Makes about 3 dozen.

CHOCOLATE LASSIES

¾ cup shortening
¾ cup sugar
1 egg, unbeaten
½ cup molasses
2½ cups sifted all-purpose flour
1½ teaspoons baking soda
½ teaspoon powdered ginger
½ teaspoon cinnamon
1 package (6 ounces) semisweet chocolate
    pieces
½ cup chopped walnuts

Cream shortening and sugar until fluffy. Beat in egg and molasses. Mix and sift flour, baking soda, and spices; add; mix well. Stir in semisweet chocolate pieces and walnuts. Drop by teaspoons onto ungreased cookie sheets. Bake at 375° for 10 to 12 minutes. Makes about 5 dozen.

CHOCOLATE DATE MERINGUE COOKIES

½ cup egg whites (about 4 egg whites)
¼ teaspoon salt
1¼ cups sugar
½ teaspoon vanilla
2 squares unsweetened chocolate, melted and
    cooled
1 cup chopped fresh California dates
1 cup chopped nuts

Beat egg whites and salt until soft peaks form. Gradually beat in sugar, 1 tablespoon at a time, until mixture is stiff and glossy. Fold in vanilla and chocolate. Fold in dates and nuts. Drop by heaping teaspoons, 2 inches apart, onto greased foil on baking sheets. Bake at 325° for 20 minutes or until firm and dry to the touch. Cool on racks. Makes about 4 dozen.

SOFT SUGAR COOKIES

½ cup butter or margarine
1½ cups sugar
2 eggs
1 teaspoon vanilla
3 cups sifted all-purpose flour
1 teaspoon salt
½ teaspoon baking powder
½ teaspoon baking soda
1 cup dairy sour cream
Cinnamon-sugar

Cream butter to consistency of mayonnaise; add sugar gradually, while continuing to cream. Add eggs one at a time, beating well after each addition. Add vanilla. Beat until light and fluffy. Mix and sift flour, salt, baking powder, and baking soda. Add to creamed mixture alternately with sour cream, beginning and ending with dry ingredients. Drop by heaping teaspoons onto well-greased cookie sheets, well apart. With spatula, flatten into circles about 2 inches in diameter. Sprinkle with cinnamon-sugar. Bake at 400° for 10 to 12 minutes. Makes about 2½ dozen.

Chocolate Sugar Cookies: Add 2 squares (1 ounce each) unsweetened chocolate, melted and cooled, to creamed mixture. Continue as above.

Raisin Sugar Cookies: Add 1 cup seedless raisins to creamed mixture. Continue as above.

LEMON WAFERS

2 cups sifted all-purpose flour
2 teaspoons baking powder
½ teaspoon salt
½ cup shortening
1 cup sugar
1 egg, unbeaten
1 tablespoon grated lemon peel
½ teaspoon vanilla
¼ cup lemon juice
½ cup water

Mix and sift flour, baking powder, and salt. Cream shortening; add sugar gradually while creaming; continue creaming until light and fluffy. Blend in egg, lemon peel, and vanilla; beat well. Add dry ingredients alternately with lemon juice and water; blend smooth after each

addition. (Dough will be very soft.) Drop by teaspoons, 2 inches apart, onto greased cookie sheets. Bake at 375° for about 10 minutes or until edges are light brown. Remove cookies to wire cake racks to cool. Makes about 5 dozen.

QUICK LEMON CRISPS

2 cups sifted all-purpose flour
¾ teaspoon baking soda
Few grains salt
¾ cup shortening
1 cup sugar
2 packages (3¾ ounces each) instant lemon
    pudding mix
3 eggs, slightly beaten

Sift flour with baking soda and salt. Cream shortening. Add sugar and pudding mix; cream until light and fluffy. Add eggs; mix thoroughly. Add flour mixture; beat thoroughly until well blended. Drop from teaspoon onto greased baking sheets, about 2½ inches apart. Bake at 375° for 8 to 10 minutes. Makes about 6 dozen.

FRUITCAKE DROPS

4 tablespoons butter or margarine
¾ cup firmly packed brown sugar
1 egg
¼ cup orange juice
1 teaspoon lemon juice
1 cup sifted all-purpose flour
¼ teaspoon baking soda
¼ teaspoon salt
½ teaspoon cinnamon
½ teaspoon allspice
¼ teaspoon ground cloves
⅛ teaspoon nutmeg
1 cup diced candied fruits, chopped
½ cup raisins
½ cup chopped apples
1 cup chopped walnuts
Confectioners' Sugar Icing (page 240) and
    candy sprinkles (optional)

Cream butter to consistency of mayonnaise; add brown sugar while continuing to cream. Add egg; beat well. Combine orange and lemon juices; add gradually to creamed mixture. Mix and sift flour, baking soda, salt, and spices; stir in. Stir in fruits and walnuts. Drop by teaspoons onto lightly greased baking sheets. Bake at 375° for about 10 minutes. Remove at once to wire racks to cool. Decorate with Confectioners'

Sugar Icing and candy sprinkles before serving, if desired. Makes 4 dozen.

PINEAPPLE COOKIES

½ cup shortening
½ cup sugar
½ cup firmly packed brown sugar
1 egg, beaten
1¾ cups sifted all-purpose flour
½ teaspoon baking powder
½ teaspoon baking soda
½ teaspoon salt
½ cup sugar 'n' honey wheat germ (plus some for decoration)
½ teaspoon vanilla
½ cup drained crushed pineapple

Cream shortening and sugars until light and fluffy. Add egg; mix well. Mix and sift flour, baking powder, baking soda, and salt; stir in ½ cup wheat germ. Combine vanilla and pineapple. Add dry ingredients and pineapple alternately to sugar mixture; mix well. Drop by spoonfuls onto greased cookie sheets. Sprinkle tops with a little additional sugar 'n' honey wheat germ. Bake at 375° for 10 to 12 minutes or until light golden brown. Makes about 4 dozen.

BANANA NUGGET COOKIES

1½ cups sifted all-purpose flour
1 cup sugar
½ teaspoon baking soda
1 teaspoon salt
¼ teaspoon nutmeg
¾ teaspoon cinnamon
¾ cup shortening
1 egg, well beaten
1 cup mashed ripe bananas (2 to 3 bananas)
1¾ cups quick-cooking rolled oats, uncooked
1 package (6 ounces) semisweet chocolate pieces

Sift together flour, sugar, baking soda, salt, nutmeg, and cinnamon into mixing bowl. Cut in shortening. Add egg, bananas, rolled oats, and chocolate pieces. Beat until thoroughly blended. Drop by spoonfuls onto ungreased cookie sheets. Bake at 400° for about 15 minutes or until cookies are done. Remove from sheets immediately. Makes about 3 dozen.

BANANA HONEY COOKIES

2 cups sifted all-purpose flour
¾ teaspoon baking soda
¼ teaspoon salt
1 teaspoon cinnamon
¼ teaspoon nutmeg
⅔ cup soft shortening
¾ cup firmly packed brown sugar
1 egg
¼ cup honey
½ cup mashed ripe banana
2 cups 100% natural cereal (plus some for decoration)
Honey Butter Frosting*

Mix and sift flour, baking soda, salt, cinnamon, and nutmeg into a large bowl. Add shortening, brown sugar, egg, honey, and mashed banana. Beat together until thoroughly combined. Stir in 2 cups cereal. Cover and chill dough 1 hour. Drop dough by teaspoons onto greased cookie sheets. Bake at 350° for 12 to 15 minutes. Cool on wire rack. Frost cooled cookies with Honey Butter Frosting and sprinkle with additional cereal. Makes 5 dozen.

*HONEY BUTTER FROSTING

¼ cup butter or margarine
¼ cup honey
2 cups sifted confectioners' (powdered) sugar
1 teaspoon water

Beat together butter and honey. Gradually beat in confectioners' sugar and water.

COCONUT MACAROONS

2 egg whites
1 cup sugar
2 cups cornflakes
1 can flaked coconut
⅛ teaspoon salt
½ teaspoon almond extract

Beat egg whites stiff but not dry. Beat sugar gradually into egg whites. Fold in remaining ingredients. Drop by spoonfuls onto greased baking sheet. Bake at 350° for 10 to 12 minutes. Makes about 2 dozen.

CRANBERRY-COCONUT JUMBLES

3 cups sifted all-purpose flour
2 teaspoons baking powder

¼ teaspoon salt
1½ cups fresh cranberries, coarsely chopped
1 can (3½ ounces) flaked coconut
½ cup shortening
½ cup butter or margarine
1½ cups sugar
3 eggs, well beaten
1 tablespoon grated lemon peel
1 tablespoon lemon juice

Mix and sift flour, baking powder, and salt; stir in cranberries and coconut. Cream shortening and butter; gradually add sugar. Add eggs; beat well. Add lemon peel and juice. Gradually stir in flour mixture. Drop from teaspoon onto lightly greased cookie sheets. Bake at 375° for about 10 minutes or until lightly browned. Makes about 5 dozen 2-inch cookies.

CRANBERRY COOKIES

½ cup butter or margarine
1 cup sugar
¾ cup firmly packed brown sugar
1 teaspoon vanilla
⅓ cup milk
1 egg
3 cups sifted all-purpose flour
1 teaspoon baking powder
¼ teaspoon baking soda
½ teaspoon salt
1 cup mixed diced candied fruits
1 tablespoon grated orange peel
2½ cups fresh cranberries, coarsely chopped

Cream butter, sugars, and vanilla together. Beat in milk and egg. Mix and sift flour, baking powder, baking soda, and salt; stir into creamed mixture. Blend well. Stir in candied fruit, orange peel, and cranberries. For each cookie, mound 2 level tablespoons on well-greased cookie sheet. Space mounds about 2 inches apart. Bake at 375° for 15 to 18 minutes. Makes approximately 3½ dozen cookies, 3 inches in diameter.

DATE-AND-APPLE COOKIES

1 package (14 ounces) date bar mix
¼ cup hot water
1 egg
1 cup finely chopped apple
½ cup chopped walnuts

Mix date filling from date bar mix with hot water until crumbly. Blend in egg, chopped apple, and

walnuts. Drop by teaspoons onto lightly greased baking sheet. Bake at 400° for 8 to 10 minutes. Makes about 4 dozen.

SOUR CREAM COOKIES

½ cup shortening
1 cup firmly packed brown sugar
1 egg, beaten
½ cup raisins
2 cups sifted cake flour
½ teaspoon salt
½ teaspoon baking soda
2 teaspoons baking powder
½ teaspoon nutmeg
½ cup dairy sour cream
½ cup broken walnut meats

Cream shortening and sugar. Add egg with raisins. Mix and sift flour, salt, baking soda, baking powder, and nutmeg. Add alternately with sour cream to raisin mixture. Stir in walnuts. Drop by teaspoons onto greased cookie sheet. Bake at 400° for 12 to 15 minutes. Makes about 3 dozen.

GUMDROP COOKIES

1 cup butter or margarine, softened
1 cup granulated sugar
½ cup firmly packed brown sugar
1 egg
1 teaspoon vanilla
1½ cups sifted all-purpose flour
½ teaspoon baking powder
½ teaspoon salt
¾ cup quick or old-fashioned oats, uncooked
1 cup chopped assorted gumdrops

Beat together butter, sugars, egg, and vanilla until creamy. Mix and sift flour, baking powder, and salt; add to creamed mixture, blending well. Stir in oats and gumdrops. Drop by teaspoons onto ungreased cookie sheets. Bake at 375° for 10 to 12 minutes. Makes about 4 dozen.

SCOTCHIES

⅓ cup shortening
2 tablespoons sugar
1 package butterscotch pudding mix (not instant)
1 egg, unbeaten
⅓ cup milk
¼ cup finely cut pitted dates or chopped raisins

1 package (6 ounces) semisweet chocolate pieces
¼ cup chopped nutmeats
1 cup plus 2 tablespoons sifted cake flour
1 teaspoon baking powder
¼ teaspoon salt

Cream together thoroughly the shortening, sugar, and pudding mix, using a spoon or electric mixer at high speed. Add egg; beat vigorously. Stir in milk and dates or raisins. Blend well, using a spoon or electric mixer at slowest speed. Add semisweet chocolate pieces and nutmeats. Mix and sift flour, baking powder, and salt; sift into first mixture a little at a time, stirring after each addition. Drop by small spoonfuls onto greased cookie sheets. Bake at 350° for 12 to 15 minutes. Cool. Makes about 4 dozen.

BREAKFAST COOKIES

1¼ cups unsifted all-purpose flour
⅔ cup sugar
½ cup Grape-Nuts
1 teaspoon baking powder
½ pound bacon, cooked and crumbled
½ cup soft-type margarine
1 egg
2 tablespoons frozen orange juice concentrate, thawed, undiluted
1 tablespoon grated orange peel

Measure flour, sugar, Grape-Nuts, and baking powder into mixing bowl; mix well. Add bacon, margarine, egg, orange juice concentrate and peel. Mix until well blended. Drop by level tablespoons 2 inches apart onto ungreased baking sheets. Bake at 350° for 10 to 12 minutes or until edges of cookies are lightly browned but cookies are still soft. Remove from baking sheet immediately. Makes 2½ dozen.

CORNFLAKE KISSES

2 egg whites
1 cup sugar
⅛ teaspoon salt
½ teaspoon orange extract
2 cups cornflakes
1 cup flaked coconut

Beat egg whites stiff but not dry. Beat sugar into egg whites gradually. Add salt and orange extract. Fold in cornflakes and coconut. Drop by teaspoons onto greased cookie sheet. Bake at 350° for 10 to 12 minutes. Makes 2½ dozen.

OATMEAL NUT BARS

1 cup sifted all-purpose flour
¼ teaspoon baking soda
¼ teaspoon salt
⅓ cup soft shortening
⅔ cup firmly packed brown sugar
1 egg
⅓ cup milk
½ teaspoon vanilla
1 cup quick-cooking rolled oats, uncooked
½ cup chopped walnuts
½ cup flaked coconut
Orange Glaze*

Mix and sift flour, baking soda, and salt into bowl; add shortening, sugar, egg, milk, and vanilla. Beat until smooth (about 2 minutes). Blend in oats, walnuts, and coconut; spread in greased 11 x 7-inch baking pan. Bake at 350° for 25 to 30 minutes. Remove from oven; pour hot Orange Glaze evenly over top. Cool; cut in 12 bars.

*ORANGE GLAZE

½ cup sugar
3 tablespoons orange juice
1 teaspoon grated orange peel

Combine sugar and orange juice in saucepan. Bring to boil; boil 3 minutes; add grated orange peel.

MOLASSES-CHOCOLATE BARS

1 egg, beaten
½ cup sugar
½ cup light molasses
¼ cup shortening
½ teaspoon vanilla
1 cup sifted all-purpose flour
½ teaspoon salt
¼ teaspoon baking soda
⅔ cup chopped walnuts
1 package (6 ounces) semisweet chocolate pieces

Combine egg, sugar, molasses, shortening, and vanilla. Sift in flour, salt, and baking soda. Add nuts and semisweet chocolate pieces. Spread in greased and lightly floured 9-inch square pan. Bake at 350° for 45 minutes. Cut in bars 1½ x 3 inches. Makes 1½ dozen.

MOLASSES-COCONUT LUNCH-BOX BARS

3 eggs
½ cup sugar
½ cup light molasses
½ cup butter or margarine, melted and cooled
2 cups sifted all-purpose flour
½ teaspoon salt
½ teaspoon baking soda
½ teaspoon cinnamon
½ teaspoon nutmeg
¼ teaspoon ground cloves
¼ teaspoon mace
1 can flaked coconut
1 cup raisins
Glaze* and flaked coconut *or* toasted coconut
    or chopped nuts (optional)

Beat eggs with sugar until well mixed. Gradually beat in molasses and melted butter. Mix and sift flour, salt, baking soda, and spices; blend into molasses mixture. Stir in coconut and raisins. Turn into greased 15 x 10 x 1-inch jelly roll pan. Bake at 350° for 15 minutes or until cake tester inserted in center comes out clean. Cool. If desired, spread with Glaze and sprinkle with flaked coconut, toasted coconut, or chopped nuts. Cut in 36 bars.

°GLAZE

Gradually blend 2 cups confectioners' (powdered) sugar and 3 tablespoons milk into 2 tablespoons soft butter or margarine. Beat until smooth.

MOLASSES FRUIT-NUT SQUARES

2 cups sifted all-purpose flour
¼ teaspoon baking soda
½ teaspoon salt
1 teaspoon cinnamon
¼ teaspoon nutmeg
½ teaspoon allspice
¼ teaspoon powdered ginger
½ teaspoon ground cloves
⅔ cup shortening
⅓ cup sugar
¼ cup dark molasses
2 tablespoons water
1 tablespoon vinegar
1 egg
1½ cups raisins
¾ cup chopped pecans
Frosting of choice (optional)

Mix and sift flour, baking soda, salt, and spices. Cream shortening and sugar; beat in molasses, water, vinegar, and egg. Blend in dry ingredients, raisins, and nuts. Spread in jelly roll pan (15½ x 10½ x 1 inch), smoothing top carefully. Bake at 375° for 20 minutes or until lightly browned. Cool slightly. Mark in approximately 2-inch squares. Cool thoroughly; cut in squares; frost, if desired. Makes about 35.

CHOCOLATE CINNAMON BARS

2 cups sifted all-purpose flour
1 teaspoon baking powder
1⅓ cups sugar, divided
4 teaspoons cinnamon, divided
½ cup softened butter or margarine
½ cup shortening
1 egg
1 egg, separated
1 package (6 ounces) semisweet chocolate
    pieces
½ cup chopped walnuts

Mix and sift flour, baking powder, 1 cup sugar, and 3 teaspoons cinnamon. Add butter or margarine, shortening, 1 egg, and 1 egg yolk. Blend well with wooden spoon or on low speed of electric mixer. Turn into a lightly greased 15½ x 10½ x 1-inch jelly roll pan; spread evenly with spatula. Beat egg white slightly; brush over mixture. Combine remaining ⅓ cup sugar, 1 teaspoon cinnamon, chocolate pieces, and walnuts; sprinkle over top. Bake at 350° for 25 minutes. Cool; cut in bars. Makes 18 to 20.

CRISPY FUDGE SQUARES

1 package (6 ounces) semisweet chocolate
    pieces
½ cup softened butter or margarine
¾ cup firmly packed brown sugar
1 teaspoon vanilla
1½ cups sifted all-purpose flour
1 teaspoon baking powder
½ teaspoon salt
¾ cup finely chopped nuts (plus extra for
    topping)

Melt chocolate pieces over hot, not boiling, water. Cream together butter and sugar; stir in vanilla. Mix and sift flour, baking powder, and salt; stir into creamed mixture. Add melted chocolate and ¾ cup finely chopped nuts; mix well. Press mixture evenly in ungreased 9 x 13-inch baking pan. Sprinkle additional chopped nuts over top; press in gently. Bake at 350° for 18 to 20 minutes. Cool. Makes 2 dozen squares.

PEBBLE-TOP CHOCOLATE BARS

1½ cups flaked coconut
2 tablespoons melted butter or margarine
½ cup plus 2 tablespoons sugar
¼ cup graham cracker crumbs
½ cup soft butter or margarine
¼ cup firmly packed brown sugar
1 egg
1 teaspoon vanilla
2 tablespoons milk
1 cup all-purpose flour
½ teaspoon baking soda
½ teaspoon salt
1 package (6 ounces) semisweet chocolate
    pieces
½ cup chopped pecans
1 package (8 ounces) diced candied fruits and
    peels

Combine coconut, melted butter, 2 tablespoons sugar, and graham cracker crumbs. Press on bottom of a 9-inch square pan. Combine soft butter, brown sugar, egg, vanilla, milk, flour, baking soda, salt, and ½ cup sugar in mixer bowl. Blend at medium speed until smooth. Stir in chocolate pieces and pecans. Spoon evenly over base. Scatter candied fruits and peels on top. Bake at 350° for 35 to 40 minutes. Cool, then cut in 16 squares.

CHOCOLATE-BUTTERSCOTCH BROWNIES

⅓ cup butter or margarine
½ cup sugar
2 tablespoons milk
1 package (6 ounces) semisweet chocolate
    pieces
1 teaspoon vanilla
2 eggs
¾ cup sifted all-purpose flour
¼ teaspoon baking soda
½ teaspoon salt
½ cup chopped nuts
2 cups miniature marshmallows
1 package (6 ounces) butterscotch pieces
1 tablespoon shortening

Melt butter in 2½-quart saucepan; stir in sugar and milk. Bring to a boil; remove from heat. Add semisweet chocolate pieces and vanilla. Stir

until smooth. Beat in eggs one at a time. Sift in flour, baking soda, and salt. Stir in nuts; mix until blended. Turn into greased 9-inch square pan. Bake at 350° for 25 minutes. Immediately cover top with miniature marshmallows; cool in pan. Melt butterscotch pieces and shortening over hot, not boiling, water; pour over marshmallows, spreading if necessary. Chill. Cut in squares and remove from pan. Makes about 18.

BUTTERSCOTCH COOKIES

1 package (6 ounces) butterscotch pieces
¼ cup butter or shortening
1 cup firmly packed brown sugar
2 eggs
½ teaspoon vanilla
¾ cup sifted all-purpose flour
1 teaspoon baking powder
¾ teaspoon salt
1 package (6 ounces) semisweet chocolate
    pieces
½ cup raisins
½ cup chopped walnuts

Melt together butterscotch pieces and butter over hot, not boiling, water. Remove from heat; stir in brown sugar; cool. Stir in eggs and vanilla. Mix and sift flour, baking powder, and salt; stir in. Stir in semisweet chocolate pieces, raisins, and chopped nuts. Spread mixture in greased 13 x 9 x 2-inch pan. Bake at 350° for 25 minutes. Cut in bars while still warm. Makes 2 dozen.

DOUBLE-SCOTCH PECAN BARS

¾ cup softened butter or margarine
1 cup firmly packed dark brown sugar
1 egg
½ teaspoon vanilla
2 cups sifted all-purpose flour
¾ teaspoon salt
½ teaspoon baking powder
¼ cup milk
1 package (6 ounces) butterscotch pieces
1 can (3½ ounces) flaked coconut
1 cup chopped pecans
Butterscotch Topping* (optional)

Cream together butter and sugar; stir in egg and vanilla. Mix and sift flour, salt, and baking powder. Add alternately to creamed mixture with milk. Fold in butterscotch pieces, coconut, and pecans. Spread evenly on greased cookie sheet into a 14 x 10-inch rectangle. Bake at 350° for 15 minutes. Cool. Spread with Butterscotch Topping, if desired. Cut in bars 2½ x 1 inch. Makes approximately 60 bars.

*BUTTERSCOTCH TOPPING

1 package (6 ounces) butterscotch pieces
1 teaspoon vegetable oil
2 tablespoons water

Melt butterscotch pieces with oil over hot, not boiling, water. Add water; stir vigorously until smooth.

TAFFY DOMINO BARS

1 can (6 ounces) thawed frozen orange juice concentrate, divided
½ cup shortening
½ cup sugar
½ cup molasses
1 egg
1½ cups sifted all-purpose flour
¼ teaspoon salt
1 teaspoon each baking soda, powdered ginger, and cinnamon
1 package (6 ounces) semisweet chocolate pieces, divided
½ cup chopped walnuts
1 cup rolled oats, quick or old-fashioned, uncooked
Orange Butter Frosting*

Reserve 2 tablespoons thawed undiluted concentrate for Orange Butter Frosting. Cream together shortening and sugar. Add remaining concentrate, molasses, and egg; blend well. Sift in flour, salt, baking soda, and spices; mix thoroughly. Stir in ⅔ cup semisweet chocolate pieces, walnuts, and rolled oats. Turn into greased and floured 9 x 13-inch baking pan; spread evenly. Bake at 325° for 40 minutes. Turn out of pan; cool. Frost with Orange Butter Frosting. Cut in 3 x 1-inch bars. Decorate with remaining semisweet chocolate pieces to resemble dominoes. Makes about 3 dozen bars.

*ORANGE BUTTER FROSTING

1 tablespoon butter
2 tablespoons reserved orange concentrate
1 cup sifted confectioners' (powdered) sugar

Cream together butter and orange concentrate. Gradually blend in confectioners' sugar.

SNOWFLAKE SQUARES

⅓ cup shortening
1 cup extra-fine (instant) sugar
1⅓ cups sifted cake flour
1½ teaspoons baking powder
¼ teaspoon salt
½ cup milk
½ teaspoon almond extract
3 egg whites
Frosting of choice

Cream shortening; add sugar slowly while creaming. Mix and sift flour, baking powder, and salt. Combine milk and almond extract. Add flour and milk alternately to creamed mixture. Beat egg whites stiff but not dry; fold in. Pour into 10-inch square, shallow cake pan. Bake at 375° for 30 minutes. Cool. Frost as desired. Cut in 9 squares.

DATE BARS

4 cups miniature marshmallows
1½ cups snipped pitted dates
2 tablespoons butter or margarine
1 box (6 ounces) *or* 4 boxes (1⅜ ounces each) Cracker Jack, coarsely crushed

In 3-quart saucepan, combine marshmallows, dates, and butter. Stir over medium heat just until all marshmallows are melted. Remove from heat. Quickly stir in crushed Cracker Jack. Stir until mixture is well combined. Press Cracker Jack mixture firmly into well-buttered 9-inch square pan with spoon or rubber spatula. Let stand until completely cooled (2 to 3 hours). Cut in squares. Makes about 3 dozen.

BANANA BARS

1¾ cups sifted all-purpose flour
2 teaspoons baking powder
½ teaspoon salt
½ cup shortening
1 cup sugar
1 teaspoon lemon extract
3 eggs, well beaten
2 tablespoons instant coffee (dry)
1 cup mashed bananas (3 fully ripe bananas)
½ cup broken walnut meats
Canned lemon frosting and chopped walnuts (optional)

Mix and sift flour, baking powder, and salt. Cream shortening and sugar; add lemon extract, eggs, and instant coffee; mix well. Add flour mixture alternately with mashed bananas. Stir in walnuts. Bake in greased pan, 8 x 12 x 2 inches, at 350° for 30 minutes. Cool in pan; cut in bars. If desired, frost with canned lemon frosting; sprinkle with chopped walnuts. Makes 24 bars, 4 inches long and 1 inch wide.

ORANGE BROWNIES

½ cup butter or margarine
2 squares unsweetened chocolate
2 eggs
1 cup sugar
1 cup sifted cake flour
¼ teaspoon baking powder
¼ teaspoon salt
1 cup walnut meats, coarsely chopped
¼ cup grated orange peel
3 tablespoons orange juice

Melt butter and chocolate together over hot water. Beat eggs; add sugar gradually while beating. Add chocolate and shortening to egg mixture; beat hard 1 minute. Mix and sift flour, baking powder, and salt; add. Add walnut meats, orange peel and juice. Pour into greased 8-inch square cake pan. Bake at 350° for 50 minutes or until done. Cut in squares. Makes about 12.

PRUNE BAR COOKIES

1 cup pitted prunes, uncooked
1 cup chopped walnuts
1 cup firmly packed brown sugar
¾ cup all-purpose flour
1½ teaspoons baking powder
¼ teaspoon salt
3 eggs, well beaten
Confectioners' (powdered) sugar (optional)

Chop prunes. Add to chopped nuts with brown sugar, flour, baking powder, and salt. Mix. Fold into well-beaten eggs. Spread in greased 9-inch square pan. Bake at 325° for 25 to 30 minutes. Cool in pan 5 to 10 minutes. Cut in 24 pieces (1 x 3 inches). Roll in confectioners' sugar, if desired. Makes about 24 bars.

TROPICAL PEAR BARS

1 can (1 pound) sliced Bartlett pears
1¼ cups unsifted all-purpose flour, divided
¾ cup firmly packed brown sugar, divided
¼ cup butter or margarine
2 eggs, well beaten
½ teaspoon cinnamon
½ teaspoon baking powder
¼ teaspoon salt
1 can (3½ ounces) flaked coconut
½ cup chopped macadamia nuts*
2 teaspoons grated lemon peel

Drain pears thoroughly; dice. Combine 1 cup flour and ¼ cup brown sugar. Cut in butter until mixture resembles coarse meal. Pat firmly into buttered 9-inch square pan. Bake at 350° for 15 minutes. Beat remaining ½ cup brown sugar gradually into eggs. Sift together remaining ¼ cup flour, cinnamon, baking powder, and salt. Stir into egg mixture. Add diced pears, coconut, nuts, and lemon peel. Mix thoroughly. Spread over warm baked mixture; return to oven. Bake 20 to 25 minutes longer or until lightly browned. Cool; cut in bars. Makes 2 dozen.

*Or salted almonds or cashew nuts.

OATMEAL COOKIES

2½ cups sifted all-purpose flour
1 teaspoon baking soda
1 teaspoon salt
1½ teaspoons cinnamon
½ teaspoon nutmeg
¾ cup shortening, soft
½ cup granulated sugar
1 cup firmly packed brown sugar
2 eggs
¼ cup milk
2½ cups rolled oats, quick or old-fashioned, uncooked
1 cup raisins, chopped
Granulated sugar (optional)

Sift first 5 ingredients together into bowl. Add shortening, sugars, eggs, and milk. Mix until smooth (about 2 minutes). Stir in oats and raisins. Chill. Roll out on lightly floured board or canvas to ¼-inch thickness; cut with floured 3-inch cookie cutter. Place on greased cookie sheets; sprinkle lightly with granulated sugar, if desired. Bake at 375° for 10 to 12 minutes. Remove from cookie sheets at once. Makes 5 dozen.

RAISIN COOKIES

1 cup raisins
2¼ cups sifted all-purpose flour
1 teaspoon salt
½ teaspoon baking soda

1½ teaspoons cinnamon
½ teaspoon nutmeg
1 cup soft shortening
1½ cups firmly packed brown sugar
1 egg
2 tablespoons water
2 cups rolled oats, quick or old-fashioned,
    uncooked

Cover raisins with boiling water; let stand 10 minutes; drain. Mix and sift flour, salt, baking soda, cinnamon, and nutmeg into bowl. Add shortening, sugar, egg, and water. Beat until smooth (about 2 minutes). Stir in oats and raisins. Chill several hours. Work with ¼ of dough at a time, keeping remainder in refrigerator. Roll out on lightly floured board or canvas to ¼-inch thickness. Cut with floured 3-inch round cutter. Place on ungreased cookie sheets. Bake at 375° for 10 to 12 minutes. Makes about 2½ dozen.

WAGON WHEEL COOKIES

1½ cups shortening
1½ cups sugar
2 eggs
2 teaspoons vanilla
4 cups sifted all-purpose flour
2 teaspoons salt
1½ teaspoons baking powder
½ cup wheat germ
⅓ cup milk
½ cup raisins

Cream shortening and sugar until light and fluffy. Beat in eggs and vanilla. Mix and sift flour, salt, and baking powder; stir in wheat germ; add alternately with milk to shortening mixture. Stir in raisins. Chill thoroughly. Roll out thin on lightly floured surface. Use standard coffee can (about 5 inches in diameter), dipped in flour, as a cutter. Bake on greased cookie sheets at 375° for 12 minutes. Makes about 18. For smaller cookies use any preferred-size cookie cutter.

NOTE: To make spokes and hubs of wheels, if desired, use pressurized cake and cookie decorator or frosting put through pastry tube.

JOE FROGGERS

4⅓ cups sifted all-purpose flour
1 teaspoon baking soda
½ teaspoon salt

1½ teaspoons powdered ginger
¾ teaspoon cloves
¾ teaspoon nutmeg
¼ teaspoon allspice
¾ cup shortening
¾ cup sugar
1 cup light molasses
1 tablespoon rum extract
⅓ cup water

Mix and sift flour, baking soda, salt, and spices. Cream shortening and sugar. Add molasses and rum extract; beat well. Add flour mixture and water alternately, beating until well blended after each addition. Wrap dough in foil; chill overnight. Roll half of dough at a time, about ¼ inch thick. Cut with floured 4-inch round cookie cutter.* Bake on lightly greased cookie sheets at 375° for 8 to 9 minutes or until just done but not browned around edges. Cool on racks. Store in airtight can or jar. Makes 2 dozen.

*If a cutter this size is not available, use the edge of an opened, empty can or cut around an inverted saucer.

MAY BASKET COOKIES

½ cup shortening
½ cup sugar
½ cup light molasses
1 egg yolk
2 cups sifted all-purpose flour
½ teaspoon salt
½ teaspoon baking soda
1 teaspoon baking powder
½ teaspoon ground cloves
¼ teaspoon allspice
1½ teaspoons cinnamon
½ teaspoon mace
Decorations (see below)

Cream shortening, sugar, and molasses. Add egg yolk; mix well. Mix and sift flour, salt, baking soda, baking powder, and spices; sift into creamed mixture. Mix well. Wrap dough in foil; chill. Roll out dough, a small portion at a time, to ⅛-inch thickness (keep remaining dough chilled until ready to roll out). Cut out cookies with round scalloped cookie cutters or flower-shaped cookie cutters. Place on ungreased baking sheets. Bake at 350° for 8 to 10 minutes. Cool. Decorate cookies with pressurized cake and cookie decorator. Makes about 6 dozen small cookies.

CHOCOLATE CAT COOKIES

¾ cup shortening
1½ cups sugar
2 eggs
2 teaspoons vanilla
3 to 3½ cups sifted all-purpose flour
2½ teaspoons baking powder
½ teaspoon salt
Chocolate Glaze*
Ornamental Frosting**

Cream together shortening, sugar, eggs, and vanilla until light and fluffy. Sift in flour, baking powder, and salt. Mix well. Chill dough until easy to handle. Roll out ¼ inch thick on lightly floured board or pastry cloth. Cut equal number of 2½-inch rounds and 1¼-inch diamonds with cookie cutters. Place rounds on lightly greased cookie sheets, leaving enough space between cookies for "ears." To make ears, cut diamonds in half crosswise and press the 2 triangles into each round about ¼ inch apart. Bake at 375° until light brown (about 10 minutes). Cool. Spread surface with Chocolate Glaze. When glaze has set, make cat face with Ornamental Frosting. Makes about 4 dozen.

*CHOCOLATE GLAZE

1 large package (12 ounces) semisweet
    chocolate pieces
1 small can (⅔ cup) evaporated milk
1½ cups confectioners' (powdered) sugar

Combine chocolate pieces and evaporated milk in saucepan. Stir over low heat until smooth. Add confectioners' sugar; beat until smooth. If frosting becomes too stiff, place over boiling water until of spreading consistency.

**ORNAMENTAL FROSTING

1½ cups confectioners' (powdered) sugar
⅛ teaspoon cream of tartar
1 egg white

Sift confectioners' sugar and cream of tartar into bowl. Add egg white; beat until stiff. Force through decorating tube to make eyes, whiskers, nose, mouth.

BUTTER MINT PATS

1 cup butter or margarine, softened
1 cup butter mints, crushed*

2 cups all-purpose flour
1 tablespoon sugar

Cream butter at medium speed in large mixing bowl until light; add crushed mints. Add flour; blend well at low speed. If necessary, chill dough for easier handling. Roll out or pat dough into a 9-inch square on waxed paper. Sprinkle with sugar. Cut in 1½-inch squares. Using tiny cutters, press a design on each square. Place on ungreased cookie sheets. Bake at 300° for 18 to 20 minutes, until pale golden brown. Do not overbake. Makes 3 dozen.

*To crush mints, place in heavy plastic bag and crush with rolling pin. Or, using a spoon, crush mints against sides of mixing bowl.

COCONUT CIRCLES

¾ cup butter or margarine
½ cup sugar
1 egg yolk
2 cups sifted cake flour
½ teaspoon vanilla
1 can (3½ ounces) flaked coconut
Lemon Butter Filling*

Cream butter until soft; add sugar gradually; cream together until light and fluffy. Add egg yolk; beat well. Add flour, a small amount at a time, mixing thoroughly after each addition. Add vanilla and coconut. Mix well. Chill several hours. Roll out ⅛ inch thick on lightly floured board; cut with round cookie cutter, 1½ inches in diameter. Bake on ungreased baking sheets at 400° for 8 to 10 minutes or until edges are lightly browned. Cool. Spread half the cookies with Lemon Butter Filling. Top each with second cookie; press down lightly. Makes about 3 dozen.

*LEMON BUTTER FILLING

¼ cup butter or margarine
½ teaspoon grated lemon or orange peel
1¾ cups sifted confectioners' (powdered)
    sugar
4 teaspoons lemon juice
Dash of salt
¾ teaspoon vanilla

Cream together butter and lemon peel. Add part of the confectioners' sugar gradually, blending after each addition. Then add remaining sugar, alternately with lemon juice, until of right consistency to spread. Add salt and vanilla; blend.

FLOWER COOKIES

4 to 4½ cups sifted all-purpose flour
2 teaspoons baking powder
½ teaspoon salt
¾ cup butter or margarine
1½ cups sugar
2 eggs
1 teaspoon vanilla
¼ cup milk
Confectioners' Sugar Icing (page 240)
Semisweet chocolate pieces

Mix and sift 4 cups flour, baking powder, and salt. Cream butter and sugar until light and fluffy. Add eggs; beat thoroughly. Add vanilla. Add flour mixture to creamed mixture alternately with milk. Mix thoroughly. Add more flour, if necessary, to form a soft dough. Wrap dough in foil or waxed paper. Chill in refrigerator for several hours or overnight. Roll out half of dough to ¹⁄₁₆-inch thickness. Cut with 3-inch scalloped cookie cutter. Roll second half; cut with 3-inch daisy cookie cutter. Place scalloped cookies on ungreased baking sheets. Brush lightly with milk. Lay a daisy cookie over each scalloped cookie. Press cookies together lightly to seal. Bake at 400° for 8 to 10 minutes. Cool. Frost daisies with Confectioners' Sugar Icing tinted pink. Make centers with semisweet chocolate pieces. Makes about 4 dozen.

HEART COOKIE CAKES

Cookie Dough

1 cup soft butter or margarine
1 cup sugar
2 eggs
1 teaspoon vanilla
½ teaspoon almond extract
2½ cups sifted all-purpose flour
¾ teaspoon salt
½ teaspoon baking powder
2 cups rolled oats, quick or old-fashioned, uncooked

Beat butter and sugar together until creamy. Beat in eggs, vanilla, and almond extract. Sift together flour, salt, and baking powder; add to creamed mixture, beating well. Stir in oats. Chill dough thoroughly. Roll out on lightly floured board or canvas to ⅛-inch thickness. Cut with a floured heart-shaped cookie cutter. Place on greased cookie sheets. Bake at 350° for 12 to 15 minutes. Remove from cookie sheets; cool on racks.

Butter Frosting:

¾ cup soft butter or margarine
4 cups sifted confectioners' (powdered) sugar
1 egg white, unbeaten
1 teaspoon vanilla
Pink-tinted coconut*

Beat butter until fluffy. Add 2 cups sifted confectioners' sugar gradually. Blend in egg white and vanilla. Beat in remaining confectioners' sugar. Put 2 cookies together with frosting; press together. Repeat with remaining cookies. Frost tops and sides of all cookies. Sprinkle with pink-tinted coconut. Makes about 5 dozen.

*Pink-tinted coconut: Put flaked coconut in glass jar with cover; add few drops red food coloring. Cover jar. Shake until all coconut is tinted evenly.

OLD-FASHIONED LEMON CRACKERS

½ ounce (about 2 tablespoons pulverized) ammonium carbonate
1 cup milk
½ cup shortening
1¼ cups sugar
1 egg, well beaten
½ ounce (1 tablespoon) oil of lemon *or* 1 ounce (2 tablespoons) lemon extract
5 cups sifted all-purpose flour

Pulverize ammonium carbonate with rolling pin; add milk; let stand ½ hour or until dissolved, stirring often. Cream shortening and sugar; add egg, lemon flavoring, and milk mixture. Stir in flour. Chill. Roll ¼ inch thick on floured board. Cut in 3-inch squares. Prick with floured fork. Bake on greased baking sheets at 375° for 15 minutes or until lightly browned. Makes 3½ dozen.

LEMON CRISPS

1 cup soft butter or margarine
1¼ cups sugar
1 egg
½ teaspoon lemon extract
½ teaspoon vanilla extract
Grated peel of 1 lemon
3 cups sifted all-purpose flour
1 teaspoon baking powder
½ teaspoon baking soda
½ teaspoon salt
½ cup dairy sour cream
2 cups quick-cooking rolled oats, uncooked
Granulated sugar

Beat butter until creamy. Gradually beat in sugar. Add egg, extracts, and lemon peel; beat well. Sift together flour, baking powder, baking soda, and salt. Add alternately with sour cream to creamed mixture; blend well. Beat in oats. Cover dough; chill several hours. Roll dough out on lightly floured board or canvas to ¼-inch thickness. Cut with floured 2-inch or 3-inch round cutter. Place on lightly greased cookie sheets, about 2 inches apart. Sprinkle with granulated sugar. Bake at 375° for 10 to 12 minutes. Remove from cookie sheets immediately. Makes approximately 3½ dozen 3-inch cookies or 7 dozen 2-inch cookies.

DATE ROLL-OUTS

- 1 cup shortening
- 1 cup confectioners' (powdered) sugar
- 2 eggs
- 2 teaspoons vanilla
- 2½ cups all-purpose flour
- ½ teaspoon salt
- ½ cup finely chopped walnuts
- ½ cup finely chopped fresh California dates

Cream shortening and sugar. Add eggs and vanilla; beat well. Add flour and salt gradually, mixing well after each addition. Stir in nuts and dates. Roll out ¼ inch thick on lightly floured board. Cut in fancy shapes. Bake on greased baking sheets at 375° for 10 to 12 minutes or until lightly browned. Cool on racks. Makes about 5 dozen small cookies.

FRUIT-FILLED COOKIES

- 2½ cups unsifted all-purpose flour
- 1½ cups sifted confectioners' (powdered) sugar
- ½ cup wheat germ
- ½ teaspoon salt
- ¼ teaspoon nutmeg
- ½ cup butter or margarine
- ½ cup shortening
- 1 egg, beaten
- 1 tablespoon vanilla
- 1 tablespoon lemon juice
- Apricot Filling*

Combine flour, sugar, wheat germ, salt, and nutmeg; mix together. Cut butter or margarine and shortening into dry ingredients with pastry blender until mixture resembles fine meal. Combine egg, vanilla, and lemon juice; stir into wheat germ mixture. Shape into 2 flat patties. Wrap and chill. Roll dough on a lightly floured board to ⅛-inch thickness. Cut in 3-inch rounds with cookie cutter. Spread Apricot Filling on half the cookies to within ⅛ inch of edge. Cut a small hole in center of remaining cookies using a small cookie cutter or knife. Place plain rounds on fruit-topped rounds and press edges together to seal. Place on ungreased baking sheet. Bake at 375° for 12 to 15 minutes, until lightly browned. Makes approximately 16 filled cookies.

*APRICOT FILLING

- 1 cup dried apricots
- 1 cup water
- ½ cup sugar
- 1 tablespoon lemon juice
- Dash salt

Combine apricots and water in saucepan; cover; cook slowly until apricots are tender (about 30 minutes). Mash apricots; add remaining ingredients; cook over low heat until thickened, stirring constantly. Let cool before spreading on cookies. Makes about 1 cup.

JOHNNY APPLESEED'S FILLED COOKIES

- ½ cup soft shortening
- 1 cup sugar
- 2 eggs
- 2 tablespoons cream
- 1 teaspoon vanilla
- 2½ cups sifted all-purpose flour
- ¼ teaspoon baking soda
- ½ teaspoon salt
- Thick apple butter

Mix shortening, sugar, and eggs thoroughly. Stir in cream and vanilla. Stir flour, baking soda, and salt together until thoroughly blended. Stir into egg mixture. Chill at least 1 hour. Heat oven to 400°. Roll dough about ⅛ inch thick on lightly floured pastry cloth or board. Cut rounds with floured cookie cutter 2½ inches in diameter. Place half the rounds on lightly greased baking sheet. Top each with rounded teaspoon of thick apple butter. Make slits in remaining rounds; place these over filled rounds. Press edges together with tines of fork. Bake 8 to 10 minutes. Makes about 2 dozen cookies.

SPICY JAM-FILLED COOKIES

1 cup butter or margarine
¾ cup firmly packed light brown sugar
1 teaspoon vanilla
2¼ cups sifted all-purpose flour
1 teaspoon salt
½ cup raspberry jam
¼ teaspoon cinnamon
⅛ teaspoon nutmeg
1 tablespoon lemon juice
Sugar to taste

Cream butter; add brown sugar gradually; cream until light and fluffy. Add vanilla. Stir in flour and salt; knead until ingredients hold together. Chill until easy to handle. Meanwhile, combine remaining ingredients in saucepan. Boil 5 minutes, stirring often. Chill. Roll cookie dough ¼ inch thick on lightly floured board. Cut equal number of cookies with doughnut cutter and round cookie cutter of same size. Put together with doughnut-shaped cookie on top. Fill centers with jam mixture. Press edges together. Bake at 350° for about 12 minutes or until light brown. Cool. Makes about 1½ dozen.

JAM STRIP CHEESERS

2 cups sifted all-purpose flour
½ teaspoon salt
¾ cup butter or margarine
1½ packages (3-ounce size) cream cheese
Jam or jelly

Mix and sift flour and salt. Cream butter and cream cheese thoroughly. Blend in flour mixture. Roll out on floured pastry cloth or board to ½-inch thickness. Cut into 3 x 1-inch strips. Make a deep groove lengthwise down center of each cookie with handle of knife, keeping ends closed. Place ½ teaspoon jam or jelly in each groove. Place on ungreased baking sheet. Bake at 350° for 15 to 20 minutes, until delicately browned. Makes 2 dozen.

OLD-FASHIONED MOLASSES COOKIES

1 cup shortening
1½ cups molasses
¼ cup sugar
4 cups sifted all-purpose flour
1½ teaspoons salt
2 teaspoons baking soda
2 teaspoons cinnamon
1½ teaspoons ginger
½ teaspoon cloves
1 egg

Melt shortening in saucepan large enough for mixing cookies. Add molasses and sugar; mix well. Sift together flour, salt, baking soda, and spices. Add 1 cup flour mixture to molasses mixture. Beat in egg. Add remaining flour mixture; blend smooth. Chill. Shape into 1½-inch balls. Place 2 inches apart on cookie sheets. Bake at 350° for 15 minutes. Makes about 4 dozen.

SHAPE-A-WAFER COOKIES WITH CREAMY FILLING

½ cup light molasses
½ cup butter or margarine
1 cup sifted all-purpose flour
⅔ cup sugar
1 teaspoon powdered ginger
3½ cups whipped topping
⅓ cup crushed lemon or peppermint candy

Heat molasses to boiling point in saucepan. Add butter. Sift together and stir in flour, sugar, and ginger. Arrange by teaspoons on ungreased cookie sheets, 3 inches apart, to allow for spreading. Bake at 300° for 15 minutes or until cookies are dry on top. Let stand 3 minutes before removing from cookie sheets. Roll baked wafers while still warm* over the handle of a wooden spoon. Combine whipped topping and crushed candy. Fill each roll with small amount of this mixture. Makes about 5 dozen.

*If cookies should become too cool to shape, return to oven for a short time.

GINGER CRACKLES

2 cups sifted all-purpose flour
1 tablespoon powdered ginger
2 teaspoons baking soda
1 teaspoon cinnamon
½ teaspoon salt
¾ cup shortening
1 cup sugar
1 egg, unbeaten
¼ cup molasses
Granulated sugar

Measure flour, ginger, baking soda, cinnamon, and salt into sifter; sift twice; return to sifter. Cream shortening; add sugar gradually, creaming after each addition. Beat in egg and molasses.

Sift dry ingredients over creamed mixture; blend well. Form dough into balls about 1 inch in diameter. Roll in granulated sugar; place 2 inches apart on ungreased cookie sheets. Bake at 350° for 12 to 15 minutes or until tops are slightly rounded, crackly, and lightly browned. Makes about 4 dozen.

TOM THUMB COOKIES

¾ cup shortening
½ cup firmly packed light brown sugar
½ cup peanut butter
½ teaspoon salt
1 egg
1 teaspoon vanilla
1¾ cups sifted all-purpose flour
Jelly for filling

Cream shortening and sugar; blend in peanut butter, salt, egg, vanilla, and flour. Shape into balls about 1 inch in diameter. Make a deep "well" in center of each with the thumb. Bake on ungreased cookie sheet at 350° for 12 to 15 minutes. Cool on racks. Fill centers with tart jelly, such as red currant. Makes about 3 dozen.

MAPLE-PEANUT YUMMIES

1¾ cups sifted all-purpose flour
½ teaspoon baking soda
½ teaspoon salt
¼ teaspoon baking powder
½ cup shortening
½ cup peanut butter
½ cup firmly packed brown sugar
½ cup maple syrup
1 unbeaten egg yolk

Sift together flour, baking soda, salt, and baking powder. Cream together shortening and peanut butter. Gradually add brown sugar, creaming well. Add maple syrup and egg yolk; beat well. Blend in dry ingredients gradually; mix thoroughly. If desired, chill for easier handling. Shape dough into balls, using a rounded teaspoonful for each. Place on ungreased baking sheets; flatten with fork, crisscross-fashion. Bake at 350° for 12 to 15 minutes. Makes about 3½ dozen.

PEANUT BUTTER DROPS

1 cup sifted all-purpose flour
1 teaspoon baking powder

½ teaspoon salt
½ cup shortening
½ cup creamy peanut butter
¾ cup firmly packed light brown sugar
2 eggs
2 cups rolled oats, quick or old-fashioned, uncooked
½ cup semisweet chocolate pieces
½ cup Spanish peanuts

Mix and sift flour, baking powder, and salt. Cream shortening and peanut butter; add sugar while continuing to cream. Add eggs one at a time, beating well after each. Stir in oats and chocolate pieces. Stir in dry ingredients. Shape dough into balls about 1 inch in diameter. Place on greased cookie sheets; flatten balls with palm of hand. Decorate each cookie with a few peanuts. Bake at 350° for 10 to 12 minutes. Makes about 3 dozen.

PEANUT STICKS

¾ cup butter or margarine
½ cup sifted confectioners' (powdered) sugar
¼ cup firmly packed brown sugar
1 teaspoon vanilla
2 cups sifted all-purpose flour
1 cup peanuts, chopped
Frosting of choice and chopped peanuts (optional)

Cream butter or margarine; gradually add confectioners' sugar, brown sugar, and vanilla, creaming well. Add flour gradually; mix well. Stir in 1 cup peanuts. If necessary, chill for easier handling. Shape into sticks 3 inches long and ½ inch in diameter. Place on ungreased baking sheets. Bake at 350° for 15 to 18 minutes or until lightly browned. Cool. If desired, frost and sprinkle with chopped peanuts. Makes about 5 dozen.

BROWNIE-PEANUT COOKIES

1 egg
½ cup chopped peanuts
3 tablespoons peanut butter
1 package brownie mix

Add egg, chopped peanuts, and peanut butter to mix. Blend with hands, adding a few drops of water if necessary. Press and shape into long roll, about 2 inches in diameter. Slice ⅛ inch thick. Bake at 375° for about 5 minutes on ungreased baking sheets. Cool slightly before removing from baking sheets. Makes about 4 dozen.

CHOCOLATE RUM SNOWBALLS

   3 cups (about 8 ounces) finely crushed vanilla
      wafers
   1 cup sifted confectioners' (powdered) sugar
   3 tablespoons cocoa (not instant)
   ¼ teaspoon salt
   1 cup finely chopped pecans
   ½ cup light corn syrup
   ¼ cup rum
   Additional confectioners' (powdered) sugar
   Halved pecans (optional)

Combine crushed wafers and next 3 ingredients. Mix in pecans, corn syrup, and rum, blending well. (Mixture will be stiff.) Dust hands with confectioners' sugar and shape cookie dough into 1-inch balls. Let stand, uncovered, 1 hour. Roll in confectioners' sugar. If desired, press a pecan meat half into top of each ball. For best flavor, store in a tightly covered container 3 days before serving. Makes about 5 dozen.

CRISSCROSS BUTTER COOKIES

   1 cup butter or margarine
   ⅔ cup sugar
   2 egg yolks
   1 teaspoon lemon extract
   2⅔ cups sifted all-purpose flour

Cream butter or margarine; add sugar gradually, beating well. Beat in egg yolks one at a time. Stir in lemon extract and flour, working with a wooden spoon to make a smooth, stiff dough. Shape into ½-inch balls. Place 2 inches apart on ungreased cookie sheet. Flatten each cookie to desired thickness by pressing, crosswise, with lightly floured fork. Bake at 375° for 10 minutes or until pale brown. Remove from sheet; cool on wire rack. Makes about 2 dozen.

BUTTER CRISPS

   1 pound soft butter or margarine
   2 cups flour
   1 cup confectioners' (powdered) sugar
   1 cup cornstarch*

Cream butter. Add flour, confectioners' sugar, and cornstarch slowly while continuing to cream. Divide in 4 portions. Wrap each portion in foil. Chill thoroughly. Shape in 1-inch balls, working quickly with 1 portion of dough at a time, keeping other portions in the refrigerator. Place balls 2 inches apart on ungreased cookie sheet. Flat-

ten with floured tines of fork. Bake at 325° for 18 to 20 minutes or until lightly browned. Makes about 7 dozen.

   *This amount of cornstarch is correct!

LEMON-COCONUT COOKIES

   1 cup shortening
   ½ cup sifted confectioners' (powdered) sugar
   1 teaspoon vanilla
   2 cups sifted all-purpose flour
   ¼ teaspoon salt
   Lemon Filling*
   Flaked coconut

Cream shortening and confectioners' sugar. Add vanilla, flour, and salt; mix well. For each cookie, measure 1 level measuring tablespoon of dough; round into a ball; flatten slightly. Place about 1 inch apart on ungreased baking sheet. Bake 8 to 10 minutes or until edges are lightly browned. Cool. Top each cookie with Lemon Filling; sprinkle with flaked coconut. Makes about 3 dozen.

ANGEL WHISPERS

   1 cup butter or margarine
   ½ cup sifted confectioners' (powdered) sugar
   1 teaspoon lemon extract
   2 cups sifted all-purpose flour
   ¼ teaspoon salt
   Lemon Filling*

Cream butter to consistency of mayonnaise. Add sugar gradually while continuing to cream. Add remaining ingredients except Lemon Filling; blend well. Chill. Measure level teaspoon of dough; round into ball; flatten slightly. Place about 1 inch apart on ungreased baking sheet. Bake at 400° for 8 to 10 minutes or until edges are lightly browned. Put together with Lemon Filling. Makes about 5 dozen double cookies.

*LEMON FILLING

   1 egg, slightly beaten
   Grated peel of 1 lemon
   ⅔ cup sugar
   2 tablespoons lemon juice
   1½ tablespoons soft butter or margarine

Blend all ingredients in top of double boiler. Cook over hot water, stirring constantly, until thick. Chill until firm.

PINEAPPLE MACAROONS

1 can (8 ounces) crushed pineapple
1½ cups sifted all-purpose flour
1 teaspoon baking soda
¾ cup butter or margarine
¾ cup firmly packed brown sugar
¼ cup sugar
1 teaspoon vanilla
2 cups cornflakes
¼ cup finely chopped walnuts
Maraschino cherries, sliced (optional)

Drain pineapple; reserve syrup. Sift flour and baking soda together. Cream butter and sugars until light and fluffy; add flour mixture, vanilla, and 1 tablespoon pineapple syrup. Stir in cornflakes. Shape into balls 1¼ inches in diameter, using round measuring tablespoon as a guide. Place on cookie sheet 2 inches apart and make an indentation in each one with thumb. Fill with drained crushed pineapple. Sprinkle with walnuts. If desired, top with slice of maraschino cherry. Bake at 350° for about 20 minutes. Makes about 2½ dozen.

CHERRY CHIP COOKIES

½ cup butter or margarine, softened
1 package (3 ounces) cream cheese, softened
1 egg
½ cup finely chopped candied cherries
1 teaspoon almond extract
½ cup sugar
1¼ cups sifted all-purpose flour
½ teaspoon salt
½ teaspoon baking powder
¾ cup rolled oats, quick or old-fashioned, uncooked
Candied cherries, sliced (optional)

Beat butter and cream cheese together. Stir in egg, chopped cherries, and almond extract. Mix and sift sugar, flour, salt and baking powder. Add to butter mixture; beat well. Stir in oats; blend thoroughly. Chill; shape mixture into small balls about ¾ inch in diameter. Place on greased cookie sheets; flatten with bottom of glass dipped in flour. If desired, press a slice of candied cherry on top of each cookie. Bake at 375° for 10 to 12 minutes. Makes about 4 dozen.

CHINESE ALMOND COOKIES
(HANG-YEN-BANG)

2½ cups sifted all-purpose flour
¾ cup sugar
¼ teaspoon salt
1 teaspoon baking powder
¾ cup shortening
1 egg, beaten
2 tablespoons water
1 teaspoon almond extract
30 (about) whole almonds (unblanched)
1 egg yolk
1 tablespoon water

Mix and sift flour, sugar, salt, and baking powder. Blend in shortening with pastry blender. Combine egg, 2 tablespoons water, and almond extract; sprinkle on dry mixture; stir with fork until mixture comes away from sides of bowl. Knead smooth; chill 1 hour (no longer). Form into balls about 1 inch in diameter. Flatten to about ⅛-inch thickness. Press almond in center of each. Beat egg yolk and remaining water together; brush over cookies. Place on baking sheet. Bake at 350° for 20 to 25 minutes or until pale golden brown. Makes about 2½ dozen.

CHERUB COINS

¾ cup butter or margarine
1½ cups firmly packed light brown sugar
1 egg, unbeaten
2 cups sifted cake flour
⅛ teaspoon baking soda
½ teaspoon salt
¼ cup finely chopped pecans

Cream butter or margarine and sugar; add egg; mix well. Mix and sift flour, baking soda, and salt; add gradually; mix well after each addition. Stir in chopped pecans. Chill overnight. Shape in tiny balls ½ inch in diameter. Place on greased cookie sheets; flatten slightly with thumb. Bake at 375° for 8 to 10 minutes. Let stand a few minutes before removing from cookie sheets. Makes about 10 dozen.

POLKA-DOT COOKIES

½ cup butter or margarine
1 cup sugar
2 eggs
½ cup flaked coconut
2¼ cups sifted all-purpose flour

1 teaspoon baking powder
¼ pound shelled Brazil nuts

Cream butter or margarine; gradually add sugar and cream well. Beat in eggs one at a time. Stir in coconut. Sift in flour and baking powder; mix well. Form dough on waxed paper into two 8-inch rolls about 1½ inches in diameter. Place Brazil nuts end to end lengthwise on top of each roll. Push into center of dough; pinch dough together and reshape roll. Repeat two more times on either side of each roll. Chill in refrigerator overnight or place in freezer for several hours. When ready to bake, cut in ⅛-inch-thick slices; place on lightly greased baking sheet. Bake at 350° for 10 to 12 minutes. Makes about 8 dozen.

HALLOWEEN MOLASSES-PEANUT COOKIES

    1 cup shortening
    ½ cup sugar
    1 cup molasses
    1 egg
    3½ cups sifted all-purpose flour
    1½ teaspoons baking soda
    1 teaspoon each cinnamon and powdered
        ginger
    1 can (6½ ounces) salted peanuts
    Orange Icing*

Cream together shortening, sugar, molasses, and egg. Sift in flour, baking soda, and spices; mix only until blended. Stir in peanuts. Chill. Form into 1½- or 2-inch balls. Place on ungreased baking sheet. Flatten to ¼-inch thickness by pressing with spatula dipped in sugar. Bake at 375° for 8 minutes. Cool. Decorate with Orange Icing. Store in tightly covered container. Makes 3½ dozen 3-inch cookies or 2½ dozen 4-inch cookies.

*ORANGE ICING

    1 cup sifted confectioners' (powdered) sugar
    4 teaspoons orange juice

Mix together confectioners' sugar and orange juice until smooth. Force through decorating tube to make cat faces and jack-o'-lanterns on cookies.

EASY HOLIDAY COOKIES

    2 cups sifted all-purpose flour
    ¾ teaspoon baking soda

½ teaspoon baking powder
¼ teaspoon salt
½ cup butter or margarine
½ cup peanut butter
½ cup firmly packed brown sugar
½ cup sugar
1 egg
¼ cup orange juice
1 egg white
Coconut, sprills, red hots, tiny candies, and
    colored sugar

Measure flour, baking soda, baking powder, and salt into a sifter. Cream butter and peanut butter with sugars until fluffy; beat in egg. Sift in flour mixture, adding alternately with orange juice and blending well to make a stiff dough. Chill until firm enough to handle. Roll dough into balls about 1 inch in diameter; place 3 inches apart on ungreased cookie sheets; flatten, criss-cross-fashion, with fork. Bake at 375° for 10 to 12 minutes or until golden. Remove from cookie sheets; brush with slightly beaten egg white; sprinkle with coconut, sprills, red hots, tiny candies, and colored sugar; cool completely on wire racks. Makes about 3 dozen.

3-WAY CHRISTMAS COOKIES— BASIC RECIPE

    1 cup butter or margarine
    ½ cup confectioners' (powdered) sugar
    2 teaspoons vanilla
    2 cups sifted all-purpose flour
    ½ teaspoon salt
    1 cup quick-cooking oats, uncooked

Beat butter until creamy; add confectioners' sugar gradually; beat until fluffy. Stir in vanilla, flour, and salt. Blend in oats. (Dough will be quite stiff.) Vary in any of the following ways. Bake on ungreased cookie sheets at 325° for 20 to 25 minutes. Makes 3 to 4 dozen.

Coconut Dreams: Shape dough into balls. Bake as directed. Cool on wire racks. Frost with thin Confectioners' Sugar Icing (page 240); sprinkle lightly with coconut before the frosting dries.

Spicy Tom Thumbs: To half of the dough add ½ teaspoon cinnamon, ¼ teaspoon each ground cloves and nutmeg. Shape dough into balls. Make depression in each with thumb. Bake about 25 minutes as directed. When cool, fill centers with jam or jelly.

Cookie Wreaths: To half of the dough, add ½ square unsweetened chocolate, melted. Shape ropes about 3 inches long; coil into circles. Bake about 25 minutes as directed. Frost; top with coconut; place half a candied cherry in center of each wreath.

CHRISTMAS COOKIES I

½ cup shortening
1 cup sugar
2 well-beaten eggs
2 tablespoons cream
1 tablespoon vanilla
3½ cups sifted cake flour
2 teaspoons baking powder
½ teaspoon salt
Confectioners' (powdered) sugar

Cream shortening and sugar together; beat until light and fluffy. Add eggs, cream, and vanilla; beat well. Mix and sift flour, baking powder, and salt; stir in. Shape into mound; wrap in waxed paper; chill. Roll on board lightly "floured" with confectioners' sugar until dough is about ¼ inch thick. Dip cutter* in sugar each time before cutting cookie, then place cookie on lightly greased baking sheet. Bake at 375° for about 8 minutes or until delicately browned. Decorate as desired. Makes 4 to 5 dozen.

*Use cutters that are shaped like stars, Christmas trees, stockings, etc.

CHRISTMAS COOKIES II

½ cup butter or margarine
1 cup sugar
½ teaspoon vanilla
1 egg, unbeaten
2 cups sifted all-purpose flour
1 teaspoon baking powder
¼ teaspoon salt
Decorations of choice (see below)

Cream butter to consistency of mayonnaise. Add sugar gradually while continuing to cream. Add vanilla and egg; beat until light. Mix and sift flour, baking powder, and salt; blend in. Chill several hours or until firm enough to roll. Roll out about ¼ at a time on lightly floured board or canvas to ⅛-inch thickness. Cut into Christmas shapes. Make a hole with a skewer at top of each cookie so that a ribbon can be put through after baking, if desired. Bake at 325° for 12 to 15 min-

utes. Cool on racks. When cool, decorate with pressurized cake and cookie decorator or frosting put through pastry tube, using Christmas colors. Finish with cinnamon red hots, candy sprills, colored sugar, dragées, tiny gumdrops, striped peppermint drops, leaves and stems cut from green gumdrops, etc. Makes approximately 3½ to 4 dozen assorted cookies.

CHRISTMAS COOKIES III

5 cups sifted all-purpose flour
3 teaspoons baking powder
1 teaspoon salt
1 cup shortening
2 cups sugar
2 eggs
2 teaspoons vanilla
2 tablespoons cream or milk

Sift together flour, baking powder, and salt. Cream shortening and sugar. Add eggs, vanilla, and cream. Stir in flour mixture. Chill thoroughly. Roll out on lightly floured board ¼ inch thick. Cut in desired shapes. Bake on greased cookie sheets at 375° for 10 minutes. Makes 5 to 6 dozen.

CHRISTMAS TREE COOKIES

⅓ cup butter or margarine
⅓ cup sugar
1 egg
⅔ cup honey
½ teaspoon lemon extract
½ cup chopped red maraschino cherries
    (about 20 cherries)
2¾ cups all-purpose flour
1 teaspoon salt
1 teaspoon baking soda
Frosting and decorations of choice

Cream butter and sugar until light and fluffy; beat in egg, honey, lemon extract, and cherries. Mix and sift dry ingredients; stir in. Wrap dough in foil; chill. Roll ¼ inch thick on lightly floured surface. Cut out with Christmas cookie cutters; pierce holes for ribbons so cookies may be hung on Christmas tree. Place on greased cookie sheets. Bake at 350° for 8 to 10 minutes. Cool on racks; frost and decorate as desired. Makes about 5 dozen.

CHAPTER 18

Desserts

YOU ARE now entering a chapter full of heavenly desserts that will end any meal with applause. Here are the things dreams are made of: delicious puddings, cream puffs, tortes, ice creams, and more—tasty treats that will please everyone, adults and children alike.

STEAMED PUMPKIN PUDDING

1¾ cups sifted all-purpose flour
1 teaspoon baking powder
½ teaspoon each salt, baking soda, ground
    cinnamon, ginger, and cloves
½ cup shortening
1 cup firmly packed brown sugar
2 eggs
¼ cup buttermilk
½ cup canned pumpkin

Mix and sift flour, baking powder, salt, baking soda, and spices. Cream shortening and sugar. Add eggs; beat well. Add flour mixture alternately with buttermilk and pumpkin to creamed mixture. Pour into greased 1½-quart mold. Cover mold tightly. Steam 1¾ hours or until wooden pick stuck in center comes out clean. Cool a few minutes; loosen from sides of mold; remove; serve warm. Makes 8 to 10 servings.

ACCOMPANIMENT: Hard sauce (molded into small "pumpkins").

BAKED PUMPKIN WHIP

1½ cans pumpkin
½ cup sugar
½ teaspoon cinnamon
¼ teaspoon nutmeg
8 cooked chestnuts, ground (or save 4 halves
    for garnish, if desired)
4 egg whites
½ teaspoon salt
¼ teaspoon lemon juice

Combine pumpkin, sugar, cinnamon, nutmeg, and ground chestnuts; set aside. Beat egg whites until foamy; add salt and lemon juice; whip until stiff. Fold into pumpkin mixture. Spoon into 4 individual ungreased baking dishes; set in pan of hot water. Bake at 300° for 40 minutes. Makes 4 servings.

QUEEN OF RICE PUDDING

⅓ cup raw regular rice
1 quart milk
½ cup sugar

Few grains salt
3 eggs, separated
½ cup strawberry jam
6 tablespoons sugar

Add rice to milk in top of double boiler; set over medium heat; bring to scalding point. Cook over hot water until rice is tender, stirring often. Add ½ cup sugar and salt; stir until sugar dissolves. Beat egg yolks slightly; pour hot rice mixture slowly on egg yolks; mix well. Pour into greased 1½-quart casserole. Set in pan of hot water; bake at 325° about 1 hour and 15 minutes or until knife inserted near edge comes out clean. Cool. Spread surface with jam. Beat egg whites until stiff; add remaining 6 tablespoons sugar gradually, beating until stiff and glossy. Swirl meringue around rim. Bake at 425° for 3 to 4 minutes, until meringue is gold-tipped. Makes 8 servings.

HEIRLOOM CHOCOLATE RICE PUDDING

¼ cup uncooked regular rice
2 cups milk
½ teaspoon salt
2 eggs, separated
2 tablespoons butter or margarine
½ cup sugar
2 squares unsweetened chocolate, melted
1 teaspoon vanilla
¾ cup seedless raisins
½ cup whipping cream

Soak rice in milk ½ hour in top of double boiler; add salt; cook over hot water until rice is tender, stirring often. Beat egg yolks slightly; add a little of the hot rice mixture to yolks; return to rice mixture in double boiler; cook and stir about 2 minutes. Cream butter and sugar; blend in melted chocolate and vanilla. Stir in raisins. Add to rice mixture; blend well. Whip cream; fold in. Beat egg whites until they form soft peaks; fold in. Turn into buttered 1-quart casserole. Bake at 325° about 20 minutes or until pudding is set. Makes 6 servings.

ACCOMPANIMENT: Plain or whipped cream, if desired.

RICE PUDDING CALIFORNIA

1½ cups cold cooked rice
1½ cups miniature marshmallows
¾ cup halved Tokay grapes, seeded
2 tablespoons grated orange peel
2 tablespoons canned chopped toasted almonds
1 small can (⅔ cup) evaporated milk
2 tablespoons lemon juice
½ cup sifted confectioners' (powdered) sugar
Garnish: whole grapes

Mix rice, marshmallows, grapes, orange peel, and almonds in bowl. Chill evaporated milk in refrigerator tray until soft ice crystals form around edges of tray (15 to 20 minutes). Whip until stiff (about 1 minute). Add lemon juice and whip very stiff (about 2 minutes longer). Beat in confectioners' sugar. Fold whipped evaporated milk into rice mixture. Garnish each serving with whole grapes. Makes 6 servings.

MAPLE RICE PUDDING

2½ cups cold milk
¼ cup maple syrup
¼ teaspoon maple flavoring
1 package (3¾ ounces) instant vanilla pudding mix
2 cups cooked rice
½ cup raisins

Pour milk into large bowl; add maple syrup, flavoring, and instant pudding mix; whip rapidly with rotary beater 30 seconds, until smooth. Combine rice and raisins in ungreased baking dish; pour maple mixture over this mixture; bake at 350° for 25 minutes. Makes 8 servings.

MINCEMEAT BREAD PUDDING

1½ cups canned mincemeat, divided
6 slices day-old bread
2 eggs
¼ cup sugar
¼ teaspoon salt
2 cups milk, scalded
1 tablespoon butter or margarine

Spread ¾ cup mincemeat on 3 slices bread. Top with remaining slices. Cut in cubes. Place in greased 1½-quart casserole. Beat eggs slightly. Add sugar and salt. Gradually add milk, mixing well. Pour into casserole. Dot with butter. Top with remaining mincemeat. Bake at 375° for 35 to 40 minutes or until inserted knife comes out clean. Makes 4 to 6 servings.

ACCOMPANIMENT: Hard sauce if served warm; cream if served cold.

CHOCOLATE-WALNUT BREAD PUDDING

1 package (6 ounces) semisweet chocolate
  ·   pieces
3 cups milk, divided
½ teaspoon salt
3 eggs, slightly beaten
¾ cup sugar
1 teaspoon vanilla
¾ teaspoon cinnamon
8 slices dry bread
½ cup broken walnuts
Garnish (optional): whipped cream

Melt semisweet chocolate pieces in 1 cup milk over medium heat. Stir in remaining 2 cups milk; reserve. Combine remaining ingredients except bread and walnuts; stir in reserved milk mixture. Trim crusts from bread; cut in ½-inch cubes. Pour bread cubes into ungreased 1½-quart casserole. Pour milk-egg mixture over bread cubes, being sure that all cubes are saturated. Scatter walnuts over surface. Set casserole in pan of warm water. Bake at 350° for 1 hour to 1 hour and 15 minutes. Pudding is done when knife inserted in center comes out clean. When cool, garnish with a frill of whipped cream, if desired. Makes 6 to 8 servings.

WEST INDIAN BREAD PUDDING

4 slices thick toasting bread, lightly toasted
3 tablespoons melted butter or margarine
½ cup raisins
1 teaspoon grated lemon peel
4 eggs
2 cups half-and-half or light cream
½ cup light molasses
⅛ teaspoon salt
½ teaspoon nutmeg
Cream, plain or whipped (optional)

Brush both sides of toasted bread with melted butter or margarine. Cut slices in quarters and arrange on bottom of shallow baking dish. Sprinkle bread with raisins and lemon peel. Beat together eggs, half-and-half, molasses, salt, and nutmeg. Pour mixture into baking dish; let stand 5 minutes. Bake at 350° for about 40 minutes or until inserted knife comes out clean. Serve warm or cold topped with plain or whipped cream, if desired. Makes 4 to 6 servings.

CUSTARD CRUMB PUDDING

1 quart milk
2 cups soft bread crumbs
2 eggs, slightly beaten
½ cup sugar
½ teaspoon salt
1 teaspoon vanilla
¼ cup butter or margarine, melted
¼ teaspoon nutmeg

Scald milk; add crumbs. Combine eggs, sugar, and salt in 1½-quart baking dish; mix well. Add milk and crumbs, vanilla, and butter; mix well. Sprinkle with nutmeg. Set in pan of warm water. Bake at 325° for 1 hour and 15 minutes or until knife inserted near edge comes out clean. Chill. Makes 6 servings.

Cinnamon Crunch-Top Pudding: Cut cinnamon-raisin bread in small cubes; add the melted butter and toss with a fork. Add 2 tablespoons of the sugar mixed with ½ teaspoon cinnamon. Place in baking dish; add scalded milk, eggs mixed with remaining sugar and salt, and vanilla. Omit nutmeg. Bake as directed.

Chocolate-Walnut Crumb Pudding: Heat 2 squares unsweetened chocolate with milk and 2 tablespoons butter or margarine over hot water until chocolate is melted; blend well. Add crumbs, ½ cup chopped walnuts, egg mixture, and vanilla. Omit nutmeg. Bake as directed.

Mocha Walnut Pudding: Substitute 2 cups strong coffee and 2 cups light cream for the milk. Add ½ cup chopped walnuts to crumbs. Bake as directed.

Fruit Crumb Pudding: Add ½ cup seedless raisins or snipped pitted dates. Top with flaked coconut, if desired. Bake as directed.

NERO'S WAY

3 tablespoons butter or margarine
½ cup firmly packed brown sugar
¼ teaspoon baking soda
1¾ cups milk
¼ cup Marsala
2 large eggs
½ teaspoon salt
2 cups soft bread crumbs
1½ cups minced walnuts, divided
Whipped cream

Melt butter in skillet; add brown sugar, stirring over low heat to avoid burning. Add baking soda to milk and wine; add gradually to melted sugar. Simmer for 2 to 3 minutes. Remove from heat; cool. Beat eggs; sprinkle with salt; add to the milk-sugar mixture. Butter a 1½-quart baking dish; spread bread crumbs evenly over bottom of dish. Sprinkle with ½ cup minced walnuts. Pour in custard; sprinkle top with ½ cup walnuts. Bake at 350° for 40 to 45 minutes. Serve with whipped cream and remaining walnuts. Makes 6 servings.

DIXIE PUDDING

2 cups milk
1 cup soft bread crumbs
½ cup light cream, divided
½ cup creamy peanut butter
1 egg, beaten
¼ cup sugar
¼ teaspoon salt
1 teaspoon vanilla
Garnish (optional): whipped cream

Scald milk; add bread crumbs; let stand 15 minutes. Add ¼ cup cream slowly to peanut butter; beat smooth. Add remaining cream; beat smooth. Add peanut butter mixture to bread crumb mixture. Combine egg, sugar, salt, and vanilla; mix well; add. Spoon into 6 greased custard cups; set in pan of warm water. Bake at 350° for 1 hour or until knife inserted near edge comes out clean. Chill. Garnish with whipped cream, if desired. Makes 6 servings.

COLONIAL STEAMED PUDDING

½ cup light molasses
1 can (6 ounces) frozen orange juice concentrate, thawed, undiluted
1 cup raisins
1½ cups mixed candied fruit and peels
2 eggs, slightly beaten
1 cup chopped nuts
½ cup (2 ounces) ground suet
¾ cup packaged fine dry bread crumbs
½ cup sifted all-purpose flour
1 teaspoon baking powder
½ teaspoon baking soda
¼ cup sugar
½ teaspoon each salt and cinnamon
¼ teaspoon each allspice and ground cloves
2 tablespoons rum flavoring
Hard Sauce "Apples"*

Blend molasses and orange juice. Add raisins and candied fruit; let stand 1 hour. Combine eggs, nuts, suet, and bread crumbs; stir into molasses mixture. Sift in dry ingredients; mix well. Stir in rum flavoring. Turn into well-greased 2-quart pudding mold with tight-fitting cover or cover with foil and tie securely. Place on rack in deep kettle; pour in boiling water to half the depth of mold. Cover; steam 5 hours, adding more boiling water during steaming if necessary. Serve warm with Hard Sauce "Apples." Makes 12 servings.

*HARD SAUCE "APPLES"

Shape hard sauce to resemble apples. Insert cloves for blossom ends. Cut stems and leaves from angelica; insert in tops. Tint one side of the "apple" with red food coloring.

HOLIDAY STEAMED PUDDING

1¼ cups sifted all-purpose flour
1 teaspoon baking soda
½ teaspoon baking powder
½ teaspoon salt
½ teaspoon cloves
½ teaspoon nutmeg
1 teaspoon cinnamon
⅓ cup diced candied citron
⅓ cup diced candied lemon and orange peel, mixed
⅓ cup candied cherries, sliced
1 cup raisins
1 cup coarsely chopped walnut meats
½ cup shortening
1 cup sugar
¼ cup molasses
2 eggs, well beaten
1 cup drained crushed pineapple
1 cup grated raw carrot
1 cup grated raw potato
Sugar

Mix and sift dry ingredients. Add fruits and walnuts. Cream shortening and sugar until fluffy; add molasses, eggs, and pineapple (mixture will look curdled). Grate carrots and potatoes; add. Stir in flour-fruit mixture; mix until "curdling" disappears. Grease pudding molds; sprinkle with sugar. Fill molds ⅔ full; cover snugly; set on rack in kettle. Pour in boiling water to ⅓ depth of molds. Cover; boil 1 to 3 hours, depending on size of molds. Serve warm. Makes about 12 servings.

CHRISTMAS PLUM PUDDING

1¼ cups seedless raisins
¾ cup dried currants
¾ cup finely chopped mixed candied fruits
½ cup chopped nutmeats
1 cup sifted all-purpose flour, divided
2 eggs, beaten
¾ cup light molasses
¾ cup buttermilk
½ cup finely chopped suet
¼ cup fruit juice
1 cup packaged fine dry bread crumbs
¾ teaspoon baking soda
¼ teaspoon each cloves, allspice, cinnamon,
    nutmeg
¾ teaspoon salt

Combine raisins, currants, candied fruits, nut-meats, and ½ cup flour; mix well. Combine eggs, molasses, buttermilk, suet, and fruit juice. Combine remaining flour, crumbs, baking soda, spices, and salt; add to egg mixture. Add floured fruits and nuts; mix well. Pour into greased 1½-quart mold; cover; set on rack in deep kettle; add boiling water to about 1 inch below cover of mold. Cover. Steam 1½ to 2 hours. Serve warm. Makes 10 to 12 servings.

ACCOMPANIMENT: Hard sauce.

PLUM PUDDING WITH BRANDIED ICE CREAM SAUCE

1 canned plum pudding
1 pint vanilla ice cream
1 tablespoon brandy flavoring
Nutmeg

Heat canned plum pudding according to directions on can. Just before serving break up ice cream with a fork; add brandy flavoring; beat with rotary or electric beater until smooth; turn into chilled serving dish; sprinkle with nutmeg. Serve with heated pudding. Makes 8 servings.

BRAZIL-NUT PLUM PUDDING

¾ cup orange juice
¾ cup seedless raisins
½ pound pitted dates, cut up
½ cup finely cut citron
2 apples, peeled and chopped
1½ tablespoons grated orange peel
3 eggs, slightly beaten
¾ cup molasses

1½ cups ground Brazil nuts
¾ cup (3 ounces) ground suet
1 cup plus 2 tablespoons packaged fine dry
    bread crumbs
¾ cup sifted enriched flour
1½ teaspoons baking powder
¾ teaspoon baking soda
6 tablespoons sugar
¾ teaspoon each salt and cinnamon
¼ teaspoon each allspice and ground cloves

Pour orange juice over raisins, dates, citron, apples, and orange peel; let stand 1 hour. Combine eggs and molasses; stir in Brazil nuts, suet, and bread crumbs. Mix and sift remaining ingredients; sift into egg mixture; blend well. Add fruit mixture; mix well. Turn into greased 2¼-quart pudding mold with tight-fitting cover (or cover with aluminum foil and tie securely). Place on rack in deep kettle; pour in boiling water to half the depth of the mold. Cover; steam 5 hours, adding more boiling water during steaming if necessary. Serve warm. Makes 10 to 12 servings.

ACCOMPANIMENT: Whipped cream or hard sauce.

EGGNOG TAPIOCA

2 eggs, separated
4 tablespoons sugar, divided
2 cups milk
3 tablespoons quick-cooking tapioca
⅛ teaspoon salt
1 teaspoon rum flavoring
Nutmeg

Beat egg yolks; add 2 tablespoons sugar and ½ cup milk. Add tapioca, salt, and remaining milk. Cook over low or medium heat, stirring constantly, until mixture boils (about 5 minutes). (The mixture will be thin.) Remove from heat; cool. Add flavoring. Beat egg whites until foamy; add remaining sugar gradually, beating constantly; fold into tapioca mixture. Pour into serving dish; chill. Sprinkle with nutmeg. Makes 6 servings.

TANGERINE TAPIOCA PARFAIT

¼ cup quick-cooking tapioca
⅓ cup sugar
Few grains salt
2½ cups tangerine juice
1 tablespoon finely cut tangerine peel,
    divided

1 cup whipping cream, divided
1 cup tangerine sections

Combine tapioca, sugar, salt, tangerine juice, and 2 teaspoons peel in saucepan. Let stand 5 minutes. Bring to boil over medium heat, stirring occasionally. Remove from heat; let stand 20 minutes; stir. Chill. Whip ½ cup cream; fold in. In 6 parfait glasses arrange layers of tapioca and tangerine sections. Whip remaining cream; swirl on top. Garnish with remaining peel. Makes 6 servings.

MINCEMEAT CREAM DESSERT

2 cups cold milk
1 cup prepared mincemeat
½ teaspoon lemon juice
1 package instant vanilla pudding mix

Pour milk into large bowl; add mincemeat, lemon juice, and pudding mix; whip rapidly with rotary beater 30 seconds, until smooth. Let stand until set. Chill. Makes 6 servings.

MINCEMEAT-BUTTERSCOTCH PARFAIT

1 package butterscotch pudding mix (instant or regular)
1 cup whipping cream
1 cup mincemeat

Prepare pudding mix as directed on package; chill. Whip cream; fold in mincemeat. Spoon both mixtures alternately into 8 parfait glasses, holding glasses on a slant for diagonal effect. Makes 8 servings.

DOUGHNUT CUSTARD

2 tablespoons butter or margarine
3 eggs
1 quart milk
½ cup sugar
¼ teaspoon salt
¼ teaspoon nutmeg
¼ teaspoon vanilla
4 doughnuts

Melt butter or margarine; cool slightly. Beat eggs slightly; add melted butter. Scald milk; add to eggs with sugar, salt, nutmeg, and vanilla; stir to dissolve sugar; pour into 1½-quart casserole. Slice doughnuts crosswise; float on casserole. Set casserole in pan of hot water. Bake at 350° for 1 hour or until inserted knife comes out clean. Makes 8 servings.

TAFFY CAKE PUDDING

2¼ cups sifted all-purpose flour
¾ cup sugar
1½ teaspoons cinnamon
¾ teaspoon nutmeg
¼ teaspoon salt
½ cup butter or margarine
¾ cup molasses
1 tablespoon instant coffee (dry)
1½ cups water
1 teaspoon baking soda
Cream Cheese Fluff*
Orange Sauce**

Mix and sift flour, sugar, cinnamon, nutmeg and salt; cut in butter or margarine finely with pastry blender or 2 knives. Combine molasses, coffee, water, and baking soda in 1-quart measure or bowl. Press ⅓ of flour mixture (about 1 cup) firmly and evenly into bottom of greased 8-inch square cake pan; spoon in half the molasses mixture; sprinkle in half the remaining flour mixture; spoon in rest of molasses; top with remaining flour mixture. Run fork gently through batter, being careful not to touch bottom flour-crumb layer. Bake at 350° about 1 hour or until top is set. Cut in squares; top with Cream Cheese Fluff and warm Orange Sauce. Serve warm. Makes 9 servings.

*CREAM CHEESE FLUFF

Whip 2 tablespoons milk or cream into 2 packages (3 ounces each) cream cheese until soft and fluffy.

**ORANGE SAUCE

½ cup sugar
1 tablespoon cornstarch
¼ teaspoon salt
1 cup orange juice
1 tablespoon grated orange peel
1 teaspoon lemon juice
1 tablespoon butter or margarine

Combine sugar, cornstarch, and salt in small saucepan. Stir in orange juice. Cook and stir until thick and clear. Stir in remaining ingredients. Serve warm.

OZARK PUDDING

1 egg
¾ cup sugar
2 tablespoons flour
1¼ teaspoons baking powder
⅛ teaspoon salt
½ cup chopped nutmeats
½ cup chopped apples
1 teaspoon vanilla

Beat egg and sugar together until very smooth. Combine flour, baking powder, and salt; stir into egg mixture. Add nutmeats, apples, and vanilla. Bake in greased 8-inch pie pan at 350° for 35 minutes. Makes 4 servings.

ACCOMPANIMENT: Whipped cream or ice cream.

PEACH TRIFLE

4 eggs, separated
½ cup extra-fine (instant) granulated sugar
½ cup sauterne, divided
Juice of 1 lemon
½ cup whipping cream, whipped
1 package ladyfingers
6 large canned peach halves

Beat egg yolks until thick and lemon-colored; beat in sugar gradually. Cook and stir over hot water about 10 minutes. Add ¼ cup sauterne and lemon juice slowly; stir to blend. Remove from heat. Chill. When ready to serve, fold in stiffly beaten egg whites and whipped cream. Line shallow serving bowl with split ladyfingers. Sprinkle with remaining ¼ cup sauterne. Arrange peach halves over ladyfingers. Top with wine custard, almost covering peach halves. Arrange more ladyfingers around rim of bowl. Makes 6 servings.

MARASCHINO TRIFLE

2 cups milk
1 package (3¾ ounces) butterscotch pudding mix
1 package ladyfingers (10 to 12)
Raspberry jam
1 can (8¼ ounces) pineapple tidbits
½ cup chopped walnuts
⅓ cup slivered maraschino cherries
¼ cup sherry
2 tablespoons maraschino cherry juice
Garnish: ½ pint whipping cream, whipped; whole maraschino cherries

Add milk gradually to pudding mix. Cook, stirring constantly, until pudding bubbles and thickens. Remove from heat. Split ladyfingers in half lengthwise. Spread one half of each with raspberry jam; press other half on top, sandwich-fashion. Cut in half; place in 4 to 6 dessert dishes. Drain pineapple tidbits, reserving juice. In a bowl, combine tidbits, walnuts, and maraschino cherries. Combine sherry, maraschino cherry juice, and juice drained from pineapple (about ⅓ cup). Divide fruit-and-nut mixture among the dishes and pour combined juices over all. Pour partially cooled pudding over this in a smooth layer; chill several hours or overnight. Garnish with whipped cream and whole cherries. Makes 4 to 6 servings.

APPLE BROWN BETTY

⅓ cup melted butter or margarine
2 cups soft corn bread crumbs (toasted in recipe)
3 cups pared, sliced tart apples
⅔ cup firmly packed brown sugar
¼ teaspoon salt
1 teaspoon cinnamon
¼ teaspoon nutmeg
2 tablespoons lemon juice
⅓ cup water

Add melted butter to corn bread crumbs; toss with fork to mix thoroughly; toast in skillet over low heat until golden brown. Combine apples, sugar, salt, and spices; mix well. Spread a layer of toasted crumbs in bottom of 1½-quart greased casserole. Add layer of apple mixture. Continue until all ingredients are used, ending with crumbs. Combine lemon juice and water; pour over all. Bake at 350° for 1 hour. Makes 5 to 6 servings.

ACCOMPANIMENT: Plain cream.

RHUBARB BETTY

4 cups thinly sliced rhubarb
2 cups firmly packed light brown sugar
4 cups soft bread crumbs
4 tablespoons butter or margarine
⅓ cup cold water
Cinnamon for top

Butter bottom and sides of a 1½- or 2-quart baking dish. Arrange in it a layer of rhubarb; cover with sugar, then with bread crumbs, and dot with bits of butter. Repeat until you have 3 layers of each. After arranging the third layer of rhubarb and sugar, add the water. Then cover top thickly with bread crumbs, dot with butter, and sprinkle with cinnamon. Bake, covered, at 350° about 30 minutes. Remove cover; if top has not browned, continue baking, uncovered, 10 minutes longer until light brown. Serve hot or cold. Makes 6 servings.

ACCOMPANIMENT: Light cream, custard sauce, or ice cream.

POT DE CRÈME

2 cups light cream
6 ounces grated sweet cooking chocolate
2 tablespoons sugar
6 egg yolks, slightly beaten
1 teaspoon vanilla
Garnish (optional): whipped cream

Combine cream, chocolate, and sugar. Cook and stir over very low heat until chocolate melts and cream is scalded. Remove from heat. Pour a little of the hot mixture on egg yolks; blend; return to remaining hot mixture; add vanilla; mix well. Strain into pot de crème or custard cups. Cover. (If custard cups are used, cover with foil.) Set in pan of warm water. Bake at 300° for 20 minutes. Chill. Top with whipped cream, if desired. Makes 6 servings.

THRIFTY POT DE CRÈME

1 cup evaporated milk, undiluted
2 eggs
⅛ teaspoon salt
1 package (6 ounces) semisweet chocolate pieces
1 teaspoon vanilla

Combine evaporated milk, eggs, and salt in top of double boiler; beat with rotary beater. Add chocolate. Place over boiling water, stirring frequently, until chocolate is melted and mixture is blended smooth (about 6 to 8 minutes). Remove from heat; stir in vanilla. Pour into pot de crème cups or small dessert dishes; chill several hours. Makes 6 servings.

3-WAY DESSERT

CHOCOLATE FLUFF

½ cup semisweet chocolate pieces
3 eggs, separated
1 teaspoon vanilla

Melt chocolate over hot water; add egg yolks one at a time, beating well after each addition. Add vanilla. Beat egg whites stiff but not dry; fold in chocolate mixture. Spoon into 4 sherbet glasses; chill. Makes 4 servings.

ACCOMPANIMENT: Light cream or whipped cream.

CHOCOLATE ROLL

Use above recipe as filling for jelly roll (page 265). Top with whipped cream and finely chopped semisweet chocolate pieces. Makes 8 servings.

CHOCOLATE REFRIGERATOR CAKE

Double Chocolate Fluff recipe. Line a small loaf pan with strips of aluminum foil or waxed paper. Split ladyfingers; place a layer on bottom and around sides of pan. Spoon in Chocolate Fluff. Top with ladyfingers. Chill several hours. Use paper lining to lift out cake; remove paper. Top with whipped cream and chopped semisweet chocolate pieces. Makes 8 servings.

CREAMY CHOCOLATE CELESTE

1 package (8 squares, 1 ounce each) semisweet chocolate
1 square (1 ounce) unsweetened chocolate
2 tablespoons butter or margarine
2 tablespoons strong coffee
Few grains salt
2 eggs, separated
1 tablespoon brandy
2 cups whipping cream
Garnish (optional): whipped cream; shaved chocolate; chopped walnuts

Melt chocolates with the butter over hot, not boiling, water, stirring to blend until smooth. Remove from heat; stir in coffee, salt, egg yolks, and brandy. Cool slightly. Beat egg whites stiff; fold into chocolate mixture slowly but thoroughly. Whip cream until it mounds softly but is not stiff. Fold in until a marbled effect is obtained. Spoon into 8 dessert dishes, mounding high. Chill several hours. If desired, garnish with small swirls of additional whipped cream, shaved chocolate, and a sprinkle of finely chopped walnuts. Makes 8 servings.

FRUITED COFFEE CREAM

½ package (9 ounces) condensed mincemeat
¼ cup cold water
1 cup strong hot coffee
1 cup miniature marshmallows
1 cup whipping cream
Garnish (optional): whipped cream; walnut
    halves

Break mincemeat into pieces. Add cold water. Stir over medium heat until all lumps are thoroughly broken up. Bring to brisk boil; continue boiling for 3 minutes or until mixture is practically dry. Cool. Pour coffee over marshmallows; stir until marshmallows are dissolved. Chill until almost set; beat until frothy. Whip cream; fold in with cooled mincemeat. Spoon into sherbet glasses; chill until firm. Garnish lightly with additional whipped cream and walnut halves, if desired. Makes 6 servings.

BAKED ALASKA

Cake:

½ cup sifted all-purpose flour
6 tablespoons sugar
1 teaspoon baking powder
¼ teaspoon salt
2 tablespoons vegetable oil
2 egg yolks
3 tablespoons water
1 teaspoon vanilla
2 egg whites
⅛ teaspoon cream of tartar

Sift flour, sugar, baking powder, and salt into a mixing bowl. Make a well in the middle and add oil, egg yolks, water, and vanilla; beat until smooth. Beat egg whites and cream of tartar until very stiff. Fold in egg yolk mixture until blended. Turn into 8 x 8 x 2-inch pan; bake at 350° for 25 minutes. Cool; remove from pan. Chill thoroughly.

Topping and Filling:

⅛ teaspoon salt
4 egg whites
1 teaspoon vanilla
½ cup sugar
2 pints strawberry ice cream

Preheat oven to 550°. Add salt to egg whites; beat until stiff; add vanilla. Add sugar gradually; continue beating until very stiff. Remove cake from refrigerator. Top with ice cream. Pile meringue on ice cream and sides of cake. Bake exactly 1 minute. Remove to serving plate. Serve at once. Makes 6 to 8 servings.

ALASKA IGLOOS

Cups:

⅓ cup butter or margarine
2 squares unsweetened chocolate
½ teaspoon salt
½ cup firmly packed brown sugar
⅓ cup sifted all-purpose flour
1 cup rolled oats, quick or old-fashioned,
    uncooked
1 teaspoon vanilla

Melt butter and chocolate in double boiler. Remove from heat. Mix together salt, sugar, flour, and rolled oats; blend into melted butter and chocolate mixture. Add vanilla. Pack into 8 greased large muffin cups, covering the bottom and extending ½ inch up onto the sides. Bake at 375° about 12 minutes. Cool; remove from cups. Place on small baking sheet covered with heavy paper.

Topping and Filling:

¼ teaspoon salt
4 egg whites
½ cup sugar
½ teaspoon vanilla
1 quart ice cream

Add salt to egg whites. Beat until frothy. Add sugar, 1 tablespoon at a time, beating after each addition. Add vanilla; continue beating until meringue stands in peaks. Fill each chocolate cup with generous scoop of ice cream. Spread meringue over top and sides, completely covering ice cream. Place 4 inches below broiler heat for a few seconds to brown meringue. Serve immediately. Makes 8.

PEARS ALASKA

3 ripe Anjou pears
3 egg whites
6 tablespoons sugar
Few grains salt
1 pint ice cream (peppermint, strawberry, or
    vanilla)
Canned slivered blanched almonds

Wash, halve, and core pears. Beat egg whites; gradually add sugar and salt, continuing to beat until meringue will stand in peaks. Place scoop of ice cream on cut side of each pear half. Spread meringue over ice cream and top of pear, covering completely. Sprinkle with almonds. Bake at 450° for 2 to 3 minutes or until meringue has browned. Serve immediately. Makes 6 servings.

FLAMING BAKED ALASKA

¾ cup sifted all-purpose flour
½ teaspoon baking powder
½ teaspoon salt
⅓ cup shortening
2 squares unsweetened chocolate
2 eggs
1 cup sugar
¼ cup chopped walnuts
⅓ cup chopped maraschino cherries, drained (about 15)
3 egg whites
¼ teaspoon cream of tartar
6 tablespoons sugar
1 pint vanilla ice cream

Mix and sift flour, baking powder, and salt. Melt shortening with chocolate over low heat. Beat eggs until thick; gradually beat in 1 cup sugar. Add chocolate mixture; mix well. Add sifted ingredients; mix well. Fold in nuts and cherries. Spread in greased 8-inch square pan. Bake at 350° for 30 to 35 minutes or until done. Cool slightly and turn out in one piece onto cake rack. Cool thoroughly. Beat egg whites and cream of tartar until frothy. Beat in 6 tablespoons sugar, 1 tablespoon at a time, beating until stiff. Place cake on a baking sheet. Slice ice cream; arrange on cake, leaving ½-inch border. Spread meringue over ice cream and cake, being careful to cover completely. Bake at 450° about 5 minutes or until lightly browned. Serve immediately. Makes 6 servings.

To Serve Flaming: Pour a few drops of lemon extract over several sugar cubes. Arrange cubes on Baked Alaska. Ignite cubes with match just before serving.

GOLDEN CARAMEL SHELLS

½ pound packaged caramels (28 caramels)
2 tablespoons water
8 cups ready-to-serve cereal flakes
1 quart peach ice cream
Spicy Blueberry Sauce*

Combine caramels and water in top of double boiler. Heat, stirring frequently, until caramels are melted and mixture smooth. Pour over the cereal flakes in a large bowl; toss until well coated. Divide into 8 portions. Moisten hands slightly with cold water; lightly form each portion into the shape of a shell. Place on lightly greased cookie sheet; let stand until firm. Fill with ice cream. Serve Spicy Blueberry Sauce separately. Makes 8 servings.

*SPICY BLUEBERRY SAUCE

1 cup cultivated blueberries
¼ cup sugar
½ teaspoon cinnamon
⅛ teaspoon nutmeg

Combine blueberries, sugar, cinnamon, and nutmeg. Bring to boiling point; boil 5 minutes, stirring occasionally. Chill. Makes 8 servings.

EASTER DESSERT RING

½ cup sugar
½ teaspoon salt
1 cup light corn syrup
4 teaspoons butter or margarine
5 cups cornflakes
1 cup salted peanuts
3 pints assorted ice cream
Black Magic Sauce*

Combine sugar and salt; add corn syrup slowly, stirring to blend. Stir over low heat until sugar dissolves. Then stir occasionally, cooking to 242° or until a little forms a soft ball when dropped into cold water. Remove from heat; add butter or margarine; pour over mixed cornflakes and peanuts; toss lightly with a fork until well blended. When cool enough to handle, shape in a ring on serving plate. Fill with egg-shaped scoops of assorted ice cream. Serve with Black Magic Sauce. Makes 6 servings.

*BLACK MAGIC SAUCE

2 squares unsweetened chocolate
¾ cup light corn syrup
1 teaspoon vanilla

Melt chocolate over hot water; blend in corn syrup. Add vanilla. Makes about 1 cup.

ORANGE LOVELY

Orange Filling:

    6 egg yolks
    3 tablespoons sugar
    1 can (6 ounces) frozen orange juice
        concentrate, thawed, undiluted
    1 tablespoon grated orange peel
    2 cups whipping cream

Beat egg yolks; add sugar and undiluted orange juice concentrate. Cook over boiling water until thickened, stirring constantly. Add grated orange peel. Remove from heat; chill. Whip cream; fold in orange mixture. Spoon into meringue shell (below). Chill 12 to 24 hours in refrigerator. Makes 12 servings.

Meringue Shell:

    6 egg whites
    ½ teaspoon cream of tartar
    ¼ teaspoon salt
    1½ cups sugar

Beat egg whites until foamy; add cream of tartar and salt. Beat until stiff but not dry. Beat in sugar gradually, beating until very stiff. Cover baking sheet with aluminum foil. Spread layer of meringue in circle about 9 inches in diameter on baking sheet. With tablespoon or pastry tube shape puffs of meringue on top of circle to form a wall for the filling. Bake at 275° for 1 hour. Cool before adding orange filling (above).

SUNDAE IN A PIE SHELL

    9-inch baked or crumb pie shell
    1½ to 2 quarts ice cream
    Fresh fruit or berries, sweetened if necessary
    Chopped nuts
    Whipped cream

Fill pie shell with ice cream, packing firmly and heaping as high as desired. Scatter berries or chopped fresh fruit and nuts over ice cream. Top with deep swirls of whipped cream. Makes 8 servings.

SUGGESTED COMBINATIONS

Ice Cream	Fruit or Berries	Nuts
Pistachio	Raspberries	Pistachio
Coffee	Crushed Pineapple	Almonds
Peach	Strawberries	Cashews
Vanilla	Cantaloupe Balls	Walnuts
Strawberry	Mandarin Oranges	Pecans
Vanilla Fudge	Nectarines	Almonds
Cherry Vanilla	Black Cherries	Walnuts
Butter Pecan	Peaches	Pecans
Burnt Almond	Canned Apricots	Almonds
Chocolate	Preserved Kumquats	Peanuts

ICE CREAM SPONGE RING

    2 eggs, separated
    ⅓ cup sugar
    ⅓ cup sifted cake flour
    Few grains salt
    ⅛ teaspoon cream of tartar
    ½ teaspoon vanilla
    Orange Syrup*
    Ice cream

Beat egg whites stiff; add sugar gradually, beating constantly. Beat yolks until thick and lemon-colored; fold into egg white mixture. Mix and sift flour, salt, and cream of tartar, fold in gradually. Add vanilla. Bake in greased 9-inch ring mold at 350° for 45 minutes. Invert on cake rack; cool; remove from pan. Pour hot Orange Syrup evenly over cake. Fill center with ice cream. Makes 8 servings.

*ORANGE SYRUP

    ⅓ cup sugar
    ⅓ cup orange juice
    1 teaspoon grated orange peel

Combine all ingredients in a saucepan; stir over low heat until sugar dissolves; simmer 3 minutes.

PASTEL MERINGUES

    3 eggs, separated
    ⅛ teaspoon salt
    ¼ teaspoon cream of tartar
    ¾ cup sugar, divided

½ cup quick strawberry-flavor beverage mix
4 tablespoons lemon juice
1½ teaspoons grated lemon peel
1 cup heavy cream, whipped
Garnish (optional): sliced fresh strawberries

In small bowl of electric mixer, beat egg whites on high speed with salt and cream of tartar until stiff peaks form. Combine ½ cup of the sugar and quick strawberry-flavor beverage mix. Add 2 tablespoons at a time, beating well after each addition. Beat until very stiff. Put meringue mixture through star tube in pastry bag to make 6 shells on foil-lined baking sheet. Bake at 250° for 1½ hours. When shells are cool, remove from foil. For the filling, beat the egg yolks in top of double boiler. Stir in remaining ¼ cup sugar, lemon juice and peel. Cook over boiling water, stirring constantly, until thickened. Remove from heat; chill. Fold in whipped cream. Fill meringue shells. Chill 6 to 12 hours. Garnish with fresh strawberry slices, if desired. Makes 6 servings.

COFFEE-RASPBERRY SQUARES

Remove cube partition from double ice cube tray. Spread 1 pint coffee ice cream on bottom of tray. Top with 1 pint raspberry sherbet. Freeze firm. Cut in squares. Serve with fresh or frozen raspberries and whipped cream, if desired. Makes 6 to 8 servings.

FROSTY DESSERT SQUARES

Crumb Crust:

1½ cups crushed crunchy, sweet peanut
    butter cereal
⅓ cup firmly packed brown sugar
⅓ cup butter or margarine, melted
1 quart vanilla ice cream

Combine cereal, brown sugar, and butter. Press half of mixture into ungreased 8-inch square pan. Chill about 1 hour. Set aside remaining crumb mixture for topping. Soften ice cream; spread over crumb crust. Freeze until firm.

Chocolate Layer:

⅓ cup butter or margarine
1 cup sifted confectioners' (powdered) sugar
2 egg yolks
1 square unsweetened chocolate, melted and
    cooled
2 egg whites, stiffly beaten

Beat butter and confectioners' sugar together until creamy. Blend in egg yolks and chocolate. Fold in beaten egg whites. Spread evenly over ice cream layer. Sprinkle with remaining crumb topping. Freeze thoroughly, several hours or overnight. Makes 9 servings.

BONBON ICE CREAM LOAF

1 pint each of 4 different flavors ice cream and
    sherbet
2 quarts chocolate ice cream
½ pint whipping cream
Colored sugar

Chill 9 x 5 x 3-inch loaf pan. With a small ice cream scoop, shape balls of ice cream and sherbet (except chocolate) and place them in freezer trays; chill until very firm. Soften chocolate ice cream; whip until fluffy. Place a layer of ice cream balls in assorted colors in bottom of chilled loaf pan. Fill spaces with whipped chocolate ice cream. Repeat until pan is filled. Freeze several hours or overnight. Invert on platter by applying moist warm cloths to bottom and sides of pan (this takes patience) until ice cream loaf slips out. Return to freezing section until very firm again. Frost top and sides with whipped cream, putting some of it through a pastry tube for garnish. Sprinkle with colored sugar. Keep in freezing compartment until ready to serve. Makes 12 to 16 slices.

FROSTY CHOCOLATE LOG

4 cups puffed rice
½ cup chopped nutmeats
28 large marshmallows
2 squares (1 ounce each) unsweetened
    chocolate
3 tablespoons butter or margarine
1 teaspoon vanilla
1 quart ice cream, any flavor

Heat puffed rice in shallow pan at 350° for 10 minutes. Pour into large greased bowl; stir in chopped nutmeats. Combine marshmallows, chocolate, and butter in top of double boiler. Heat over boiling water until melted, stirring occasionally. Stir in vanilla. Pour marshmallow mixture over cereal and nutmeats, stirring until all kernels are evenly coated. Butter hands and, working quickly, shape mixture around well-greased rolling pin. Chill until firm. Remove rolling pin, being careful not to break chocolate shell. Fill hollow center with ice cream. Freeze until firm. Let stand at room temperature a few minutes, then slice crosswise with sharp knife. Makes 6 to 8 servings.

ICE CREAM SANDWICHES

1 package piecrust mix
2 eggs
½ cup sugar
½ cup light corn syrup
1½ cups milk
1 teaspoon grated lime peel
½ cup light cream
¼ cup lime juice
Green food coloring
2 cups sliced, sweetened strawberries

Prepare piecrust mix as directed on package. Roll out very thin. Cut in 12 squares or oblongs to fit ice cream slices. Prick thoroughly with tines of fork. Bake at 450° for about 10 minutes or until golden brown. Cool. Beat eggs until light and lemon-colored. Add sugar gradually while beating. Add corn syrup, milk, lime peel, cream, and lime juice; mix well. Tint delicate green. Freeze to a firm mush. Turn out into chilled bowl. Beat until light and creamy. Return to tray. Freeze until firm. Cut in slices about 1 inch thick. Put each slice between 2 squares of pastry. Return to freezer trays until needed. Serve with strawberries. Makes 6 sandwiches.

FRUITED ICE CREAM SANDWICHES

3 pints ice cream, any flavor
Packaged sugar wafers
Raspberry-Peach Sauce*

Soften ice cream until spreadable. Spread to a depth of about ¾ inch in bottom of any shallow pan that will fit into freezing compartment of refrigerator. Freeze firm. Shortly before serving time cut in pieces 3 x 2½ inches. Press 4 sugar wafers gently on top of each piece. Invert on aluminum foil. Top each with 4 more sugar wafers; press gently. Return to freezer until ready to serve. Place each sandwich on small plate; top with Raspberry-Peach Sauce. Makes 8 servings.

*RASPBERRY-PEACH SAUCE

1 pint red raspberries
3 ripe peaches
1 jar (3 ounces) Bar Le Duc (optional)
Extra-fine (instant) granulated sugar
Rum flavoring to taste

Wash raspberries gently in ice water; drain. Peel peaches; slice; combine with raspberries and Bar Le Duc. Add sugar and rum flavoring to taste. Chill until ready to serve. Makes 8 servings.

BROWNIE ICE CREAM SANDWICHES

1 package semisweet chocolate pieces
⅓ cup shortening
½ cup sugar
2 eggs
1 teaspoon vanilla
½ cup sifted all-purpose flour
½ teaspoon baking powder
¼ teaspoon salt
1 cup coarsely chopped nuts
1 quart vanilla ice cream

Put semisweet chocolate and shortening in top of double boiler; cook over hot water, stirring occasionally, until chocolate is melted; mix smooth. Remove from heat. Add sugar; mix thoroughly. Add eggs one at a time, beating well after each addition. Stir in vanilla. Mix and sift flour, baking powder, and salt; add to chocolate mixture; mix until blended. Stir in chopped nuts. Turn into a greased 15 x 10 x 1-inch jelly roll pan; spread with spatula. Bake at 375° for 15 minutes. Cool. Cut in oblongs, 2½ x 3¼ inches. Spread ice cream between 2 brownie squares. Freeze firm. Makes 9 sandwiches.

NOTE: If desired, ice cream sandwiches may be freezer-wrapped and kept in freezing compartment of refrigerator for later use.

CHOCOLATE-COOKIE ICE CREAM SANDWICHES

⅔ cup butter or margarine
6 tablespoons sugar
1 egg yolk
½ teaspoon vanilla
1 package (6 ounces) semisweet chocolate pieces
1¾ cups sifted enriched flour
¼ teaspoon baking powder
Vanilla ice cream
Chocolate Sauce (optional; page 223)

Cream butter and sugar; stir in egg yolk and vanilla. Melt semisweet chocolate pieces over hot, not boiling, water. Remove from heat; cool 2 minutes. Stir into creamed mixture. Sift in flour and baking powder; beat until smooth. Put dough into empty 1-pound-4-ounce can from which both ends have been removed. Chill thoroughly. Push dough out of can; slice ¼ inch thick. Place cookies about 1 inch apart on ungreased cookie sheets. Bake at 375° for 10 to 12 minutes. Remove from oven; cool. Put together, sandwich-fashion, with slightly softened vanilla ice cream. Wrap in foil; freeze until ready to use. Serve with Chocolate Sauce, if desired. Makes 18 cookies.

BLUEBERRY TORTE

½ cup butter or margarine
1 cup sugar
3 eggs
¾ cup milk
2 cups fresh blueberries
1½ cups graham cracker crumbs
1 cup all-purpose flour
1 teaspoon baking powder
1 teaspoon baking soda
Sweetened whipped cream

Cream butter; beat in sugar. Beat in eggs one at a time. Stir in milk. Combine blueberries, graham cracker crumbs, flour, baking powder, and baking soda. Add all at once; mix until well blended. Pour into greased and floured 8-inch springform pan. Bake at 375° for 50 to 60 minutes or until cake tests done and top is richly browned. Remove springform rim. Cut in wedges; serve warm or cold topped with sweetened whipped cream. Makes 6 to 8 servings.

STRAWBERRY-WALNUT TORTE

5 eggs, separated
1 cup confectioners' (powdered) sugar
1 cup ground walnuts
7 unsalted soda crackers
2 tablespoons baking powder
Sweetened whipped cream (for filling and topping)
Sliced strawberries (at least 1 cup)
Garnish: whole strawberries

Beat yolks until thick and lemon-colored; gradually beat in confectioners' sugar. Add ground walnuts, crushed crackers, and baking powder

(the amount is correct). The mixture will be very stiff. Fold in beaten egg whites slowly and carefully. Bake at 375° for 15 minutes in three 9-inch layer-cake pans. Remove from pans at once (layers will be thin and very soft). Cool. Fill with sweetened whipped cream and sliced strawberries. Top with whipped cream; garnish with whole berries. Makes 10 servings.

CHOCOLATE MERINGUE TORTE

Meringue:

5 egg whites, at room temperature
¼ teaspoon cream of tartar
¾ cup sugar
½ teaspoon vanilla
1 package (1 cup) semisweet chocolate pieces, chopped

Place egg whites in large bowl; add cream of tartar; beat at high speed of electric mixer until foamy. Beat in sugar, about 1 tablespoon at a time; beat until very stiff. Beat in vanilla; fold in chopped semisweet chocolate. Place four 7-inch circles of greased waxed paper on baking sheet, greased side down. Grease tops well. Spread with meringue. Bake at 200° for 1 hour. Turn off heat; cool in oven about 2 hours. Carefully peel off paper.

Chocolate Filling:

16 large marshmallows
⅓ cup water
⅛ teaspoon salt
3 egg yolks, beaten
1 package (6 ounces) semisweet chocolate pieces
½ cup whipping cream, whipped
1 teaspoon vanilla
½ cup chopped pistachio nuts

Combine marshmallows, water, and salt in medium saucepan. Stir constantly over low heat until marshmallows melt and mixture is smooth. Remove from heat. Stir a small amount of hot mixture into beaten egg yolks, then stir into marshmallow mixture in saucepan. Stir over low heat 1 minute. Remove from heat; stir in semisweet chocolate. Stir until chocolate melts and mixture is smooth. Cool 5 minutes. Fold in whipped cream and vanilla; chill until thick enough to spread. Spread filling on each meringue circle; sprinkle each layer with pistachio nuts. Stack circles. Chill several hours. Makes 8 to 10 servings.

CHOCOLATE CROWN TORTE

½ cup sugar
⅛ teaspoon cream of tartar
4 egg whites
¾ cup finely chopped walnuts
1 package (6 ounces) semisweet chocolate
    pieces
1 small can (⅔ cup) evaporated milk
16 marshmallows (¼ pound)
1 cup whipping cream

Make very stiff, glossy meringue with first 3 ingredients. Reserve about ¼ of meringue for crown. Fold walnuts into remaining meringue. Place three 8-inch waxed-paper circles on ungreased baking sheets. Spread each circle with even layer of walnut meringue. Drop reserved plain meringue from teaspoon or force through pastry tube onto additional waxed paper to form 10 to 12 small meringues. Bake meringues and layers at 300° for 45 minutes. Cool. Peel off paper carefully. Heat semisweet chocolate, evaporated milk, and marshmallows over hot water; stir until smooth. Remove from heat. Chill. Whip cream; fold in. Spread 1 meringue layer almost to edge with ⅓ chocolate mixture. Top with second layer; spread with chocolate; repeat. Place small meringues around edge of top layer. Chill 12 hours. Makes 10 to 12 servings.

ORANGE BLINTZES

Pancakes:

3 eggs
2 egg yolks
½ cup milk
½ cup orange juice
2 tablespoons vegetable oil
1 cup unsifted all-purpose flour
¾ teaspoon salt
1 tablespoon sugar
1 teaspoon grated orange peel

Beat eggs and egg yolks together. Add remaining ingredients; beat until smooth. Let stand at room temperature for at least 1 hour. Lightly brush hot 7- or 8-inch skillet with oil. Add 2 tablespoons batter to skillet; turn and tip skillet so mixture covers bottom evenly. Batter will set immediately into thin lacy pancake. When it browns (in about 15 to 20 seconds), loosen with spatula and flip over. Brown other side (in just a few sec-

onds); turn pancake out onto foil or waxed paper. Repeat with remaining batter. Makes 18 pancakes, or 6 servings of 3 blintzes each.

Filling:

1½ cups creamed cottage cheese
1 teaspoon grated orange peel
1 tablespoon sugar

Combine cottage cheese, orange peel, and sugar. Put a tablespoon of cheese mixture in center of each pancake; fold over ends; roll up.

Sauce:

½ cup softened butter or margarine
½ cup confectioners' (powdered) sugar
1 tablespoon grated orange peel
3 tablespoons orange liqueur
⅓ cup orange juice
1 cup orange sections

Cream butter with confectioners' sugar and orange peel. Gradually blend in orange liqueur. Blend with orange juice in large skillet or chafing dish over direct heat. Cook until bubbly. Add filled blintzes; heat, spooning sauce over. Add orange sections; heat 2 or 3 minutes longer. Makes 6 servings.

WHOLE WHEAT BLINTZES WITH FRESH PLUM SAUCE

2 cups whole wheat flour
2 cups milk
4 eggs, beaten
¼ cup dairy sour cream
½ teaspoon salt
1 pound creamed cottage cheese
2 teaspoons sugar
1 teaspoon grated orange peel
Butter or margarine
Fresh Plum Sauce*
Dairy sour cream

Combine first 5 ingredients; beat until smooth. Let stand ½ hour. Meanwhile, make the filling by combining the next 3 ingredients; blend well; set aside. To make the blintzes, heat a buttered 7-inch skillet over medium heat. Pour ¼ cup of batter into skillet and swirl quickly to cover bottom of pan. When underside is golden brown and top is set, remove to paper towel. Repeat, buttering each time, until all of batter is used. It makes 12 to 14 pancakes. Place equal amounts of filling in center of browned side of each pancake. Fold in ends and roll jelly-roll fashion or shape like envelopes. Melt additional butter in skillet and place a few blintzes folded side down in skillet. Brown on both sides. Serve warm with Plum Sauce and dairy sour cream. Makes 6 to 7 servings of 2 blintzes each.

*FRESH PLUM SAUCE

2 cups water
1½ cups sugar
¼ teaspoon nutmeg
4 cups stoned sliced
    California plums

Combine water, sugar, and nutmeg in heavy saucepan. Bring to boil, stirring until sugar dissolves. Lower heat; simmer, uncovered, about 12 minutes until liquid is somewhat reduced. Add plums; simmer until plums are tender but have not lost their shape (about 10 minutes). Remove from heat; cool to room temperature. Serve with blintzes. Makes about 4 cups.

DESSERT PANCAKES

2¼ cups milk
2 cups pancake mix
2 tablespoons melted butter or margarine
1 egg, beaten
½ cup chopped pecan meats
Mocha Sauce*

Add milk to pancake mix all at once; stir lightly. Fold in melted butter or margarine, egg, and nutmeats. Pour 1 measuring tablespoon of batter for each pancake onto a hot, lightly greased griddle. Bake to a golden brown, turning only once. Serve with Mocha Sauce. Makes 6 to 8 servings.

*MOCHA SAUCE

1 cup sugar
1 cup firmly packed brown sugar
¾ cup strong coffee
2 tablespoons butter or margarine

Combine sugar, brown sugar, and coffee in saucepan. Stir over low heat until sugar dissolves. Bring to boil; cook 5 minutes. Add butter or margarine; mix well. Serve hot. Makes 6 to 8 servings.

SNOW-CAPPED PANCAKES

Cherry Filling:

1 can (1 pound) pitted sour red cherries
⅔ cup cherry juice from can
½ cup sugar
3 tablespoons cornstarch
⅛ teaspoon salt
2 tablespoons butter or margarine
Red food coloring

Drain cherries, saving ⅔ cup of juice; combine juice, sugar, cornstarch, and salt. Heat slowly until smooth and thickened. Add butter and coloring. Stir until butter melts. Add cherries; cool.

Pancakes:

½ teaspoon baking soda
2¼ cups buttermilk
1 egg
2 tablespoons melted shortening
2 cups pancake mix

Dissolve baking soda in buttermilk; add with egg and shortening to pancake mix; mix lightly. Slightly lumpy batter makes light, fluffy pancakes. Pour ¼ cup batter for each pancake onto hot, lightly greased griddle. Bake golden brown, turning once. Cool. When cool, fill with cherry filling; roll up. Wrap in foil; freeze. Freeze extra filling to serve with pancakes later. When ready to serve, unwrap pancakes; place on cookie sheet. Heat at 350° for 10 minutes. Makes 6 servings.

Meringue:

2 egg whites
¼ teaspoon salt
¼ cup sugar
½ teaspoon vanilla

Beat egg whites and salt until frothy. Add sugar slowly, beating until stiff and glossy. Add vanilla. Remove pancakes from oven; top each with meringue; bake about 15 minutes longer. Serve with hot extra cherry filling.

NOTE: If you do not wish to freeze the pancakes, they may be topped with meringue, baked, and served at once.

TROPICAL PANCAKES

1 can (30 ounces) fruit cocktail
2 packages (3 ounces each) cream cheese

1 egg, beaten
2 cups milk
2 cups pancake mix
2 tablespoons melted shortening
1 ripe banana, finely diced

Drain syrup from can of fruit cocktail; save syrup. Cream the cheese until light and fluffy; slowly add 2 tablespoons syrup from can while beating. Fold fruit lightly into cheese. Combine egg and milk; add to pancake mix all at once, stirring lightly. (The batter should be somewhat lumpy.) Fold in melted shortening and banana. Pour ¼ cup batter for each pancake onto hot, lightly greased griddle. Bake golden brown, turning only once. Serve with cheese-fruit sauce. Makes 6 to 8 servings.

SWEDISH PANCAKES WITH CRANBERRIES

2 cups fresh cranberries
1 cup sugar
¾ cup water
2 cups sifted flour
½ teaspoon baking powder
½ teaspoon salt
2 tablespoons sugar
3 eggs, separated
3 cups milk
Confectioners' (powdered) sugar

Chop or grind cranberries coarsely. Combine 1 cup sugar and water; stir until sugar dissolves. Add cranberries; simmer until berries are done and mixture is quite thick. Chill. Mix and sift flour, baking powder, salt, and 2 tablespoons sugar. Beat egg yolks; combine with milk; add to dry ingredients; beat until smooth. Beat egg whites stiff; fold in. Bake quickly in hot greased 7-inch skillet, 1 cake at a time, or in a special griddle (*plett*) containing several small pancake molds. Spread large cakes with cranberry mixture and stack in fours; sprinkle top cake with confectioners' sugar. Cut each stack in 4 wedges to serve. Serve small cakes with cranberry mixture at the side. Makes 8 to 10 servings.

APRICOT-ALMOND PANCAKES

1 cup dried apricots
2 cups water
⅓ cup sugar
½ teaspoon rum flavoring
1 cup milk

1 egg
1 tablespoon vegetable oil
1 cup buttermilk pancake mix
Garnish: ⅓ cup canned toasted slivered
   almonds

Bring apricots and water to boil; cook in uncovered saucepan about 25 minutes. Add sugar and flavoring; stir well; cook 5 minutes longer; cool. Place milk, egg, and oil in shaker or glass jar. Add buttermilk pancake mix; shake vigorously 10 to 15 times or until batter is fairly smooth. Pour 1 measuring tablespoon of batter for each pancake onto hot, lightly greased griddle. Bake to a golden brown, turning once. Makes about 30 pancakes. For each serving, overlap 5 or 6 pancakes. Top with apricot sauce; garnish with toasted almonds. Makes 5 or 6 servings.

PINEAPPLE DESSERT PANCAKES

1 can (20 ounces) crushed pineapple
1 tablespoon cornstarch
3 eggs, beaten
½ cup milk
½ cup pancake mix
Butter
½ pint dairy sour cream
Toasted flaked coconut

Combine pineapple and cornstarch in saucepan. Stir over low heat until thickened. Continue cooking a few minutes; stir occasionally. Set aside; keep warm. Combine beaten eggs and milk. Add pancake mix, stirring until smooth. Place 1 teaspoon butter in frying pan (6-to-7-inch bottom diameter); heat until butter bubbles. Pour in enough batter to coat bottom of pan with thin layer. Bake until delicately browned on underside; turn; bake on other side. To serve, place hot pineapple filling across center of each pancake. Roll up jelly-roll fashion. Top each serving with spoonful of sour cream. Sprinkle with toasted coconut. Makes 6 servings.

APPLE PANCAKE PIE

2 cups pancake mix
¼ teaspoon cinnamon
2 tablespoons sugar
1 cup finely chopped apples
2 cups milk
2 tablespoons melted shortening
Butter
Garnish: crisp bacon slices
Maple-blended syrup

Combine pancake mix and cinnamon. Add sugar to apples; let stand 5 minutes. Add milk to pancake mix; fold in apples; stir in shortening. Bake 1 large pancake (about 8 inches in diameter) at a time on hot greased griddle until golden brown underneath. Turn and bake other side. Keep warm in slow oven while baking remaining pancakes (6 in all). Spread pancakes with butter and stack. Cut in pie-shaped wedges to serve. Garnish with crisp bacon slices. Serve with maple-blended syrup. Makes 6 servings.

CHOCOLATE-CREAM DESSERT PANCAKES

3 eggs, beaten
½ cup milk
½ cup pancake mix
½ teaspoon almond flavoring
Butter
¼ cup sugar
2 teaspoons sifted cocoa (not instant)
1 teaspoon instant coffee (dry)
½ cup chopped nutmeats
1 cup whipping cream, whipped

Combine beaten eggs and milk. Add pancake mix and almond flavoring, stirring until smooth. Place about a teaspoon of butter in 6-inch frying pan; heat until butter bubbles. Pour in enough batter to coat bottom of pan with a thin layer. Bake until delicately browned on underside; turn and bake on other side. Continue until batter is all used. Cool pancakes. Fold sugar, cocoa, instant coffee, and nutmeats into whipped cream. Place a small amount of cream mixture on edge of each pancake. Roll up jelly-roll fashion. Makes 6 servings.

JULY 4TH DOUGHNUTS

¾ cup apricot nectar
¾ cup sherry
1¼ cups sugar
2 teaspoons lemon juice
6 doughnuts (unsugared)
Vanilla ice cream
Garnish: sweetened raspberries

Combine apricot nectar, sherry, and sugar in saucepan. Bring to boil, stirring until sugar is dissolved; simmer 5 minutes. Add lemon juice. Arrange doughnuts in single layer in shallow pan or dish; pour hot syrup over them. Let cool, basting doughnuts frequently with the syrup. To serve, place doughnuts on dessert plates and spoon any syrup remaining in the pan over them. Heap ice cream in center of doughnuts; garnish each serving with sweetened raspberries. Makes 6 servings.

NOTE: Doughnuts may be prepared several hours ahead, except for ice cream and berries.

CREAM PUFFS

These tasty puffs are just as delicious frozen.

½ cup butter or margarine
1 cup boiling water
1 cup sifted all-purpose flour
4 eggs
Sweetened, vanilla-flavored whipped cream
    or Chocolate Filling*
Canned chocolate frosting *or* confectioners'
    (powdered) sugar (optional)

Melt butter or margarine in boiling water in saucepan; bring to boil; lower heat. Add flour all at once, stirring rapidly. Cook and stir until mixture leaves sides of pan and gathers smoothly around spoon. Remove from heat. Add eggs one at a time; beat thoroughly after each. Keep beating until mixture looks satiny and breaks off when spoon is raised. Drop by spoonfuls onto ungreased baking sheet, making 12 large or 18 medium mounds. Bake at 425° for 30 minutes or until puffed, dry, and golden brown. Cool. Cut puffs partway through crosswise. Fill with whipped cream or Chocolate Filling. If desired, frost tops with canned chocolate frosting or sprinkle with confectioners' sugar. Makes 12 large or 18 medium cream puffs.

*CHOCOLATE FILLING

1 package (6 ounces) semisweet chocolate
    pieces
½ cup milk
¼ cup sugar
16 marshmallows (¼ pound)
1 teaspoon vanilla
1 cup whipping cream

Place chocolate pieces, milk, sugar, and marshmallows in top of double boiler. Cook over hot water, stirring constantly, until mixture is smooth. Remove from heat; add vanilla; chill. Whip cream. Fold chocolate mixture into whipped cream. Fill cream puffs.

CREAM PUFF DESSERT

Miniature Cream Puffs*
1 quart vanilla ice cream
1 quart raspberry sherbet
Chocolate Sauce (optional; page 223)

Make and cool Miniature Cream Puffs. Place a layer of puffs in ungreased 10-inch angel food pan with removable bottom. Top with layer of softened ice cream (1 quart). Repeat with layer of puffs, then sherbet, then puffs. Freeze until firm, preferably overnight. Remove from freezer about 15 minutes before serving. Remove from pan by running spatula around the outside edge of mold and around tube; push bottom up and out of the tube pan. With two large spatulas, one on each side of mold, lift from bottom of pan; place on serving plate. Serve in slices, with Chocolate Sauce, if desired. Makes 16 servings.

*MINIATURE CREAM PUFFS

Follow recipe for Cream Puffs (page 352). Drop by scant teaspoons onto ungreased baking sheet. Bake at 425° for about 15 minutes or until puffed, dry, and golden brown. Remove from baking sheet with spatula; cool. Makes about 90 to 100 miniature puffs.

SHERRY CREAM PUFFS

Cream Puffs (page 352)
Sherry Filling*
Chocolate Sauce (page 223)

Make one batch of Cream Puffs; fill with Sherry Filling. Serve with Chocolate Sauce. Makes 12 large or 18 medium cream puffs.

*SHERRY FILLING

½ cup butter or margarine
½ cup all-purpose flour
⅔ cup sugar
Dash of salt
1½ cups milk
2 eggs, slightly beaten
½ cup sherry
1 cup whipping cream, whipped

Melt butter or margarine; stir in flour, sugar, and salt. Add milk; cook, stirring constantly, until mixture boils and thickens. Stir a little hot mixture into slightly beaten eggs; add to mixture in saucepan; cook and stir 1 minute longer. Remove from heat; add sherry. Cool. Fold in whipped cream. Use to fill puff shells.

ÉCLAIRS

Cream Puffs (page 352)
Cream Filling*
Caramel Glaze**

Follow recipe for Cream Puffs. Drop rounded tablespoons about 2 inches apart in rows 6 inches apart on ungreased baking sheets. With small spatula, spread each mound into a rectangle about 4 inches long by 1 inch wide, rounding sides and piling dough on top. Bake as directed for Cream Puffs. Cool on racks. Cut éclairs in half lengthwise and put together with Cream Filling between halves. Spread tops with Caramel Glaze. Makes about 18.

Chocolate Éclairs: Use cooked chocolate pudding mix for filling. Frost with Chocolate Glaze.***

Butterscotch Éclairs: Use cooked butterscotch pudding mix for filling. Frost with either Caramel** or Chocolate Glaze.*** Sprinkle with chopped walnuts.

*CREAM FILLING

1 package vanilla pudding mix (not instant)
1½ cups milk
½ cup whipping cream

Prepare vanilla pudding mix according to package directions, but use 1½ cups milk instead of 2. Cool. Whip the cream; fold in.

**CARAMEL GLAZE

½ pound vanilla caramels
¼ cup water

Put caramels in top of double boiler. Add water. Cook over boiling water, stirring often, until caramels melt and blend with water to make a smooth glaze. Spoon over tops of éclairs and spread thin.

***CHOCOLATE GLAZE

2 squares (1 ounce each) unsweetened chocolate
2 tablespoons butter
2 tablespoons hot water

1 to 1½ cups confectioners' (powdered) sugar
½ teaspoon vanilla

Melt chocolate with butter and hot water. Stir to blend. Stir in confectioners' sugar and vanilla. Beat until smooth. Spread thinly on éclairs.

PARFAIT PERFECTION

In addition to the suggestions below, don't forget other fruits of the summer—strawberries, chopped and sweetened; red currants, sugared; sweet red or black cherries, chopped and sweetened; homemade or canned applesauce, spiced to taste; diced pears combined with melted red currant jelly. And your choice of ice cream or pudding makes for other interesting parfait combinations.

TAPIOCA PUDDING PARFAIT

Arrange in parfait glasses alternate layers of tapioca pudding (made with quick-cooking tapioca), sweetened cultivated blueberries spiced with cinnamon (or blueberries folded into blueberry preserves), and frozen whipped topping. Garnish with a few berries.

PEACHY PARFAIT

Layer in parfait glasses peach ice cream, sweetened fresh red raspberries (or raspberries folded into raspberry preserves), and whipped cream. Garnish with a few berries. (Another suggestion: Peach or lemon ice cream, chopped sweetened peaches or nectarines, and whipped cream.)

VANILLA PUDDING PARFAIT

Spoon into parfait glasses layers of vanilla pudding, thick fudge sauce with finely diced bananas or well-drained crushed pineapple folded into it, and chopped walnuts combined with whipped cream.

COTTAGE PARFAIT

1 cup creamed cottage cheese
1 cup whipping cream, whipped
1 egg white, stiffly beaten
½ teaspoon salt
½ teaspoon almond extract
Crushed fruit (fresh, canned, or frozen)

Beat cottage cheese with rotary egg beater until smooth and fluffy. Fold whipped cream, beaten egg white, salt, and almond extract into cheese; blend well. Place alternate spoonfuls of cheese mixture and fruit in parfait glasses. Chill until ready to serve. Makes 8 servings.

RASPBERRY TAPIOCA PARFAIT

1 egg white
2 tablespoons sugar
1 egg yolk
2 cups milk, divided
3 tablespoons quick-cooking tapioca
3 tablespoons sugar
⅛ teaspoon salt
¼ teaspoon nutmeg
½ teaspoon vanilla
2 teaspoons lemon juice
1 teaspoon grated lemon peel
1 cup whipping cream, whipped
1 cup sweetened fresh raspberries
Garnish (optional): whipped cream

Beat egg white until foamy. Beat in 2 tablespoons sugar, 1 tablespoon at a time; beat until mixture stands in soft peaks. Mix egg yolk with ¼ cup of the milk in saucepan. Add remaining milk, tapioca, sugar, salt, and nutmeg. Stir over medium heat until mixture comes to a boil (5 to 8 minutes). Pour small amount of hot mixture on egg-white meringue; blend. Add remaining mixture quickly, stirring constantly. Add vanilla, lemon juice, and grated lemon peel. Cool, stirring once after 15 to 20 minutes. Fold into whipped cream. Fill parfait glasses with alternate layers of pudding and raspberries. Top with additional whipped cream, if desired. Makes 8 servings.

LEMON TAPIOCA PARFAIT

¼ cup quick-cooking tapioca
¾ cup sugar
¼ teaspoon salt
2¼ cups water
¼ cup lemon juice
2 teaspoons grated lemon peel
½ cup whipping cream
1 cup crushed, sweetened red raspberries
Garnish (optional): whipped cream

Combine tapioca, sugar, salt, and water. Let stand 5 minutes. Bring to a boil over medium heat, stirring occasionally. Remove from heat.

Stir in lemon juice and peel. Cool. Whip cream; fold in. Chill. Spoon tapioca and raspberries alternately into parfait glasses, ending with raspberries. Garnish with whipped cream, if desired. Makes 6 servings.

ORANGE SOUFFLÉ

    2 envelopes unflavored gelatin
    1 cup cold water
    8 eggs, separated
    ½ teaspoon salt
    2 can (6 ounces each) frozen orange juice
        concentrate, thawed, undiluted
    1 cup sugar, divided
    1 cup whipping cream, whipped
    Garnish (optional): orange sections; fresh
        mint

Sprinkle gelatin on cold water in top of double boiler. Beat together egg yolks, salt, 1 can of the orange concentrate, and ¼ cup sugar; stir into gelatin mixture. Set over boiling water. Stir constantly until gelatin is dissolved and mixture thickens slightly (about 6 to 8 minutes). Remove from heat; stir in remaining can of orange concentrate. Chill until mixture mounds slightly when dropped from spoon. Beat egg whites until stiff but not dry. Gradually beat in remaining ¾ cup sugar and continue beating until very stiff. Fold gelatin mixture into egg whites; fold in whipped cream. Turn into 2-quart soufflé dish with 2-inch collar.* Chill until firm. If desired, garnish with orange sections and fresh mint. Makes 12 servings.

*To make collar: Fold foil into 4 thicknesses 3 inches wide and long enough to go around soufflé dish with generous overlap. Attach to dish with sealing tape, leaving 1 inch of foil around dish to make collar 2 inches high. Carefully remove collar to serve.

CHOCOLATE SOUFFLÉ

    3 tablespoons butter or margarine
    ⅓ cup flour
    ⅓ cup sugar
    1 cup light cream
    3 egg yolks, well beaten
    2 squares unsweetened chocolate, melted
    1 teaspoon vanilla
    4 egg whites
    Butter
    Sugar
    Confectioners' (powdered) sugar

Melt 3 tablespoons butter; blend in flour and ⅓ cup sugar; mix well. Add cream; cook and stir over medium heat until thick. Beat in egg yolks; cook 1 minute longer. Cool slightly. Stir in melted chocolate and vanilla. Beat egg whites stiff but not dry; fold in chocolate mixture. Butter a 1½-quart soufflé dish; coat with granulated sugar. Spoon soufflé mixture into prepared dish; set in pan containing 1 inch of hot water. Bake at 350° for about 30 minutes or until firm. Sprinkle top with sifted confectioners' sugar; serve at once. Makes 6 to 8 servings.

ACCOMPANIMENT: Slightly sweetened whipped cream flavored with a dash of your favorite liqueur.

PEACH DUMPLINGS

    3 cups sliced fresh peaches
    2 cups water
    1 cup sugar
    2 tablespoons lemon juice
    1 cup pancake mix
    ¼ cup firmly packed brown sugar
    ¼ teaspoon nutmeg
    ½ cup milk
    2 tablespoons melted shortening

Combine peaches, water, sugar, and lemon juice in 3-quart saucepan. Bring to a boil. Combine remaining ingredients, stirring lightly. Drop batter from tablespoon onto hot peach mixture. Reduce heat; cover tightly; cook 15 minutes without lifting cover. Serve warm. Makes 6 to 8 servings.

ACCOMPANIMENT: Plain cream or peach or vanilla ice cream.

HEIRLOOM STRAWBERRY LOAF

    1 large loaf unsliced white bread
    1 quart fresh strawberries
    ⅓ to ½ cup sugar
    Butter or margarine
    ½ pint whipping cream
    Garnish (optional): whole strawberries

Trim crusts from bread; cut lengthwise in 3 slices. Wash berries in ice water; hull. Place berries in saucepan with sugar. Set over low heat; crush gently. Butter bottom bread layer; top with half the warm berries. Butter middle slice; set in place; top with remaining berries. Set top slice of bread on berries. Cover loaf with foil or plastic wrap. Chill several hours or overnight. Just before serving, whip cream; spread on top and sides of loaf. Garnish with whole strawberries, if desired. Slice crosswise. Makes 8 servings.

STRAWBERRY SHORTCAKE

2 cups biscuit mix
2 tablespoons butter or margarine
1 quart strawberries, sliced and sweetened to taste
Plain or whipped cream

Prepare biscuit mix as directed for shortcake on package. Roll out ½ inch thick on lightly floured board. Cut in 6 rounds with 2½-inch cutter. Place on ungreased baking sheet. Dot with butter. Bake at 450° for 12 to 15 minutes or until golden brown. Split while hot; spread cut surfaces with additional butter or margarine. Put together with strawberries between and on top. Serve with plain or whipped cream. Makes 6 servings.

FROSTY PEACH SHORTCAKE

2 cups sifted all-purpose flour
3 teaspoons baking powder
¾ teaspoon salt
⅓ cup sugar
½ cup butter or margarine
1 egg, beaten
⅓ to ½ cup milk
Melted butter
3 cups peeled, sliced fresh peaches
4 tablespoons sugar
1 quart peach ice cream

Mix and sift flour, baking powder, salt, and ⅓ cup sugar. Cut in butter or margarine with 2 knives or pastry blender. Stir in egg and enough milk to make dough easy to handle. Knead lightly on lightly floured board 10 strokes. Grease an 8 x 8 x 2-inch pan. Pat out half the dough into a square slightly smaller than pan. Transfer to pan; pat out to fit; brush lightly with melted butter. Roll out remaining dough; pat and fit over first layer; brush with milk. Bake at 400° for 15 to 20 minutes. Combine peaches and 4 tablespoons sugar. Spoon half the peaches and ice cream between shortcake layers. Top with remaining peaches and ice cream. To serve, cut in 9 squares.

PEACH BUTTERCRUST SHORTCAKE

1 package piecrust mix
3 tablespoons butter or margarine
Sliced peaches, fresh (sweetened) or frozen
1 cup whipping cream
2 tablespoons sugar (or to taste)
½ teaspoon vanilla (or to taste)

Prepare piecrust mix as directed on package. Roll out very thin on a lightly floured board. Cut in twelve 3-inch squares with knife or pastry wheel. Place on baking sheet. Dot with butter or margarine. Bake at 450° for about 10 minutes or until puffed and golden brown. Put together, sandwich-fashion, with sliced peaches. Whip cream; sweeten to taste with sugar and vanilla; swirl on shortcakes; top with more peaches. Makes 6 servings.

BLUEBERRY-PEACH SHORTCAKE

1 package piecrust mix
1 cup whipping cream
Kirsch
Extra-fine (instant) sugar
1 cup fresh blueberries
1 cup fresh sliced peaches
Garnish (optional): additional fresh blueberries

Prepare piecrust mix as directed on package. Roll out very thin on lightly floured board or canvas. Cut out three 9-inch circles (use a 9-inch layer-cake pan or pie plate as a guide). Place on ungreased baking sheet. Prick each circle with tines of fork. Bake at 425° for 12 to 15 minutes or until golden brown. Cool. Whip cream; fold in kirsch and sugar to taste. Fold in blueberries and peaches. Place one pastry circle on serving dish, top with ⅓ whipped cream mixture and second pastry circle. Spread this circle with ⅓ whipped cream mixture. Top with third pastry circle; frost with remaining whipped cream mixture. Garnish center with a mound of additional berries, if desired. Cut in wedges to serve. Makes 6 servings.

BLUEBERRY–GRAHAM-CRACKER SHORTCAKES

½ pint whipping cream
2 tablespoons sugar
½ teaspoon vanilla
18 sugar-honey graham crackers
Blueberries, fresh (sweetened) or frozen

Whip cream; add sugar and vanilla. Put 3 graham crackers together with whipped cream between and on top. Repeat with remaining graham crackers. Cover; chill 1 hour. Top generously with blueberries. Makes 6 servings.

"GOLD RUSH" PEACH COBBLER

Filling:

2 cans (1 pound 13 ounces each) cling peach slices
⅓ cup firmly packed brown sugar
⅓ cup granulated sugar
2 tablespoons cornstarch
¼ teaspoon each cinnamon and nutmeg
Few grains salt
3 tablespoons cider vinegar
1 cup peach syrup (from cans)
1 tablespoon butter or margarine

Drain peaches, reserving 1 cup syrup; put peaches in shallow baking dish rounded side up. Combine sugars, cornstarch, spices, and salt in saucepan; mix well. Add vinegar, reserved syrup, and butter or margarine. Bring to boil; stir and simmer until thickened and clear (about 5 minutes). Pour over peaches.

Topping:

1 cup sifted all-purpose flour
1 teaspoon baking powder
½ teaspoon salt
2 tablespoons sugar
¼ cup butter or margarine
¼ cup light cream
2 teaspoons grated orange peel
2 tablespoons sugar

Mix and sift the first 4 ingredients; cut in butter or margarine; stir in cream. Pat out about ¼ inch thick; cut in 3-inch squares, then cut each square in halves on the diagonal to make triangles. Place around edge of baking dish of peach filling. Combine peel and remaining sugar; sprinkle on biscuits. Bake at 450° for 15 minutes or until biscuits are golden. Serve warm. Makes 8 servings.

ACCOMPANIMENT: Cream or ice cream.

CRUNCHY PEAR DESSERT

Crust:

½ cup butter or margarine
¼ cup firmly packed brown sugar
1 cup sifted all-purpose flour
½ cup flaked coconut

Combine all ingredients; mix with hands. Spread in oblong pan, 13 x 9½ x 2 inches. Bake at 400° for 15 minutes. Remove from oven; stir with spoon. Press 2 cups of this hot crunch mixture against bottom and sides of 9-inch pie pan, using fork. Cool. Reserve remaining crunch mixture.

Filling and Topping:

½ cup firmly packed brown sugar
⅓ cup all-purpose flour
¼ teaspoon salt
¾ cup pear syrup, from canned pears
¾ cup milk
2 eggs, slightly beaten
2 tablespoons butter or margarine
½ teaspoon vanilla
1 cup whipping cream
¼ cup sugar
1 teaspoon cinnamon
6 canned pear halves, well drained

Combine brown sugar, flour, and salt. Blend in pear syrup and milk until smooth. Cook over medium heat, stirring constantly, until mixture thickens and comes to a boil. Boil 1 minute. Remove from heat. Gradually stir hot mixture into beaten eggs until all is added. Return to heat. Boil 1 minute longer. Blend in butter and vanilla. Pour into crunchy crust. Chill thoroughly. Just before serving, whip cream; spread over top. Mix sugar and cinnamon; dip pear halves in mixture; arrange on whipped cream. Sprinkle reserved crunch over all. Makes 8 servings.

BLUEBERRY TARGET DESSERT

3 packages (6 ounces each) marshmallows
½ cup light cream
1 baker's jelly roll
3 egg whites
2 cups cultivated blueberries, washed and well drained
Garnish (optional): additional blueberries

Place marshmallows and cream in saucepan. Cook over low heat until marshmallows are melted. Cool. Cut jelly roll in 6 slices about ½ inch thick. Line the sides of a 9-inch springform pan with jelly roll slices. Beat egg whites until stiff; fold into cooled marshmallow mixture. Fold in blueberries. Pour carefully into pan. Chill until firm; remove from pan. Garnish with additional blueberries, if desired. Makes 12 servings.

GINGER DATE ROLL

1½ cups fine gingersnap crumbs
¾ cup finely cut pitted dates
¼ pound marshmallows, cut fine
1 cup broken walnut meats
¼ cup strong coffee
Golden Sauce*

Reserve ½ cup gingersnap crumbs. Combine remaining 1 cup crumbs with dates, marshmallows, walnuts, and coffee; mix well. Form into a roll about 3 inches in diameter; cover with reserved crumbs. Wrap in waxed paper or aluminum foil; chill several hours. Slice crosswise in pieces about 1 inch thick. Serve with Golden Sauce. Makes 8 slices.

*GOLDEN SAUCE

1 cup sugar
⅓ cup water
2 egg yolks
2 tablespoons vanilla**
1 cup whipping cream

Boil sugar and water to 238° (or until syrup forms "threads") in a small saucepan. Meanwhile, beat egg yolks until thick and light. Pour syrup slowly on yolks while continuing to beat. Continue beating until creamy; chill. Add vanilla. Whip cream; fold in. Makes 8 to 10 servings.

**This may seem a lot, but it is correct.

TROPICAL DATE ROLL

2 cans (1 pound each) date-nut roll
1 cup whipping cream, divided
2 tablespoons sugar, divided
1 teaspoon grated orange peel, divided
½ teaspoon rum flavoring, divided
Flaked coconut
Garnish: maraschino cherries

Cut each date-nut roll in 8 slices. Whip ½ cup cream; blend in 1 tablespoon sugar, ½ teaspoon orange peel, and ¼ teaspoon rum flavoring. Spread slices with whipped cream; put together to form 1 long roll. Hold in place with wooden picks. Wrap in aluminum foil. Chill 3 or 4 hours. Just before serving remove picks; whip remaining cream; add remaining sugar, orange peel, and flavoring; frost top and sides of roll. Sprinkle generously with coconut. Garnish with maraschino cherries. Slice diagonally. Makes 8 to 10 servings.

BANANA RUM FRITTERS

6 firm bananas
½ cup rum
½ cup orange juice
3 egg whites, slightly beaten
2 tablespoons cornstarch
2 tablespoons flour
¼ cup butter or margarine
¼ cup sugar

Peel bananas; cut in half lengthwise and then in half again. Place in shallow dish. Pour rum and orange juice over bananas. Let stand for ½ hour. In small bowl mix egg whites, cornstarch, and flour. Heat butter in large skillet. Dip bananas in cornstarch mixture; arrange in skillet. Brown on all sides. Remove to serving platter. Pour rum marinade into skillet; add sugar; stir over high heat until sugar dissolves. Pour over bananas. Makes 6 servings.

PINEAPPLE FRITTERS

1 cup sifted all-purpose flour
1½ teaspoons baking powder
¼ teaspoon salt
3 tablespoons confectioners' (powdered) sugar
1 egg, slightly beaten
⅓ cup milk
2 teaspoons vegetable oil or melted shortening
1 can (20 ounces) pineapple chunks
Vegetable oil for frying
Pineapple-Coconut Sauce (page 225)

Mix and sift first 4 ingredients. Combine egg, milk, and oil or shortening; add gradually to dry ingredients, stirring, to make a stiff batter. Drain pineapple chunks (save syrup for sauce). Pour additional oil into skillet to a depth of about 1 inch; heat to 375°. Coat each pineapple chunk with batter; fry until golden brown, turning once. Drain on absorbent paper. Serve hot with Pineapple-Coconut Sauce. Makes 6 servings.

FRUIT BETTY, BRAZIL

1 can (1 pound) fruit cocktail
¼ cup sugar
3 tablespoons flour
¼ teaspoon salt
½ teaspoon cinnamon
¼ teaspoon nutmeg
3 tablespoons butter or margarine

¾ cup chopped Brazil nuts
1 tablespoon grated orange peel
Cream

Pour fruit cocktail into 8-inch square cake pan. Mix and sift sugar, flour, salt, and spices. Cut in butter or margarine with 2 knives or pastry blender until mixture resembles coarse meal. Mix in Brazil nuts and orange peel. Sprinkle over fruit. Bake at 375° for 30 minutes. Serve warm with cream. Makes 6 servings.

CHERRY FLOATING ISLAND

½ cup sugar, divided
2 teaspoons cornstarch
¼ teaspoon salt
2 cups milk
2 eggs, separated
1 teaspoon vanilla
Few grains nutmeg
2 bananas, sliced
2 cups drained pitted canned black cherries
Few grains salt

Mix ¼ cup sugar, cornstarch, and ¼ teaspoon salt. Add milk gradually. Cook over hot water, stirring constantly, until slightly thickened. Beat egg yolks; add hot milk mixture. Return to double boiler; cook, stirring constantly, until mixture coats spoon. Cool. Add vanilla and nutmeg. Chill. Place fruits in serving dish; add custard. Meanwhile, beat egg whites stiff but not dry. Add remaining ¼ cup sugar and a few grains salt gradually while beating. Heap 6 mounds of meringue in shallow dish; set in shallow pan of warm water. Bake at 325° for 20 minutes or until golden brown. Cool. Transfer to top of custard. Makes 6 servings.

FIG MERINGUES MELBA

8 fig bars
Syrup drained from canned peaches
8 canned peach halves
1 egg white
Few grains salt
½ teaspoon almond flavoring
3 tablespoons sugar

Crumble fig bars; add ⅓ cup peach syrup and let stand 10 minutes. Fill peach halves with this mixture. Beat egg white with salt until stiff but not dry; gradually beat in the almond flavoring and sugar; swirl on peaches. Place peaches on heatproof platter; pour remaining syrup around them. Bake at 350° for 15 to 20 minutes or until meringue is golden brown. Makes 8 servings.

BAKED APPLE SURPRISE

1 package lemon-flavor pudding and pie
    filling mix (not instant)
6 large baking apples
Sugar
1 egg white
2 tablespoons sugar

Prepare lemon-flavor mix as directed on package for pie filling. Chill until firm. Core apples almost through to blossom end, making cavities larger than usual. Pare about ⅓ of the way down from stem end. Place in baking pan. Add enough boiling water to cover bottom of pan. Cover pan (use foil if you do not have a cover to fit). Bake at 350° for about 20 minutes. Remove cover. Sprinkle tops of apples and cavities lightly with sugar. Bake 20 to 25 minutes longer, uncovered, or until apples are tender. Remove from pan. Chill. Fill centers with lemon mixture. Beat egg white until stiff but not dry. Add 2 tablespoons sugar gradually while beating until meringue will stand in stiff peaks. Place spoonful of meringue on each apple. Run under broiler for a few seconds to brown meringue. Makes 6 servings.

NOTE: Serve any remaining lemon mixture with the apples to those who would like a little more. Or use it for tart filling for filled cookies.

STRAWBERRIES IN THE SNOW

1 quart strawberries
Extra-fine (instant) granulated sugar
3 cups milk
2 tablespoons sugar
6 eggs, separated
Few grains salt
⅔ cup extra-fine (instant) granulated sugar
Garnish: 6 whole strawberries

Wash strawberries in ice water; hull; slice, reserving 6 whole berries for garnish. Spread sliced strawberries in bottom of shallow serving dish; sprinkle with a little extra-fine (instant) sugar; chill. Scald milk with 2 tablespoons sugar in top of double boiler over direct low heat. Beat 6 egg yolks slightly; add a little scalded milk; add to remaining scalded milk. Cook over hot, not boiling, water, stirring until mixture coats spoon. Chill. Beat 4 egg whites to a froth; add salt; beat until stiff. Add ⅔ cup extra-fine (instant) sugar gradually, continuing to beat until very stiff and glossy. Drop by tablespoons into barely simmering water, making 6 mounds. Cook exactly 2 minutes. Turn carefully; cook 2 minutes longer. Remove with slotted spoon to foil-lined tray. Cool. Spoon chilled custard sauce over sliced strawberries; top with meringues. Garnish with whole strawberries. Makes 6 servings.

NOTE: Make extra meringues with the 2 leftover egg whites, using ⅓ cup extra-fine (instant) sugar, or store the egg whites, tightly covered, in the refrigerator to use later in making cake, frosting, fruit whips, glazes, etc.

CRANBERRY CUSTARDS

2 cans (1 pound each) whole-berry cranberry sauce
4 large eggs, lightly beaten
1 cup coconut milk
2 tablespoons cornstarch
1 tablespoon dark rum

Drain cranberry sauce; reserve the liquid. Combine drained sauce with eggs. Scald coconut milk; stir a little at a time into egg-and-cranberry mixture. Pour into 6 custard cups. Set custard cups in a pan of water; bake at 350° for 45 minutes or until a wooden pick inserted in custard comes out clean. Dissolve cornstarch in a little of the reserved cranberry juice. Combine with remaining juice in small saucepan. Cook, stirring constantly with a wooden spoon, until thickened. Stir in rum. Serve warm or cold with the custards. Makes 6 servings.

YANKEE DOODLE APPLE DESSERT

½ cup sifted cake flour
¾ cup firmly packed light brown sugar
1 teaspoon baking powder
¼ teaspoon salt
Dash of mace
Dash of cinnamon
1 egg
½ teaspoon vanilla
1 cup chopped tart apples
½ cup chopped walnuts
Garnish: whipped cream sprinkled with cinnamon *or* vanilla ice cream

Mix and sift first 6 ingredients. Stir in unbeaten egg and vanilla. Fold in apples and walnuts.

Turn into well-greased 8-inch pie pan. Bake at 350° for 25 to 30 minutes or until brown and crusty. Garnish with whipped cream sprinkled with cinnamon or top with small scoops of vanilla ice cream. Makes 6 servings.

BAKED APPLES CANTONESE

6 large baking apples
1 cup coarsely chopped walnuts
½ cup chopped pitted dates
⅓ cup chopped candied ginger
1 cup light corn syrup
1 teaspoon powdered ginger
Red food coloring
Sugar

Core apples almost through. Pare about ⅓ of the way down from stem end. Combine walnuts, dates, and candied ginger. Fill centers of apples. Combine corn syrup and powdered ginger. Tint red with food coloring; simmer 5 minutes. Brush apples thickly with this mixture. Place apples in baking dish; add enough boiling water to cover bottom of baking dish. Bake at 350° about 40 minutes or until tender, basting frequently with syrup. Remove from oven. Sprinkle with sugar. Broil with surface of apples 4 inches below source of heat, basting with remaining syrup and sprinkling with additional sugar until glazed (about 15 minutes). Makes 6 servings.

BAKED APPLES GRENADA

4 large baking apples
Grenadine syrup
½ cup whipping cream
2 tablespoons orange marmalade
Nutmeg

Core apples, being careful not to cut through blossom end. Pare about ⅓ of the way from stem to blossom end. Fill centers with grenadine syrup and brush cut surfaces with this syrup also. Place apples in baking dish; add hot water to a depth of about ½ inch; cover. Bake at 350° about 45 minutes or until apples are tender, brushing cut surface once or twice with grenadine during this time. Chill. When ready to serve, whip cream; fold in orange marmalade; fill centers of apples; sprinkle lightly with nutmeg. Makes 4 servings.

PEARS IN CHOCOLATE SAUCE

6 large winter pears
3 cups water
1¼ cups sugar, divided
1 piece lemon peel
1 stick cinnamon (2 inches)
3 squares (1 ounce each) semisweet chocolate
¾ cup coffee, divided
8 egg yolks, slightly beaten
2 tablespoons cognac (optional)
1 cup whipped cream*

Peel the pears, leaving 1 inch around stem. Leave the pears whole. Combine water, 1 cup sugar, lemon peel, and cinnamon stick. Stir over low heat until sugar is dissolved. Add pears; poach them, covered, over low heat until tender. (The cooking time varies a great deal, depending on the ripeness of the fruit.) Remove from heat. Let pears and liquid cool completely. Refrigerate, undrained, until serving time. Just before serving, make the sauce. Combine chocolate and 2 tablespoons coffee. Cook over low heat, stirring often, until chocolate is completely melted and smooth. Combine ¼ cup sugar and egg yolks. Add to chocolate mixture. Add remaining coffee. Whisk over simmering water until mixture is creamy and thick. Do not let it come to a boil or the sauce will curdle. Remove from heat; add cognac, if desired. Drain pears. Place in serving dish and pour warm sauce over them. Serve whipped cream on the side or pipe around pears. Makes 6 servings.

*If desired, garnish with 1 cup whipped cream sweetened with 2 tablespoons extra-fine granulated sugar, and 2 tablespoons cognac.

CRANBERRY CREAM

¼ pound marshmallows
1 can (16 ounces) whole cranberry sauce
1 cup drained crushed pineapple
2 tablespoons lemon juice
⅛ teaspoon salt
1 cup whipping cream, whipped

Snip marshmallows in small pieces; combine with cranberry sauce, pineapple, lemon juice, and salt. Fold in the whipped cream; chill thoroughly. Makes 6 servings.

OLYMPIAN ORANGES

6 large seedless oranges
2 cups sugar
1 cup water
¼ cup light corn syrup
Yellow food coloring
Red food coloring
¼ cup slivered orange peel
1 teaspoon orange extract
Flaked coconut

Remove a thin layer of peel from one orange, being careful not to cut into the white layer. Cut this thin peel into ¼ cup of slivers for the syrup. Now remove peel from all oranges, cutting deep enough to remove every bit of the white membrane. Leave oranges whole. Combine sugar, water, and corn syrup; boil to 228° on candy thermometer or until thick. Tint deep orange with yellow and red food coloring. Stir in slivered peel and orange extract. Dip oranges in syrup; remove to shallow pan. Keep basting with syrup at intervals until oranges are well glazed. Chill thoroughly, basting often. Place each orange in shallow fruit saucer; surround with syrup. Top with flaked coconut. Serve with fruit knives (or any small sharp knives) and dessert forks. Makes 6 servings.

PEACHES AND CREAM

6 to 8 fresh peaches
¼ cup lemon juice
¼ cup kirsch
½ cup sugar
2 cups fresh blueberries
1 cup whipping cream
1½ teaspoons (½ envelope) unflavored gelatin
¼ cup cold water
1 cup dairy sour cream
2 tablespoons brandy
Garnish (optional): sprigs of mint

Peel and slice peaches; toss with lemon juice; add kirsch. Sprinkle with ½ cup of sugar. Wash blueberries in ice water; add to peaches; toss gently; chill. Heat cream until bubbles form around rim (do not let it boil). Soften gelatin in cold water; add to cream; stir until dissolved. Blend in sour cream and brandy; whisk thoroughly; chill 3 to 4 hours. When ready to serve, whisk vigorously until mixture attains consistency of thick sour cream. Garnish fruits with mint, if available, and serve cream mixture separately. Makes 6 to 8 servings.

MINTED PEACHES

1 can (29 ounces) cling peach halves
¼ cup granulated sugar
2 tablespoons lemon juice
⅓ cup orange juice
1 tablespoon chopped fresh mint leaves *or*
few drops mint extract

Drain peaches, reserving syrup. Combine syrup and sugar; boil 2 minutes. Remove from heat; add fruit juices and mint. Cover; let stand until cool. Strain over peach halves. Chill. Makes 4 to 6 servings.

PINEAPPLE-WALNUT DESSERT

2 cups vanilla wafer crumbs
1 cup butter or margarine
1 cup extra-fine (instant) granulated sugar
2 eggs
2 teaspoons vanilla
2 cups well-drained crushed pineapple
1 cup finely chopped walnuts
Garnish (optional): whipped cream;
maraschino cherries

Reserve 2 tablespoons crumbs. Cream butter to consistency of mayonnaise; add sugar gradually while continuing to cream. Add eggs one at a time, beating well after each addition. Add vanilla; mix well. Combine pineapple and walnuts; stir in until well mixed. Line a loaf pan, 8 x 5 x 3 inches, with aluminum foil, leaving overhang so loaf can be lifted out easily. Press ½ cup crumbs on bottom of pan. Add about ¼ pineapple mixture, spreading evenly. Repeat until crumbs and pineapple mixture are used up, ending with latter. Scatter reserved crumbs on top. Chill 24 hours or longer (or freeze). Garnish with whipped cream and maraschino cherries, if desired. Slice to serve. Makes 10 to 12 servings.

RHUBARB-BANANA DESSERT

Cook fresh or frozen rhubarb; sweeten to taste. While rhubarb is still warm, add sliced bananas (3 bananas to 4 cups cooked rhubarb). Chill. Serve with cream, if desired.

CANTALOUPE À LA MODE WITH BLUEBERRY SAUCE

½ cup sugar
½ cup water
⅛ teaspoon salt
1 tablespoon cornstarch
1 cup cultivated blueberries
1 teaspoon grated lemon peel
1 tablespoon lemon juice
3 small cantaloupes
1 quart vanilla ice cream

Combine sugar, water, salt, and cornstarch. Cook, stirring frequently, until mixture boils and is thickened. Add blueberries; heat to boiling; simmer 5 minutes. Stir in lemon peel and juice. Let sauce cool slightly. Cut cantaloupes in halves. Scoop out seeds. Spoon vanilla ice cream into cantaloupe halves; top with warm blueberry sauce; serve immediately. Makes 6 servings.

PEACH MELBA

1 quart vanilla ice cream
12 small canned cling peach halves
Melba Sauce*

Place a scoop of ice cream in each of 6 deep dessert dishes. Arrange a peach half on either side of ice cream. Pour Melba Sauce over all. Makes 6 servings.

*MELBA SAUCE

1 package (10 ounces) frozen red raspberries,
thawed
⅔ cup sugar
⅛ teaspoon cream of tartar

Press raspberries through very fine sieve into small saucepan. Stir sugar and cream of tartar into purée. Heat quickly to boiling point. Boil 3 minutes, stirring constantly. Cover. Chill thoroughly. (Sauce will thicken as it chills.) Makes 6 servings.

LEMON CREAM WITH APRICOT SAUCE

1 envelope unflavored gelatin
⅔ cup sugar, divided
¼ teaspoon salt
2 eggs, separated
6 tablespoons cold water
6 tablespoons lemon juice
2 teaspoons grated lemon peel

1 cup whipping cream
Apricot Sauce*
Garnish (optional): apricot halves

Combine gelatin, ⅓ cup sugar, and salt in saucepan. Beat egg yolks, then beat in water and lemon juice, and add to gelatin mixture. Mix well. Cook over low heat, stirring constantly, until gelatin dissolves and mixture thickens slightly (about 5 minutes). Remove from heat; add lemon peel. Chill, stirring occasionally, until mixture mounds slightly when dropped from a spoon. Beat egg whites stiff but not dry. Add remaining ⅓ cup sugar gradually and beat until very stiff. Fold into gelatin mixture. Whip cream; fold in. Turn into ungreased 4-cup mold or serving bowl. Chill until firm; unmold; serve with Apricot Sauce. Garnish with apricot halves, if desired. Makes 6 servings.

NOTE: Lemon Cream mixture may be turned into 9-inch baked pie shell or crumb crust. Garnish with apricot halves and sprigs of mint.

*APRICOT SAUCE

Drain 1 can (1 pound) apricot halves. Purée drained halves with ¼ cup apricot syrup in electric blender or press through strainer. Chill. Makes 1 cup sauce.

HONEY-PECAN BAVARIAN

  2 packages (3 ounces each) mixed-fruit–flavor
    gelatin
½ teaspoon salt
2 cups boiling water
1 cup cold water
4 teaspoons lemon juice
⅔ cup honey
⅔ cup whipping cream
⅔ cup chopped pecans
Garnish (optional): pecan-stuffed dates

Dissolve gelatin and salt in boiling water. Add cold water, lemon juice, and honey. Pour about 1 cup into 6-cup mold; chill until set. Chill remaining gelatin mixture until syrupy. Whip cream until thick and shiny but not stiff; fold in. Fold in pecans. Spoon into mold on top of clear gelatin. Chill until firm. Unmold. Garnish with pecan-stuffed dates, if desired. Makes 8 servings.

MAYFLOWER CHARLOTTE

1 envelope unflavored gelatin
1¼ cups orange juice, divided
⅔ cup sugar
1 tablespoon flour
¼ teaspoon salt
1 tablespoon grated orange peel
2 tablespoons lime juice
⅔ cup *icy-cold* evaporated milk, whipped
½ cup flaked coconut, toasted
1 cup orange sections
Strawberries

Sprinkle gelatin on ¾ cup orange juice in saucepan to soften. Blend together sugar, flour, and salt. Add to softened gelatin; mix thoroughly. Stir over medium heat until gelatin is dissolved and mixture is thickened. Remove from heat; add orange peel, remaining ½ cup orange juice, and lime juice. Chill until mixture is slightly thicker than unbeaten egg white. Fold into whipped evaporated milk. Turn into 1½-quart serving dish; chill until firm. When ready to serve, mound coconut in center. Arrange orange sections, flower-fashion, around edge of serving dish, using whole strawberries for center of "flowers." Makes 8 servings.

STRAWBERRY FESTIVAL DESSERT

1 envelope unflavored gelatin
½ cup sugar, divided
⅛ teaspoon salt
2 eggs, separated
1¼ cups milk
1 teaspoon vanilla
1 cup whipping cream, whipped
1 pint strawberries
Strawberry Sauce*

Combine gelatin, ¼ cup sugar, and salt in saucepan. Beat egg yolks and milk together; add to gelatin mixture. Stir constantly over low heat until gelatin is dissolved (about 6 minutes). Remove from heat; add vanilla. Chill until mixture mounds slightly when dropped from spoon. Beat egg whites until stiff but not dry. Beat in remaining ¼ cup sugar gradually; beat until very stiff. Fold into gelatin mixture; fold in whipped cream. Turn ⅓ of the gelatin mixture into serving dish. Slice ⅔ of the strawberries; save remainder for garnish. Alternate layers of gelatin mixture and sliced berries. Garnish with whole berries.

Chill until firm. Serve with Strawberry Sauce. Makes 6 servings.

*STRAWBERRY SAUCE

Crush 1 cup strawberries. Cut another cup of berries in slices (or leave whole). Combine; sprinkle with 2 tablespoons sugar. Chill until ready to serve.

DOUBLE-RING DESSERT

   3 envelopes unflavored gelatin
   ¾ cup cold water
   3 cups sliced, sweetened strawberries
   3 cups stewed sweetened rhubarb
   2 cups rosé wine
   1 cup whipping cream
   Garnish: whole strawberries

Soften gelatin in cold water; dissolve over hot water. Purée strawberries and rhubarb in electric blender or put through food mill or sieve. Add wine. Add dissolved gelatin, stirring constantly until thoroughly blended. Chill until slightly thickened. Whip cream until soft peaks form; fold in. Spoon into two 6-cup ring molds. Chill until set. Unmold onto serving platter side by side or interlocked. Garnish with whole strawberries. Makes 16 servings.

   ACCOMPANIMENT: Whipped cream.

DOUBLE-DELIGHT ORANGE DUET

   1 cup evaporated milk
   1 envelope unflavored gelatin
   1 cup water, divided
   1 cup sugar
   ¼ teaspoon salt
   2 cans (6 ounces each) frozen orange juice
      concentrate
   Ginger ale

Chill evaporated milk in freezer tray until ice crystals form around edges. Meanwhile, sprinkle gelatin on ½ cup of the water in saucepan to soften. Place over medium heat; stir until gelatin is dissolved. Remove from heat; stir in remaining water, sugar, and salt. Stir until sugar is dissolved. Add concentrate; stir until blended. Turn evaporated milk into chilled bowl; whip until stiff. Pour orange mixture in thin stream into evaporated milk, continuing to whip. Turn half the mixture into refrigerator tray; freeze. Chill remaining mixture until firm. For dessert, spoon chilled mixture into 4 sherbet glasses. For drinks, spoon frozen mixture into 6 tall glasses; fill to top with ginger ale, stirring briskly.

COFFEE JELLY

   1 envelope unflavored gelatin
   ¼ cup cold strong coffee
   2 cups hot strong coffee
   ⅓ cup sugar
   1 teaspoon vanilla
   Cream

Soften gelatin in cold coffee. Add hot coffee; stir until gelatin dissolves. Add sugar and vanilla. Stir until sugar dissolves. Mold as desired. Chill until firm. Serve with cream. Makes 4 to 6 servings.

SERVING SUGGESTIONS

1. Mold in a ring; fill center with whipped cream sprinkled with chopped walnuts. Serve extra chopped walnuts, if desired.
2. Pour the jelly into a shallow pan to a depth of about ½ inch. Chill until firm. Cut in cubes. Layer cubes with whipped cream in tall glasses.
3. Chill jelly until it reaches the consistency of unbeaten egg white. Fold in 1 cup sliced bananas and 1 cup pineapple tidbits. Spoon mixture into mold; chill until firm.
4. Flavor jelly with 1 teaspoon rum extract instead of vanilla. Chill as above. Whip with rotary beater until light and fluffy. Beat 2 egg whites; beat in 2 tablespoons sugar; fold gently but thoroughly into jelly. Spoon into 6 to 8 individual molds. Chill until firm.

CHOCOLATE BAVARIAN

   1 envelope unflavored gelatin
   ½ cup sugar, divided
   ⅛ teaspoon salt
   2 eggs, separated
   1 cup milk
   1 package (6 ounces) semisweet chocolate
      pieces
   ½ teaspoon vanilla
   1 cup whipping cream

Mix gelatin, ¼ cup sugar, and salt in medium-sized saucepan. Beat egg yolks and milk together; stir into gelatin mixture. Add chocolate.

Cook over medium heat, stirring constantly, until gelatin is dissolved and chocolate melted (5 to 8 minutes). Remove from heat. Beat with rotary beater until chocolate is blended. Stir in vanilla. Chill until mixture mounds slightly when dropped from a spoon. Beat egg whites until stiff but not dry. Beat in remaining ¼ cup sugar gradually; beat until very stiff. Fold into chocolate mixture. Whip cream; fold in. Turn into 6-cup mold (allow room for expansion during freezing). Cover with freezer wrap. Freeze. Thaw several hours or overnight in refrigerator before unmolding. Keep chilled until just before serving. Makes 6 servings.

BUTTERSCOTCH-RUM CHARLOTTE RUSSE

1 envelope unflavored gelatin
½ cup water
2 eggs, separated
1 package (6 ounces) butterscotch pieces
2 teaspoons rum flavoring
¼ cup sugar
2 cups whipping cream
Ladyfingers (packaged)
Garnish: chocolate curls

Sprinkle gelatin over water in saucepan. Add egg yolks and butterscotch pieces; mix well. Cook over low heat, stirring constantly, until gelatin is dissolved and butterscotch pieces are melted and smooth (about 5 minutes). Remove from heat; stir in rum flavoring. Cool, stirring occasionally. Beat egg whites until stiff but not dry. Beat in sugar gradually; beat until very stiff. Fold into butterscotch mixture. Whip cream; fold in. Fill dessert glasses about ⅓ full. Arrange split ladyfingers around glass, letting them extend about ¾ inch above rim of glass. Fill glasses with remaining butterscotch mixture, mounding at least as high as ladyfingers. Chill. Garnish with chocolate curls. Makes 8 to 12 servings, depending on size of dessert glasses.

STRAWBERRY MOUSSE

2 envelopes unflavored gelatin
1 cup cold water
1 cup sugar
1 quart strawberries, washed and hulled
1 tablespoon lemon juice
1 teaspoon vanilla
2 cups whipping cream

Sprinkle gelatin over water in saucepan. Stir over low heat until gelatin dissolves (about 5 minutes). Remove from heat; stir in sugar. Stir until sugar dissolves. Mash berries (or purée in electric blender). Add to dissolved gelatin with lemon juice and vanilla. Chill, stirring occasionally, until mixture mounds slightly when dropped from spoon. Whip cream; fold in. Chill, stirring occasionally, until mixture will pile in a high mound. Makes 6 to 8 servings.

MOLASSES CHIFFON MOLD

2 envelopes unflavored gelatin
1 cup cold strong coffee, divided
⅛ teaspoon cream of tartar
½ cup molasses
⅛ teaspoon cinnamon
½ teaspoon salt
3 eggs, separated
3 tablespoons sugar
1 cup finely chopped walnuts
Garnish (optional): whipped cream; grated
    chocolate

Soften gelatin in ½ cup cold coffee. Stir cream of tartar into molasses; add cinnamon, salt, and remaining coffee. Beat egg yolks until thick; add molasses mixture. Cook over hot water, stirring constantly, until slightly thickened; add softened gelatin; stir until dissolved. Chill until syrupy. Beat egg whites stiff; beat sugar into egg whites, 1 tablespoon at a time; fold into gelatin mixture with chopped walnuts. Spoon into 5-cup mold; chill until set. Unmold. Garnish with whipped cream and grated chocolate, if desired. Makes 8 servings.

LIME DELLA ROBBIA

1 envelope unflavored gelatin
½ cup sugar
1¼ cups cold water
1 teaspoon grated lime peel
3 tablespoons fresh lime juice
Green food coloring
3 egg whites
½ cup whipping cream, whipped
Garnish: fruits and berries in season

Combine gelatin and sugar in a small saucepan. Stir in water; heat just to boiling point, stirring constantly. Stir in lime peel and juice. Add just enough green food coloring to tint pale green. Chill until mixture becomes syrupy. Beat egg whites until soft peaks form, then fold gelatin mixture into egg whites. Fold in whipped cream. Turn into a 1-quart mold; chill until firm. Unmold onto serving dish; surround with a wreath of small fruits and berries in season. Makes 6 servings.

MACADAMIA MOUSSE

2 envelopes unflavored gelatin
½ cup cold milk
½ cup milk, heated to boiling
4 teaspoons instant coffee (dry)
¼ cup boiling water
2 eggs
¾ cup sugar
¼ teaspoon salt
1 cup whipping cream
¾ cup macadamia nuts*
1½ cups ice cubes
Garnish: whipped cream

Sprinkle gelatin over cold milk in blender container to soften. Add boiling milk. Cover and process at low speed until gelatin dissolves. Dissolve instant coffee in boiling water; add with eggs, sugar, and salt to mixture in blender; cover; process at high speed. Remove cover; add whipping cream and nuts; whip mixture in the blender. Add ice cubes one at a time and continue to process until ice is melted. Turn into 4-cup mold; chill until firm (about 30 minutes). To serve, unmold; garnish with whipped cream. Makes 6 servings.

*Cashews may be used if macadamia nuts are not available.

SHERRY CHARLOTTE

First Layer:

1 envelope unflavored gelatin
1 cup cold water, divided
⅓ cup sugar
¼ cup orange juice
1 tablespoon lemon juice
½ cup sweet sherry or port, divided

Soften gelatin in ½ cup water. Stir over boiling water until gelatin dissolves. Remove from heat; add sugar; stir until dissolved. Add remaining ½ cup water, orange juice, lemon juice, and sherry or port. Turn into 6-cup mold; chill until almost firm.

Second Layer:

1 envelope unflavored gelatin
¼ cup sugar
⅛ teaspoon salt
1¼ cups milk
¼ cup sweet sherry or port
½ pint whipping cream
Garnish (optional): frosted grapes

Combine gelatin, sugar, and salt in top of double boiler. Stir in milk. Cook over hot water until gelatin dissolves; remove from heat. Add sherry or port. Chill until mixture is slightly thicker than unbeaten egg white. Whip cream; fold in. Spoon on top of first layer; chill until firm. Unmold. If desired, garnish with frosted grapes. Makes 8 servings.

STRAWBERRY CREAM MOLD WITH STRAWBERRY SAUCE

1 envelope unflavored gelatin
¼ cup red wine
1 pint whipping cream
1 cup sifted confectioners' (powdered) sugar
1 teaspoon vanilla
1 teaspoon lemon juice
2 cups sliced strawberries
Red food coloring
Strawberry Sauce*

Sprinkle gelatin on wine; dissolve over hot water; cool. Whip cream until stiff, adding the sugar gradually as cream begins to thicken. Fold in cooled gelatin, vanilla, lemon juice, and strawberries. Tint delicate rose color with food coloring. Turn into 6-cup mold; chill until firm. Unmold; serve with Strawberry Sauce. Makes 8 servings.

*STRAWBERRY SAUCE

¾ cup sugar
½ cup red wine
1½ cups lightly crushed strawberries

Combine sugar and red wine in a saucepan; bring to boil; simmer 10 minutes. Cool slightly; add lightly crushed strawberries. Cover; chill at least 1 hour before serving.

FRUIT CHIFFON

1 envelope unflavored gelatin
⅔ cup sugar, divided

½ cup water
1 container (about 1 cup) junior fruit (any
    variety)
6 tablespoons lemon juice, divided
½ cup ice water
½ cup instant nonfat dry milk

Combine gelatin and ⅓ cup sugar in saucepan; add water. Cook over low heat, stirring constantly, until gelatin dissolves. Remove from heat; stir in fruit and 4 tablespoons lemon juice. Chill, stirring occasionally, until mixture is the consistency of unbeaten egg white. While mixture is chilling, pour ice water into mixing bowl; add instant nonfat dry milk. Beat until soft peaks form (3 to 4 minutes). Add remaining 2 tablespoons lemon juice. Continue beating until firm peaks form (3 to 4 minutes longer). Gradually beat in remaining ⅓ cup sugar. Fold in gelatin mixture. Turn into a 4-cup mold. Chill until firm. Makes 6 servings.

PEACH-COCONUT MOLD

1 package (3 ounces) mixed-fruit–flavor
    gelatin
1 cup boiling water
1 cup milk
1 cup sugar
Dash salt
2 cups whipping cream
1⅓ cups flaked coconut
1 teaspoon vanilla
6 fresh peaches, peeled, sliced, and sugared
    to taste*

Dissolve gelatin in boiling water. Cool to lukewarm. Scald milk; add sugar and salt; stir until dissolved. Cool until lukewarm. Add milk mixture to gelatin very gradually, stirring constantly. (Mixture may look slightly curdled, but this disappears when beaten.) Chill until syrupy. Beat until thick and fluffy. Whip cream stiff. Fold with coconut and vanilla into whipped gelatin. Spoon into 2-quart ring mold; chill until firm. Unmold onto large plate; spoon peaches into center. Makes 12 servings.

*Or use 3 packages (10 ounces each) frozen sliced peaches, thawed; or 2 cans (1 pound each) sliced peaches.

MOLASSES FLUFF

1 envelope unflavored gelatin
¼ cup cold water

½ cup molasses
⅛ teaspoon cinnamon
½ teaspoon salt
½ cup water
3 eggs, separated
3 tablespoons sugar
1 cup dried macaroon crumbs
Whipped topping
Garnish (optional): grated unsweetened
    chocolate

Sprinkle gelatin on cold water. Combine molasses, cinnamon, salt, and water. Beat egg yolks; add molasses mixture. Cook over hot water, stirring constantly, until thickened. Add gelatin mixture; stir until gelatin is dissolved. Chill until syrupy. Beat egg whites stiff; beat in sugar gradually. Fold egg whites into gelatin mixture with macaroon crumbs. Chill until firm. Pile in sherbet glasses. Serve with whipped topping. Grated unsweetened chocolate may be sprinkled over pudding just before serving. Makes 4 to 6 servings.

EMPRESS RICE MOLD

½ cup uncooked long-grain rice
2½ cups milk, divided
½ teaspoon salt
1 envelope unflavored gelatin
¼ cup cold water
2 eggs, separated
½ cup sugar, divided
¼ cup finely chopped diced candied fruits
    and peels
2 teaspoons grated lemon peel
1 cup whipping cream, whipped
Garnish: whipped cream; candied fruit

Combine rice, 2 cups milk, and salt in heavy saucepan. Slowly bring to a boil. Reduce heat; cover; cook over very low heat, stirring frequently, until rice is tender (about 30 minutes). Sprinkle gelatin over cold water in small cup; let stand until gelatin granules are moistened. Stir into hot rice mixture. Beat egg yolks with ¼ cup sugar and remaining ½ cup milk. Add small amount of hot rice mixture to egg yolks; mix well; stir into saucepan. Cook over low heat for 2 or 3 minutes, until slightly thickened. Add candied fruits and lemon peel. Chill, stirring occasionally, until mixture mounds slightly when dropped from a spoon. Beat egg whites until stiff but not dry; gradually beat in remaining ¼ cup sugar; beat until very stiff. Fold into rice mixture.

Fold in whipped cream. Turn into 6-cup mold; chill until firm (several hours or overnight). Unmold; serve garnished with additional whipped cream and candied fruit. Makes 8 servings.

STRAWBERRY RICE CREAM

2 cups sliced strawberries
1 cup sugar
2 envelopes unflavored gelatin
½ cup cold water
2 cups cooked rice
1 cup whipping cream
1 teaspoon vanilla
Garnish (optional): whole strawberries;
    whipped cream

Combine strawberries and sugar; let stand, stirring occasionally with fork, until sugar dissolves. Soften gelatin in cold water; dissolve over hot water; add to strawberries; mix well. Stir in rice. Whip cream; add vanilla; fold into strawberry mixture. Turn into 5-cup mold; chill until set. Unmold; garnish with whole strawberries and additional whipped cream, if desired. Makes 8 to 10 servings.

TROPICAL CREAM

2 tablespoons unflavored gelatin
2½ cups chocolate milk
3 eggs, separated
¼ cup sugar
⅔ cup mashed ripe banana
1 cup whipping cream
Garnish (optional): fresh mint; banana slices

Soften gelatin in ¾ cup chocolate milk. Beat egg yolks; combine with remaining chocolate milk; beat well. Cook over low heat, stirring constantly, until slightly thickened. Add gelatin mixture; stir until gelatin is dissolved. Chill until slightly thickened. Meanwhile, beat egg whites stiff; gradually add sugar, beating constantly, until very stiff. Fold egg whites and banana into gelatin mixture. Whip cream; fold in. Turn into 6-cup mold; chill until firm. Unmold; garnish with fresh mint and banana slices, if desired. Makes 8 servings.

SOFT FRUITED GELATIN

1 package (3 ounces) raspberry-flavor gelatin
1 cup boiling water
1½ cups ice water*

1 cup diced fresh peaches
1 cup cultivated blueberries
Garnish: whipped topping

Dissolve gelatin thoroughly in boiling water; add ice water; mix well. Chill until syrupy; fold in fruits. Spoon into dessert dishes. Chill until ready to serve. Garnish with whipped topping. Makes 4 to 5 servings.

*Because an extra ½ cup of water is used in making the gelatin dessert, it will not be stiff enough to mold, but it will "set" and the softer consistency is delightful.

GRAPEFRUIT-GINGER DESSERT

2 grapefruit, sectioned
½ cup grapefruit juice (from grapefruit)
1 envelope unflavored gelatin
¼ cup sugar
1 cup dry ginger ale
6 maraschino cherries, sliced
1 egg white

To section grapefruit, cut off peel in strips from top to bottom, cutting deep enough to remove all white membrane. Then cut slice from top and bottom. Cut along side of each dividing membrane from outside to middle, or core. Remove section by section over bowl to save juice. Cut enough sections to make 1 cup, diced; drain well. Measure ½ cup juice. Reserve remaining whole grapefruit sections for garnish. Soften gelatin in grapefruit juice; dissolve over boiling water. Add sugar; stir until dissolved; cool. Add ginger ale; chill until consistency of unbeaten egg white. To half of the mixture add diced grapefruit and cherries; spoon into oiled 5-cup mold. Beat egg white until stiff; fold in remaining gelatin mixture; beat until mixture begins to hold shape. Spoon on top of clear gelatin; chill until firm. Unmold. Makes 6 servings.

PARFAIT MEDLEY

1 envelope unflavored gelatin
½ cup sugar, divided
⅛ teaspoon salt
2 eggs, separated
1¼ cups milk, divided
½ teaspoon vanilla
1 cup whipping cream
Sliced bananas or berries *or* diced peaches *or*
    crushed pineapple *or* any dessert sauce

Combine gelatin, ¼ cup sugar, salt, and egg yolks in saucepan. Stir in ½ cup milk. Cook over low heat, stirring constantly, until mixture thickens slightly and gelatin dissolves (about 5 minutes). Remove from heat; stir in remaining ¾ cup milk and vanilla. Chill, stirring occasionally, until mixture is slightly thicker than the consistency of unbeaten egg white. Beat egg whites until stiff but not dry. Gradually add remaining ¼ cup sugar; beat until very stiff. Fold in gelatin mixture; whip cream; fold in. In parfait glasses, alternate layers of gelatin mixture with sliced bananas or berries, diced peaches, crushed pineapple, or any dessert sauce. Chill 1 hour or until ready to serve. Makes 6 servings.

JELLIED WINE DESSERT

    2 envelopes unflavored gelatin
    1 can (15½ ounces) pineapple chunks
    1½ cups boiling water
    2 cups Concord grape sweet wine
    2 cups diced seeded watermelon
    Whipped cream

Soften gelatin in syrup drained from pineapple; dissolve in boiling water; add wine. Pour a little of this mixture into 5-cup mold to a depth of about 1 inch. Chill until set. Chill remaining mixture until consistency of unbeaten egg white; fold in pineapple chunks and watermelon; spoon into mold; chill until set. Unmold; serve with whipped cream. Makes 8 servings.

PEACH MELBA MOLD

Clear Layer:

    1 can (29 ounces) sliced cling peaches
    1 envelope unflavored gelatin
    ¼ cup sugar
    ⅛ teaspoon salt
    ¼ cup cold water
    ¼ cup lemon juice

Drain syrup from peaches; reserve. Sprinkle gelatin over ½ cup peach syrup in medium saucepan. Stir over low heat until gelatin dissolves (2 to 3 minutes). Remove from heat; stir in sugar and salt. Add remaining peach syrup, water, and lemon juice. Pour thin layer of gelatin mixture into 6-cup mold. Chill until slightly thickened. Make pattern with several peach slices; spoon a little clear gelatin mixture over them; chill until thickened but not firm. Dice remaining peach

halves; reserve 1 cup for cream layer. Fold remainder into clear gelatin mixture; spoon into mold over layer of peach slices. Chill until almost but not completely firm. Meanwhile, prepare cream layer.

Cream Layer:

    1 envelope unflavored gelatin
    ⅓ cup sugar
    ⅛ teaspoon salt
    1 cup milk
    1 teaspoon vanilla
    1 cup whipping cream
    1 cup diced peaches (reserved from clear
        layer)
    Melba Sauce*

Combine gelatin, sugar, and salt in medium saucepan. Stir in milk. Stir over low heat until gelatin dissolves completely (about 4 minutes). Remove from heat; add vanilla. Chill until mixture mounds slightly when dropped from spoon. Whip cream; fold in gelatin mixture. Fold in diced peaches. Turn into mold over almost-firm clear layer. Chill until firm. Unmold onto serving plate. Serve with Melba Sauce. Makes 8 servings.

*MELBA SAUCE

    2 teaspoons cornstarch
    2 packages (10 ounces each) frozen
        raspberries, thawed

Measure cornstarch into saucepan; blend with a little syrup from raspberries. Add remaining syrup and berries. Cook over medium heat, stirring constantly, until mixture thickens and comes to a boil. Mash berries with spoon. Put through strainer or food mill; chill. Makes approximately 1½ cups.

VALENTINE STRAWBERRY MOUSSE

    2 envelopes unflavored gelatin
    1 cup milk
    2 packages (10 ounces each) frozen
        strawberries, thawed
    6 egg whites
    ¼ teaspoon salt
    ½ cup sugar
    2 cups whipping cream, whipped

Sprinkle gelatin over milk in 2½-quart saucepan to soften. Place over low heat; stir constantly until gelatin dissolves (3 to 5 minutes). Remove from heat; stir in strawberries. Beat egg whites with salt in large bowl until stiff but not dry. Gradually beat in sugar until very stiff. Fold in strawberry mixture; fold in whipped cream. Turn into 12-cup mold. Chill until firm. Unmold. Makes 12 servings.

CHOCOLATE MINT ICE CREAM

1 package chocolate pudding mix (not instant)
¼ cup sugar
2 cups milk
¼ teaspoon peppermint extract
1 cup whipping cream

Combine pudding mix and sugar in saucepan. Add milk gradually, stirring constantly. Cook and stir over medium heat until mixture comes to a boil and is thickened (about 5 minutes). Remove from heat. Stir in peppermint extract. Cool slightly. Turn into freezer tray. Chill in freezer ½ hour. Remove to bowl; whip cream; fold in; return to tray. Freeze 1 hour longer; return to bowl; beat with rotary beater until smooth but not melted. Return to tray; freeze until firm (at least 3 to 4 hours). Makes about 1 quart.

LEMON ICE CREAM

2 eggs
½ cup sugar
½ cup light corn syrup
1½ cups milk
⅔ cup whipping cream
½ cup lemon juice
1 tablespoon grated lemon peel

Beat eggs thoroughly; add sugar gradually while beating. Add corn syrup, milk, cream, lemon juice and peel. Freeze firm. Turn out into chilled bowl. Beat with rotary beater until light. Freeze firm. Makes 6 servings.

BANANA MEDLEY ICE CREAM

1 cup sugar
2 tablespoons flour
¼ teaspoon salt
4 cups light cream or half-and-half
4 eggs, beaten
4 large ripe bananas, peeled and mashed
    (about 2 cups)
1 tablespoon lemon juice
½ teaspoon almond extract

3 or 4 drops yellow food color
½ cup chopped almonds
1 cup miniature marshmallows
1 square (1 ounce) semisweet chocolate,
    grated

Combine sugar, flour, and salt in saucepan. Gradually stir in cream. Bring to a boil, stirring constantly, over low heat. Simmer 2 minutes. Add small amount of hot mixture to eggs; mix well; return egg mixture to pan. Simmer and stir over low heat 1 minute; remove from heat; add bananas, lemon juice, almond extract, and food color; mix well. Pour into 2 freezer trays; freeze until firm around edges but soft in center. Turn into large chilled bowl. Beat until creamy. Stir in almonds, marshmallows, and grated chocolate. Return to freezer trays; freeze until firm. Makes about 2 quarts.

COFFEE-WALNUT ICE CREAM

1 large can (1⅔ cups) evaporated milk
1 tablespoon lemon juice
2 tablespoons instant coffee (dry)
½ cup water
1 cup sugar
⅛ teaspoon salt
1 teaspoon vanilla
½ cup finely chopped walnuts

Chill evaporated milk in freezer tray until ice crystals form around edges. Turn into large chilled bowl; whip with cold rotary beater or on high speed of electric mixer until milk is stiff. Add lemon juice; beat until well blended. Dissolve instant coffee in water; add sugar, salt, vanilla, and walnuts; fold into whipped mixture. Turn into 2 freezer trays; freeze until firm. Makes about 2 quarts.

Chocolate-Mint Ice Cream: Substitute ½ cup chopped semisweet chocolate morsels, ½ teaspoon peppermint flavoring, and ¼ teaspoon green food coloring for instant coffee, vanilla, and walnuts. Reduce sugar to ¾ cup.

Banana-Pecan Ice Cream: Increase lemon juice to 3 tablespoons; substitute 2 cups (4 to 6) mashed ripe bananas and ½ cup chopped pecans for instant coffee, water, vanilla, and walnuts.

FROZEN LEMON VELVET

1 can (15 ounces) sweetened condensed milk
½ cup lemon juice
1 teaspoon grated lemon peel
2 eggs, separated
¼ cup sugar

Combine condensed milk, lemon juice, lemon peel, and egg yolks; stir until mixture thickens. Beat egg whites until almost stiff enough to hold a peak. Add sugar gradually, beating until stiff but not dry. Slowly pour condensed milk mixture over beaten egg whites, folding in carefully. Pour mixture into freezer tray. Freeze until firm (about 2 to 3 hours). Makes 6 servings.

WATERMELON SHERBET

4 cups (about 3 pounds) diced seeded
    watermelon
1 package unflavored gelatin
1½ cups light corn syrup
2 tablespoons lemon juice
Few drops red food coloring (optional)

Crush watermelon through a strainer or with electric blender. This will make about 3 cups liquid. Soften gelatin in ½ cup watermelon juice. Place over boiling water; heat until gelatin is dissolved. Combine corn syrup, lemon juice, and food coloring: add dissolved gelatin and remaining watermelon liquid. Turn into freezer trays. Freeze until almost firm (1 to 2 hours). Turn into chilled bowl; break up with spoon; beat until smooth. Return to trays; freeze until firm (about 3 hours). Makes about 1 quart.

EASY ORANGE SHERBET

1 envelope unflavored gelatin
½ cup cold water
¾ cup sugar
1 can (6 ounces) frozen orange juice
    concentrate, thawed
2¼ cups buttermilk

Soften gelatin in cold water. Stir over boiling water until gelatin dissolves. Add sugar; stir until dissolved. Combine concentrate and buttermilk; mix well. Stir in gelatin mixture. Pour into freezer tray. When mixture is partially frozen, break up with a spoon; beat with rotary or elec-

tric beater until smooth. Return to freezer compartment; freeze until firm. Makes about 1 quart.

APPLESAUCE SHERBET

1 can or jar (1 pound) applesauce
¾ cup light corn syrup, divided
¼ teaspoon salt
1 tablespoon lemon juice
1 tablespoon grated orange peel
¼ cup orange juice
2 egg whites, stiffly beaten

Combine applesauce, ½ cup corn syrup, salt, lemon juice, orange peel and juice. Beat remaining corn syrup gradually into stiffly beaten egg whites; fold into applesauce mixture. Pour into freezer tray; freeze until firm. Makes 6 servings.

FROZEN GRAPE FLUFF

¾ cup water
2 teaspoons lemon juice
¾ cup nonfat dry milk
1 can frozen grape juice concentrate, thawed

Pour water and lemon juice into large bowl. Sprinkle nonfat dry milk powder over surface of water; beat with rotary beater or electric mixer until mixture stands in stiff peaks (8 to 10 minutes). Beating constantly, slowly add thawed grape juice; blend well. Spoon into refrigerator tray; freeze until firm (2 to 3 hours). Makes 6 servings.

AVOCADO SHERBET

2 cups pineapple juice
½ cup sugar
Few grains salt
2 ripe avocados
2 tablespoons lemon juice
Garnish: mint leaves

Combine pineapple juice, sugar, and salt; stir over medium heat until sugar is dissolved (do not boil). Cool. Purée peeled and stoned avocados with lemon juice; add to pineapple mixture; mix well. Freeze. Garnish with mint leaves, if desired. Makes 4 to 5 servings.

BANANA-ORANGE SHERBET

2 tablespoons lemon juice
1 cup orange juice
4 ripe medium-sized bananas
2 tablespoons sugar
⅔ cup nonfat dry milk
⅔ cup water

Combine lemon and orange juices; pour over bananas while forcing through sieve or food mill.

Stir sugar into banana mixture. Sprinkle dry milk over water; beat with rotary beater ½ minute; scrape down sides of bowl; beat ½ minute longer. Stir into banana mixture. Pour into freezer tray. Cover with aluminum foil. Freeze to firm mush. Turn into chilled bowl; beat with rotary beater or electric mixer until fluffy but not melted. Quickly return to freezer tray; cover with foil. Return to freezing unit. Freeze until firm. Makes 4 servings.

CHAPTER 19
Candies and Confections

THE RECIPES that follow are simple and uncomplicated—and yet they make delicious candies. An assortment of two or three, attractively packed, would be a charming hostess gift or a welcome bit of cheer for a shut-in.

Make up a few batches to have around for the holiday season, or for school vacations. Tuck a few pieces in a lunch box for a surprise dessert. You'll find many happy uses for these easy-to-make sweets.

STRAWBERRY JELLY APPLES

    12 red apples
    12 wooden skewers
    1½ cups quick strawberry-flavor beverage mix
    1½ cups sugar
    2 teaspoons vinegar
    ⅔ cup water

Wash apples thoroughly; dry; remove stems. Place wooden skewer in stem end of each apple. In 1-quart saucepan, combine quick strawberry-flavor mix, sugar, vinegar, and water. Place over medium heat, stirring constantly, until sugar is dissolved. Boil without stirring to 300° (hard crack stage). Remove from heat. Dip apples quickly into syrup. Twirl above pan to let excess syrup drip back into pan. Set apples on greased cookie sheet. Makes 12.

SUGAR PLUMS

    2 cups firmly packed brown sugar
    1 cup sugar
    ½ cup light corn syrup
    ½ cup water
    ¼ teaspoon salt
    2 egg whites
    ½ teaspoon vanilla
    ½ cup diced candied fruits and peels

Combine sugars, corn syrup, water, and salt in saucepan. Stir over low heat until sugars dissolve. Bring to boil, stirring often. Lower heat; cover pan for a minute or two to dissolve sugar on sides of pan. Remove cover; cook without stirring to 248° or until a little dropped in cold water forms a firm ball. Beat egg whites stiff but not dry. Pour syrup in fine stream over egg whites while beating constantly. Add vanilla. Continue beating until candy will form peaks. Drop by teaspoons onto greased waxed paper. Decorate with diced candied fruits and peels. Let stand until cool. Makes about 50 pieces.

WALNUT BUTTER CRUNCH

1 pound (2 cups) butter or margarine
2 cups sugar
¼ cup water
2 tablespoons light corn syrup
2 cups coarsely chopped walnuts
1 package (6 ounces) semisweet chocolate
    pieces
½ cup finely chopped walnuts

Melt butter over low heat in 2-quart saucepan. Add sugar; stir constantly until sugar is melted. Add water and corn syrup. Continue cooking over low heat until syrup, dropped in very cold water, becomes brittle or candy thermometer reaches 290°. Remove from heat; stir in coarsely chopped walnuts. Spread in a greased jelly roll pan, 15 x 10 x 1 inch. Cool until hardened. Melt chocolate over hot, not boiling, water; spread on crunch. Sprinkle with finely chopped walnuts. Break in pieces. Makes 2 pounds.

STUFFED PRUNES

Combine finely chopped walnuts and minced candied ginger in any desired proportion with enough honey to hold ingredients together. Use to stuff pitted dried prunes.

POPCORN BALLS

3 quarts freshly popped corn*
1 cup light corn syrup
1 cup sugar
½ teaspoon salt
1 teaspoon vanilla
¼ teaspoon red or green food coloring

Keep popped corn warm in a 275° to 300° oven. Combine corn syrup, sugar, and salt in heavy 2-quart saucepan. Cook and stir over medium heat until mixture comes to a boil. Cook without stirring 4 minutes. Remove from heat. Stir in vanilla and food coloring; mix well. Pour syrup slowly over popped corn in a fine stream, mixing with a wooden spoon. When cool enough to handle but still quite warm, shape into 2- to 2½-inch balls. Makes 12 to 18.

Chocolate Popcorn Balls: Follow basic recipe adding semisweet chocolate pieces to corn syrup mixture.

Peppermint Popcorn Balls: Follow basic recipe adding ¼ teaspoon peppermint flavoring to syrup just before pouring over popped corn.

Spicy Popcorn Balls: Follow basic recipe adding few drops oil of cloves just before pouring over popped corn.

Polka-Dot Popcorn Balls: Follow basic recipe adding ½ cup raisins and ½ cup peanuts to popped corn before adding syrup.

*POPCORN

If you do not have a corn popper, pour ¼ cup vegetable oil into heavy 4-quart saucepan. Set over medium high heat. Add 1 kernel of popcorn. When kernel pops, remove it and add ½ cup popcorn. Stir to mix. Cover, leaving a small air space at edge of cover. Shake pan frequently until popping stops. Makes about 3 quarts. If you need more, make up the recipe again.

FIVE-WAY FUDGE

½ cup miniature marshmallows
½ cup broken walnuts
2½ cups sugar
¾ cup evaporated milk
⅓ cup light corn syrup
3 tablespoons butter or margarine, divided
1 large package (12 ounces) *or* 2 small
    packages (6 ounces each) semisweet
    chocolate pieces
1 teaspoon vanilla
Walnut halves, chopped walnuts, flaked
    coconut

Line 8-inch square pan with aluminum foil. Cover bottom of pan with marshmallows and walnuts. Combine sugar, evaporated milk, corn syrup, and 2 tablespoons butter in 3-quart saucepan. Bring to full, all-over boil, stirring constantly. Continue to boil 5 minutes, stirring constantly. Remove from heat. Add semisweet chocolate pieces and vanilla; stir until smooth. Pour half of chocolate mixture into prepared pan. When firm, cut in squares. Turn remaining mixture onto greased cookie sheet; let stand until cool enough to handle. Grease hands and work additional butter or margarine (about 1 tablespoon) into fudge until smooth and pliable. Divide mixture in 4 parts and shape as follows: (1) Shape into 1½-inch patties and press walnut half on each patty. (2) Shape into cornucopias and press wide ends into chopped walnuts. (3) Shape into logs and roll in chopped nuts. (4) Work in ¼ cup chopped walnuts and shape into 1-inch balls; roll in flaked coconut or chopped walnuts. Makes approximately 2½ pounds.

SPARKLING CHRISTMAS CANDY JELLS

1 bottle (6 fluid ounces) liquid fruit pectin*
2 tablespoons water
½ teaspoon baking soda
1 cup sugar
1 cup light corn syrup
Flavoring and coloring (see suggestions below)
Sugar
Decorations (see below)

Combine fruit pectin and water in 2-quart saucepan. Stir in baking soda. (Mixture will foam slightly.) Mix sugar and corn syrup in another saucepan. Place both saucepans over high heat and cook, stirring alternately, until foam has thinned from pectin mixture and sugar mixture is boiling rapidly (3 to 5 minutes). Pour pectin mixture in slow, steady stream into boiling sugar mixture, stirring constantly. Boil and stir 1 minute longer. Remove from heat. Add flavoring and coloring. Pour at once into buttered 9-inch square pan. Let stand at room temperature until cool and firm (about 3 hours). Invert pan onto waxed paper that has been sprinkled with granulated sugar. Cut in squares or other shapes (using tiny cutters), dipping knife or cutters in warm water. Roll in sugar, white or tinted. Let candy stand a while; roll again in sugar to prevent stickiness. Then, if desired, roll in gold or silver dragées, chopped coconut, or finely chopped nuts. Let stand overnight, uncovered, at room temperature, before packing or storing. Do not refrigerate. Makes 2 to 3 dozen.

*Candy jells may also be made with powdered fruit pectin, using 1 box (1¾ ounces). Increase water to ¾ cup.

SUGGESTIONS FOR FLAVORING AND COLORING

1. Increase boiling time to 2 minutes. After removing from heat stir in ¼ cup green crème de menthe.
2. Add ½ cup finely chopped crystallized ginger, 1 tablespoon lemon juice, and 10 drops red food coloring.

3. Add 1 tablespoon vanilla and no coloring, or 10 drops yellow food coloring.
4. Do not roll jells in sugar. Let stand overnight. Partially melt 2 or 3 one-ounce semisweet chocolate squares over hot, not boiling, water. Remove from water; stir rapidly until entirely melted. Let chocolate stand until it feels cool to the touch (83°). Dip candies quickly in melted chocolate. Place on waxed paper until firm.

CHRISTMAS WELCOME WREATH

You'll need about 5 dozen candies, plastic wrap, gift-wrapping wire (or fine florists' wire), one wire coat hanger, a red ribbon bow, artificial holly leaves, and a pair of small blunt scissors.

1. Wrap each candy in a square of plastic wrap at least 2 inches bigger than the candy.
2. Secure each wrap with a twist of wire, making sure a plastic wrap "handle" remains.
3. Shape the wire coat hanger into a rough circle, leaving the hook in place.
4. Take about a 20-inch length of wire, wrap one end around a candy's plastic wrap "handle," then twist wire and candy around hanger circle. Take another piece of candy, wrap, attach. Continue this process with 20-inch lengths of wire until candies are clustered thickly around wreath.
5. Hide wreath handle under red bow.
6. Attach holly leaves, and tie scissors to bottom of wreath for easy snipping of candies.
7. Wrap leftover candies and use as replacements as candies are eaten.

POPCORN WREATHS

12 cups popped corn (page 374)
½ cup chopped candied fruits
¾ cup light corn syrup
¾ cup sugar
½ teaspoon vanilla
Sliced candied cherries

Combine popped corn and candied fruits; set aside. Mix corn syrup and sugar. Cook over medium heat, stirring occasionally, until sugar has completely dissolved (about 8 to 10 minutes). Stir in vanilla. Remove from heat. Stir syrup into popped corn mixture. Return to heat; stir until popcorn kernels begin to stick together. Shape quickly into wreaths. (Rubber gloves will prevent burned fingers!) Decorate tops with sliced candied cherries. Makes 12 wreaths.

FOUR-WAY CHRISTMAS FUDGE

1 jar (7 ounces) marshmallow cream
1½ cups sugar
1 small can (⅔ cup) evaporated milk
¼ cup butter or margarine
¼ teaspoon salt
2 packages (6 ounces each) *or* 1 large package
   (12 ounces) semisweet chocolate pieces
1 teaspoon vanilla
Whole nutmeats
Chopped nuts

Combine marshmallow cream, sugar, evaporated milk, butter, and salt in 2-quart saucepan. Bring to a full, all-over boil, stirring constantly. Continue to boil over moderate heat, stirring constantly, 5 minutes. Remove from heat; stir in semisweet chocolate pieces and vanilla; beat until smooth. Turn into greased 8-inch square pan. Chill in refrigerator until firm. Cut in squares; top half the squares with whole nutmeats. Cut remaining squares in half; roll between palms of hands to make patties or logs or balls; roll logs and balls in chopped nuts; press whole nut into top of patties. Makes 2⅛ pounds.

CRISPY PEANUT SQUARES

1½ cups cornflakes
1½ cups crisp rice cereal
1 cup flaked coconut
½ cup salted peanuts
½ cup cream
½ cup light corn syrup
½ cup sugar

Combine cereals, coconut, and peanuts in large mixing bowl. Combine cream, corn syrup, and sugar in saucepan; bring to boil, stirring until sugar dissolves. Boil to 240° (soft ball stage). Pour syrup over cereal mixture; mix well. Press into well-buttered 9-inch square pan. Cool. Cut into 12 squares.

HONEY CRISP BARS

1 large package (12 ounces) semisweet
   chocolate pieces (or two 6-ounce
   packages)
⅔ cup honey
1 package (6 ounces) crisp rice cereal

Melt chocolate over hot, not boiling, water. Add honey; mix well. Remove from heat. Pour over rice cereal; stir until each kernel is coated. Press into buttered shallow oblong pan. Cool. Cut in 12 to 18 bars.

SUGARED CRUNCH

5½ cups crisp rice cereal
1½ cups firmly packed light brown sugar
3 tablespoons butter or margarine

Measure cereal into buttered bowl. Combine sugar and butter in heavy frying pan; cook, stirring, until melted and smooth. Pour at once over cereal, stirring to coat each kernel. Form into small balls. Makes about 2 dozen.

PEANUT BUTTER CLUSTERS

1 package (8 ounces) semisweet chocolate for
   baking and candy making
3 tablespoons peanut butter
3 cups wheat flakes

Heat chocolate and peanut butter over hot water, stirring constantly, until chocolate is melted. Remove from heat; add wheat flakes. Mix thoroughly. Drop from teaspoon onto waxed paper. Cool until firm. Makes about 36 clusters.

CALIFORNIA FRUIT FUDGE

2 squares (2 ounces) unsweetened chocolate
¾ cup milk
2 cups sugar
Dash of salt
2 tablespoons butter or margarine
1 teaspoon vanilla
½ cup chopped dried figs
½ cup chopped seedless raisins
¼ cup flaked coconut

Add chocolate to milk; cook over low heat, stirring constantly, until mixture is smooth and blended. Add sugar and salt; stir until sugar is dissolved and mixture boils. Continue boiling, without stirring, to 232°, or until a small amount of the mixture forms a very soft ball in cold water. Remove from heat. Add butter or margarine and vanilla. Cool to lukewarm (110°); beat until mixture begins to thicken and loses its gloss. Add fruits and coconut; turn at once into greased 8-inch square pan. When fudge is cold, cut in squares. Makes 24.

CHOCOLATE DREAMBOATS

1 package (8 ounces) semisweet chocolate for
   baking and candy making
1½ cups salted cashew nuts or salted peanuts

Heat chocolate over boiling water until partly
melted. Remove from heat; stir rapidly until
completely melted. Add nutmeats, whole or broken, and mix well. Drop from teaspoon onto
waxed paper. Place whole nutmeat on each. Let
stand in cool place until firm. Makes about 32.

BLACK MAGIC BUNDLES

1 package (6 ounces) semisweet chocolate
   pieces
2 tablespoons shortening
¼ teaspoon cinnamon
⅛ teaspoon nutmeg
24 spoon-size shredded-wheat cereal
Candy sprills, small gumdrops, candy orange
   slices

Melt chocolate and shortening together. Add cinnamon and nutmeg; mix well. Coat each small
shredded-wheat biscuit with chocolate. Place on
waxed paper. Decorate with multicolored candy
sprills, small gumdrops, candy orange slices, etc.
Let stand until chocolate has hardened. Makes
24.

BUTTERSCOTCH BRITTLE

½ pound butter
1 cup sugar
1 package (6 ounces) butterscotch pieces
¾ cup very finely chopped nuts

Line jelly roll pan, 15 x 10 x 1 inch, with aluminum foil; set aside. Put butter in 2-quart saucepan; melt over low heat; add sugar. Put candy
thermometer in pan. Stir over moderate heat
until mixture becomes pale-caramel color and
candy thermometer reaches 300° (about 10 minutes). Remove from heat; spoon evenly into foil-
lined pan. Cool 5 minutes; scatter butterscotch
pieces evenly over candy. As soon as they are
soft (about 4 minutes), spread with back of teaspoon over entire surface. Sprinkle evenly with
chopped nuts. Chill until firm. Break into pieces.
Makes about 1⅔ pounds.

BRANDIED CITRUS PEEL

6 oranges *or* 2 grapefruit
2 cups water
½ cup sugar
½ cup light corn syrup
¼ cup brandy
Sugar

Remove outer peel from oranges or grapefruit
with vegetable peeler or sharp knife, cutting it
off in pieces as large as possible. It is important
to cut away only the peel and not the white pith,
which tends to be bitter. Place in a saucepan
with water; simmer; covered, 40 minutes. Drain;
reserve 1 cup of the liquid. Return reserved liquid to saucepan with sugar, corn syrup, and
brandy. Simmer over low heat until sugar is dissolved. Add peel; cook over low heat 20 minutes.
Drain, reserving syrup. Toss peel in additional
sugar to coat completely. Place pieces on cake
racks; dry for at least 24 hours. Store in a tightly
covered container. Use reserved syrup as a sauce
for candied vegetables, pancakes, or ice cream.

Chocolate-Dipped Brandied Peel: Prepare brandied citrus peel but do not coat with sugar. Melt
1 cup (6 ounces) semisweet chocolate pieces
with 2 tablespoons vegetable shortening in top
of double boiler over hot, not boiling, water. Remove from heat; keep over water. Dip pieces of
branded citrus peel in melted chocolate; place
on waxed paper to harden. Store in cool place.

PEPPERMINT PATTIES

Make fondant base, using 2 tablespoons evaporated milk, ½ teaspoon peppermint extract, and
2½ cups sifted confectioners' (powdered) sugar.
After kneading until smooth and shiny, shape
mixture into balls; flatten balls to form patties.
Makes 2 to 3 dozen.

CHERRY PECAN LOGS

Fondant Base:

2 tablespoons evaporated milk
½ teaspoon rum flavoring
2½ cups sifted confectioners' (powdered)
   sugar

Combine evaporated milk and rum flavoring in
mixing bowl. Stir in sugar until blended; knead
until smooth and shiny.

Logs:

1 cup coarsely chopped candied cherries
Sifted confectioners' (powdered) sugar (if
  necessary)
14 caramels (¼ pound)
3 tablespoons evaporated milk
1½ cups coarsely chopped pecans

Knead cherries into Fondant Base, adding more
sugar if necessary. Shape into two 6-inch logs;
roll in waxed paper; chill until firm. Combine
caramels and evaporated milk; heat over boiling
water until melted, stirring often. Turn caramel
mixture into pie pan. Quickly roll logs in caramel
mixture, then in pecans. Roll in waxed paper;
chill until firm. Slice.

EASY PECAN PRALINES

2 cups firmly packed light brown sugar
1 cup sugar
¾ cup milk
2 cups pecan halves

Combine sugars and milk; cook over low heat to
soft ball stage (240°). Beat until almost cool. Add
pecans. Drop by tablespoons onto waxed paper;
flatten and let cool and harden slightly. Makes
about 18 large patties.

CHOCOLATE MILK POPS

1 cup quick chocolate-flavor drink mix
2 cups instant nonfat dry milk
2½ cups cold water
Flat wooden sticks

Combine quick chocolate-flavor drink mix and
instant dry milk. Stir in cold water. Pour into
eight 5-ounce paper cups. Put in freezer; when
frozen enough to hold spoon upright, press stick
in center of each cup. Freeze firm. When ready
to serve, peel off cups. Makes 8 pops.

"FIRECRACKERS"

6 cups puffed rice
½ cup butter or margarine
½ pound fresh marshmallows
¼ cup red cinnamon candies
Few drops red food coloring
Shredded coconut

Heat puffed rice in shallow pan at 350° for 10
minutes; pour into large greased bowl. Melt butter, marshmallows, and red cinnamon candies in
top of double boiler. Tint bright red with food
coloring; stir until smooth. Pour marshmallow
mixture over puffed rice, mixing until all kernels
are evenly coated. Grease hands; form candy into
"firecrackers" about 3 inches long and 1 inch in
diameter. With a fork or skewer, push a long
strand of coconut into one end of each for a fuse.
Makes 2 dozen.

CHOCOLATE CRUNCH

½ cup evaporated milk
¾ cup sugar
2 tablespoons butter or margarine
1 package (6 ounces) semisweet chocolate
  pieces
1 teaspoon vanilla
2 cups O-shaped puffed oat cereal
1 cup salted peanuts
1 cup broken pretzel sticks

Combine evaporated milk, sugar, and butter in
medium saucepan. Bring to a full boil, stirring
constantly. Continue to boil, stirring constantly,
for 2 minutes. Remove from heat. Add chocolate
pieces and vanilla; stir until smooth. Combine
cereal, peanuts, and pretzels in mixing bowl.
Add chocolate mixture; toss lightly until well
coated. Drop quickly by heaping teaspoons onto
waxed paper or foil. Let stand until set. Makes 3
to 4 dozen pieces.

PEANUT BUTTER NOUGATS

⅔ cup peanut butter
⅔ cup light molasses
1 cup nonfat dry milk
Colored candy shot *or* chocolate sprills *or*
  semisweet chocolate pieces

Combine peanut butter and molasses. Gradually
stir in nonfat dry milk; mix well. Turn onto
waxed paper; knead until well blended. Chill
about 1 hour. Shape into a square block, ½ inch
thick. Cut in squares, then shape some of the
squares into balls. Roll in colored candy shot or
chocolate sprills, or top with semisweet chocolate pieces. Makes about 1 pound.

POPCORN PADDLE POPS

2 quarts unsalted popped corn (page 374)
1 cup firmly packed brown sugar
½ cup light corn syrup

⅓ cup water
1 teaspoon salt
⅛ teaspoon cream of tartar
¼ cup butter or margarine
1 quart vanilla ice cream
8 to 10 flat wooden spoons

Place popcorn in buttered bowl. Combine sugar, corn syrup, water, salt, cream of tartar, and butter or margarine in heavy saucepan. Cook to the hard crack stage (280° to 285°), stirring frequently. Pour syrup in a fine stream over popcorn and stir until corn is evenly coated. Spread out on greased baking sheet; separate kernels. Cool. Cover bottom of 2 refrigerator trays or 1 double tray with half the popcorn; top with layer of slightly softened ice cream. Top with remaining popcorn. Put in freezing compartment to harden. Cut in slices. Insert wooden spoons. Makes 8 to 10 servings.

STUFFED APRICOT CANDY

36 large dried apricots
½ cup ground walnuts
½ cup ground mixed diced candied fruits and peels
¼ cup sweet sherry
Dash each of cinnamon and nutmeg
Dash of salt
Granulated sugar

Place apricots in colander over boiling water; cover; steam 10 to 15 minutes or until soft. Dry well. Press 2 apricots together with edges overlapping slightly to make 18 "double-length" apricots. Mix walnuts, fruits, sherry, spices, and salt. Stuff the "double" apricots with this mixture. Roll apricots in sugar. "Ripen" in tightly covered container for 3 or 4 days. Makes 18.

CHOCOLATE FUDGE

3 squares (1 ounce each) unsweetened chocolate
4 tablespoons butter or margarine
⅓ cup unseasoned mashed potato*
⅛ teaspoon salt
1 teaspoon vanilla
1 pound confectioners' (powdered) sugar
Nutmeats (optional)

Melt chocolate and butter together over hot water. Blend in mashed potato, salt, and vanilla. Mix well. Sift sugar. Add a small amount at a time, blending until no sugar is visible. When a spoon is no longer equal to the task of mixing, knead in the balance of the sugar with well-buttered hands. Turn out onto board and continue to knead until mixture is smooth, glossy, and pliable, buttering hands as necessary. No crumbs should remain. Press into buttered 8-inch square pan and cut in squares, or shape into balls and top each ball with a nutmeat. Makes 1¼ pounds.

*It is best to cook and mash a medium potato especially for this purpose. Omit any seasoning, butter, or milk.

RASPBERRY MALLOWS

2 packages (3 ounces each) raspberry-flavor gelatin
¾ cup boiling water
¾ cup light corn syrup
¼ cup cornstarch
¼ cup confectioners' (powdered) sugar

Empty gelatin into small saucepan. Pour boiling water over gelatin; stir well. Stir over very low heat until gelatin is completely dissolved. Pour corn syrup into large bowl of electric mixer. Add dissolved gelatin; beat 15 minutes on high speed or until mixture is thick and of marshmallow consistency. Combine cornstarch and confectioners' sugar; sprinkle 2 tablespoons in bottom of 10-inch square pan. Pour marshmallow mixture into pan; smooth top. Sprinkle with 2 tablespoons cornstarch mixture. Let stand in cool place (not refrigerator) about 1 hour. Loosen around edges with knife dipped in cold water. Turn out onto board sprinkled with 2 tablespoons cornstarch mixture. Cut in 1½-inch squares with wet knife; sprinkle cut edges with cornstarch mixture. Makes 42 squares.

CHOCOLATE-DIPPED FRUIT

24 bite-size chunks fresh pineapple (about ¼ medium pineapple)
24 seedless grapes
2 ripe bananas, peeled and cut in 12 slices each
24 Bing cherries with stems
1 package (12 ounces) or 2 packages (6 ounces each) semisweet chocolate pieces
⅔ cup vegetable shortening (not oil)

Stick wooden picks or tiny metal skewers into pineapple chunks, grapes, and banana slices.

Place with cherries in a single layer in waxed-paper-lined shallow pan so that pieces do not touch. Place in freezer for 2 or more hours, until frozen solid. Put chocolate pieces and shortening in 2-cup measure (that's right—it all melts down to 2 cups and doesn't run over). Place cup in pan of hot, not boiling, water until melted; stir until smooth. Leave chocolate mixture in pan of hot water, but remove from heat. Dip pieces of frozen fruit into chocolate mixture to coat. Do not put fruit back in pan until coating hardens (the chocolate hardens almost immediately on frozen fruit). Cover pan with foil; return to freezer until ready to serve. Fruit is best served as soon as possible after dipping. Do not remove from freezer until ready to serve; fruit will thaw for eating in 5 to 12 minutes. Makes 6 servings of 4 pieces of each fruit.

CHOCOLATE-MARSHMALLOW VELVET

    1 cup evaporated milk
    2 cups sugar
    1 package (12 ounces) or 2 packages (6 ounces
        each) semisweet chocolate pieces
    1 teaspoon vanilla
    1½ cups miniature marshmallows

Combine evaporated milk and sugar in saucepan. Place over low heat; stir until sugar is dissolved and mixture comes to a boil. Increase heat; boil 2 minutes, stirring constantly. Remove from heat; add semisweet chocolate pieces and vanilla; stir until smooth. Turn about ½ the chocolate mixture into waxed-paper-lined 8-inch square pan. Cover with miniature marshmallows, pressing them gently into the chocolate. Top with remaining chocolate mixture. Chill. Cut into 12 squares.

JIFFY FUDGE

    1 package (12 ounces) or 2 packages (6 ounces
        each) semisweet chocolate pieces
    ¾ cup sweetened condensed milk
    1 teaspoon vanilla

Melt semisweet chocolate pieces over hot, not boiling water. Remove from heat; stir in milk and vanilla. Mix well. Turn into pan or shape as desired. Let stand several hours or overnight. Makes about 1¼ pounds.

Chocolate Nut Squares: Turn chocolate mixture into an 8-inch square pan. Cut in squares. Press whole almond or pecan or walnut half into each square.

Pralines: Cool chocolate mixture thoroughly. Measure 1 tablespoon of mixture. Place on piece of waxed paper. Place another piece of waxed paper on top. Press with bottom of a water glass to make a 2-inch circle. Continue until all of chocolate mixture is used. Press pecans in center of each praline.

Peanut or Coconut Balls: Shape chocolate mixture into ¾-inch balls; roll in chopped peanuts or coconut.

Chocolate Nut Rolls: Add ½ cup coarsely chopped nuts to chocolate mixture. Divide mixture in half. Make 2 rolls about 1½ inches in diameter. Lightly press rolls into additional chopped nuts, covering all surfaces. Cut in 16 slices.

CHOCOLATE MARSHMALLOWS

    1 envelope unflavored gelatin
    ⅓ cup cold water
    ½ cup sugar
    ⅔ cup light corn syrup
    1 teaspoon vanilla
    3 squares (1 ounce each) unsweetened
        chocolate
    ¾ cup finely chopped peanuts

Soften gelatin in cold water; place over boiling water; stir until dissolved. Add sugar; stir until dissolved. Remove from heat. Place corn syrup and vanilla in large bowl of electric mixer. Add gelatin-sugar mixture; beat on highest speed until mixture becomes thick and of soft marshmallow consistency (about 15 minutes). While mixture is being beaten, melt chocolate; cool. When marshmallow consistency is reached, fold in cooled, melted chocolate by hand. Pour into greased pan, preferably about 7 x 10 x 1½ inches. Smooth off top with spoon or knife. Let stand in a cool place (not refrigerator) until well set (about 1 hour). To remove from pan, loosen around edges and invert onto waxed paper. Cut in 1-inch squares with knife moistened with cold water. Roll in finely chopped peanuts. Makes about 1½ pounds.

MARZIPAN

1 pound canned almond paste
½ cup light corn syrup
1 jar (1 pint) marshmallow topping
2 teaspoons vanilla
6 cups sifted confectioners' (powdered) sugar
Artificial leaves
Food coloring
Cocoa
Cinnamon
Red sugar

Combine almond paste, corn syrup, marshmallow topping, and vanilla; mix thoroughly. Add sugar, 1 cup at a time, mixing well after each addition (knead in the last 2 or 3 cups by hand) until marzipan is satiny. Mold small pieces into fruit or vegetable shapes. Insert tiny artificial leaves where needed while the marzipan is still soft. Let stand several hours to permit the surface to dry before painting. Paint with food coloring, diluted and mixed as necessary, using artist's brushes. Roll "potatoes" in a mixture of cocoa and cinnamon instead of painting. Roll "strawberries" and "raspberries" in red sugar after painting. Store in tightly covered metal boxes. Will keep indefinitely. Makes about 5 dozen pieces.

SANTA'S SWEETS

1 package (12 ounces) or 2 packages (6 ounces each) semisweet chocolate pieces
½ cup dairy sour cream
¾ cup confectioners' (powdered) sugar
¼ teaspoon salt
2 cups fine vanilla wafer crumbs
½ cup broken walnuts

Melt semisweet chocolate pieces over hot, not boiling, water. Remove from water; stir in sour cream, confectioners' sugar, and salt. Blend in vanilla wafer crumbs. Spread in foil-lined 8-inch square pan. Press walnuts into surface. Chill until firm. Cut in 1-inch squares. Makes 64 pieces.

CHAPTER 20

Grace Notes

A PRETTY crystal dish of sparkling jelly, a compote holding a very special conserve, relish dishes with spicy concoctions to enliven the main course—what a difference these grace notes make in a dinner menu that is otherwise run-of-the-mill.

You can find many products of this type on supermarket shelves, but unless you try your hand at making some of them once in a while you are missing out on a lot of fun. When you see sunlight slanting through a row of glasses holding jewel-colored jelly, when your nose is titillated by the pungent aroma of pickles or relishes ready to be packed into jars, when you proudly serve a bowl of homemade chutney with your next batch of curry, you will experience the thrill that comes only with the creation of your own grace notes for your table.

RASPBERRY JELLY

To Prepare the Juice:

2½ quarts (about) fully ripe red raspberries
¼ cup lemon juice (optional)

Cook thoroughly about 2½ quarts fully ripe red raspberries. Place in jelly cloth or bag and squeeze out juice. Measure 4 cups juice into a very large saucepan. (If berries lack tartness, use only 3¾ cups prepared juice and add ¼ cup lemon juice.)

To Make the Jelly:

4 cups raspberry juice (from above)
7½ cups sugar
1 bottle (6 ounces) fruit pectin

Add sugar to juice in saucepan; mix well. Place over high heat; bring to a boil, stirring constantly. At once stir in bottled fruit pectin. Bring to full, rolling boil; boil hard 1 minute, stirring constantly. Remove from heat; skim; pour quickly into clean, scalded glasses. Paraffin at once. Makes about eleven 6-ounce glasses.

STRAWBERRY JELLY

To Prepare the Juice:

3 quarts (about) fully ripe strawberries
¾ cup water

Crush thoroughly about 3 quarts fully ripe strawberries in a very large saucepan. Add ¾ cup water; mix well. Cover; place over medium heat; bring just to the simmering point. (Do not boil.)

Place in large sieve lined with double thickness of cheesecloth. Drain; measure 2 cups juice into a large saucepan. Remove cheesecloth and use fruit remaining in sieve for Strawberry Jam (page 384).

To Make the Jelly:

  2 cups strawberry juice (from above)
  3½ cups sugar
  2 tablespoons lemon juice
  ½ bottle (3 ounces) fruit pectin

Add sugar and lemon juice to juice in saucepan; mix well. Place over high heat; bring to a boil, stirring constantly. At once stir in pectin. Then bring to a full, rolling boil; boil hard 1 minute, stirring constantly. Remove from heat; skim; pour quickly into clean, scalded glasses. Cover jelly at once with ⅛-inch hot paraffin. Makes about five 6-ounce glasses.

APPLE MINT JELLY

  1½ cups packed mint leaves and stems
  3¼ cups bottled apple juice
  1 box (1¾ ounces) powdered fruit pectin
  3½ cups sugar
  Green coloring

Wash mint; place in saucepan; crush thoroughly with a wooden masher. Add apple juice and pectin. Place over high heat; bring quickly to boil. Remove from heat; cover; let stand 10 minutes. Strain through a fine sieve or double thickness of cheesecloth into large saucepan. Place saucepan holding juice over high heat. Stir in sugar. Bring to a full, rolling boil and boil hard 1 minute, stirring constantly. Remove from heat; add enough green food coloring to give desired shade. Skim off foam with metal spoon; pour quickly into clean, scalded glasses. Paraffin at once. Makes about six 6-ounce glasses.

GRAPE JELLY I

(Made with bottled grape juice.)

  2 cups bottled grape juice
  3 cups sugar
  ½ bottle (3 ounces) liquid fruit pectin

Measure grape juice and sugar into a large saucepan; mix well. Bring quickly to boiling point over high heat. At once add pectin, stirring constantly. Bring to a full, rolling boil; boil hard

exactly ½ minute. Remove from heat; skim. Pour quickly into clean, scalded jelly glasses. Paraffin at once. Makes five 6-ounce glasses.

GRAPE JELLY II

  5½ pounds ripe Concord grapes
  ½ cup water
  7 cups sugar
  ½ bottle (3 ounces) liquid fruit pectin

Stem grapes; crush well. Add water; simmer, covered, 5 minutes. Strain through double cheesecloth. Measure 4 cups juice into large saucepan; add sugar; mix. Bring to boil, stirring constantly. At once stir in liquid pectin. Bring to full, rolling boil; boil 1 minute, stirring constantly. Remove from heat; skim; pour quickly into clean, scalded glasses. Paraffin at once. Makes about ten 6-ounce glasses.

PLUM-AND-GRAPE JELLY

To Prepare the Juice:

  1½ pounds fully ripe grapes
  2 pounds (about) fully ripe plums
  ¾ cup water

Stem and crush fully ripe grapes; crush thoroughly fully ripe plums. (Do not peel or pit.) Combine fruits. Add ¾ cup water; bring to boil; cover; simmer 10 minutes. Place in jelly cloth or bag; squeeze out juice. Measure 3½ cups into large saucepan.

To Make the Jelly:

  3½ cups juice (from above)
  1 box (1¾ ounces) powdered fruit pectin
  4½ cups sugar

Place saucepan holding juice over high heat. Add powdered fruit pectin; stir until mixture comes to a hard boil. At once stir in sugar. Bring to a full, rolling boil and boil hard ½ minute, stirring constantly. Remove from heat; skim; pour quickly into clean, scalded glasses. Paraffin at once. Makes about eight 6-ounce glasses.

NECTAR-ORANGE JELLY

  1 cup apricot whole-fruit nectar
  ½ cup orange juice
  2 tablespoons lemon juice
  3½ cups sugar
  ½ bottle (3 ounces) liquid pectin

Combine nectar, orange and lemon juices, and sugar. Cook and stir over high heat until sugar is dissolved and mixture reaches boiling point. Stir in pectin; bring to full, rolling boil; boil hard 1 minute. Remove from heat; skim foam from surface; pour at once into clean, scalded glasses. Seal with paraffin. Makes about four 6-ounce glasses.

CHABLIS WINE JELLY

2 cups Chablis
¾ cup apple cider
¼ cup lemon juice
1 package (¾ ounces) powdered fruit pectin
3½ cups sugar
Candied ginger *or* dried sweet basil,
    rosemary, or tarragon

Combine Chablis, cider, and lemon juice in 4-quart kettle. Add fruit pectin; bring to hard boil over high heat, stirring constantly. Stir in sugar. Bring to full, rolling boil; boil hard 2 minutes. Remove from heat; skim off foam; pour into hot sterilized glasses, leaving ½-inch space at top of glass. To each glass add 1 tablespoon chopped candied ginger or ¼ teaspoon of any preferred dried herb. Push into jelly with back of spoon. Paraffin at once. Makes six 6-ounce glasses.

PINK CHAMPAGNE JELLY

2 cups pink champagne
¾ cup apple cider
¼ cup lemon juice
1 package (1¾ ounces) powdered fruit pectin
3½ cups sugar
Red food coloring

Combine champagne, cider, and lemon juice in 4-quart kettle. Add fruit pectin. Bring to hard boil over high heat, stirring constantly. Stir in sugar and few drops red food coloring. Bring to full, rolling boil and boil hard 1 minute. Remove from heat; skim off foam; pour into hot sterilized glasses, leaving ⅓-inch space at top of each.

To Make Champagne Bubbles: Let jelly cool (about 3 hours) until it is partially set. Then insert a teaspoon into center of jelly and rotate the bowl of the spoon several times. This allows air to come in and creates the bubbles. (To avoid breaking up the jelly, do not remove spoon during stirring.) Seal with paraffin. Makes six 6-ounce glasses.

STRAWBERRY JAM

To Prepare the Fruit:

Use strawberries remaining from Strawberry Jelly (page 383) or prepare as directed for that recipe. Measure 4 cups into very large saucepan.

To Make the Jam:

4 cups prepared strawberries (from above)
7 cups sugar
2 tablespoons lemon juice
½ bottle (3 ounces) fruit pectin

Add sugar and lemon juice to fruit in saucepan; mix well. Place over high heat; bring to a full, rolling boil; boil hard 1 minute, stirring constantly. Remove from heat; at once stir in pectin. Then stir and skim by turns for 5 minutes to cool slightly and to prevent floating fruit. Ladle quickly into clean, scalded glasses. Cover at once with paraffin. Fills about ten 6-ounce glasses.

STRAWBERRY-RHUBARB JAM

1 pound rhubarb
1 quart ripe strawberries
7 cups (3 pounds) sugar
½ bottle (3 ounces) liquid fruit pectin

Slice rhubarb (do not peel). Chop or crush strawberries. Combine fruits; measure 4 cups into large saucepan or kettle. Add sugar; mix well. Place over high heat; bring to full, rolling boil; boil hard exactly 1 minute. Remove from heat; stir in fruit pectin. Ladle quickly into clean, scalded self-sealing half-pint jars, leaving about ⅛-inch head space. Remove lids from hot water; place on jars. When all jars are filled, screw bands tight. Let stand 30 minutes; shake each jar gently to distribute fruit through syrup. Fills about 6 half-pint jars.

PEACH-AND-GINGER JAM

2½ pounds soft, ripe peaches
4½ cups sugar
½ cup sliced candied ginger
1 box (1¾ ounces) powdered fruit pectin

Pare and pit peaches; chop very fine or grind. Measure 3½ cups into large saucepan. Measure sugar; add ginger; set aside. Place saucepan holding fruit over high heat. Add pectin; stir until mixture comes to a hard boil. At once stir in sugar. Bring to a full, rolling boil; boil hard 1 minute, stirring constantly. Remove from heat; skim; ladle quickly into clean, scalded glasses. Paraffin at once. Makes about eight 6-ounce glasses.

SPICED PEACH JAM

3 pounds soft, ripe peaches
¼ cup lime juice
7½ cups sugar
1 teaspoon cinnamon
½ teaspoon allspice
¼ teaspoon cloves
1 bottle (6 ounces) liquid fruit pectin

Pare and pit peaches; chop fine or grind. Measure 4 cups into large saucepan. Add lime juice. Mix sugar and spices; add. Place over high heat. Bring to full, rolling boil; boil hard 1 minute, stirring constantly; remove from heat; stir in pectin. Stir and skim by turns 5 minutes. Ladle into clean, scalded glasses. Paraffin at once. Makes eleven 6-ounce glasses.

PLUM-BANANA JAM

To Prepare the Fruit:

3 ripe bananas
1½ pounds (about) fully ripe plums

Mash bananas to fine pulp. Pit (do not peel) about 1½ pounds fully ripe plums. Cut in small pieces; chop. Combine fruits; measure 3½ cups into large saucepan.

To Make the Jam:

3½ cups prepared fruit (from above)
4½ cups sugar
1 box (1¾ ounces) powdered fruit pectin

Measure sugar; set aside. Place saucepan holding fruit over high heat. Add powdered fruit pectin; stir until mixture comes to a hard boil. At once stir in sugar. Bring to a full, rolling boil; boil hard 1 minute, stirring constantly. Remove from heat; skim; ladle quickly into clean, scalded glasses. Paraffin at once. Makes eight 6-ounce glasses.

PLUM-PEACH JAM

To Prepare the Fruit:

1½ pounds (about) soft, ripe peaches
1 pound (about) fully ripe plums

Peel and pit about 1½ pounds soft, ripe peaches. Grind or chop very fine. Pit (do not peel) about 1 pound fully ripe plums. Cut in small pieces; chop. Combine fruits; measure 4½ cups into large saucepan.

To Make the Jam:

4½ cups prepared fruit (from above)
7½ cups sugar
1 bottle (6 ounces) fruit pectin

Add sugar to fruit in saucepan; mix well. Place over high heat; bring to full, rolling boil; boil hard 1 minute, stirring constantly. Remove from heat; at once stir in fruit pectin. Stir and skim by turns for 5 minutes to cool slightly and to prevent floating fruit. Ladle quickly into clean, scalded glasses. Paraffin at once. Makes about twelve 6-ounce glasses.

RASPBERRY JAM

To Prepare the Fruit:

2 quarts (about) fully ripe red raspberries

Crush thoroughly about 2 quarts fully ripe red raspberries. (If desired, sieve half of pulp to remove some of seeds.) Measure 4 cups into very large saucepan.

To Make the Jam:

4 cups prepared raspberries (from above)
6½ cups sugar
½ bottle (3 ounces) fruit pectin

Add sugar to fruit in saucepan; mix well. Place over high heat; bring to full, rolling boil; boil hard 1 minute, stirring constantly. Remove from heat; stir in bottled fruit pectin. Stir and skim by turns for 5 minutes to cool slightly and to prevent floating fruit. Ladle quickly into clean, scalded glasses. Paraffin at once. Makes about ten 6-ounce glasses.

GINGER-PEAR JAM

To Prepare the Fruit:

3 pounds (about) fully ripe pears
1 to 2 teaspoons powdered ginger

Peel and core about 3 pounds fully ripe pears. Grind or chop very fine. Measure 4 cups into large saucepan. Add powdered ginger to taste.

To Make the Jam:

4 cups prepared pears (from above)
7½ cups sugar
1 bottle (6 ounces) liquid fruit pectin

Add sugar to fruit in saucepan; mix well. Place over high heat; bring to full, rolling boil; boil hard 1 minute, stirring constantly. Remove from heat; at once stir in pectin. Stir and skim by turns for 5 minutes to cool slightly and to prevent floating fruit. Ladle quickly into clean, scalded glasses. Paraffin at once. Makes about eleven 6-ounce glasses.

Spiced Pear Jam: In place of ginger, substitute ½ to 1 teaspoon each cinnamon, cloves, and allspice or any combination of spices to pears before cooking.

RIPE RASPBERRY MARMALADE

To Prepare the Fruit:

2 medium oranges
2 medium lemons
1 cup water
⅛ teaspoon baking soda
1 quart fully ripe raspberries

Peel off yellow rind of oranges and lemons with sharp knife, leaving as much of white part on fruit as possible. Put yellow peels through food chopper; add water and baking soda; bring to a boil; cover; simmer 10 minutes. Cut off tight skin of peeled fruit and slip pulp out of each section. Add pulp and juice to cooked peel; simmer, covered, 20 minutes longer. Crush or grind raspberries; combine with orange mixture.

To Make the Marmalade:

7 cups sugar
4 cups prepared fruit (from above)
1 bottle (6 ounces) fruit pectin

Measure sugar and prepared fruit into large saucepan, filling up last cup of fruit with water if necessary. Mix well. Place over high heat; bring to a full, rolling boil; boil hard 1 minute, stirring constantly. Remove from heat; at once stir in bottled fruit pectin. Stir and skim by turns for 5 minutes to cool slightly and to prevent floating fruit. Pour quickly into clean, scalded glasses. Paraffin at once. Makes about 11 medium-sized glasses.

MYSTERY MARMALADE

2 cups peeled, seeded, finely chopped
    cucumbers
4 cups sugar
2 tablespoons grated lime peel
Few drops green food coloring (optional)
½ bottle (3 ounces) liquid fruit pectin

Peel cucumbers; remove seeds; chop. Pour chopped cucumbers into large saucepan. Add sugar, lime juice, and lime peel; mix well. Place over high heat; add food coloring, if desired; bring to full, rolling boil. Boil hard exactly 1 minute, stirring constantly. Remove from heat; at once stir in pectin. Skim off foam; then stir and skim 5 minutes to cool slightly and to prevent floating particles. Ladle quickly into clean, scalded jelly glasses. Paraffin at once. Makes about 5 medium-sized glasses.

CONCORD CONSERVE

To Prepare the Fruit:

3 pounds (about) fully ripe Concord grapes
2 medium-sized lemons

Slip skins from about 3 pounds fully ripe Concord grapes; reserve the skins. Bring pulp to a boil and simmer, covered, 5 minutes. Sieve to remove seeds. Chop or grind skins; add to pulp. Measure 4 cups into very large saucepan. Grate the peel from lemons. Measure 1 tablespoon peel into saucepan with grapes. Squeeze the juice from the lemons and add ¼ cup juice to fruit.

To Make the Conserve:

4 cups prepared grapes (from above)
7 cups sugar
½ pound seeded raisins
1 cup finely chopped nutmeats
½ bottle (3 ounces) fruit pectin

Add sugar, raisins, and nutmeats to fruit in saucepan; mix well. Place over high heat; bring to full, rolling boil; boil hard 1 minute, stirring constantly. Remove from heat; at once stir in pectin. Stir and skim by turns for 5 minutes to prevent floating fruit. Ladle quickly into clean, scalded glasses. Paraffin at once. Makes about eleven 8-ounce glasses.

APRICOT-FIG CONSERVE

2 cups dried apricots
2 cups dried figs
1 lemon
5 cups water
3 cups sugar
⅛ teaspoon salt
½ cup canned slivered blanched almonds

Rinse apricots and figs (remove stems); cut in small pieces. Cut lemon in thin slices. Combine fruits, water, sugar, and salt; boil about 1 hour or until lemon peel is clear, stirring frequently. Add almonds; boil 5 minutes. Pour into clean, scalded glasses. Paraffin at once. Makes about twelve 6-ounce glasses.

SNAPPY CRANBERRY RELISH

1⅔ cups sugar
1 cup water
4 cups fresh cranberries
1 cup raisins
1½ teaspoons powdered ginger
¼ teaspoon ground cloves
1 cinnamon stick, 2 inches long
1 onion, thinly sliced
1 apple, chopped
½ cup thinly sliced celery

Combine sugar, water, cranberries, raisins, and spices in saucepan. Cook until berries pop and mixture starts to thicken (about 20 minutes). Add remaining ingredients; simmer 15 to 20 minutes longer or until relish is as thick as desired. Discard cinnamon stick. Ladle into clean, scalded jelly glasses; seal at once with paraffin. Makes about five 8-ounce glasses.

RAISIN-CRANBERRY RELISH

1 pound fresh cranberries
3 cups water
2 cups golden raisins
2¼ cups sugar
1 teaspoon grated orange peel
¼ cup orange juice

Rinse and drain cranberries; add water; boil about 10 minutes. Rub through sieve. Rinse and drain raisins. Combine strained cranberries, raisins, sugar, orange peel and juice; boil 10 minutes. Pour into clean, scalded glasses; paraffin at once. Makes six 6-ounce glasses.

CRANBERRY-PINEAPPLE RELISH

Combine 1 can (20 ounces) whole-berry cranberry sauce with 1 can (9 ounces) crushed pineapple, drained. Mix well. Chill thoroughly. Makes about 2¼ cups.

PEACH RELISH

To Prepare the Fruit:

4 pounds (about) soft, ripe peaches

Peel and pit about 4 pounds soft, ripe peaches. Grind. Measure 4 cups into large saucepan.

To Make the Relish:

4 cups prepared peaches (from above)
½ cup vinegar
1 box (1¾ ounces) powdered fruit pectin
5 cups sugar

Add vinegar to fruit in saucepan; place over high heat. Add powdered fruit pectin; stir continuously until mixture comes to a hard boil. At once stir in sugar. Bring to a full rolling boil; boil hard 1 minute, stirring constantly. Remove from heat. Stir and skim by turns for 5 minutes to cool slightly and to prevent floating fruit. Ladle quickly into clean, scalded glasses. Paraffin at once. Makes about nine 6-ounce glasses.

Spiced Peach Relish: Add ½ to 1 teaspoon each cinnamon, cloves, and allspice or any desired combination of spices to peaches before cooking.

RIPE PLUM RELISH

To Prepare the Fruit:

2 pounds (about) fully ripe plums
¼ to 1 teaspoon each cinnamon, cloves, and allspice (to taste)

Pit (do not peel) about 2 pounds fully ripe plums. Cut in pieces; chop fine. Add cinnamon, cloves, and allspice or any desired combination of spices. Measure 3½ cups fruit into very large saucepan.

To Make the Relish:

3½ cups prepared plums (from above)
6½ cups sugar
½ cup vinegar
½ bottle (3 ounces) fruit pectin

Add sugar and vinegar to fruit in saucepan; mix well. Place over high heat; bring to a full, rolling boil; boil hard 1 minute, stirring constantly. Remove from heat; at once stir in bottled fruit pectin. Stir and skim by turns for 5 minutes to cool slightly and prevent floating fruit. Ladle quickly into clean, scalded glasses. Paraffin at once. Makes about ten 6-ounce glasses.

BEET RELISH

1 can (1 pound) shoestring beets
½ cup sugar
6 teaspoons vinegar
¼ cup prepared horseradish

Drain beets; combine with remaining ingredients; chill several hours. Makes 6 servings.

CARAWAY BEET RELISH

1 medium onion, sliced thin
2 cans (1 pound each) diced beets, drained
     (reserve juice)
½ cup reserved beet juice
1 cup sugar
1 cup wine vinegar
1 teaspoon caraway seeds
½ teaspoon salt
Few grains black pepper

Separate onion slices into rings; combine with beets. Combine remaining ingredients; heat to boiling. Pour over beets and onions. Cool. Refrigerate overnight. Makes about 4 cups.

CORN RELISH

3 cans (12 ounces each) kernel corn
1 cup chopped onion
1 cup thinly sliced celery
½ cup chopped green pepper
1 can (4 ounces) pimiento, drained and diced
1 cup sugar
1 tablespoon salt
1 teaspoon crushed dried sweet red pepper
     (optional)
1 large garlic clove, minced (optional)
1 tablespoon celery seed
1 tablespoon mustard seed
½ teaspoon ground ginger
3 cups white vinegar, divided
1½ tablespoons dry mustard
1 teaspoon turmeric
¼ cup flour
¼ cup corn liquid from can

Drain corn thoroughly; reserve ¼ cup liquid. Combine onion, celery, green pepper, pimiento, sugar, salt, red pepper, garlic, seeds, ginger, and 2½ cups of the vinegar. Boil 5 minutes. Blend mustard, turmeric, and flour with corn liquid until smooth. Thin with the remaining ½ cup vinegar. Add to hot mixture; cook 5 or 6 minutes or until liquid thickens to consistency of cream. Add corn. Boil 5 minutes. Pour boiling-hot relish to within ¼ inch of top of clean, scalded half-pint jars. Cover and seal as directed for jars being used. Makes about 8 half-pint jars.

QUICK CORN RELISH

1 can (1 pound) whole kernel corn
½ cup sweet pickle relish
½ teaspoon celery seed
½ cup cider vinegar

Drain liquid from corn. Reduce liquid by boiling to about half. Add corn and other ingredients; simmer 10 minutes. Serve hot or cold. Makes 8 servings.

CUCUMBER-DILL RELISH

3 medium cucumbers
¼ cup grated onion
½ teaspoon pepper
1½ teaspoons salt
¼ cup cider vinegar
1 teaspoon dillweed

Put cucumbers through food chopper, using medium blade. Drain well. Stir in remaining ingredients. Chill several hours. Makes about 2 cups.

ONION RELISH

3 medium onions
1 green pepper
1 tomato
1 cucumber
½ teaspoon salt
¼ teaspoon cayenne
3 teaspoons sugar
Juice of 1 lemon
½ cup vinegar
2 tablespoons vegetable oil

Cut onions, green pepper, tomato, and cucumber in thin slices. Combine remaining ingredients; mix well; pour over vegetables; toss until thoroughly mixed. Makes 6 to 8 servings.

UNCOOKED TOMATO RELISH

1 quart chopped tomatoes
½ cup thinly sliced celery
½ cup finely chopped onion
¼ cup diced green pepper
4½ teaspoons sugar
1 teaspoon salt
1½ teaspoons mustard seed
⅛ teaspoon ground nutmeg
⅛ teaspoon ground cinnamon
Dash ground cloves
½ cup vinegar

Combine all ingredients; mix thoroughly. Turn into clean, scalded half-pint jars. Cover tightly. Store in refrigerator. Relish will keep 2 to 3 weeks. Makes about 2½ pints.

CHOP-CHOP RELISH

1 cup finely chopped cabbage
½ cup finely diced tomato
¼ cup finely chopped onion
¼ cup finely chopped green pepper
¼ cup finely chopped celery
¼ cup chopped radishes
½ teaspoon salt
Few grains pepper
1 tablespoon sugar
2 tablespoons tarragon vinegar

Combine all ingredients. Chill thoroughly before serving. Makes 2½ cups.

BARBECUE RELISH

1 package (3 ounces) lemon-flavor gelatin
1¼ cups hot water
1 can (8 ounces) tomato sauce
1½ tablespoons vinegar
Few drops hot-pepper sauce
1 green pepper, minced
1 cup finely chopped raw cabbage
½ cup finely diced celery
2 tablespoons cut chives
1 tablespoon prepared horseradish
Vegetable oil

Dissolve gelatin in hot water; add tomato sauce, vinegar, and hot-pepper sauce. Chill until mixture begins to thicken. Fold in green pepper, cabbage, celery, chives, and horseradish. Turn into oiled refrigerator tray. Insert oiled ice cube divider. Chill (do not freeze) until set. Unmold

squares. Makes about 16 squares, depending on size.
ACCOMPANIMENT: Cold cuts.

SWEET-SOUR CUCUMBERS

2 medium cucumbers
3 medium onions
½ cup white vinegar
½ cup sugar
½ teaspoon salt

Do not peel cucumbers; score lengthwise with tines of fork; slice paper-thin. Slice onions; separate into rings; combine with cucumbers. Combine vinegar, sugar, and salt; stir over low heat until sugar dissolves; bring to boil; pour over cucumbers and onions; chill. Makes 6 to 8 servings.

WATERMELON PICKLES

4 pounds watermelon rind
2 quarts cold water
1 tablespoon slaked lime*
2 tablespoons whole allspice
2 tablespoons whole cloves
10 2-inch pieces stick cinnamon
1 quart cider vinegar
1 quart water
4 pounds sugar

Remove all pink pulp from watermelon rind; peel. Weigh. Cut in 1-inch circles or cubes. Combine 2 quarts cold water and lime; pour over rind. Let stand 1 hour. Drain. Cover with fresh cold water. Simmer 1½ hours or until tender; drain. Tie spices in cheesecloth. Combine vinegar, remaining 1 quart water, and sugar. Heat until sugar dissolves; add spice bag and rind; simmer gently 2 hours. Discard spice bag. Pack rind in clean, hot sterile jars. Fill jars with boiling-hot syrup. Seal. Makes about 12 half pints.

*Powder #40 lime (slaked), Eli Lilly & Co.

CUCUMBER CHUNK PICKLES

½ peck young cucumbers
¼ cup salt
½ teaspoon powdered alum
Grape leaves (optional)
Seedless white grapes
Dill seed
2½ cups cider vinegar
2½ cups water

2½ cups sugar
1 tablespoon mixed pickling spices

Wash cucumbers; do not peel or seed. Cut in 1-inch chunks. Sprinkle with salt; cover with cold water. Let stand 24 hours; drain, saving brine. Heat brine to boiling; add alum. Pour over cucumbers; let stand 12 hours; drain. Place sterilized pint jars in pan of hot water. Place a grape leaf in bottom of each jar. Fill jars with cucumber chunks; pack firmly. Add 3 to 4 grapes and ⅛ teaspoon dill seed (or sprig of fresh dill) to each jar. Heat until cucumbers are warmed through. Combine remaining ingredients; bring to boil. Pour into containers. Place grape leaf on top. Seal. Makes about 8 pints.

BAKED APPLESAUCE

5 pounds tart apples
1 cup currant jelly
⅓ cup sugar
⅔ cup water
⅓ cup lemon juice
¼ teaspoon nutmeg

Pare and core apples; slice in eighths; place in casserole. Combine jelly, sugar, and water; heat until jelly is partially melted. Remove from heat; stir in lemon juice and nutmeg; pour over apples. Cover; bake at 350° for 45 minutes to 1 hour or until apples are soft; stir to desired consistency. Serve hot. Makes about 5 cups.

HOLIDAY APPLESAUCE

1 jar (about 1 pound) applesauce
Few drops green food coloring
½ teaspoon mint extract
6 maraschino cherries, chopped

Remove cap from jar. Add green food coloring (enough to get color desired) and stir into applesauce. Add mint extract; stir in thoroughly. Add chopped cherries; stir through applesauce. Recap jar; store in refrigerator until ready to use. Makes 6 to 8 servings as a relish with meat, 4 servings as a dessert.

SPICED PEACHES

1 can (29 ounces) cling peach halves
2 teaspoons whole cloves, divided
3-inch piece stick cinnamon
⅔ cup firmly packed brown sugar
3 tablespoons vinegar

Drain peach syrup into saucepan. Add 1 teaspoon cloves and stick cinnamon. Stud peach halves with remaining cloves; return to peach can. Bring syrup to boil; boil rapidly until reduced to about ½ cup. Add brown sugar and vinegar. Simmer 5 minutes. Pour over peaches in can. Let stand several hours. Reheat; drain; use to garnish roast chicken or turkey.

PEACH CHUTNEY

2 cans (29 ounces each) cling peach slices
1 green pepper
1 large onion
½ cup light or dark raisins
1 cup firmly packed brown sugar
1½ cups vinegar
¼ cup chopped preserved ginger
½ teaspoon salt
¼ teaspoon cloves
¼ teaspoon nutmeg
½ teaspoon cayenne
¼ teaspoon black pepper

Drain peaches. Remove membrane and seeds from green pepper. Chop pepper and onion. Rinse and drain raisins. Combine all ingredients; simmer 1 to 1½ hours, until thick. Store in covered jars in refrigerator. Makes about 1 quart.

PEAR CHUTNEY

1 small onion, chopped
1 medium apple, peeled and chopped
2 tablespoons crystallized ginger
½ teaspoon salt
¼ teaspoon mustard seeds
⅓ cup cider vinegar
2 tablespoons lemon juice
½ cup firmly packed brown sugar
3 whole cloves
¼ cup raisins
1 jar (20 ounces) whole pears

Peel onion; chop fine. Peel apple; chop. Cut ginger in small pieces. Mix together onion, apple, ginger, salt, mustard seeds, vinegar, lemon juice, sugar, cloves, and raisins. Slowly bring mixture to a boil, stirring occasionally. Reduce heat; cook gently for 25 minutes or until mixture thickens. Meanwhile, remove cap from jar and drain liquid from pears. Core pears; cut in small pieces. Add pears to mixture; cook 5 minutes longer. Pack hot in original glass container. Recap tightly. Store in refrigerator.

PRUNE MINCEMEAT

1 pound pitted prunes
1 pound lean boneless chuck steak
¼ pound suet
¼ pound citron
2 cans (20 ounces each) pie-sliced apples
1 pound raisins
1 quart apple juice
3½ cups sugar
1½ teaspoons nutmeg
1½ teaspoons cinnamon
¼ teaspoon cloves

Cover prunes with cold water. Let stand 24 hours. Drain. Cover meat with boiling water; simmer until tender. Let cool in broth. Remove meat (use broth for soup). Put meat, suet, citron, and prunes through fine blade of food chopper. Chop apples fine; add to prune mixture. Combine this mixture with raisins, apple juice, sugar, nutmeg, cinnamon, and cloves. Simmer over low heat 1½ hours or until thick, stirring often to prevent sticking. Pour into hot sterilized jars; seal. Makes 3 quarts, or enough for three 9-inch pies.

CLARET PRUNES

1 jar (approximately 1 pound) stewed prunes
⅔ cup claret
⅓ cup prune liquid from jar
¼ cup brown sugar
¼ teaspoon powdered cinnamon
⅛ teaspoon powdered allspice
6 whole cloves

Remove lid from jar; set lid aside. Drain liquid from prunes; save liquid. Place ⅓ cup liquid, wine, sugar, and spices in saucepan. Cook, stirring occasionally, until mixture comes to a boil. Reduce heat; cook gently for 5 minutes. Remove from heat; cool slightly before pouring over prunes. Recap jar tightly. Store in refrigerator until ready to use.

CRANBERRIES CLARET

4 cups cranberries
2 cups sugar
1 cup claret
1 cup water

Pick over and wash cranberries; combine sugar, wine, and water in deep saucepan; stir over low heat until sugar dissolves; boil 5 minutes. Add cranberries; cook until skins pop open (about 10 minutes). Chill. Makes about 1 quart.

MAPLE-JELL

1 tablespoon lemon juice
1 bottle (12 ounces) maple-blended syrup
1 bottle (6 ounces) liquid fruit pectin

Place lemon juice in medium bowl. Pour in maple-blended syrup and fruit pectin; stir well. Pour into 2 sterilized 8-ounce jelly glasses. Cover at once with tight lids or seals. Let stand at room temperature 3 days to set. Serve as an accompaniment to waffles or other hot breads or with meats.

BANANA SCALLOPS I

1¾ cups grated Swiss cheese
1 tablespoon flour
¼ teaspoon salt
½ teaspoon Worcestershire sauce
3 egg whites, stiffly beaten
2 bananas
Packaged cornflake crumbs
Vegetable oil for frying

Combine cheese, flour, salt, and Worcestershire sauce. Fold in egg whites. Cut bananas in ½-to-¾-inch slices. Coat each slice with cheese mixture (don't dip; pat around banana slice to coat evenly); roll in crumbs. Pour oil in skillet to depth of 1½ inches; heat to 375°. Fry scallops in oil until golden brown. Drain on absorbent paper. Serve immediately as meat or fish accompaniment. Makes 10 to 15 scallops.

BANANA SCALLOPS II

1½ teaspoons salt
¼ cup undiluted evaporated milk
6 firm bananas
¾ cup fine cornflake crumbs
Fat for frying
Peanut butter

Add salt to milk. Peel bananas; cut in ¾-to-1-inch crosswise slices. Dip in evaporated milk; drain. Roll slices in crumbs. Fry in shallow fat, 1 inch deep, heated to 375° for 1½ to 2 minutes or until golden brown. Drain on absorbent paper. Pick up 2 scallops on wooden picks; put together with dab of peanut butter. Serve as accompaniment to ham.

CHAPTER 21

Outdoor Cooking

Of one thing there is no doubt: outdoor cooking grows in importance and popularity with every year. House buyers are demanding an outdoor living area, and the manufacturing of barbecuing equipment has become very big business, with prices for such equipment varying from the inexpensive to thousands of dollars.

What of the future? It's easy to predict that there will be more and more outdoor cookery. More meats will be merchandised specifically for this purpose, and more and more women will get into the act.

So join the outdoor cooking fans. Learn to barbecue with expertise. Delight your family, friends, and neighbors with well-planned, well-cooked barbecue menus, and enjoy the pleasures of the rich, hearty flavor that outdoor cooking bestows.

How to Barbecue with Charcoal

Always use charcoal briquettes of good quality made from oak, maple, beech, or birch wood, all of which are hardwoods with low resin content. Store the briquettes in a dry place or they will absorb moisture and be difficult to ignite.

Choose a fire starter that best suits your needs.

Electric starters are practical because they are reusable, but they are expensive and they must be plugged into an electrical outlet. Safe liquid and jelly fire starters are readily available. Follow the manufacturer's directions for use, and follow them *exactly*. Never add a starter to a fire that is burning or to warm briquettes. *Never* use gasoline or alcohol.

As the briquettes burn, a fine gray ash will form on the surface. Just before starting to cook, tap off the ash with a fire rake or poker. Repeat this tapping occasionally during cooking.

Allow plenty of time to prepare a good bed of coals before beginning to cook. If you are using an electric fire starter, allow about fifteen minutes; for other starters, allow at least forty-five minutes.

Put some extra briquettes at the edge of the barbecue to warm up, and add them to the fire about fifteen minutes before they are needed for additional heat. Cold briquettes lower the temperature and slow up the cooking.

When the coals are ash-covered, spread them over a gravel base (see manufacturer's directions) or foil lining about a half inch apart, or if a spit is being used, heap them toward the rear of the unit and set a foil drip pan in front of them (page 394).

All of the recipes in this book can be used with various types of barbecue units. Prepare the food as directed in the recipe; then follow the manufacturer's directions for using the appliance.

BARBECUING ON A HIBACHI

Any of the kabob recipes in this book, small steaks, chops, and so forth, can be grilled on a hibachi for a small group of people. Use short skewers, smaller portions, and foods that adapt themselves to a small cooking area, such as hors d'oeuvres.

Follow manufacturer's directions for the use and care of this cooking device.

Never use a hibachi inside the house unless you set it in a fireplace with a good draft to carry the fumes up and out. Burning charcoal gives off carbon monoxide, which is odorless, invisible—and deadly. Use a hibachi on a porch or patio where there is plenty of fresh air.

COOKING ON A GAS GRILL

Cooking on a gas-fired grill is similar to cooking with charcoal. Instead of charcoal, a pumice-type rock, ceramic briquettes, or volcanic rock "coals" are used, and the gas can be either natural or liquefied petroleum. These appliances are self-contained and cook primarily by radiant heat. As the food cooks, fat drops onto the coals and the smoke produces a barbecued look and flavor. For a stronger smoked flavor, sprinkle hickory chips over the coals.

In the majority of gas-fired grills the heat source is below the cooking surface. When the heat source is above, the unit is called an enclosed grill. Both types should be preheated for about ten minutes.

There are three types of gas-fired grills. In one, the grill is mounted on a permanent post and the gas line runs underground. The second type has a pedestal base that makes for a semipermanent installation and the gas line may be below or above the ground. The third type has a quickly connected flexible gas line. These three types are referred to as post, patio, and portable.

Today, gas grills are getting larger. Several manufacturers make single-hearth models with more than 450 square inches of cooking area. Some manufacturers make double-hearthed grills. One model has separate baking and broiling compartments, both of which are temperature-controlled. Another double-grilled model makes it possible to grill and do rotisserie cooking at the same time. Still another has a grill plus an oven, a warming shelf, and a smoke box.

Split grills are growing in popularity. By a simple adjustment of racks, rare and well-done portions can be prepared at the same time.

A warming shelf, a front or side service shelf, and a protective cover are standard with most grills. Other available equipment includes a rotisserie, quick-connect gas line assembly, automatic ignition, hickory chips, and griddle.

HOW TO USE A GAS GRILL

Follow the manufacturer's directions for use and care. An A.G.A. seal on the gas grill indicates that it complies with national safety standards.

To light: Open grill cover. Be sure the briquettes are in an even layer. Unless the grill has an automatic ignition, use a long wooden match, hold it near the ignition location, and turn control to high setting.

Leave the grill open and preheat at high setting for five to fifteen minutes.

If the cover is left closed during cooking there is more concentration of heat and smoke. This method is usually best for large cuts of meat such as hams, roasts, or turkeys.

A moderate amount of flaring and smoking is to be expected; this provides flavor and deep browning. If flaring is excessive, move food to another part of the grill and sprinkle a little water on the flaring briquettes. To avoid excess flaring, do not preheat too long or use briquettes that are coated with drippings. Trim excess fat from meat before grilling.

To clean: After each use, leave the burner at a medium setting, lower cover, and let food particles cook off for about fifteen minutes. Then use a wire brush on the grid. After several uses, remove the grid for washing in hot suds. Turn the briquettes every few weeks to keep all surfaces clean. Occasionally, brush the burner with a stiff brush, open any clogged parts with a wire, take out all interior parts, brush any food ash from bottom, wash outside and inside with hot suds, rinse, and dry thoroughly.

Your local gas company can undoubtedly supply you with helpful booklets on using an outdoor gas grill.

COOKING WITH WOOD FIRES

On camping or fishing trips, knowing how to build and use a wood fire is necessary. A wood fire should be started with small dry sticks and paper. When the small sticks are burning well, gradually add larger pieces of wood. Wait until these burn down to a good bed of coals before cooking. This will take about an hour. On a windy day improvise a fireplace with rocks and stones.

Aromatic wood fires can be built with oak, hickory, or fruitwoods, such as apple or wild cherry. Do not use pine, cedar, fir, spruce, or eucalyptus wood. They impart an unpleasant flavor to foods. On a beach, pick up driftwood of various sizes for your fire.

Caution: Before you leave be sure the fire is completely dead and cold. Use a fire extinguisher, dirt, or plenty of water, and be sure no sparks remain.

If you prefer, there are excellent portable camp stoves on the market. Follow carefully the instructions that come with the model you select and don't try to improvise with fuel or methods.

USING ALUMINUM FOIL IN BARBECUING

Heavy-duty aluminum foil is extremely helpful. The grill may be lined with foil and the fire built directly on it. Or, if the grill has a grate for holding the coals, the ash pit may be lined.

Foil reflects heat back on the food and speeds up cooking. It also catches drippings and makes cleanup easier. When the cooking is finished and the fire is dead, gather up the remaining ashes in the foil and throw in the trash can. Or, if there are partially burned briquettes that can be used again, close the foil over the fire to smother it, protecting your hands with asbestos mitts.

If a grill does not have a hood and the day is windy, use extra-long lengths of foil to line the grill. Bring the foil up and partially over the food to shield it and hold in the heat.

Wrap water-soaked hickory chips in foil. Punch a few holes in the foil and place directly on hot coals. No flare-up—just lots of smoke.

Cook foil-wrapped foods on the grill. Drip pans made of heavy-duty foil are essential for rotisserie cooking. To make one, tear two sheets from an eighteen-inch-wide roll of heavy-duty aluminum foil about five inches longer than the meat to be spit-roasted. Place the sheets one on top of the other. Fold in half lengthwise. Make a rim all around, one and one-half inches high. Pull out the corners, then fold them back against the sides, leaving the inside seams tight and smooth.

PLANNING A BARBECUE

Plan ahead.
Keep the menu simple.
Make out a complete market order.
Make desserts, juice cocktails, and so forth, ahead of time.
Prepare salad ingredients ahead of time.
Check barbecuing and serving equipment.
Make cleanup easy with paper supplies.

EQUIPMENT YOU WILL NEED

(Depending on the type of grill in use.)

For Fire Building and Cooking:

Gravel
Briquettes of good quality
Safe fire starter
Small fire rake
Fire tongs
Water (to quench flare-ups or briquettes)
Asbestos gloves
Small shovel
Hickory chips (optional)
Long matches
Skewers
Heavy-duty aluminum foil
Meat thermometer (for spit-roasting)
Basting brush
Fork, spatula, and tongs with long handles

For Seasoning and Serving:

Salt, pepper, and condiments
Carving board and carving knife and fork
Platters
Salad bowl and servers
Coffeepot
Trays
Plastic-coated paper plates
Paper cups for hot and cold beverages
Sturdy paper napkins
Paper towels
Paper or plastic garbage bags
Plastic knives, forks, and spoons to spare your fine silver
Ice bucket
Vacuum bottle or jug
Cellulose sponge and water for cleanup

HELPFUL HINTS

Brush the grill with vegetable oil or rub a piece of fat or suet from the meat across the grill to keep meat from sticking.

Trim excess fat from meat to prevent flare-ups.

Plan on two servings per person. For really hearty eaters, plan on three!

Buy three-quarters to one pound of meat with bone in for each person, a half pound if the meat is boneless.

Use natural meat tenderizer according to directions on label if you have reason to believe the meat may not be tender.

GRILL-ROASTED BEEF

1 roast of beef (see below)
Salt and pepper
Canned beef consommé

Choose a standing rib, a boned and rolled rib, or a top sirloin roast. A rib eye, the bone-out eye of a rib roast, is luxurious and wonderful eating, but available only on special order. Season beef with salt and pepper. Build the fire at one end of the grill pit. Line a shallow pan with heavy-duty aluminum foil and place under the rack that will hold the meat. When the hot coals are ready, place the roast on the rack. Insert meat thermometer in thickest part of roast. Close the grill cover; adjust dampers so fire burns slowly. Look at the roast occasionally; if it is overbrown, protect with a piece of foil. Add additional briquettes toward the end of the roasting time. Add hickory chips at this time, if desired. Roast will be cooked when the meat thermometer registers 140° for rare meat, 160° for medium, and 170° for well done. Remove roast to carving board. Remove pan with drippings; skim off excess fat; add canned beef consommé to make amount of gravy desired. Simmer; season to taste; serve without thickening.

BARBECUED RIB ROAST WITH CLASSIC KRAUT RELISH

3½ cups undrained sauerkraut
½ cup vegetable oil
¼ cup each wine vinegar and soy sauce
2 teaspoons Worcestershire sauce
2 small onions, thinly sliced
2 garlic cloves, crushed
1 teaspoon each coarsely ground pepper and dry mustard
Eye of rib roast, about 5 to 6 pounds
½ cup vinegar
1½ cups sugar
1 cup chopped celery
1 green pepper, chopped
1½ cups chopped sweet onion
1 jar (4 ounces) pimiento, drained and chopped

Drain kraut, reserving liquid; set kraut aside. Combine kraut liquid, oil, wine vinegar, soy sauce, Worcestershire sauce, sliced onions, garlic, ground pepper, and mustard in large shallow dish. Add roast; roll until coated on all sides. Cover; marinate several hours, turning occasionally. Combine kraut, vinegar, sugar, celery, green pepper, chopped sweet onion, and pimiento. Toss lightly; cover; chill several hours. Remove meat from marinade; balance securely on rotisserie spit. Insert meat thermometer parallel to spit; roast meat to desired degree of doneness, brushing occasionally with marinade. Just before serving, drain kraut relish; serve with meat. Makes 8 servings.

ROTISSERIED RUMP ROAST WITH BARBECUE SAUCE

1 rolled rump roast, 5 to 8 pounds
Barbecue Sauce*

Tie roast securely. Thread meat onto spit exactly through center. Make sure the roast is balanced on the spit to ensure smooth turning. Roast to the desired degree of doneness over coals. Allow 15 to 20 minutes per pound of meat for rare beef, 20 to 25 minutes per pound for medium, and 25 to 30 minutes per pound for well done. If meat thermometer is used, insert at a slight angle so the bulb is centered in the thickest part of the roast, but not resting in fat or on the rotisserie rod. Thermometer should register an internal temperature of 140° for a rare roast, 160° for a medium roast, or 170° for a well-done roast. Brush surface of roast with Barbecue Sauce 2 or 3 times during last 20 minutes of roasting. Slice and serve with additional Barbecue Sauce. Makes 12 to 15 servings.

*BARBECUE SAUCE

2 cans (8 ounces each) tomato sauce
½ cup firmly packed brown sugar
1 cup water
½ cup vinegar
1 cup coarsely chopped onion
1 garlic clove, minced
2 teaspoons chili powder
½ teaspoon salt

½ teaspoon pepper
2 teaspoons Worcestershire sauce

Combine all ingredients in saucepan. Simmer slowly over low heat 20 to 25 minutes to blend flavors. Makes about 3 cups sauce.

BARBECUED BEEF ON THE ROCKS

4-to-5-pound beef chuck roast, bone in
1 cup (about) prepared mustard
3 cups (about) rock salt

Trim any fat from edges of beef. Spread roast with mustard, coating top and sides completely. Pack rock salt onto mustard as thick as it will stick. Turn beef roast over. Coat reverse side with mustard and rock salt. Place beef directly on bed of glowing coals. Cook about 30 minutes, depending on thickness of chuck roast. Using a small baking sheet and a broad spatula, turn beef. Continue cooking for an additional 30 minutes. To determine degree of doneness, make a small, deep cut into the roast near the bone. Remove beef from charcoal. Knock off any salt that has not come off in the turning. Slice beef diagonally across the grain. Makes 6 to 8 servings.

CHUCK ROAST BARBECUE

1 chuck roast, 3 to 5 pounds
1 tablespoon salt
1 large onion, sliced
5 peeled potatoes
10 peeled carrots
Barbecue Sauce*

Rub beef with salt. Brown on grill over medium coals 15 minutes per side. Place on large sheet of heavy-duty aluminum foil. Top with onion. Place potatoes and carrots around sides. Cover with Barbecue Sauce. Wrap tightly in foil. Grill over low coals 2 hours, turning several times. Makes 5 to 6 servings.

*BARBECUE SAUCE

¼ cup vegetable oil
½ teaspoon garlic powder
½ cup catchup
¼ cup steak sauce
1 teaspoon salt
½ teaspoon pepper
1 teaspoon dry mustard
1 tablespoon brown sugar
2 tablespoons wine vinegar

Combine all ingredients. Cook, stirring constantly, over low heat until mixture boils. Makes about 1¼ cups sauce.

CHARCOAL-BROILED SIRLOIN STEAK WITH ONION RINGS AND FLAVORED BUTTER

1 sirloin steak (see below)
Choice of basting sauce, melted butter, *or* vegetable oil
Canned or frozen French fried onion rings
Chili-Onion Butter* *or* Ginger Butter**

Select a sirloin steak of the thickness desired. A 1½-to-2-inch-thick steak is best when serving a group or when a rare steak is desired. Trim any excess fat from outside edge of steak; save for greasing grids. Slash fat around edge of steak diagonally, with slashes 1 to 2 inches apart, to keep steak from curling during broiling. Grease hot grids with reserved fat. Grill steak 1½ to 2 inches thick 5 to 6 inches above hot coals. Grill first side; turn with tongs and grill second side. See chart below for suggested cooking times. Brush with favorite basting sauce, melted butter, or oil during grilling. To check steak for doneness, cut a small slash in center of steak with sharp-pointed knife, examine color, and continue broiling, if desired. Serve steak with hot canned or frozen French fried onion rings and Chili-Onion Butter or Ginger Butter.

SUGGESTED COOKING TIMETABLE

Thickness of Steak (inches)	Approximate Weight (pounds)	Inches Between Grill and Coals	MINUTES PER SIDE FOR		
			Rare	Medium	Well Done
2	3–3½	6	8–9	10–15	19–20
1½	2½–3	5	6–7	8–9	12–15
1	2½	4	5–6	6–8	9–10

*CHILI-ONION BUTTER

⅓ cup chopped onion
1 garlic clove, minced
½ cup butter or margarine, divided
2 tablespoons lemon juice
1 teaspoon chili powder
¼ teaspoon salt
¼ teaspoon pepper

Sauté onion and garlic in 2 tablespoons butter until onion is soft. Add lemon juice, chili powder, salt, and pepper; heat to simmering stage. Cool to room temperature. Cream remaining butter; add onion mixture gradually; cream well. Spread over hot steak. Makes about ¾ cup.

**GINGER BUTTER

⅓ cup orange juice
¼ cup sherry
2 tablespoons finely chopped preserved
    ginger
1 tablespoon preserved ginger syrup
1 tablespoon soy sauce
1 tablespoon lemon juice
½ cup butter or margarine

Combine first 6 ingredients; simmer until mixture is reduced to about ¼ cup. Cool to room temperature. Cream butter; add ginger mixture gradually; cream well. Spread over hot steak. Makes about ¾ cup.

SIZZLING RIB OR STRIP STEAKS

3 beef rib steaks, about 1½ pounds each, cut 1
    inch thick, *or* 4 to 6 loin strip steaks, ¾ to
    1 pound each, cut 1 inch thick
Marinade* (optional)
Basting Sauce and Spread for Steaks**
Sour-Cream Steak Sauce*** (optional)

Trim any excess fat from steaks; save fat pieces for greasing grill. Slash remaining fat around edge of steaks so the meat will remain flat and cook evenly. If desired, marinate steaks before broiling. This is done easily by placing steaks in a large plastic bag in a shallow pan. Pour Marinade over steaks; close bag. Refrigerate several hours, turning bag 2 or 3 times. Drain steaks; place on greased grill 3 to 4 inches above bed of glowing coals. Broil to doneness desired. Turn steaks with long tongs; brush with Basting Sauce. Count on about 4 minutes per side for rare steaks, 5 minutes for medium, 7 minutes for

well done. To check doneness, make a slash near center of steaks with knife point; examine color. Serve or continue cooking. Serve hot with Basting Spread or Sour-Cream Steak Sauce. Makes 6 to 8 servings. Count on ½ to ¾ pound raw steak per adult serving, ⅓ to ½ pound for children.

*MARINADE

¾ cup chopped onions
½ cup lemon juice or wine vinegar
½ cup vegetable oil
1½ teaspoons seasoned salt
½ teaspoon leaf thyme
½ teaspoon rosemary
1 garlic clove, minced

Combine ingredients; mix. Let stand at room temperature 1 hour to blend flavors; pour over steaks. Makes about 1¼ cups marinade, enough for 3 rib or 6 strip steaks.

**BASTING SAUCE AND SPREAD FOR STEAKS

½ cup wine or cider vinegar
½ cup water
½ cup chopped onions
3 tablespoons brown sugar
1 teaspoon prepared mustard
1 teaspoon Worcestershire sauce
½ teaspoon salt
¼ teaspoon tarragon leaves
½ cup butter or margarine, divided

Combine all ingredients except butter in saucepan. Simmer to blend flavors (10 to 15 minutes); strain. Add 2 tablespoons butter and let melt. Reserve and cool ¼ cup of sauce for making steak spread. Use remaining sauce for basting steaks while broiling. Cream reserved butter; add reserved ¼ cup sauce gradually; beat well. Keep cool until used. Makes about ¾ cup basting sauce and ½ cup spread.

***SOUR-CREAM STEAK SAUCE

½ pint dairy sour cream
2 tablespoons lemon juice or vinegar
¼ cup chopped onion
½ teaspoon paprika
¼ teaspoon each salt and garlic salt
Dash of pepper

Combine all ingredients; mix. Serve with steaks. Makes about 1¼ cups sauce.

GADO-GADO FAMILY STEAK

½ cup peanut butter
¾ cup hot water
¾ teaspoon crushed red chili pepper
1 tablespoon molasses
1 tablespoon soy sauce
2 garlic cloves, minced
½ teaspoon lemon juice
3-to-3½-pound boneless top round, cut 2 inches thick
Seasoned natural meat tenderizer

Combine peanut butter with hot water in a small saucepan; add all remaining ingredients except meat and tenderizer; simmer 5 minutes. Slash fat edges of meat. Use meat tenderizer as directed on label. Grill 2 inches above coals, 25 minutes for rare steak or 30 minutes for medium, turning frequently. When steak is done, place on meat board to carve. Using a sharp knife, cut steak in thin diagonal slices across the grain, holding knife at a 30° angle rather than perpendicular. To serve, pour peanut butter sauce over slices. Three or more slices make a generous portion. Makes 5 to 6 servings.

WIKIWIKI STEAK HAWAIIAN

1 foil packet (0.8 ounces) 15-minute meat marinade
⅔ cup pineapple juice
2 tablespoons soy sauce
1 garlic clove, minced
½ teaspoon ground ginger
4 to 6 steaks, from eye, top round, or shoulder, cut about 1 inch thick
2 slices pineapple, drained and cut in quarters
4 to 6 slices banana, cut diagonally about 1 inch thick

Blend package contents of meat marinade with pineapple juice, soy sauce, garlic, and ginger in shallow pan. Place steaks in marinade. Pierce all meat surfaces deeply and thoroughly with a fork to carry flavor deep down and to lock in natural juices. Marinate 15 minutes, turning several times. Remove steaks from marinade; drain. Reserve remaining marinade for basting. Grill 4 inches above coals 6 minutes per side for rare meat. The last 3 minutes, place pineapple on broiler grill. Baste steaks and pineapple frequently with marinade. To serve, top each steak with pineapple and banana slices skewered on a wooden pick. Or if you prefer, bananas may be dipped in pineapple juice and grilled along with pineapple slices during last 3 minutes. Makes 4 to 6 servings.

BARBECUED STEAK ORIENTAL

1 foil packet (0.8 ounces) 15-minute meat marinade
1 cup lemon-lime carbonated beverage
3 tablespoons soy sauce
2 tablespoons vegetable oil
¼ teaspoon ginger
1 tablespoon sesame seeds
1 teaspoon minced dried onion
2-to-2½-pound round, chuck, or sirloin tip steak, cut 1 inch thick

Thoroughly blend all ingredients except steak in shallow pan. Place steak in marinade. Pierce all meat surfaces deeply and thoroughly with a fork to carry flavor deep down and to retain natural meat juices. Marinate 15 minutes, turning several times. Remove meat from marinade, reserving marinade for sauce. Grill 3 inches above coals 6 to 7 minutes per side for rare steak or longer for further degrees of doneness. Makes 4 to 6 servings.

For Sauce: Pour remaining marinade into small saucepan; add about ⅓ cup additional lemon-lime carbonated beverage. Bring to a boil; simmer 5 minutes.

TOP ROUND WITH CHEESE

2-to-3-pound top round, cut 2 inches thick
1 foil packet (0.8 ounce) 15-minute meat marinade
⅔ cup cold water
4 to 6 sourdough French rolls
½ pound sliced Muenster cheese
Powdered cumin

Slash fat edges of meat to prevent curling. Thoroughly blend package contents of marinade and water in a shallow glass dish. Place meat in marinade. Pierce all surfaces of the meat deeply and thoroughly with a fork to carry flavor deep down and to lock in natural juices. Marinate only 15 minutes, turning several times. Remove meat from marinade; drain; reserve remaining marinade for basting. Grill 2 inches from heat 12 to 15 minutes for rare meat or until cooked to desired degree of doneness, turning frequently. Carve on the diagonal in very thin slices. Arrange hot steak strips on top of split sourdough French rolls as open-face sandwiches, alternating and overlapping steak with thin slices of Muenster cheese. Sprinkle with powdered cumin. Makes 4 to 6 servings.

KOREAN BARBECUED BEEF
(BUL-KOGI)

1 tablespoon sesame seeds
2 pounds lean beef, sirloin or top round, cut 1½ inches thick
3 scallions, finely chopped
3 to 4 garlic cloves, minced
5 tablespoons soy sauce
2 tablespoons vegetable oil
¼ cup sugar
2 tablespoons dry sherry
⅛ teaspoon black pepper

Brown the sesame seeds lightly over low heat; set aside. Slice the steak on the diagonal in very thin slices. Score each slice with an X. Combine remaining ingredients; mix well. Pour mixture over steak slices. Let stand about 30 minutes. Drain meat. Strain marinade; reserve. Grill steak slices (a hinged grill with a long handle makes this easier) as near to the source of heat as possible for 30 seconds to 1 minute; turn; sprinkle with sesame seeds. Grill 30 seconds longer. Serve with rice and reserved marinade. Makes 4 to 6 servings.

RUSTLER'S ROUND STEAK

1 foil packet (0.8 ounce) 15-minute meat marinade
⅔ cup tomato sauce
1 garlic clove, minced
1 teaspoon sweet basil, divided
2½-to-3-pound top or bottom round, or rump steak, cut 1 inch thick

In a shallow pan, thoroughly blend marinade, tomato sauce, garlic, and ½ teaspoon sweet basil. Place meat in marinade. Pierce all surfaces thoroughly and deeply with a fork. Marinate 15 minutes, turning several times. Use remaining marinade for basting. Toss remaining sweet basil on coals. Place meat on barbecue grill about 1 or 2 inches above glowing coals. (Coals are ready when gray, shot with a ruddy glow.) Grill a total of 12 to 15 minutes for rare, basting and turning frequently. To serve, carve across the grain of meat in thin slices. Makes 6 servings.

CIRCLE "A" CHUCK WAGON SPECIAL

2 blade chuck or round bone arm steaks, cut 1 inch thick
1 foil packet (0.8 ounce) 15-minute meat marinade
⅔ cup cold water
1 tablespoon Worcestershire sauce
2 tablespoons catchup
½ teaspoon liquid smoke
1 garlic clove, pressed
1 tablespoon brown sugar
Water
Catchup
1 can (4 ounces) mushroom stems and pieces

Slash fat edges of meat to prevent curling. Blend package contents of instant meat marinade with water, Worcestershire sauce, catchup, liquid smoke, garlic, and brown sugar in a shallow pan. Place meat in marinade. Pierce all surfaces of meat deeply and thoroughly with a fork to carry flavor deep down and to lock in natural juices. Marinate only 15 minutes, turning several times. Remove meat from marinade; drain; reserve remaining marinade for basting. Grill 1 to 2 inches above coals 10 to 12 minutes. Turn and baste frequently with marinade. Remove meat to hot platter. To serve, carve meat across grain at a slight angle in thin slices. Add additional water and catchup in equal amounts to any remaining marinade; bring to boil. Add mushroom stems and pieces. Use as sauce for the steak. Makes 4 to 6 servings.

BARBECUED CHUCK STEAK

1 boneless chuck steak, about 2 pounds, cut 1½ inches thick
Seasoned natural meat tenderizer
2 tablespoons vegetable oil
Paprika
Garlic powder
Coarse black pepper

Treat steak with seasoned tenderizer as directed on label. Brush oil on all sides of steak; sprinkle generously with paprika, garlic powder, and pepper. Grill 6 or 7 inches from source of heat 20 minutes on each side or until cooked to desired degree of doneness. Makes 6 servings.

BARBECUED CHUCK STEAK ROMANO

2 tablespoons olive oil
1 medium garlic clove, minced or pressed
2 cans (8 ounces each) tomato sauce
½ teaspoon sweet basil
3 chuck steaks, round bone or blade bone, cut
    1 to 1¼ inches thick
Seasoned natural meat tenderizer
½ cup grated Parmesan cheese

Heat oil in medium saucepan; brown garlic. Add next 2 ingredients; simmer 10 minutes. Slash fat edges of steaks. Use meat tenderizer according to label directions. Grill 1 inch above coals 10 to 12 minutes for rare steaks, or to desired degree of doneness, turning frequently. About 4 to 5 minutes before steaks are done, brush sauce generously over the top, then sprinkle with ½ cup grated Parmesan cheese. Makes 6 servings.

STEAK IN CHILI MARINADE

1 arm or blade chuck steak, about 3 to 3½
    pounds, cut about 1½ inches thick
1 to 2 tablespoons chili powder
1 garlic clove, sliced
½ teaspoon oregano leaves
½ cup sliced pimiento-stuffed olives
⅓ cup vegetable oil
¼ cup lemon juice
Unseasoned natural meat tenderizer*

Place steak in shallow dish; sprinkle with chili powder, garlic, oregano, and olives. Combine oil and lemon juice; pour over steak. Cover; chill several hours or overnight, turning steak once. Remove steak from marinade; use tenderizer as label directs. Grill 4 inches from source of heat 10 to 15 minutes per side or to desired degree of doneness. Brush steak with marinade frequently during grilling. Place steak on heated platter; top with olive slices drained from marinade. Makes 4 servings.

*For more tender cuts of meat, omit tenderizer.

BEEF CARBONADE GRILL

1 good-quality chuck steak, about 3 pounds,
    cut 1½ inches thick
Seasoned natural meat tenderizer
1 garlic clove, cut in slivers
1½ cups beer
¼ cup molasses
1 onion, sliced

1 teaspoon grated orange peel
2 tablespoons butter
2 tablespoons flour

Treat meat with tenderizer as label directions indicate. Cut slits in meat and press in slivers of garlic. Place steak in shallow pan. Add next 4 ingredients and let stand 2 hours. Turn steak occasionally in liquid. Place steak 4 inches above hot coals; grill 10 to 12 minutes on each side, brushing steak with marinade every few minutes during cooking. Remove onions from marinade. In a saucepan placed over coals, melt butter; stir in flour. Gradually stir in remaining marinade. Cook, while stirring, until sauce bubbles and thickens. Slice steak; spoon sauce over each serving. Makes 6 to 8 servings.

OLIVE STEAK MIRABEAU

1 arm or blade chuck steak, 3 to 3½ pounds,
    cut about 1½ inches thick
½ cup sliced pimiento-stuffed olives
2 garlic cloves, sliced
⅓ cup lemon juice
3 tablespoons vegetable oil
Unseasoned natural meat tenderizer*
1 can (2 ounces) anchovy fillets, drained

Place steak in large shallow dish; top with olives. Combine garlic, lemon juice, and oil; pour over steak. Cover; chill overnight, turning steak once. Remove steak from marinade. Use tenderizer as label directs. Grill steak 4 inches from source of heat 10 to 15 minutes on each side or to desired degree of doneness. Meanwhile, marinate anchovies in remaining olive marinade. Place steak on heated platter. Arrange anchovies in a pattern of squares on steak and place olive slices in each square. Slice to serve. Makes 4 to 6 servings.

*For more tender cuts of steak, omit tenderizer.

CHUCK WAGON PEPPER STEAK

1 round bone arm, chuck roast, or boneless
    round roast, about 3 pounds, cut about 2
    inches thick
2 teaspoons natural meat tenderizer
1 cup wine or cider vinegar
½ cup olive oil or vegetable oil
3 tablespoons lemon juice
1 small onion, chopped
2 teaspoons oregano
1 bay leaf, crushed

¼ cup peppercorns, coarsely crushed, *or* 2
    tablespoons bottled cracked pepper

Slash fat edges of meat. Treat with tenderizer as directed on label. Place meat in shallow glass or plastic pan. Mix vinegar, oil, lemon juice, onion, oregano, and bay leaf in a 2-cup measure; pour over and around meat. Chill in refrigerator about 2 hours, turning meat every ½ hour to marinate well. When ready to grill, remove meat from marinade, letting marinade drain back into dish. (Save marinade, if you wish, for another cookout.) Place meat on a cutting board; pound half the crushed peppercorns into each side (a wooden mallet makes a handy tool). Grill 4 inches above coals 15 minutes or until juice begins to show on top. Turn; grill 15 to 20 minutes longer for rare roast or until meat is done as you like it. (Time will depend on heat of coals and distance of meat from coals.) To serve, place meat on a carving board and cut diagonally in ¼-to-½-inch-thick slices. Makes 6 servings.

LONDON BROIL

1 flank steak
California Marinade*

Marinate flank steak in California Marinade 3 to 4 hours or overnight. Grill 4 inches above coals 25 to 30 minutes, turning once. Slice very thin diagonally across the grain.

*CALIFORNIA MARINADE

1 cup vegetable oil
¾ cup soy sauce
½ cup lemon juice
¼ cup Worcestershire sauce
¼ cup prepared mustard
1½ tablespoons salt
1 teaspoon pepper
1 garlic clove

Blend all ingredients together. Makes about 2½ cups marinade.

MAI TAI STEAK

1 foil packet (0.8 ounce) 15-minute meat
    marinade
⅔ cup pineapple juice
2 tablespoons dark rum
½ teaspoon ground ginger
1½ to 2 pounds flank steak
Mai Tai Sauce*

Blend package contents of meat marinade with pineapple juice, rum, and ginger in a shallow pan. Place steak in marinade. Pierce all surfaces of meat deeply and thoroughly with a fork to carry flavor deep down and to lock in natural juices. Marinate 15 minutes, turning several times. Remove steak from marinade; drain, reserving remaining marinade for Mai Tai Sauce. Grill 2 inches above coals 5 to 8 minutes, turning once. Transfer steak to carving board; carve meat in very thin, diagonal slices. Pour hot Mai Tai Sauce over sliced steak. Makes 4 servings.

*MAI TAI SAUCE

Marinade (from above)
¾ cup pineapple juice
1 tablespoon dark rum
1 teaspoon cornstarch

Combine all ingredients; blend well. Bring to a boil; reduce heat; simmer 5 minutes. Makes 4 servings.

BARBECUED FLANK STEAK

1 foil packet (0.8 ounce) 15-minute meat
    marinade
⅓ cup water
⅓ cup tomato juice
⅓ cup catchup
¼ teaspoon basil
¼ teaspoon rosemary
1 garlic clove, minced or pressed
1¾-pound flank steak
2 tablespoons vegetable oil
1 can (4 ounces) sliced mushrooms, with juice

Blend meat marinade with water, tomato juice, and catchup in shallow pan. Add basil, rosemary, and garlic. Blend well. Marinade will be quite thick. Place meat in marinade. Pierce all meat surfaces deeply and thoroughly with a fork to carry flavor deep down and to lock in natural juices. Marinate only 15 minutes, turning several times, coating all surfaces thoroughly. Remove meat from marinade. Pour marinade into measuring cup; add oil. Save for basting. Grill 2 inches above coals 7 to 8 minutes, turning and brushing frequently with marinade. Do not overcook. Meat should be crusty-brown outside and pink inside. Place remaining marinade in saucepan with mushrooms, including juice. Bring to boil; simmer 5 minutes. Remove from heat; serve with steak which has been sliced diagonally across the grain. Makes 4 servings.

STUFFED FLANK STEAK

1 flank steak
2 tablespoons finely chopped scallions
¼ cup finely chopped celery
¼ cup finely chopped fresh mushrooms
½ cup grated carrot
2 tablespoons butter or margarine
1 can (8 ounces) oysters
2 tablespoons chopped parsley
¼ cup fine soft bread crumbs
½ cup grated Swiss cheese

Have meat dealer make lengthwise pocket in flank steak, leaving tapering ends of steak uncut. Sauté scallions, celery, mushrooms, and carrot in butter until tender-crisp. Drain oysters; cut in quarters. Combine with vegetables and remaining ingredients. Fill steak with vegetable-oyster mixture; secure with long skewer. Grill about 4 inches above coals until crisp on the outside. Cut into crosswise slices to serve. Makes 6 servings.

FLANK STEAK ROULADES

1 flank steak
¼ cup soy sauce
¼ cup tarragon wine vinegar
¼ cup dry sherry
½ cup finely chopped fresh mushrooms
¼ cup finely chopped scallions
1 tablespoon butter or margarine

Trim fat from flank steak. Marinate steak in soy sauce mixed with vinegar and sherry for several hours or overnight. Sauté mushrooms and scallions in butter a few minutes. Remove steak from marinade; spread mushrooms and onions lengthwise down center of steak. Starting at narrow end, roll steak over filling; secure rolled steak with skewers at 1¼-inch intervals. With sharp knife, slice between skewers into roulades. Insert skewer in each roulade to hold in position. Grill 4 inches above hot coals to desired degree of doneness, turning once. Makes 5 to 6 roulades.

HAWAIIAN SHORT RIBS OONA LOA

6 to 8 pounds lean beef short ribs
Seasoned natural meat tenderizer
1 can (1 pound) pineapple slices
½ cup soy sauce
½ cup honey
1 cup water
2 tablespoons brown sugar

1 large garlic clove, pressed or minced
2 teaspoons ground ginger *or* 1 piece fresh
    ginger root, 1 inch long, grated

Prepare all surfaces of the meat with tenderizer as directed on label. Place ribs in bowl. Drain pineapple slices; save syrup. Set slices aside; combine syrup with remaining ingredients to make a Luau Sauce; pour over ribs. Cover ribs loosely with waxed paper; refrigerate 4 hours or overnight. Half an hour before serving time remove ribs from sauce; place on barbecue grill set 4 inches above coals. Cook until well browned, 20 to 25 minutes, turning frequently and basting with Luau Sauce during grilling. About 10 minutes before the ribs are done, dip pineapple slices in Luau Sauce; place on grill with ribs and brown quickly on both sides. Makes 6 to 8 servings.

SWEET 'N' SOUR SHORT RIBS

4 pounds beef short ribs
2 teaspoons unseasoned natural meat
    tenderizer
⅓ cup garlic wine vinegar
1 cup papaya nectar or pineapple juice
⅓ cup firmly packed brown sugar
1 tablespoon soy sauce
1 tablespoon catchup
1½ teaspoons salt
½ teaspoon pepper

Have meat dealer trim off excess fat and cut short ribs in 2-inch squares. Sprinkle tenderizer evenly on beef and pierce all surfaces deeply with a fork. Place in shallow pan; let stand 10 minutes. Meanwhile, combine vinegar, fruit juice, brown sugar, soy sauce, and catchup. Simmer 10 minutes. Pour over beef; marinate 1 hour or longer. Drain; reserve marinade. Sprinkle beef with salt and pepper. Grill slowly about 4 inches above hot coals 1 to 1½ hours or until tender. Brush with remaining marinade during cooking. Makes 4 or 5 servings.

FRONTIER SHORT RIBS

1 medium onion, minced
¼ cup celery, chopped very fine
2 tablespoons vegetable oil
2 tablespoons brown sugar
1 tablespoon molasses
2 tablespoons prepared mustard
1 tablespoon Worcestershire sauce

½ cup water
½ cup catchup
1 can (8 ounces) tomato sauce
⅛ teaspoon rosemary
4 pounds lean beef short ribs
Seasoned natural meat tenderizer

Cook onion and celery in hot oil until soft and slightly browned. Add all remaining ingredients except meat and tenderizer; mix thoroughly. Use meat tenderizer as directed on label. Grill ribs 4 to 6 inches above coals until well browned (25 to 30 minutes), turning several times and basting frequently with sauce. Serve topped with remainder of sauce. Makes 4 servings.

BARBECUED SHORT RIBS

4 pounds short ribs of beef, cut in serving pieces
Natural meat tenderizer
1 can (8 ounces) tomato sauce
1 small onion, finely chopped
3 tablespoons brown sugar
2 tablespoons water
1 tablespoon each vinegar and vegetable oil
⅛ teaspoon salt
2 teaspoons Worcestershire sauce
Dash garlic powder

Treat short ribs with meat tenderizer as directed. Meanwhile, combine tomato sauce, onion, sugar, water, vinegar, oil, and seasonings. Cover; simmer 30 minutes, stirring occasionally. Place ribs on grill, 4 inches from source of heat. Grill 10 minutes; turn; brush with barbecue sauce; grill about 5 minutes longer. Turn ribs again. Brush with sauce; grill 5 minutes longer or until meat is browned. Serve with remaining sauce. Makes 4 servings.

BUCKAROO SHORT RIBS

2 foil packets (0.8 ounce each) 15-minute meat marinade
⅔ cup tomato purée
⅔ cup red wine
2 tablespoons vinegar
2 garlic cloves, minced
2 tablespoons brown sugar
2 tablespoons prepared mustard
5 pounds lean, meaty beef short ribs
Hickory chips, soaked
Dried rosemary leaves

Combine meat marinade, tomato purée, wine, vinegar, garlic, brown sugar, and mustard in shallow pan. Blend thoroughly. Pierce all surfaces of ribs deeply and thoroughly with a fork; place ribs in marinade. Marinate for 15 minutes, turning several times. Remove meat from marinade; drain; reserve remaining marinade for basting. Toss hickory chips and a generous pinch of rosemary on barbecue coals. Place ribs on grill about 4 or 5 inches from hot coals. Grill 35 to 40 minutes, turning and basting frequently with marinade. Makes 6 servings.

DEVILED GRILLED RIBS

4 pounds beef chuck short ribs or flat ribs
Instant natural unseasoned meat tenderizer
2 tablespoons tarragon vinegar
½ cup fine soft bread crumbs
Devil Sauce*

Treat ribs with meat tenderizer as directed. Dip ribs in vinegar; roll in bread crumbs. Grill 6 to 8 inches above hot coals for 20 to 25 minutes, turning occasionally. Serve with Devil Sauce. Makes 6 servings.

*DEVIL SAUCE

6 scallions, finely chopped
2 tablespoons butter or margarine
1½ tablespoons flour
1 tablespoon Dijon mustard
½ cup consommé
½ cup white wine
2 tablespoons Worcestershire sauce
¼ teaspoon tarragon
½ teaspoon cracked pepper
2 tablespoons chopped parsley
1 tablespoon lemon juice

Sauté scallions in butter until tender. Stir in flour; brown. Blend in all remaining ingredients except last two. Simmer 10 minutes, stirring until smooth. Add parsley and lemon juice just before serving.

GOLDEN GIANT ONION BURGERS ON ITALIAN BREAD WITH CHEESE SAUCE

1 can (3½ ounces) French fried onion rings
2 pounds ground beef, chuck or round
1 egg, beaten
1 tablespoon Worcestershire sauce
1½ teaspoons salt

½ teaspoon garlic salt
¼ teaspoon pepper
6 big oval Italian bread slices, ¾ inch thick
Cheese Sauce*
6 tomato slices

Reserve ⅓ cup French fried onions for garnishing burgers. Chop remaining onions; combine with next 6 ingredients; mix well. Shape mixture into 6 oval patties about 2½ inches wide, 5 inches long, and ¾ inch thick. Grill on lightly greased grill, 3 to 4 inches above coals, to desired degree of doneness (12 to 15 minutes). Broil on first side about 7 minutes; turn and continue broiling 4 to 8 minutes on second side. While burgers are grilling, toast bread slices on grids and prepare Cheese Sauce. To serve, top each bread slice with a burger, tomato slice, onion rings, and Cheese Sauce. Makes 6 servings.

*CHEESE SAUCE

2 tablespoons butter or margarine
2 tablespoons flour
½ teaspoon salt
Dash of pepper
1 cup milk
1½ cups shredded Cheddar cheese
1 teaspoon Worcestershire sauce
½ teaspoon prepared mustard
4 drops hot-pepper sauce

Melt butter in heavy saucepan. Stir in flour, salt, and pepper. Add milk; cook, stirring constantly, until thickened. Add remaining ingredients; stir gently until cheese melts. Makes about 1½ cups sauce.

ZESTY HAMBURGERS

⅓ cup water
2 slices whole wheat bread
2 pounds ground beef
2 teaspoons salt
Zesty Barbecue Sauce*

Pour water on bread; let stand 2 to 3 minutes. Mix ground beef, bread, and salt. Shape mixture into 6 patties, about 1 inch thick. Grill at a moderate temperature until browned on both sides, allowing 6 to 8 minutes per side. Serve topped with Zesty Barbecue Sauce. Makes 6 servings.

*ZESTY BARBECUE SAUCE

⅓ cup finely chopped onion
1 tablespoon vinegar
1 tablespoon brown sugar
2 tablespoons lemon juice
½ cup catchup
1 tablespoon Worcestershire sauce
⅓ cup water
2 tablespoons chopped green pepper

Combine all ingredients. Cook, stirring occasionally, 15 minutes. Makes approximately 1 cup sauce.

BEEF BURGERS WITH A CHOICE OF TOPPINGS

Prepare and serve Beef Burgers as presented below or use any of the variations that follow.

BEEF BURGERS

2 pounds ground beef, round or chuck
½ cup finely chopped onion
2 teaspoons salt
¼ teaspoon pepper
2 eggs
Melted butter or margarine

Combine all ingredients except butter or margarine; mix well. Shape into 8 large patties; brush with melted butter or margarine and grill slowly until brown on both sides, turning once. Cook to desired degree of doneness, 10 to 20 minutes. If cooked on outdoor gas grill, preheat on high flame 5 minutes, then reduce flame and broil meat as desired. If cooked over charcoal, broil on rack 4 to 4½ inches above coals. Makes 8 large burgers.

PEANUT BUTTER BURGERS

Follow recipe for Beef Burgers, reducing salt to 1¾ teaspoons. Mix in ⅔ cup finely chopped salted peanuts. Proceed as for Beef Burgers. Serve each topped with a dill pickle slice and a dollop of peanut butter. Serve on buns or as an entrée. Makes 8 large burgers.

GUACAMOLE-TOPPED BURGERS

Pulp of 1 avocado
½ cup chopped tomato
¼ cup chopped onion

1 tablespoon lemon juice
¼ teaspoon each salt and garlic salt
Dash of pepper
4 to 6 drops hot-pepper sauce
8 Beef Burgers

Mash avocado; stir in tomato, onion, lemon juice, salt, garlic salt, pepper, and hot-pepper sauce. Spoon mixture over sizzling-hot Beef Burgers; heat. Makes about 1¼ cups topping, enough for 8 large burgers.

HAWAIIAN BURGERS

3 tablespoons each prepared mustard and catchup
1½ tablespoons soy sauce
8 Beef Burgers
8 slices canned pineapple

Combine mustard and catchup; stir in soy sauce. Brush Beef Burgers with this sauce instead of butter or margarine. Top each burger with a heated canned pineapple slice. Makes 8 large burgers.

BURGER DOGS

2½ pounds ground beef
1 small onion, minced
2 eggs
½ cup ice water
6 to 8 frankfurter rolls
Seasoned natural meat tenderizer
Garnish: 6 large stuffed green olives, sliced; 1 tablespoon chopped parsley

Blend together, lightly but thoroughly, ground beef, onion, eggs, and water. Form into 6 to 8 log-shaped patties to fit frankfurter rolls. Just before cooking, sprinkle all surfaces of the patties with meat tenderizer as you would salt; do not add salt. Grill 1 inch above coals 8 to 10 minutes. Serve in hot frankfurter rolls and garnish with sliced olives and chopped parsley. Makes 6 to 8 servings.

DOUBLE CHEESEBURGERS

2 pounds ground beef
¼ cup finely chopped onion
2 teaspoons Worcestershire sauce
2 teaspoons salt
¼ teaspoon pepper
2 eggs

1½ cups shredded Cheddar cheese
3 tablespoons salad dressing
4 teaspoons prepared mustard
2 teaspoons drained pickle relish
6 large onion slices, ⅛ inch thick
6 toasted buttered hamburger buns
Garnish: 6 cherry tomatoes or tomato slices (optional)

Combine first 6 ingredients; mix well. Shape into 12 flat patties about 4 inches in diameter. Broil 3 to 3½ inches from heat source 8 to 10 minutes or to the desired degree of doneness, turning once. Combine cheese, salad dressing, mustard, and pickle relish; mix. Top each onion slice with a patty and spread each with cheese mixture, using ⅔ of the cheese mixture. Top each with a second patty and ⅙ of remaining cheese. Return burgers to grill just until cheese softens. Arrange in buns; garnish each with a cherry tomato or tomato slice, if desired. Makes 6 double cheeseburgers.

BONANZA CHEESEBURGERS

Hamburgers:

1 pound ground beef
½ cup quick or old-fashioned oats, uncooked
¼ cup chili sauce
2 tablespoons milk
2 teaspoons minced dried onion
2 teaspoons Worcestershire sauce

Combine all ingredients thoroughly; shape to form 12 thin patties.

Filling:

½ cup grated Cheddar cheese
1 tablespoon mayonnaise
½ teaspoon seasoned salt
½ teaspoon Worcestershire sauce
¼ teaspoon prepared mustard

Combine all ingredients thoroughly.

Spread about 1½ teaspoons filling on center of 6 patties. Cover with remaining patties; pinch edges together to seal. Cook over hot coals or in broiler about 4 inches from source of heat (about 5 minutes). Turn and cook about 5 minutes longer. Serve on toasted buns. Makes 6 cheeseburgers.

BACON BURGERS

3 pounds lean beef, ground
2 cups soft raisin bread crumbs

1 teaspoon salt
Few grains pepper
2 eggs
½ cup catchup
2 tablespoons chopped parsley
6 slices crisp bacon, crumbled
12 hamburger rolls
Sliced tomatoes
6 slices Swiss cheese, halved
Sliced onions
Pickles
Condiments (see below)

Combine first 8 ingredients; mix thoroughly. Shape into 12 large patties. Grill, with meat 4 inches above hot coals, to desired degree of doneness, turning once. Serve in heated hamburger rolls, with slices of tomato, Swiss cheese, onions, and pickles. Serve with condiments, such as mustard, chili sauce, steak sauce, catchup, and prepared horseradish. Makes 12 servings.

BARBECUED RACK OF LAMB

3 tablespoons finely chopped parsley
1 teaspoon salt
1 teaspoon dried leaf thyme
1 teaspoon dried leaf oregano
½ teaspoon hot-pepper sauce
½ cup olive oil
¼ cup dry red wine
1 bay leaf
2 racks of lamb, 8 ribs each

Mix parsley, salt, thyme, and oregano. Add hot-pepper sauce, oil, wine, and bay leaf; mix well. Pour over racks of lamb in shallow glass or enamel pan; cover and marinate in refrigerator 4 hours or overnight. Remove from marinade and place on grill set 4 to 6 inches from heat. Cook, turning occasionally and brushing with marinade, to desired degree of doneness (45 minutes to 1½ hours). Makes 8 servings.

SPIT-ROASTED LEG OF LAMB

½ cup lemon juice
¼ cup vegetable oil
1 large garlic clove, crushed
½ teaspoon each coarse ground pepper,
    thyme, and basil leaves
1 leg of lamb, 6 to 8 pounds
Salt

In large shallow dish combine lemon juice, oil, garlic, pepper, thyme, and basil. Add lamb; turn until coated with marinade. Refrigerate several hours, turning lamb occasionally. Remove leg and reserve marinade. Balance leg of lamb on rotisserie spit so it will rotate evenly. Sprinkle with salt. Cook on rotisserie according to manufacturer's directions 25 to 30 minutes per pound, or until meat thermometer registers 175°, for medium doneness. Baste occasionally with reserved marinade during roasting. Makes 8 to 12 servings.

BARBECUED SHOULDER LAMB CHOPS

1 can (8 ounces) tomato sauce
1 tablespoon minced onion
1 tablespoon brown sugar
½ teaspoon salt
Dash pepper
1½ teaspoons vegetable oil
½ teaspoon vinegar
Seasoned natural meat tenderizer
6 shoulder lamb chops, cut 1 inch thick

Combine tomato sauce, onion, sugar, salt, pepper, oil, and vinegar in small saucepan; cover; cook over low heat 30 minutes, stirring occasionally. Meanwhile, treat chops with tenderizer as directed. Grill chops 4 to 5 inches from source of heat 8 to 10 minutes on each side, brushing with sauce. Pour remaining sauce over chops before serving. Makes 6 servings.

ALOHA PORK ROAST

1 pork loin roll, 6 to 8 pounds, *or* 1 boneless
    leg of pork, 9 to 11 pounds
1 can (13 ounces) crushed pineapple
2 tablespoons brown sugar
1 tablespoon cornstarch
¼ tablespoon ginger
¾ teaspoon garlic salt
¼ cup soy sauce

Insert rotisserie rod through center of roast. Insert meat thermometer at an angle so that its tip is in center of roast but not resting on fat or on rod. Place on rotisserie and cook at low to moderate temperature to 170° (well done). Allow 2½ to 3½ hours for pork loin roll and 3½ to 4½ hours for leg of pork. Meanwhile, combine remaining ingredients; mix well. Cook 5 minutes, stirring occasionally. Brush pork roast frequently with this glaze during last 30 minutes of cooking. Makes at least 12 servings.

BONELESS PORK LOIN ROAST

Pork loin roast, 4 to 6 pounds, boned, rolled,
    and tied
Salt
Pepper
Italian salad dressing

Insert rotisserie rod, lengthwise, through center
of roast; secure rod. Test for balance by rotating
rod in hands. When roast is balanced on rod, it
should turn as rod turns without slipping or stop-
ping. Insert a meat thermometer at a slight angle
so its tip is in center of roast but not resting in fat
or on rotisserie rod. Make certain thermometer
clears cooking unit and drip pan while meat
turns. Season roast with salt and pepper. Roast
approximately 3½ to 4½ hours or until thermometer registers 170°. If grill thermometer is used,
keep temperature as close to moderate (350°) as
possible. During last 30 minutes of cooking time,
brush roast with Italian salad dressing 2 or 3
times. Makes 8 to 12 servings.

SPITTED PORK ROAST VIRGINIA

1 tablespoon dry mustard
1½ teaspoons cornstarch
¾ cup beer
3 tablespoons lime or orange marmalade or
    tart jam
2 tablespoons molasses
1 garlic clove, crushed or pressed
¼ teaspoon seasoned natural meat tenderizer
1½ teaspoons liquid smoke
Seasoned natural meat tenderizer
Pork shoulder roast, 4 to 5 pounds, boned and
    rolled

Combine dry mustard and cornstarch in saucepan, adding just enough beer to work into
smooth paste. Add marmalade, molasses, garlic,
and the ¼ teaspoon meat tenderizer, blending
thoroughly. Add remaining beer and simmer
until sauce is slightly thickened. Remove from
heat; stir in liquid smoke. Set aside. Use meat
tenderizer on roast as directed on label. When
barbecuing, place foil pan beneath roast and arrange coals around it. Secure roast on spit, making sure it is balanced to turn evenly. Cook 30 to
35 minutes per pound, 2 to 2½ hours. One hour
before end of cooking time, brush generously
with the sauce. Baste frequently with sauce for
the balance of cooking time. Add a few fresh
coals when necessary to maintain constant temperature. Let finished roast rest about 15 minutes

before carving, for more attractive and uniform
slices. Delicious au jus gravy can be made from
pan drippings. Simply skim the fat and add remaining sauce with water to thin if necessary.

GRILLED PORK SLICES

Simmer boned and rolled smoked pork butt 45 to
60 minutes. Let cool in broth. Drain. Refrigerate
until ready to cook. Cut in slices about ½ inch
thick. Grill over charcoal until brown on both
sides. Top with grilled pineapple slices.

CHINESE PORK SHOULDER STEAKS

1 beef bouillon cube
⅓ cup hot water
1 teaspoon ginger
2 teaspoons salt
1 tablespoon sugar
¼ cup honey
¼ cup soy sauce
4 to 6 pork arm or blade steaks, cut ¾ inch
    thick

Dissolve bouillon cube in hot water. Combine
ginger, salt, sugar, honey, and soy sauce; add to
bouillon. Marinate steaks in soy sauce mixture in
refrigerator 2 hours, turning occasionally. Remove steaks from marinade and place on grill
over glowing coals, 3 inches from heat. Grill 30
to 45 minutes. Brush frequently with marinade.
Turn after grilling 15 minutes; continue cooking
until done. Makes 4 to 6 servings.

PATIO PORK STEAKS

4 to 6 pork blade or arm steaks, cut ½ inch
    thick
1 cup bottled barbecue sauce
1 cup beer
1 teaspoon Worcestershire sauce
2 teaspoons salt

Place steaks in flat dish. Combine remaining ingredients; pour over steaks. Chill 4 hours. Place
steaks on grill as far as possible above hot coals,
brushing with marinade and turning occasionally. Grill for 35 to 45 minutes or until well done.
Makes 4 to 6 servings.

GRILLED PORK CHOPS

6 pork chops, cut 1 to 1½ inches thick
Salt
Pepper

Place pork chops on grill about 5 inches from heat. (This distance allows the chops to become well done inside by the time they are browned on the surface.) Grill at moderate temperature (350° measured by grill thermometer) 10 minutes on each side. Continue grilling, turning occasionally, about 20 minutes longer or until well done. Season with salt and pepper. Makes 6 servings.

CHARCOAL-GRILLED PORK CHOPS

Pork chops
Vegetable oil *or* melted butter or margarine
Spicy Honey Sauce*

Arrange pork chops on well-greased grill or in hinged rack 5 inches above a bed of low-glowing coals or on gas grill above low heat. Brown well on first side; turn. Brown second side; cook until done. Cook chops 1 to 1¼ inches thick 15 minutes on first side, 12 to 15 minutes on second side. Cook chops ¾ inch thick about 12 minutes on first side, 10 to 12 minutes on second side. Season as desired; brush chops frequently during grilling with vegetable oil or melted butter or margarine. Brush with Spicy Honey Sauce during last 10 minutes of cooking.

*SPICY HONEY SAUCE

½ cup honey
½ cup lime or lemon juice
¼ cup sugar
1 tablespoon soy sauce
½ teaspoon grated lime or lemon peel
¼ teaspoon powdered cloves
¼ teaspoon nutmeg

Combine ingredients; mix. Bring to a boil; boil 1 minute. Makes about 1 cup sauce.

BARBECUE BUFFET

3 to 5 pounds spareribs, cut in serving pieces
Barbecue Sauce*
1 or 2 ducklings, quartered
4 to 8 minute steaks or cube steaks
Brown 'n' serve sausages

The spareribs go on the grill first, about 4 inches above hot coals. Turn them often, brushing with Barbecue Sauce each time. Allow 1 to 1½ hours' cooking time. Spareribs are done when meat shrinks from ends of bones. Grill duckling next. Place pieces skin side down on ungreased grill. Cook 15 minutes on each side. Brush with Barbecue Sauce. Grill 2 to 5 minutes longer or until duckling is done. Do minute or cube steaks and brown 'n' serve sausages last. If steaks are lean, the grill should be oiled or greased. Grilling time depends on degree of rareness desired. For medium-rare steaks, grill 5 minutes; turn; brush with Barbecue Sauce if you wish, and grill 5 minutes longer. Makes 4 to 8 servings.

*BARBECUE SAUCE

1 garlic clove, crushed
¼ cup wine vinegar
2 teaspoons dry mustard
½ teaspoon savory
¼ teaspoon coarse black pepper
½ teaspoon salt
1 can (8 ounces) tomato sauce
1 envelope instant beef broth mix
1 tablespoon butter or margarine
½ teaspoon Worcestershire sauce
½ teaspoon sugar

Combine garlic, vinegar, mustard, savory, pepper, and salt. Simmer 10 minutes; strain. Combine tomato sauce, broth mix, butter, Worcestershire sauce, sugar, and strained vinegar mixture. Stir over low heat until well blended. Makes about 1¼ cups sauce.

SPARERIBS WITH COLA

4 pounds spareribs (2 racks)
Seasoned natural meat tenderizer
1 large onion, chopped
1 bottle or can (12 ounces) cola beverage
Barbecue sauce of choice

Treat meat with tenderizer as directed on label. Place in roasting pan with onion; cover tightly. Bake at 350° for 15 minutes. Add cola; bake 30 minutes longer. Grill 4 inches above coals for 45 minutes, turning frequently, until crispy and golden brown. Serve with your favorite barbecue sauce. Makes 4 servings.

SPARERIBS IKINA (ORIENTAL)

1 foil packet (0.8 ounce) 15-minute meat
    marinade
⅔ cup pineapple juice
¼ cup soy sauce
1 teaspoon garlic salt
3 to 3½ pounds spareribs
¼ cup toasted sesame seeds

Blend meat marinade with pineapple juice, soy
sauce, and garlic salt in a shallow pan. Place
spareribs in marinade in a single layer. Pierce all
surfaces of meat deeply and thoroughly with a
fork to carry flavor deep down and to lock in natural juices. Marinate only 15 minutes, turning
several times. Remove ribs from marinade;
drain, reserving remaining marinade for basting.
Grill 4 to 6 inches above coals 40 to 50 minutes,
turning and basting frequently with marinade.
During the last 10 minutes of cooking, brush ribs
with marinade; sprinkle generously with sesame
seeds and "toast" to set the sesame. Repeat on
other side of ribs. Use kitchen shears to cut ribs
into pieces for serving. Makes 4 to 6 servings.

SNAPPY SPARERIBS

4 pounds spareribs
½ cup chopped onion
1 large garlic clove, minced
2 tablespoons butter or margarine
½ cup catchup
1 can (10½ ounces) condensed beef broth
1 tablespoon Worcestershire sauce
1 tablespoon brown sugar
1 teaspoon dry mustard

Have spareribs cut in serving-size pieces at meat
market. Place in large pot of boiling water; cover;
simmer 1 hour. Drain. Meanwhile, prepare
sauce. Cook onion and garlic in butter until
onion is tender. Stir in remaining ingredients.
Cook over low heat about 15 minutes or until
sauce is slightly thickened, stirring now and
then. Place spareribs on grill about 4 inches
above hot coals; brush with sauce. Cook about 30
minutes or until meat pulls away from bones,
basting and turning every 5 minutes. Makes 4 to
6 servings.

BARBECUED SPARERIBS WITH FRUIT

6 pounds (2 racks) spareribs, cut in serving
    pieces

1½ teaspoons salt
1 lemon, thinly sliced
⅓ cup light molasses
⅓ cup prepared mustard
⅓ cup vinegar
2 tablespoons soy sauce
1 tablespoon celery seed
2 tablespoons Worcestershire sauce
Green-tipped bananas
Pineapple chunks
Maraschino cherries

Place spareribs, meaty side up, on shallow foil-
lined baking pan. Sprinkle with salt. Top with
lemon slices. Bake at 350° for 1 hour. Remove
from oven; pour off fat. Refrigerate. When ready
to grill, combine all but last 3 ingredients. Place
spareribs on grill 6 to 8 inches above coals. Brush
with sauce after 15 minutes. Cook 15 minutes
longer, brushing with sauce. Alternate chunks of
banana, pineapple, and cherries on skewers.
Brush with barbecue sauce; grill last 10 minutes
of cooking time, until fruit is heated. Makes 4 to
6 servings.

SPICY BARBECUED SPARERIBS

2 foil packets (0.8 ounce each) 15-minute meat
    marinade
1½ cups apple cider
½ teaspoon cinnamon
¼ teaspoon each cloves and nutmeg
5 pounds meaty spareribs, cut in serving
    portions

Thoroughly blend meat marinade with cider and
spices in shallow pan. Place ribs in marinade;
pierce all surfaces thoroughly with fork. Marinate 15 minutes, turning several times. Remove
from marinade; drain. Pour remaining marinade
into small saucepan; keep handy for basting.
Place ribs on grill set 6 inches above glowing
coals; barbecue total of 1 to 1½ hours (until
done), turning often and brushing frequently
with marinade during last 30 minutes. Serve any
remaining marinade with ribs. Makes 8 servings.

GLAZED SPARERIBS

2 racks fresh pork spareribs, whole or cut in
    serving-size pieces, as desired
2 cups cranberry juice cocktail
1 large sweet onion, sliced
Juice of 1 lemon
¼ cup firmly packed light brown sugar

4 whole cloves
1 teaspoon salt
¼ teaspoon black pepper

Place spareribs in shallow pans. Combine remaining ingredients in saucepan. Bring to boil; let simmer 5 minutes. Pour over spareribs; marinate in refrigerator several hours or overnight. Drain, reserving marinade. Place on grill about 6 inches above coals; grill 45 to 60 minutes, brushing meat with reserved marinade every 5 minutes. Turn frequently. Makes 6 to 8 servings.

FRUITED PORK ROLL WITH HERBS

6 pounds boned fresh ham
1½ cups seedless white grapes, divided
1 cup seedless raisins, light or dark, divided
1 teaspoon dried marjoram
½ teaspoon dried sage
½ teaspoon dried mint
Salt
2 nectarines
1 cup water

Have meat boned and rolled, but not tied, at the market. When charcoal fire is ready, flatten meat on a board and sprinkle with ½ cup each grapes and raisins. Roll again and tie securely with clean white string, then skewer. Score outside fat and rub with herbs. Sprinkle with salt. Roast on rotating spit over charcoal, allowing 45 minutes per pound. During last half hour, peel nectarines; slice into saucepan. Add water; simmer until liquid has consistency of light corn syrup. Add remaining raisins; simmer until plump. Remove from heat; add remaining grapes. To serve, slice pork and top with fruit sauce. Makes 8 to 10 servings.

GLAZED SPIT-ROASTED CANNED HAM

1 canned ham (8 to 10 pounds)
Basting Sauce*
Cherry-Almond Sauce**

Remove ham from can. Scrape off gelatin and save it for preparing Basting Sauce. Score surface of ham lightly, if desired. Carefully push spit through center of ham, lengthwise. Make certain ham is perfectly balanced on spit. Tie ham securely with string. Cook over low-glowing coals that give off an even heat. Baste ham frequently with Basting Sauce during last 30 minutes of roasting. It takes about the same time to spit-

roast a canned ham as it does to bake it in the oven. Check the label for length of baking time and use it as a guide. Since canned hams have been thoroughly cooked, they need only heating. To serve, slice ham; pour Cherry-Almond Sauce over slices; serve any extra sauce separately. Makes 10 to 12 servings.

*BASTING SAUCE

Gelatin from canned ham (above)
Water
2 tablespoons butter or margarine
2 tablespoons honey
½ teaspoon each ground cloves, mustard, and cinnamon

Melt gelatin reserved from ham. Add water as needed to make ¾ cup liquid. Add remaining ingredients. Heat and use for basting ham during last 30 minutes of roasting time.

**CHERRY-ALMOND SAUCE

1 can (1 pound) pitted sour red cherries
1 cup light corn syrup
3 tablespoons cornstarch
2 tablespoons lemon juice
4 teaspoons grated orange peel
¼ teaspoon almond extract
¼ cup slivered almonds

Drain cherries. Combine cherry juice, syrup, cornstarch, and lemon juice. Blend. Cook, stirring constantly, until clear and thickened. Stir in orange peel, extract, almonds, and cherries. Heat. Serve over hot ham slices. Makes about 3 cups sauce.

CHARCOAL-BROILED HAM SLICES WITH ASPARAGUS TOPPING

2 packages (10 ounces each) frozen asparagus spears, defrosted
2 tablespoons butter or margarine
½ teaspoon salt
6 slices fully cooked ham, ⅜ inch thick
Herb Butter*
Mock Hollandaise Sauce**

Arrange asparagus spears in aluminum-foil pan. Add butter or margarine in small pieces; sprinkle with salt. Cover pan with aluminum foil and crimp tightly to edges of pan. Heat on grill over coals about 40 minutes. About 12 minutes before end of heating time, brush ham slices with Herb Butter. Arrange ham slices on grill 4 to 5 inches above hot coals. Brown slices on both sides, turning once. Total time will vary with heat and placement of slices on grill. To serve, arrange asparagus spears on ham slices and spoon Mock Hollandaise Sauce over ham and asparagus. Makes 6 servings.

*HERB BUTTER

¼ cup butter or margarine
1 tablespoon minced parsley
1 teaspoon dry mustard

Combine ingredients in a saucepan; heat to melt butter or margarine. Makes about ¼ cup.

**MOCK HOLLANDAISE SAUCE #2

¼ cup butter or margarine
3 tablespoons flour
½ teaspoon salt
1 cup milk
½ cup salad dressing
3 tablespoons lemon juice
½ teaspoon grated lemon peel

Melt butter or margarine; stir in flour and salt. Add milk; cook, stirring constantly, until thick and smooth. Stir in remaining ingredients. Heat. Makes 1⅔ cups sauce.

HAM SLICES WITH PEANUT BUTTER BARBECUE SAUCE

½ cup peanut butter
¼ cup honey
2 teaspoons soy sauce
1 teaspoon brown gravy seasoning sauce
1 onion, grated
1 garlic clove, chopped fine
1 cup chicken broth
¼ teaspoon fresh ground black pepper
2 fully cooked center ham slices, about 1½ inches thick

Combine peanut butter, honey, soy sauce, seasoning sauce, onion, garlic, broth, and pepper; stir to blend. Place ham slices in flat pan and spread with half the sauce. Let stand several hours in refrigerator. Place on grill. Cook over glowing charcoal for 30 to 40 minutes. Baste with sauce. Cut in inch-wide slices. Serves 8 to 10.

BARBECUED PICKLE HAM STEAK

⅓ cup sweet pickle liquid
¼ cup sweet mixed pickles, coarsely chopped
½ cup currant jelly, melted
1 fully cooked ham steak, cut ¾ inch thick

Combine pickle liquid, pickles, and jelly; blend. Place ham on grill, 3 to 4 inches from source of heat. Grill 6 to 8 minutes. Turn; top with pickle mixture; grill 8 to 10 minutes longer. Makes 4 servings.

CHARCOAL-GRILLED LIVER STEAKS

2 slices beef liver, about 2 pounds, 2 inches thick
Seasoned natural meat tenderizer
2½ cups barbecue sauce of choice
⅓ cup vegetable oil
3 Bermuda onions, thickly sliced

It is not necessary to wash or scald liver. Treat liver with meat tenderizer as directed on label. Pour 2½ cups of your favorite barbecue sauce into bowl; add vegetable oil. When ready to grill, brush meat generously with barbecue sauce. Place on barbecue grill, about 2 inches above coals; cook a total of 45 minutes for well-done meat, 35 to 40 minutes for medium-rare meat, turning frequently and brushing with sauce. During last 10 or 15 minutes, brush thick slices of onion with sauce and place on grill. Makes 4 servings.

COOKOUT WITH SAUSAGES

Precooked sausages are the greatest for a cookout. All they need is a quick warming, just enough to add that wonderful char-broiled flavor. Cook them until they look the way you like them best. Doneness is no problem since they're already cooked.

You can please everybody at a cookout if you grill a variety of sausages. Include all the favorites—bratwurst, knockwurst, frankfurters, smoked sausage links, and others. Then each person can choose his favorites.

Sausages should be grilled gently, over well-burned-down coals. If the fire is too hot, the sausages will burst. Use tongs for turning the links on the grill. If the casings are pierced with a fork, the flavorful juices will be lost.

RED-HOT SANDWICH ROLLS

1 pound frankfurters, cut in ½-inch cubes
¾ pound sharp Cheddar cheese, cut in ½-inch cubes
3 tablespoons minced scallions
⅓ cup chopped stuffed olives
3 hard-cooked eggs, chopped
¼ cup chili sauce
3 tablespoons mayonnaise
12 frankfurter buns, split

Combine franks, cheese, scallions, olives, eggs, chili sauce, and mayonnaise; mix thoroughly. Open buns; fill each with about ⅓ cup of frank mixture. (Buns will close only partially.) Wrap each bun in heavy-duty or broiler foil, twisting ends tightly. Store in refrigerator until ready for use. Before serving, place wrapped buns on grill over hot coals for 15 to 20 minutes. Makes 12 servings.

MEXI-FRANKS

1 pound frankfurters*
1 can (12 ounces) whole kernel corn, drained
2 tablespoons pickle relish
1 onion, chopped
1 can (8 ounces) tomato sauce
¼ cup chopped green pepper
¼ teaspoon hot-pepper sauce
½ teaspoon chili powder or oregano
Frankfurter rolls

Cut frankfurters lengthwise, being careful not to cut completely through. Place on grill. While frankfurters are roasting, make relish by combining next 7 ingredients in small saucepan. Simmer 10 to 15 minutes. Serve franks in hot rolls with relish spooned down middle. Makes 6 to 8 servings.

*Knockwurst may be substituted for frankfurters, if desired.

PICKLE-BARBECUED BOLOGNA

4-pound piece of bologna, unsliced
1 can (8 ounces) tomato sauce
1 cup catchup
½ cup barbecue relish
½ teaspoon Worcestershire sauce
2 tablespoons butter or margarine
1 tablespoon prepared mustard

Remove casing from bologna; score in diamond pattern with ¼-inch-deep lines. Push spit rod through center of bologna; attach to rotisserie about 12 inches from source of heat. Grill until nicely browned (about 1 hour). Meanwhile, combine remaining ingredients in saucepan; bring to a boil, stirring constantly. Simmer 10 minutes, stirring occasionally. Brush sauce onto bologna 10 minutes before end of cooking period. Slice meat about ¼ inch thick; serve with remaining sauce. Makes 12 to 16 servings.

ROTISSERIE CHICKEN WITH SPANISH BARBECUE SAUCE

2 whole broiler-fryer chickens, about 3 pounds each
Vegetable oil
Salt
Pepper
3 cans (8 ounces each) tomato sauce with onions
1 cup chopped pimiento-stuffed olives
⅓ cup seedless raisins
6 tablespoons each water and honey
1½ tablespoons vinegar
2 teaspoons soy sauce
2 garlic cloves, crushed

Tie legs of chickens together; fold wings under back. Brush with oil; sprinkle with salt and pepper. Balance chickens on rotisserie rod; secure with skewers. Place pan under chickens to catch drippings. Roast chickens, 9 inches from source of heat, about 1½ hours (or follow rotisserie manufacturer's directions) or until meat thermometer registers 185°. Meanwhile, combine remaining ingredients in saucepan and cook over low heat 20 minutes, stirring occasionally. Brush chickens with sauce during last 15 minutes of roasting time. Heat remaining sauce and serve with chickens. Makes 8 servings.

ROTISSERIE BARBECUED CHICKEN WITH ORANGE GLAZE

2 whole broiler-fryer chickens, about 3 pounds each
1½ teaspoons salt, divided
1 can (6 ounces) frozen orange juice concentrate, thawed, undiluted
2 tablespoons soy sauce
1 teaspoon minced dried onion
½ teaspoon celery seed
¼ teaspoon ginger
¼ teaspoon hot-pepper sauce

Sprinkle cavity of each chicken with ½ teaspoon salt. Tie legs together, then to tail. Secure on revolving spit. Cook over medium heat 1 hour and 15 minutes. Combine orange juice concentrate, soy sauce, onion, celery seed, ginger, hot-pepper sauce, and remaining ½ teaspoon salt. Brush chickens with sauce. Cook chickens another 15 minutes, brushing frequently with sauce. Makes 8 servings.

CHICKEN COOKOUT

    2 whole broiler-fryer chickens, about 3
        pounds each
    1½ teaspoons salt, divided
    1 can (6 ounces) frozen orange juice
        concentrate, thawed and undiluted
    1 can (8 ounces) tomato sauce
    1 tablespoon soy sauce
    ½ teaspoon ginger

Sprinkle cavity of each chicken with ½ teaspoon salt. Tie legs together, then tie to tail. Place chickens close together on rotisserie spit. Secure with spit forks. Grill over glowing coals about 1 hour and 15 minutes. Remove string. Combine orange juice concentrate with tomato sauce, soy sauce, ginger, and remaining ½ teaspoon salt; mix thoroughly. Brush chickens with sauce. Cook chickens another 15 minutes or until done, brushing frequently with sauce. Heat remaining sauce; serve with chickens. Makes 8 servings.

BARBECUED CHICKEN WITH KRAUT RELISH

    3½ cups undrained sauerkraut
    2 large tomatoes, chopped
    1 large onion, finely chopped
    ¼ cup French dressing
    1 teaspoon pepper, divided
    ½ cup catchup
    ¼ cup vegetable oil
    1½ teaspoons salt
    3 broiler-fryer chickens, about 2 pounds each,
        halved

Drain kraut; reserve juice. Combine kraut, tomatoes, onion, French dressing, and ½ teaspoon pepper. Combine kraut juice, catchup, oil, salt, and remaining ½ teaspoon pepper; mix well. Brush chickens with catchup mixture. Grill 5 to 6 inches from source of heat about 45 minutes or until chickens are tender. Turn and brush with catchup mixture frequently. Serve with kraut mixture. Makes 6 servings.

TEXAS BARBECUED CHICKEN

    1 foil packet (0.8 ounce) 15-minute meat
        marinade
    ¼ cup water
    ¼ cup vegetable oil
    3 tablespoons dry white wine
    2 tablespoons gin (optional)
    2 tablespoons lemon juice
    ½ teaspoon ground ginger
    1 teaspoon minced dried onion
    1 teaspoon chopped parsley
    2 broilers, about 1½ pounds each, cut in
        halves

Blend package contents of meat marinade with remaining ingredients except chicken. Place chicken pieces in marinade. Pierce all surfaces deeply and thoroughly with a fork to carry flavor deep down and to lock in natural juices. Marinate 15 minutes, turning several times. Remove chicken from marinade; reserve remaining marinade for basting. Grill about 4 to 6 inches above hot coals 35 to 45 minutes, turning and basting frequently with marinade. To test for doneness, cut slit near the leg bone—meat should not be pink. Makes 4 servings.

BARBECUED CHICKEN U.S.A.

Place broiler-fryer chicken halves on grate set 4 to 6 inches from heat. Brush with any of the following barbecue sauces. Cook slowly until tender, turning and basting frequently. Allow 45 to 60 minutes' total cooking time. When done, leg should twist easily out of thigh joint and pieces should be fork-tender.

NORTH

    ½ cup molasses
    ½ cup prepared mustard
    ½ cup tarragon vinegar
    2 tablespoons Worcestershire sauce
    1 teaspoon dried tarragon

Combine all ingredients; beat with rotary beater. Allow ¼ cup sauce for 2 broiler-fryer chicken halves. Makes approximately 1½ cups sauce.

SOUTH

    ¼ cup melted butter or margarine
    2 tablespoons sugar
    ¼ teaspoon hot-pepper sauce

½ teaspoon dry mustard
½ cup vegetable oil
¼ cup catchup
1 tablespoon Worcestershire sauce
1 medium onion, chopped fine
2 tablespoons vinegar

Combine as above. Makes approximately 1½ cups sauce.

EAST

⅔ cup vegetable oil
1 cup lemon juice
½ teaspoon celery seed
2 tablespoons salt
¼ teaspoon cayenne
2 tablespoons minced onion
¼ teaspoon thyme

Combine as above. Makes 1¾ cups sauce.

WEST

¼ cup vegetable oil
½ cup lemon juice
1 garlic clove, minced
1 medium onion, chopped
2 tablespoons soy sauce
¼ teaspoon pepper
1 teaspoon thyme, marjoram, or rosemary

Combine as above. Makes approximately 1 cup sauce.

SAVORY BARBECUED CHICKEN

1 can (8 ounces) tomato sauce
1 can water
1 tablespoon grated onion
⅛ teaspoon powdered sage
¼ teaspoon dry mustard
Juice of 1 lemon
1 teaspoon salt
Dash cayenne
1 teaspoon sugar
1 garlic clove
Few grains pepper
½ cup vegetable oil
¼ teaspoon rosemary
4 broilers, halved

Measure first 11 ingredients into a saucepan. Simmer 20 minutes. Remove garlic. Slowly heat oil and rosemary. Brush broilers on both sides with this mixture. Place chicken on grill, about 4 inches above hot coals, skin side down. Grill 5 minutes; turn; grill 5 more minutes. Add any remaining oil mixture to barbecue sauce; baste broilers. Continue grilling and basting for ¾ to 1 hour, turning frequently. When chicken is done, serve piping-hot. Makes 8 servings.

BARBECUED CHICKEN

3 broiler-fryer chickens, halved
Salt and pepper
¼ cup vegetable oil
⅓ cup catchup
½ cup tomato juice
¼ cup lemon juice or vinegar
½ cup water
1 teaspoon each salt and paprika
2 teaspoons sugar
1 teaspoon Worcestershire sauce
1 small onion, finely chopped
¼ teaspoon hot-pepper sauce

Sprinkle each chicken half with salt and pepper. To make barbecue sauce, combine remaining ingredients in saucepan; heat. Place chicken, skin side up, on grate set about 6 inches above hot coals. Brush chicken with barbecue sauce. Cook chicken slowly until tender, turning and basting occasionally. Allow 1 to 1¼ hours' total cooking time. To test for doneness, leg should twist easily out of thigh joint and pieces should be fork-tender. Makes 6 servings.

HERB BARBECUED CHICKEN

4 broiler-fryer chickens, halved or quartered
Herb Barbecue Sauce*

Place broiler-fryer halves or quarters skin side up on a grate set at least 4 inches above hot coals. Cook, turning occasionally and basting frequently with Herb Barbecue Sauce. Allow 45 minutes' to 1¼ hours' total cooking time, depending on weight of chicken and distance from heat. To test for doneness, leg should twist easily out of thigh joint and pieces should be tender when probed with a fork. Makes 8 to 10 servings.

*HERB BARBECUE SAUCE

⅔ cup vegetable oil
⅔ cup lemon juice or vinegar
¼ cup water
1 tablespoon sugar
2 teaspoons salt

1 teaspoon paprika
1½ teaspoons dried leaf tarragon
½ teaspoon dried leaf rosemary
¼ teaspoon hot-pepper sauce
1 tablespoon minced onion

Combine all ingredients. Mix well. Let stand at least 1 hour for flavors to blend. Makes 1⅔ cups sauce, enough for 4 broiler-fryer chickens.

LEMON BARBECUED CHICKEN

1 teaspoon grated lemon peel
1½ teaspoons salt
½ teaspoon dry mustard
½ teaspoon dried leaf oregano
1 teaspoon Worcestershire sauce
½ cup lemon juice
½ cup vegetable oil
2 tablespoons chopped scallions
2 broiler-fryer chickens, halved or quartered

Combine lemon peel, salt, dry mustard, oregano, and Worcestershire sauce in bowl. Gradually stir in lemon juice, then gradually stir in oil. Add scallions. Pour over chicken in large bowl or baking dish; marinate in refrigerator 2 hours. Remove chicken from marinade and place skin side down on grill set 3 to 6 inches above coals. Cook until tender, turning and basting occasionally with marinade 45 minutes to 1 hour and 15 minutes. Makes 4 to 8 servings.

ORIENTAL BARBECUED CHICKEN

4 broiler-fryer chickens, halved or quartered
Salt
Pepper
Oriental Barbecue Sauce*

Sprinkle broiler-fryer chicken halves or quarters with salt and pepper. Let stand 10 to 15 minutes. Place chicken, skin side up, on grate set 3 to 6 inches above coals. Cook until tender, turning and basting occasionally. Allow 45 minutes' to 1¼ hours' total cooking time, depending on weight of chicken and distance from heat. About 15 minutes before chicken is done, begin brushing frequently with Oriental Barbecue Sauce. To test for doneness, leg should twist easily out of thigh joint and pieces should feel tender when probed with a fork. Makes 8 to 10 servings.

*ORIENTAL BARBECUE SAUCE

1 can (6 ounces) frozen orange juice
    concentrate, thawed, undiluted
¼ cup light molasses
¼ cup soy sauce
¼ cup vegetable oil
1 teaspoon ground ginger
1 teaspoon dry mustard
1 teaspoon minced dried onion
1 teaspoon minced dried green onion
½ teaspoon celery seed
1 teaspoon minced dried garlic

Combine all ingredients in saucepan. Simmer 10 minutes. Makes 1½ cups sauce, enough for 8 broiler-fryer chicken halves.

FAVORITE BARBECUED CHICKEN

3 broiler-fryer chickens, halved or quartered
Tomato Barbecue Sauce*

Place chicken halves or quarters on grill set 3 to 6 inches above coals. Cook until tender, 45 minutes to 1 hour and 15 minutes, turning occasionally. Brush frequently with Tomato Barbecue Sauce during last 10 to 15 minutes' cooking time. Makes 6 to 12 servings.

*TOMATO BARBECUE SAUCE

1 tablespoon sugar
1½ teaspoons salt
½ teaspoon grated lemon peel
2 tablespoons chopped scallions
1 tablespoon lemon juice
1 tablespoon Worcestershire sauce
1 cup chili sauce
1 cup water

Combine all ingredients in a large saucepan. Bring to a boil over medium heat, stirring occasionally. Remove from heat. Makes about 2 cups sauce, enough for 3 broiler-fryer chickens.

NOTE: For more highly seasoned sauce, double amount of lemon peel, lemon juice, and Worcestershire sauce.

BROILERS IN WINE MARINADE

½ cup vegetable oil
½ cup Rhine wine
¼ cup lemon or lime juice
½ teaspoon dried rosemary
1 tablespoon prepared mustard

½ cup liquid honey
½ teaspoon hot-pepper sauce
1 teaspoon Worcestershire sauce
2 broiler chickens, quartered

Blend well, with rotary beater, all ingredients except chicken. Pour mixture over broilers in deep dish; chill several hours, turning chicken occasionally. Warm remaining marinade in small saucepan; place near grill with small pastry brush and use to baste broilers while cooking. Serve extra marinade as sauce or store in covered jar for next barbecue. Makes 4 to 6 servings.

BARBECUED CHICKEN IN SAUCE

2 frying chickens, fresh or frozen, cut up
½ cup chopped green pepper
1 tablespoon minced onion
1 tablespoon brown sugar
½ teaspoon salt
1 teaspoon prepared mustard
2 teaspoons thick steak sauce
¼ teaspoon hot-pepper sauce
1 tablespoon lemon juice
1 can (8 ounces) tomato sauce
½ cup water

Thaw frozen chicken according to package directions. Combine remaining ingredients for sauce. Place chicken, skin side down, on barbecue grill over glowing coals. Broil about 4 minutes or until brown. Turn chicken; broil about 4 minutes longer. Make a 12-inch square pan of doubled heavy-duty aluminum foil by turning edges up all around. Put chicken pieces in this pan; pour sauce over chicken. Simmer over glowing coals, turning occasionally, 45 minutes to an hour or until tender. Makes 4 to 6 servings.

BARBECUED CHICKEN BREASTS

3 whole broiler-fryer chicken breasts, halved
Salt
¾ cup lemon juice
¼ cup water
1½ teaspoons salt
1½ teaspoons dried leaf tarragon
2 tablespoons finely chopped onion
2 tablespoons sugar
¼ teaspoon hot-pepper sauce

Sprinkle chicken with salt; place skin side up on grill set 6 inches above coals. Combine remaining ingredients and brush onto chicken. Cook until tender, 40 to 50 minutes, turning and brushing occasionally. Makes 6 servings.

DO-EASY DRUMSTICKS

12 broiler-fryer drumsticks
Salt
Paprika
¼ cup melted butter or margarine
2 tablespoons lemon juice
1 teaspoon dried leaf tarragon
½ teaspoon dried dillweed

Sprinkle drumsticks with salt and paprika. Combine melted butter, lemon juice, tarragon, and dillweed. Place drumsticks on grill 4 inches above coals. Brush with herb mixture. Cook until tender, 45 minutes to 1 hour, turning and brushing occasionally. Makes 6 servings.

CHARCOAL-GRILLED CHICKEN LEGS

¼ cup vegetable oil
½ cup Rhine wine
1 garlic clove, peeled and grated
1 medium onion, peeled and grated
½ teaspoon salt
½ teaspoon celery salt
½ teaspoon coarsely ground black pepper
¼ teaspoon each dried thyme, oregano, and
    rosemary
12 chicken legs

Combine all ingredients except chicken legs; mix well. Chill several hours in covered container. Arrange chicken legs in shallow pan or refrigerator dish. Shake chilled sauce; pour evenly over chicken legs. Cover; chill about 3 hours, turning pieces at least once. Drain. Pour remaining sauce into small pan. Cover each leg bone with a frill of doubled heavy-duty aluminum foil. Grill about 4 inches above hot coals, turning often and basting with sauce. Grill about 30 minutes or until thoroughly done. Makes 6 servings.

GRILLED CORNISH HENS À L'ORANGE

3 or 4 Rock Cornish hens
1 teaspoon salt
½ teaspoon ginger
1 garlic clove, crushed
2 tablespoons lemon juice
4 tablespoons vegetable oil

½ cup frozen orange juice concentrate, undiluted
½ cup giblet broth (page 107)
2 teaspoons soy sauce

Wash thawed Rock Cornish hens. Blend remaining ingredients; let hens stand in this marinade at least 1 hour before placing on spit. Pull neck skin back; secure wings against body; tie tail and legs together. Follow manufacturer's directions for securing hens on spit. Start motor. Grill 45 to 60 minutes, brushing occasionally with reserved marinade until golden brown and done. Makes 3 to 4 servings.

To Barbecue on Grill: Place halved birds on grill, breast side down, about 4 inches above hot coals. Baste well; turn when brown. Baste again; cook until fork-tender and golden crisp.

SMOKED TURKEY

12-to-15-pound turkey
Salt
1 stalk celery with leaves, cut up
¼ cup chopped onions
¼ cup chopped parsley
2 sprigs of fresh thyme *or* ½ teaspoon dried herbs
½ cup vegetable oil
1 cup cider or dry white wine with sprinkling of herbs
Pepper
Giblet broth (page 107)
1 tablespoon cornstarch

If turkey is frozen, defrost until pliable. Sprinkle cavity with salt and fill with mixture of celery, onion, and herbs. Close openings with skewers; truss. Combine oil, cider with herbs, salt, and pepper; brush over turkey. Place turkey right on grill with foil pan underneath. If the fire seems quite hot, place foil around the sides of the bird for protection. Cover the grill with its own cover or a foil hood. Adjust damper so fire will burn slowly. If a foil hood is used, adjust opening in the top. Let turkey cook and brown very slowly, allowing about 5 hours for a 12-to-15-pound bird. Lift the cover and brush with the herb-cider-oil mixture once or twice. Add 3 or 4 damp hickory chips to the fire when first started, about halfway through the cooking, and toward the end. Add additional briquettes once. The turkey is done when the second joint moves easily and the breast meat is soft to the touch. A meat thermom-

eter inserted in the thickest part of the thigh should read 185°. Remove turkey to serving plank or platter. Slip the foil pan with juices carefully onto a cookie sheet; then pour the juices into a saucepan. Add any remaining basting sauce. Skim off the fat. Taste; add broth made from cooking giblets to make 3 cups. Add additional salt and pepper if needed and thicken with 1 tablespoon cornstarch mixed with ¼ cup of broth. Serve a little of this sauce over each serving of turkey. Makes 12 to 15 servings.

DUCKLING ON A SPIT À L'ORANGE

1 5-pound duckling
Salt
Pepper
1 stalk celery with leaves
2 to 3 sprigs parsley
1 small onion, quartered
½ small orange with peel, cut up
Orange Barbecue Sauce*
1 orange, peeled and sliced

Remove pinfeathers, excess fat, and skin of duck. Rinse inside and out; pat dry. Prick lightly all over to allow for escape of excess fat during cooking. Salt and pepper the cavity and stuff with the celery, parsley, onion, and ½ orange. Rub outside with salt. Truss securely with skewers and string. Insert the spit through the duck and secure it firmly. Make a pan of heavy-duty aluminum foil about 1½ inches deep and 5 inches longer than the duckling; place at the front of the fire to catch drippings. Set the spit in motion and roast the duck slowly. Baste every 15 minutes with Orange Barbecue Sauce, using either a bulb-type baster or a brush. Roast about 2 hours. Duckling is done when drumstick meat is soft when pressed between protected fingers. When duck is done, transfer to hot platter. Remove foil drip pan; pour drippings into saucepan. Pour off fat; add remaining barbecue sauce and sliced orange to saucepan. Heat to serving temperature. Add salt and pepper to taste. Makes about 4 servings.

*ORANGE BARBECUE SAUCE

3 oranges
½ cup vinegar
Sprig of rosemary
Sprig of fresh tarragon
¼ cup light brown sugar
1 tablespoon prepared mustard

Peel the thin outer peel from 1 orange. Squeeze the other two. Add peel and juice to the vinegar with the rosemary, tarragon, brown sugar, and mustard. If fresh tarragon and rosemary are not available, use ½ cup tarragon vinegar and ¼ teaspoon dried rosemary. Heat almost to the boiling point, but do not boil. Keep hot for 10 minutes. Strain to use.

BARBECUED DUCKLING HALVES

2 frozen ready-to-cook ducklings, 4 to 5
    pounds each
¼ cup honey
1 teaspoon brown gravy seasoning sauce
½ teaspoon salt
½ teaspoon ginger

Thaw ducklings in warmest place in the refrigerator, 24 to 36 hours. Cut ducklings in half, removing backbone and wing tips. Place skin side down on ungreased grill at highest position above the coals. Grill 15 minutes on each side. Combine last 4 ingredients; brush generously over skin side of ducklings. Broil 2 minutes longer. Makes 8 servings.

WHOLE FISH GRILLED IN FOIL

Butter or margarine
1 medium onion, sliced thin
1-to-3-pound fish, cleaned, head and tail
    removed
Salt
Pepper
Fresh tarragon, parsley, dill, thyme, rosemary
Softened butter
Chopped parsley
Lemon juice

Tear off a suitably sized piece of heavy-duty foil. Spread a little butter or margarine in center of foil and arrange several onion slices on it. Place the fish over onion slices. Sprinkle inside of fish with salt and pepper. Arrange remaining onion slices over fish and sprinkle with salt, pepper, and herbs; dot with butter. Bring foil up over fish, sealing edges with a double fold. Seal both ends with double fold. Place on grate 4 inches above coals. Cook about 30 to 45 minutes, turning two or three times. To serve, transfer foil with fish to a serving dish; turn back the foil and crimp edges. Fish may be lifted right off the bones. Serve with softened butter to which chopped parsley and lemon juice to taste have been added.

FISH FILLETS IN FOIL

6 or more small fish fillets
Melted butter
Lemon slices
Onion slices
Salt
Pepper
Sour-Cream Tartar Sauce*

Dip fish fillets in melted butter and roll up each one. Have squares of heavy-duty foil ready. Place one or two rolled fillets in center of each square. Add a very thin lemon slice and 1 or 2 slices of onion. Season with salt and pepper. Seal the foil to make a tight package. Place on the grill 4 inches above coals. Cook about 20 minutes, turning one or two times. Serve each person a package, or turn back foil and arrange packages on a large heatproof platter. Serve with Sour-Cream Tartar Sauce.

°SOUR-CREAM TARTAR SAUCE

1 cup mayonnaise
2 tablespoons minced old-fashioned dill
    pickle
1 tablespoon minced onion
1 tablespoon lemon juice
1 tablespoon parsley
1 teaspoon each minced fresh thyme,
    tarragon, and dill *or* 1 teaspoon mixed
    dried herbs
Freshly ground pepper
4 tablespoons dairy sour cream

Add to the mayonnaise, pickle, onion, lemon juice, parsley, and herbs. Then add a generous sprinkling of freshly ground black pepper. Just before serving, fold in sour cream. Makes about 1¼ cups sauce.

BARBECUED HADDOCK FILLETS

2 pounds haddock fillets or other fish fillets,
    fresh or frozen
¼ cup chopped onion
2 tablespoons chopped green pepper
1 garlic clove, finely chopped
2 tablespoons vegetable oil
1 can (8 ounces) tomato sauce
2 tablespoons lemon juice

1 tablespoon Worcestershire sauce
1 tablespoon sugar
2 teaspoons salt
¼ teaspoon pepper

Thaw frozen fillets. Cook onion, green pepper, and garlic in oil until tender. Add remaining ingredients; simmer 5 minutes, stirring occasionally. Cool. Cut fillets into serving-size portions and place in a single layer in a shallow dish. Pour sauce over fish; let stand for 30 minutes, turning once. Remove fish, reserving sauce for basting. Place fish in well-greased hinged wire grill. Cook about 4 inches above coals 8 minutes. Baste with sauce. Turn and cook 7 to 10 minutes longer or until fish flakes easily when tested with a fork. Makes 6 servings.

SCAMPI IN FOIL PACKETS

2 pounds uncooked large shrimp (15 to 20 to a
    pound)
2 garlic cloves
¾ cup butter or margarine
½ teaspoon each tarragon, rosemary, and
    thyme
3 tablespoons lemon juice
1½ teaspoons salt
Freshly ground pepper
French bread

Remove shells from shrimp, leaving tails in place; devein. Mince or crush the garlic; combine with the butter or margarine and the herbs in a small saucepan. Let stand over heat for a few minutes to blend flavors, then add lemon juice. Tear six 12-inch squares of heavy-duty aluminum foil and arrange 4 or 5 shrimp on each. Pour garlic butter mixture over shrimp; sprinkle with salt and freshly ground pepper. Bring foil up over shrimp, gathering edges together, and twist at top. Place on grill 4 inches above coals; grill 10 to 20 minutes. Wrap French bread in foil; heat on grill 5 minutes, turning once. Makes 6 to 8 servings.

BARBECUED LOBSTER TAILS

Frozen lobster tails
Seasoned natural meat tenderizer
Melted butter
Garnish: parsley; lemon wedges

Allow one 6-ounce frozen lobster tail per person. Sprinkle seasoned natural meat tenderizer

evenly, like salt, on partially thawed lobster tail. Do not use salt. Pierce generously with a fork right down to shell. Cut membrane down edges and remove. To keep tails flat, bend backward toward shell side to crack in 3 places or insert skewer lengthwise through tails. Brush meat side with melted butter; place meat side down on grill. Set about 4 inches above coals. When meat is nicely browned (about 5 minutes), turn and cook shell side down for 9 to 12 minutes longer, basting frequently with melted butter. Serve in shell, garnished with parsley and lemon wedges.

EASY PICNIC FOR FOUR

Cold Broiled Chicken: Have broiler-fryer chicken quartered. Brush with melted butter or margarine. Broil skin side down 3 to 4 inches below source of heat for 15 minutes; turn. Brush with butter again; broil 15 minutes longer. Chill. Sprinkle with salt and pepper; dot with butter or margarine. Wrap in aluminum foil.

Corn on the Cob: Brush each ear of corn with melted butter or margarine; sprinkle with salt and pepper. Wrap in aluminum foil; twist ends.

Relishes: Prepare celery, carrot sticks, radish roses. Pack with ice in covered plastic container.

French Bread: Cut loaves almost through in 1-inch slices. Spread cut surfaces with relish sandwich spread. Wrap each loaf in aluminum foil.

Final Cooking: Place foil-wrapped chicken and corn on grate over glowing coals; cook 15 to 20 minutes, turning once. Place wrapped bread on grate for last 10 minutes, turning once. The ice-packed relishes will be brittle-crisp; just pour off water and serve them from the container.

BARBECUE BANQUET

Each of the recipes below is easy to prepare and when put together they truly form a banquet.

Heavenly Barbecue Sauce

1½ cups light molasses
1 cup prepared yellow mustard
⅓ cup Worcestershire sauce
1½ cups vinegar
1 teaspoon hot-pepper sauce
¼ teaspoon each marjoram and oregano

Pour molasses into large mixing bowl; gradually blend in mustard. Stir in remaining ingredients. Store in tightly covered jar in refrigerator. (It keeps.) Makes about 1 quart sauce.

Golden Gate Barbecued Chicken

Buy broiler-fryer chickens, quartered. Brush with melted butter or margarine; brown on both sides over hot coals; place in foil pan. Grill with pan about 3 inches above hot coals about 45 minutes, basting often with Heavenly Barbecue Sauce (use about ¾ cup sauce for 2 chickens).

Luscious Potatoes

Baking potatoes
Soft butter or margarine
Dairy sour cream
Cut chives, fresh or freeze-dried

Scrub baking potatoes; rub with soft butter or margarine; double-wrap in foil; place directly on coals; roast 1 hour, turning several times. Break open; top with sour cream and cut chives.

Savory Zucchini

Zucchini squash
1 can (8 ounces) tomato sauce
1 tablespoon minced dried onion
Butter or margarine
Salt and pepper

Slice zucchini squash ½ inch thick. Combine tomato sauce and onion. Place enough squash for each serving in double square of foil; top with 2 or 3 tablespoons tomato sauce, 1 teaspoon butter or margarine, salt, and pepper. Gather up foil; twist top. Grill 25 minutes.

Onion Bread Cuts

½ cup butter or margarine
1 tablespoon minced dried onion
1 loaf French bread

Melt butter or margarine; add onion; let stand over low heat 10 minutes. Cut bread loaf almost through lengthwise, then crosswise. Brush all cut surfaces with onion butter; wrap in foil; set on grill where heat is not too intense.

BASIC BARBECUE SAUCE

1 cup light molasses
1 cup prepared mustard
¾ cup vinegar

Blend molasses and mustard. Add vinegar; mix well. Cover tightly; store at room temperature or in refrigerator. Sauce will store indefinitely. Makes 2¾ cups sauce.

Tangy Tomato Barbecue Sauce: Add ¼ cup catchup and ½ teaspoon hot-pepper sauce to 1 cup Basic Barbecue Sauce.

Herb Barbecue Sauce: Add 1⁄16 teaspoon each marjoram, oregano, and thyme to 1 cup Basic Barbecue Sauce.

Curry Barbecue Sauce: Add 1 tablespoon curry powder, 1 tablespoon Worcestershire sauce, and ½ teaspoon hot-pepper sauce to 1 cup Basic Barbecue Sauce.

TANGY BARBECUE SAUCE

½ cup finely diced celery
2 tablespoons vegetable oil
2 cups catchup
½ cup dark corn syrup
2 tablespoons Worcestershire sauce
3 teaspoons mustard-with-horseradish
2 teaspoons vinegar
½ teaspoon dried rosemary leaves
½ teaspoon dried thyme leaves
½ teaspoon dried oregano leaves
½ teaspoon dried savory leaves

Cook celery in oil in saucepan over medium heat until tender. Stir in catchup, corn syrup, Worcestershire sauce, mustard-with-horseradish, vinegar, rosemary, thyme, oregano, and savory. Reduce heat; simmer, uncovered, 10 minutes. Makes about 3 cups.

DILL-FLAVORED BARBECUE SAUCE

1½ cups vegetable oil
½ cup lemon juice
1 to 2 tablespoons sugar (to taste)
1 teaspoon paprika
Few drops hot-pepper sauce
½ teaspoon salt
½ teaspoon dried dillweed

Combine all ingredients. Stir well before using. Makes about 2 cups.

SPICY BARBECUE SAUCE

2 cans (8 ounces each) tomato sauce
2 tablespoons Worcestershire sauce
1 tablespoon prepared horseradish
Dash hot-pepper sauce
1 tablespoon sugar
1 tablespoon grated onion
½ teaspoon oregano
⅛ teaspoon cloves
2 tablespoons butter or margarine

Combine all ingredients; stir over low heat until butter melts. Use to baste meat while broiling, or as an accompaniment.

COUNTRY TERRACE BARBECUE SAUCE

¾ cup diced scallions
½ cup chopped celery
¼ cup butter, margarine, or vegetable oil
2 cans (15 ounces each) tomato sauce with tomato bits *or* 4 cups chopped fresh tomatoes
¼ cup chopped parsley
4 tablespoons brown sugar
4 tablespoons vinegar
1½ teaspoons salt
2 tablespoons Worcestershire sauce

Sauté scallions and celery in butter or oil. Add tomato sauce or fresh tomatoes; simmer until vegetables are tender. Add remaining ingredients. Makes about 1 quart sauce.

CARIBBEAN BARBECUE SAUCE

¼ cup light molasses
¼ cup prepared mustard
¼ cup vinegar
2 tablespoons Worcestershire sauce
1 teaspoon hot-pepper sauce
1⁄16 teaspoon each powdered marjoram, oregano, and thyme

Put molasses, then mustard, into 1-cup measure. Stir to blend. Add remaining ingredients; mix well. Makes approximately ¾ cup, or enough for 3 broiler-fryer chickens or for 12 to 18 hamburgers or frankfurters.

VARIATIONS

1. Add 1 can (8 ounces) tomato sauce or ½ cup catchup and ¼ cup vegetable oil.

2. Add 2 tablespoons finely chopped onion and 2 tablespoons finely chopped green pepper.
3. Add 1 garlic clove, minced.
4. Add ¼ cup red wine.

STEAK MARINADE

½ cup vegetable oil
¼ cup lemon juice
½ teaspoon hot-pepper sauce
½ cup dry red wine
1 teaspoon dry mustard
½ teaspoon salt
⅛ teaspoon each dried leaf marjoram and thyme

Measure oil, lemon juice, and hot-pepper sauce into shallow dish. Stir in wine, dry mustard, salt, and herbs. Add steak; marinate in refrigerator for at least 5 or 6 hours, turning once. Makes enough for one 4-pound steak.

ROQUEFORT STEAK SPREAD

½ teaspoon hot-pepper sauce
2 tablespoons butter or margarine
1 package (3 ounces) Roquefort cheese

Cream together all ingredients until blended. Spread over broiled steak. Makes enough for two 4-pound steaks.

TABASCO BUTTER

½ cup butter or margarine
½ teaspoon Tabasco
2 tablespoons lime or lemon juice

Cream together butter, Tabasco, and lime juice. Spread over broiled steak. Makes enough for two 4-pound steaks.

OLIVE DIABLO BUTTER

½ cup softened butter or margarine
½ cup finely chopped onion
¼ cup finely chopped stuffed olives
⅓ cup Dijon mustard
2 tablespoons prepared horseradish

Melt 2 tablespoons of the butter. Add onion; cook 5 minutes. Beat into remaining butter with rest of ingredients. Serve with meat as desired. Makes about 1 cup.

SEAFOOD SAUCE

¾ cup chili sauce or catchup
3 tablespoons lemon juice
2 tablespoons prepared horseradish
2 teaspoons Worcestershire sauce
1 teaspoon grated onion
¼ teaspoon salt
3 drops hot-pepper sauce

Combine all ingredients; chill. Makes about 1 cup sauce.

BANANAS WITH CINNAMON

Bananas
Lemon juice
Brown sugar
Cinnamon
Butter or margarine

Peel bananas; place each on double thickness of heavy-duty or broiler foil. Brush with lemon juice. Sprinkle generously with brown sugar; dust with cinnamon. Dot with butter or margarine. Wrap foil securely around bananas, twisting ends. Grill over hot coals 7 to 9 minutes. Serve piping-hot.

GRILLED BANANAS IN FOIL

4 firm, green-tipped bananas
½ cup lemon juice
¼ cup melted butter or margarine
½ cup packaged flavored bread crumb mix

Dip bananas in lemon juice; roll in melted butter, then in flavored bread crumbs. Wrap in heavy foil; grill 10 minutes about 4 inches above hot coals. Makes 4 servings.

BARBECUED STUFFED PEAR HALVES

1 can (1 pound) Bartlett pear halves
¼ cup bottled all-purpose barbecue sauce
¼ cup sweet pickle relish
¼ cup finely diced celery
1 teaspoon minced pimiento

Drain pears, reserving ½ cup pear syrup for marinade. Combine syrup with barbecue sauce. Place pears cut side up in baking dish. Pour marinade over pears; let stand several hours or overnight. Drain. Combine pickle relish, celery, and pimiento; spoon into pears. To serve hot, place stuffed pears on aluminum foil plate; cover with foil; heat on grill about 5 minutes. Makes 4 servings.

STRING BEANS

Serve beans alone or in combinations. A good combination is string beans, tomatoes, and onion. Sliver the beans; add tomato wedges and wafer-thin slices of onion. Place individual portions on squares of heavy-duty foil. Add salt, pepper, and butter or margarine. Basil is a good herb seasoning for all vegetable combinations when tomato is included. Seal foil into airtight package. Grill 4 inches above coals 35 to 40 minutes, turning once or twice.

FROZEN BABY LIMAS WITH CREAM SAUCE

1 package (10 ounces) frozen small lima beans
3 tablespoons water
2 tablespoons butter or margarine
½ teaspoon salt
Pepper
1 can (10¾ ounces) condensed cream of celery soup

Partially thaw lima beans. Place in center of a square of heavy-duty foil. Add water, butter or margarine, salt, and a sprinkling of pepper. Close the foil, twisting at top to seal. Place on grill and cook gently about 30 minutes, shaking occasionally. Open package and pour condensed cream of celery soup over beans. Stir to combine; continue cooking until sauce is hot. Makes 4 servings.

CHUCK WAGON BEANS

½ pound Canadian-style bacon
½ cup diced onion
1 garlic clove, minced
¼ teaspoon salt
4 cans (1 pound each) red kidney beans
1 teaspoon dry mustard
½ cup light molasses

Fry bacon in skillet over outdoor grill or campfire until brown and slightly crisp. Add onion and garlic; cook until onion is just tender (about 5 minutes). Turn into deep casserole. Stir in remaining ingredients. Cover; cook over low heat at back of grill about 30 minutes. Remove cover; cook 15 minutes longer, stirring often. Makes 6 to 8 servings.

CARROTS AND CELERY IN FOIL

Scrape carrots; cut in strips. Cut celery in small pieces. Combine enough for all on a large square of heavy-duty foil. Add butter or margarine and seasonings. Sprinkle with a little chopped parsley or mint. Bring corners of foil together and twist to make packet. Grill 4 inches above coals 35 to 40 minutes, turning once. Serve right from the packet.

CORN CHUNKS

Select tender, young ears of corn. Break each ear into 3 to 4 chunks. Roll in melted butter or margarine; sprinkle with salt and coarse black pepper. Wrap individual portions securely in double thickness of heavy-duty aluminum foil. Grill directly on hot coals 10 to 12 minutes, turning once. Keep hot on grill. Use metal meat skewers for holders.

ROAST CORN ON THE COB

Method 1: Select 1 or 2 good, full ears of corn for each person. Pull husks partway down; remove as much silk as possible; trim off any imperfect parts; re-cover corn with husks. Place ears in a tub of cold water for about ½ hour. When fire has burned down to gray coals, place corn on grill. Turn ears frequently as they cook. Cooking takes 30 to 45 minutes. When done, strip off husks; dip corn into melted butter and season with salt and pepper.

Method 2: Remove husks and silk. Spread corn with butter; sprinkle with salt and pepper; wrap securely in aluminum foil. Roast 15 to 20 minutes on the grill. Turn several times.

NOTE: For a gourmet treat, try spreading each ear of corn with peanut butter. Wind a bacon strip around ear before wrapping in foil. You'll find no butter or salt is needed when the corn is prepared in this manner, and the flavor is terrific.

GRILLED EGGPLANT

Cut unpared eggplant in ¾-inch slices. Brush both sides of slices with vegetable oil, then coat with packaged seasoned fine dry bread crumbs. Place on grill set 4 inches above coals. Grill 10 to 15 minutes or until tender, turning once.

BERMUDA ONIONS ROASTED IN FOIL

Select good-sized Bermuda onions. Do not peel. Prick through with a long-tined fork several times so onions won't burst when cooking. Place each on a square of heavy-duty foil and wrap, twisting at the top to seal. Place on grill and cook, rolling onions around and turning them several times. When soft, open and turn back foil. Slit each onion with a sharp knife as you would a potato; add butter, salt, and pepper.

GARDEN PEAS IN FOIL

1 pound fresh young peas
1 tablespoon butter or margarine
½ teaspoon sugar
¼ teaspoon salt
Pepper
Nutmeg
2 teaspoons chopped fresh mint

Shell peas and place on heavy-duty foil. Add butter or margarine, sugar, salt, a sprinkling of pepper and nutmeg, and chopped fresh mint. Close the foil, twisting at the top to seal. Place on the grill and cook gently about 20 minutes, shaking occasionally. Makes 2 servings.

STUFFED BAKED POTATOES

Good-sized baking potatoes
Hot milk
Butter
Salt
Pepper
Choice of flavoring (see below)
Paprika
Melted butter

Prepare potatoes ahead; store in refrigerator or freezer. Wrap good-sized baking potatoes in heavy-duty foil; bake. Remove foil; divide potatoes lengthwise, allowing about ⅔ for the lower half. Scoop out centers and whip to feathery lightness with hot milk, butter, and seasoning. Add any of the following: minced onion, cut chives, crisp bacon bits, small cubes of cheese. Heap the filling in the large potato-skin shell, discarding the smaller one. Sprinkle with paprika and melted butter. Wrap stuffed potatoes in foil; store in refrigerator or freezer. To serve, place on grill where heat is moderate; heat for 20 minutes if chilled, 45 minutes if frozen. Turn back foil about 5 minutes before potatoes are done. If grill is covered, tops will brown from reflected heat.

GRILLED TOMATOES

Ripe tomatoes
French or Italian dressing
Salt
Pepper
Sugar
Dried basil

Cut washed ripe tomatoes in half. Do not peel. Brush the cut side with French or Italian dressing. Sprinkle each with salt and pepper, ¼ teaspoon sugar, and about ⅛ teaspoon dried basil. Place cut side up on a sheet of heavy-duty aluminum foil. Place on grill for about 10 minutes. Do not turn. Use a wide spatula to remove the tomatoes from the foil.

SPANISH CREOLE YAMS

2 cans (1 pound each) Louisiana yams
½ cup butter or margarine
½ cup chopped onion
½ cup diced green pepper (about 1 medium pepper)
½ cup sliced stuffed olives
½ teaspoon salt
Dash pepper
Dash paprika

Drain yams on paper towels; cut in half. Melt butter in large skillet on grill. Sauté yams, a few at a time, until lightly browned. Remove yams to warm serving dish; keep warm. In same skillet, sauté onion and green pepper just until tender. Stir in olives and seasonings; spoon mixture over yams and serve at once. Makes 4 to 6 servings.

ZUCCHINI CREOLE

6 small zucchini
3 medium tomatoes
1 teaspoon salt
¼ teaspoon coarse black pepper
½ teaspoon sugar
2 tablespoons butter or margarine

Slice zucchini crosswise in ¼-inch slices. Cube tomatoes; add to zucchini with salt, pepper, and sugar. Mix well. Divide into 4 portions on 4 large squares of doubled heavy-duty aluminum foil. Place ½ tablespoon butter on each portion. Wrap

foil securely around food. Grill 4 inches above hot coals 20 to 25 minutes, turning once. Makes 4 servings.

SAVORY ITALIAN BREAD

1 round loaf Italian bread
½ cup mayonnaise
¼ teaspoon garlic powder
⅓ cup minced parsley
2 tablespoons prepared mustard
½ teaspoon herb seasoning
Dash cayenne

Slash bread into 8 wedges, almost to bottom crust. Combine remaining ingredients; mix well. Spread cut surface of bread with mayonnaise mixture. Wrap in heavy-duty aluminum foil. Heat on grill 12 to 15 minutes. Makes 8 servings.

CAMPFIRE STEW

2 pounds lean beef, ground
2 cans (10½ ounces each) beef gravy
1 can (8 ounces) tomato sauce
½ cup strong coffee
1 can (1 pound) small white potatoes
1 can (1 pound) baby carrots
1 can (1 pound) onions
1 can (1 pound) green beans

Shape beef into 6 large patties. Brown well on both sides. Combine beef gravy, tomato sauce, and coffee. Drain potatoes; discard liquid. Drain carrots, onions, and green beans, saving liquids. Combine liquids from these 3 vegetables; measure 1 cup; add to gravy mixture; blend well. Fill 3 coffee cans with equal amounts of vegetables and 2 meat patties; pour an equal amount of gravy mixture into each can. Cover. Pack in portable ice chest to carry to camping grounds. Replace plastic covers on coffee cans with foil before heating. Heat on camp stove or over campfire until bubbling hot. Each can holds 2 servings.

BEEF 'N' BARLEY MULLIGAN

1½ pounds ground beef
1 medium-sized green pepper, chopped
1 medium-sized onion, chopped
1 small garlic clove, crushed
1 can (1 pound) whole tomatoes with juice
1 can (6 ounces) tomato paste
⅔ cup water

1 beef bouillon cube
2 teaspoons salt
¼ teaspoon pepper
1 tablespoon firmly packed brown sugar
1 tablespoon vinegar
1 cup quick pearled barley

Lightly brown meat in large kettle set on grill. Drain off excess fat. Add green pepper, onion, and garlic. Sauté lightly. Add remaining ingredients. Bring to boil on camp stove or over campfire. Cover; simmer 30 minutes, stirring occasionally. Makes 6 servings.

BEEF-AND-MACARONI SUPPER

1 pound ground beef
2 cans (10¾ ounces each) condensed tomato
    soup
2 soup cans water
1½ teaspoons oregano
½ teaspoon salt
½ cup sliced stuffed olives
2 cups elbow macaroni, uncooked

Brown ground beef in a large skillet or Dutch oven on camp stove or over campfire, stirring frequently. Add soup, water, oregano, salt, and olives. Heat until boiling. Stir in macaroni; cook, covered, over low heat 30 minutes or until macaroni is tender. Makes 4 servings.

SAFARI FRIED CHICKEN

½ cup enriched corn meal
½ cup pancake mix
2 teaspoons salt
¼ teaspoon pepper
2 tablespoons sesame seeds, toasted
2 frying chickens, about 2½ pounds each, cut
    in pieces
½ cup evaporated milk
½ cup shortening

In a paper bag, combine corn meal, pancake mix, salt, pepper, and sesame seeds. Dip chicken in evaporated milk, then shake a few pieces at a time in bag to coat thoroughly. Slowly heat shortening in skillet on camp stove or over campfire. Brown chicken on all sides; cover; cook about 35 minutes or until tender. Uncover; cook 5 minutes longer to crisp. Makes 8 servings.

OPEN SKIES SPAGHETTI SKILLET

1 can (1 pound) small whole onions
1 can (18 ounces) tomato juice
1 can (1 pound) stewed tomatoes with juice
1 envelope garlic salad dressing mix
1 package (8 ounces) spaghetti
½ cup sweet fresh cucumber pickles
1 can (12 ounces) frankfurters with juice

Drain liquid from onions into large skillet. Stir in tomato juice, tomatoes, and salad dressing mix; bring to boil on camp stove or over campfire. Gradually add spaghetti; cover; cook slowly, stirring occasionally, 20 minutes or until tender. Mix in onions, pickles, and frankfurters; heat to serving temperature. Makes 6 servings.

CURRIED FRANKFURTER SKILLET

1 quart water
5 chicken bouillon cubes
1 teaspoon curry powder
1 can (1 pound) green peas, undrained
1 medium onion, minced
1 package (8 ounces) spaghetti
1 pound frankfurters, cut in 1-inch pieces

Combine water and bouillon cubes in large skillet. Stir over high heat on camp stove or over campfire until water boils and cubes dissolve. Add curry powder and liquid from peas (reserve peas). Bring to boil; stir in onion, spaghetti, and frankfurters. Cover; cook over low heat 30 minutes or until spaghetti is tender, stirring occasionally. Add peas; mix lightly; heat to serving temperature. Makes 4 servings.

FRANKFURTER-NOODLE SKILLET

1 can (1 pound) tomatoes with juice
1 can (6 ounces) tomato paste
1 quart water
4 beef bouillon cubes
1 medium onion, chopped
2 garlic cloves
2 teaspoons salt
⅛ teaspoon pepper
¼ teaspoon crushed oregano
¼ teaspoon crushed basil
1 package (8 ounces) medium egg noodles
    (about 4 cups)
1 can (12 ounces) frankfurters, cut in 1-inch
    pieces
Grated Parmesan cheese

Combine tomatoes, tomato paste, water, bouillon cubes, onion, garlic, and seasonings in large skillet. Cover; cook on camp stove or over campfire over low heat 1 hour, stirring occasionally; discard garlic. Gradually add noodles; cover; cook 20 minutes or until noodles are tender, stirring frequently. Stir in frankfurters; heat thoroughly. Serve with Parmesan cheese. Makes 4 to 6 servings.

CAMPFIRE SKILLET

1 can (1 pound) tomatoes
3 cups water
2 tablespoons parsley flakes
1 tablespoon salt
½ teaspoon basil leaves
¼ teaspoon garlic powder
Dash pepper
1 package (8 ounces) medium egg noodles
1 can (12 ounces) frankfurters with juice
¼ cup grated American cheese

Combine undrained tomatoes, water, parsley, and seasonings in large skillet; bring to boil on camp stove or over campfire. Add noodles gradually; cook, covered, stirring occasionally, until tender. Add frankfurters. Sprinkle with cheese. Heat gently. Makes 4 servings.

WOODSMAN'S NOODLES

1 can (1 pound) sliced bacon, cut in half
1 can (11 ounces) condensed Cheddar cheese soup, undiluted
3 soup cans water
¼ teaspoon dry mustard
1 can (1 pound) sliced carrots with juice
1 package (8 ounces) fine egg noodles (about 4 cups)

Cook bacon in large skillet until crisp on camp stove or over campfire; remove from pan; drain off drippings. Stir in soup, water, and mustard; bring to boil. Add carrots and noodles gradually; cook, covered, 10 minutes. Return bacon to skillet; cook 5 minutes longer or until noodles are tender and bacon is heated through. Makes 4 servings.

SPAGHETTI CAMPER-STYLE

1 medium onion, sliced
2 garlic cloves, minced
2 tablespoons vegetable oil

1 can (28 ounces) pear-shaped tomatoes with juice
1½ teaspoons salt
1 bay leaf
¼ teaspoon marjoram
⅛ teaspoon crushed red pepper
1 can (6 ounces) broiled sliced mushrooms
¼ cup raisins
1 tablespoon salt
3 quarts boiling water
1 package (8 ounces) spaghetti
Grated Parmesan cheese

Sauté onion and garlic in oil until lightly browned on camp stove or over campfire. Add tomatoes, 1½ teaspoons salt, bay leaf, marjoram, red pepper, and mushroom broth. Simmer, uncovered, 1 hour, stirring occasionally. Remove bay leaf. Add mushrooms and raisins; heat 5 to 10 minutes. Add 1 tablespoon salt to rapidly boiling water. Gradually add spaghetti so that water continues to boil. Cook, uncovered, stirring occasionally, until tender. Drain. Serve with mushroom sauce and cheese. Makes 4 servings.

MACARONI-VEGETABLE SKILLET

1 can (1 pound) cut green beans
1 can (3 ounces) broiled sliced mushrooms
1 quart water
1 envelope onion soup mix
1 teaspoon salt
½ teaspoon crushed marjoram
2 cups uncooked elbow macaroni
1⅓ cups (2 small cans) undiluted evaporated milk
2 tablespoons dry white wine (optional)

Drain green bean and mushroom liquids into skillet; add water, soup mix, and seasonings. Mix well; bring to boil on camp stove or over campfire. Gradually add macaroni so that water continues to boil. Cover; cook over low heat 20 minutes or until tender, stirring occasionally. Stir in evaporated milk, wine, and vegetables; heat to serving temperature. Makes 4 to 6 servings.

CAMPFIRE BACON PANCAKES WITH PEACHY CINNAMON SYRUP

¾ cup maple-flavored pancake syrup
½ teaspoon cinnamon
1 tablespoon butter or margarine
1 can (16 ounces) sliced cling peaches, drained

1 pound sliced bacon
1 cup pancake mix
1 cup milk*
1 egg
2 tablespoons bacon drippings or vegetable
   oil

Combine pancake syrup, cinnamon, and butter in small saucepan; heat slowly on camp stove or over campfire, stirring occasionally, until butter is melted and syrup hot; add peaches. Keep warm. Dice 6 slices of bacon; fry until crisp in heavy frypan over moderate heat. Fry remaining whole bacon slices in same manner. Keep warm. Save drippings. Combine pancake mix, milk, egg, and bacon drippings or oil in mixing bowl; mix well. Stir in crisp, diced bacon pieces. Bake pancakes on hot griddle using ¼ cup batter for each one. Cook first side until underside is brown and top is full of bubbles. Turn; brown second side. For each serving, stack pancakes. Serve with warm peachy cinnamon syrup over pancakes and add bacon slices to each plate. Makes 4 servings.

*Or ½ cup evaporated milk and ½ cup water.

CAMPFIRE CORN BREAD

1 cup enriched corn meal
½ cup sifted all-purpose flour
¼ cup sugar
2 teaspoons baking powder
1 teaspoon salt
1 cup milk*
1 egg
2 tablespoons vegetable oil

Mix and sift corn meal, flour, sugar, baking powder, and salt. Beat together milk, egg, and oil; add to dry ingredients. Stir just enough to moisten. Do not overmix. Pour batter into hot, lightly greased 10-inch skillet. Cover; cook over hot coals or on camp stove about 20 minutes or until bottom is brown and top is set. To turn corn bread over, place plate over top of skillet and invert. Return corn bread to skillet and cook, covered, about 15 minutes on other side. Makes 8 servings.

*Or ½ cup evaporated milk and ½ cup water.

OUTDOOR BLUEBERRY BAKE

1 pint fresh blueberries
½ cup water

1 cup sugar
1 tablespoon lemon juice
½ teaspoon cinnamon
3 tablespoons biscuit mix
¼ cup butter or margarine
2 cups biscuit mix
Garnish (optional): dairy sour cream

Put berries in 9-inch pan made of foil. Place over hot coals. Combine water, sugar, lemon juice, cinnamon, and 3 tablespoons biscuit mix; stir into blueberries. Cook, stirring frequently, until thick. Meanwhile, melt butter in second foil pan. Make drop biscuit dough, following directions on package. Drop 6 large spoonfuls into melted butter. Place on camp stove or on grill over hot coals; brown on both sides. Top blueberries with butter-browned biscuits and serve. If desired, use dairy sour cream for topping. Makes 6 servings.

KABOBS

Cooking meat on a stick undoubtedly originated with primitive man, soon after he learned how to build and light a fire. Perhaps he dropped a chunk of raw meat into the fire, fished it out and liked the taste so much that he began to spear chunks with sticks and hold the meat over the fire.

In any event, the custom of grilling meat and vegetables—even fruits—spread throughout the world. Skewered foods are known by various names. You will find them in Russia as *shashlik*, often grilled on a sword and flamed before serving. In the Near East the term is *şiş kebabi*. In Japan *yakimono* means broiled food, while in Indonesia and other parts of Southeast Asia the term is *saté*. In Hungary *rablo-hus* and in Serbia *ražnjići* and *ćevapčići* all mean skewered foods. The South Africans say *sasaties*. In England the savories following dessert are sometimes skewered foods. The Greeks have a word for tidbits cooked on a skewer—*souvlakia*.

In this country the kabob is king! It has grown in popularity until today it is the favorite of all alfresco foods. And no wonder, because the necessary equipment is inexpensive and kabobs are easy to make. Much of the work can be done before it is time to cook, and everybody always enjoys them!

EQUIPMENT NEEDED FOR MAKING KABOBS

Brushes of different sizes are needed for basting kabobs as they grill. A small paintbrush of good quality is recommended, but be sure the bristles are not plastic.

Bunches of fresh herbs tied to a long stick add aromatic flavor when used for basting.

Skewers are available in many sizes. In an emergency, long, peeled green sticks with pointed tips may be used. The best skewers are made of steel and come in different lengths; some have decorative handles. Two-tined skewers help to hold food securely. Bamboo or wooden skewers should be thoroughly soaked before using, and one end of each should be sharpened.

Skewer racks placed on the grid support the skewers and make them easier to turn. Long-handled hinged grills adapt to kabobs of various thicknesses and make turning easy.

HELPFUL HINTS

Start your fire at least forty-five minutes before you begin to cook (see page 392).

Grease skewers either by running them through a piece of suet or oiling them lightly, so that the cooked food will slide off easily.

Cut onions from the stem down to keep them from falling apart.

Parboil certain vegetables such as small whole onions, potatoes, sweet potatoes, zucchini, etc., before broiling or grilling.

Kabobs need a hot fire, so be sure coals are glowing under the coating of ash.

Balance the foods by weight on the skewers as you thread them.

Remember to rotate the skewers often and brush the kabob each time with a sauce or marinade.

APPETIZERS

1. Cooked shrimp, 1-inch slices cooked rock lobster tails, raw scallops, half strips of bacon. Wrap each piece of seafood with bacon and thread 3 or 4 onto short skewers. Grill 4 or 5 inches above coals until bacon is crisp and brown.
2. Halved sautéed chicken livers, chunks of cooked chicken, water chestnuts, and pineapple chunks. Wrap in half slices of bacon; skewer and grill as above.
3. Vienna sausages, watermelon pickles, artichoke hearts, canned mushroom crowns. Proceed as in item 1.
4. Cooked turkey cubes, stuffed olives, Vienna sausages, canned mushroom crowns. Proceed as in item 1.

MARINATED BEEF AND PINEAPPLE KABOBS

1½ pounds tender lean beef
2 cups tomato juice
½ cup wine vinegar
¼ cup prepared mustard
2 teaspoons salt
2 teaspoons sugar
¼ teaspoon hot-pepper sauce
Pineaple chunks
½ pound fresh medium mushrooms

Cut beef in 1-inch cubes. Combine remaining ingredients except pineapple and mushrooms; pour over beef cubes. Cover; refrigerate for 2 hours. Drain beef, saving marinade. Alternate beef cubes and pineapple chunks on skewers; end with mushrooms. Grill 4 inches above coals for 12 to 15 minutes, turning often and basting with marinade. Makes 4 servings.

HERB BEEF KABOBS

¼ cup finely chopped onion
½ cup lemon juice
¼ cup vegetable oil
½ teaspoon salt
¼ teaspoon celery salt
¼ teaspoon pepper
½ teaspoon oregano
½ teaspoon thyme
1 garlic clove, minced
2 pounds beef sirloin tip, cut in 1½-inch cubes
8 eggplant wedges, cut 2 inches long
4 small cooked onions
4 cherry tomatoes

Combine onion, lemon juice, oil, salt, celery salt, pepper, oregano, thyme, and garlic. Pour marinade over meat in shallow dish. Cover tightly; refrigerate overnight. Pour off marinade; reserve. Thread each of four 12-inch skewers with meat, eggplant, meat, onion, meat, eggplant, and meat. Brush with marinade. Place on grill 3 to 4 inches from heat. Cook 10 to 12 minutes. Turn. Brush with marinade. Cook 8 to 10 minutes or until done. Place cherry tomato on each skewer about 2 minutes before meat is done. Makes 4 servings.

BEEF AND VEGETABLE KABOBS

1½ pounds lean beef, cut in cubes
Unseasoned natural meat tenderizer
1 cup red wine
½ cup soy sauce
1 cup pineapple juice
1 teaspoon thyme
1 teaspoon rosemary
¼ cup Worcestershire sauce
1 onion, finely chopped
½ teaspoon pepper
3 tomatoes, cut in eighths, if large, *or* 24
    whole cherry tomatoes
3 onions, cut in 1-inch wedges
12 whole mushrooms
1 small eggplant, peeled and cut in 1-inch
    pieces
1 green pepper, cut in large squares
12 small peeled whole potatoes, fresh-cooked
    or canned

Place meat in bowl and treat with tenderizer as directed on package. Combine next 8 ingredients to make a marinade. Pour marinade over meat in a bowl. Let stand 2 hours at room temperature or overnight in the refrigerator. Alternate the beef on skewers with the vegetables. Grill over glowing charcoal for about 15 minutes, turning frequently and basting with marinade. Makes 8 servings.

WEST INDIAN SKEWERED BEEF

4 small onions, finely chopped
Dash cayenne
2 garlic cloves, minced
1 tablespoon dark brown sugar
1 teaspoon lime juice
2 teaspoons curry powder
½ teaspoon ground cloves
½ teaspoon ground ginger
3 tablespoons warm water
3 tablespoons soy sauce
1½ pounds round steak, cut in ¾-inch cubes
Peanut Sauce*

Combine onions, cayenne, garlic, brown sugar, lime juice, curry powder, cloves, and ginger; blend well. Combine water and soy sauce; blend with spice mixture. Add meat; stir thoroughly with fork. Chill for 6 hours. Drain meat, saving

marinade. Thread 5 or 6 pieces of meat onto each skewer. Broil with skewers 3 inches below heat for 15 to 20 minutes, turning frequently and brushing meat with remaining marinade. Serve with Peanut Sauce. Makes 4 to 5 servings.

*PEANUT SAUCE

2 tablespoons grated onion
2 tablespoons vegetable oil
1 tablespoon dark brown sugar
1 teaspoon lime juice
¼ cup creamy peanut butter
1 cup water
Dash of salt

Sauté onion in oil 5 to 10 minutes until clear. Add brown sugar, lime juice, peanut butter; blend well. Gradually add water, stirring constantly. Add salt. Cook slowly until sauce is thick and smooth. Makes 1¼ cups.

STEAK-AND-APPLE KABOBS

3 pounds top round, ½ inch thick
Red Wine Marinade*
2 large green peppers, cut in 1½-inch squares
4 baking apples, cut in sixths

Cut beef in 1½-inch squares; cover with Red Wine Marinade; refrigerate for at least 12 hours, turning meat cubes several times. Drain, saving marinade. Alternate beef cubes, green pepper squares, and apple slices on skewers, using 3 squares of meat to 1 each of peppers and apples. Brush with marinade. Grill 4 inches above coals for 20 to 25 minutes, turning often and basting with marinade. Makes 6 servings.

*RED WINE MARINADE

½ cup vegetable oil
¼ cup soy sauce
½ cup dry red wine
1½ teaspoons ground ginger
2 garlic cloves, minced
1 tablespoon curry powder
2 tablespoons catchup
½ teaspoon hot-pepper sauce

Combine all ingredients; beat with electric or rotary egg beater until smooth.

SAYBROOK SHISH KABOB

Tenderized lean round steak
Strips of bacon
Celery stalks
Onion
Toasted frankfurter rolls

Cut tenderized lean round steak in 1-inch cubes. Cut bacon strips crosswise in 1-inch pieces. Cut celery stalks crosswise in ½-inch pieces. Dice onion in ½-inch pieces. Use 8-inch skewers. Skewer steak, bacon, celery, and onion and repeat until skewer is filled, beginning and ending with steak. Grill 3 inches above coals, turning often to cook on all sides; slip off skewers into toasted frankfurter rolls.

COUNTRY CLUB KABOBS

3 pounds top round, cut 1 inch thick
Natural meat tenderizer
1½ cups claret
½ cup soy sauce
1 cup vegetable oil
1½ teaspoons powdered ginger
¼ teaspoon garlic powder
¼ cup minced dried onion
2 teaspoons salt
½ teaspoon coarse black pepper
24 small cooked or canned onions
4 green peppers, cut in 24 squares
8 cherry tomatoes
8 fresh medium mushroom caps

Remove excess fat from beef. Cut beef in cubes (you will need 32). Treat with tenderizer as directed on label. Combine next 8 ingredients; mix well; pour over beef cubes. Let stand for at least 2 hours. Drain, saving marinade. Alternate 4 beef cubes, 3 onions, and 3 green pepper squares on each of 8 long skewers, beginning and ending with beef cubes. Broil over charcoal for about 15 minutes, turning often to brown on all sides, brushing frequently with marinade. During last 5 minutes put a cherry tomato and mushroom cap on end of each skewer. Makes 8 servings.

BARBECUED BEEF KABOBS

2 pounds packaged stew meat or top or
  bottom round, cut 1½ inches thick
1 foil packet (0.8 ounce) 15-minute meat
  marinade
Cold water

8 small onions, parboiled 5 minutes
1 green pepper, parboiled and cut in 8
  squares
8 small fresh mushrooms
4 cherry tomatoes

If meat was not purchased already cubed, cut in ¾-to-1-inch cubes. Blend contents of packet of meat marinade and amount of water called for in directions in a shallow pan. Place meat cubes in marinade. Pierce all surfaces of meat thoroughly with fork to carry flavor deep down and to lock in natural juices. Marinate for only 15 minutes, turning several times. Remove meat from marinade; drain. Reserve marinade for basting. Lace meat alternately with vegetables (except tomato) onto skewers. Allow 4 cubes of meat per skewer. Brush entire skewer with marinade or roll entire skewer in marinade. Place on barbecue grill 3 inches from hot coals. Barbecue for 8 to 12 minutes, turning and brushing frequently with marinade. During last 5 minutes of cooking, top each skewer with cherry tomato. Makes 4 servings.

PATIO BEEF CHUCK STRIPS

1 chuck steak (about 1½ pounds)
½ cup soy sauce
2 tablespoons brown sugar
1 tablespoon lemon juice
⅛ teaspoon garlic powder
½ teaspoon ground ginger
2 tablespoons white dinner wine
1 teaspoon natural meat tenderizer

Trim fat from beef. Cut beef crosswise in ½-inch slices. Cut each slice lengthwise in 2 strips, removing white membrane. Combine all remaining ingredients except tenderizer. Blend or shake well in covered jar to dissolve sugar. Pour marinade over beef strips. Cover; refrigerate several hours. When ready to cook, drain; save marinade. Sprinkle beef with tenderizer. Thread strips on each of 6 skewers. Grill 4 inches above coals to desired degree of doneness, turning often and brushing with marinade. Makes 6 servings.

HEARTY BEEF KABOBS

2 pounds lean, boneless beef chuck
Unseasoned natural meat tenderizer
Beef Basting Sauce*
Zucchini, green pepper, cherry tomatoes
French dressing

Remove excess fat from beef. Cut beef in 1½-to-2-inch cubes. Treat with meat tenderizer, following label directions. Thread beef onto skewers. Grill to desired degree of doneness. Brush often with Beef Basting Sauce after beef begins to brown. Turn to brown all sides. Cut zucchini lengthwise, then crosswise. Cut green pepper in chunks; leave tomatoes whole. Thread vegetables onto skewers and grill to desired degree of doneness. Baste with French dressing. Makes 4 servings.

*BEEF BASTING SAUCE

¼ cup vinegar
1 tablespoon Worcestershire sauce
2 tablespoons catchup
2 tablespoons dry sherry
1 tablespoon brown sugar
1 teaspoon prepared mustard
¼ cup maple-flavored syrup

Combine all ingredients, stirring to blend well. Heat and stir until sauce simmers. Makes about ¾ cup.

KABOBS CALIFORNIA

1½ pounds beef chuck, cut in 1½-inch cubes
Unseasoned natural meat tenderizer
1 teaspoon dry mustard
½ teaspoon salt
½ teaspoon peppercorns
¼ teaspoon oregano
1 bay leaf
1 tablespoon minced onion
½ cup vegetable oil
1 cup beer
1 green pepper, cut in 1-inch squares
3 tomatoes, quartered
12 small whole onions, parboiled
12 whole mushrooms

Treat beef with meat tenderizer according to label directions. Combine dry mustard, salt, peppercorns, oregano, bay leaf, onion, oil, and beer; pour over beef. Marinate in refrigerator for 5 hours or overnight. Drain, saving marinade. Alternate beef and vegetables on skewers. Place on grill about 4 inches above coals. Grill 10 minutes on each side, using marinade for basting. Makes 6 servings.

HAMBURGER KABOBS

Meat loaf mixture
Slices of bacon
Onions
Hamburger Sauce*
Toasted frankfurter rolls

Form your favorite, firm meat loaf mixture into small balls, about 1½ inches in diameter. Thread the end of a slice of bacon onto skewers. String skewer with 4 meatballs and 4 pieces of onion. Weave bacon strip in and out around skewer and run skewer through the other end. Brush with Hamburger Sauce. Grill until bacon is crisp, turning often and basting with sauce. Slide off skewers into toasted frankfurter rolls.

*HAMBURGER SAUCE

2 tablespoons butter or margarine, melted
⅓ cup vegetable oil
½ cup catchup
1 tablespoon prepared mustard
Dash hot-pepper sauce
1 teaspoon onion powder
1 tablespoon lemon juice
1 teaspoon sugar

Combine all ingredients; mix well. Makes about 1 cup.

BURGUNDY KABOBS

2 pounds ground beef
1 cup quick or old-fashioned oats, uncooked
2 teaspoons salt
¼ teaspoon seasoned pepper
2 tablespoons prepared mustard
2 tablespoons prepared horseradish
2 eggs
48 small stuffed olives
Burgundy Marinade*
32 canned broiled mushroom crowns

Combine first 7 ingredients. Shape around olives to make 48 small balls. Cover with Burgundy Marinade. Chill for several hours. Drain, saving marinade. Thread onto skewers, using 3 meatballs and 2 mushroom crowns on each. Grill 4 inches above heat to desired degree of doneness, turning once carefully, and brushing with marinade several times. Makes 8 servings.

*BURGUNDY MARINADE

1 tablespoon cornstarch
2 tablespoons cold water
3 tablespoons wine vinegar
1½ tablespoons light brown sugar
1 cup Burgundy
1 small onion, sliced thin
2 peppercorns, crushed
1 small bay leaf, crushed
¼ teaspoon oregano
¼ teaspoon salt

Blend cornstarch and cold water. Add vinegar, sugar, and wine. Cook and stir over low heat until thickened and clear. Remove from heat. Add remaining ingredients; cool. Pour over meatballs. Chill.

MAUI KABOBS

1½ pounds veal
Sauce*

Cut veal in 1½-inch cubes. Marinate for 2 hours in Sauce. Drain meat, saving marinade. Thread meat onto skewers. Broil about 4 inches above coals for 20 to 25 minutes, turning often and basting with marinade. Makes 4 servings.

*SAUCE

3 tablespoons minced dried onion
1 teaspoon chili powder
1 teaspoon turmeric
½ teaspoon ground ginger
1 teaspoon salt
¼ cup lemon juice
1 tablespoon honey

Combine all ingredients; mix well.

VEAL-AND-BACON KABOBS

3 pounds boneless veal
Salt
Pepper
2 garlic cloves, minced
½ cup vegetable oil
½ pound bacon
Melted butter or margarine

Cut veal in 1-inch cubes. Sprinkle with salt and pepper. Add garlic and vegetable oil; stir to coat veal. Refrigerate for 2 hours. Cut bacon in 1-inch squares. Drain veal; thread veal and bacon alter-nately on skewers. Grill 4 inches above heat, turning often, for about 20 minutes or until veal is done and bacon is crisp. Before serving, brush with melted butter or margarine. Makes 6 serv-ings.

LAMB AND CHICKEN LIVERS EN BROCHETTE

2 pounds lean lamb
Marinade*
12 bacon slices, halved
8 chicken livers, cut in 24 pieces
16 medium mushroom caps

Cut lamb in 24 cubes. Pour Marinade over lamb; refrigerate for about 3 hours. Wrap a half strip of bacon around each piece of chicken liver. Drain lamb, saving marinade. Alternate 3 lamb cubes, 3 wrapped chicken livers, and 2 mushrooms on each of 8 skewers. Brush with marinade. Grill 4 inches above heat for about 15 minutes, turning often and basting with marinade. Makes 4 serv-ings.

*MARINADE

½ cup vegetable oil
1 cup dry red wine
1 medium onion, minced
1 garlic clove, minced
1 teaspoon tarragon
1 teaspoon salt
¼ teaspoon hot-pepper sauce

Combine all ingredients; mix well.

LAMB-AND-SALAMI KABOBS

6 lamb steaks, 1 inch thick
1 pound salami, unsliced
2 large onions, sliced
2 garlic cloves, crushed
⅓ cup vegetable oil
3 tablespoons soy sauce
3 tablespoons vinegar
2 teaspoons sugar
Dash hot-pepper sauce

Cut lamb and salami in 1-inch cubes. Place in shallow pan. Arrange onions on top. Combine remaining ingredients; pour into pan. Cover. Re-frigerate for several hours or overnight. Remove onions. Drain meat, saving sauce; string onto skewers. Broil over hot coals for about 15 minutes, turning often. Cook onions in remaining sauce until golden brown. Serve with kabobs. Makes 6 to 8 servings.

LAMB-AND-EGGPLANT KABOBS

12 cubes (1 inch) lean lamb, about 1 pound
4 small onions, halved
4 medium mushrooms
1 green pepper, cut in 1-inch squares
1 small eggplant, cut in chunks
French dressing

Marinate meat and vegetables in French dressing for at least 1 hour. Drain, saving marinade. Thread 4 skewers, beginning and ending with meat. Broil or grill about 4 inches from source of heat for 20 to 25 minutes, turning often and basting with marinade. Makes 4 servings.

LAMB-AND-VEGETABLE KABOBS

2 pounds boneless lamb, cut in 1-inch cubes
2 medium zucchini, sliced and parboiled
1½ cups cauliflower flowerettes, parboiled
12 canned baby carrots
12 small canned white potatoes
Paprika
⅓ cup catchup
1 tablespoon prepared mustard
3 tablespoons vegetable oil

Thread lamb and vegetables onto 6 long skewers. Sprinkle cauliflower and potatoes with paprika. Combine last 3 ingredients; mix well; brush on skewered foods. Grill 4 inches above coals for about 15 minutes, turning often and basting with catchup mixture. Makes 6 servings.

LAMB KABOBS WITH FRUITS

2 pounds boneless lamb
16 pineapple chunks
2 large apples, cut in eighths
16 preserved kumquats
16 maraschino cherries
¼ cup butter or margarine, melted
½ teaspoon salt
½ teaspoon paprika

Cut lamb in 1-inch cubes. On each of 8 skewers alternate lamb cubes, 2 pineapple chunks, 2 apple slices, 2 kumquats, and 2 maraschino cherries. Combine melted butter, salt, and paprika; blend well; brush skewered foods with this mixture. Grill 4 inches above coals for about 15 minutes, turning often and brushing with butter mixture. Makes 4 servings (2 skewers per person).

CURRIED LAMB KABOBS

1 tablespoon curry powder
1 cup applesauce
1 teaspoon salt
⅛ teaspoon hot-pepper sauce
2 tablespoons lime juice
1 teaspoon sugar
2 pounds boneless lamb, cut in 1-inch cubes

Stir curry powder into applesauce, mixing thoroughly. Add all remaining ingredients except lamb. Pour applesauce mixture over lamb. Chill for several hours. Thread lamb onto skewers; brush with marinade. Grill 4 inches above coals for about 20 minutes, turning often and brushing with marinade. Makes 6 servings.

EAST INDIAN KABOBS

2 pounds boneless lamb
¾ cup yogurt
1 teaspoon powdered ginger
¼ teaspoon hot-pepper sauce
2 teaspoons powdered coriander
¼ teaspoon powdered cloves
½ teaspoon powdered cinnamon
¼ teaspoon turmeric
1 medium onion, minced
2 teaspoons lime juice
Salt and sugar to taste

Cut lamb in 1½-inch cubes. Combine remaining ingredients; pour over lamb. Marinate for 3 hours; drain lamb, saving marinade. Thread lamb onto skewers. Brush with marinade. Grill 4 inches above coals for about 20 minutes, turning often and brushing with marinade. Makes 4 to 6 servings.

LAMB SATÉ

2 garlic cloves, minced
2 medium onions, finely chopped
¼ cup creamy peanut butter
2 tablespoons brown sugar
¼ teaspoon hot-pepper sauce
¼ cup soy sauce
3 tablespoons lime juice
2 pounds boneless lamb, cut in 1-inch cubes

Combine all ingredients except lamb; mix well; pour over lamb. Chill for several hours. Drain lamb; save marinade. Thread lamb onto skewers; brush with marinade. Grill 3 inches above coals for 20 minutes, turning once and brushing often with marinade. Makes 4 or 5 servings.

SKEWERED LAMB TERIYAKI

½ cup pineapple juice
¼ cup soy sauce
2 teaspoons brown sugar
½ teaspoon Worcestershire sauce
½ small garlic clove, minced
¼ teaspoon ground ginger
⅛ teaspoon thyme
1 pound boned lamb shoulder
6 bacon strips
8 mushroom caps
8 pineapple chunks
Hot cooked rice

Combine first 7 ingredients; mix well. Cut lamb in 12 cubes. Cut bacon strips in halves; fold each piece in two. On each of 4 long skewers, string 3 pieces of lamb, 3 bacon folds, 2 mushroom caps, and 2 pineapple chunks, beginning and ending with lamb. Place in shallow pan; pour pineapple juice mixture over. Chill for several hours. Drain, saving sauce. Broil for 10 minutes with surface of meat 3 inches below heat; brush twice with sauce. Turn; broil for 10 minutes longer, brushing twice with sauce. Serve on rice; heat any remaining sauce; pour over all. Makes 4 servings.

LAMB, CORN, AND TOMATO KABOBS

1 cup vegetable oil
½ cup lemon juice
2 garlic cloves, crushed
1 tablespoon salt
2 teaspoons dried dillweed
¼ teaspoon coarsely ground black pepper
3 pounds boneless lamb
8 cherry tomatoes
4 ears of corn, cut crosswise in 2-inch pieces

Combine first 6 ingredients; mix well. Cut lamb in 1-to-1½-inch cubes; pour marinade over cubes. Chill for 4 hours, turning meat occasionally. Drain meat, saving marinade. Thread meat, tomatoes, and corn onto skewers, beginning and ending with meat. Brush with marinade. Grill 4 inches above coals for 15 to 20 minutes, turning

once and basting with marinade. To serve, slip food off skewers onto plates. Makes 8 servings.

FRUITED LAMB KABOBS

2 pounds lean boneless lamb
Celery
1 cup pineapple juice
½ cup white wine
½ teaspoon rosemary
1 can (about 1 pound) pineapple chunks
4 firm, green-tipped bananas, cut in 1½-inch slices

Cut lamb in 1½-inch pieces. Slice an equal number of celery pieces in 1½-inch lengths. Combine pineapple juice, wine, and rosemary; pour over lamb and celery. Let stand for at least 1 hour, turning meat occasionally. Drain, saving marinade. Alternate meat, celery, pineapple chunks, and banana slices on long skewers. Grill 4 inches above coals for about 15 minutes, turning frequently and basting with marinade. Makes 4 to 6 servings.

SAVORY SKEWERED LAMB

3 pounds lean boneless lamb
1 cup dry sherry
⅓ cup vegetable oil
1 teaspoon salt
Dash hot-pepper sauce
½ teaspoon thyme
½ teaspoon caraway seed
1 tablespoon snipped parsley
2 garlic cloves, sliced
2 bay leaves, crumbled
1 can (1 pound) small white potatoes
3 firm medium tomatoes, quartered

Cut lamb in 1½-inch chunks. Combine next 9 ingredients; pour over lamb. Let stand for several hours. Drain, saving marinade. Thread lamb, potatoes, and tomatoes onto long skewers. Grill 4 inches above coals for about 15 minutes, turning often and brushing with marinade. Makes 6 servings.

SHASHLIK CAUCASIAN

2 pounds boneless lamb
1 large onion, minced
1 tablespoon vegetable oil
1 teaspoon salt
¼ teaspoon coarsely ground black pepper

1 tablespoon lemon juice
¼ cup dry red wine
2 medium onions, cut in chunks
Brandy for flaming (optional)

Cut lamb in 1½-inch cubes. Combine next 6 ingredients; pour over lamb. Marinate for several hours, turning lamb several times. Thread lamb and onion chunks alternately onto skewers. Grill 4 inches above coals for 10 to 15 minutes, turning often and brushing with marinade. Flame with warmed brandy, if desired. Makes 4 servings.

TURKISH ŞIŞ KEBABI

1 large onion, chopped
2 tablespoons olive oil
¼ cup lemon juice
1 tablespoon salt
½ teaspoon freshly ground black pepper
2 pounds lean boneless lamb
2 tablespoons whipping cream

Place the onion in a deep bowl; sprinkle with oil, lemon juice, salt, and pepper. Trim any excess fat from lamb; cut in 1½-inch cubes. Add to onion mixture; turn to coat well. Chill for 4 hours, turning occasionally. Thread lamb onto 4 long skewers; brush evenly with cream. Grill or broil 4 inches from heat for about 15 minutes. Slip meat off skewers onto serving plates. Makes 4 servings.

SPICY LAMB KABOBS

2 pounds boneless lamb
1 large onion, minced
1 garlic clove, crushed
½ teaspoon coarsely ground black pepper
1 tablespoon cumin
1 teaspoon ground cardamom
1 teaspoon chili powder
½ teaspoon ground ginger
2 teaspoons salt
1 cup dry white wine
⅓ cup vegetable oil

Cut lamb in 1½-inch cubes. Combine remaining ingredients; pour over lamb. Refrigerate for several hours, turning lamb occasionally. Drain lamb, saving marinade. Thread lamb onto skewers; brush with marinade. Grill 4 inches above coals for about 20 minutes, turning often and brushing with marinade. Makes 4 to 6 servings.

CURRIED PORK KABOBS

2 pounds lean boneless pork
2 garlic cloves, minced
⅓ cup butter or margarine, melted
1 can (8 ounces) tomato sauce
1 teaspoon turmeric
1 teaspoon salt
½ teaspoon coarsely ground black pepper
2 teaspoons curry powder
1 cup dry sherry
1 can (1 pound) small white onions, drained

Cut pork in 1-inch cubes. Cook garlic in butter in a large skillet. Add tomato sauce, turmeric, salt, pepper, and curry powder; mix well. Stir and simmer for 5 minutes. Add sherry; heat. Pour over pork. Let stand for 2 hours. Drain, saving marinade. Thread pork and onions onto skewers. Brush with marinade. Grill 4 inches above coals until pork is well done, turning several times and basting with marinade. Makes 4 servings.

JAVANESE KABOBS

2 pounds pork tenderloin
1 cup finely chopped onion
2 garlic cloves, minced
2 tablespoons coriander
3 tablespoons brown sugar
¼ cup lime juice
¼ cup soy sauce
¼ cup vegetable oil
1 tablespoon chili powder
4 preserved kumquats

Cut pork in 1-inch cubes. Combine all remaining ingredients except kumquats. Pour over pork; marinate for 2 hours; thread pork cubes onto skewers, ¼ inch apart. Grill 3 inches above coals for about 25 minutes, turning three or four times and brushing with marinade. During last 5 minutes, thread a preserved kumquat onto end of each skewer. Makes 4 servings.

CRANBERRY KABOBS

1 small smoked boneless pork butt
2 cups fresh cranberries
1 cup water
¾ cup sugar
1 teaspoon minced dried onion
1 tablespoon grated lemon peel
1 teaspoon dry mustard
18 mushroom caps
18 pineapple chunks

Simmer smoked pork butt in water to cover for about 1 hour; cool; cut in 1½-inch cubes. Meanwhile, combine cranberries, water, sugar, onion, lemon peel, and dry mustard; cook over low heat, stirring often, until thick. String pork cubes, mushrooms, and pineapple chunks onto skewers. Brush with cranberry mixture; grill with surface of food 4 inches above coals until mushrooms are done, turning often and basting with cranberry mixture. Serve remaining cranberry mixture with finished kabobs. Makes 4 to 6 servings.

GLAZED SMOKED PORK CHOPS WITH FRUIT KABOBS, POLYNESIAN STYLE

½ cup honey
½ cup lime or lemon juice
2 tablespoons sugar
1½ tablespoons soy sauce
½ teaspoon cloves
½ teaspoon grated lime or lemon peel
   (optional)
½ teaspoon salt
6 thick (1 to 1¼ inches) smoked pork chops*
2 large oranges, peeled and sliced
½ medium cantaloupe, peeled and seeds
   removed, cut in chunks
½ medium honeydew melon, peeled and
   seeds removed, cut in chunks

Combine first 7 ingredients in saucepan; mix and heat. Thread chops onto double-pronged kabob skewers. If double-pronged skewers are unavailable, broil chops in greased hinged rack or directly on greased grill. Grill about 5 inches above coals until well browned on first side (about 15 minutes). Turn; grill until well done (12 to 15 minutes). Brush chops with sauce frequently during grilling. Thread fruit onto double-pronged or single-pronged kabob skewers. Brush with glaze; warm, do not brown, on grill for 3 to 5 minutes. Makes 6 servings. For hearty eaters allow 2 chops per person.

*If smoked pork chops are not available, fresh pork loin or rib chops may be substituted.

PORK-AND-APPLE KABOBS

2 pounds boneless pork shoulder
Claret Marinade*
Apples, sliced thick

Cut boneless pork shoulder in 1½-inch cubes. Cover with Claret Marinade; refrigerate 12 hours or longer, turning cubes several times. Drain pork, saving marinade. Alternate cubes of pork and thick slices of apple on skewers. Grill 4 inches above coals, turning often and basting with marinade, until pork is thoroughly done (about 30 minutes). Makes 4 to 6 servings.

*CLARET MARINADE

½ cup vegetable oil
½ cup claret
2 tablespoons minced candied ginger
2 garlic cloves, grated
1 tablespoon curry powder
¼ teaspoon coarsely ground black pepper
¼ cup soy sauce
2 tablespoons catchup

Combine all ingredients; mix well.

PORK-ROAST KABOBS

3 cups cubed cooked pork roast
⅓ cup wine vinegar
⅓ cup olive oil
1 garlic clove, minced
⅛ teaspoon oregano leaves
1 medium green pepper
1 medium red apple
12 small white onions

Combine first 5 ingredients in large shallow baking dish. Refrigerate, covered, turning occasionally. Cut pepper and apple in chunks. Drain pork, reserving marinade. On 6 skewers, arrange pork, onion, pepper, and apple chunks. Grill 4 inches above coals 10 minutes, turning once and brushing occasionally with marinade. Makes 6 servings.

TERIYAKI HAM CUBES

2 pounds fully cooked ham steak, cut in ¾-
   inch cubes
Salt
Pepper
1 cup grape jelly
½ cup lemon juice
1 tablespoon grated onion
1 garlic clove, minced
2 teaspoons dry mustard
3 drops hot-pepper sauce

Dampen 16 small bamboo skewers. Spear 3 meat cubes on each of the small bamboo skewers; sprinkle with salt and pepper. Place kabobs in a shallow pan in a single layer. Combine remaining ingredients; heat until jelly melts and sauce is smooth. Pour hot sauce over skewered meat. Let stand at room temperature for 1 hour. Turn meat several times to coat evenly. Drain meat; grill 3 to 5 minutes on each side. Serve immediately. Makes 16 appetizers.

SWEET-AND-PUNGENT HAM KABOBS

Cooked ham
Pineapple chunks (reserve syrup for sauce)
Maraschino cherries
Eggplant, parboiled, peeled, cubed
Sweet-and-Pungent Sauce*

Cut ham in 1½-inch cubes. Alternate on skewers with pineapple chunks, maraschino cherries, and cubes of eggplant. Brush with Sweet-and-Pungent Sauce. Grill 3 inches above coals for 8 to 10 minutes or until eggplant is tender, turning often and basting with sauce.

*SWEET-AND-PUNGENT SAUCE

3 tablespoons vegetable oil
1 teaspoon salt
½ cup wine vinegar
1½ teaspoons soy sauce
Syrup from 1-pound can pineapple chunks
    with enough water to make ⅔ cup
½ cup firmly packed brown sugar

Combine all ingredients in saucepan. Simmer for 15 minutes, stirring often.

CALF'S LIVER KABOBS

1½ pounds calf's liver, sliced 1 inch thick
1 garlic clove, crushed
½ cup yogurt
¼ teaspoon hot-pepper sauce
1 teaspoon powdered ginger
½ teaspoon powdered cinnamon
¼ teaspoon powdered cloves
1 tablespooon ground coriander
Squares of bacon, partially cooked (optional)
Melted bacon drippings or butter

Cut liver in 1-inch cubes. Combine all remaining ingredients except bacon and drippings; pour over liver. Marinate for several hours. Drain

liver; thread onto skewers. If desired, partially cooked squares of bacon may be inserted between cubes of liver. Brush with melted drippings. Grill 4 inches above coals to desired degree of doneness, turning often and brushing with drippings. Makes 4 to 6 servings.

BREADED CHICKEN LIVER KABOBS

12 chicken livers
Salt and pepper
12 slices bacon
⅔ cup melted butter or margarine
1 cup fine bread crumbs
1 cup chicken broth
2 tablespoons lemon juice
1 teaspoon nutmeg
¼ cup medium sherry
¼ cup minced parsley

Cut chicken livers in fourths. Sprinkle with salt and pepper. Cut bacon in 1-inch pieces. Alternate chicken livers and bacon on skewers. Brush with some of the melted butter; roll in crumbs. Grill 4 inches above coals for 10 to 12 minutes or until bacon is crisp, turning often. Meanwhile, bring broth to a boil; add remaining melted butter; beat with rotary egg beater until well blended. Add remaining ingredients except parsley. Slide livers and bacon from skewers onto saffron rice on 4 plates. Pour broth mixture over all. Sprinkle with parsley. Makes 4 servings.

LAMB KIDNEYS AND BACON EN BROCHETTE

Use 2 lamb kidneys, 1 slice bacon, and 3 mushroom caps per skewer. Wash kidneys in cold water. Remove outer membrane; split; remove white veins and fat. Simmer until tender in water to which a little lemon or lime juice has been added. Cool slightly; cut in quarters. Thread bacon slice onto skewer, then a piece of kidney, then a mushroom, then the bacon strip. Repeat, with bacon running like a ribbon on the skewer. Repeat until all ingredients are used. Grill 3 inches above coals for about 7 minutes. Turn; broil for 5 to 7 minutes longer. Sprinkle with salt and pepper. Makes 4 servings.

MIXED GRILL EN BROCHETTE

6 lamb kidneys
6 bacon slices

18 cherry tomatoes
12 medium whole mushrooms
3 brown 'n' serve sausages, halved crosswise
6 small lamb chops, boned and rolled
Salt
Pepper
Melted butter or margarine

Split lamb kidneys lengthwise but do not separate into halves. Remove cores; wrap each kidney in a slice of bacon. Thread 6 skewers with 3 cherry tomatoes, 2 mushrooms, ½ sausage, 1 lamb chop, and 1 lamb kidney, arranged alternately as desired. Season with salt and pepper; brush with melted butter or margarine. Grill 4 inches above coals 10 to 15 minutes, turning often and brushing with melted butter. Makes 6 servings.

ACCOMPANIMENT: Mint sauce or mint jelly.

MIXED GRILL KABOBS

4 lamb kidneys
1 calf's heart
½ pound calf's liver
6 loin lamb chops
½ pound bacon
Bottled Italian dressing

Remove membranes and fat from kidneys and heart. Cut in 1-inch pieces. Cut liver in 1-inch pieces. Cut lean section of each chop in 3 pieces (use bones and remaining meat for making soup or stew). Cut bacon in 1-inch pieces. Cover meats, except bacon, with dressing. Chill for at least 3 hours. Drain, saving dressing. Thread meats alternately onto skewers. Brush with dressing. Grill 4 inches above coals until bacon is crisp and meats are done (about 15 minutes), turning often and brushing with dressing. Makes 6 servings.

BRUNCH KABOBS

Brown 'n' serve sausages
Canned apricot or small peach halves
Canned broiled mushroom crowns
Melted butter or margarine

String halved brown 'n' serve sausages, apricot or peach halves, and mushroom crowns on skewers. Brush with melted butter or margarine. Grill 3 inches above coals for about 5 minutes; turn; brush again with melted butter; grill 5 minutes longer.

FRANKFURTER-BACON KABOBS

3 slices bacon
6 frankfurters
Sweet-Sour Sauce*
4 frankfurter rolls

Cut each bacon slice in 6 pieces. Cut frankfurters crosswise in fourths. Thread 4 skewers with alternate pieces of bacon and frankfurters. Grill 4 inches above coals until light brown, turning often. Brush with Sweet-Sour Sauce; turn; grill for 5 minutes; turn; brush again with sauce; grill 5 minutes longer. Slide off skewers into frankfurter rolls. Makes 4 servings.

*SWEET-SOUR SAUCE

1 cup chili sauce
3 tablespoons vinegar
Few drops hot-pepper sauce
1 tablespoon brown sugar
1 small onion, sliced

Combine all ingredients; simmer for 5 minutes.

HOT DOGS ON A STICK

Frankfurters
Slices of bacon
Pineapple chunks
Frankfurter rolls

Cut frankfurters in fourths, crosswise. Thread end of bacon slice onto skewer, then alternate frankfurter pieces and pineapple chunks onto skewer, weaving bacon strip over and under, skewering at the other end. Grill 4 inches above coals for about 15 minutes, turning often. Slide off into hot frankfurter rolls.

WIENER SPECIAL

1 pound frankfurters, cut in 1-inch slices
1 cup celery, cut in 1-inch slices
1 cup onions, cut in 1-inch slices
1 cup green pepper, cut in 1-inch squares
Soy-and-Herb Marinade*
6 large pitted black olives
6 toasted frankfurter rolls

Combine frankfurter pieces and vegetables. Cover with Soy-and-Herb Marinade. Let stand for about 3 hours; drain, saving marinade. Alternate frankfurter pieces and vegetables on 6 skewers, ending with a black olive. Broil 4 inches above glowing coals for 5 minutes on each side, brushing often with marinade. Slide off skewers into toasted frankfurter rolls. Makes 6 servings.

*SOY-AND-HERB MARINADE

½ cup soy sauce
⅓ cup catchup
¼ cup vegetable oil
¼ cup wine vinegar
½ teaspoon thyme
½ teaspoon savory
¼ cup minced chives, fresh or freeze-dried
1 teaspoon prepared mustard

Combine all ingredients; mix well.

CAMPFIRE KABOBS

8 frankfurters
1 pound sharp Cheddar cheese, unsliced
8 slices bacon, halved
16 sweet gherkins
16 cherry tomatoes

Cut each frankfurter in 3 pieces. Cut cheese in 1½-inch pieces and wrap each piece in bacon. String onto 8 skewers, alternating 3 frankfurter pieces, 2 gherkins, 2 tomatoes, and 2 cheese-and-bacon chunks on each, ending with frankfurter. Grill 4 inches above coals until bacon is crisp, turning often. Makes 4 servings.

CHICKEN KABOBS

Chicken meat, cut in 1½-inch chunks
Italian sausage, cut in 1-inch pieces
Medium mushroom caps
Halved chicken livers
Melted butter or margarine

String onto skewers, alternating chicken, sausage, mushrooms, and chicken livers. Brush with melted butter. Grill 4 inches above heat for 7 minutes. Turn; brush again with melted butter; grill for 7 or 8 minutes longer. (Using fresh rosemary as a brush adds delightful flavor.)

HIBACHI CHICKEN KABOBS
(See page 393.)

4 whole broiler-fryer chicken breasts, uncooked
2 medium zucchini, cut in ¾-inch slices

2 green peppers, cut in pieces about 1½ inches square
16 small white onions, parboiled for 5 minutes
2 teaspoons salt
½ cup butter or margarine, melted
1 tablespoon dried leaf tarragon
1 tablespoon lemon juice
2 tomatoes, cut in 8 wedges each

Bone chicken breasts; remove skin. Cut each breast half in 6 to 8 chunks, about 1½ inches square. Alternate chunks on 16 skewers with zucchini, green pepper pieces, and onions. Sprinkle with salt. Combine melted butter, tarragon, and lemon juice. Brush over kabobs; grill 3 inches above coals for 5 to 10 minutes. Turn; add tomato wedge to ends of skewers and grill for 5 minutes longer, brushing occasionally with butter mixture, until chicken and vegetables are tender. Makes 8 servings.

CHICKEN WINGS LEE

12 chicken wings (2½ pounds)
1 foil packet (0.8 ounce) 15-minute meat marinade
⅔ cup liquid (pineapple juice from can plus water)
2 tablespoons soy sauce
1 garlic clove, minced or pressed
1 tablespoon chopped parsley
3 tablespoons vegetable oil
2 medium green peppers, cut in chunks, parboiled 5 minutes
1 can (13¼ ounces) pineapple chunks (36 chunks)

Cut wings in 2 pieces after removing wing tips. (Freeze wing tips for soup later.) Thoroughly blend contents of package of marinade with ⅔ cup liquid in shallow pan. Add soy sauce, garlic, and parsley. Place wings in marinade. Pierce all surfaces of meat deeply and thoroughly with a fork to carry flavor deep down and to lock in natural juices. Marinate 15 minutes, turning several times. Remove from marinade. Pour remaining marinade into cup; add oil; blend; use for basting. On four 10-inch skewers, lace 6 chicken wing parts alternately with pineapple chunks and green pepper; brush with marinade. Grill 4 to 6 inches above coals 15 to 20 minutes or until well done (meat should not be pink inside), turning several times and basting with marinade. Makes 4 servings.

FISH KABOBS

2 pounds firm white fish
Marinade*
2 cucumbers
½ pound bacon
Cherry tomatoes
Toasted frankfurter rolls

Cover fish with Marinade; chill for several hours; drain, saving marinade; cut in 1-inch squares. Peel cucumbers; cut in ½-inch slices. Cut bacon in 1-inch pieces. Alternate fish, cucumber slices, and bacon on skewers. End with a cherry tomato. Grill 4 inches above coals for about 8 minutes, turning often and basting with marinade. Slide off skewers into toasted frankfurter rolls. Makes 4 servings.

*MARINADE

½ cup vinegar
1 crushed bay leaf
½ teaspoon chervil
1 teaspoon salt
Dash hot-pepper sauce
⅓ cup vegetable oil

Combine all ingredients; mix well.

SEA SCALLOP KABOBS

1 medium onion, finely grated
3 tablespoons lime juice
½ teaspoon salt
1 teaspoon sugar
¼ teaspoon coarse black pepper
2 pounds sea scallops
Melted butter or margarine
Garnish: lime wedges

Combine onion, lime juice, salt, sugar, and pepper; pour over scallops; stir until scallops are coated. Cover; chill for 2 hours, turning scallops several times. Thread scallops close together onto skewers. Brush generously with melted butter. Broil or grill 4 inches from heat for about 10 minutes, turning often and basting with melted butter. Slide off skewers to serve. Garnish with lime wedges. Makes 6 servings.

Variation: Thread squares of partially cooked bacon between scallops.

SEABOARD KABOBS

2 pounds sea scallops
Melted butter or margarine
Salt
Paprika
½ cup wheat germ
1 pound shrimp, cooked, peeled, and
    deveined
1 can (about 1 pound) pineapple chunks
4 slices bacon, cut in 1½-inch pieces

Dip scallops into melted butter; sprinkle with salt and paprika; roll in wheat germ. Alternate scallops, shrimp, pineapple chunks, and bacon on 6 skewers. Brush shrimp with melted butter. Wrap each skewer in strip of heavy-duty aluminum foil. Grill 4 inches above coals for 10 to 12 minutes, turning once. Makes 6 servings.

KABOBS NEPTUNE

1 pound shrimp
Lemon Butter Sauce*
1 pound sea scallops
12 large stuffed olives

Cook, shell, and devein shrimp. Marinate for about 1 hour in Lemon Butter Sauce. Drain, saving sauce. Alternate shrimp, scallops, and olives on skewers. Grill 3 inches from heat for about 3 minutes on each side, brushing with sauce and turning often. Do not overcook. Makes 6 kabobs.

*LEMON BUTTER SAUCE

¼ cup butter or margarine
¼ cup lemon juice

Melt butter; stir in lemon juice; keep warm. Makes ½ cup sauce.

SHRIMP-FRUIT KABOBS

1 cup orange juice
½ cup vinegar
½ cup vegetable oil
½ cup soy sauce
1 teaspoon salt
1 pound fresh shrimp, shelled and deveined,
    or 1 package (10 or 12 ounces) frozen
    shrimp, thawed
16 thin slices lime or lemon
16 maraschino cherries
2 bananas, cut in thick slices

Combine orange juice, vinegar, oil, soy sauce, and salt; blend. Add remaining ingredients. Chill for 1 hour. Arrange shrimp, lime or lemon slices, cherries, and banana slices on 8 skewers. Reserve marinade. Grill 4 inches above coals for 3 to 4 minutes on each side. Heat remaining marinade and serve as a sauce with kabobs. Makes 4 servings.

SKEWERED SHRIMP

Raw shrimp, shelled and deveined
French dressing
Cherry tomatoes
Lemon slices

Marinate raw shrimp in French dressing. Thread shrimp onto skewers, alternating with cherry tomatoes, with lemon slice on end. Broil or grill 3 inches from heat for 3 minutes on each side. Brush with additional French dressing after the first turning.

CAPE COD KABOBS

Large raw clams
Bacon slices
Onion chunks
Canned white potatoes, halved
Melted butter or margarine

Skewer clams wrapped in bacon alternately with onion chunks and halved white potatoes. Brush with melted butter or margarine. Grill 4 inches above coals until bacon is crisp, turning occasionally and brushing with melted butter. To serve, slide off skewers onto plates.

FRUIT KABOBS

Select any combination of the following fruits and thread onto small skewers. Brush with melted butter or margarine and broil, or grill 4 inches above coals just long enough to heat through and lightly brown. These fruits lend themselves particularly well to this treatment: banana chunks, small firm apricot halves, orange sections, grapefruit sections, apple chunks, pineapple chunks, chunks of fresh peaches, or halves of pitted plums. All are good accompaniments to pork or ham.

VEGETABLE KABOBS

Select any combination of the following vegetables and thread onto skewers. Brush with melted butter or margarine and broil or grill until vegetables are soft and golden brown, turning and basting often. Use small canned white potatoes, chunks of parboiled sweet potatoes, small canned white onions, mushroom crowns, zucchini slices, cherry tomatoes, parboiled eggplant chunks, 1-inch slices of celery. If desired, 1-inch squares of bacon may be skewered between pieces of vegetables. If you wish, a marinade of bottled Italian dressing (in which vegetables have been soaked 1 hour before cooking) may be used in place of butter or margarine.

Variation: Parboil sweet potatoes; cool; peel; cut in cubes; alternate on skewers with fresh or canned pineapple cubes. Brush with melted butter or margarine; grill.

KABOB COMBINATIONS

Use your favorite marinade, barbecue sauce, or melted butter or margarine for brushing and basting. Grill as usual.
1. One-inch slices of knockwurst, cherry tomatoes, onion chunks.
2. Chunks of knockwurst or frankfurters wrapped in a bacon spiral.
3. Small fish balls, bacon squares, crisp pickle slices.
4. Chunks of rock lobster tails, mushroom crowns, bacon squares, pitted black olives.
5. Oysters, bacon squares, shrimp, cocktail onions.
6. Cheese sandwiches cut in 1½-inch squares, dill pickle slices, pineapple chunks, 1-inch beef cubes.
7. Vienna sausages, apple wedges, cubes of French bread drenched in melted butter or margarine.
8. Chunks of cooked chicken or turkey, 1-inch slices of celery, watermelon pickles, cherry tomatoes.

CHAPTER 22

Foreign Dishes

IN THIS melting pot called the United States of America, there is hardly a nation in the world whose people are not represented among our citizens. They came here for various reasons, bringing with them their customs and their native cookery. Their dishes, adapted for use in American kitchens, have enhanced the variety and flavor of the foods we serve today. Examples of these dishes, which had their origin in far-off lands but which you can easily prepare in your own home, are included in this chapter.

FRENCH ONION SOUP

5 cups thinly sliced yellow onions (1½ pounds)
3 tablespoons butter or margarine
1 tablespoon vegetable oil
1 teaspoon salt
¼ teaspoon sugar
3 tablespoons flour
3 cans (10½ ounces each) condensed beef bouillon, boiling
3 cups boiling water
½ cup dry white wine
Salt and pepper to taste
2 ounces Swiss cheese cut in thin slivers
1 tablespoon grated onion
16 slices hard-toasted French bread*
½ cup grated Parmesan cheese
1 tablespoon melted butter or margarine

Cook onions slowly with butter and oil in heavy, covered 4-quart saucepan for 15 minutes. Stir in salt and sugar; raise heat to moderate; cook, uncovered, 35 to 40 minutes, stirring often, until onions are a deep golden brown. Sprinkle with flour; stir 3 minutes. Remove from heat; add boiling bouillon and boiling water; blend well. Add wine; season to taste. Simmer, partly covered, about 35 minutes longer.** Bring to boil; pour into ovenproof tureen. Stir in slivered cheese and grated onion. Float toast rounds on top of soup; spread grated cheese over toast. Sprinkle with melted butter. Bake 20 minutes at 325°. Set under broiler for a minute or two to brown top lightly. Serve at once. Makes 8 servings.

*Cut bread ½ to 1 inch thick; place in one layer on cookie sheet and bake at 325° about 30 minutes or until thoroughly dried out and golden brown.

**Preparation may end here. Pour over toast rounds and pass grated Parmesan cheese separately.

SPANISH GAZPACHO

1 large sweet onion, chopped
2 medium cucumbers, peeled and chopped
4 large *or* 6 medium-sized tomatoes, peeled and chopped (save juice)
1 medium green pepper
2 cups coarsely crumbled French bread (trimmed of crusts)
1 garlic clove
1 can (4 ounces) pimientos with juice
3 cups chicken broth or bouillon
2 tablespoons olive oil
¼ cup red wine vinegar
1 teaspoon sugar
2 teaspoons salt (or to taste)
Ice cubes

Blend onion, cucumbers, tomatoes, green pepper, bread crumbs, garlic, and pimientos in electric blender until fairly smooth, or put through food chopper, using fine blade. Add chicken broth, oil, vinegar, sugar, and salt. Mix well; chill thoroughly. When ready to serve, place an ice cube in each soup bowl. Ladle in the soup. Makes 6 generous servings.

ACCOMPANIMENTS: Pass small bowls holding 3 or 4 of the following: garlic croutons (packaged or homemade), diced unpeeled cucumber, chopped parsley, sliced scallions, diced green pepper, chopped sweet onion, peeled and chopped tomatoes.

SWEDISH SEAFOOD BISQUE

Fish Stock:

2 tablespoons butter or margarine
2 medium onions, chopped
1 garlic clove
1 carrot, cut up
3 stalks celery with leaves, chopped
1 tomato, chopped
10 sprigs fresh dill (optional)
2 quarts water
1 lemon slice
1 bay leaf
10 peppercorns
1 tablespoon salt
1 pound shrimp, uncooked
3 pounds fish fillets (any firm white fish)

Melt butter or margarine in large saucepan. Add onions and garlic. Simmer gently for a few minutes. Remove garlic. Add vegetables, dill, and water. Bring to boil. Add lemon slice, bay leaf,

peppercorns, and salt. Simmer, covered, 30 minutes. Add shrimp. Cover; cook for 5 to 7 minutes. Remove shrimp; peel and devein; reserve for bisque. Cut fish into chunks; add; cook 10 minutes; remove and reserve for bisque. Simmer stock 30 minutes longer; strain; reserve for bisque.

Bisque:

2 tablespoons butter or margarine
3 tablespoons all-purpose flour
Fish stock (from above)
¼ cup chopped fresh dill or chives, fresh or freeze-dried
2 egg yolks, slightly beaten
½ cup whipping cream
1 can (4 ounces) button mushrooms
Cooked fish (from above)
Cooked shrimp (from above)

Melt butter or margarine; stir in flour; stir in fish stock slowly; stir and cook until smooth and thickened. Combine dill, egg yolks, and cream. Bring fish stock to boiling point; add slowly, beating vigorously. Add mushrooms, fish, and shrimp. Serve immediately. Makes 8 servings.

GREEK EGG AND LEMON SOUP

The Stock:

1½ to 2 pounds lean lamb
2 quarts water
3 tablespoons salt
4 carrots, sliced or diced
1 onion, sliced or diced
2 potatoes, sliced or diced
1 celery root (celeriac) if available, sliced or diced

Cut lamb in pieces; add water, salt, and vegetables. Simmer until meat is tender; strain off stock; chill.

The Soup:

Soup stock (from above)
⅓ to ½ cup raw regular rice
3 egg yolks
1 tablespoon cornstarch
1 cup milk
Juice of 1 large lemon (or more, according to taste)
1 tablespoon butter or margarine, melted
1 teaspoon chopped parsley
Salt and pepper to taste

Remove fat from chilled stock; measure stock; add water to make 8 cups. Heat to boiling. Add rice; cook until tender (about 20 minutes). Mix egg yolks with cornstarch and milk; stir slowly into stock. When mixture has thickened slightly, remove from heat; stir in lemon juice slowly to avoid curdling. Add butter, chopped parsley, salt and pepper. Makes 8 to 12 servings.

HOLLANDAISE BIEFSTUK

¼ cup butter or margarine
4 individual steaks (8 ounces each)
4 fried eggs

Brown butter or margarine in skillet. Cook steaks quickly in browned butter, turning to brown both sides to desired degree of doneness. Top each steak with a fried egg. Serve with home-fried potatoes and tiny green peas, well seasoned with salt and pepper. Makes 4 generous servings.

STEAK SICILIANO

1 cup Burgundy
1 small garlic clove, minced
1 tablespoon Worcestershire sauce
¼ teaspoon oregano
1 small onion, minced
1 teaspoon salt
¼ teaspoon pepper
2 tablespoons prepared horseradish
2 tablespoons minced parsley
2 tablespoons prepared mustard
1 tablespoon sugar
2 tablespoons butter or margarine
2½ pounds round steak, cut about 1½ inches thick
Seasoned natural meat tenderizer

Combine first 12 ingredients; heat until butter melts. Cool to room temperature. Meanwhile, treat meat with tenderizer as directed on label. Pour sauce over steak. Chill several hours, turning steak several times. Remove steak from sauce. Strain sauce, keeping solid material as well as liquid. Broil steak on one side, basting occasionally with liquid. Turn; spread top surface with solids from sauce. Broil to desired degree of doneness (5 minutes on each side for rare, 7 minutes medium rare, 8 minutes medium). Slice to serve. Makes 6 servings.

CHINESE PEPPER STEAK

1½ tablespoons vegetable oil
1 garlic clove, crushed
1 pound lean beef, cut in small, thin slices
Pepper
1 cup bouillon
2 tablespoons cornstarch
1 tablespoon soy sauce
2 tablespoons water
1 cup green peppers, cut in 1-inch squares
¼ teaspoon powdered ginger
2 tablespoons dry sherry (optional)

Heat pan; add oil and garlic. When garlic turns brown, remove. Add beef; fry a few minutes (2 to 4 minutes or until meat slices are no longer red). Season with pepper. Add bouillon; continue to cook for a few seconds. Combine cornstarch, soy sauce, and water; add. Cook, stirring, until sauce thickens. Add peppers, ginger, and sherry. Heat thoroughly. Makes 4 servings.

SUKIYAKI I

½ cup soy sauce
¾ cup canned chicken broth (or chicken bouillon)
3 tablespoons sugar
1 2-inch square suet
3 cups Chinese cabbage, cut in ½-inch diagonal slices
12 scallions, cut in 2-inch lengths
3 large mushrooms, sliced
2 medium Spanish onions, cut in half lengthwise, then in ¼-inch slices
4 celery stalks, sliced
1 can (5 ounces) bamboo shoots, drained
8 small cubes canned bean curd (optional)
3 cups snipped fresh spinach (about ½ pound) pounds)
1 pound beef tenderloin or sirloin, very thinly sliced

Combine soy sauce, chicken broth, and sugar; mix well; set aside. Heat suet in heavy skillet to grease thoroughly, then discard any remaining suet. Add cabbage, scallions, mushrooms, onions, celery, bamboo shoots, and bean curd. Pour soy sauce mixture over vegetables. Cook over high heat for 8 minutes. Add spinach and meat; reduce heat and simmer for 2 minutes. Push all solid ingredients down into sauce and cook for 3 minutes longer. Makes 6 servings.

SUKIYAKI II

2 tablespoons vegetable oil
1 pound tender beef, sliced very thin (or
  boned chicken breasts or meatballs)
2 medium onions, sliced
1 bunch scallions, cut in 1-inch pieces
1 bunch radishes, cut in halves
1 tablespoon sugar (optional)
½ cup sake *and* ½ cup soy sauce, mixed (dry
  sherry may replace sake if necessary
1 head Chinese cabbage, cut crosswise in 1-
  inch pieces
1 green pepper, cored, seeded, and sliced
10 to 15 mushrooms, cut in halves
1 box frozen snow peas, thawed
1 can (5 ounces) water chestnuts, drained
  (optional)
1 can (5 ounces) bamboo shoots, drained
  (optional)
1 bunch watercress, trimmed

Heat skillet; grease lightly with oil. Cook sliced beef quickly; push over to one side of skillet. Add onions, scallions, and radishes. Add sugar. Combine sake and soy sauce; pour half of mixture into skillet. Stir. After a few minutes add cabbage, green pepper, and mushrooms. Drain snow peas; add to skillet. Add water chestnuts and bamboo shoots. Pour rest of sake-soy mixture over vegetables. After a few minutes add watercress. When cress begins to wilt, the dish is ready to serve. Be sure to include some of each of the vegetables in each serving. Makes 6 servings.

SUKIYAKI FAMILY-STYLE

1½ cups beef bouillon
¾ cup soy sauce
3 tablespoons sake
3 tablespoons sugar
1½ pounds flank steak
½ can bamboo shoots, drained
1 bunch green onions, cut in 2-inch lengths
4 stalks celery, cut diagonally in 1-inch pieces
1 medium onion, cut lengthwise
1 cup fresh sliced mushrooms
½ pound fresh spinach (steamed to reduce
  bulk)

Combine first 4 ingredients to make a sauce; set aside. Place beef in freezer for about 30 minutes to make it easier to slice. With a heavy, sharp knife, cut lengthwise in 1½-inch strips and then cut crosswise against the grain into ⅛-inch slices about 2 inches long. Arrange vegetables and meat on a large platter in an attractive pattern. Cover; refrigerate until ready to cook. Simmer sauce about 5 minutes. Arrange vegetables attractively in large frying pan and add sauce. Place meat over the vegetables to act as a "cover" so the vegetables will be steamed. Cook on medium heat 10 to 12 minutes. Turn meat; cook for 2 to 3 minutes longer. Serve with rice. Makes 4 or 5 servings.

BOEUF PROVENÇAL

6 pounds lean beef (chuck or round)
Unseasoned natural meat tenderizer
1 cup flour
2 teaspoons salt
¾ cup butter or margarine, divided
4 cups dry red wine
2 cans (6 or 8 ounces each) whole mushroom
  crowns
¼ teaspoon coarsely ground black pepper
2 bay leaves, crushed
1 teaspoon dried leaf thyme
3 cans (1 pound each) whole white potatoes,
  drained
2 cans (1 pound each) whole white onions,
  drained
2 teaspoons sugar
¼ cup chopped parsley

Cut beef in strips about 3 inches long and ¾ inch wide. Treat with meat tenderizer as directed on label. Combine flour and salt; coat beef cubes. Melt ½ cup butter in large skillet or heatproof casserole. Add beef ⅓ at a time; brown on all sides. Return all meat to skillet. Add wine, liquid from mushrooms, pepper, bay leaves, and thyme. Simmer or bake at 350° for 3 hours or until meat is tender. Add mushrooms and potatoes. Drain onions well on paper towels. Heat remaining ¼ cup butter in skillet; add onions; sprinkle with sugar; cook over high heat until lightly browned; add to beef mixture. Sprinkle with parsley just before serving. Makes 12 servings.

STROGANOFF MARSALA

2 pounds lean boneless sirloin
¼ pound butter or margarine, divided
6 medium onions, thinly sliced
2 pounds fresh mushrooms, thinly sliced
2 tablespoons tomato paste

2 cups dairy sour cream
1½ teaspoons salt
½ teaspoon freshly ground pepper
½ cup Marsala
3 cups cooked wild rice

Slice steak at angle in ¼-inch strips (partially freeze steak for easier slicing). Melt half the butter in extra-large skillet; sauté beef until brown. Remove beef. Melt half the remaining butter in skillet; sauté onions for 10 minutes over medium heat. Remove onions; melt remaining butter; sauté mushrooms for 5 minutes over medium heat. Return beef and onions to skillet. Add tomato paste, sour cream, and seasonings; mix thoroughly. Cover; cook over low heat 30 minutes or until beef is tender. Add wine; simmer 5 minutes longer. Serve over bed of wild rice. Makes 6 generous servings.

ECONOMY NOTES: Use a less expensive cut of beef, such as round steak, with meat tenderizer applied as directed on label. One pound of mushrooms or 1 can (6 ounces) broiled sliced mushrooms will be enough—using 2 pounds is really lavish! Serve with noodles, plain rice, or a packaged mixture of wild rice, plain rice, and seasonings instead of costly wild rice.

ENGLISH STEAK-AND-KIDNEY PIE

⅛ pound beef suet
1 large onion, coarsely chopped
2 pounds top round, cut 1 inch thick
1 pound lamb kidneys, quartered
1 teaspoon salt
Few grains pepper and cayenne
1½ teaspoons Worcestershire sauce
1½ cups beef bouillon
Pastry for 1-crust pie
1 egg yolk
2 tablespoons water

Cook suet until golden brown. Remove suet from pan. Fry onion in drippings until soft and brown; remove from pan. Cut beef in 1-inch cubes; add to pan with kidneys; cook in drippings until well browned. Return onion to pan; add seasonings and beef bouillon. Stir well; cover; simmer 2 hours, adding more broth if necessary. Thicken gravy, if desired. Transfer to baking dish. Cool. Meanwhile, roll out pastry ⅛ inch thick; place over meat mixture. Trim; crimp edges with floured fork. Cut slits in center of pastry. Beat egg yolk slightly; add water; brush over pastry.

Bake at 425° for 10 minutes. Lower heat to 350°; bake 20 minutes longer or until pastry is deep golden brown. Makes 6 servings.

VIENNA GOULASH

1 foil packet (0.8 ounce) 15-minute meat marinade
⅔ cup cold water
1 medium onion, thinly sliced
1 teaspoon paprika
3 pounds stewing beef, cubed
⅔ cup dairy sour cream

Blend meat marinade, water, onion, and paprika in Dutch oven or large casserole. Arrange meat in single layer in marinade. Pierce all surfaces thoroughly and deeply with a fork. Marinate 15 minutes, turning several times. Cover tightly; bake at 325° for 1½ to 2 hours or until meat is tender. Just before serving, blend in sour cream. Makes 6 servings.

MOUSSAKA

4 medium eggplants (about 1 pound each)
Salt
2 pounds lean beef, ground
3 medium onions, chopped
½ cup butter or margarine, divided
½ cup dry red wine
2 teaspoons salt
¼ teaspoon coarse black pepper
1 teaspoon oregano
2 eggs, lightly beaten
1 cup grated sharp Cheddar cheese, divided
½ cup soft bread crumbs, divided
Vegetable oil
2 cans (about 1 pound each) plum tomatoes, drained
6 tablespoons flour
3 cups milk
Salt and pepper
Dash nutmeg
4 eggs, lightly beaten

Peel eggplants; cut crosswise in ¼-inch slices. Sprinkle lightly with salt; arrange in stacks; place heavy plate on top of each stack; let stand to drain. Cook beef and onions in 2 tablespoons butter until beef is browned. Add wine, 2 teaspoons salt, ¼ teaspoon pepper, and oregano. Simmer until liquid is absorbed. Stir in 2 beaten eggs, ¾ cup grated cheese, and ¼ cup bread crumbs. Brown eggplant slices quickly on both sides in vegetable oil. Grease large casserole or baking dish (3½ to 4 quart). Sprinkle bottom of casserole with remaining crumbs. Fill with alternate layers of eggplant, meat mixture, and tomatoes, ending with eggplant, leaving 1-inch head space. Melt remaining butter; blend in flour; add milk slowly, stirring constantly. Season to taste with salt, pepper, and nutmeg. Pour a little hot milk mixture on 4 lightly beaten egg yolks; return to remaining hot milk mixture. Cook about 2 minutes over low heat, stirring constantly, until thickened. Pour sauce into casserole. Sprinkle with remaining cheese. Bake at 350° for 45 to 60 minutes or until top is golden brown and eggplant is tender. Makes 10 to 12 servings.

GRAPE-LEAF ROLLS

1 pound ground beef
¼ cup butter or margarine
1 cup canned tomatoes
½ cup uncooked long-grain rice
1 onion, chopped
2 tablespoons crushed mint leaves *or* chopped
    parsley
Salt
Pepper
Canned grape leaves *or* cooked cabbage
    leaves
1½ cups hot water

Combine all ingredients except grape leaves and water. Rinse leaves several times in cool water to remove brine. Lay out grape leaves with leaf veins up, stem toward you. Put 1 teaspoon meat mixture in center of leaf close to the stem. Turn in sides of leaf; roll from stem toward top of leaf to form an oblong roll. Arrange rolls in saucepan with seam side down to keep leaves from opening while cooking. If desired, place a small plate over the rolls to guarantee their remaining intact. Add water; turn heat high until water starts to boil; reduce heat to medium for 25 minutes. As a main dish, this serves 4 to 5.

KALB GUYLASCH (Veal Paprika)

1½ pounds boneless veal
¼ cup flour
1 teaspoon salt
Dash pepper
¼ cup chopped onion
1 tablespoon paprika
½ cup vegetable oil
2 medium tomatoes
½ cup hot water
½ cup dairy sour cream

Cut veal in 1-inch cubes. Dredge with flour mixed with salt and pepper. Cook onion, veal cubes, and paprika in oil until meat is well browned, stirring frequently. Cut tomatoes into small pieces; add hot water and run through sieve. Add to meat; cover; simmer 1½ hours or until veal is tender. Add sour cream; simmer 15 minutes longer. More paprika may be added to taste. Serve with buttered noodles. Makes 4 servings.

OSSO BUCO ALLA MILANESE

4 veal knuckles (1½ pounds each)
Seasoned flour
¼ pound butter or margarine
1 medium onion, diced
1 carrot, sliced
1 bay leaf
2 stalks celery, sliced
1 garlic clove, minced
2 cups dry white wine
4 tablespoons tomato paste
3 cups beef bouillon (approximately)
Cooked mixed vegetables to serve 4

Have veal knuckles cut in 2- or 3-inch pieces at meat market. Dredge in seasoned flour. Sauté in butter or margarine until well browned on both sides. Add next 7 ingredients with enough beef bouillon to cover knuckles halfway. Bring to boil; lower heat; simmer, covered, for 1 hour or until meat is tender. Remove knuckles. Simmer sauce until reduced by about ¼ its original volume. Strain. Add to freshly cooked mixed vegetables. Bring to boil; pour over knuckles. Serve very hot with saffron rice. Makes 4 servings.

SWEDISH LAMB

8 lamb shanks
Boiling water
Salt
4 peppercorns
1 bay leaf
5 fresh dill sprays *or* ½ teaspoon dried
    dillweed
Dill Sauce*
Garnish: fresh dill

Cover lamb shanks with measured boiling water. Add 1 tablespoon salt for each quart of water used. Add peppercorns, bay leaf, and dill. Cover; simmer 1 hour or until lamb is tender. Drain; reserve 1½ cups of the broth for preparing the Dill Sauce. To serve, arrange lamb shanks on serving dish and pour Dill Sauce evenly over them. Garnish with fresh dill. Makes 4 generous servings.

*DILL SAUCE

3 tablespoons butter or margarine
3 tablespoons flour
1½ cups hot reserved broth (from above)
½ cup milk
2 tablespoons chopped fresh dill *or* 2
    teaspoons dried dillweed
2 tablespoons vinegar
2 teaspoons sugar
Salt to taste
1 egg yolk, slightly beaten

Melt butter; blend in flour. Combine broth and milk; stir into flour mixture gradually; cook and stir over medium heat until smooth and thickened; simmer 10 minutes. Add dill, vinegar, sugar, and salt. Pour a little of the hot sauce on egg yolk; return to remaining sauce; blend. Heat, stirring, for 1 minute (do not boil). Makes about 2 cups sauce.

BOMBAY CURRY

1 pound stewing lamb (weight after boning)
3 tablespoons vegetable oil
1 onion, chopped fine
1 garlic clove, minced
1 tart apple, chopped
2 teaspoons Worcestershire sauce
1 tablespoon curry powder
1 teaspoon paprika
½ teaspoon powdered ginger
2 teaspoons brown sugar
¼ teaspoon chili powder
1 can (6 ounces) tomato paste
1 package (7 ounces) precooked rice
¼ teaspoon powdered turmeric

Cut lamb in 1-inch pieces. Heat oil in skillet. Sauté onion, garlic, and apple in oil until golden brown. Add Worcestershire sauce, curry powder, paprika, ginger, brown sugar, and chili powder; cook till quite brown. Add lamb; brown on all sides. Add tomato paste and enough boiling water to cover. Cover; cook about 30 minutes. Meanwhile, cook rice according to package directions, adding powdered turmeric to the water to tint the rice deep yellow. Makes 4 servings.

EGGPLANT ARMENIAN

1 large eggplant
Salt
1 pound ground lamb shoulder
½ cup finely chopped onion
½ cup finely chopped parsley
½ teaspoon salt
Few grains pepper
10 slices bacon
Tomato Sauce*

Pare eggplant; slice lengthwise in ¼-inch slices. Sprinkle slices liberally with salt. Stack slices and let stand ½ hour or until slices are limp enough to roll. Rinse in cold water. Combine lamb, onion, parsley, salt, and pepper. Place a large spoonful of this mixture on each slice of eggplant. Roll up; wrap bacon slice around each roll; fasten with wooden picks. Place in shallow baking pan; bake at 375° for 1½ hours. Serve with Tomato Sauce. Makes 10 rolls.

*TOMATO SAUCE

¼ cup chopped celery
¼ cup chopped onion
1 can (1 pound) tomatoes with juice
½ teaspoon salt
1 teaspoon sugar
Few grains pepper
2 teaspoons Worcestershire sauce
2 tablespoons butter or margarine
2 tablespoons flour

Combine celery, onion, tomatoes, salt, sugar, few grains pepper, and Worcestershire sauce. Cover; simmer 10 minutes; put through fine sieve or food mill. Heat butter or margarine; blend in flour. Gradually add tomato mixture. Cook, stirring constantly, until thickened.

EASY MOUSSAKA

3 medium-sized eggplants
1 cup butter or margarine, divided
3 large onions, finely chopped
2 pounds ground lamb
3 tablespoons tomato paste

½ cup dry red wine
½ cup chopped parsley
¼ teaspoon cinnamon
Salt to taste
Freshly ground pepper to taste
6 tablespoons flour
1 quart milk
4 eggs, beaten until frothy
Nutmeg to taste
2 cups ricotta cheese
1 cup packaged fine dry bread crumbs
1 cup freshly grated Parmesan cheese

Peel eggplants; slice ½ inch thick. Brown slices quickly in large, heavy skillet in 4 tablespoons butter (more as needed). Set aside. Heat 4 tablespoons butter in same skillet. Cook onions until lightly browned. Add ground meat. Cook 10 minutes. Combine tomato paste with wine, parsley, cinnamon, salt, and pepper; stir into meat; simmer, stirring frequently, until all liquid has been absorbed. Remove from heat. Melt 8 tablespoons butter in large saucepan; blend in flour with wire whisk. Meanwhile, bring milk to a boil; add gradually to butter-flour mixture, stirring constantly. When mixture is thickened and smooth, remove from heat. Cool slightly; stir in beaten eggs, nutmeg, and ricotta cheese. Grease an 11 x 16-inch ovenproof pan (2½ inches deep at least). Sprinkle bottom lightly with bread crumbs. Arrange alternate layers of eggplant and meat in the pan. Sprinkle each layer with Parmesan cheese and bread crumbs (about 2 layers each of meat and eggplant). Pour ricotta cheese sauce over the top. Bake 1 hour or until golden. Remove from oven; cool slightly before cutting into squares to serve. Makes 8 to 10 servings.

DANISH BLACK POT

2 pounds fresh pork tenderloin
3 tablespoons butter or margarine
1½ cups light cream
Salt and pepper
1½ cups green peas, cooked or canned
1 pound fresh mushrooms, sliced

Cut pork in slices about 1 inch thick; brown well in butter or margarine. Add cream, salt, and pepper. Simmer ½ hour. Add peas and mushrooms; bring to boil; simmer 15 minutes or until vegetables are tender. Thicken gravy, if desired. Serve with mashed potatoes. Makes 4 to 6 servings.

NOTE: Instead of pork tenderloin, you may use boned and rolled fresh pork shoulder butt, which is less expensive.

KARELIAN ROAST
(Karjalanpaisti)

1½ pounds lean pork
1 pound boned lamb
1 pound beef round
1 pound boned veal
¼ cup cooking oil
Salt and pepper to taste
18 small onions
8 carrots, diced

Cut meat in bite-size chunks; brown in hot oil. Place in heavy kettle in alternate layers with salt and pepper, whole small onions, and diced carrots. Pour boiling water over contents of kettle until well covered. Bake at 350° for about 3 hours, adding more water if necessary. When done, meat should be tender enough to cut with a fork. Serve with mashed potatoes and green peas. Makes 8 to 10 servings.

SCANDINAVIAN MEAT LOAF

2 eggs, slightly beaten
1 pound ground beef
½ pound ground veal
½ pound ground pork
1 cup packaged fine dry bread crumbs
1 teaspoon salt
¼ teaspoon pepper
1 tablespoon minced dried onion
1 tablespoon chopped parsley
¼ teaspoon nutmeg
½ teaspoon dried dillweed
1 tablespoon lemon juice
1 cup evaporated milk
½ cup dairy sour cream

Combine all ingredients except sour cream. Mix well. Press meat loaf mixture into well-greased 8- or 9-inch ring mold. Bake at 375° for 1 hour and 15 minutes. Remove from oven. Loosen edges with knife; turn out onto serving dish. Fill center with Harvard beets; surround with cooked Italian green beans. Spread sour cream over top of loaf. Makes 6 hearty servings.

MEXICAN CHICKEN I

1 roasting chicken, about 4 pounds, disjointed
3 tablespoons vegetable oil
1 tablespoon butter or margarine
2 red onions, chopped
1 cup diced green tomatoes*
1 cup blanched slivered almonds
½ cup chopped parsley
2 garlic cloves, minced
1½ cups chicken broth
½ cup dry vermouth
2 oranges, peeled and sectioned
1 teaspoon cumin

Brown chicken on all sides in mixture of oil and butter (about 15 minutes). Remove chicken. Cook onions in same pan until soft. Purée tomatoes, almonds, and parsley in blender or mince very fine. Combine all ingredients. Simmer, covered, for 45 minutes or until chicken is done. Makes 6 servings.

*If green tomatoes are not available, use underripe red tomatoes.

MEXICAN CHICKEN II

1 roasting chicken, about 5 pounds
Salt, cayenne
¼ cup vegetable oil
¼ cup blanched almonds
⅓ cup seedless raisins
½ cup pineapple chunks
⅛ teaspoon cinnamon
⅛ teaspoon cloves
1½ cups orange juice
2 tablespoons flour
¼ cup water
Garnish: avocado wedges; orange sections;
    watercress

Season chicken with salt and cayenne; brown on all sides in oil. Add almonds, raisins, pineapple, cinnamon, cloves, and orange juice. Cover; simmer 1 hour or until chicken is tender. Remove chicken to platter. Make a smooth paste of flour and water; add to gravy. Cook, stirring constantly, until thickened. Pour over chicken. Garnish with avocado wedges, orange sections, and watercress. Makes 6 servings.

PAELLA VALENCIANA

2 broiler-fryer chickens, cut up
¼ cup vegetable oil
½ teaspoon salt
¼ teaspoon coarsely ground black pepper
2 or 3 garlic cloves
1 Italian sausage, hot or sweet
2 medium onions, chopped
2 cups raw long-grained rice
1 can (1 pound) tomatoes with juice
1 can (10½ ounces) whole clams
2 cups water or giblet broth (page 107)
1 envelope saffron
1 pound shrimp, shelled and deveined
1 large green pepper, diced
1 can (4 ounces) pimientos, diced
1 cup fresh or frozen peas
Garnish: 2 tablespoons chopped parsley

Brown chicken pieces in oil in large skillet until skin is crisp and brown. Sprinkle with salt and pepper. With garlic press squeeze garlic over chicken. Place chicken in 4-quart baking dish or Dutch oven. Slice sausage ½ inch thick; brown slices in oil left in skillet. Add slices to baking dish. Cook onions in skillet until soft but not brown, adding more oil if necessary; add to baking dish. Combine rice, tomatoes, juice from clams, water or giblet broth, and saffron; mix well; turn into baking dish. Cover; bake at 375° for 45 minutes. Remove cover. Halve clams; add to baking dish with shrimp, green pepper, pimientos, and peas. Stir well. Add more giblet broth if necessary. Cover baking dish. Bake ½ hour longer. Serve on a platter, garnished with chopped parsley. Makes 8 servings.

CHICKEN BENGAL

1 frying chicken, about 3½ pounds, cut up
3 tablespoons butter or margarine, divided
1 cup sliced onion
1 medium garlic clove, minced
½ cup chicken broth
¼ cup lemon juice
1 teaspoon salt
¼ teaspoon powdered ginger
⅛ teaspoon ground cumin
⅛ teaspoon pepper
4 cups cooked rice
1 cup plain yogurt
½ cup grape jam

Brown chicken in 2 tablespoons butter; remove from skillet. Add remaining 1 tablespoon butter to skillet; sauté onion and garlic until tender. Return chicken to skillet. Add chicken broth, lemon juice, salt, and spices. Cover; simmer about ½ hour or until chicken is tender. Remove chicken to bed of rice on serving plate. Stir yogurt and jam into onion mixture in skillet. Cook 5 minutes, stirring until jam dissolves; pour over chicken. Makes 4 servings.

CHICKEN TIKKA

1 cup plain yogurt
½ teaspoon ground coriander
1 tablespoon chili powder
½ teaspoon coarse black pepper
½ teaspoon salt
1 teaspoon sugar
1 to 4 garlic cloves, minced (to taste)
2 broiler-fryer chickens, cut up

Combine all ingredients except chicken; mix well. Pierce chicken pieces thoroughly with tines of fork. Brush generously with yogurt mixture on all sides. Let stand 30 minutes. Place on foil-lined broiler pan. Broil slowly at moderate temperature (350°) 30 to 40 minutes, depending on size of chicken pieces, with surface of chicken 3 to 4 inches below source of heat (the coating burns if too near heat). Serve with plain or saffron rice, or a mixture of rice and green peas. Makes 8 servings.

BREAST OF CHICKEN NORMANDY

4 to 6 whole broiler-fryer chicken breasts, boned and flattened
Salt, pepper
½ teaspoon powdered thyme
½ cup butter or margarine, divided
½ pound chicken livers, chopped
2 tablespoons finely chopped onion
1 teaspoon salt
1 can (3 or 4 ounces) chopped mushrooms, drained
1 cup (4 ounces) grated Swiss cheese
1 egg, beaten
Packaged fine dry bread crumbs
Supreme Sauce*

Have chicken breasts boned at market unless you know how to do it yourself. To flatten, place between 2 pieces of foil and pound with broad side of cleaver or rolling pin. Sprinkle insides with salt, pepper, and powdered thyme. To prepare stuffing, heat ¼ cup butter in skillet. Add chicken livers and onion; sprinkle with salt. Sauté gently about 5 minutes or until livers are cooked. Remove from heat; stir in mushrooms

and grated cheese. Divide stuffing into 4 to 6 portions and place in center of chicken breasts. Fold sides of breasts over stuffing and fasten with skewers or wooden picks. Roll first in beaten egg, then in bread crumbs. Chill, uncovered, in refrigerator for at least 2 hours to allow coating to dry. Heat remaining ¼ cup butter in large skillet. Add chicken breasts and brown on both sides. Remove to ungreased shallow pan. Bake at 350° for 45 minutes. Pour a little Supreme Sauce over chicken breasts. Serve remaining sauce separately. Makes 4 to 6 servings.

*SUPREME SAUCE

¼ cup butter or margarine
¼ cup flour
2 cups chicken stock or canned chicken broth
1 tablespoon lemon juice
½ cup light cream

Melt butter in saucepan; blend in flour. Add chicken stock. Cook, stirring constantly, until mixture thickens and comes to a boil. Boil gently for 3 to 5 minutes longer, stirring constantly. Add lemon juice. Stir in cream. Heat, but do not allow to boil. Makes approximately 3 cups.

CHICKEN KIEV

Breast meat from 2 small chickens
Butter
1 garlic clove, chopped
2 teaspoons rosemary *or* finely chopped mixed fresh herbs
Salt and pepper
¼ cup flour
1 egg, beaten
½ cup packaged fine dry bread crumbs
Fat for frying
Garnish: watercress

Remove bones from chicken breasts; carefully remove skin; cut breasts in halves. Place between 2 sheets of waxed paper on chopping board. Beat with wooden mallet until very thin. Remove paper. Cut ¼-pound stick of butter in half lengthwise, then cut one half into 4 "fingers." Place butter finger in center of each piece of chicken; sprinkle each with garlic, rosemary, salt, and pepper. Roll up; tuck in ends. Dust with flour; dip in beaten egg, then in crumbs. Fry in shallow fat (1½ to 2 inches deep) heated to 350° until golden brown (5 to 8 minutes). Drain on paper toweling. Garnish with watercress. Makes 4 servings.

MIDDLE EAST CHICKEN PAPRIKA

2 chicken breasts, halved
4 second joints or thighs
4 drumsticks
1 teaspoon salt
½ teaspoon turmeric
Paprika
¼ cup butter or margarine
½ cup sliced scallions
1 can (about 14 ounces) chicken broth
1 tablespoon cornstarch
2 tablespoons water
1 cup plain yogurt

Remove skin from chicken parts; rinse chicken; pat dry with paper towels. Sprinkle with salt and turmeric; sprinkle generously with paprika. Heat butter in large pan until it foams. Add half of chicken at a time and brown on both sides. Remove pieces from pan as they brown. Pour all butter from pan, leaving only a film. Add scallions; sauté 1 or 2 minutes. Return chicken pieces to pan; add chicken broth. Bring to a boil; cover; reduce heat; simmer 30 minutes. Remove lid; continue to simmer until broth is reduced by half. Mix cornstarch with water. Remove chicken from pan; keep warm. Stir cornstarch into broth. Cook, stirring, until thick and clear. Stir in yogurt. Serve with chicken. Makes 4 to 6 servings.

CHICKEN LASAGNE

1 cup chopped onion
2 garlic cloves, crushed
⅓ cup vegetable or olive oil
½ pound chicken livers, cooked and chopped
¼ pound prosciutto ham,* chopped
2 cups diced cooked chicken
4 cans (8 ounces each) tomato sauce
2 cans (6 ounces each) tomato paste
1 cup chicken broth
1 cup dry white wine
1 teaspoon salt
½ teaspoon each pepper, basil leaves, oregano leaves
1 pound curly lasagne
1 pound ricotta (Italian cottage cheese)
2 cups grated Parmesan cheese
½ pound mozzarella cheese, sliced

Cook onion and garlic in oil until soft but not brown. Stir in chicken livers, prosciutto, chicken, tomato sauce and paste, broth, wine, salt, pepper, basil, and oregano. Cover; simmer gently 30 minutes. Meanwhile, cook lasagne as directed on package. Drain in colander. Rinse with cold water; drain again. Cover bottom of oblong 4½-to-5-quart baking dish with about ¼ of the sauce. Top with a layer of cooked lasagne. Spread with ⅓ of the ricotta and sprinkle with ⅓ of the Parmesan cheese; top with another ¼ of the sauce. Repeat these layers twice. Arrange sliced mozzarella cheese on top. Bake at 350° for 30 minutes or until sauce is bubbly and cheese has melted. Makes 8 to 10 servings.

*Or cooked ham of any kind.

EGGS FOO YUNG

4 to 5 eggs, beaten
1 medium onion, minced
1 green pepper, minced
1 tablespoon soy sauce
½ cup minced celery
¼ teaspoon salt
1 can (16 ounces) bean sprouts, drained
Vegetable oil
3 tablespoons flour
2 cups water
Soy sauce to taste

Combine eggs, onion, green pepper, 1 tablespoon soy sauce, celery, and salt. Chop bean sprouts slightly; add; mix well. Cover bottom of frying pan with oil to a depth of about 1 inch. Heat. Drop egg mixture from large spoon into hot oil. Cook until golden brown, turning once. Drain on absorbent paper. Makes 6 to 8 patties. Drain off all but 3 tablespoons oil. Blend flour with oil in pan. Add water; cook over low heat, stirring, until thickened. Add soy sauce to taste. Serve sauce with egg patties. Makes 3 to 4 servings.

EGG ROLLS

Egg Roll "Skins":

3 eggs
½ cup milk
½ cup pancake mix
Butter

Beat together eggs, milk, and pancake mix until smooth. Pour small amount of batter into hot, lightly buttered small frypan; immediately tilt to coat bottom evenly with thin layer. Heat only until delicately browned on underside and dry on top. (Do not turn.) Remove from pan. Cool. Repeat until batter is used (18 "skins"). Chill.

Filling:

¼ pound finely ground raw pork
2 tablespoons vegetable oil, divided
1 tablespoon soy sauce
¼ teaspoon sugar
1 can (5 ounces) shrimp, drained and finely
    chopped
¼ cup finely chopped mushrooms
2 cups finely chopped celery
1 teaspoon salt
1 can (1 pound) bean sprouts, drained
1½ teaspoons cornstarch
3 tablespoons chicken broth

Fry pork in 1 tablespoon vegetable oil in large skillet until all pink color disappears. Add soy sauce, sugar, shrimp, and mushrooms; cook an additional minute. Transfer pork mixture to bowl; set aside. Cook celery in 1 tablespoon vegetable oil 5 minutes. Add salt and bean sprouts; mix thoroughly. Return pork mixture to skillet; stir to combine. Cook over medium heat about 5 minutes. Combine cornstarch and chicken broth; add to skillet. Cook until slightly thickened, stirring occasionally. Cool just to room temperature before using.

To Assemble:

Place 1 tablespoon of filling in the center of the browned side of each "skin." Fold the edges of each "skin" in, one at a time, to form an oblong package; secure with a wooden pick. Fry the egg rolls in deep fat or oil heated to 375° until golden brown and crisp (about 2 minutes). Drain on absorbent paper. Makes 18 egg rolls.

ACCOMPANIMENTS: Hot mustard and bottled sweet-and-sour sauce.

SPINACH-CHEESE GNOCCHI

1 pint ricotta cheese
1 package (10 ounces) frozen chopped spinach
¼ cup grated Parmesan cheese
1 egg, lightly beaten
½ teaspoon nutmeg
¼ to ½ cup packaged unseasoned fine dry
    bread crumbs
Salt and pepper
Flour
Melted butter or margarine
Grated Parmesan cheese

Put ricotta in a strainer over a bowl; let drain in refrigerator for at least 3 hours. Cook frozen spin-

ach as suggested on box. Drain well in a strainer. Let cool; squeeze out as much liquid as possible. Place squeezed spinach in mixing bowl; add drained ricotta; mix well. Add ¼ cup Parmesan cheese, egg, and nutmeg. Mix well; add bread crumbs gradually. Add only enough so that mixture can be shaped into balls. It must not be too firm, just firm enough to handle. Season with salt and pepper to taste. Form into 1-inch balls; roll balls in flour and place on waxed paper. Sprinkle with flour. Bring 2 quarts unsalted water to a rolling boil and drop in the little balls a few at a time so that water does not stop boiling. When they rise to top, boil 3 minutes longer. Remove with slotted spoon to a serving dish. Pour melted butter over all. Serve with additional grated Parmesan cheese. Makes 6 servings.

TORTA DI PARMA

1¼ cups sifted all-purpose flour
½ teaspoon salt
2 eggs, unbeaten
3 tablespoons lukewarm water
1 medium head Savoy cabbage
2 medium onions
½ cup butter or margarine
1 package (3 ounces) cream cheese
1 cup grated Parmesan cheese
4 cups cooked rice
¼ teaspoon salt
Few grains pepper
3 eggs, slightly beaten

Sift flour and salt together. Add 1 unbeaten egg; mix well. Add lukewarm water a little at a time. Now work the dough vigorously, lifting it up and "crashing" it down on a heavily floured board until it becomes elastic and cleans the board. Grease an aluminum tray or jelly roll pan about 15 x 10 x 1 inch. Roll dough paper-thin in a rectangle at least 4 inches longer and wider than the pan. Place in pan. Chop cabbage fine; wash thoroughly. Chop onions fine; add to cabbage; sauté in butter or margarine until soft but not brown. Add cheeses; stir until melted. Add rice, salt, pepper, and beaten eggs; mix well; spread on dough in pan. Bring overhanging pastry up and over filling; pierce with tines of fork; pull away from sides of pan with fork. Break remaining egg on top; "scrub" over entire surface with a pastry brush. Bake at 375° for 45 minutes or until golden brown. Cool; then chill. Serve cut in 12 squares.

LINGUINE CARBONARA

5 eggs
1 cup grated Parmesan cheese (freshly grated
    preferred)
3 tablespoons freshly chopped parsley
Black pepper (freshly ground), to taste
12 slices bacon, chopped
1 small onion, chopped fine
1 pound linguine
Grated Parmesan cheese

Combine eggs, 1 cup cheese, parsley, and pepper in a mixing bowl; mix thoroughly with a wire whisk or rotary beater. Sauté bacon until crisp, and onion until clear. Pour off most of the drippings; set bacon and onion aside. Cook linguine according to package directions. Meanwhile, warm a large bowl or serving pan thoroughly, and warm the serving plates or bowls you plan to use. Lift some of the cooked linguine from the water with 2 forks or serving spoons, letting the water run off for just a moment, then drop it into the egg-and-cheese mixture and stir. The hot pasta will cook the eggs. Repeat this process until all the linguine has been added. Add bacon and onions; mix well. Serve immediately in heated bowls or plates. Serve additional grated cheese at the table. Makes 6 servings.

LASAGNE ROLL

10 lasagne noodles
1 cup (8 ounces) cream-style cottage cheese
1 large package (8 ounces) cream cheese
1 large garlic clove, minced, divided
½ teaspoon salt
¼ teaspoon pepper, divided
2 tablespoons grated Parmesan cheese,
    divided
2 cans (10¾ ounces each) condensed tomato
    soup
½ cup water
½ teaspoon oregano
Grated Parmesan cheese (optional)

Cook lasagne noodles according to package directions; drain. Arrange noodles, overlapping ½ inch, in rectangle. Meanwhile, combine cottage cheese, cream cheese, ½ of the minced garlic, salt, ⅛ teaspoon of the pepper, and 1 tablespoon of the Parmesan cheese. Spread mixture on noodles; roll as for jelly roll. Place roll in ungreased shallow baking dish (10 x 6 x 2 inches). Combine soup, water, oregano, and remaining garlic and

pepper; pour over noodles. Sprinkle with remaining Parmesan cheese. Bake at 350° for 30 minutes. If desired, serve with additional Parmesan cheese. Makes 4 servings.

KASHA

2 cups medium kasha (buckwheat groats)
2 eggs, beaten
¼ cup vegetable oil
2 medium onions, sliced thin
1 can (6 ounces) broiled sliced mushrooms
3¾ cups water
2 teaspoons salt
½ cup golden raisins

Combine kasha and eggs. Heat oil in deep frying pan. Add onions; cook until soft but not brown. Drain mushrooms, saving broth. Add mushrooms to onions; cook until onions are lightly browned. Add kasha mixture, water, salt, and mushroom broth; bring to boil; cover. Cook over low heat 10 minutes. Stir in raisins; cook 5 minutes longer. Makes 8 generous servings.

DUTCH HUTSPUT

8 California long potatoes
4 carrots
4 medium-sized onions
Salt and pepper
½ cup evaporated milk
Grated sharp Cheddar cheese

Peel potatoes, cut in quarters; peel and dice carrots and onions. Cook, covered, in boiling salted water until tender. Drain; shake vegetables over low heat to dry. Mash vegetables, adding salt, pepper, and hot evaporated milk. Beat until light and fluffy. Heap in individual ramekins; sprinkle generously with grated sharp Cheddar cheese. Broil with surface of food 4 inches below heat until cheese melts and browns. Makes 6 servings.

HUZAREN SALADE

1 cup (about) diced cooked veal or beef
1 large sour pickle, minced
1 large apple, peeled and diced
1 cup diced cooked potatoes
1 small onion, minced
1 tablespoon vegetable oil
1½ tablespoons vinegar
2 tablespoons mayonnaise

Garnish: mayonnaise; sliced hard-cooked
    eggs; shredded pickled beets

Combine first 5 ingredients. Mix oil, vinegar, and
mayonnaise; add to meat mixture; mix well. Garnish with mayonnaise, sliced hard-cooked eggs,
and shredded pickled beets. Makes 4 servings.

YOGURT WITH CUCUMBER AND TOMATO

1 small firm ripe tomato
1 medium-sized cucumber
1 tablespoon minced onion
1 tablespoon salt
1 tablespoon finely chopped fresh coriander
    (cilantro) (optional)
1 cup plain yogurt

Cut tomato crosswise in ½-inch-thick rounds,
slice in ½-inch-wide strips, then in ½-inch
cubes. Peel cucumber; cut in half lengthwise;
scoop out seeds. Cut cucumber halves lengthwise in ⅛-inch-thick slices, then crosswise in ½-
inch pieces. Combine cucumber, onion, and salt;
mix well. Let stand at room temperature for 5
minutes. Squeeze gently between fingers to remove excess liquid. Combine with tomato, coriander, and yogurt. Makes 6 servings.

AUSTRIAN COFFEECAKE

½ cup milk, scalded
½ cup cold water
⅓ cup butter or margarine
½ cup sugar
2 eggs
2 cups sifted all-purpose flour
1¾ teaspoons salt
¾ teaspoon mace
2 packages active dry yeast
1½ cups quick or old-fashioned oats,
    uncooked
½ cup golden raisins
2 teaspoons grated lemon peel
Melted butter
Packaged fine dry bread crumbs
Blanched whole almonds
Confectioners' Sugar Icing (optional; page
    240)
Candied cherry (optional)

Combine milk and water; cool to lukewarm. Beat
butter and sugar together until creamy; add eggs
one at a time, beating after each addition. Add
lukewarm liquid. Sift together flour, salt, and

mace; add to creamed mixture. Stir in yeast. Beat
until smooth (about 2 minutes). Stir in oats, raisins, and lemon peel. Cover; let rise in warm
place (85°) until double in size (about 1½ hours).
Brush bottom and sides of 2-quart mold generously with melted butter; coat with bread
crumbs. Arrange almonds in a decorative design
in bottom of mold. Stir batter down; spoon carefully into mold. Let rise in warm place until
nearly double in size (about 1 hour). Bake at 350°
about 25 minutes. Cool on wire rack 10 minutes.
Unmold; cool. If desired, decorate with thin
Confectioners' Sugar Icing and a candied cherry.
Makes 1 coffeecake.

PANETTONE

½ cup milk
½ cup butter or margarine
¼ cup sugar
1 teaspoon salt
¼ cup warm water (105° to 115°)
1 package active dry yeast
2 eggs, beaten
3 cups all-purpose flour (about)
⅓ cup raisins
¼ cup mixed diced candied fruits
¼ cup canned diced roasted almonds
1 tablespoon grated lemon peel
Shortening

Scald milk; cool to lukewarm. Cream butter or
margarine with sugar and salt. Measure warm
water into large mixing bowl. Sprinkle yeast on
water; stir until dissolved. Stir in lukewarm milk
and creamed mixture. Add beaten eggs and
about ½ the flour. Beat until smooth. Blend in
fruits, almonds, and lemon peel. Add enough remaining flour to make very soft dough. Turn out
onto lightly floured surface; knead until smooth
and elastic. Place in greased bowl; brush top
with shortening. Cover; let rise in a warm place
(85°) until double in bulk (about 1½ hours).
Punch down. Turn out onto lightly floured board.
Let rest 10 minutes. Shape into round loaf. Place
in greased deep round pan. Cover; let rise in
warm place until double in bulk (about 1 hour).
Bake at 375° for 50 to 60 minutes. Turn out and
cool on rack. Makes 1 round loaf.

BATH BUNS

2 packages active dry yeast
½ cup warm water (105° to 115°)
2 teaspoons sugar

1 cup butter or margarine
1 cup sugar
1 teaspoon salt
4 eggs
⅔ cup milk, scalded and cooled to lukewarm
4 cups sifted all-purpose flour (about)
⅔ cup mixed diced candied fruits*
Raisins (optional)
1 egg yolk, slightly beaten
1 teaspoon water
Sugar

Soften yeast in warm water; stir in 2 teaspoons sugar; let stand about 15 minutes. Cream butter to consistency of mayonnaise; add 1 cup sugar slowly, continuing to cream until light and fluffy. Add salt. Beat eggs with milk; add to butter-sugar mixture; mix well. Stir in yeast. Stir in flour and candied fruits, using enough flour to make a soft dough. Place in greased bowl; turn to bring greased side of dough up; cover; let rise in warm place (85°) free from drafts until doubled. Punch down. Divide into 16 equal pieces. Shape into buns. Press a few pieces of candied fruit or raisins into tops of each. Brush with egg yolk diluted with water; sprinkle with a little sugar. Let rise in warm place until doubled. Place on greased baking sheets. Bake at 375° for 15 to 20 minutes or until deep golden brown. Makes 16 buns.

*Or use shredded or chopped citron, raisins, or dried currants.

FASTNACHTS

1½ cups milk
¼ cup light molasses
1 teaspoon salt
¼ cup soft butter or margarine
1 package active dry yeast
½ cup warm water (105° to 115°)
1 egg, beaten
4¼ to 4½ cups sifted all-purpose flour
Vegetable oil for frying
Granulated sugar

Heat milk until bubbles form around edge of pan. Add molasses, salt, and butter, stirring until butter is melted. Remove from heat; cool to lukewarm. Sprinkle yeast over warm water; stir until dissolved. Add milk mixture, egg, and 2 cups flour; beat until smooth and light. Beat in 2¼ cups of flour with spoon. Dough will be soft. Cover with damp towel. Let rise in warm place

(85°) until double in bulk. Punch down dough. If dough seems too soft to handle, work in additional ¼ cup flour. Turn out onto well-floured surface, rolling over to coat lightly with flour. Knead 10 times to make a smooth dough. Cover with mixing bowl; let rest 10 minutes. Divide dough in half. Roll out ½ inch thick. Cut with floured 3-inch doughnut cutter. Roll out and cut remaining dough. Cover with towel; let rise until double in bulk. Meanwhile, heat vegetable oil (2 inches deep) to 375°. Gently drop fastnachts, 3 or 4 at a time, into hot oil. As they rise to surface, turn over with slotted spoon. Fry until golden on both sides (about 3 minutes). Drain well on paper towels. Roll in granulated sugar. Makes about 2 dozen.

HOLIDAY BREADS

Make up a batch of Basic Sweet Dough, then use the dough as the basis for any of the 4 recipes that follow.

BASIC SWEET DOUGH

2 packages active dry yeast
½ cup warm water (105° to 115°)
1½ cups lukewarm milk
½ cup sugar
2 teaspoons salt
2 eggs
½ cup soft shortening
7 to 7½ cups sifted all-purpose flour

Dissolve yeast in warm water. Stir in milk, sugar, and salt. Add eggs, shortening, and half the flour; mix with spoon. Add enough of the remaining flour to make a soft dough; mix with hands. Turn onto lightly floured surface. Knead until smooth and blistered (about 5 minutes). Round up in greased bowl; bring greased side up. Cover with damp cloth. Let rise in warm place (85°) until double in bulk (about 1½ hours). Punch down; round up; let rise again until almost double in bulk (about 30 minutes). Divide dough for desired breads.

STOLLEN

½ Basic Sweet Dough
½ cup cut-up blanched almonds
¼ cup each cut-up citron and candied cherries
1 cup seedless raisins
1 tablespoon grated lemon peel
Soft butter

After Basic Sweet Dough has risen twice, knead in almonds, citron, cherries, raisins, and lemon peel. Roll or pat out dough into oval about 12 x 8 inches. Spread with soft butter. Fold in half the long way. Form into a crescent. Press folded edge down firmly. Place on greased baking sheet. Brush top with butter. Let rise until double (35 to 45 minutes). Bake at 375° for 30 to 35 minutes or until golden brown. Frost.

BAVARIAN BRAID

Basic Sweet Dough
1 teaspoon grated lemon peel
⅛ teaspoon mace
½ cup raisins
½ cup chopped blanched almonds
Icing of choice
Decorations of choice

After Basic Sweet Dough has risen twice, knead in the lemon peel, mace, raisins, and almonds. Divide dough in 4 equal parts. Shape 3 of the parts into strands each 14 inches long. Place about 1 inch apart on lightly greased baking sheet. Braid loosely, beginning at middle, working toward either end. Do not stretch. Seal ends by pressing firmly together and tucking under. Divide remaining portion of dough into 3 equal parts; shape into 3 strands each 12 inches long. Make another braid and place on top of the large braid, pinching ends into large braid. Cover; let rise until double in bulk (45 to 60 minutes). Bake at 350° for 30 to 40 minutes. Ice and decorate as desired.

SWISS FRUITED BREAD

Basic Sweet Dough
¼ teaspoon nutmeg
¼ teaspoon mace
⅛ teaspoon cloves
¼ cup raisins
¼ cup cut-up candied cherries
2 tablespoons chopped nuts
2 tablespoons chopped citron

Follow Basic Sweet Dough recipe except with the last half of the flour add the remaining ingredients. Let rise in warm place (85°) until double in bulk. Punch down. Divide in half and shape into 2 loaves. Place in 2 greased 9 x 5 x 3-inch loaf pans. Cover and let rise until center is a little higher than edges of pan. Bake at 375° about 40 minutes.

ITALIAN HOLIDAY BREAD

Basic Sweet Dough
¼ cup raisins
¼ cup diced candied fruit
¼ cup chopped nuts
¾ teaspoon anise
¼ teaspoon vanilla
Frosting of choice
Decorations of choice

Follow Basic Sweet Dough recipe except with the last half of the flour add the raisins, candied fruit, nuts, anise, and vanilla. Divide dough into 2 equal portions. Place each portion in a greased 1-pound coffee can. Let rise in warm place (85°) until double in bulk (15 to 20 minutes). Bake at 375° about 40 minutes. Frost and decorate as desired.

CHRISTMAS BREADS

After preparing a batch of Sweet Dough, choose one or several ways to shape your Christmas loaves.

SWEET DOUGH

2 packages active dry yeast
½ cup warm water (105° to 115°)
1½ cups lukewarm milk
1 cup sugar
1 teaspoon salt
1 teaspoon ground cardamom
4 eggs, beaten
8 cups all-purpose flour (approximate)
½ cup melted butter or margarine

Sprinkle yeast on warm water; let stand a few minutes; stir to blend. Stir in milk, sugar, salt, cardamom, eggs, and 2 cups flour. Beat smooth. Add 3 more cups of flour; beat until smooth. Stir in melted butter. Add enough of the remaining flour to make a soft dough that can be handled. Cover. Let rest 15 minutes. Turn out onto floured surface; knead until smooth and elastic. Place in greased bowl; turn greased side up. Cover with damp towel. Let rise in warm place (85°) until double in bulk (about 1 hour). Punch down. Cover. Let rise again until almost double (about ½ hour). Turn out onto lightly floured surface; shape in any of the following ways. *Important:* After shaping loaves, let rise about 20 minutes, until puffy but not doubled, then bake at 375° for 20 to 25 minutes or until lightly browned.

LUCIA'S CROWN

Use ⅓ of Sweet Dough. Divide in 9 portions. Roll each portion into a strand about 15 inches long. Twist 2 strands together to form a rope and arrange in a curve on a lightly greased baking sheet. Curl up remaining strands and place along outside edge of curved rope. Cover; let rise and bake. Frost with Confectioners' Sugar Icing (page 240) and decorate with whole glacé cherries and colored sugar.

CHRISTMAS STAR

Use ⅓ of Sweet Dough. Divide in 5 equal portions. Roll each portion into 12-inch strip. Shape each strip into a triangle (without a base) on a lightly greased baking sheet to form one point of the star. Arrange in a star shape. Let rise and bake.

GOLDEN CHARIOT

Use ⅓ of Sweet Dough. Divide in 4 portions. Roll each portion into a strand about 12 inches long. Arrange like the spokes of a wheel on a lightly greased baking sheet. Curl up the outer end of each spoke. Brush with beaten egg; cover; let rise and bake.

PULLA (COFFEE BRAID)

Use ⅓ of Sweet Dough. Divide in 3 equal portions. Shape each portion into a rounded strip about 16 inches long. Braid the 3 strips together; pinch ends and tuck under. Place on a lightly greased baking sheet; cover; let rise. Brush with beaten egg; sprinkle with 3 tablespoons each crushed loaf sugar and slivered blanched almonds. Bake.

BISHOP'S WIG

Use ⅓ of Sweet Dough. Divide in 3 equal portions. Roll each portion into a rounded strip about 18 inches long. Fold one strip in the middle and place on a lightly greased baking sheet. Curl each end upward. Place second strand above first; curl ends. Repeat with third strand; cover; let rise. Brush with beaten egg. Bake. When cool, decorate with white icing, trim with candied cherries.

GUGELHUPF

1 cup sweet butter
2 cups sugar
6 eggs, separated
1½ cups sifted all-purpose flour
½ teaspoon salt
2 teaspoons baking powder
6 tablespoons milk
Flavoring*
Confectioners' (powdered) sugar

Cream butter to consistency of mayonnaise. Add sugar slowly while continuing to cream. Beat until light and fluffy. Beat in egg yolks one at a time. Mix and sift flour, salt, and baking powder. Combine milk and flavoring. Add flour mixture and milk alternately to butter mixture, stirring in gently but thoroughly. Beat egg whites stiff but not dry; fold in thoroughly. Spoon into well-greased 12-cup gugelhupf pan (Turk's head mold). Bake at 350° for about 1 hour and 10 minutes or until cake tests done. Cool in pan 10 minutes. Loosen cake gently around rim and tube. Invert on cake rack. Finish cooling. Dust with confectioners' sugar.

*1 teaspoon vanilla or ½ teaspoon almond extract or 2 teaspoons grated lemon peel.

CHOCOLATE-CHERRY KUCHEN

¾ cup butter or margarine
3 squares (1 ounce each) unsweetened chocolate
1½ cups sugar
3 eggs, beaten
1½ cups sifted cake flour
½ teaspoon baking powder
½ teaspoon salt
1 can (1 pound) pitted sour red cherries
1½ teaspoons vanilla
1 cup whipping cream

Melt butter or margarine and chocolate together over hot water. Add sugar to beaten eggs gradually while beating. Add chocolate mixture to egg mixture; beat hard 1 minute. Mix and sift flour, baking powder, and salt. Drain cherries thoroughly; add to flour mixture; stir into chocolate-egg mixture. Stir in vanilla. Divide batter evenly between 2 greased and floured 9-inch layer-cake pans. Bake at 350° for 35 to 40 minutes. Cool. Whip cream; spread between layers and on top of cake. Chill. Makes 8 servings.

BÛCHE DE NOËL

½ teaspoon salt
4 eggs
¾ cup sugar
2 tablespoons dry cocoa (not instant)
1 teaspoon vanilla
¾ cup pancake mix
Confectioners' (powdered) sugar
2 cans ready-to-use chocolate frosting
White or green frosting (optional)
Cinnamon red hots (optional)
Flaked coconut

Grease bottom and sides of jelly roll pan, 10 x 15 x 1 inch; line with waxed paper; grease paper thoroughly. Add salt to eggs; beat until thick and lemon-colored. Combine sugar and cocoa; add gradually to eggs, beating well after each addition. Stir in vanilla and pancake mix; beat until smooth. (Batter will be quite thin.) Spread batter evenly in pan; bake at 400° for 12 minutes. Sprinkle dry tea towel generously with confectioners' sugar; loosen edges of cake; turn out onto towel; peel off waxed paper. Roll up cake in towel; let stand 20 minutes. Unroll. Spread with some of the frosting; roll up. Cut a thin slice from one end; unroll slice; cut in half; reroll each half to resemble stumps of cut-off branches. Frost log with remaining frosting, using pastry tube with serrated tip, or marking with a fork or spatula to resemble bark. Place "stumps" on top. If desired, decorate with vine and leaves made with white or green frosting, using a pastry tube with appropriate tips, and cinnamon red hots for berries. Sprinkle with flaked coconut to resemble drifts of snow. Chill or freeze until ready to serve. Makes 12 servings.

GÂTEAU SANS SOUCI

2 eggs
¼ teaspoon salt
1 cup sugar
1 teaspoon rum flavoring
½ cup milk
1 tablespoon butter or margarine
1 cup all-purpose flour
1 teaspoon baking powder
Coffee Syrup*
Cream Filling**
½ cup drained apricot preserves
½ cup whipping cream

Beat eggs until thick and light. Beat in salt, sugar, and flavoring. Heat milk and butter to boiling point; beat in. Mix and sift flour and baking powder; beat in. Turn into well-greased and floured 9-inch layer-cake pan 1½ inches deep. Bake at 350° for 35 to 40 minutes. Remove from pan. Spoon Coffee Syrup slowly and evenly over surface of warm cake until all is absorbed. Let stand until cold. Split crosswise, carefully, to make 2 layers. Fill with Cream Filling. Spread top with drained apricot preserves. Whip cream. Force through cake decorator to make lattice pattern. Makes 10 servings.

*COFFEE SYRUP

½ cup strong coffee
½ cup sugar
1 teaspoon rum flavoring (or to taste)

Combine coffee and sugar. Stir over low heat until sugar dissolves. Boil 3 minutes. Add rum flavoring to taste.

**CREAM FILLING

⅓ cup sugar
¼ cup flour
⅛ teaspoon salt
1 cup milk
2 egg yolks, slightly beaten
1 teaspoon rum flavoring

Combine sugar, flour, and salt in saucepan. Add milk; cook and stir over low heat until thickened. Cover; cook 10 minutes longer. Add a little hot mixture to egg yolks; combine with remaining hot mixture; cook 2 minutes longer, stirring constantly. Add flavoring. Chill.

MEXICAN FIESTA CONFECTION

1 package piecrust mix
¼ cup granulated sugar
½ cup dry cocoa (not instant)
¼ cup cold water
3 ounces sweet cooking chocolate
2 tablespoons butter or margarine
1 cup sifted confectioners' (powdered) sugar
1 teaspoon cinnamon
¼ teaspoon salt
1 egg
1 teaspoon vanilla
1 cup whipping cream

1 package (6 ounces) semisweet chocolate
    pieces
2 teaspoons vegetable shortening

Combine first 3 ingredients; blend well. Stir in cold water, a little at a time, with a fork, until dough clings together and leaves sides of bowl clean. Divide into 4 portions. Roll each portion ¼ inch thick and press each on bottom of an inverted 8-inch square pan to within ¼ inch of edge. (If you do not have 4 pans, let remaining pastry stand at room temperature while first layers bake.) Bake at 425° for 6 to 8 minutes, until almost firm. Loosen while warm with wide spatula. Remove to cake racks to cool. Melt sweet cooking chocolate with butter over simmering (not boiling) water. Without removing from hot water, beat in confectioners' sugar, cinnamon, salt, and egg. Continue beating 1 minute longer. Remove from heat. Fill bottom of double boiler with ice and water; set top in place. Beat 1 minute or until slightly cool. Beat in vanilla. Add cream very slowly, a little at a time, while beating. Continue beating until mixture is fluffy and spreadable (at least 5 minutes). A portable electric mixer makes this easier and faster. Spread each pastry layer with ¼ of the filling. Stack evenly on serving plate. Chill overnight. Melt semisweet chocolate pieces and shortening over hot, not boiling, water; blend well. Spread evenly in a paper-thin layer on baking sheet. Chill until firm. Break into large chips; heap on top pastry layer. Cut in 2-inch squares to serve. Makes 16 squares.

CUERNITOS
(Little Horns)

2½ cups sifted all-purpose flour
1 teaspoon salt
¾ cup butter or margarine
2 egg yolks
2 to 3 tablespoons cold water
Thick jam or preserves
1 egg, beaten
⅓ cup finely chopped blanched almonds
Extra-fine (instant) granulated sugar

Measure flour, salt, and butter into mixing bowl. Work butter into flour until finely divided, as for piecrust. Add egg yolks and water. Mix to a stiff dough. Divide dough into 24 even-sized pieces; shape into balls. Roll each ball on floured board (or pat with floured fingers) into a small round about 2½ to 3 inches in diameter. In center of each round, place about 1 teaspoon jam or preserves; fold pastry over; press edges together to prevent jam from running out. Place on ungreased baking sheets. Shape filled rolls into small horns or crescents. Brush each with beaten egg and sprinkle top with almonds. Bake at 375° for 12 to 15 minutes. Remove from sheets; dust with extra-fine sugar. Cool before storing. Makes 2 dozen.

NOTE: This is very short, rich dough. Handle gently to prevent breaking or tearing.

LEBKUCHEN

2¾ cups sifted all-purpose flour
½ teaspoon baking soda
½ teaspoon salt
½ teaspoon cloves
1 teaspoon cinnamon
1 teaspoon allspice
1 cup light molasses
¾ cup sugar
1 egg
1 teaspoon grated lemon peel
½ cup chopped walnuts
1 jar (8 ounces) diced mixed candied fruits

Sift together flour, baking soda, salt, and spices. Heat molasses to boiling in saucepan deep enough for mixing dough. Add sugar; cool. Beat in egg; add lemon peel. Gradually stir in flour mixture. Add nuts and mixed fruits; mix well. Chill dough overnight. Divide dough in half. Roll each half into a 6 x 12-inch rectangle on a greased baking sheet, using a lightly greased rolling pin. Bake at 400° for 12 to 15 minutes. While still hot, trim edges and cut in bars 1½ x 2½ inches. Cool. Frost with white frosting; decorate as desired. Makes about 40.

SUSPIROS
(Sighs)

3 egg whites
1 cup sugar
½ teaspoon lemon juice
½ cup slivered blanched almonds

Beat egg whites until very stiff but not dry. Add sugar gradually while continuing to beat. Add lemon juice. Fold in almonds. Line a cookie sheet with foil. Drop mixture by teaspoons onto foil and bake at 350° for 12 minutes or until slightly brown. Makes about 12.

MORAVIAN CHRISTMAS COOKIES

1 cup light molasses
½ cup shortening
1 teaspoon baking soda
2¼ cups sifted all-purpose flour
1¾ teaspoons baking powder
1 teaspoon salt
1 teaspoon powdered ginger
½ teaspoon each cloves, cinnamon, and
    nutmeg

Heat molasses to boiling in saucepan deep enough for mixing dough. Remove from heat; stir in shortening and baking soda. Sift together flour, baking powder, salt, and spices; add to molasses mixture. Chill overnight. Roll out dough ⅟₁₆ inch thick on lightly floured board or pastry cloth. Cut with Christmas cookie cutters. Place on a lightly greased baking sheet; bake at 350° for 7 minutes. Makes about 6½ dozen cookies.

SPRINGERLE

4 eggs
1 pound extra-fine (instant) sugar
1 teaspoon lemon extract
4½ cups sifted cake flour
1 teaspoon baking powder
Aniseeds

Beat eggs until light. Stir in sugar; beat until thoroughly combined. Add lemon extract. Mix and sift flour and baking powder; add to sugar mixture; mix thoroughly. Chill 1 hour; roll out ½ inch thick on floured board; cut in fancy shapes with cookie cutters or use springerle board to press designs in dough, then cut out cookies with a sharp knife. Grease cookie sheets; sprinkle with aniseeds. Arrange cookies on sheets. Bake at 350° for 30 minutes. Cool; store in covered jar for 2 or 3 weeks before serving. Makes about 42.

ISCHLER COOKIES

1½ cups sifted all-purpose flour
⅓ cup sugar
2½ cups finely grated walnuts*
¾ cup (1½ sticks) cold sweet butter
1 cup raspberry jam
1 package (6 ounces) semisweet chocolate
    pieces

Mix flour, sugar, and walnuts. Add butter; knead until smooth and firm. Work quickly to keep but-

ter from melting. Chill dough 1 hour. Roll out ¼ of dough at a time on floured board to ⅛-inch thickness. Cut in 2-inch rounds. Repeat until all dough is used, making 72 circles. Place on ungreased cookie sheets; bake at 350° for 10 to 15 minutes or until cookies are lightly browned. Cool on cookie sheets. Spread half the cookies with raspberry jam. Melt chocolate pieces over hot water. Spread thin layer of chocolate over remaining cookies. Place chocolate-covered cookies chocolate side up on top of cookies spread with jam. Makes about 3 dozen.

*An electric blender makes this easy; grate about ¼ cup at a time.

LUKSHEN KUGEL
(Noodle Pudding)

½ pound broad noodles, broken
2 eggs, separated
2 tablespoons vegetable oil
2 tablespoons sugar
½ teaspoon salt
½ cup chopped raisins
½ cup chopped apples
½ cup broken walnuts
¼ teaspoon cinnamon
⅛ teaspoon nutmeg

Cook noodles in boiling salted water until tender; drain (not too dry! moist noodles make the pudding more tender). Beat egg yolks; beat in oil, sugar, and salt. Fold into noodles. Combine fruits and nuts with spices; mix well. Fold in. Beat egg whites stiff but not dry. Fold in. Pour into a well-greased 1½-quart casserole. Bake at 350° for 45 minutes or until the top is browned. Makes 6 servings.

WEST INDIES PUDDING

2¼ cups sifted all-purpose flour
¾ cup sugar
¾ teaspoon nutmeg
1½ teaspoons cinnamon
¼ teaspoon salt
½ cup butter or margarine
1 cup molasses
1 cup water
1 teaspoon baking soda
1 tablespoon rum flavoring
1 large package (8 ounces) cream cheese
2 tablespoons milk or light cream
Lemon Sauce*

Mix and sift flour, sugar, nutmeg, cinnamon, and salt. Add butter and cut with 2 knives or pastry blender until mixture resembles coarse meal. Combine molasses, water, baking soda, and rum flavoring. Alternate layers of flour mixture and liquid in a greased 11-inch pie pan or 8 x 8 x 2-inch square pan or baking dish that has a volume of at least 6 cups. Begin and end with the flour mixture. Stir gently only 3 or 4 times with a fork. The surface should look marbled. Bake at 350° for 50 minutes. When ready to serve, blend cream cheese and milk or cream. Garnish top of pudding with cheese mixture. Serve with Lemon Sauce. Makes 10 servings.

*LEMON SAUCE

    2 tablespoons cornstarch
    ½ cup sugar
    ¼ teaspoon salt
    2 cups water
    3 tablespoons lemon juice
    1 tablespoon grated lemon peel
    ¼ cup butter or margarine

Combine cornstarch, sugar, and salt in saucepan. Gradually stir in water. Cook, stirring constantly, until mixture boils and is thickened and clear. Remove from heat and stir in remaining ingredients. Serve hot. Makes 2¼ cups.

SACHER TORTE

    ¾ cup butter or margarine
    ¾ cup sugar
    6 eggs, separated
    1 teaspoon vanilla
    1 package (6 ounces) semisweet chocolate
        pieces, melted and slightly cooled
    2 cups sifted cake flour
    Apricot jam
    Chocolate frosting

Cream butter to consistency of mayonnaise. Add sugar slowly while continuing to cream until light and fluffy. Add egg yolks one at a time, beating well after each addition. Add vanilla; mix well. Beat egg whites stiff but not dry. Fold into egg yolk mixture alternately with chocolate; fold in flour a little at a time. Spoon into 2 well-greased and floured 9-inch layer-cake pans. Bake at 325° for 25 minutes or until top of cake springs back when touched with fingertip. Spread one layer with apricot jam; top with second layer; spread with apricot jam. Frost top and sides with chocolate frosting. Makes 12 servings.

VIENNESE TORTE

    1 package chocolate cake mix
    ¾ cup apricot preserves
    3 tablespoons boiling water
    1 package (6 ounces) semisweet chocolate
        pieces
    1 tablespoon shortening
    3 tablespoons light corn syrup
    2 tablespoons milk
    Garnish: ½ cup chopped almonds or pistachio
        nuts

Prepare and bake cake mix as directed on package for two 8-inch layers. Cool. Cut each layer in half crosswise to make 4 thin layers. Break up preserves with fork; add water; beat smooth. Spread between layers, on sides, and on top. Chill thoroughly. Melt chocolate and shortening over hot, not boiling, water. Remove from heat; blend in corn syrup and milk. Pour warm frosting over chilled torte; smooth with spatula. Garnish with chopped nuts. Makes 8 servings.

ICELANDIC PANCAKES

    1 cup flour
    2 eggs
    ½ cup milk, divided
    2 tablespoons butter or margarine, melted
    2 teaspoons vanilla
    ¼ cup jam
    ⅓ cup whipping cream, whipped

Sift flour into small bowl. Beat eggs; add ¼ cup milk. Stir egg mixture, melted butter, and vanilla into flour. Add enough more milk to make a batter the thickness of whipping cream. Cover bottom of hot, lightly buttered small (5- or 6-inch) skillet with thin layer of batter by tilting skillet slightly. Brown lightly on both sides. When baked, spread teaspoon of jam and tablespoon of whipped cream over pancake. Fold twice; remove to a warm serving plate. Makes 12 pancakes, or 6 servings.

SICILIAN CREAM PUFFS

    ½ cup butter or margarine
    1 cup boiling water
    1 cup flour
    Few grains salt
    4 eggs
    Ricotta Filling*
    Orange-flavored confectioners' (powdered)
        sugar icing (optional)

Put butter or margarine and water in saucepan; bring to boiling point. Mix flour and salt; add to saucepan all at once; mix well. Cook, stirring constantly, until mixture forms smooth, compact mass. Remove from heat. Add unbeaten eggs one at a time, beating vigorously after each addition. Drop by tablespoons onto greased baking sheet 2 inches apart. Bake at 400° for 35 minutes or until thoroughly browned and set. Cool. Make slit with sharp-pointed knife near bottom of puff. Fill with Ricotta Filling. If desired, glaze lightly with orange-flavored confectioners' sugar icing. Makes about 12 puffs.

*RICOTTA FILLING

1 pound ricotta or farmer's cheese
½ cup sugar
2 squares unsweetened chocolate, grated
Few drops almond extract

Combine ricotta and sugar. Mix thoroughly. Stir in grated chocolate and flavoring.

APPLE CHARLOTTE

Kuchen Dough:

1 cup sifted all-purpose flour
½ teaspoon baking powder
¼ teaspoon salt
2 tablespoons sugar
2½ tablespoons butter or margarine
2 eggs, beaten
2 tablespoons milk

Mix and sift flour, baking powder, salt, and sugar. Work butter into mixture smoothly with wooden spoon. Beat in eggs. Stir in milk. Grease 8-inch springform pan. With rubber spatula or spoon, spread dough on bottom and partway up the side of springform pan (top edge of crust will be ragged).

Apple Filling:

5 cups sliced apples
½ cup golden raisins
⅔ cup sugar
1 teaspoon cinnamon
1 tablespoon grated lemon peel
Almond-flavored sweetened whipped cream

Cook apple slices and raisins in enough water to cover until apples are just tender but have not lost their shape; drain. Combine sugar, cinnamon, and lemon peel; stir gently into apples and raisins. Spoon into dough-lined springform pan. Bake at 425° for 50 to 60 minutes or until crust is deep golden brown and filling is firm. Serve hot, topped with almond-flavored and sweetened whipped cream. Makes 8 servings.

Index